PSYCHOLOGISTS & THEIR THEORIES
for Students

PSYCHOLOGISTS & THEIR THEORIES
for Students

VOLUME 1: A-K

Kristine Krapp, Editor

THOMSON

GALE

Detroit • New York • San Francisco • San Diego • New Haven, Conn. • Waterville, Maine • London • Munich

Psychologists and Their Theories for Students

Product Manager
Meggin Condino

Project Editor
Kristine Krapp

Editorial
Mark Springer

Indexing Services
Katherine Jensen

Rights and Aquisitions
Margaret Abendroth, Ann Taylor

Imaging and Multimedia
Robyn Young, Lezlie Light, Dan Newell

Product Design
Pamela A. Galbreath

Manufacturing
Evi Seoud, Lori Kessler

LIBRARY OF CONGRESS CATALOGING-IN-PUBLICATION DATA

Psychologists and their theories for students / Kristine Krapp, editor.
    p. cm.
      Includes bibliographical references and index.
      ISBN 0-7876-6543-6 (set : hardcover : alk. paper) —
      ISBN 0-7876-6544-4 (v. 1) —
      ISBN 0-7876-6545-2 (v. 2)
      1. Psychologists.   2. Psychology.   I. Krapp, Kristine M.

BF109.A1P72 2004
150'.92'2—dc22
                                        2004011589

Printed in the United States of America
10 9 8 7 6 5 4 3 2 1

Table of Contents

INTRODUCTION vii

ADVISERS ix

CONTRIBUTORS xi

HISTORICAL OVERVIEW xiii

CHRONOLOGY xxiii

MARY SALTER AINSWORTH 1
    Further analysis: Setting up the strange
    situation 7
    Biography: John Bowlby 9
    Further analysis: Japanese attachment
    theory 13

ANNE ANASTASI 15
    Biography: James Cattell 28
    Biography: Hans Eysenck 34

ALBERT BANDURA 39
    Further analysis: Personality theories . . 63
    Further analysis: Self-esteem 64

AARON TEMKIN BECK 67
    Biography: Albert Ellis 77
    Biography: David Barlow 89

ALFRED BINET 93
    Biography: David Wechsler 113
    Biography: Robert Sternberg 117

KENNETH BANCROFT CLARK 119
   Biography: Gordon Allport 133
   Biography: Claude Steele 140

SIGMUND SCHLOMO FREUD 145
   Further analysis: Hypnosis 151
   Biography: Anna Freud 170

KAREN CLEMENTINE HORNEY 175
   Biography: Women of Freudian
   psychology 192
   Biography: Mary Whiton Calkins . . . 198

CARL GUSTAF JUNG 201
   Further analysis: Dream symbolism . . 209
   Biography: Marie von Franz 226

GEORGE ALEXANDER KELLY 229
   Biography: Susan Fiske 245
   Biography: Elizabeth Loftus 250

LAWRENCE KOHLBERG 253
   Further analysis: The case of Heinz . . . 256
   Biography: Carol Gilligan 267

KURT LEWIN 279
   Group leadership models 294
   Biography: Fritz Heider 300

ABRAHAM MASLOW 303
   Biography: Viktor Frankl 316
   Biography: Rollo May 322

IVAN PAVLOV 325
   Biography: John Watson 332

   Biography: Clark Hull and Kenneth
   Spence 339

JEAN PIAGET 345
   Table of Erik Erikson's stages of
   development 362
   Table of Piaget's stages of
   development 369

CARL ROGERS 373
   Further analysis: Sample questions of
   the Q sort 394
   Biography: Hazel Markus 397

BURRHUS FREDERIC (B.F.) SKINNER 399
   Further analysis: Operant chamber . . . 402
   Further analysis: Baby box—Myth and
   reality 423

MAX WERTHEIMER 425
   Biography: Kurt Koffka 429
   Biography: Wolfgang Köhler 437

WILHELM WUNDT 447
   Biography: G. Stanley Hall 452
   Biography: William James 464

ROBERT YERKES 473
   Biography: Konrad Lorenz 483
   Biography: Harry Harlow's monkey
   infant experiment 494

GLOSSARY 499

INDEX 507

Introduction

Purpose of the book

The purpose of *Psychologists and Their Theories for Students* is to provide readers with in-depth information on major psychological theories, past and present, as well as the people who developed them. *Psychologists* explains each psychologist's theories in detail, then analyzes the historical context and critical reaction to the theories. Biographical information is also included. *Psychologists* is designed to meet the needs of high school and college students in the first two years of study.

Psychologists contains entries on 20 of the most frequently studied or most pertinent psychologists in history. Each entry is accompanied by sidebars containing information on related theories or other psychologists who were close to the subject of the entry, either through proximity or ideology. Photos and charts are included. Entries follow a standard structure and include a personal chronology, list of the subject's principal publications, sources, and bibliographic information on materials for a student's further exploration of the subject. The entries are accompanied by a historical overview of the science of psychology, chronology, glossary of terms used in the book, and a general index.

Selection criteria

Many individuals had input into the final content of *Psychologists*. A preliminary list of most-studied psychologists and theories was compiled from the suggestions of librarians who regularly receive requests from students for further information on psychologists studies in their classes. Another group of high school librarians and psychology teachers gave input on the list of entries and made suggestions for accompanying sidebars. Two academic advisers gave final approval on the list of topics and reviewed the content of every entry. Writers also gave input on the content of sidebars and complementary graphics.

How each entry is organized

Each entry, or chapter, in *Psychologists* focuses on one psychologist and his or her most important theories. Each entry heading lists the full name of the psychologist, birth and death dates, nationality, and occupation. The following elements are contained in each entry:

- **Brief overview:** An overview of the psychologist, his or her life, and introduction to the nature of his or her work.

- **Biography:** This section includes basic facts about the psychologist's life, including family background, education, positions held, and information on marriage and family.

- **Theories:** Detailed account of the psychologist's main theory(s). Each is broken down into sections on main points of the theory, explanations, and examples.

- **Historical context:** Analysis of the political, social, and scientific events in play during the psychologist's life, many of which may have influenced his or her career.

- **Critical response:** A summary of criticism of the theories, both during the psychologist's time and since. Related theories that other psychologists developed as a response to the main subject's theories are addressed here.
- **Theories in action:** A summary of how the theory is used in study or treatment. Sections on research and case studies are included. A final section explains the relevance of the psychologist's work to modern readers.
- **Sources:** Bibliographic citations of sources the writer used compile the entry.
- **Further readings:** Bibliographic citations of sources that readers, can go to for further information on the subject.
- **Sidebars:** Related topics are included in "Further analysis" sidebars. "Biography" sidebars are devoted to those psychologists close to the entry's subject.

Additional features

Psychologists further benefits readers with these features:

- Photos and charts within the entries give the reader more information on the topics being discussed.

- Lists of every psychologist's principal publications are included in the entries.
- A personal chronology in every psychologist's entry gives the important events in his or her life.
- A collective chronology of the psychologists' lives included in the frontmatter, in addition to selected world events, gives reader context for the psychologists' lives.
- A brief essay on the history of psychology gives the reader historical context and discusses major schools of psychological thought.
- A glossary of terms used in the book explains important concepts.
- A general index allows easy access to entry information.

We welcome your suggestions

The editor of *Psychologists and Theories for Students* welcomes your comments and suggestions. Please direct all correspondence to:

Editor, *Psychologists and Their Theories
    for Students*
Thomson Gale
27500 Drake Road
Farmington Hills, MI 48331-3535

Advisers

Three high school faculty members were consulted about the initial scope and nature of the book. Two university psychology professors finalized the entry list and review the entry content. The content review advisers include:

Bonnie Ruth Strickland, PhD: former President, American Psychological Association; Professor Emeritus of Psychology, University of Massachusetts, Amherst, Massachusetts.

William O'Donohue, PhD: Nicholas Cummings Professor of Organized Behavioral Healthcare Delivery, Department of Psychology, University of Nevada Reno, Reno, Nevada; adjunct faculty, University of Hawaii, Manoa; Distinguished Practitioner, National Academies of Practice.

High school scope advisers include:

Virginia Chaussee: Librarian, Compadre High School, Tempe, Arizona.

Charlie Jones: Library media specialist, Plymouth High School, Plymouth, Michigan.

Dana Serlin: Psychology teacher, North Farmington High School, Farmington Hills, Michigan.

Contributors

Linda Wasmer Andrews, MS: Science writer specializing in psychology, Albuquerque, New Mexico. Wrote entries on Albert Bandura, Alfred Binet, and Robert Yerkes.

Paula Ford-Martin, MA: Clinical and consumer medical writer, Wordcrafts, Warwick, Rhode Island. Wrote entries on Ivan Pavlov and Mary Ainsworth.

Rebecca Frey, PhD: Science and medical freelance writer, New Haven, Connecticut. Wrote entries on Aaron Beck, Carl Jung, Lawrence Kohlberg, and Kurt Lewin.

Gary Gilles, MA, LCPC: Psychologist and freelance writer, Chicago, Illinois. Wrote entries on Sigmund Freud and B.F. Skinner.

Clare Hanrahan, BS (Psychology): Author and researcher, CelticWordCraft, Asheville, North Carolina. Wrote entries on Kenneth Bancroft Clark and Jean Piaget.

Denise Schmutte, PhD (Clinical psychology): Freelance writer, Edmonds, Washington. Wrote entry on Abraham Maslow.

Joan Schonbeck, RN: Nurse and freelance writer, Marlborough, Massachusetts. Wrote entries on Karen Horney, Carl Rogers, and Max Wertheimer.

J.E. Spehar: Freelance biographer and science writer, Canton, Ohio. Wrote entries on George Kelly, Wilhelm Wundt, and Anne Anastasi.

Historical Overview

In a very real sense, psychology is probably as old as humanity. In fact, some scientists have argued that one of the defining characteristics of human beings is the ability to study the behavior of others, imagine oneself in their positions and make predictions about their future behavior based on these insights. Certainly, there is evidence that humans have done just that at least since the dawn of recorded history. Ancient writings from China, Egypt, India, Persia, and Greece all display an intense curiosity about the nature of thought, memory, emotion, sensation, and motivation.

The scientific study of psychology is a much more recent development, however. Many historians date the birth of modern psychology from the founding of the first experimental psychology laboratory by Wilhelm Wundt in 1879. As a science, then, psychology is still relatively young. Yet, over the course of little more than 120 years, it has managed to make a tremendous impact on both the academic world and society at large. Psychology has given rise to influential schools of thought ranging from psychoanalysis to behaviorism, and from Gestalt psychology to cognitive psychology.

Forerunners of psychology

Philosophical roots Questions about mental life and human behavior have fascinated philosophers through the centuries. In seventeenth-century France, the great philosopher and mathematician René Descartes conceived of a system of true knowledge that was modeled on mathematics and supported by a philosophical approach called rationalism. This approach held that knowledge was derived from the use of reason and

logic. Descartes' system was summed up in his famous pronouncement: "I think, therefore I am." Descartes also viewed the mind and body as two separate entities. The mind belonged to the spiritual sphere, while the body belonged to the physical world of science.

Descartes was an intellectual giant, but his was not the only voice of the day. Toward the end of the Renaissance period in Europe, some philosophers were starting to look at the world from a more science-based perspective. It was a heady time for science. In Italy, Galileo proposed a sun-centered theory of the solar system to replace the older earth-centered model. In England, Francis Bacon argued for use of the scientific method to solve problems, and William Harvey demonstrated that the heart was actually nothing more than a pump for circulating blood.

The stage was set for the rise of a philosophical approach called empiricism, which held that all factual knowledge came from experience. One of the founders of English empiricism was Thomas Hobbes, who, not coincidentally, served briefly as Bacon's secretary and numbered Galileo among his friends. Hobbes saw the world and everything in it as bodies in motion. For him, mental processes were merely the byproducts of motion inside the brain. In addition, Hobbes believed that all knowledge was derived through the senses. Although Hobbes' writings were sometimes incomplete or inconsistent, he succeeded in planting the seed of empiricism.

The approach soon blossomed into a more organized school of thought, thanks to John Locke, a seventeenth-century English philosopher. Locke believed that the mind at birth was like a blank slate, just waiting to be written upon by experience. Therefore, there were no innate ideas. Instead, all ideas came from two forms of experience: sensation, which referred to information received from the senses; and reflection, which referred to the mental processes involved in sifting through all that sensory information. Much later, Locke's influence could still be seen in behaviorism, a twentieth-century school of psychology that focused on conditioning and learning—in other words, experience—as the determining factors in behavior.

In addition, Locke introduced the term "association of ideas." In the eighteenth and nineteenth centuries, a group of British philosophers took up the term and applied it to a new theory called associationism. This theory started with the notion that knowledge is acquired through experience, but it then went a step further, attempting to explain how that knowledge is organized. Associationism held that the process involved the association of ideas within the mind. Proponents believed that the way these associations were formed could be described by fundamental laws.

Associationism reached its height in the work of British philosopher James Mill and his son, John Stuart Mill. James Mill believed that ideas were added together to form more complex ideas. However, there was a basic flaw with this philosophy: It required that consciousness be able to hold an implausibly large number of ideas, since even a not-too-complex idea such as "brick" would require a vast number of ever-simpler ideas to define it. To address this flaw, John Stuart Mill revised his father's position. He described a process called mental chemistry, by which complex ideas could be greater than the sum of the simpler ideas making them up. This concept was later echoed by Gestalt psychology. The younger Mill also was enthusiastic about the prospect of establishing a true science of human behavior, and his enthusiasm may have influenced Wundt, who founded his lab just six years after Mill's death.

Physiological roots For centuries, as we have seen, philosophers had mused over the nature of the mind and its relationship to outward behavior. Yet their musings were pure speculation, since the technology to study the inner workings of the brain and nervous system was not yet available. In the nineteenth century, however, physiologists made great advances in the tools and techniques for studying the nervous system. These advances laid the groundwork for the development of a new discipline: psychophysics, or the study of the relationship between the physical properties of stimuli and the psychological impressions that those stimuli produce.

One of the scientific giants of the era was Hermann von Helmholtz, a German physicist. Helmholtz rejected the common idea that physiological and psychological processes in organisms needed to be explained in terms of mysterious forces or energies. Instead, he believed that the processes within a living thing could be explained by the same kinds of laws that applied to nonliving matter. Among other contributions, Helmholtz measured the speed of nerve impulses, conducted important research on sound perception, revised a theory of color vision, and invented the ophthalmoscope, an instrument used to examine the interior of the eyes. By achieving such impressive results, Helmholtz showed that the nervous system was indeed amenable to scientific study.

Around the same time, other scientists were making discoveries about the localization of specific functions in particular parts of the brain. For example, French neurologist Paul Broca came across a patient who apparently understood everything that was said to him, but who could only reply by saying "tan, tan." When the man died of an infection in 1861, Broca's autopsy revealed that there was a large lesion on the left side of the frontal lobe of his brain. Thus, this area of the brain, which became known as Broca's area, was identified as important for speech production. A little more than a decade later, German neurologist Carl Wernicke identified another area in the temporal lobe of the brain that was crucial for speech comprehension.

Still another pioneering figure was Ernst Weber, an anatomist and physiologist at the University of Leipzig in Germany. Weber studied the sense of touch by mapping what became known as the two-point threshhold. This was the smallest distance at which touching the skin at two different points was felt as two sensations rather than just one. Weber found that touch sensitivity varied for different parts of the body, with the tongue, for instance, being much more sensitive than the back.

One of Weber's younger colleagues at the University of Leipzig was Gustav Fechner. In 1860, Fechner published a book called *Elements of Psychophysics*, which was destined to become a classic. In the book, he described several methods of measuring responses to stimuli. The development of a practical research methodology paved the way for the first experimental studies in psychology.

Birth of a science

German beginnings German scientists—such as Hermann von Helmholtz, Ernst Heinrich Weber, and Gustav Theodor Fechner—had already developed many of the tools and techniques that would be needed if psychology were ever to stand on its own as a science. It is little wonder, then, that the first experimental psychology lab was established at the University of Leipzig. In this hotbed of scientific discovery, Wundt found fertile ground for his studies on topics such as attention, sensation, perception, and reaction time—the split-second needed for mental processing between the time when an event occurs and the time when the muscles start responding to it.

Wundt was trained in medicine and physiology, and he held professorships in philosophy. Yet, more than any of his predecessors, he not only melded these interests, but also expanded on them to create a brand-new science of psychology. In addition to actively pursuing research in his lab, he founded a journal and trained a steady stream of graduate students. He also wrote an influential two-volume book entitled *Principles of Physiological Psychology*.

American beginnings

The birth of psychology in Germany was closely watched in the United States. No one observed the developments with keener fascination than William James, an American scholar who went on to make his mark on both psychology and philosophy. Like Wundt, James had been trained in medicine and physiology, but his true calling lay elsewhere. In 1890, he published *Principles of Psychology*, a lengthy text that became an instant success and influenced generations to come. In this book, James argued the psychologists should base their studies not on isolated sensations, but on complete conscious experiences. Thus, he expanded the rather narrow borders of early German psychology to include a much wider range of mental processes.

Another towering figure of the same period was G. Stanley Hall. During his career, Hall racked up an impressive number of firsts. As a young man, he received the first U.S. doctoral degree in psychology. He earned the degree at Harvard University, where he studied with James. Afterward, Hall also studied for a time in Germany, where he was the first American student in Wundt's lab. Returning to the United States, Hall founded the *American Journal of Psychology*, the first English-language journal devoted exclusively to the new field. He also set up the first experimental psychology lab in the United States at Johns Hopkins University. Soon after, in 1889, he was named the first president of Clark University in Worcester, Massachusetts, where he promptly established a world-class psychology department. The glory days at Clark were short-lived, since most of the outstanding faculty and students left a few years later over a dispute with the university and Hall. Yet Hall still had enough clout to become the driving force behind the founding of the American Psychological Association (APA), and it should come as no surprise that he served as that group's first president. Finally, Hall's last graduate student was also a notable first: Francis Sumner, the first African American student to earn a PhD in psychology in the United States.

It is perhaps less remembered that Hall was instrumental in giving the American public its first taste of Sigmund Freud's psychoanalysis. In 1909, Hall invited Freud to give a series of five lectures at a conference held at Clark. The lectures were well received by both fellow psychologists and the press. Hall also published Freud's lectures in the journal he edited, reaching an even wider audience. As an interesting sidelight, a second speaker at the same conference was a then-obscure psychologist who also went on to make a name for himself: Carl Jung.

Psychoanalysis

Freud's theory Modern psychology began as an experimental science. However, it was not long before a clinical offshoot of the new science appeared. Today, clinical practice is a very important part of the field. No figure looms larger in the history of clinical psychology than Freud. His method of psychoanalysis had an enormous impact, both on those who loved it and on those who hated it, some of whom reacted by offering up equally influential alternatives.

Freud was an Austrian physician whose ideas came out of his clinical experiences rather than a lab. When he first began presenting his ideas in the 1890s, they met with harsh criticism, in part because of his heavy emphasis on sexuality. By the early 1900s, however, he had attracted an international following. Freud theorized that there were three aspects of personality—id, ego, and superego—that existed at different levels of consciousness. He believed that instincts in general, and sexual instincts in particular, were at the heart of human behavior. He also thought that personality development proceeded through five stages: oral, anal, phallic, latency, and genital. Failure to successfully pass through the early stages in childhood could lead to emotional problems later in life.

Before Freud, there had been philosophical discussions of the differences among people. However, there was no psychological theory to explain exactly what made individuals who they were. As the first to advance such a theory, Freud opened the door to a host of other personality theorists who followed.

Psychoanalysis was not only a theory, however, but also a treatment approach. As such, it was the first true form of psychotherapy. Freud developed a therapeutic technique called free association, in which a patient was encouraged to say anything that came into his or her conscious mind without trying to censor the thoughts first. Freud also stressed the importance of dream interpretation for understanding a patient's mental life. In fact, many consider *The Interpretation of Dreams*, published in 1900, to be his most important book.

Neo-Freudian approaches   Since Freud's day, a number of followers have attempted to pick up where he left off. Perhaps his most devoted disciple was his own daughter, Anna Freud. She became one of the leading figures in psychoanalysis after her father's death. Her major contribution was the detailed description of defense mechanisms, which are methods that the ego uses to defend itself when faced with conflicting demands from the id and superego.

Among Anna Freud's notable contemporaries was Karen Horney, a German-born psychoanalyst who moved to the United States in 1932. While Horney accepted many of Sigmund Freud's ideas, she criticized his views on the psychology of women. Freud had claimed that women felt inferior to men because of penis envy, and that this inevitably had a negative effect on their personality development. Horney disagreed strongly. She believed that, when women did lack self-esteem, it was due to their experiences living in a male-dominated culture rather than to their sexual anatomy.

One thing on which Freud and his followers all agreed was that the interactions between children and their parents played a critical role in molding the children's personalities. This led to research on how children form healthy emotional attachments. For example, Canadian psychologist Mary Ainsworth conducted studies in which she placed a mother and her infant in an unfamiliar room with toys. The mother would twice leave the room briefly and then return, and a researcher would observe the infant's reaction. Ainsworth noted that securely attached infants were distressed when their mothers left and comforted when their mothers returned. Other reactions signaled less healthy attachments.

Beyond psychoanalysis   Psychoanalysis was just the start, of course. Numerous other theories of personality and schools of psychotherapy have emerged over the past century. Two early members of Freud's inner circle who eventually broke away to found their own analytic psychologies were Alfred Adler and Carl Jung.

Adler was an Austrian psychiatrist who joined Freud's discussion group in 1902. In 1911, however, he had left the fold to pursue his own theory of psychology. Called individual psychology, Adler's theory downplayed sexual instinct. Instead, it emphasized the importance of overcoming early feelings of inferiority. By focusing on the individual and the positive, goal-directed nature of humanity, Adler was a forerunner of the later movement known as humanistic psychology.

Jung was a Swiss psychiatrist who began an active correspondence with Freud in 1906. By 1913, however, the once-friendly relationship between the two men had turned into a bitter rift. Jung developed his own school of thought, which he called analytical psychology. Like Freud, he stressed the impact of unconscious ideas on behavior. However, Jung expanded this notion to include not only a personal unconscious, but also a collective unconscious—a deeper level of unconsciousness that he believed to contain emotionally charged symbols that were common to all peoples and had existed since the dawn of time.

In addition, Jung introduced a system for classifying personality types. He classified people based on their tendency toward an inward focus, called introversion, or an outward focus, called extroversion. In addition, Jung identified four functions of the mind: sensing, thinking, feeling, and intuiting. He believed that, while everyone used all four functions, people normally used one more than the others. Therefore, people could be grouped into categories based on their dominant mental function.

Legacy of psychoanalysis   Freud was a rationalist in the tradition of Descartes, and he avoided experimental research. While this approach led to some brilliant insights, it also was a serious limitation. Some of Freud's specific concepts have not held up well to scientific study. Nevertheless, the psychoanalytic system as a whole has had an enduring and far-reaching impact on theory, therapy, and society in general. Terms such as id, ego, unconscious, Freudian slip, and Oedipus complex have become part of our everyday language.

In addition, modern versions of psychoanalysis continue to be used for treating mental illness. These modern therapies, often called psychodynamic therapies, all share a common focus on past experiences as an important cause of present problems. Using various techniques, therapists aim to help individuals gain insight into their emotional life, including influences from the past. Therapists also try to help people uncover their unconscious conflicts and understand how these conflicts may be affecting their current experiences.

Behaviorism

Animal learning Adler and Jung devised alternatives to psychoanalysis, but their approaches still were based on the invisible and sometimes unconscious workings of the mind. From a scientific perspective, such approaches posed a big problem, since there was no objective way for scientists to validate the subjective thoughts and feelings that people reported having. In the early 1900s, the desire for greater objectivity led to the rise of behaviorism, a school of psychology that completely rejected the study of inner mental processes and focused instead on observable behaviors.

Like other schools of thought, behaviorism did not arise in a vacuum. Instead, it grew out of animal research on learning and conditioning. Early on, Wundt had written a book titled *Lectures on Human and Animal Psychology*, which helped establish animal research as a legitimate area of study for psychologists. By the turn of the twentieth century, animal research was a booming field. Around this time, William S. Small began using mazes to study lab rats, and Edward L. Thorndike tested the ability of cats to escape from puzzle boxes. Thanks to such creative experimental designs, a practical method for studying animal learning was rapidly developed.

One particularly prominent animal researcher was American psychologist Robert Yerkes. Although Yerkes later became known for his work with primates, he studied a wide range of species early in his career. In 1907, he published a book about the behavior, learning, and sensory capabilities of a particular type of mutant mouse. The next year, he coauthored a paper that presented the so-called Yerkes-Dodson Law, which originally related the strength of a stimulus to the speed of avoidance learning.

Meanwhile, a Russian physiologist named Ivan Pavlov had been studying the digestive process in dogs. He noticed that the dogs salivated when their keeper entered the room, apparently because they had come to associate the keeper's arrival with food. This led Pavlov to conduct his famous experiments on classical conditioning, the first form of learning to be studied experimentally. In classical conditioning, an association is formed by pairing a previously neutral stimulus (such as a bell) with an unconditioned stimulus (such as food) to produce an unconditioned response (such as salivation). Over time, the previously neutral stimulus becomes able to bring on the response all by itself.

Watson's theory Yet another scientist who was drawn to the study of animal learning around this time was American psychologist John B. Watson. In early work, Watson studied matters such as the cues used by rats to learn their way through a maze. Unlike most psychologists before him, however, Watson completely rejected the study of inner mental processes, even in humans. Instead, he believed that the only way to turn psychology into a truly objective science was to focus strictly on observable behavior. In a 1913 paper, Watson laid out his ideas forcefully. It was the opening shot in what became the behaviorist revolution.

Watson argued that the proper goal of psychology was the prediction and control of behavior. He believed that the same principles of learning and conditioning that were being used in animal research could also be used to explain all of human personality and behavior. For example, he believed that most fears were the result of unfortunate conditioning experiences. In one famous study, he showed how fear could be instilled through classical conditioning. The study involved an 11-month-old boy called Little Albert. Before the study began, Albert showed no fear of a white rat, but he appeared frightened and started to cry when a loud sound was made. In the study, researchers showed Albert the rat. Whenever Albert reached for the rat, however, they made the scary sound. After the researchers repeated this procedure several times, Albert began to cry as soon as he saw the rat, even without the loud noise. Afterward, Albert also began avoiding other objects—such as a rabbit and a fur coat—that resembled the rat in some way. It seemed that his conditioned fear response had generalized from the original stimulus to other similar stimuli.

Locke had described the mind of a newborn infant as a blank slate. Watson took this idea quite literally. He once boasted that, given a dozen healthy infants and his own specific world in which to raise them, he could pick any child at random and train that child to become anything. In other words, Watson believed that people were entirely products of their environment. It was an extreme position, but one that had a lasting impact on psychology. For decades after Watson, students were taught that the definition of psychology was "the study of behavior."

Radical behaviorism For half a century, behaviorism remained the dominant school of psychology in the United States. As had happened earlier with psychoanalysis, however, different factions soon developed within the ranks of the true believers. The most celebrated champion of behaviorism in the mid-twentieth century was B.F. Skinner. While Skinner was often controversial, he was also extremely influential. His approach, dubbed radical behaviorism, helped define the course of modern experimental psychology.

Skinner is perhaps best remembered for his discovery of what he called operant conditioning. This type of conditioning occurs when a behavior is shaped by its immediate consequences. If the consequences are positive, the behavior is more likely to occur again in the future, given the same environment. If the consequences are negative, the behavior is less likely to occur again. To study operant conditioning in animals, Skinner developed the Skinner box. This was a special box in which the rate of some behavior, such as pressing a bar, could be continuously recorded. Skinner found that an organism's behavior could be shaped by providing positive consequences for actions that came closer and closer to a desired behavior.

Legacy of behaviorism   Skinner envisioned a world in which behavioral techniques could be used to improve childrearing, education, and society as a whole. In his book *Walden Two*, he described a utopian community based on operant conditioning, in which government rewarded socially appropriate behavior, and life was trouble-free. Skinner actually designed both a special crib and a teaching machine based on behaviorist principles, but neither achieved commercial success. Nevertheless, his ideas are still widely used in education, business, and other settings where the aim is to encourage appropriate behavior using rewards.

Behaviorism also gave rise to a popular form of psychotherapy, known as behavior therapy or behavioral modification. This type of therapy is based on the assumption that maladaptive behavior is caused by faulty or inadequate learning. The aim of the therapy is to reduce or halt the unwanted behavior by rewarding more helpful responses.

Gestalt psychology

Three founders   While behaviorism was the dominant school of American psychology for much of the twentieth century, it was far from the only one. Gestalt psychology, founded in Germany and imported to the United States in the 1930s, offered an important alternative. This school of psychology dealt with organized wholes that could not be explained by breaking them down into their component parts. As such, it was opposed to behaviorism, which sought to reduce complex human experiences to simple behavioral explanations.

Three German psychologists are credited with founding Gestalt psychology: Max Wertheimer, Kurt Koffka, and Wolfgang Köhler. *Gestalt* is a German

word that can be loosely translated as "a structured whole." The story goes that Gestalt psychology had its beginnings one day in 1910, as Wertheimer was taking a trip by train. Gazing out the train window, he was struck by the apparent movement of stationary objects, such as poles and buildings. Once back home, he began conducting experiments of apparent motion, which he called the phi phenomenon. His subjects were two younger colleagues, Koffka and Köhler. In 1912, Wertheimer published a paper about his experiments that is said to mark the official start of Gestalt psychology. Wertheimer and his two colleagues later moved to the United States to escape the Nazi regime.

Gestalt psychology flourished in the first half of the twentieth century. The three founders and their followers used Gestalt ideas to develop basic principles of perception, learning, and thinking. For example, the principle of proximity stated that elements that were close together in time or space would be seen as belonging together. The principle of similarity stated that similar elements would also be seen as going together in the mind. The principle of closure stated that, if there were gaps in an element, people would tend to mentally close those gaps to make the element complete.

Field theory   Other psychologists sought to apply Gestalt ideas to areas such as motivation, personality, and social relationships. Among those who wanted to broaden Gestalt psychology was Kurt Lewin, a Prussian-born psychologist who was educated in Germany. Lewin also immigrated to the United States in the 1930s.

Lewin soon developed his own theory, known as field theory, first published in 1935. It stood out from earlier approaches that had focused single-mindedly on either internal mental processes or external rewards and punishments. Instead, Lewin's theory stressed the interaction of the person and the environment. In this way, it anticipated some popular approaches of the late twentieth century, such as Bandura's social-cognitive theory.

One of Lewin's key concepts was life space, which consisted of all the influences acting on a person at any given time. These influences might include personal and biological facts (a memory, fatigue), physical events (an aroma, a room), and social facts (another person, being a member of a family). Lewin referred to the positive or negative features of objects in the life space as valences. In general, objects that met a need had a positive valence, while those that gave rise to frustration or fear had a negative valence. The concept of valences helped explain people's behavior in the face of interpersonal conflict. In an approach-avoidance conflict, for instance, people had to decide what to do when a goal had both positive and negative valence. Lewin believed that their decision would be based on which of the two forces—the one pulling them toward the goal or the one pushing them away—turned out to be more powerful.

Psychometrics

Intelligence testing   From its beginnings, psychology was grounded in basic lab research. However, it was not long before psychologists began seeking real-world applications for their research findings. After all, there was no better way to show psychology's value to society than by offering up practical solutions to vexing social problems. However, these practical applications often required classifying people into groups based on particular abilities, skills, or other characteristics. Such classification, in turn, required valid and reliable tests for measuring the characteristic in question. Thus was born the field of psychometrics, which involves the construction of psychological tests using statistical methods.

Intelligence testing, one very visible branch of psychometrics, began in France around the turn of the twentieth century. At that time, the French government enacted laws requiring that all children be given a public education. For the first time, mentally "subnormal" children—those who today might be called mentally retarded or developmentally disabled—were to be provided with special classes. However, this raised the question of how to identify those children who would benefit from special education. French psychologist Alfred Binet set out to solve the problem by devising a test for measuring mental abilities. In 1905, he introduced the Binet-Simon Scale, the world's first practical test of intelligence.

Binet's groundbreaking test soon attracted interest in the United States. When World War I arrived, an APA committee set out to devise a similar test that could be used by the U.S. Army to assess recruits. Yerkes, the noted animal researcher who had a side interest in intelligence testing, was APA president at the time. He headed up the committee, which eventually developed the first intelligence tests designed to be given in a group rather than individually. While the hastily thrown-together Army tests had many flaws, they introduced the idea of mass testing to the American public. Over the next several decades, standardized testing of vast numbers of people became common in schools and businesses nationwide.

Validity and reliability   Through the years, test development methods have become much more sophisticated. Statistical techniques have been developed for assessing a test's validity and reliability. Validity refers to the extent to which a test measures what it is supposed to measure. Reliability refers to the extent to which the measurements are consistent or repeatable over time. Several psychologists have played key roles in refining the methods that are currently used for testing the tests to make sure they meet acceptable standards.

One innovator in the field was American psychologist Anne Anastasi, whose contributions included work on test construction and the proper use of psychological tests. Anastasi also had a deep interest in the way that psychological development was affected by the environment and individual experience. This interest undoubtedly shaped her views on testing as well, making her especially sensitive to the role that culture played in test results. Today, test fairness and culture loading—the extent to which a test reflects the vocabulary, knowledge, and traditions of one culture more than another—are still subjects of lively debate.

Humanistic psychology

The Third Force   By the mid-twentieth century, many psychologists were growing disenchanted with behaviorism. They were looking for an alternative to what some saw as the bleak behaviorist view of humans as little more than two-legged lab rats. In addition, they were eager to study psychological health rather than focus on emotional maladjustment, the way psychoanalysis did. With behaviorism and psychoanalysis as the first two forces in American psychology, the time was ripe for what became known as the Third Force. This approach, also called humanistic psychology, focused more on positive rather than negative aspects of the self. It was also more concerned with present choices than past events. Among the central concerns of humanistic psychology were free will, the lifelong search for meaning, and each person's potential to achieve self-fulfillment.

At the forefront of this movement was American psychologist Abraham Maslow. He is best remembered for the hierarchy of needs that he proposed. This was often depicted as a pyramid, with the most basic needs on the bottom. These included physiological needs, such as food and water, and safety needs. Only after those needs had been satisfied was a person free to focus on the next level, which consisted of needs for belonging and love. Once those needs, in turn, had been met, a person could move on to addressing esteem needs, such as achievement and independence. Finally, after all of the lower needs had been met, a person could begin working on self-actualization, the feeling of fulfillment that comes from realizing one's potential.

Maslow believed that there was more to be gained by studying self-actualized individuals than by studying maladjusted people or nonhuman animals. This shift in focus opened the door to the psychological study of many subjects that had previously been considered off-limits, but that were clearly important aspects of the human experience. Such subjects included play, humor, love, aesthetics, personal values, and spiritual growth, among others.

Client-centered therapy   Carl Rogers was another member of the humanistic movement who helped change the face of American psychology. In the 1950s, he described a new therapeutic approach that he named client-centered therapy. This approach called for the therapist to show congruence, empathetic understanding, and unconditional positive regard. Congruence meant that the therapist would be honest and willing to express his or her true feelings. Empathetic understanding meant that the therapist would really listen to the client (not patient) and then share his or her understanding of what the client had communicated. Unconditional positive regard meant that the therapist would respect the client as an individual and accept whatever the client had to say.

The therapist's job, in short, was to create an atmosphere that was conducive to change. However, responsibility for the change itself rested squarely on the client. Rogers had great faith in people's ability to take control of their own lives. His ideas still affect the way that psychotherapy is conducted today.

Humanistic psychology gave rise to the human potential movement of the 1960s and 1970s. People were encouraged to get in touch with their inner selves and realize their potential through such activities as encounter groups, meditation, and communing with nature. At the time, these were considered fringe activities, more suitable to hippie communes than middle-class living rooms. Today, however, they have gone mainstream along with the notion that people should strive for self-knowledge and personal fulfillment.

Social psychology

Race and gender   Humanistic psychology placed individual fulfillment above all else. However, humans are also social creatures who are influenced by those around them. Social psychology, which looks at the way that individuals are affected by social trends and events, provided another valuable perspective on the human condition.

Social psychologists study a wide range of topics, including societal norms, group conflicts, obedience to authority, and social roles. In addition, they have made key contributions to the study of race and gender issues. Such issues came to the forefront of psychology after World War II. Even before that, however, American psychologist Kenneth Clark had conducted studies of racial identity and self-concept. In a famous study from the late 1930s, Clark and his wife found that African American preschoolers preferred white dolls to black ones. Clark went on to become the first African American president of the APA in 1971.

In the area of gender studies, social psychologist Sandra Bem has challenged widely held notions about what it means to be male or female. Bem is best known for the Bem Sex Role Inventory, a popular scale for measuring how well a person conforms to traditional sex-role stereotypes. Historically, masculinity and femininity were viewed as opposite poles on a single dimension. However, research in the 1970s showed that masculinity and femininity were actually two separate traits. Bem used her scale to classify individuals of either sex as high in masculinity only, high in femininity only, high in both traits, or low in both.

Social-cognitive theory   Another important topic in social psychology is observational learning, in which people learn to do something merely by watching others, without performing the behavior themselves or being directly rewarded for it. Pioneering work in this area was done by Canadian-born psychologist Albert Bandura of Stanford University. In the 1960s, Bandura conducted classic studies that looked at how observational learning affected aggressive behavior in children. A group of children were shown a film in which an adult punched, hammered, and kicked an inflatable doll, called a Bobo doll. These children were more likely to behave aggressively themselves when given a chance to play with the doll later. More than 40 years later, this research is still very relevant to the ongoing debate over violence in the media.

Bandura's Bobo doll experiments contained elements of both social psychology and learning theory. In the intervening years, Bandura has cast an even wider net in his research and theoretical interests. In the 1980s, he put forth a social-cognitive theory of human functioning that added elements of cognitive psychology, an approach that many consider to be the dominant school of psychology today. According to social-cognitive theory, human functioning results from the interplay of three forces: personal factors (such as thoughts, feelings, and physical states), the environment, and behavior. Cognition, or thought, plays a big role in people's ability to effectively manage their own responses to other people and the environment as a whole.

Cognitive psychology

Cognitive development   Psychologists have long been fascinated by cognitive processes, such as thought, perception, memory, and attention. Many noted psychologists, including G. Stanley Hall and Kurt Koffka, theorized about the development of such processes in children. However, no name became more closely linked to the study of cognitive development than that of Swiss psychologist Jean Piaget.

In the 1930s, Piaget developed his stage theory of child development. Piaget believed that infants were born with simple cognitive structures, called schemas. As children matured, they built new schemas on the existing ones. Piaget also described two mental processes for dealing with new information: assimilation and accommodation. If a new experience fit the child's existing schemas, then it was assimilated, or taken into the mind. On the other hand, if the experience did not match existing schemas, the schemas were altered to accommodate the perceived reality.

Piaget believed that cognitive development passed through four stages: sensorimotor, preoperational, concrete operational, and formal operational. Later research has not always supported Piaget's descriptions of the stages in every specific detail. Nevertheless, Piaget's general concepts are still quite influential. It is now widely accepted that the mind of a young child differs from that of an older child or adult not only in the quantity of knowledge, but also in the quality of the thought processes.

While Piaget also wrote about the development of moral reasoning, it was American psychologist Lawrence Kohlberg who became the most influential figure in that field. According to Kohlberg's theory, there were three stages of moral development: preconventional, conventional, and postconventional. At the lowest stage, moral behavior was motivated by punishments or rewards. At the next stage, it was motivated by social rules. At the highest stage, however, people's moral behavior was guided by ethical principles that had become internalized.

Personal constructs   Yet another take on the structure of the mind was offered by American psychologist George Kelly. In the 1950s, he put forth a personal construct theory, which stated that people construct their own theories about human behavior as they actively work to understand the world around them. As Kelly saw it, we are all personality theorists, developing a set of ideas for explaining and predicting our own behavior and that of other people.

Kelly's work foreshadowed some of the most important themes in modern cognitive and personality psychology. In recent decades, increasing attention has been paid to individual explanatory styles, or the habitual ways that people interpret the events in their lives. For example, some researchers have compared people with an optimistic explanatory style to those with a pessimistic one. In related research, Bandura has stressed the importance of self-efficacy beliefs, or people's beliefs about how capably they will be able to perform a specific behavior in a particular situation.

Cognitive therapy   Cognitive theory has also produced a popular form of psychotherapy, known as cognitive therapy. Originally developed by American psychiatrist Aaron Beck in the 1960s to treat depression, it has since been applied to a wide range of emotional and behavioral problems. Among other things, cognitive therapy has been used to treat chronic stress, anxiety disorders, substance abuse, marital conflicts, and personality disorders.

The basic concept behind cognitive therapy is that people's feelings and behaviors are influenced by how they perceive situations. When people are in distress, their thoughts may be irrationally negative or otherwise distorted. Cognitive therapy aims to help people identify distorted thinking patterns and replace irrational thoughts with more rational ones. In practice, cognitive therapy is often combined with behavior therapy in what is called cognitive-behavioral therapy.

Now and then   In the second half of the twentieth century, some cognitive researchers began using concepts from computer science to explain information processing inside the human brain. They soon discovered that the metaphor of the brain as computer could only be taken so far. It became apparent that there were fundamental differences between the inners workings of the human brain and those of computers. Nevertheless, the combination of cognitive psychology and computer science has led to some fruitful models for describing how information is processed within the brain.

In the twentieth-first century, cognitive psychology continues to evolve. Physiology is once again at the forefront of psychology, thanks to the development of sophisticated brain imaging technology that allows scientists to study the structure and function of the brain as never before. Such advanced technology is already providing fresh insights into age-old questions, such as how humans perceive sensory information, store information in memory, and use information to make decisions and solve problems. Such findings have recently given rise to a high-tech specialty known as cognitive neuroscience.

It is interesting to note that this technological specialty has a pedigree going all the way back to psychology's earliest days. Wundt and Wertheimer, among others, used what were then cutting-edge tech-niques to study mental processes such as perception, memory, and thought. It seems that the science of psychology keeps returning to the same traditional themes with the latest tools and techniques. The complexities of thought, feeling, and behavior will undoubtedly remain a never-ending source of fascina-tion and investigation.

Linda Wasmer Andrews, M.S.

Chronology

1832: Wilhelm Wundt born in Neckarau, Baden, Germany, outside of Leipzig, on August 16.

1849: Ivan Pavlov born in the village of Ryazan, Russia.

1852: Napoleon III founded the Second Empire in France.

1856: Sigismund Freud is born (changes his name to Sigmund at age 22).

1857: Alfred Binet born on July 8 in Nice, France.

1857: Louis Pasteur introduces his germ theory of fermentation.

1857: Wilhelm Wundt begins a seven-year position as lecturer in physiology at Heidelberg. During this time he serves as an assistant Hermann von Helmholtz.

1859: Charles Darwin presents his theory of evolution in *On the Origin of Species*.

1861–65: The Civil War is fought in the United States.

1864: Wilhelm Wundt appointed associate professor in physiology at University of Heidelberg.

1870–71: Prussia defeats France in the Franco-Prussian War. The Third Republic is founded in France.

1873: Sigmund Freud receives a summa cum laude award on graduation from the Gymnasium. He is already able to read in several languages.

1873–74: Wilhelm Wundt publishes first edition of *Principles of Psychology*.

1875: Carl Jung born in a country parsonage at Kesswil in Canton Thurgau, Switzerland.

1875: Wilhelm Wundt appointed one of two fellow professors at Leipzig University, focusing on practical-scientific theories.

1876: Robert Yerkes born on May 26 in Breadysville, Pennsylvania.

1876: Alexander Graham Bell patents the telephone.

1877: Sigmund Freud joins Brücke's laboratory.

1878: Alfred Binet receives a license in law, a career he chose not to pursue.

1879: Ivan Pavlov graduates from the Medical Academy; wins a gold medal in student competition.

1879: Wilhelm Wundt established the first laboratory for experimental psychology.

1880: Max Wertheimer born on April 15, 1880, in Prague.

1880: Alfred Binet publishes his first article, "On the Fusion of Similar Sensations."

1881: Sigmund Freud awarded a delayed doctor's degree in medicine.

1883–84: Wilhelm Wundt's laboratory receives official status at Leipzig as an institution of its department of philosophy.

1884: Francis Galton sets up a laboratory in London to measure individual differences in mental abilities.

1884: Sigmund Freud discovers the analgesic properties of cocaine.

1885: Karen Horney is born outside Hamburg, Germany.

1886: Alfred Binet publishes his first book, *The Psychology of Reasoning.*

1886: Sigmund Freud starts private practice.

1887: Sigmund Freud starts using hypnosis.

1890: Kurt Lewin born in Germany, now a part of Poland.

1890: James McKeen Cattell publishes a paper in which he coined the term "mental test."

1894: Alfred Binet receives a doctoral degree in natural science from the Sorbonne.

1895: Alfred Binet helps found the first French psychological journal.

1896: Sigmund Freud for the first time uses the term "psychoanalysis."

1896: Wilhelm Wundt dies in Groábothen, German, near Leipzig, August 31. His book, *Outlines of Psychology,* was published the same year.

1896: Alfred Binet publishes a paper outlining "individual psychology" with Victor Henri.

1896: Jean Piaget born in Neuchatel, Switzerland.

1897: Ivan Pavlov publishes "Lectures on the Work of the Main Digestive Glands."

1897: Sigmund Freud postulates Oedipus complex.

1898: Marie and Pierre Curie discovered the element radium.

1899: Alfred Binet began working with Théodore Simon.

1899: Sigmund Freud's *The Interpretation of Dreams* is published on November 4.

1900: After finishing medical school at the University of Basel, Carl Jung travels to Zurich to study psychiatry under Eugen Bleuler, a world-famous expert on schizophrenia.

1900: Gregor Mendel's basic laws of heredity, which went unnoticed when first set forth in the 1860s, are rediscovered.

1900–09: Carl Jung works as a psychiatric resident at the Burghölzli, a famous mental hospital in Zurich.

1900–20: Wilhelm Wundt's *Volkerpsychologie (Folk Psychology)* published in 10 volumes.

1901: Guglielmo Marconi sends the first long-wave radio signals across the Atlantic Ocean.

1902: Robert Yerkes receives a PhD in psychology from Harvard and begins teaching comparative psychology at Harvard.

1902: Sigmund Freud begins the Wednesday Psychological Society meetings at his home.

1902: Carl Rogers is born in Oak Park, Illinois.

1903: The Wright Brothers make the first successful airplane flight.

1904: Max Wertheimer receives his doctorate in philosophy at the University of Würzburg.

1904: Ivan Pavlov awarded the Nobel Prize in Physiology or Medicine.

1904: B.F. Skinner born March 20.

1905: George Alexander Kelly born on a farm near Perth, Kansas.

1905: Alfred Binet, along with Theodore Simon, introduces the first version of the Binet-Simon Scale.

1905: Albert Einstein publishes his special theory of relativity.

1906: Carl Jung publishes a book on schizophrenia that applies Sigmund Freud's psychoanalytic approach to the study of psychosis.

1906: Carl Jung starts his correspondence with Sigmund Freud.

1906: Jean Piaget publishes first article in local journal.

1908: Anne Anastasi born on December 19 in New York City.

1908: Robert Yerkes publishes the Yerkes-Dodson law, developed with John Dodson, which related the strength of a stimulus to the speed of avoidance learning.

1908: Abraham Maslow born in Manhattan.

1909: Publication of Sigmund Freud's *Analysis of a Phobia in a Five-Year-Old Boy (Little Hans).*

1909: Carl Jung travels with Sigmund Freud to the United States to give lectures at Clark University in Massachusetts.

1910: Max Wertheimer discovers the phi phenomenon on a train ride and published his groundbreaking paper "Experimental Studies of the Perception of Movement" two years later.

1910: Construction of Ivan Pavlov's "Towers of Silence" begins.

1911: Marie Curie wins her second Nobel Prize for her discovery and study of radium.

1911: Robert Yerkes founds the *Journal of Animal Behavior,* the first U.S. scientific journal devoted solely to animal behavior research.

1911: Alfred Binet makes the last revision of the Binet-Simon Scale. Dies on October 18.

1912: The ocean liner *Titanic* sinks after hitting an iceberg on her maiden voyage.

1913: Sigmund Freud publishes *Totem and Taboo.*

1913: Mary Salter (later Ainsworth) born in Glendale, Ohio.

1913: Carl Jung breaks with Sigmund Freud. Publishes *Psychology of the Unconscious,* the first account of his analytical psychology as an approach to therapy distinct from psychoanalysis.

1913–14: Carl Jung experiences a midlife crisis or period of psychological turmoil that resolves with the outbreak of World War I in July 1914.

1913–17: Robert Yerkes works half-time as a psychologist in the Psychopathic Department at Boston State Hospital.

1914: Kenneth Bancroft Clark born in Panama.

1914: Kurt Lewin volunteers to serve in World War I.

1914–18: World War I in Europe.

1915: Robert Yerkes introduces a point scale for measuring intelligence, developed with J. W. Bridges.

1916: Lewis Terman introduced the Stanford-Binet Intelligence Scales, a U.S. version of the Binet-Simon Scale that modified it substantially.

1917: The October Revolution occurs. The Bolsheviks take power, and Vladimir Lenin becomes new Soviet leader. The United States enters World War I.

1917: Kurt Lewin wounded in war.

1917: Robert Yerkes elected president of the American Psychological Association. Becomes a member of the National Research Council.

1917–18: Robert Yerkes chairs a committee that developed the U.S. Army Alpha and Beta intelligence tests during World War I.

1918: Jean Piaget receives PhD in Natural Sciences, University of Neuchatel. He works in Eugen Bleuler's psychiatric clinic at the University of Zurich and develops his technique of the clinical interview.

1919: Kenneth Bancroft Clark comes to America with mother and sister.

1919: Prohibition begins in the United States.

1919–24: Robert Yerkes works for the National Research Council.

1920: Women win the right to vote in the United States.

1920: Sigmund Freud publishes *Beyond the Pleasure Principle.*

1920: Wilhelm Wundt publishes autobiography entitled *Erlebtes und Erkanntes.*

1921: Sigmund Freud publishes *Group Psychology and the Analysis of the Ego.*

1921: Aaron Temkin Beck born in Providence, Rhode Island.

1921: Carl Jung publishes *Psychological Types,* a major work that secures his reputation as an original thinker.

1921: Jean Piaget appointed research director of the *Institut Jean-Jacques Rousseau* in Geneva, and publishes article in the *Archives de Psychologie* stating that logic is not innate but develops over time through interactive processes of self-regulation.

1923: Jean Piaget publishes *The Language and Thought of the Child.* Four more books follow, bringing him worldwide fame before the age of 30.

1923: Sigmund Freud diagnosed with cancer of the jaw. Publication of *The Ego and the Id.*

1924: The first Olympic Winter Games are played.

1924–44: Robert Yerkes holds a post as professor of psychobiology at Yale University.

1925: Jean Piaget begins the study of the intellectual development of his three children from infancy through their teenage years.

1925: Albert Bandura born on December 4, 1925, in Mundare, Alberta, Canada.

1925: Hitler publishes "Mein Kampf."

1926: Carl Brigham introduced the forerunner of the SAT.

1927: Lawrence Kohlberg born in Bronxville, New York.

1927: Ivan Pavlov publishes "Lectures on the Work of the Large Hemispheres of the Brain."

1928: Albert Einstein and Jean Piaget meet. Einstein suggests that Piaget study the origins in children of the notions of time and simultaneity.

1929: Stock market crash on Wall Street marks the beginning of the Great Depression.

1929: Robert Yerkes publishes *The Great Apes: A Study of Anthropoid Life*, coauthored with his wife, Ada Watterson Yerkes.

1929: Jean Piaget teaches the history of scientific thought at the University of Geneva until 1939. Begins 35-year tenure as director of the International Bureau of Education in Geneva.

1929–41: Robert Yerkes founds and directs the Yale Laboratories of Primate Biology, the first laboratory for nonhuman primate research in the United States.

1930: Anne Anastasi awarded a PhD from Columbia University. Hired as instructor of psychology at Barnard College.

1930: B.F. Skinner initiates research in reflexes.

1931: George Alexander Kelly receives his PhD from the University of Iowa.

1931–34: Abraham Maslow conducts primate research with Harry Harlow. Completes a masters thesis and doctoral dissertation on primate behavior.

1932: Karen Horney moves to United States.

1933: Kurt Lewin moves to United States to escape the rise of Hitler.

1933: Sigmund Freud has a letter exchange with Albert Einstein on the topic Why the War? The Nazis publicly burn Freud's work in Berlin.

1933: Adolf Hitler became dictator of Germany.

1934: Max Wertheimer arrives in New York and begins teaching at the "University in Exile" for the next 10 years.

1934: Kenneth Bancroft Clark earns his bachelor's degree from Howard University. Gains his master's the following year.

1934: Karen Horney takes teaching position at Washington-Baltimore Society for Psychoanalysis.

1935–37: Abraham Maslow completes postdoctoral fellowship at Columbia University. Research on sexuality and dominance in humans.

1936: Ivan Pavlov dies on February 27 after developing pneumonia at the age of 86.

1936: Karen Horney publishes *Feminine Psychology*.

1936: Jean Piaget publishes *The Origins of Intelligence in Children* based on his observations of his three children.

1937: Carl Jung invited by Yale University to deliver the Terry Lectures on psychology and religion.

1937: Anne Anastasi publishes her first major work, *Differential Psychology*, through Macmillan Publishing, New York.

1937–51: Abraham Maslow obtains a faculty position at Brooklyn College. Eventually reaches rank of associate professor.

1937–61: Carl Jung continues to practice medicine in Küssnacht, a suburb of Zurich, until his death in 1961.

1938: March 13th: Austria is annexed by Germany. Sigmund Freud's house and the headquarters of the Vienna Association of Psychoanalysis are searched. Anna Freud is arrested and interrogated by the Gestapo. In June, Freud and his family emigrate to Great Britain.

1938: B.F. Skinner's *The Behavior of Organisms* published.

1939: Mary Salter Ainsworth receives her PhD from the University of Toronto.

1939: Sigmund Freud dies. *Moses and Monotheism* is published.

1939: David Wechsler published the Wechsler Bellevue Scale, an adult-oriented intelligence test.

1939: Anne Anastasi appointed assistant professor of psychology and department chair, Queens College of the City University of New York.

1939–45: World War II in Europe.

1940: Jean Piaget appointed Chair of Experimental Psychology, University of Geneva (until 1971).

1940: Carl Rogers receives a full professorship at Ohio State University.

1941: The Japanese attack Pearl Harbor. The United States enters World War II.

1941–45: George Alexander Kelly serves during World War II as a Navy aviation psychologist, and teaches at the University of Maryland.

1942: B.F. Skinner awarded the Warren Medal by the Society of Experimental Psychologists.

1942: Jean Piaget lectures at the College of France during Nazi occupation. Lectures compiled into *The Psychology of Intelligence* published in 1963.

1942: Karen Horney publishes *Self-Analysis*.

1942: Mary D. Salter Ainsworth enters the Canadian Women's Army Corps.

1943: Max Wertheimer dies at his home after suffering a heart attack.

1944: Kurt Lewin invited to set up research institute at MIT.

1944: D-Day invasion occurs.

1945: United States drops the first atomic bombs. Liberation of the concentration camps in Europe.

1945: B.F. Skinner takes over the psychology department at the University of Indiana, where he developed the Teaching Machine and Aircrib.

1945: Mary D. Salter Ainsworth serves as Director of Women's Rehabilitation at Veteran Army Services Hospital.

1945: Carl Rogers joins faculty at the University of Chicago. Elected president of the American Psychological Association.

1945: Max Wertheimer publishes his only book, *Productive Thinking*.

1946: Aaron Temkin Beck graduates with a medical degree from Yale University.

1946: Mary D. Salter Ainsworth returns to University of Toronto to teach.

1946: George Alexander Kelly accepted the position as director of clinical programs for the school of psychology at the Ohio State University, following Carl Rogers.

1947: Kurt Lewin dies of heart attack.

1947: Anne Anastasi joins the faculty at Fordham University as associate professor, where she would be appointed to a full professorship in 1951.

1948: The state of Israel is founded and Gandhi is assassinated.

1948: B.F. Skinner's *Walden Two* published.

1949: NATO is established.

1949: David Wechsler introduced the Wechsler Intelligence Scale for Children.

1950: Kenneth Bancroft Clark publishes "Effect of Prejudice and Discrimination on Personality Development" for the Mid-Century White House Conference on Children and Youth.

1950: Mary D. Salter Ainsworth moves to London.

1950: Jean Piaget publishes his three volume book, *Introduction a l'epistemologie genetique*.

1951: Korean War breaks out. Aaron Temkin Beck takes a position at Valley Forge Field Hospital and treats soldiers with post-traumatic stress disorder.

1951–69: Abraham Maslow obtains a faculty position at Brandeis University. Serves as department chair until 1961.

1952: Polio vaccine is developed.

1952: Albert Bandura receives a PhD in clinical psychology from the University of Iowa.

1952: Karen Horney dies of stomach cancer at age 67.

1953: Albert Bandura takes a job as a psychology instructor at Stanford University.

1953: DNA is discovered.

1954: The publication of Abraham Maslow's *Motivation and Personality* brings national prominence.

1954: Mary Salter Ainsworth moves to Africa; starts Uganda mother-infant studies.

1954: *Brown v. Board of Education* uses Kenneth Bancroft Clark's studies as a basis for school desegregation.

1954: Anne Anastasi publishes *Psychological Testing*, Macmillan, New York.

1954: Aaron Temkin Beck joins the Department of Psychiatry of the University of Pennsylvania.

1955: Mary Salter Ainsworth hired as lecturer at Johns Hopkins in Baltimore.

1955: W. W. Norton & Company publishes George Alexander Kelly's groundbreaking, two-volume work, *The Psychology of Personal Constructs.*

1955: Jean Piaget's International Center for Genetic Epistemology opens at the University of Geneva.

1955: First edition of Kenneth Bancroft Clark's book *Prejudice and Your Child* published as Clark's first public scientific commentary.

1956: Fixed interval schedule of reinforcement described by B.F. Skinner.

1956: Robert Yerkes dies on February 3.

1957: The Soviet Union launches Sputnik, its first satellite, into Earth's orbit.

1958: Angelo Roncalli elected Pope; he takes the name John XXIII.

1958: Lawrence Kohlberg graduates from University of Chicago with a doctoral degree.

1959: Fidel Castro expels the dictator Fulgencio Batista and becomes premier of Cuba.

1959: Albert Bandura publishes his first book, *Adolescent Aggression*, with Richard Walters.

1959: Kenneth Bancroft Clark elected president of the Society for the Psychological Study of Social Issues.

1961: The first issue of *The Journal of Humanistic Psychology*, founded by Abraham Maslow, is published.

1961: Kenneth Bancroft Clark awarded the Spingarn Medal by the NAACP.

1961: The East German government builds the Berlin Wall. The Bay of Pigs Invasion occurs.

1962: Abraham Maslow publishes *Toward a Psychology of Being*.

1962: Mary D. Salter Ainsworth begins Baltimore replication study of mother-infant dyads.

1962–63: Abraham Maslow consults with Andy Kay at Non-Linear Systems.

1963: Albert Bandura publishes *Social Learning and Personality Development*, which summarized his research on observational learning and the Bobo doll experiments.

1963: President John F. Kennedy is assassinated while riding in a motorcade through Dallas.

1964: Carl Rogers elected "Humanist of the Year" by the American Humanist Association.

1964: Civil Rights Act passes in U.S. Congress.

1964: Albert Bandura becomes a full professor at Stanford.

1965: George Alexander Kelly begins research position at Brandeis University, where Abraham Maslow is also working at the time.

1965: Kenneth Bancroft Clark publishes *Dark Ghetto*.

1966: Abraham Maslow is elected president of the American Psychological Association.

1966: B.F. Skinner introduces the concept of critical period in reinforcing an event.

1966: Jean Piaget publishes *The Psychology of the Child* with Barbel Inhelder.

1967: Israelis fight the Six Days War.

1967: George Alexander Kelly dies on March 6.

1967: Mary Salter Ainsworth publishes *Infancy in Uganda*.

1968: Assassination of Martin Luther King, Jr.

1968: Lawrence Kohlberg becomes a full professor at Harvard University. Later founds the Center for Moral Devlopment and Education there.

1968: B.F. Skinner identifies the critical characteristics of programmed instruction.

1968: Robert Kennedy is assassinated.

1969: Lawrence Kohlberg studies moral development in an Israeli kibbutz.

1969: Jean Piaget awarded distinguished Scientific Contribution Award by the American Psychological Association. He is the first European to receive the award.

1969: The first human beings set foot on the Moon.

1970: Protesting students at Kent State University are shot.

1970: Carl Rogers' *On Encounter Groups* published. He would publish two more books before his death.

1970: Abraham Maslow dies of a heart attack at his home in Menlo Park, California.

1971: Lawrence Kohlberg coauthors "The Adolescent as Philosopher" with Carol Gilligan. Kohlberg also contracts a parasitic illness in Central America, which afflicts him for 16 years.

1971: Kenneth Bancroft Clark elected president of the American Psychological Association. Clark has been the only African American to serve in that capacity.

1971: B.F. Skinner publishes *Beyond Freedom and Dignity*.

1972: B.F. Skinner receives the Humanist of the Year Award by the American Humanist Association.

1972: Terrorists attack and kill athletes at the Munich Olympic games.

1973: Abortion is legalized in the United States.

1974: Kenneth Bancroft Clark publishes *Pathos of Power*.

1974: Albert Bandura serves as president of the American Psychological Association.

1974: Aaron Temkin Beck publishes *The Prediction of Suicide*.

1975: Mary Salter Ainsworth leaves Johns Hopkins for University of Virginia.

1975–95: Kenneth Bancroft Clark serves on the New York Board of Regents.

1976: North and South Viet Nam re-join.

1977: Albert Bandura publishes *Social Learning Theory*, which aroused interest in social learning and modeling.

1978: Mary D. Salter Ainsworth publishes *Patterns of Attachment*.

1979: Anne Anastasi named professor emeritus at Fordham.

1979: The Iranians under Khomeini take Americans as hostages.

1980: Jean Piaget dies at the age of 84 in Geneva, Switzerland.

1981: Sandra Day O'Connor becomes the first woman appointed to the United States Supreme Court.

1983: B.F. Skinner publishes *Enjoying Old Age*.

1984: The virus that causes AIDS is identified by two groups of scientists in France and the United States.

1984: Mary Salter Ainsworth retires from the University of Virginia as Professor Emeritus.

1985: Robert Sternberg presents his three-part theory of intelligence in *Beyond IQ*.

1986: The Challenger Space Shuttle explodes, killing all on board.

1986: Albert Bandura publishes *Social Foundations of Thought and Action: A Social Cognitive Theory*, which described his social-cognitive theory of human functioning.

1986: Carl Rogers travels to Russia to facilitate conflict resolution.

1987: Carl Rogers dies of heart attack.

1987: Lawrence Kohlberg commits suicide by drowning in Winthrop, Massachusetts.

1988: Aaron Temkin Beck publishes *Love is Never Enough*.

1990: B.F. Skinner dies on August 18.

1992: President George Bush of the United States and President Boris Yeltsin of Russia jointly declare an end to the Cold War.

1994: Kenneth Bancroft Clark receives the APA Award for Outstanding Lifetime Contribution to Psychology.

1997: Albert Bandura publishes *Self-Efficacy: The Exercise of Control*, which set forth his ideas about self-efficacy beliefs.

1998: Mary Salter Ainsworth receives APA Gold Medal Award for Life Achievement in the Science of Psychology.

1999: Mary Salter Ainsworth dies in Charlottesville, Virginia.

2000: Yassir Arafat launches the second Palestinian intifada (uprising) against Israel.

2001: Anne Anastasi dies on May 4.

2003: Space shuttle *Columbia* explodes on reentry, killing the seven astronauts on board.

2004: 50th anniversary of *Brown v. Board of Education*. Kenneth Bancroft Clark and Mamie Phipps-Clark awarded honorary degrees from Earlham College to mark their "historic contributions to the cause of equal rights for all Americans."

2004: Aaron Temkin Beck publishes *Cognitive Therapy of Personal Disorders*, second edition.

Mary D. Salter Ainsworth

BRIEF OVERVIEW

If John Bowlby was the father of attachment theory, Mary Ainsworth could certainly be considered its mother. Together the two started a rich field of study that has changed the face of developmental psychology and profoundly influenced theories of parenting.

In brief, attachment theory is based on the concept that all infants have a fundamental need to develop a close relationship, or attachment, to their mother (or primary caregiver). They initiate attempts at attachment through attachment behaviors such as smiling at, hugging, and moving toward their caregiver. If the mother or caregiver answers consistently and appropriately with sensitive and responsive behavior such as comforting, holding, hugging, and stroking, the attachment bond is strengthened and secure. When responses are inconsistent, insensitive, or inappropriate, an insecure attachment is formed.

Although it was Ainsworth's London colleague John Bowlby who first theorized that there was something beyond the mother-infant bond than a fulfillment of basic physical needs (i.e., food and shelter), Ainsworth provided attachment theory with both the empirical data and the psychological scales and methods for validating Bowlby's hypotheses. She also further refined attachment theory with concepts such as mother as secure base and organizations of attachment.

Ainsworth pioneered the concept of longitudinal, systematic, yet naturalistic observation in the home.

1913–1999

CANADIAN DEVELOPMENTAL PSYCHOLOGIST

UNIVERSITY OF TORONTO, Ph.D., 1939

Mary Salter Ainsworth. (*Photo courtesy of Mary Salter Ainsworth.*

Reproduced by permission.)

Her field studies of mother-infant dyads and narrative data collection, first in Uganda and later in Baltimore, were unprecedented, although they were at first frequently criticized as having too "unscientific" a tone. Ainsworth's "strange situation" laboratory procedure is still used in developmental research today.

The "strange situation" technique involves a series of separations and reunions between an infant and his or her mother, which take place in a laboratory setting. A stranger is also introduced at several points in the protocol. As with all of Ainsworth's clinical studies, observers carefully monitor and transcribe how the procedure unfolds. The infant's reaction to the separation and behavior towards his or her mother upon reunion provides a framework for determining the type of attachment he or she has to the mother. Ainsworth had determined three main categories of infant attachment: secure, insecure-avoidant, and insecure-resistant.

Finally, throughout Ainsworth's lengthy academic and teaching career, she mentored dozens of students who would go on to make significant contributions to broadening the field of attachment theory in their own right. One of these, student Mary Main, summed up what made Ainsworth such a remarkable mentor:

First, she required rather than simply recommended independence on the part of her students, meaning that rather than utilizing her already-collected data for a thesis, each student had to design and carry out a complete project, bringing in their own research participants and drawing their own new conclusions. Second, she believed that a person's academic life was not the whole of their life, but only a portion. . . . Third, she wrote our better ideas down in an endeavor not to become confused later and think that she herself had come up with them. Fourth, she worked very hard on helping us with our work.

Her love of both teaching and research kept Ainsworth working well past her official retirement at age 80. She was a co-recipient of the APA's first mentoring award in 1998, the same year she was also honored with one of the APA's highest recognitions— the Gold Medal Award for Life Achievement in the Science of Psychology.

BIOGRAPHY

Mary Dinsmore Salter Ainsworth was born in Glendale, Ohio, in 1913, the oldest of three daughters of Charles and Mary Salter. Ainsworth showed a talent for academics early in life, reportedly learning to read at the age of three. The Salters valued education; both Charles and Mary were graduates of Dickinson College in Pennsylvania. Ainsworth recalls the weekly visits the family took to the library and the high academic expectations her parents had for all three of their girls to attend college.

Charles Morgan Salter was employed by a Cincinnati-based manufacturing firm, and when Ainsworth was five the family moved to Toronto after his company relocated him to a branch office. Her father eventually became branch President of Aluminum Goods, Ltd., and in 1931 Ainsworth and her parents became naturalized Canadian citizens.

Mary Main, a behavioral psychologist and student of Ainsworth's, recounts that Ainsworth described a contentious relationship with her mother that was characterized by her mother's interference in personal matters and jealousy of the closeness she had with her father. Ainsworth herself never commented publicly on any disharmony within the family, stating they were "a close-knit family, with a not unusual mixture of warmth and tensions and deficiencies."

Ainsworth excelled in school and entered the University of Toronto in 1929 at the age of 16, entering the psychology program in her second year. In an autobiographical essay published in the 1983 book *Models of Achievement: Reflections of Eminent Women in*

Psychology, Ainsworth recalls her first realization that she wanted to enter the field of psychology:

> When I was 15 and in my final year in high school, one of the books brought home was William McDougall's *Character and the Conduct of Life* (1927), which I read with great excitement. It had not previously occurred to me that one might look within oneself for some explanation of how one felt and behaved, rather than feeling entirely at the mercy of external forces. What a vista that opened up! I decided thereupon to become a psychologist.

Remaining at the University of Toronto for graduate school, Ainsworth earned her master's degree in 1936 and her Ph.D. in 1939. She worked as a teaching assistant to Professor Edward Bott, head of the Psychology Department and one of Ainsworth's mentors. Later, she would cite Bott as the influence who helped her develop the attitude that science is a "state of mind."

Another influential mentor during her graduate years was Professor William Blatz, who had developed a personality theory called security theory. Security theory was based on the idea that children who feel secure in their dependence on their parents are better equipped to adjust and cope with experiences in the outside world, because they are assured that their parent(s) will always be there for them. Those who are insecure in the parent-child relationship will not be as willing to act independently of their parents and explore the world around them.

As children grow into adults, the relationship evolves and the person(s) with whom they find security changes; children become less dependent on their parents and more on their peers, until as adults they become securely dependent on a spouse or partner. The concept of security theory would help to shape Ainsworth's later work in attachment theory in several important ways. With Blatz's guidance and urging, Ainsworth wrote her doctoral dissertation, "An Evaluation of Adjustment Based on the Concept of Security," which involved creating and testing new psychometric scales (or tests) for young adults that quantitatively evaluated their relationships with their parents and peers.

Ainsworth also credits Professor Sperrin Chant with shaping her future destiny as both a psychologist and later a teacher and mentor for her own students. Chant oversaw her master's thesis, an investigation into emotions and galvanic skin response (GSR). GSR is a measurement of the electrical properties of the skin, which change in response to stress and anxiety. It is one of the same technologies used in today's polygraph, or lie detector test. Ainsworth also coauthored a 1937 article with Chant on the topic in the *Journal of Educational Psychology* entitled "The Measurement of Attitude Toward War and the Galvanic Skin Response."

After completing her doctoral dissertation and graduating with a Ph.D., Ainsworth continued on at the University of Toronto as a lecturer beginning in the fall of 1939. Shortly thereafter with the advent of World War II, many of her Toronto colleagues and mentors left the University to assist in the war effort. Ainsworth herself joined them in 1942, enlisting in the Canadian Women's Army Corps. She first served as an army examiner in Kitchener, Ontario, using her background in psychology and personality development to work in personnel selection, which involved interviewing and assessing recruits and recommending a placement based on the results. After several months in Kitchener, Ainsworth transferred to Ottawa, where she attained the rank of major in less than a year. She also spent several months abroad working with the personnel service of the British Army.

At the conclusion of the war, Ainsworth was tapped for a post at the Department of Veteran's Affairs. She served as the Superintendent for Women's Rehabilitation for about a year, and then, longing to return to her alma mater and tiring of the heavy load of administrative work her position required, she accepted a post as assistant professor at the University of Toronto, teaching introductory psychology and experimental psychology to undergrad students.

In preparation for teaching a graduate-level course on personality assessments, Ainsworth began to study psychometric and neuropsychiatric tests—including the Rorschach (i.e., 'inkblot test') and the thematic apperception test (TAT)—in earnest, taking several workshops and volunteering her clinical services at the local Department of Veterans Affairs hospital. She took several workshops with well-known psychologist Bruno Klopfer, who had developed a scoring and administration technique for the Rorschach. Ainsworth would later collaborate with Klopfer on the revision of his book on the subject, *Developments in the Rorschach Technique: Vol. 1.*

Over the next several years Ainsworth taught and, along with mentor William Blatz, co-directed a research team developing psychological testing scales associated with Blatz's security theory. In 1950, she married one of the graduate students on that team, Leonard Ainsworth, and the newlyweds moved to London, where Leonard had been accepted at University College to do his doctoral work after receiving his master's degree at Toronto.

A former colleague of Ainsworth's from her days in the Canadian armed services told her about a

PRINCIPAL PUBLICATIONS

- "The Effects of Maternal Deprivation: A review of findings and controversy in the context of research strategy." *Deprivation of Maternal Care: A Reassessment of its Effects.* World Health Organization, Public Health Papers 14 (1962): 97–165.

- With J. Bowlby. *Child Care and the Growth of Love,* 2nd ed. London: Penguin, 1965.

- *Infancy in Uganda: Infant Care and the Growth of Love.* Baltimore: Johns Hopkins University Press, 1967.

- With S. M. Bell. "Attachment, Exploration, and Separation: Illustrated by the behavior of one-year-olds in a strange situation." *Child Development* 41: 49–67, 1970.

- With M. C. Blehar, E. Waters, and S. Walls. *Patterns of Attachment: A Psychological Study of the Strange Situation.* Hillsdale, NJ: Lawrence Erlbaum, 1978.

- "Attachments Beyond Infancy." *American Psychologist* 44 (1989): 709–16.

- With J. Bowlby. "An Ethological Approach to Personality Development." *American Psychologist* 46 (1991): 331–41.

research position at London's Tavistock Clinic under Dr. John Bowlby, who was investigating the impact of early separation from one's mother on childhood personality development (see sidebar). Ainsworth was hired, marking the beginning of a lifelong professional association with Bowlby, and worked at Tavistock through the end of 1953 while her husband Leonard completed his Ph.D.

The Ainsworths moved to Africa in 1954 after Leonard was hired as a research psychologist at the East African Institute of Social Research in Kampala, Uganda. It was here where Ainsworth performed observational studies on infant-mother interaction and gathered the data that would later become her landmark book *Infancy in Uganda.*

In 1955 Leonard Ainsworth landed a position in Baltimore, Maryland as a forensic psychologist, and Ainsworth quickly found an appointment as a lecturer at Johns Hopkins and a part-time clinical psychologist at Sheppard and Enoch Pratt Hospital.

Mary and Leonard Ainsworth divorced in 1960. Ainsworth continued to work in earnest, but as a result of what she called "a depressive reaction to divorce," she also entered long-term personal psychoanalysis. Retrospectively, Ainsworth credits her eight years of psychoanalysis as improving her productivity and exposing her to Freudian theory that expanded her knowledge and understanding as a psychologist.

Looking for an opportunity to delve back into research, Ainsworth shifted focus at Johns Hopkins, leaving the part-time clinical work at the hospital in 1961 and becoming first an associate professor and then a full professor in developmental psychology. In 1962 Ainsworth embarked on what is perhaps her most significant and influential contribution to developmental psychology—short-term longitudinal research into the development of infant-mother attachment sometimes referred to as "the Baltimore study."

Ainsworth and her research team went into the homes of 26 area women and observed their interaction with their infants in approximate four-hour blocks every three weeks, totaling up to 80 hours on observation over the first year of life. The method built on her previous work in Uganda. In fact, the Baltimore study was designed as a "replication" study for the Uganda work, to validate its findings. But the experience would prove to broaden the scope of that study and ultimately spur Ainsworth to develop one of attachment theory's most useful clinical tools—the "strange situation" technique.

Although her observations of the maternal-infant relationship were quite astute, Ainsworth herself never had any children of her own. This was more a factor of timing than anything else; she often spoke of her wish to have become a mother herself, but she married late (at age 37) and divorced a decade later. Ainsworth never remarried, and according to student Mary Main, her next serious relationship didn't occur until she was in her 80s.

After over a decade at Johns Hopkins, Ainsworth was nearing the usual retirement age at that institution (60) but was as professionally productive as ever. After investigating her options, she moved on to the University of Virginia in the fall of 1975 as a visiting professor. There she helped to develop the University's psychology training program, which gave students the opportunity to do clinical casework under supervision.

The Mary D. Ainsworth Psychological Clinic continues to provide mental health services to the University of Virginia community today.

Ainsworth retired in the capacity of professor emeritus in 1984, but remained active in research until the early 1990s, coauthoring several more papers with Bowlby and others and providing the assistance of her own insight and opinions on the attachment research of her former students and colleagues. She was awarded two of the APA's highest honors in 1998—the Mentor Award in Developmental Psychology and the Gold Medal Award for Life Achievement in the Science of Psychology. Ainsworth lived the remainder of her life in Charlottesville, Virginia, where she died in 1999 after a lengthy illness following a stroke.

In addition to the APA awards, Ainsworth was bestowed with numerous honors, awards, and official appointments throughout her career, including: Distinguished Contribution Award, Maryland Psychological Association (1973); President of the Society for Research in Child Development (1977–79); Distinguished Scientific Contribution Award, Virginia Psychological Association (1983); Distinguished Scientific Contribution Award, Division 12, APA (1984); G. Stanley Hall Award, Division 7, APA (1984); Salmon Lecturer, Salmon Committee on Psychiatry and Mental Hygiene, New York Academy of Medicine (1984); William T. Grant Lecturer in Behavioral Pediatrics, Society for Behavioral Pediatrics (1985); Award for Distinguished Contributions to Child Development Research, Society for Research in Child Development (1985); Award for Distinguished Professional Contribution to Knowledge, APA (1987); C. Anderson Aldrich Award in Child Development, American Academy of Pediatrics (1987); Distinctive Achievement Award, Virginia Association for Infant Mental Health (1989); Honorary Fellowship, Royal College of Psychiatrists (1989); Distinguished Scientific Contribution Award, APA (1989); American Academy of Arts and Sciences (1992); Distinguished Professional Contribution Award, Division 12, APA (1994); and International Society for the Study of Personal Relationships Distinguished Career Award (1996).

THEORIES

Mary Ainsworth's work in attachment theory had its roots in her research with John Bowlby at Tavistock. Bowlby and another colleague, James Robertson, first introduced her to the naturalistic method of observation and descriptive statistics that would later become her trademark.

Before Bowlby, the prevailing view among psychologists and psychoanalysts was that infants bonded with their mothers simply because the mother fed the child and met his or her physical needs. Bowlby was also a maverick in his belief that evolutionary and ethological theory both influenced personality development and the attachment process (see sidebar). Ethology, or the study of animal (and human) behavior and adaptation in natural surroundings, particularly influenced Ainsworth's work. While Ainsworth initially questioned the place of ethology in attachment formation, she later came to embrace the idea. Bowlby's theory of attachment was based on the idea that a child's development is tied closely to the bond he or she has with the mother, which was ultimately either a secure or an insecure one. From an ethological standpoint, attachment was necessary for infant survival—the mother being the source of the infant's food, security, and shelter.

Ainsworth took Bowlby's theories and put them to the empirical test, using innovative new field and laboratory techniques to do so. Along the way, she refined attachment theory further and contributed the concept of infant defense systems, mother as secure base, and organizations or patterns of attachment.

Patterns of attachment
Main points   Central to Ainsworth's work on attachment is the concept of mother as "a secure base." As early as 1940, influenced by mentor William Blatz and his security theory, she wrote about the essential role of family security to provide a secure base for individual growth. Later, in her writings on the Uganda home studies, she describes infants using their mothers as a secure base for their own exploration. The secure child is able to leave his or her mother's side and investigate surroundings because he or she knows through experience that the mother is there if needed.

Ainsworth's home studies of mother-infant dyads (i.e., couples) first in Uganda and then in Baltimore were unique in that they were longitudinal (i.e., longterm; nine months for Uganda and 12 months for Baltimore), and used carefully compiled narrative data gathered by trained observers over a substantial amount of home visit time (i.e., an average of 72 hours over one year in Baltimore).

Ainsworth's Uganda studies found three classifications or patterns of infant attachment—secure, insecure, or non-attached. Later, in her Baltimore replication studies, she refined the classifications based on additional data from the "strange situation" laboratory procedure, resulting in three categories—secure, avoidant (also called anxious-avoidant or insecure-avoidant), and resistant (also called anxious-resistant or insecure-ambivalent/resistant).

Avoidant infants (a.k.a. Group A) became focused on exploration to the exclusion of all else (including mother) in the strange situation environment. At home, however, they were anxious and often angry, and wouldn't tolerate separation from their mother, who rejected their advances through her words and actions. Ainsworth explained that the seemingly incongruous exploratory behavior of avoidant infants in the strange situation setting was a defensive (or adaptive) reaction to their life experience of their mother's rejection. She outlined specific qualities of maternal behavior that were associated with avoidant attachments—rejection, physical rejection (i.e., pulling away from kisses or hugs), submerged anger (i.e., holding anger in), and a lack of awareness of infant cues.

Secure infants (a.k.a. Group B) were those with the strongest mother-infant attachment. They considered their mother what Ainsworth called a secure base, meaning that they would return to her for reassurance and comfort while they explored both familiar and unfamiliar environments. They were happy and responsive to her, and did not become upset during brief separations in the home environment. However, they did experience separation anxiety when put in the strange situation environment, but they were easily calmed and reinvolved in exploration once the mother returned.

Resistant infants (a.k.a. Group C) tended to cling to their mothers and become overly preoccupied with her whereabouts in the strange situation environment. They also avoided exploration in her absence. Ainsworth theorized this was due to the mother's insensitive and inconsistent reactions to the child at home. These children either became unusually distant and detached (i.e., ambivalent) or expressed anger (i.e., resistant) in the home environment.

Ainsworth saw all of these attachment patterns as the result of defensive behaviors formed through the child's life experience with the mother (or other attachment figure). She developed a series of scales that rated maternal behavior in four areas: sensitivity vs. insensitivity to infant signals, cooperation vs. interference with ongoing behavior, psychological and physical availability vs. neglect, and acceptance vs. rejection of infant's needs. Based on these scales, secure infants had mothers who scored high in sensitivity, cooperation, availability, and acceptance.

Explanation   In *Infancy in Uganda*, Ainsworth first describes attachment behaviors in infants that are cues

for maternal response. They include smiling, crying, adjusting posture, suckling, looking at the mother, listening to the mother, vocalizing in response to her voice, "scrambling" (i.e., climbing) over her, moving nearer, following her, and clinging to her. Ainsworth is quite clear in explaining that these behaviors are not signs of attachment in and of themselves:

> They are the patterns of behavior *through which attachment grows*. The baby is not attached to anyone at first. He does not somehow become attached and *then* show it by smiling at the loved person and crying when she leaves him. He gradually becomes attached.

In other words, secure attachment isn't inherent at birth, but develops through an interplay of infant cues and maternal response.

In everyday encounters with new experiences, the mother acts as what Ainsworth called the secure base for the child. For children with a secure attachment, the mother serves as a provider of safety and comfort, whom the child can turn to for help in situations where he or she feels in danger (such as when the stranger enters in the strange situation protocol.) Having access to a secure base also allows the infant to engage in exploratory behavior, with the knowledge that his or her mother will be there to help if needed. Again, whether or not the child perceives the mother as a secure base depends on their interaction and whether the child's attachment behavior is responded to. Ainsworth believed the first year of life was most crucial in this relationship.

Infants who do not have a secure base, and therefore don't have a strong and secure attachment with their mother or primary caregiver, won't explore their surroundings as readily as secure children and therefore miss out on important cognitive stimuli, or "hands on" learning experiences. Insecure attachment in infancy has been linked to later problems in childhood and adolescence, including conduct disorder, anxiety disorders, and reactive attachment disorder. In addition, stress associated with insecure attachments has been shown to negatively impact neurological development of the limbic system of the brain and can also trigger the chronic release of potentially damaging stress hormones.

Ainsworth's patterns or classifications of attachment were developed from two main data sources—home visits to the mother-infant study subjects, and a laboratory-based procedure she developed known as the strange situation method.

The strange situation protocol measured infant attachment behavior by exposing an infant to a series of separations and reunions from its mother, performed in a laboratory. It was originally designed for children

FURTHER ANALYSIS:

Setting up the strange situation

Mary Ainsworth developed the strange situation protocol with the assistance of colleague and clinical psychologist Barbara Wittig in 1969. The technique was first used on 23 of the 26 mother-infant pairs involved in Ainsworth's Baltimore studies, right around the time of each infant's first birthday. In brief, the strange situation is a 20-minute test that brings an infant into an unfamiliar laboratory environment with an array of new and interesting toys, and exposes him or her to a series of separations from and reunions with the mother.

Initially, the procedure was created as a litmus test for secure attachment of one-year-olds. The goal was two-fold: first, the test would observe a child's exploratory behaviors with the new toys in an unfamiliar environment; secondly, it would assess the nature of attachment the child was thought to have to his mother based on his reactions to a stressful situation (i.e., being separated from his mother).

John Bowlby's evolution-based theory of human attachment as a survival mechanism influenced the creation of Ainsworth's strange situation. Bowlby believed that secure attachments are created by necessity; infants develop proximity-seeking behavior towards their mother because she provides protection against danger. Ainsworth incorporated stressors into the protocol that had been identified by colleague John Bowlby as cues to danger (much like predators) that would activate attachment behavior in infants—an unfamiliar environment (i.e., the lab where the strange situation takes place) and separation from the mother. A third stressor, the entrance of a stranger, was also added.

Ainsworth also had great interest in the work of Harry Harlow, a University of Wisconsin research psychologist who had published a provocative study on the role of emotion and attachment in rhesus monkeys in 1961. Harlow had placed infant monkeys in cages with fabricated "surrogate" mothers. When given the choice of a cold, wire wrapped "mother" that was equipped with a bottle of food, and a soft, cloth wrapped "mother" that had none, the infants preferred snuggling with the latter. His finding flew in the face of conventional psychological beliefs that the mother-infant relationship was built solely on the basis of the mother satisfying physical drives for hunger and other basic needs.

Harlow's work foreshadowed Ainsworth's strange situation results in his subsequent discovery that infant monkeys would use their cloth surrogate mother as a secure base from which to explore frightening or unusual stimuli that were introduced to their environment. Ainsworth would report the same behaviors in securely attached infants in her 1978 work, *Patterns of Attachment: A Psychological Study of the Strange Situation*, co-authored with Mary Blehar, Sally Wall, and Everett Waters. The book analyzed the findings of four separate studies involving a total of 106 infants placed in the strange situation. Ainsworth combined this data with information gathered from extensive home observations of the infants to classify them as either securely attached, insecure-avoidant, or insecure-resistant.

---

up to one year of age, although later refinements pushed the age limit to 18 months.

In the procedure, a mother and baby are brought into a room that contains a variety of new toys. Over a period of approximately 20 minutes, the child is periodically separated from the mother, left with a stranger, and then reunited with his mother. Observers gauge the infant's interest in the toys, reaction to separation and reunion, and interaction with the stranger.

The strange situation technique uses the following protocol:

- Mother, baby, and observer enter the room (30 seconds).

- Observer leaves and mother lets baby explore toys and surroundings (three minutes).

- Stranger enters the room quietly, converses with the mother, and then approaches the baby while the mother leaves (three minutes).

- Stranger remains with the baby (three minutes).

- Mother enters and stranger leaves, mother interests baby in the toys again (three minutes).

- Mother says goodbye to baby and leaves baby alone (three minutes).

- Stranger enters and visits with baby (three minutes).

- Mother returns and picks baby up and stranger leaves quietly (three minutes).

How the child deals with the separations, his or her response to the stranger and the mother, and his or her willingness to explore the unfamiliar surroundings and use mother as a secure base are observed, and provide insight into the relationship between mother and child and their pattern of attachment.

Ainsworth devised a scoring system that examined six dimensions of behavior in the infant:

- *Proximity-seeking and contact-seeking behavior.* Child moves close to the mother or seeks physical contact with her (i.e., grabbing her hand).

- *Contact-maintaining behavior.* Clinging, getting back up on lap after being set down.

- *Avoidance.* Ignoring mother and/or stranger.

- *Resistance.* Squirming away from, hitting, pushing away adult-initiated contact.

- *Searching.* Looking around for the mother, approaching the door after she leaves the room, staring or approaching her empty chair.

- *Distance interaction.* Smiling across the room, vocalizing to the mother or stranger.

Based on the scoring criteria from these measurements, infant attachments are categorized as avoidant, secure, or resistant.

While Ainsworth performed some of the Baltimore home visits herself, she also sent many graduate and undergrad students out as trained observers. She required her students to make an advance visit to mother-infant pairs to clearly explain the nature of the research, and obtain informed consent. All observers were carefully trained to recognize and document attachment behaviors. Throughout her career, Ainsworth believed in the absolute value of this type of home-visit field work, and expressed disdain for strange situation studies that didn't include an account of additional home observation.

Examples   In her narratives of the Uganda mother-child pairs, Ainsworth offered some illustrative cases of secure and insecure attachment relationships. William was one memorable example of a securely attached child.

> William was the youngest of 10 children, and there was also a foster child. The mother, single-handed, had reared all of these children, grown their food and prepared it, made many of their clothes, and looked after a large mud and wattle house, which was tastefully decorated and graced by a flower garden. She was a relaxed, serene person, who could talk to us in an unhurried way, devote time to playful, intimate

interchange with William, and also concern herself with the other children according to their needs. . . . She used a wheelbarrow as a pram, and there lay William, nested amid snowy white cotton cloths. The wheelbarrow could be moved from place to place—out to the garden where his mother worked, or under the shade tree where the other children were playing, and never out of the earshot of some responsible person.

In contrast, Ainsworth offers this description of an insecure infant.

> Sulaimani's mother was a slip of a girl, still in her teens. This was her first baby, and both she and he were unhappy. She had to do most of the garden work, but had no satisfactory arrangement for Sulaimani's care while she was gone. He cried so much that his mother was at her wit's end, and could not behave consistently. Sometimes she was tender and indulgent, and sometimes she was rough and angry in the way she picked him up, slung him over her back, and rocked him. Sometimes she just let him cry and cry.

Mothers who form secure attachments with their infants tend to be at ease and secure in their own life relationships. Long-term research has indicated that those infants who start life with secure attachments are more likely to perpetuate the behavior when they have children of their own. Conversely, those with insecure attachments in childhood often grow up to form insecure attachments with their children unless they are able to develop healthier attachment relationships later in life and in adulthood.

HISTORICAL CONTEXT

The very fact that Mary Ainsworth entered the University of Toronto at age 16 was a testament to her remarkable will and intelligence. For it wasn't until that year (1929) that Canada would recognize women officially and by law as "persons" and grant them the right to serve in the Senate. Fortunately Ainsworth had chosen a more progressive institution for her studies; the University of Toronto's Psychology Department was known for its large number of female graduate students and equal treatment of both genders. While the University opened its doors to women many years earlier (1884), all of its facilities would not be fully accessible to women until as late as the 1970s.

The advent of World War II did allow a number of prominent women in psychology the opportunity to move into important and high-profile academic and clinical positions as men left to contribute to the war effort. Although Ainsworth initially stayed at the University of Toronto and continued her work there, she soon followed the path of her male colleagues. Interestingly,

BIOGRAPHY:

John Bowlby

Mary Ainsworth's colleague and friend, John Bowlby (1907–1990), is considered the father of attachment theory. He strongly believed that a child's personality development was influenced heavily by early home experiences. At a time when other developmental psychologists and psychoanalysts described the mother's relationship with her child as one of meeting physical drives, Bowlby's idea that infants would form secure family relationships and feel confident enough to explore their surroundings if they had a mother who responded sensitively to their actions and verbalizations was controversial, to say the least.

John Bowlby was born in 1907, and followed his surgeon father's footsteps towards a career in the sciences, studying medicine at Cambridge University and eventually graduating in 1928 with a Ph.D. in psychology. His early work with young boys led him to conclude that it was a child's early experiences with (or without) caregivers that most profoundly affected their character, and he decided on a career as a child psychiatrist.

Bowlby also was unique in his belief that the key to helping a child was addressing the problems of the child's parents, and that parenting styles could be passed down between generations. He also wrote a paper analyzing case studies of 44 boys he had encountered while working at the London Child Guidance Center. Bowlby linked their delinquent behavior with a lack of maternal guidance and/or affection. He was later appointed the head of the Children's Department at London's Tavistock Clinic, which he renamed the Children and Parents Department to reflect his theory that family experience and interactions shape a child's emotional development.

In 1948, Bowlby and colleague James Robertson began a research study into mother and child separation and its impact on children. Robertson, a former employee at Anna Freud's clinic, had gained considerable training in child observation and data collecting that Bowlby found valuable. He was dispatched to observe children in area hospitals. Robertson and Bowlby would eventually produce the film "A Two-Year-Old Goes to Hospital" together. The work was a chronicle of the destructive emotional impact of forced separation of a hospitalized child from the parent. The film and its findings played a major impetus in changing hospital policy in the UK to allow parents to stay with their sick children.

As his work on childhood psychology became more well known, Bowlby was commissioned by the World Health Organization (WHO) to produce a report analyzing the mental health situation of the large population of homeless children in post-WW II Europe. *Maternal Care and Mental Health* was published in 1951, and would eventually be translated into 14 languages.

Around this time Bowlby read a paper by Konrad Lorenz on the concept of imprinting in geese. This piqued Bowlby's interest in the field of ethology (the study of animal behavior), a discipline that he would draw on heavily for his work on attachment theory. His work was also grounded in evolutionary theory; Bowlby admired Charles Darwin and wrote a biography entitled *Charles Darwin: A New Life* (1990).

In 1958 Bowlby presented his first written work on attachment theory—"The Nature of the Child's Tie to His Mother." He presented the paper at the British Psychoanalytic Society where it was met with much controversy among the psychoanalytic community. Two other seminal papers—"Separation Anxiety" (1959) and "Grief and Mourning in Infancy and Early Childhood" (1960) would follow. Over the next two decades, Bowlby would develop his theory further in a trilogy of books entitled "Attachment" (1969), "Separation" (1973), and "Loss" (1980). Bowlby passed away in 1990 at the age of 83.

---

her future colleague John Bowlby was doing the same type of work for the armed forces overseas. Both did active duty in the field of personnel selection during World War II. Ainsworth credits her work with the Canadian Women's Army Corps during the war as providing her with practical skills in both administration and clinical psychology (e.g., test administration, clinical interviews) that would serve her well later in her career.

The war also set the stage for John Bowlby's initial work in attachment and separation theory that would later inspire Ainsworth to delve deeper into maternal-infant separation. During the incessant bombing of the Battle of Britain, children from London and other urban centers were evacuated and sent to the safety of estates in the countryside, where they were cared for by healthcare professionals and childcare experts. Bowlby studied the impact of this sudden parental separation on the children (particularly the younger ones), many of whom had become withdrawn and depressed and had ceased to engage in play and other natural childhood behaviors. Soon after his focus turned to the plight of children in hospitals, at which point Ainsworth would join his research team at Tavistock.

Climbing the academic ladder at a time when women generally had a significant disadvantage in terms of pay and opportunity to their male counterparts, Ainsworth herself minimizes the significance of her accomplishments in academics, saying that the only time in her career that she ever experienced gender discrimination was when the senate of Queens University vetoed her nomination as head of their psychology department based on her sex (a position she wasn't especially keen on accepting to begin with).

However, Ainsworth student Mary Main recounts that Ainsworth was the first woman to break the "men only" rule for dining in the Johns Hopkins Club:

> Without fanfare, she succeeded in integrating this facility simply by—wearing, as she later reported, her best suit and a rose corsage—sitting alone one day at a center table until she was, very eventually, waited on. After that, as she knew, the precedent had been set, and she began taking her many female graduate students to dinner there.

Ainsworth also took the initiative for breaking down gender barriers in regards to salary at that institution.

Attachment theory was coming into its own in the 1960s and '70s, coinciding with the women's liberation movement. Ainsworth and Bowlby both faced criticism on their emphasis of mother as primary caregiver from those who believed that women had been relegated to that role for far too long. Ainsworth herself had this to say about the theoretical impact of her work on the women's movement:

> By some it has been viewed as a stroke against women's liberation, since it has highlighted the importance of sensitive responsiveness to infant behavioral cues on the part of the mother figure and the desirability of continuity of the infant's relationship with that figure, unbroken by separations that are unduly long or frequent. It has been assumed that I believe in full-time mothering during the child's earliest years, and indeed this does seem to be the most usual way of ensuring adequate responsiveness and continuity. I acknowledge that satisfactory supplementary mothering arrangements can and have

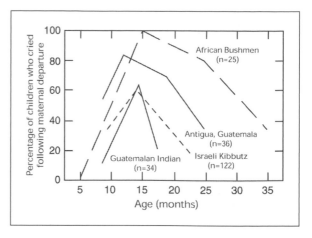

Children who cried during separation, shown as a percentage. Note the differences between babies of different cultures. (Courtesy Thomson Gale.)

been made by a not inconsiderable few. Had I myself had the children for whom I vainly longed, I like to believe that I could have arrived at some satisfactory combination of mothering and a career, but I do not believe that there is any universal, easy, ready-made solution to the problem.

CRITICAL RESPONSE

The field observation techniques of Mary Ainsworth were perhaps the most unorthodox, and thus most criticized, aspect of her research among contemporaries. In fact, after her Baltimore study, Ainsworth had difficulty getting a grant for another longitudinal study of the same type because most funding entities considered her original sample size too small and her clinically focused interview technique too far afield.

Ainsworth was also initially taken to task for "non-objective" language in case reports describing mother-infant interaction. Descriptive terms such as "sensitive" and "tender" were considered too subjective by many scientists, who believed that there was only value in concrete, measurable phenomena.

Unlike other research psychologists of her era, Ainsworth looked at all of her observational data in context in order to uncover its meaning, and sought to identify relationship patterns. That is, instead of counting the number of infant smiles and steps towards the mother and using this "frequency" data as a barometer of the level and nature of attachment, she analyzed all of the situational information with each event (e.g., maternal and infant mood, physical surroundings, and larger issues such as cultural and social influences). Student Mary Main points out that this tendency was likely a result of the value Ainsworth placed on psychoanalysis. In Ainsworth's own words from *Patterns of Attachment*:

> We do not consider measures of the strength of proximity and contact seeking—let alone measures of the frequency of smiling, vocalization, or looking—as measures of the strength of attachment. The very fact that there is such a shift in the nature and intensity of attachment behavior under different conditions and levels of activation suggests that the strength of attachment behavior reflects the situational intensity of activation rather than some postulated underlying strength of the bond between infant and attachment figure. We . . . have had difficulty in convincing others—so ingrained in various current psychological paradigms is the notion that any construct such as attachment must have a high-low dimension of strength or intensity.

Ainsworth also made a point of seeking out answers for those cases that did not "fit the pattern" that the rest of the group fell into, a tendency that was out of character for the research psychology field at the time. When a number of her mother-infant dyads in her Baltimore study group did not neatly fit preconceived behavioral patterns, she continued to analyze and re-analyze the data until she could construct sub-categorizations that explained every case in her study sample. This commitment to accounting for individual differences instead of going with the group trends was considered peculiar by some of her contemporaries.

Behavioral learning theorists also took issue with Ainsworth's conclusion, gathered from the Baltimore data, that mothers who responded sensitively to their children's cries in the first few months of life had a better and more secure relationship with the infant throughout the first year. They believed that attending to a crying child only served to reinforce the crying behavior and perpetuate it. Ultimately, Ainsworth's findings would have a major impact on parenting theory and parental attitudes towards letting an infant "cry it out" versus responding to their needs.

Among more modern theorists, developmental psychologist Jerome Kagan is a vocal opponent of attachment theory. Kagan endorses the temperament view of mother-infant interaction, espousing that a secure or insecure attachment is not the product of maternal attention, but instead of genetic predisposition that forms infant temperament or personality. In other words, babies are born already pre-coded for the type of attachments they will form.

Although researchers have brought Ainsworth's strange situation protocol to Germany, Israel, and other

CHRONOLOGY

1913: Mary Dinsmore Salter born in Glendale, Ohio.

1929: Enters the University of Toronto at age 16.

1939: Receives her Ph.D. from University of Toronto.

1942: Enters the Canadian Women's Army Corps.

1945: Serves as Director of Women's Rehabilitation at Veteran Army Services Hospital.

1946: Returns to University of Toronto to teach.

1950: Marries Leonard Ainsworth.

1950: Moves to London; meets John Bowlby at Tavistock.

1954: Moves to Africa; starts Uganda mother-infant studies.

1955: Hired as lecturer at Johns Hopkins in Baltimore.

1960: Divorces Leonard Ainsworth; begins psychoanalysis.

1962: Begins Baltimore replication study of mother-infant dyads.

1967: Publishes *Infancy in Uganda*.

1975: Leaves Johns Hopkins for University of Virginia.

1978: Publishes *Patterns of Attachment*.

1984: Retires from the University of Virginia Professor Emeritus.

1998: Receives APA Gold Medal Award for Life Achievement in the Science of Psychology.

1999: Dies in Charlottesville, Virginia.

countries, several studies have demonstrated that the strange situation does not necessarily apply across all cultures. This may be due to differences in parenting styles and family values, or (perhaps more accurately) attributable to the fact that the attachment classifications resulting from the test may reflect a Western bias.

THEORIES IN ACTION

Ainsworth's strange situation technique is still used in child development research today. Research on her classifications of secure and insecure attachments has been carried out with older children, adolescents, and adults.

Research

As a teacher, Ainsworth drew a remarkable number of talented graduate and undergrad students into her orbit, many of whom have gone on to make substantial contributions to the field of attachment research themselves—including Sylvia Bell, Mary Blahar, Inge Bretherton, Jude Cassidy, Patricia Crittenden, Alicia Lieberman, Mary Main, Robert Marvin, and Everett Waters, to name just a few.

Ainsworth's students and colleagues went on to refine her organizations of attachment. After conducting their own longitudinal studies on Bay Area infant-mother dyads, Berkeley professors Mary Main and Judith Solomon added a fourth classification—disorganized/disoriented—to Ainsworth's original three. The disorganized category, also called class D, represents those infants that have conflicted reactions to their mother (such as reaching out and then pushing away). Disorganized attachment is thought to be a result of maternal behavior that is inconsistent (i.e., sometimes loving, sometimes threatening).

Ainsworth's students also went on to broaden the field of attachment research in other ways. Marvin performed the first study of attachment in preschool-aged children; Pat Crittenden designed the Preschool Assessment of Attachment (PAA); Main researched the strange situation technique with fathers; Waters developed a Q-sort for home observations; and Blehar did work on attachment and daycare.

Main also developed the Adult Attachment Interview, which asks parents to recall interactions with their own parents. Studies have shown that an infant's performance on the strange situation test is highly correlated with the parent's personality and family relationships in childhood as recalled on the AAI.

Other research has studied dimensions of maternal-infant attachment throughout the lifespan. Klaus and Karin Grossman of the University of Regensburg, colleagues and friends of Ainsworth, embarked on a replication study of Ainsworth's Baltimore project in 1975. Their longitudinal study of mother-infant pairs from Bielefeld, Northern Germany, confirmed many of Ainsworth's findings, as did a second longitudinal study of Regensburg infants who were followed up on as six-year-olds. The Grossmans also performed follow-up studies on their original Bielefeld children as young adults, analyzing their behavior and language and gathering narrative data on their adult relationships

to determine how their early attachments impacted them in the long term.

Interestingly, the Grossman study is most well known for its finding that half of the infants in the sample were classified as "avoidant," and two-thirds of the infant subjects were insecurely attached. The Grossmans attributed this to the fact that German culture values independence at an early age (see Japanese attachment theory sidebar).

Other noted international psychologists that contributed to attachment theory included the temperament researcher Joan Stevenson-Hinde, Avi Sagi (who studied infant attachment in the communal childcare environment of the kibbutz), and adult attachment researcher Philip Shaver. All consulted with Ainsworth during their career, and she offered her feedback and insights on their attachment research directions.

Another fertile testing ground for attachment research is the University of Minnesota, where researchers embarked on the Parent-Child Interaction Project, a long-term study beginning in 1975 following high-risk (e.g., chaotic home life, low socioeconomic status, no supportive partner) mothers and their infants from birth to adulthood and has contributed a rich body of research on how infant attachment affects relationships later in life. Long-term University of Minnesota studies on these women and their children has found that "anxiously attached" infants frequently grew up to have behavioral and emotional problems, and those that were securely attached had a better quality of social interaction with their peers and better skills at forming friendships, more empathy, and higher self-esteem and self-reliance.

New focuses of attachment research include the development of preventive programs designed to break the intergenerational cycle of insecure attachment by raising parental awareness of attachment issues.

Case studies

While her early work with Uganda infants described each home setting and mother-infant dyad in detail, Ainsworth took particular care to maintain the confidentiality of her Baltimore study subjects, blinding (i.e., removing names and identifying data and assigning each case with a number for identification purposes) all the data to even her own students. In *Patterns of Attachment*, Ainsworth describes several Baltimore and Uganda infant reactions to separation from their mother, and how the infants differed in their reactions based on home experience:

> [O]ne child in Sample I could not tolerate separation in the strange situation. Throughout the first year he had been left by his working mother with a responsive

FURTHER ANALYSIS:

Japanese attachment theory

Research involving the strange situation method in other cultures has yielded some surprising results. German mothers, for example, were found to encourage early independence and separation. At the other end of the spectrum, traditional Japanese families valued interdependence and ongoing togetherness throughout childhood and into adulthood. Infants and children stayed physically as well as emotionally close to their mothers, and separation was uncommon.

The Japanese concept of *amae*, first introduced by Japanese psychiatrist Takeo Doi in his book *The Anatomy of Dependence*, describes a love relationship of deep emotional dependence. In terms of the infant-mother bond, it is often called "indulgent love." Infant amae is complete dependence and reliance on the mother, and maternal amae is meeting the infant's needs in a comprehensive and selfless way. Unlike Western societies, which encourage independence as a child grows older, the amae mother-child bond stays strong in traditional Japanese families.

Several strange situation studies with Japanese infants and their mothers illustrate the difference between Western and Eastern values in child rearing. A study by Takahashi found a large percentage of infant subjects were classified as insecure and resistant. But because Japanese infants raised in traditional households rarely separate from their mothers, much less spend time with a complete stranger, their reaction to Ainsworth's strange situation procedure was understandably stressful. Ainsworth herself designed the test with an American audience in mind, although colleagues and other developmental researchers have applied the test to other cultures. For example, scoring assessments that take into account such differences and define normative standards for different individuals (called attachment Q-sets or Q-sorting) may be useful in accounting for variances in certain population groups and cultures.

However, some Japanese attachment studies have reached an attachment classification distribution similar to those done in America. One interesting similarity that seems to span cultures is the finding that those mothers who feel more supported by their spouse or partner were more likely to have a secure attachment with their child.

---

housekeeper. Until he was about 10 months old, he accepted his mother's departures in the morning, but then began to protest them. In the strange situation, the moment his mother got up to go at the end of Episode 3 he was undone. Ganda infants . . . showed more intense distress in everyday separation situations at home than did the American babies of our Sample 1. Most of them had been left with other caregivers every day for four hours or more while their mothers worked in the garden, whereas when the mother was at home she tended to take the baby with her as she moved from room to room. It would seem that when the Ganda mother did leave the baby behind, this signified to him a much longer absence than that expected by most of our American sample babies when the mother left the room. Similarly, we found . . . that children in full-time day care, having been previously home reared, showed significantly more distress in the separation episodes of the strange situation than home-reared age peers—a finding that may be due to their having become sensitized to separation by their frequent, long absences from home. On the other hand, it would seem likely that these same day-care children might have left the mother's side voluntarily in order to approach other children when introduced to a new play group, as Ricciuti (1974) found with a sample of young children who had been reared in a daycare center

Relevance to modern readers

Mary Ainsworth's theories of attachment development have stood the test of time, and researchers still use them as a basis for further research. Today, thanks to the work of attachment pioneers Mary Ainsworth, John Bowlby, and James Robertson, hospitals recognize the importance of letting parents room-in with sick children. Infants that used to be routinely whisked away from their mothers at birth to spend those crucial first days in a hospital nursery are now able to stay in a room with the mother.

The attachment parenting movement also owes a debt of gratitude to Ainsworth and Bowlby. Pediatrician William Sears, who coined the term "Attachment Parenting," advocates infant care practices such as emotional responsiveness to infant cues, skin-to-skin contact, bed sharing, breastfeeding, avoiding separation, and what Sears calls "babywearing" (i.e., carrying the child everywhere in a body sling).

Complex child development issues such as adoption, foster care, daycare, and grief have been made clearer by the advent of attachment theory. Child service agencies now have a better understanding of how removal from the home impacts attachment processes at different ages. In the United States, long-term foster care is now preferred over group care settings whenever possible. In many places, foster parents receive training on how to be most effective in promoting attachment relationships and how to respond to the foster child's needs sensitively to become a secure base for the child.

BIBLIOGRAPHY

Sources

Ainsworth, Mary D. Salter. "The Development of Infant-Mother Interaction Among the Ganda." *Determinants of Infant Behavior,* edited by B. M. Foss. New York, Wiley: 67–103, 1963.

Ainsworth, Mary D. Salter. *Infancy in Uganda: Infant Care and the Growth of Love.* Baltimore: Johns Hopkins University Press, 1967.

Ainsworth, Mary D. Salter. "Mary D. Salter Ainsworth." *Models of Achievement: Reflections of Eminent Women in Psychology,* edited by A. N. O'Connell and N. F. Russo. New York: Columbia University Press, 1983.

Ainsworth, Mary D. Salter, and S. M. Bell. "Attachment, Exploration, and Separation: Illustrated by the Behavior of One-Year-Olds in a Strange Situation." *Child Development* 41: 49–67, 1970.

Ainsworth, Mary D. Salter, M. C. Blehar, E. Waters, and S. Walls. *Patterns of Attachment: A Psychological Study of the Strange Situation.* Hillsdale, NJ: Lawrence Erlbaum, 1978.

Bowlby, John. *Attachment and Loss: Volume I: Attachment,* 2nd ed. New York: Basic Books, 1982.

Bretherton, Inge. "Mary Ainsworth: Insightful Observer and Courageous Theoretician." *Portraits of Pioneers in Psychology,* edited by G. A. Kimble and M. Wertheimer. Hillsdale, NJ: Erlbaum, 2003.

Bretherton, Inge. "The Origins of Attachment Theory: John Bowlby and Mary Ainsworth." Unpublished.

Main, Mary. "Mary D. Salter Ainsworth: Tribute and Portrait." *Psychoanalytic Inquiry* 19 (1999): 682–776.

Miyake, K., S. Chen, and J. Campos. "Infant Temperament, Mother's Mode of Interaction, and Attachment in Japan: An interim report." *Growing Points in Attachment Theory and Research. Monographs for the Society for Research in Child Development,* edited by I. Bretherton and E. Waters, (1985) 50, (Serial No. 209): 276–97.

Rothbaum, F. et al. "Attachment and Culture: Security in the United States and Japan." *American Psychologist* 55, no. 10 (2000): 1093–104.

Schore, Allan. "The Effects of a Secure Attachment Relationship on Right Brain Development, Affect Regulation, and Infant Mental Health." *Infant Mental Health Journal* 22 (2001): 7–66.

Takahashi K. "Are the Key Assumptions of the 'Strange Situation' Procedure Universal? A View from Japanese Research." *Human Development* 33, no. 1 (1990): 23–30.

Van IJzendoorn, M. H., and P. Kroonenberg. "Cross-Cultural Patterns of Attachment: A Meta-Analysis of the Strange Situation." *Child Development* 59 (1988): 147–56.

Further readings

Bowlby, John. *A Secure Base: Parent-Child Attachment and Healthy Human Development.* New York: Basic Books, 1988.

Bowlby, J., with M. D. S. Ainsworth. *Child Care and the Growth of Love,* 2nd ed. London: Penguin, 1965.

Anne Anastasi

1908–2001

AMERICAN PSYCHOLOGIST, UNIVERSITY
PROFESSOR

BARNARD COLLEGE, NEW YORK, B.A., 1928;
COLUMBIA UNIVERSITY, Ph.D., 1930

BRIEF OVERVIEW

Anne Anastasi (1908–2001) became synonymous with psychometrics—the measurement of human characteristics—by the 1950s. As the long-touted "Test Guru," Anastasi remained the key influence for anyone who had ever administered or taken an achievement, intelligence, aptitude, personality, or creativity test. Even at the time of her death in 2001, Anastasi's 1954 textbook, *Psychological Testing,* remained the standard for students and professionals alike doing research in the design and analysis of psychological tests.

What made Anastasi unique among her contemporary research and professional community members was her keen interest that went beyond test results. She found a way to seek the underlying cause of behaviors, and to explain statistics in the simplest way possible. This gave her students a grasp of the complex principles that could prove an obstacle to understanding the crucial essence of evaluations. Anastasi's approach was that of a generalist who paid attention not only to a psychological test's results, but how results might be interpreted in regard to the influences of a person's life history, intelligence, and other variables. When evaluating hospitalized psychiatric patients, for instance, Anastasi looked to the content of their drawings as well as the statistics that might have been gleaned from her testing. The psychometric measures that emerged meant little to Anastasi without looking at their psychological content, their relationship to other psychometric tests in consideration of other areas of psychology, and the social context of the testing.

Anne Anastasi. (*Archives of the History of American Psychology—The University of Akron. Reproduced by permission.*)

Anastasi was revolutionary for her time. In 1937 when she published her first book, *Differential Psychology, Individual and Group Differences in Behavior,* what she offered the professional psychological community as well as the individual student cut through the complexity of the work that had already been done—work that was virtually incomprehensible to the average layperson. Her approach was presented as just one way of understanding behavior and was not intended to outline an entirely separate field of psychology. Her first paragraph noted that with differential psychology, it was "apparent that if we can explain satisfactorily why individuals react differently from each other, we shall understand why each individual reacts as [he] does."

Anastasi found her way through the line of earlier experimental psychologists such as Charles Edward Spearman and Wilhelm Wundt. She established her own place in that tradition by expanding on the knowledge of early researchers in order to help her shape human study within the context of a broader human history. Her research and experimentation gave her the message that people were not mechanisms reacting, or not reacting, to certain stimulus. She understood that each individual was a product of a combination of factors that included genetic, hereditary, and environmental influences. These

created an equally unique profile to be considered when creating or interpreting psychological tests.

Anastasi's work has remained especially relevant to modern questions in education and psychological evaluations because of the intensity with which she penetrated the issue of cultural bias, or fairness in testing. Anastasi seriously questioned whether or not tests could be created without cultural bias. During the 1960s and 1970s, others argued that a test could be created that was totally fair to all individuals, crossing cultural lines. She insisted that no such test could be produced.

Anastasi consequently became renowned for her work with the interaction between biology and environment. She was a critical participant in the "nature versus nurture" arguments that significantly occupied the psychological scene of the later twentieth century. Because of her work in applied psychology, such fields as industrial and consumer psychology were given a boost in prestige at a time when few academic or theoretical psychologists dealt with the practical issues of human interaction.

BIOGRAPHY

Anne Anastasi was born of Sicilian heritage in New York City on December 19, 1908. Her parents were Anthony Anastasi, who worked for the New York City Board of Education, and Theresa Gaudiosi Anastasi. Her father died when Anastasi was only a year old, and the child and her mother became estranged from her father's family. She would never get to know them. Instead, her grandmother and mother's brother would form with Anastasi and her mother a unique family—her grandmother would be responsible for her home schooling during the first nine years of her life, and her uncle would become a father figure to her. Both he and her grandmother were educated and had graduated from college—but her uncle was not skilled in such a way to earn a living. That was left to Anastasi's mother. After her husband's death, she learned bookkeeping and founded her own piano company. When that company failed, she went to work at the Italian newspaper, *Il Progresso,* one of the largest foreign newspapers in the United States, as office manager, and supported the family through her years of hard work until her retirement.

Anastasi's grandmother reportedly did not approve of the "boisterous children" she had witnessed in the nearby schoolyard. She deemed public education would be inappropriate for her granddaughter. Instead, the decision was made to school Anastasi at home with the benefit of her grandmother's "interactive, dramatic, and glamorous" approach, according to the Anastasi biography published in the online series *Women's Intellectual Contribution to the Study of Mind & Society*. The family eventually hired a local public school teacher as a private tutor for Anastasi. Because she was such an excellent student, the teacher persuaded the family to allow Anastasi to attend the neighborhood public school. At nine she entered the third grade. In only two months she was skipped to the fourth grade. Problems arose as she was seated in the back of the class and had a difficult time seeing the blackboard, and suffered the interference of a crowded and noisy classroom. She resumed her studies at home for a period when it was determined that she needed glasses. Anastasi then returned to school and entered the sixth grade. She stayed on to graduate from P.S. 33 in the Bronx, receiving the gold medal for excellence. That fall she entered Evander Childs High School but grew restless after only two months. The school was overcrowded, and Anastasi felt that she was not being properly challenged. At that time a family friend suggested she consider applying to college early. In anticipation of that, she attended Rhodes Preparatory School—a school primarily attended by adults who want to pursue a college degree—and was accepted at Barnard College within two years, entering at age 15.

Anastasi had an early interest in mathematics, having taught herself spherical trigonometry as a teenager. At Barnard her focus shifted to a major in psychology. Her mathematical skills would prove to be an asset in Anastasi's statistical calculations for her psychological research. While she was still intending to major in math, the work of Charles Edward Spearman that changed her mind. Spearman (1863–1945), a renowned British psychologist, began his career as a student in Wilhelm Wundt's (1832–1920) famed experimental laboratory in Germany at the end of the nineteenth century. He was a statistician known for his work on correlation coefficients, and the development of the "two-factor" theory of intelligence. According to Patricia Lovie and A. D. Lovie, writing a biographical profile of Spearman for the *Biographical Dictionary of Psychology*, that theory predicted a "common, or general, intellective function underlying every mental ability to some degree, as well as a function specific to the task in hand." One of Anastasi's professors, and later a colleague, Harry Hollingworth, influenced Anastasi once she was securely settled into psychology. She would later recall that it was a chance meeting in a pedestrian crossing zone a few years later during which Hollingworth would offer Anastasi an instructor position at Barnard, her first professional teaching position.

Anastasi graduated from Barnard at the age of 20, going on to complete her Ph.D. from Columbia University only two years later, in 1930. There she had studied under the supervision of H. E. Garrett. She stayed at Barnard as an instructor from 1930 until 1939. During that time, in 1937, she published her first major text, *Differential Psychology*. In his introduction to the volume, Hollingworth wrote that

> No topic has greater significance for the organization of lives among human beings than that of the nature and basis of the individual differences among those human beings. Except for individual differences among us there would be no such distinctions as right and wrong; just and unjust; health and illness. There would be no laws, no courts, no systems of ethics, no politics, and no need of government. Individual differences are responsible for such institutions as education, for such episodes as wars, and probably, if the truth were known, for culture, for science, for the church, and for nearly everything else that is characteristically human.

What was so groundbreaking in Anastasi's early work defining the importance of differential psychology was the very recognition of the human differences of which Hollingworth spoke. The field of experimental psychology was still relatively young in 1937. Anastasi was not yet 30 and had already begun to make her mark in the history of psychological evaluation. Hollingworth noted:

> It was a special privilege to introduce such a volume in the form of the present book by one whose psychological studies I have observed from their beginning; by one whom I was earlier honored to know as a student in my own classes, and am now pleased to know as a colleague of long standing.

Anastasi left Barnard to join the psychology faculty at Queens College. She left there in 1947, having served as the chair of the department by the end of her tenure. When she moved to Fordham University, a Jesuit institution back in her home territory of the Bronx, first as an assistant professor, it would be her final move in academia. She remained at Fordham through to her retirement in 1979 as a full professor and having served from 1968–74 as chair of the department. Upon her retirement Anastasi was named professor emeritus.

Personal success

While at Columbia, Anastasi met the man who would become her husband, industrial psychologist John Porter Foley, Jr. (1910–1994). Their marriage in 1933 would mark not only a domestic partnership, but a professional partnership as well. With Foley, Anastasi would broaden her own interests in applied psychology to match what he was discovering in his field. Only a year into their marriage, the marriage was severely tested. With the discovery that Anastasi was suffering

PRINCIPAL PUBLICATIONS

- *Differential Psychology.* New York: Macmillan, 1937.

- *Psychological Testing.* New York: Macmillan, 1954.

- "Heredity, Environment, and the Question 'How'" *Psychological Review* 65, 197–208, 1958.

- *Fields of Applied Psychology.* New York: McGraw-Hill, 1964.

- "Sex Differences: Historical Perspectives and Methodological Implications." *Developmental Review* 1, 187–206, 1981.

- Anastasi, Anne. "Autobiography." *Models of Achievement: Reflections of Eminent Women in Psychology,* edited by A. N. O'Connell and N. F. Russo. Vol. 2, Erlbaum, 1988.

- "The Gap Between Experimental and Psychometric Orientations." *Washington Academy of Sciences* 81, 61–73, 1991.

---

from cervical cancer, the two faced the challenge brought by such a diagnosis. Radium treatments successfully treated the cancer with a prognosis for survival—but they also left her infertile. In an American Psychological Association (APA) tribute in the Summer 2002 issue, *The Legacy of Anne Anastasi,* Agnes N. O'Connell, who considered Anastasi a lifelong mentor, noted that when Anastasi would later recall this difficult time in her life, she said that the "response to misfortune can vary from self-pity, depression, and even suicide, to enhanced motivation and a determination to show the world that it can't keep you down."

With the Depression in full force and jobs scarce, Foley was forced to take a job in Washington while Anastasi held her position at Barnard. He would later accept a job with the Psychological Corporation in New York City. They stayed in New York throughout the rest of their marriage until Foley's death in 1994.

Anastasi's and Foley's New York City home was a six-story townhouse on East 38th Street. Her mother Theresa lived with them until her death. Though she was unable to have her own children, a former student, Oliva J. Hooker, also speaking in the Anastasi tribute, noted that:

In teaching or mentoring, Anne had few peers. Every student was made to feel as if his/her career was of primary concern. Whenever a candidate needed an emergency meeting, she made time even if it meant having the student appear in the sanctity of her Manhattan home at 10 p.m.

In her daily life, Anastasi was noted for both her brilliance and her absentminded involvement with the more practical aspects of daily life. In her May 2001 obituary of Anastasi for the *New York Times,* Erica Goode related an incident told by Dr. Mary Procidano, then chair of the psychology department at Fordham. "Once, Dr. Procidano said, she heard a shriek coming from Dr. Anastasi's office. Running to see what was wrong, she found Dr. Anastasi trying to pry a plug out of an electrical outlet by using a metal letter opener," wrote Goode. When Dr. Procidano asked her if she got a shock, with the letter opener still in her hand, Anastasi replied, saying "How fascinating. How did you know it was a shock?"

Anastasi was known as a tireless friend, teacher, and colleague who in many ways was ahead of her time. Harold Takooshian wrote for the tribute that, "as early as 1937 her integrated model for cross-cultural psychology actually surpasses the Procrustean [a method named for Procrustes in Greek mythology, by which conformity was sought at any cost—including through ruthless or drastic means] models we are evolving today." Hooker also noted that, "No one who had the privilege of working with Dr. Anastasi was ever bored. Her diverse interests and firm convictions defied easy prediction." Jonathan Galente, whose father was Anastasi's colleague and who would become a psychology professional himself, recalled a lifetime of experiencing her as friend and mentor. He had spent many hours with his father working right in her townhouse office, and enjoying her company with his family at holidays. According to Galente, Anastasi was "gracious, amusing, opinionated, frugal, hard-working, dedicated to the scientific psychology, totally unpredictable in some ways and highly predictable in others," as well as a "master at telling stories."

Professional achievement   While maintaining her teaching career and family life, Anastasi continued her research, writing, and lectures. She became the third woman to be elected president of the APA—the first in 50 years at the time of her 1972 election. Procidano told Goode that, "Every psychologist has heard of Anastasi. She really defined the field." Her interest in cultural diversity was evident throughout her many writings, extending throughout her professional life. From her first work in 1937, to her next major publication, *Psychological Testing,* first published in 1954—Anastasi was acutely aware of how group differences with variations in age, gender, family, anatomy, race, and ethnicity would affect the results of psychological tests. In her lifetime, Anastasi published more than 150 scholarly books, monographs, and articles. Dr. Robert Perloff, a distinguished service professor emeritus of psychology at the University of Pittsburgh, according to Goode, said that Anastasi had "brought to the issue a balanced, deeply rational perspective and an insistence on solid science," and a consideration of how both biology and environment as a crucial part of human character formation. In one series of studies, Anastasi examined creativity in elementary and high school students. Her research interests were widely varied. According to her friends and colleagues, Anastasi was in constant contemplation of human behavior, ever fascinated by it, and continually attempting to understand it better.

In addition to *Differential Psychology* and *Psychological Testing,* Anastasi's other major publications included *Fields of Applied Psychology,* 1964; *Individual Differences,* 1965; *Testing Problems in Perspective,* 1966; and *Gap Between Experimental and Psychometric Orientation,* 1991.

Anastasi's professional honors and awards included: the APA Distinguished Scientific Award, 1971; Recipient award for distinguished service to measurement from the Educational Testing Service (ETS), 1977; distinguished contribution to research, American Educational Research Association, 1983; APA E. L. Thorndike Medal, 1983; Gold Medal for lifetime achievement, American Psychological Foundation, 1984; National Medal of Science, the nation's highest award for scientific achievement, 1987; and the James McKeen Cattell fellow of the American Psychological Society, 1993. In 1946 she was elected to the presidency of the Eastern Psychological Association. Later Anastasi would serve both the Psychonomic Society and the APA on the board of directors, in addition to her role as APA president. Among the schools that awarded Anastasi honorary doctorates were: La Salle University in Philadelphia; University of Windsor, Canada; Villanova University; Cedar Crest College; and Fordham. She was also a member of the honor societies of Phi Beta Kappa and Sigma Xi. In the Spring 1987 issue of *Psychotherapy in Private Practice,* Eileen A. Gavin reported the findings of a study of the world's most prominent women psychologists. Anastasi emerged first among 84 possible choices.

Anastasi died on May 4, 2001, in New York, at the age of 92. Friends and colleagues noted that the always-dignified, bright woman remained so even to her death. In the profile of Anastasi for the *Biographical*

Dictionary of Psychology, Colin Cooper wrote that Anastasi, in her generalist approach, did not "become mesmerized by psychometric minutiae," but paid attention instead to the "psychological content of psychometric measures, the link between psychometric tests and other areas of psychology, and the social context of mental testing." He went on to say that:

> Her books tell a compelling story of how properly constructed, well-validated, and psychologically well-founded mental tests can prove valuable in both theoretical and applied fields; provided that the underlying sociocultural, developmental, and cognitive processes are well understood. Through them she has made a real and substantial contribution to the science of psychometrics and to good testing practice.

THEORIES

Anastasi's interest in experimental psychology expanded to include her research and work in the areas of differential psychology, psychological testing, and applied psychology. Her focus revolved around the questions of heredity versus environment, and the value of psychometrics. She spent her life of research examining and reexamining her experiments and their results. The outlines of her texts provide not only her students, but anyone reading her work, a careful investigation of her theories. The basic premise of her pursuit remained the same throughout every single step she took in unraveling human behavior. The premise was that human beings were different from each other, each unique for a variety of reasons. As she begins her very first book in 1937, Anastasi says that:

> Man has always been aware of differences among his fellow-beings. He has, to be sure, entertained various theories, beliefs, or superstitions regarding the causes of such differences, and has interpreted them differently according to his own traditional background, but has at all times accepted the fact of their existence.

With this premise she gradually built an entire approach that helped determine testing methods for the next several generations of the human race. In any statistical analysis, report, or investigation, for Anastasi the key was in remembering that statistics had names, families, and a host of factors that influenced their behaviors.

Heredity and environment: Original theory
Main points   On September 4, 1957, Anastasi presented a paper to the division of General Psychology of the APA, in her address as president of that division. She said that, "Two or three decades ago, the so-called heredity-environment question was the center of lively

controversy. Today, on the other hand, many psychologists look upon it as a dead issue. It is now generally conceded that both hereditary and environmental factors enter into all behavior." Her contention was that many of the "traditional investigations," as she called them, had been inconclusive even after the controversy subsided. Whether either of those factors were considered together, or separately, or calculated for the percentages of what their contribution to the human behavior were determined to be, Anastasi found that much of the research was not successful. What she noted as a more viable hypothesis highlighted the demonstrated results of geneticists and psychologists, showing that the two factors were not an additive proposition—heredity plus environment equals character—but the interaction of the two components. For Anastasi, whose research had focused on individual differences and the question of heredity and environment from the beginning, neither was that explanation viable. "Small wonder," she exclaimed, "that some psychologists regard the heredity-environment question as unworthy of further consideration!"

In her 1937 book, Anastasi had laid out the groundwork for understanding the role that both heredity and environment played in individual human differences. As previously noted, that concept was controversial. Through extensive research, for instance, she determined at that time, that it was "obvious that any attempt to identify psychological characteristics, and especially such a manifold and ill-defined phenomenon as 'intelligence,' with unit characters," Anastasi suggested, was "entirely inconsistent with the concepts and data of genetics." She criticized the early mental tests that attempted to quantify intelligence. For her and other experimental psychologists, the work being done in genetics was crucial in understanding that there were an infinite number of gene combinations possible when considering hereditary issues in human development—with the exception of identical twins—with ongoing studies into the natural genetic phenomenon into the twenty-first century. Anastasi sought to clear up two issues of heredity at the outset.

The two major misconceptions regarding the manifestations of heredity, as expressed by Anastasi in 1937, are:

- Inheritance is indicated only by resemblance to parents or immediate ancestors.
- Hereditary factors that influence structure mean a particular behavior will occur.

Explanation   Anastasi explained the flaws of these two myths with scientific theories known at the time.

With the first myth, Anastasi argued that the "germ plasm" was continuous, from generation to generation, and not dependent simply on the two parents. (Although the theory of germ plasm in not recognized today, Anastasi saw that people inherit qualities associated with extended family members.) With the second myth, Anastasi explained that though a certain inherited structure, or lack of one, might be the underlying factor for the development of certain abilities, such structures do not mean that the activity will occur simply because of such a structure's presence or absence.

Examples   As can be easily witnessed, for example, two parents might be very short yet produce a very tall child. Barring an accidental factor or disease that could cause such height, it is likely that the gene producing it emerged from a member or members of other generations. In the same vein, by virtue of height, that child might be better able to perform certain athletic or physical behaviors—but such activity will not necessarily occur simply because the height is present.

Anastasi took other factors into consideration. A serious scientist, she looked to experimental data to support her theories. She also addressed those issues that presented a possibility of variations. The four other factors that she examined were:

- prenatal environment
- experimentally produced variations in behavior
- human children reared in abnormal environments
- differences among social or occupational groups

Heredity and environment: Theory refined

Main points   By 1957, Anastasi was continuing the particular exploration of the influence of heredity and environment and their interaction by suggesting that researchers had been asking the wrong questions. She noted:

> The traditional questions about heredity and environment may be intrinsically unanswerable. Psychologists began by asking *which* type of factor, hereditary or environmental, is responsible for individual differences in a given trait. Later, they tried to discover *How much* of the variance was attributable to heredity and how much to environment. It is the primary contention of this paper that a more fruitful approach is to be found in the question, *'How?'*

Explanation   Anastasi explained that her contemporary colleagues engaged in research had emerged with various techniques of answering the question of "How?" that offered much promise to the investigation. Some hereditary factors influencing behavior, she explained, were isolated from environmental factors in what they might produce. She used the example of such conditions as phenylpyruvic amentia and amaurotic idiocy—both considered at the time as irreversible birth defects. In the early twenty-first century, with medical advances that might eliminate those or other such genetic complications for mental capacity or direction, the issue would remain that with those genetically produced alterations, certain behaviors could not be influenced by environmental factors because of an innate lack of capability due to that so-called "defect." But Anastasi used other examples to illustrate how hereditary issues can directly affect such issues as intelligence.

Examples   Anastasi pointed out that in the situation of hereditary deafness, there was an initial possibility that intellectual growth might be stunted due to the interference that lack of hearing might cause with social interaction, language development, and schooling. This, of course, was 1957—still a time when advances in the education of the hearing-impaired lagged behind the development and change of thought that would come by the end of the century. As late as the early twentieth century, hearing- and sight-impaired people—due to their inability to communicate with people who had no such impairment—were sometimes branded as mentally insane or learning-challenged and relegated to insane asylums and other institutions. Anastasi did indicate that once adaptations occurred, such "retardation" would not be an issue.

Another example Anastasi offered was that of being susceptible to certain illnesses or diseases due to heredity. Combined with genetic susceptibility, environmental factors might indeed trigger an illness, with the possibility of various behavioral effects. As a more specific example, Anastasi explained that

> Intellectually, the individual may be handicapped by his inability to attend school regularly. On the other hand, depending upon age of onset, home conditions, parental status, and similar factors, poor health may have the effect of concentrating the individual's energies upon intellectual pursuits. The curtailment of participation in athletics and social functions may serve to strengthen interest in reading and other sedentary activities.

Other circumstances that surround the situation might further alter the influence that an illness might have on personality development. In severe cases, such as grave disfigurement of the face or other parts of the body, the physical affliction could also alter the social environ-

ment and isolate a person to the point of a psychiatric breakdown.

The case of the latter circumstance, or any inherited physical characteristics, most certainly affects human behavior—by the beginning of the twenty-first century, evidence exists that a woman who is deemed beautiful is more likely to be assisted in a roadside emergency than one who is considered unattractive. Given the possible dangerous consequences facing a woman in such a situation—from other humans, animals, or daunting weather conditions—it is possible that even the genetic or hereditary component of physical attractiveness of a person could affect his or her behavior as it reacts to positive or negative response to the individual.

Indirect relationship   The important distinction in this discussion for Anastasi was the reminder that any link of heredity on behavior was always an indirect one. No psychological trait, she explained, was ever inherited. "All we can ever say directly from behavioral observations is that a given trait shows evidence of being influenced by certain 'inheritable unknowns'," Anastasi reminded her audience. "Psychological traits are related to genes by highly indirect and devious routes," she emphasized. Geneticists and psychologists both recognize the wide range of possible variants when examining the compound of factors linking heredity, environment, and behavior.

Environmental factors

Main points   Environmental variations can be organic or behavioral. Of those that are classified as organic, the environmental factors that are indicated would be those that produce actual organic effects that might consequently influence behavior. Those considered behavioral would indicate that they serve as a direct stimulus for one or more particular psychological reactions.

Explanation   Environmental influences that are organic bear a similarity to hereditary factors. They can be set along a continuum of how much they directly or indirectly affect behavior. Those that are behavioral are considered to have a direct influence on behavior; those that are organic are considered indirect. A different sort of continuum measure the breadth of indirect influences.

Examples   As an example of an organic cause indirectly affecting behavior, Anastasi offered the actual example of the stereotypical young female secretary, usually unnoticed due to her "mousy brown hair," who becomes a glamorous blonde through the use of culturally available techniques. The possibility that others would have a different reaction to her, and that her own self-concept would change as a result of that social response, is very likely. The broader indirect result of such a response could lead to a different social poise, or perhaps even a drop in her clerical accuracy should the attention she receives cause an interference to her job.

Anastasi used the example of social class membership as a behavioral environmental factor. "Its influence upon behavior development," she determined, "may operate through many channels." Social class can direct intellectual pursuits, for example, depending on the level of education and experience that has been provided by individual families or communities. Such influence could go even deeper as it affects consequent factors as the extent of formal schooling their financial status might afford, access to cultural diversions or lessons, and even access to medical care.

Another example of a behavioral environmental influence is language, especially in the case of bilingualism, or multilingualism. An adult who moves to a country where the natives speak a different language could experience communication difficulties until some proficiency in the new language is gained. Anastasi believed such difficulties did not have a long-lasting effect, and any problems were easily overcome. She did contend that bilingualism in children had in some cases had a negative effect on learning or communication. With scholastic problems brought on by language issues, other behavior brought on from a feeling of frustration might lead further to academic discouragement or a dislike of school. She cited the example of a group of Puerto Rican children in New York City. As Anastasi explained that, she noted:

> In the case of certain groups, moreover, the child's foreign language background may be perceived by himself and his associates as a symbol of minority group status and may thereby augment any emotional maladjustment arising from such status.

The marked difference of an example from the early twenty-first century could be that of a young minority who might be well-spoken with no dialect. The youngster wants to fit in, though, and deliberately alters language to include the more acceptable slang or grammar of the desirable group.

Anastasi provided an elaboration of the issue following these examples, saying, "There is clearly a need for identifying explicitly the etiological (meaning the *cause* assigned) mechanism whereby any given hereditary or environmental condition ultimately leads to a behavioral characteristic—in other words, the 'how' of heredity and environment."

Methodological approaches

Main points   The methodological approaches to understanding the "how" of the hereditary-environment question, could be counted at seven, according to Anastasi. They were:

- extension of selective breeding investigations to permit the identification of specific hereditary conditions underlying the observed behavioral differences
- exploration of possible relationships between behavioral characteristics and physiological variables which may in turn be traceable to hereditary factors
- prenatal environmental factors
- investigation of the influence of early experience on the eventual behavioral characteristics of animals
- comparative investigation of child-rearing practices in different cultures and subcultures
- research on somatopsychological relationships—the way physical traits might influence behavior
- adaptation of traditional twin studies

Explanation: Selective breeding   Anastasi discussed the background for her advocacy of the extension of selective breeding investigations recalling that early selective breeding investigations indicated that the "maze learning ability" was inherited. What researchers would eventually learn from such experimentation was not that the actual ability had been inherited, but that the ability was being transmitted from genes. In 1957, Anastasi was years ahead of her time in believing that the actual chemical properties of the genes might ultimately explain such specific behavioral characteristics. What in fact was key to Anastasi's entire premise was the careful delineation of research methods, and questions that would cover thoroughly the questions of heredity and environment.

Examples   Anastasi cited ongoing research that was then current. L.V. Searle, following the work of R.C. Tryon in determining the ability of rats to undergo mazes, used rats with the strains of maze-bright and maze-dull that Tryon had developed. He was able to demonstrate that the "two strains differed in a number of emotional and motivational factors," according to Anastasi, "rather than in ability." That experiment represented the next step in determining the link between maze learning and genes.

Explanation: *Physiological variables* Anastasi's second proposed approach in the discussion was that of discerning relationships between behavioral characteristics and physiological variables that could be traced to hereditary factors. Anastasi said that certain research—that on EEG, autonomic balance, metabolic processes, and biochemical factors—was an illustration of that approach.

Examples The example that Anastasi provided was that of the research that traced the metabolic disorder phenylpyruvic amentia. This research process uncovered the causal chain from the defective gene, through metabolic disorder and the resulting cerebral malfunction, to the feeblemindedness and other symptoms.

Explanation: *Prenatal environmental factors* Based on the research available, Anastasi believed that prenatal environment factors could show that a link existed between socioeconomic factors, complications of pregnancy, and poor nutrition to the psychological disorders of the offspring.

Examples As an example, Anastasi cited research that had been conducted among samples of whites and blacks in Baltimore. The research showed that prenatal and infancy disorders were directly related to the level of mental defects and psychiatric disorders. Another study focused on prenatal nutrition that was observed through monitoring pregnant women in low-income groups whose diets were otherwise seriously lacking, but were given supplements through pregnancy and nursing. This control group was compared with a similar group given placebos. The control group that received the supplements produced offspring that showed significantly higher intelligence quotient ratings than the group receiving placebos.

Explanation: *Early perceptual experiences* Animal studies of the time showed the crucial link of early perceptual experiences on later performance. Anastasi believed that some of these observations were also key to understanding human behavior.

Examples Some tests were more traditional in tying an individual's maturity level and learning to behavior development. Other tests were designed to determine particular psychoanalytic theories based on the discussion of experiences in infancy. German biologist Konrad Lorenz's experiments with birds were also cited. He had studied early social stimulation of birds,

with a particular view to "imprinting"—the way that behavior was learned by the young observing the mother, in many cases.

Explanation: *Child-rearing practices* The research of child-rearing practices offered a way to determine their relationship to personality development in children from various cultures.

Example A study by Judith R. Williams and R.B. Scott conducted in 1953 observed the relationship between socioeconomic level, permissiveness, and motor development among black children. Esther Milner conducted a study of the relationships between reading readiness in grade one school children and the patterns of parent-child interaction. Milner found that lower-income children lacked two advantages that middle-class children did not. The first factor was described as "a warm positive family atmosphere or adult relationship pattern" already recognized as a motivational prerequisite. The other was involved the opportunity to verbally interact with adults in the family.

Explanation: *Somatopsychological relationships* Anastasi was unable to cite specific research available at the time on the influence of the body on psychological development (*somatopsychological*), but suggested that there could be many ways in which physical traits, both hereditary and environmental, might influence behavior.

Explanation: *Twin studies* Twin studies have continued to offer ever-evolving understanding of certain psychological traits in the hereditary versus environment discussion. Anastasi was an advocate of pursuing such investigations in order to scientifically determine what the results might indicate about all human behavior, and not simply that of twins.

Examples Some of the most interesting twin studies conducted since Anastasi's early work have involved those identical twins separated at birth and raised in very different environments. These twins frequently have similar psychological or personality traits. She cited F. J. Kallmann's research, *Heredity in Health and Mental Disorder: Principles of psychiatric genetics in the light of comparative twin studies.* Kallmann found that the hereditary factor in schizophrenia was identical between dizygotic twins (fraternal twins born from two separate eggs, as opposed to identical twins) and other siblings. Earlier findings of other research had shown that intelligence test scores varied less with dizygotic twins than they did with other siblings.

Anastasi concluded the summary of this particular address by reminding her audience that

> Such approaches are extremely varied with regard to subjects employed, nature of psychological functions studied, and specific experimental procedures allowed. But it is just such heterogeneity of methodology that is demanded by the wide diversity of ways in which heredity and environmental factors interact in behavior development.

Psychometrics

Main points Anastasi spent her career defining psychometrics. In a 1991 article for the *Journal of the Washington Academy of Sciences,* "The Gap Between Experimental and Psychometric Orientations," she began by saying that

> One of the inevitable consequences of the rapid growth of psychology is an increasing specialization in the training and functioning of psychologists. Specialization is obviously needed if one is to attain sufficient depth of knowledge and expertise to make an effective contribution to either research or practice. At the same time, specialization creates hazards which are becoming increasingly apparent in psychology. There is the likelihood of losing contact with neighboring specialties that may be relevant to one's work. And there is the danger that the methodological focus becomes too circumscribed to provide an adequate picture of so complex a phenomenon as human behavior. As a result, one's data may be incomplete and one's conclusions incorrect.

Anastasi had expressed a concern for years that the gap was widening between psychometric and experimental orientations in research. The main issue was that scientists were becoming so involved in the development of the test and the techniques, that the reason behind such tests—the behavior they were supposed to be measuring—had gotten lost.

Explanation Psychometrics can be defined as the design and analysis of research, resulting in the measurement of human characteristics. Anastasi further explained that psychometrics included psychological testing and statistical analysis, encompassing the "nature and sources" of psychological differences, as in differential psychology. Psychometrics represents the statistics of the variability of human behavior—with variability providing the essence of investigation. Such methodology was developed in order to find a place for the variability discovered in research and experiment. When any data regarding human behavior is analyzed (the wide variations of people exhibiting

that behavior as well as the widely varied specific response indicators), a valid interpretation can come only through factoring in all of the variables. Random variability in response can reflect the variables that can alter individual performance on tests over short periods of time. That would likely include changes in physical and psychological status, as well as external changes.

Anastasi pointed out that experimental psychology initially ignored any forms of random variability. The variations were considered "errors" and were seen as restricting how the general findings might be used. According to her, nineteenth-century psychologists in the early years of experimentation were simply looking for general cases of human behavior, with no focus on real, individual human behavior. As a consequence, terminology that was indicated as "standard error," or "error variance," and other such terms, were derived from that disposition. Psychometricians see only variance, not error, because all facts of human behavior are deemed as accountable and crucial to any investigation. Such variation that is gained by sampling errors and errors of measurement is not the only matter with which psychometrics is concerned. The standard deviation (a measure of variability) of the whole distribution of statistics is inextricably linked to the analysis of findings—as well as the "standard error."

Examples One example Anastasi gave was that of seeking the range of individual variation that was appropriate to consider for a particular purpose. Using the standard deviation to cover the middle 95% of the group is one way to analyze the varition. Another is to look at a wider, or perhaps, narrower range. Another example is to look at the data provided by the correlation coefficient, a measure a variation in more than one variable. This is because the relation between any two variables can vary between any two people observed. "If the same relation between two variables held for all persons, such that each person occupied the same relative position in both variables, the correlation between the two variables would be +1.00 and we would not need to compute it," Anastasi explained. But in fact one person might be high in both variables, another person high in one and only mediocre in another, with still a third person offering another variation. If only one test was given, a whole picture would not be possible either of the individual, or of how that individual compared with a group.

Experimental methodology

Explanation In further understanding the nature of psychometrics and how it can merge with experimental methodology, Anastasi offered a story that, she noted, was a common occurrence in the lives of many young researchers:

> The investigator in the story has been busy collecting an extensive body of data in the effort to test one or more hypotheses. Faced with an overabundance of numerical data, the investigator decides to consult a well-known statistician for expert advice on how to analyze the data. The statistician tried to do the best that he or she can to help, but with a sad shake of the head remarks, 'I could have been of real help if you had contacted me *before* you gathered your data.' This, of course, is the question of experimental design, which is closely linked to statistical considerations.

Examples   There are three key examples of the link between statistical and experimental methodology.

The three examples as outlined by Anastasi are:

- analysis of variance
- structural equation modeling
- factor analysis

An analysis of variance is a concept also known as ANOVA. R.A. Fisher was chief statistician at the Rothamsted Experimental Station, a British agricultural research center, when he introduced ANOVA. It has been used in experimental psychology and statistical methodology. Experimental design constituted an important premise in Fisher's treatment of ANOVA. When it was introduced to psychological researchers and adopted by them for their experimental use, it was primarily implemented to assign individuals to a group so that the effects of specific variables on them could be identified. The typical simple use of this theory is the experimental-control groups method of research. What it offered, more importantly, was to allow simultaneous study of the effects of several independent variables. An example of that is to use both sex and socioeconomic factors when analyzing the results of a mechanical aptitude test. Variables can also be manipulated within the experiment.

Structural equation modeling was an innovation from the last decades of the twentieth century. This method used what is known as regression equations to predict the dependent from the independent variables in cross-lagged correlation—for instance, when an attempt to measure the influence of an individual's attitude and ability on a math test in comparison to performance at various points in time. In structural equation modeling, all the intercorrelations among the variables are used in the measurement, with both measurement and sampling errors taken into account. Provision is made to calculate any possible additional or unmeasured causal variables, as well. When calculating a student's attitude toward math, for instance, several of the indicators would be used to define a "construct" of the individual's attitude toward math, useful in predicting future achievement in the subject. A construct represents a person's entire relationship to a subject that involves a complexity of variables.

Using factor analysis in research to determine the organization of human behavior comprises the third example of the merging of statistical and psychometric approaches. In factor analysis, the principal object of the technique is the simplification of data. This is accomplished by reducing the number of necessary variables, or dimensions. Anastasi explained that if, for instance, five factors were deemed sufficient to account for all of the common variance in a battery of 20 tests, five scores could be substituted for the original 20 in most cases without any loss of crucial information. By the end of the twentieth century, computers served the function necessary in such analysis—but Anastasi emphasized the importance of understanding the background of the analysis.

Summary

Anastasi's work in differential psychology, applied psychology, psychometrics, and psychological testing was carried through completion by a common thread: her desire for true scientific investigation, with its thorough and exhaustive approach, in uncovering both common and not-so-common human behavior. The testing was not an end in itself. Anastasi sought to make understanding human beings and the applying that understanding less complicated. She concluded her thoughts for the journal article in 1991 by saying that:

> When dealing with human behavior, in any form and from any angle, you will encounter variability—extensive and pervasive variability. If you ignore this variability, it will come back to haunt you in the form of incorrect conclusions in basic research and wrong decisions in applied research and practice. Equally serious are the consequences of becoming totally immersed in the statistics of variability, while ignoring the psychological content and context of the behavior itself. The experimental and psychometric approaches are not only intrinsically compatible but also mutually interdependent. Each depends upon the other for effective functioning in research design, in data analysis, and in the interpretation of results.

HISTORICAL CONTEXT

Anastasi and her work represented only the third generation of experimental psychology since Wilhelm Wundt opened his laboratory in Germany in 1879. His work paved the way for others, including James Cattell and William James, to create all that would be embodied in modern psychological practice and theory. It was only 50 years after Wundt that Anastasi began her own professional career—inspired by Charles Spearman, and based still on what he and those other nineteenth-century psychologist pioneers had begun to organize. The field was still foreign to all but a very particularly educated population. Even to educated classicists and philosophers, the language of psychology still represented anything but scientific validity. Only slowly was psychology merged into the study of human history as a valid academic pursuit.

Anastasi was born into a family of Sicilian immigrants in New York City in 1908. It was a time of class struggles among newly arrived immigrants to the United States and a culture that was a not unlike the blending of the psychological variables she would utilize to analyze human behavior throughout her life. The prejudice against "non-Americans" represented an obstacle to many immigrant families as they struggled to survive economically and work toward a better life through education. Many stereotypes of these immigrants designated them as mentally less fit or capable than their American counterparts. Ironically, many of the prejudices would be battled with the triumph of scientific evidence that Anastasi would help support against those stereotypes. The country was still young, really—a little over 125 years old—compared with the ancient culture of her own ancestors.

As she began her career, the horrors of the First World War were visible throughout the United States and Europe, not only in the loss of lives and the destruction of countryside, but in the scarred faces and bodies of soldiers who were the first to experience modern bombings and chemical attacks. Faces were burned beyond recognition, yet new medicinal techniques saved the soldiers who might have died in previous wars. These soldiers were left with lives that created new forms of recognized psychological trauma. Europe, especially Germany, was economically ravaged.

While Anastasi was preparing her dissertation, Wall Street experienced the collapse of the stock market on October 29, 1929. The world was plunged into a depression that would last nearly a decade. People struggled with their identities as they were often forced into lives they never would have expected to endure. Farmers in the Midwest would experience the drought of the "dust bowl" and head to California in record numbers, forming a whole new kind of immigration. Even Anastasi and her husband would be forced to live lives between two cities in order to support themselves; her husband could find work only in Washington while she had to be in New York.

Theirs was an experience repeated by thousands of others. In fact, families were torn apart when fathers and husbands left their homes to find work in massive numbers, creating a whole new class of vagabonds. They hopped on trains and walked miles simply to earn enough money for food, often just enough for a day. What was going on in the academic enclaves was not divorced from what was going on in the country outside the university walls.

The new discipline of psychology found a new role in those early years as both observer and sometimes crusader, helping to form a new consciousness of what it meant to be human. Just as the Great Depression reached a conclusion, the world was dragged into another war that would have even more dire consequences for the previously provincial people of all countries—and particularly of the United States. Farm boys would travel not only out of state for the first time, but out of the country to face the tragedy of war in a foreign landscape. Jewish people and others who had escaped to the United States and elsewhere from the horrors of Nazi Germany were themselves creating a new brand of American. Many educated and brilliant people were a part of this group, who would also begin to redefine many American universities with their own background of research and experience.

Anastasi published her first major work in 1937, when the refugees from Europe were entering the United States because a madman had an idea of developing a "perfect" race of people. In the APA tribute to Anastasi, Fordham colleague Takooshian noted the greater significance of Anastasi in view of the Nazi rise to power. He commented that:

> At precisely the time when Nazi and continental researchers were vigorously developing a race science to emphasize group differences based on genetic factors, Anne's 894-page tome casually dismissed such efforts in a few crisp words: "The array of evidence in support of this [Aryan supremacy] is incomplete and one-sided at its best and fantastic and mythical at its worst."

When Anastasi published her first edition of *Psychological Testing* in 1954, yet another phenomenon was changing the country. The post-World War II "baby boom" generation was just eight years into its 18-year reign. Suburbs were being developed at record levels to accommodate a growing population—and with them, public education was expanded to a level before unseen. Returning GIs had also taken advantage of the GI Bill for education in record numbers, and the number of college graduates in America was growing as well. Parents who had not been able to graduate from high school because of the hard years of the Depression were now preparing their own children for higher education, beginning as early as kindergarten. American education and consequently American labor were becoming the "equalizers." Old class structures were revised, and a new middle class was defined.

Prosperity also meant that greater attention could be given to both medical and psychological problems. Medications such as penicillin meant that adults and their children were not as likely to succumb to infections. Life expectancies rose as a consequence of these new medications, along with less physically demanding lifestyles for the average family. Although old racial and cultural prejudices might have been slow to subside, there was still a promise of a modern life that was coming with many technological miracles—and some new anxieties. Psychologists became standard fixtures on the landscape of America. Whether it was study after study of the impact of the baby boomers on the future, or simply determining what could be done to increase children's ability to learn, psychology had gained prominence that would never again be questioned.

Anastasi's life and legacy was embroiled in a time of great change in the social and physical sciences. Her contribution to those changes was represented by the position she chose to take professionally. She not only served as vital observer and analyst. Anastasi was a pioneer who helped in the move toward greater understanding of human behavior, embracing the good news that this understanding would bring for society as a whole.

CRITICAL RESPONSE

Anastasi was rather quiet in her revolution of ideas. She was one of many psychologists teaching and making discoveries at roughly the same time through their research. She had been inspired by her love of mathematics, and from the career of Charles Edward Spearman, whose hard work in experimental psychology and psychometrics brought about the opening of the first psychological research center in Britain. James McKeen Cattell began his work defining differential psychology in the early twentieth century. This experimental psychologist who met Francis Galton after leaving Wundt in Leipzig was inspired by Galton's work on individual differences. Anastasi is a descendent of those who first defined differential psychology.

The simple fact that Anastasi's texts remain the standard for students of psychological testing, and that

all of her books have gone into several revised editions, shows that her work has achieved critical success. She was in a different situation than some other psychologists might have been. Anastasi was a tenacious and determined researcher while also being a devoted and gifted teacher. She functioned as a messenger as well, relating and responding to as much of the work of her contemporary researchers as possible. Her own ideas were continually evolving. As research became available that might have changed what she had deemed true, Anastasi let valid scientific evidence change her perspective.

In his introduction to *Differential Psychology,* Hollingworth called attention to the necessity of the work she was doing. He wrote that the tale of human diversity needed "constantly to be rewritten." Anastasi was doing that.

> Especially it needs now to be written by one who can hold prejudice at a minimum, who is equipped with technical tools and native endowment to know and to expose sources of error, to evaluate reported data in terms of the recent refinements of statistical and mathematical method, and who has, by virtue of original contributions to this field, demonstrated a competence therein and achieved contemporary authority.

Hollingworth had more or less hand-picked his former student for her first teaching position at Barnard College of Columbia University. Although he was also her friend, he was a professional who viewed Anastasi with careful and critical consideration regarding what she brought and would continue to bring to the field of differential psychology.

What is evident in the discussion of Anastasi's work is the praise she received, especially following her death. John Hogan, of St. John's University, recalled in his tribute that, "For Anastasi, there was nothing mysterious about psychological tests. They were simply tools, and their effectiveness depended on the skill and integrity of the examiner." Anastasi herself had objections to the way some testing was done, and the way results might have been interpreted. According to Takooshian, "Far more than other psychometricians, Anne consistently emphasized the limitation of psychological tests, their environmental and cultural contexts, and the value of qualitative information."

Anastasi was still in her 20s when she entered into a debate with L.L. Thurstone (1887–1955) on the subject of personality traits. The first president of the Psychometric Society, Thurstone was a well-known psychometrician and psychologist, and almost 50 at the time. He was educated as an electrical engineer and had been offered a job with Thomas Edison in developing his motion picture techniques. However, psychology interested him enough to abandon engineering and

BIOGRAPHY:

James Cattell

James Cattell (1860–1944) became known in the early years of the second generation of experimental psychologists because he worked to establish the quantitative methods and techniques that would become recognized as the basis for all psychological study. Among his psychological testing machines, the Hipp Chronoscope would become synonymous with Cattell and his advanced methods of scientific investigation.

James McKeen Cattell was born on May 25, 1860, in Easton, Pennsylvania, to his mother Elizabeth and his father, William, president of Lafayette College. Cattell received his bachelor's degree from Lafayette in 1880 and decided to travel to Europe to study philosophy. He ended his journey at the Leipzig, Germany, laboratory of Wilhelm Wundt, the father of modern experimental psychology. Eager young men from around the world, particularly Americans, were eager to study this new science with such a prominent scholar. In addition to Wundt, he also studied with philosopher Rudolf Lotze at Göttingen and wrote a paper on him that led to a fellowship in philosophy at Johns Hopkins University in Baltimore when he returned to America in 1882.

At Johns Hopkins, Cattell completed investigations of his own regarding the timing of various psychological processes. In 1883 he returned to Leipzig to work with Wundt as his first research assistant, and stayed for three years. Cattell worked well with Wundt, but veered significantly from Wundt's theoretical stance. Whereas Wundt used introspection as a control variable in his reaction time experiments, Cattell doubted this process of utilizing such subjective controls. When he later conducted his own psychophysical studies, his approach focused on the importance of accurate observations under different conditions.

Cattell left Leipzig and studied with Francis Galton in England. Galton was known for his work in establishing the basis for the discipline of differential psychology. With Galton as his mentor, Cattell conducted a long series of scientific investigations into the nature of individual differences. One of his devoted students at Columbia University, H. H. Hollingworth, would eventually become a mentor for Anne Anastasi in her own pursuit of differential psychology.

Cattell developed a method of ranking used in psychophysics, aesthetics, and value-judgments. He used this method to create his 1906 publication, *Directory of American Men of Science.* Cattell also gained some prominence indirectly related to his position as a university professor. On October 1, 1917, he was fired from the post he had held at Columbia University since 1890. Cattell expressed his objections to World War I in letters to several members of the United States Congress, also advocating that men not be drafted into service. The controversial position got the already disliked professor fired. The newly formed union of the American Association of University Professors took up Cattell's cause as one of academic freedom. He was eventually restored to his former position, and his case has stood as a landmark decision in the area of academic freedom.

Cattell was married to Josephine Owen, who saw him through frequent bouts with depression. His other academic position was as a professor at the University of Pennsylvania, holding the first chair of psychology established at any university in the world. He served as the president of the American Psychological Association in 1895. Among the journals he served as editor were the *Psychological Review,* 1894–1903; *Popular Science Monthly,* 1900–1915; *Science,* 1904–1944; *American Naturalist,* 1907–1944; *School and Society,* 1915–1939; and *Scientific Monthly,* from 1915–1943. Cattell also founded the Psychological Corporation in 1917 and served as its president; and served as president of the Ninth International Congress of Psychology in 1929.

establish himself in a whole new career. He rejected the stimulus-centered approach in experimental psychology that many others believed was the way to conduct research. He is best known for his multiple factors theory, and his theory of the seven elements that best examine intelligence. Those included verbal comprehension, word fluency, number facility, spatial visualization, associative memory, perceptual speed, and reasoning.

Anastasi's *Psychological Testing* was not only received well in this country in its many revised editions, but was translated around the world. In 1954, the middle of the Cold War, its translation into Russian for study there was highly unusual for such textbooks. One of her colleagues remarked that it was even translated in Persia (now Iraq)—and that its translator was executed afterwards. The fact that the text was considered by academic colleagues as the best text for 47 years was another remarkable testimony of how well she was received among her peers.

At a time when few women gained prominence or even received much attention in many professional areas, Anastasi was recognized as an expert. "She was an enormously central figure in the whole area of the measurement of human abilities," offered Eva Baker, director of the University of California at Los Angeles (UCLA) Center for the Study of Evaluation. Baker also told Elaine Woo of the *Los Angeles Times* on Anastasi's death, that, "Her contribution is all the more astounding given that she was working in a field that is quantitatively oriented and not well-populated by women." Woo also wrote that, "Her success was owed, in part, to her ability to write lucidly about complex topics. Colleagues said her forthright approach to sensitive issues also contributed to her authority in the testing world."

The field of applied psychology was an area where Anastasi ventured when few in her academic circle would do so. At the time she first published *Fields of Applied Psychology* in 1964, the idea that psychology could have an impact on the diverse worlds of consumer advertising, the industrial work place, and perhaps international affairs was still held in suspicion by professionals and laypeople alike. As long as it struggled in its identity as a science, all of psychology was sometimes held apart from "real medicine" or "real science." That would change. Due in large part to people such as Anastasi and her husband, America and the rest of the world was on the verge of a big step into a whole new frontier. In her preface, Anastasi explained that, "Although applied psychology has undergone explosive development during and since World War II, it did not originate at that time." She simply stated her reason for producing the book.

> The primary aim of this book is to bring together what the well-educated person needs to know about the professional activities of psychologists in business, industry, advertising and marketing, education, clinical practice, law, government, and the military services. The book does not presume to give advice on how to treat neuroses, bring up children, handle employees, or live one's life. It seeks rather to give a comprehensive view of the work of applied psychologists, that is, all psychologists other than those engaged primarily in teaching or basic research within an academic setting. Although directed principally to the college student, the book is also appropriate for beginning graduate students in psychology, as well as for students in schools of business and possibly in schools of law and medicine. It should likewise be of special interest to personnel workers, advertisers, and businessmen in general who want an overview of what psychology has to offer in practical contexts.

In the era before language changed to reflect a modern society, Anastasi's use of the word, "businessmen" in that original edition is worth noting. This book was written in the early days of what would come to be known as the "sexual revolution," a few years away from the publication of *MS* magazine in the early 1970s, when a woman's role in the professional world became more pronounced. Up to that time in America, few women held the positions that men held in business, government, or higher posts in academia. Anastasi held to a quiet and conservative pace in her work, slowly introducing and reflecting the concepts that were emerging onto the social context of a latter twentieth-century perspective. Anastasi represented a new era in psychology. Leaders within the APA attempted to simplify its divisions, leading away from clearly defined specialties. By 1964 such distinctions were being abandoned.

Anastasi's legacy

Anastasi was known for her insight and her tireless pursuit in scientific research. She is not only remembered but revered as the person who organized crucial data and kept pace with the constant alterations that had to be made as psychological testing grew beyond anyone's imagination. Hers was the balanced view, stating in her later years that, "Intelligence is not a single, unitary ability, but rather a composite of several functions. The term denotes that a combination of abilities required for survival and advancement within a particular culture." Speculation might arise regarding just why criticism against her work seemed virtually absent from her colleagues and other professionals, especially in education. Anastasi did the work that few others did, and made known the work of other psychologists. As a generalist, her main objective was to lift psychology into the scientific realm of facts—and yet expand its possibilities to create a better world.

In the early years of the twenty-first century, testing—for intelligence and academic proficiency—was a word, a concept, that made the headlines almost daily. The accountability of educators often rested on one or two tests, and served as the basis for the "No Child Left Behind" federal legislation with the reported intention of raising educational standards. Anastasi said that no test could be a predictor of future success, but only in some small part a measure of how a child, for instance, had reacted to the experiences up to that point. For Anastasi, testing was a mere tool in education and the workplace that was meant to help define the best direction. Early in her career, she had reached the conclusion that intelligence was a product of the interaction of heredity and environment. Tests supposedly given across cultural lines were to be evaluated, contended Anastasi, within the context of the group taking the test as well as with a view to the broader perspective. Standardized tests were valid only if they were seen as part of a process, not as an end-product. In terms of intelligence tests alone, Anastasi believed they served three purposes.

- They permit a direct assessment of prerequisite intellectual skills demanded by many important tasks in our culture.

- They assess availability of a relevant store of knowledge or content also prerequisite for many educational and occupational tasks.

- They provide an indirect index of the extent to which the individual has developed effective learning strategies, problem-solving techniques, and work habits; and has utilized them in the past.

According to Anastasi, "Intelligence can be improved at any age, but the earlier one begins the greater will be the return from one's efforts." How to best measure that intelligence would be another issue.

Using psychological testing   Anastasi's strict standards for investigation remained her trademark long after her death. What she brought to the world of testing was the demand that statistical evaluation be precise when interpreting tests. What must precede that, of course, was the soundness of the test itself, and of its administration under the strictest standards. As she began the first chapter of her 1961 edition of *Psychological Testing,* she offered that

> Anyone reading this book today could undoubtedly illustrate what is meant by a psychological test. It would be easy enough to recall a test the reader [himself] has taken in school, in college, in the armed services, in the counseling center, or in the personnel office. Or perhaps the reader has served as a subject in an experiment in which standardized tests were employed. This would certainly not have been the case 50 years ago. Psychological testing is a relatively young branch of one of the youngest of the sciences.

Anastasi reminded her readers and students of the common ground they shared. This was indicative of the way in which she moved—slowly and methodically. She set out to explain each step, a subtle reminder to her audience that there were no quick and easy answers when examining such a complex matter.

Anastasi provided some examples of how careful the professional tester must be. In order to accomplish the goal, she encouraged the ethical safeguards that had been adopted by the APA to ensure against misuse.

Some of Anastasi's proposed examples of test misuse, based on real incidents, were:

- "May I have a Stanford-Binet blank? I'd like to find my little sister's I.Q. The family thinks she's precocious."

- "Last night I answered the questions in an intelligence test published in our newspaper, and I got an I.Q. of 80—I think psychological tests are silly."

- "My roommate is studying psych. She gave me a personality test and I came out neurotic. I've been too upset to go to class ever since."

Anastasi's point was that psychological tests could be misused in those and other ways that would make the test worthless. The greater consequence of such misuse would be that the supposed results of a test under the wrong circumstances could do great harm to an individual or group. She quoted two statements from the *Ethical Standards of Psychologists* that helped illustrate the potential hazards of unethical testing.

The two statements read as follows:

- "The psychologist who asks that an individual reveal personal information in the course of interviewing, testing, or evaluation, or who allows such information to be divulged to him, does so only after making certain that the person is aware of the purpose of the interview, testing, or evaluation and of the ways in which the information may be used."

- "The psychologist in industry, education, and other situations in which conflicts of interest may arise among varied parties, as between management and labor, defines for himself the nature and direction of his loyalties and responsibilities and keeps these parties informed of these commitments."

Almost 50 years after Anastasi first proposed that such ethics be strictly followed, questions arise. The early twenty-first century represented an era of the "tell-all" talk show with celebrity psychologists. Many popular magazines offer personality "tests" monthly in order to determine everything from the success of a marriage to child-raising to career direction. Certainly, her interest in spreading the value of applied psychology and the benefits of psychological testing has been served. Whether or not the commercial marketplace heeded her admonitions remains another issue.

Modern issues in testing   The question of the marketplace in the creation, administration, and interpretation of intelligence tests was an issue addressed by Robert Sternberg in his own theory of intelligence. Frank R. Yekovich, in a 1994 paper prepared for the Educational Resources Information Center (ERIC) in cooperation with the Office of Educational Research and Improvement, Washington, D.C., discussed Sternberg's theories, as well as those of Howard Gardner and John L. Horn. Yekovich noted in *Current Issues in Research on Intelligence* that the general consensus by the end of the twentieth century was that intelligence was a composite of factors, not one concept. Each of the three scholars represented distinct views, however.

Sternberg's work (1985) revealed his theory of intelligence was composed of three subtheories. They were: context, indicating that the definition of intelligence was found within a given culture or context; experience, representing the amount of experience within a class of particular tasks—with the more unfamiliar the task tackled and successfully performed indicating higher intelligence; and, cognitive components of information processing, with the idea that structure plus processes equaled intelligence. Sternberg also differentiated between various kinds of intelligence, such as academic, practical, and other similar categories.

Gardner's theory seems to have borrowed an idea from Thurstone, in that he suggested seven components in determining intelligence. Those components included logical-mathematical, linguistic, musical, spatial, bodily-kinesthetic, interpersonal, and intrapersonal.

Horn, who developed his theory in concert with another well-known psychologist, Raymond Cattell, offered a two-part determination. One component was the category of "fluid abilities," meaning the reasoning used in novel circumstances. The other was "crystallized abilities," indicating the extent to which an individual has attained the knowledge of the culture.

Anastasi's concerns were well-represented in these, and other contemporary concerns of intelligence tests, at the end of the twentieth into the twenty-first. Intelligence was not seen as a category into which a person was to be classified. Rather, professionals determined that intelligence testing was to be used as a measure of how heredity and experiences combine to provide a diagnostic tool.

In 1992, Sternberg was one of many in the professional community expressing misgivings about the current state of testing. The popularization of intelligence and personality tests were made available to anyone with Internet service, a television, radio, bookstore, or magazine stand. The easy access to both sound and unsound tests was a dictate of the marketplace, Sternberg said. Clearly, money was to be made in testing, and that would likely remain true for years to come. Even in academic circles, the demand for standardized proficiency tests was not always seen in the best interest of improving educational standards. Some would argue that tests were often being created more with an eye to profitability rather than the intense and plodding determinations to be carefully examined, for instance, when considering the future of a child's education.

Anastasi provided a standard against which psychological testing was to be measured. She gave credence to the relatively modern field of applied psychology, helping to provide guidance for creating a better workplace, school system, and government. What others would carry into the future with that legacy remains to be seen.

THEORIES IN ACTION

From the beginning of her days as a student in experimental psychology, Anastasi had an awareness of the necessity of creating the highest scientific standards. She quickly moved from the simple stimulus-response form of testing into one that represented a more highly individualized form. It was testing wherein the exceptions to the general concept became as crucial to the results as to the initial hypothesis. Her research included both animal experiments and human testing and surveys. She relied on the methods of all credible researchers. In order to understand behavior, Anastasi knew that it was important to build from the most basic realities of physiology and biology before proceeding to the more difficult aspects of determining human behaviors.

Research

Simply stated, Anastasi encouraged research most obviously in the constancy of attention she gave both to her students and fellow professionals. She was a mentor to at least two generations of future psychologists and other students. Never did she waiver from the devotion to the truth that she inspired in her own academic community, and the larger one outside of it. Though not the initiator of the heredity versus environment theories of differential psychology, her 1937 work was a herald of what was to come. It was a forerunner of the long discussion that would never seem to reach a conclusion. She asked the important questions and challenged other researchers to delve deeper in the attempt to unravel the mysteries of human behavior. Anastasi carefully examined research results in a tireless effort to determine what was valid and what was inconclusive. She was a champion of the hard-working researchers who advanced psychological testing, as well as their most sincere critic.

A vast array of intelligence, aptitude, and personality tests emerged, particularly after World War II, and Anastasi was often called to evaluate them. By the end of the 1950s, when she spoke, the psychological and academic worlds listened. In the late 1960s when proponents of so-called "culturally fair" testing came forth, Anastasi was there to argue that no totally unbiased tests existed. She usually represented the voice of caution when the professional community was deciding such matters too hastily. Anastasi provided a grounding of lofty philosophical and psychological theories with real-world situations that required practical problem-solving.

Case studies

Some of Anastasi's case studies and research are interesting as much from a historical perspective as a scientific perspective. She helped to develop and clarify experiments and testing methods. The research results fill volumes over the expanse of her 50-year academic career. Her work with intelligence tests in particular encompassed groups of individuals rather than focusing simply on the individuals themselves. The tool of testing would ultimately extend to understanding an individual and how best to determine intelligence or behavior. But the importance of Anastasi's work was based in obtaining a complete picture of how each individual fit into a culture or group, and how that would inform a study of human behavior. Those examples that follow represent only a small portion of the significance of her studies.

Individual differences Anastasi presented the results of a learning test as early as the second chapter of *Differential Psychology*. She introduces the section by explaining that:

> Since individual differences have been found to be quantitative, we may now ask how the varying degrees of each trait are distributed among people. Are individuals scattered uniformly over the entire range or do they cluster at one or more points? What are the relative frequencies with which different degrees of a trait occur?

As the basis for this evaluation of difference, Anastasi used the scores of 1,000 students on a simple learning test. The scores ranged from eight to 52 and were grouped into class-intervals (representing each score) of four points. She first organized the scores into a table revealing the data. She then was able to construct a graph in order to show the distribution curve. Such a curve was helpful in determining how to treat the results, and identify any possible trends in learning distribution.

The results of the sampling within 12 class-intervals were as follows, with each scoring range followed by the number of students who scored within that range:

- 52–55: 1
- 48–51: 1
- 44–47: 20
- 40–43: 73
- 36–39: 156
- 32–35: 328
- 28–31: 244
- 24–27: 136
- 20–23: 28
- 16–19: 8
- 12–15: 3
- 8–11: 2

The total of 1000 students were then distributed along a curve, called a frequency polygon. The results represented a norm wherein the majority of students fell within a median. The curve concept, according to Anastasi (writing in 1937), was an old one in statistics. What Anastasi was able to do was to create other kinds of distribution curves that revealed samplings and statistics of various kinds—all with the purpose of providing a simple understanding on which to build in the statistical gathering of information.

Differences among social or occupational groups In her 1937 discussion of heredity and environment on intelligence and behavior, Anastasi cited one study on the effect of the home environment and schooling on intelligence as measured by H. Gordon as early as 1923, in London, England. Gordon served as the official Inspector of Schools and based his report on his findings in that capacity, observing those known as the "canal-boat children" and those of the Gypsy children. (In twenty-first-century America, Gordon might have similarly studied homeless children, or those of the groups known as the "Irish travelers" who move their extended families to various communities often throughout the course of a year.) The actual results were based on the Stanford-Binet intelligence tests and educational test scores of various groups of children whose schooling was deficient. This was in the early days of a developing awareness that such factors as stability of home life and good health could seriously affect the academic performance of a child. Such a notion had not always been prevalent. In any case, Gordon's results of the canal-boat children came from the two special schools that were open for the purpose of educating such children. Their only chance to attend school was during the time that the canal boats were docked for loading or discharging. The average child attended school about 5% of the time. Most of them only attended school on a monthly basis, for a one or two consecutive half-day period. Their home life was not intellectually stimulating, though health and cleanliness usually met appropriate standards. Most of the adults were illiterate, with families living isolated lives, and not engaging in much social interaction, even among themselves.

The number of canal-boat children was 76. The average IQ was 69.9, a score considered to be "borderline" in 1923. A few of the children were considered "feeble-minded," which was a term used at the time for individuals of a low intelligence. (Modern-day terminology often offers profile in such instances that is not so negative in its connotation.) The correlation that Gordon calculated between age and IQ within the group was a negative .755. Such a calculation indicated that the older children were more likely to score a lower IQ than the younger children. Results should have indicated the opposite, with the older children representing more advancement. The results were interpreted in terms of specific negative environmental influences. The younger children were not too far below the normal children, a difference from their older siblings. Anastasi wrote that:

> The high negative correlation with age is corroborated by analysis of individual scores. In 22 cases, two or more children from the same family were tested. With only one or two exceptions, there was found a consistent drop in IQ from the youngest to the eldest child within each family. Most of the youngest children had IQs between 90 and 100, which would place them within the normal group; among the eldest, on the other hand, were several whose IQs were low enough to make them appear distinctly feebleminded. A further corroborative fact brought out by this analysis is that the mental ages of children within a single family tended to be very similar, even though their chronological ages differed. Such a mental age might well represent the limit of intellectual development which was made possible by the available educational opportunities and the type of home environment furnished within the given family.

Gordon's findings among the Gypsy children were similar. Though these children attended school at a higher rate than the canal-boat children—34.9% of the attendance of the average child—similar results of decreasing IQ among the older children prevailed. The average IQ score was 74.5, with those attending school more often more likely to score higher.

What emerged from such early studies was the necessity to gather the facts based on scientific methods rather than making presumptions about an

CHRONOLOGY

1908: Born on December 19 in New York City, to Anthony Anastasi and Theresa Gaudiosi Anastasi.

1928: Receives a bachelor's degree from Barnard College, New York.

1930: Awarded a Ph.D. from Columbia University. Hired as instructor of psychology at Barnard.

1933: Marries John Porter Foley, Jr., an industrial psychologist.

1937: Publishes her first major work, *Differential Psychology,* through Macmillan Publishing, New York.

1939: Appointed assistant professor of psychology, and department chair, Queens College of the City University of New York.

1947: Joins the faculty at Fordham University as associate professor, where she would be appointed to a full professorship in 1951.

1954: Publishes *Psychological Testing,* Macmillan, New York.

1979: Named professor emeritus at Fordham.

2001: Dies on May 4.

outcome. Anastasi gathered information in such a way to demonstrate that a whole new area of knowledge was opening up in areas where preconceived notions had been considered sufficient.

Cross-cultural testing Of the many forms of testing Anastasi discussed in her textbook, one was the non-language test, designed to test individuals raised in different cultures or subcultures. Some non-language tests, as Anastasi pointed out, were still inadequate at times due to the presupposition of knowledge that such tests often embody. As early as 1954, Anastasi was adamant in her argument that culturally fair tests were impossible to design. Still, one such cross-cultural test example that she offered was the Leiter International Performance Scale, by R. G. Leiter. The Leiter is a series of tests that was developed in Hawaii, using both elementary and high school students.

BIOGRAPHY:

Hans Eysenck

Hans Eysenck (1916–1997) was one of the best-known psychologists of the twentieth century. The enormously prolific writer produced more than 1,000 publications in his lifetime, and was known for his popularization of psychology for the general reader. In spite of his respected theories, he gained notoriety as well with his 1989 article for *Psychology Today,* in which he suggested that attitude was more deadly than cigarettes in causing lung cancer and contributing to heart disease.

Hans Jurgen Eysenck was born in Berlin, Germany, on March 4, 1916. Both of his parents were actors who divorced when he was only two years old. The Catholic grandmother who raised him would fall victim to Nazi terror and die in a concentration camp during World War II. Eysenck himself fled Nazi Germany when he was only 18 to study physics at the University of London. He was a Jewish sympathizer whose life would be in danger. His scorn for Nazi philosophies motivated him to abandon his native country. When he found out that he did not have the prerequisites to study physics, he turned to another available option, that of psychology. In 1938 he graduated with honors, and two years later received his Ph.D., also from the University of London where he had studied with Sir Cyril Burt.

From 1946 until 1983, Eysenck served as the director of the Psychological Department of Maudsley Hospital, having gone there after his first post-war appointment at Mint Hill Hospital to study abnormal psychology. Maudsley enjoyed the reputation as the foremost psychiatric institute in England. Throughout his years at the hospital, Eysenck developed an aversion to many of the established methods of psychology, particularly psychoanalysis and clinical psychology. His theory of personality, based in physiology and genetics, established the controversial psychologist as a key figure the studies of temperament. His primary contribution was considered to be his "conceptualization of

personality as a small number of dimensional traits," according to W. S. Terry, writing for the *Biographical Dictionary of Psychology* in 1997. He derived the two major factors of neuroticism—stability, and extraversion-introversion—by utilizing the methods of factor analysis.

Eysenck developed several standardized tests, including the Maudsley Personality Inventory, 1959; the Eysenck Personality Inventory, 1963; and, the Eysenck Personality Questionnaire, 1975, with his wife, Sybil B. G. Eysenck. These tests have been used extensively throughout the world. His theory of certain personality types being more prone to particular types of psychopathology was carried through to his later theory of suggesting a person's possible predisposition to such diseases as lung cancer.

Eysenck was honored with numerous awards that included the APA Presidential Citation in 1993 for his outstanding contributions to Psychology. Included among the more than 60 books and an estimated 1,000 journal articles he published are *Dimensions of Personality,* 1947; "The Effects of Psychotherapy: An Evaluation," for *Journal of Consulting Psychology,* 1952; *The Great Intelligence Debate,* 1980; and *Genes, Culture, and Personality: An Empirical Approach,* 1989. He was named as the most-cited British psychologist, and as the second most-cited living psychologist (after Piaget) in the mid-1970s. In a 1991 survey of historians of psychology and department chairs, Eysenck was named as one of the top 10 contemporary psychologists. His work has inspired a large number of graduate and postdoctoral students to the extent that a proliferation of scientists and scholars in psychology worldwide by the end of the twentieth century was often referred to as the "Eysenck Commonwealth," according to Terry.

Eysenck died on September 4, 1997. His son Michael is continuing his father's work in personality theory within a context of cognitive and memory research.

Another researcher, S. D. Porteus, eventually applied it to African groups, in addition to other national groups by a few other investigators. A revised version in 1948 was based on testing of American students, as well as Army recruits during World War II.

The most significant feature of the test is its lack of instructions, either verbal or through signs. Each of the tests begins with a simple task that resembles similar tasks throughout the rest of the test battery. The subject's ability to comprehend the task is a part of the test itself.

The materials include a response frame with an adjustable card holder, to which response cards can be attached. The cards each contain a printed picture. The subject chooses the blocks with the proper response pictures and puts them into the frame. The test was created in order to cover a wide range of functions, much like those found in verbal tests. Some of the tasks included: matching identical colors, shades of gray, forms, or pictures; copying a block design; picture completion; number estimation; analogies; series completion; recognition of age differences; spatial relations; footprint recognition; similarities; memory for a series; and a classification of animals according to habitat.

The test was arranged in year levels, from two to 18. Each test is administered with no time limit. Scoring is done in terms of mental age (MA) and IQ, with no guarantee that the IQ remains constant in its meaning at different ages—which in fact, data showed did represent significant variation in the standard deviation of the IQs at different age levels. The test findings were shown to have high correlations as reported by some teachers with their ratings of intelligence, and other intelligence tests, including the Stanford-Binet. The correlations range from the latter was .64 to .81. They were results obtained from heterogeneous groups, so that figure might be different were the groups of a more homogeneous composition.

Anastasi, as mentioned by her colleagues and admirers, was extremely thorough in her textbooks, particularly in *Psychological Testing*. Her survey included hundreds of tests used for various study or experimental purposes. She presented information on tests that included various intelligence tests, especially the Stanford-Binet; various industrial screening tests for adults; performance and non-language tests; testing for physically challenged; a variety of tests for infants and preschool children; the Wechsler Scales and other clinical tests; various aptitude test batteries; and a number of personality profile tests. Her text in applied psychology represented applications in various areas that included personnel development; psychology to study engineers; consumer psychology; clinical applications; counseling therapy; and the use of psychology in the fields of education, medicine, law, and government settings. Anastasi supplied dozens of cases of tests that were ultimately responsible for the changes that occurred in the workplace and even in the supermarket in the latter half of the twentieth century.

Relevance to modern readers

Anyone who has ever taken or administered a psychological or intelligence test of any kind is likely to have Anastasi to account for it. Even with the issue of the modern "pop culture" personality

Hans Eysenck using a machine for measuring eye blinks. (Hulton Archive/Getty Images. Reproduced by permission.)

tests haphazardly given or taken, all modern psychological testing owes its reliability to Anastasi. Taking tests has long been a fact of life, not unlike death or taxes. Aptitude tests are taken for early placement in college. Psychological profiles are given in clinical settings to better serve those with mental health issues. Consumer products—everything from toothpaste to microwavable sandwiches to television shows—are tested among control populations that are determined as representative of the average citizen.

In less than 100 years since the first psychological tests and experiments were conducted, Anastasi made tremendous advances in testing to the greater advantage of others. Some tests have not been reliable. Some have had faulty interpretations of their results. Many of these issues affected such areas as racial equality, economic standing, and whether or not parent were fit to raise their own children. Prejudices and ideas without scientific basis were often too successful in dismissing a person to a life that was less than desirable. People such as the famous writer and personality Helen Keller, without the faculties of sight or hearing, were cast out of normal society. They were admitted to mental institutions and left to deteriorate without regard for investigation into what their intelligence might be. In fact, the advances in medical science throughout the twentieth century helped to concur with what the advances in psychological testing indicated. One often served the other in the quest for human understanding. During the early years of the twenty-first century, society is not so far removed from the time when people were judged on the basis of a perceived deficit, without knowing the true nature of their abilities.

Anastasi said that when examining intelligence:

> Not only does the nature of one's antecedent experiences affect the degree of differentiation of "intelligence" into distinct abilities, but it also affects the particular abilities that emerge, such as verbal, numerical, and spatial abilities. Thus, experiential factors affect not only the level of the individual's development, but also the very categories in terms of which [his] abilities may be identified.

During a modern age of bombardment with stimuli such as television commercials, music videos, or elaborate Internet Web sites, Anastasi has something relevant to impart. Because of her scientific rigor, average individuals—if they exist—have been offered an alternative to superstition, prejudice, and faulty thinking in getting to know themselves better. People should not imagine that there are tests that will absolutely justify their actions or who they think they are. Instead, Anastasi has offered generations of individuals a way to manage society's ills, for instance, by understanding human behavior. She stood for nothing less than exacting scientific data to represent the widely ranging variety of humans and their abilities. Her intention was not to categorize people, or stereotype them by their abilities. She wanted to use her work as a tool to discover what those abilities could mean.

Anastasi also serves as an important reminder to young women of the twenty-first century. She might not have said she struggled in a man's world as many of her generation might have said. She seemed content enough to satisfy her intellectual curiosity and fit into her research and academic niche without regard to her gender. But Anastasi did successfully utilize her assets to transcend any barriers due to her gender—in addition to those barriers that could have befallen her due to an unusual, nontraditional family, or her inability to bear children at a time when that often proved to be a social stigma for a married woman. In so doing, she took great strides for other women as well. Her ability to turn the worst or saddest circumstance into one of fortune is an example that was not lost on her friends and colleagues. Perhaps she was born with a gene for such ability. Or perhaps she, too, was the product of heredity, environment, and a wealth of experiences enough to transform an entire discipline into one of the most valuable assets available to modern individuals—the chance to know themselves and others.

BIBLIOGRAPHY

Sources

Anastasi, Anne. *Differential Psychology*. New York: Macmillan, 1937.

Anastasi, Anne. *Fields of Applied Psychology*. New York: McGraw-Hill, 1964.

Anastasi, Anne. "The Gap Between Experimental and Psychometric Orientations." *Journal of the Washington Academy of Sciences* 81, no. 2, (June 1991): 61–73.

Anastasi, Anne. "Heredity, Environment and the Question 'How'." *Psychological Review* 65 (1958): 197–208.

Anastasi, Anne. *Psychological Testing*. New York: Macmillan, 1961.

"Anne Anastasi." *American Psychological Association*. [cited May 2004] http://www.apa.org.

"Anne Anastasi." *American Psychological Society*. [cited May 2004] http://www.psychologicalscience.org.

"Anne Anastasi" (obituary). *American Psychometric Society*. [cited May 2004] http://www.fordham.edu/aps.

Boeree, C. George. "Hans Jurgen Eysenck." *Personality Theories*. e-text, Shippensburg, Pennsylvania: Shippensburg University, 1997. http://www.ship.edu/~cgboeree/perscontents.html.

Goode, Erica. "Anne Anastasi, the 'Test Guru' of Psychology Is Dead at 92" (obituary). *New York Times* (May 16, 2001).

Sheehy, Noel, Antony J. Chapman, and Wendy A. Conroy, eds. "Anne Anastasi," "James McKeen Cattell," and "Hans Jurgen Eysenck." *Biographical Dictionary of Psychology*. London and New York: Routledge, 1997.

"What is Psychometrics?" *American Psychometric Society*. [cited May 2004] http://www.fordham.edu/aps/whatpsy.html.

Woo, Elaine. "Anne Anastasi, Author spoke of cultural, racial fairness in testing" (obituary). Los Angeles. *Sicilian Culture.* May 18, 2001. [cited May 10, 2004]. http://www.sicilianculture. com/people/anastasi.htm.

Further readings

"Current Issues in Research on Intelligence." *Educational Resources Information Center.* [cited May 2004] http://www. ericfacility.net.

Eysenck, Hans, with L. J. Eaves and H. G. Martin. *Genes, Culture, and Personality: An Empirical Approach.* Academic Press, 1989.

Eysenck, Hans, with L. J. Kamin. *The Great Intelligence Debate.* London: Lifecycle, 1980.

"James McKeen Cattell." *University of Pennsylvania.* [cited May 2004] http://www.psych.upenn.edu/history/cattelltext.htm.

Albert Bandura

1925-

CANADIAN-BORN AMERICAN PSYCHOLOGIST, RESEARCHER

UNIVERSITY OF IOWA, PhD, 1952

BRIEF OVERVIEW

When people first try a new sport, they often know what they need to do before ever stepping onto a playing field or court because they've watched other people play. Albert Bandura recognized the importance of this process, called observational learning or vicarious learning, in which people learn to do something without actually performing the behavior themselves or being directly rewarded or punished for it. The advantage of this kind of learning is that it lets people learn from the experience of others, without having to reinvent the wheel every time they do something new.

In a series of classic studies, Bandura and his colleagues looked at the way observational learning affects aggressive behavior in children. Some children were shown a film in which an adult punched, hammered, and kicked a plastic inflatable doll, called a Bobo doll. Those who viewed the film were later more likely to act aggressively themselves when given a chance to play with the doll. Furthermore, seeing the adult in the film be rewarded for aggression increased the likelihood of aggression in the children even more, while seeing the adult punished had the opposite effect. However, just watching the aggressive behavior was enough for the children to learn it, regardless of whether rewards or punishments were given. The Bobo doll experiments became some of the best-known studies in psychology.

Yet, as important as observational learning is, Bandura also stressed that people have self-control

Albert Bandura. (Archives of the History of American Psychology. Reproduced by permission.)

over which behaviors they copy and which they do not. This self-control is exercised through cognitive, or thought, processes. Bandura's other major contribution to psychology has been the description of one key cognitive process, called perceived self-efficacy. People's perceived self-efficacy refers to their beliefs about how capably they will be able to perform a behavior in a particular situation.

These two central themes in Bandura's work—observational learning and self-efficacy beliefs—have been brought together with other factors under the label "social-cognitive theory." According to Bandura's social-cognitive theory, the outer world and the inner person—including that person's beliefs, thoughts, and feelings—combine to determine an individual's actions. The results of those actions, in turn, help shape the person's future beliefs, thoughts, and feelings. In this way, a cycle is established, in which the outer world, the inner person, and the person's behavior all act on and feed off each other. However, this does not necessarily have to be a vicious cycle. In fact, by changing his or her self-efficacy beliefs, a person can potentially break free of an old, negative cycle and establish a new, positive one. This theory is the culmination of Bandura's lifetime of study and research.

In 2002, a psychologist named Steven Haggbloom and his colleagues published a paper in which they attempted to rank the 100 most eminent psychologists of the twentieth century. They based their ranking on six different variables: citations in journals, mentions in introductory psychology textbooks, a survey of American Psychological Society members, election as president of the American Psychological Association (APA) or receipt of the APA Distinguished Scientific Contributions Award, membership in the National Academy of Sciences, and use of the psychologist's surname to identify a particular theory or school of psychology. Bandura ranked number four, right behind B.F. Skinner, Jean Piaget, and Sigmund Freud.

BIOGRAPHY

Growing up in a remote village in Canada, Bandura attended a small school where teachers and textbooks were in short supply. Perhaps because of these limitations, Bandura became a self-motivated and independent learner. His curiosity and independence would serve him well throughout a long and productive career.

Childhood in Canada

Bandura was born on December 4, 1925, the youngest child and the only boy of six children. His parents were both immigrants who had come to Canada from Eastern Europe as adolescents. His mother was originally from the Ukraine, and his father, from Poland. Neither had a formal education, but they valued learning highly. For example, Bandura's father taught himself to read three languages: Polish, Russian, and German.

Bandura grew up in Mundare, a tiny community in northern Alberta, Canada, about 50 miles (80 km) east of Edmonton. There, he attended the only school in town. The little school was woefully short on both teachers and supplies. Two teachers taught all the high school classes, and the high school math class had only a single textbook for everyone, including the teacher, to share. As a result, the students were left largely to their own devices. One might expect that this situation would produce students who were ill-prepared for the larger world. Instead, it seems to have pushed the students to take charge of their own educations, and many of them went on to attend universities around the globe. As Bandura was later quoted on an Emory University Web site in his honor, "The content of most textbooks is perishable, but the tools of self-directedness serve one well over time."

The college years

When it came time for college, Bandura headed for the University of British Columbia in Vancouver.

Once there, he stumbled onto psychology by chance. Bandura was carpooling to school with a group of other students who were early risers. He signed up for an introductory psychology class just to fill the early morning time slot, but he quickly became fascinated with the subject. Within three years, in 1949, he had graduated with a prize in psychology. Years later, Bandura discussed how personal actions often place people in situations where fortunate events can then shape the future course of their lives.

For graduate school, Bandura settled on the University of Iowa. At the time, the psychology department there was a hotbed of research and scholarly activity. Among the distinguished faculty members were Kenneth Spence and Kurt Lewin. Spence was known for his research on learning and conditioning. Earlier, Spence had studied with Clark Hull, a leading figure in behaviorism, a school of psychology that posits that organisms can be trained, or conditioned, to respond in specific ways to specific stimuli. At Iowa, Spence extended Hull's theories and research in an effort to come up with a precise mathematical formula to describe the learning of behavior. The two men's research on learning became known collectively as the Hull-Spence theory.

Lewin, on the other hand, had a rather different approach to the study of human behavior—an approach he called field theory. Lewin held that a person's behavior arises from complex interactions among psychological factors inside the person, environmental factors outside the person, and the relationship between these inner and outer worlds. Lewin proposed his field theory as a method for analyzing these kinds of causal relationships.

It must have been a very exciting time and place for Bandura. As he later recalled in a book by Richard Evans:

> I found Iowa to be intellectually lively, but also very supportive. . .At Iowa we were imprinted early on a model of scholarship that combined high respect for theory linked to venturesome research. It was an excellent beginning for a career.

Bandura also found time for nonacademic interests. One day, while golfing with a friend, he found himself playing behind a pair of female golfers. Eventually, he wound up in a sand trap with one of the women, Virginia Varns, who was on the teaching staff at the College of Nursing. The two struck up an acquaintance that blossomed into a lifelong romance. Bandura and Varns were married in 1952, the same year Bandura finished his PhD in clinical psychology. The couple went on to have two daughters: Mary, born in 1954, and Carol, born in 1958.

Career at Stanford

In 1953, Bandura took a job as an instructor in the psychology department at Stanford University. He has remained at Stanford ever since, becoming a full professor in 1964. In 1974, Stanford awarded Bandura an endowed chair, a high honor in the academic world, and he became the David Starr Jordan Professor of Social Science in Psychology. The intellectual climate at Stanford has served Bandura well, providing eminent colleagues and bright students with whom to conduct research and exchange ideas.

Perhaps the first prominent colleague to influence Bandura at Stanford was Robert Sears, who was chairman of the psychology department when Bandura arrived. Among other things, Sears was studying child-rearing patterns that led to aggressiveness and dependency in children. Following this line of work, Bandura and his first graduate student, Richard Walters, began studying the family backgrounds of very aggressive delinquents. They discovered that one factor affecting aggression among teenagers was whether or not the teens' parents were hostile or aggressive. In 1959, Bandura and Walters published a book titled *Adolescent Aggression*, which described their research on this subject.

Bandura was struck by the seeming influence of parental role models on teenagers' aggressive behavior. He wanted to study this effect in more depth experimentally, but first he had to come up with a workable study design. The result was the now-famous Bobo doll experiments, which Bandura conducted with Dorothea Ross and Sheila Ross. In 1963, the findings from this research were summarized in a second book with Walters, titled *Social Learning and Personality Development*. Few areas of psychological research have ever captured the public imagination as well as the Bobo doll studies did. As Bandura told Evans, "When I'm introduced at invited lectures at other universities, the students place a Bobo doll by the lectern. From time to time I have been asked to autograph one. The Bobo doll has achieved stardom in psychological circles."

Of course, it was Bandura himself who was really the rising star. In 1964, in addition to being made a professor at Stanford, he was elected a Fellow of the APA. During the 1969–70 school year, he was awarded a fellowship at the Center for Advanced Study in the Behavioral Sciences, a center near Stanford that brings together scientists and scholars from around the world who show exceptional accomplishment or promise in their fields. In 1969, Bandura published *Principles of Behavior Modification*, the first important book in cognitive behavior therapy. In 1974, Bandura received his endowed chair at Stanford, and, during the 1976–77

PRINCIPAL PUBLICATIONS

- With R. H. Walters. *Adolescent Aggression.* New York: Ronald Press, 1959.
- With R. H. Walters. *Social Learning and Personality Development.* New York: Holt, Rinehart & Winston, 1963.
- *Principles of Behavior Modification.* New York: Holt, Rinehart & Winston, 1969.
- Editor. *Psychological Modeling: Conflicting Theories.* Chicago: Aldine-Atherton Press, 1971.
- *Aggression: A Social Learning Analysis.* Englewood Cliffs, NJ: Prentice-Hall, 1973.
- "Self-Efficacy: Toward a Unifying Theory of Behavioral Change." *Psychological Review* 84 (1977) 191–215.
- *Social Learning Theory.* Englewood Cliffs, NJ: Prentice-Hall, 1977.
- *Social Foundations of Thought and Action: A Social Cognitive Theory.* Englewood Cliffs, NJ: Prentice-Hall, 1986.
- Editor. *Self-Efficacy in Changing Societies.* New York: Cambridge University Press, 1995.
- *Self-Efficacy: The Exercise of Control.* New York: Freeman, 1997.

---

school year, he served as chairman of the psychology department there.

Meanwhile, Bandura continued his ambitious research program. In 1977, he offered a theoretical framework for his findings in *Social Learning Theory.* This book had a dramatic impact on psychology. It heralded a great upsurge in interest in social learning theory among other psychologists during the 1980s.

By this time, however, it was already growing apparent to Bandura that something was missing from his theory. In a 1977 paper, titled "Self-Efficacy: Toward a Unifying Theory of Behavioral Change," he identified the missing piece as self-beliefs. Soon, Bandura had broadened his social learning theory to include a wide range of self-beliefs and self-control abilities. He described a system in which a person's beliefs, thoughts, feelings, and physical responses

interact with both the environment and the person's behavior. He then renamed his expanded theory the "social-cognitive theory," both to distinguish it from other social learning theories of the day and to stress the central importance of beliefs and thoughts. In 1986, Bandura published *Social Foundations of Thought and Action: A Social Cognitive Theory,* which set forth his new theory of human functioning.

The linchpin of social-cognitive theory is self-efficacy. In the last few decades, Bandura has continued to explore this concept and its many practical applications. Researchers around the world have taken up the torch as well. In 1993, a scientific conference was held in Germany on young people's beliefs about their personal efficacy to meet the demands of a rapidly changing world. Bandura later edited a book, titled *Self-Efficacy in Changing Societies,* containing papers presented at the conference. Then, in 1997, he published *Self-Efficacy: The Exercise of Control,* in which he set forth his detailed ideas about the causes and effects of self-efficacy beliefs.

Lifetime of achievement

Over the years, Bandura has collected numerous awards and honors. These include a Guggenheim Fellowship (1972), the APA Distinguished Scientific Contributions Award (1980), the APA William James Award (1989), the APA Thorndike Award for Distinguished Contributions of Psychology to Education (1999), and the Lifetime Achievement Award from the Association for the Advancement of Behavior Therapy (2001). He is a member of the Institute of Medicine of the National Academy of Sciences. He has also received 14 honorary degrees from universities around the world.

In return, Bandura has given generously of his time and energy to the field of psychology. He has held a number of offices in scientific societies, including serving as APA president in 1974 and being named honorary president of the Canadian Psychological Association in 1999. He has also sat on the editorial boards of some 30 journals. In addition, he has authored seven books and edited two others. Several of his books have been translated into languages such as Polish, Spanish, Portuguese, German, Japanese, Russian, French, Italian, and Korean. Today, Bandura's name and ideas are familiar to psychologists and psychology students worldwide.

In his late seventies, at a age when most people have long since retired, Bandura continues to publish and make contributions to psychology. His most recent interests include the psychological impact of electronic media, the means by which people affect their own motivation and behavior, the way people view their self-efficacy to influence events in their lives, and the source of stress reactions and depression.

THEORIES

Perhaps the most notable aspect of Bandura's long career is the number of significant contributions he has made through the decades. In the 1960s, he published classic research on observational learning and modeling. In the 1970s, he expanded upon these findings to develop an influential theory of social learning. In the 1980s, this evolved into a social-cognitive theory of human functioning. And in the 1990s, Bandura further refined his ideas about self-efficacy. In recent years, his followers have found widespread practical uses for self-efficacy theory in education, mental health, physical health, sports, business, and politics.

Observational learning and modeling

Main points Behaviorism, the dominant school of psychology when Bandura was a student, holds that people are conditioned, or trained, to respond in certain ways by rewards and punishments. Bandura soon realized that this could not be the whole explanation for how people learn. It would take several lifetimes to learn all the complicated responses that people need to know by rewards and punishments alone. Bandura suggested that there must be a way that people can learn simply by watching others, thereby removing the need to learn everything by tedious trial-and-error.

This process of learning by watching others is called observational learning or vicarious learning. It is closely related to the concept of modeling, in which people fashion themselves after the image of another. According to Bandura, people do not just mindlessly mimic whatever they see. Instead, although people may learn a multitude of behaviors by observation, they consciously decide which ones to actually copy.

Explanation One powerful factor influencing whether or not a behavior will be copied is the expected outcome. Bandura's research showed that people are more likely to copy behavior that they expect will lead to a positive outcome. However, this expectation is not rooted only in the actual rewards and punishments that people have seen. It is also based on anticipated consequences; in other words, on people's beliefs about what will happen.

Several other factors may also affect the likelihood that an observed behavior will be imitated:

- Characteristics of the person being observed—For example, studies have found that the person's age, sex, similarity to the observer, status, skill, and power may all be important.

- Characteristics of the observer—For example, research has shown that people with low self-esteem, those who are more dependent, and those who have been rewarded in the past for imitative behavior are more likely to copy someone else. In addition, the observer obviously must have the necessary mental and physical skills to carry out the task.

- Characteristics of the behavior—For example, behavior that is simple or admired is more likely to be imitated.

Examples In the famous Bobo doll experiments, Bandura and his colleagues showed some children a film in which an adult hit, hammered, and kicked the inflatable doll. These children were more likely than ones who had not seen the film to later hit and kick the doll themselves when given a chance to play with it. This tendency was strengthened if the adult in the film was rewarded for aggressive behavior, and the tendency was weakened if the adult was punished. However, just seeing the aggressive behavior was enough for the children to learn it, even when no rewards or punishments were given.

Of course, Bandura was not the first person to note that people often learn by copying others. Anyone who has spent time around young children, for instance, has undoubtedly noticed how they mimic their parents. Two decades before the Bobo doll experiments, Neal Miller and John Dollard had published the first scholarly book about observational learning, titled *Social Learning and Imitation*. Miller and Dollard's work was still in the behaviorist mode, but they construed conditioning more broadly than had earlier theorists. They emphasized not only personal and social rewards, but also factors such as motivations and drives. Bandura took these ideas a step further. More than any other psychologist, Bandura built a solid foundation of scientific evidence about how observational learning actually occurs, with or without rewards and punishments. In so doing, he helped the study of observational learning truly break free of behaviorism.

At the same time, Bandura's findings also ran counter to another major strain in psychology: psychoanalytic theory. According to the psychoanalytic concept of catharsis, when people are given an opportunity to safely release feelings of aggression, it relieves those feelings and reduces the impulses associated with them. Based on this theory, watching the adult model pummel the Bobo doll should have drained the children's aggressive feelings and reduced their violent behavior. In fact, it had the opposite effect. Bandura's studies soundly refuted the notion that watching aggressive behavior might offer a healthy catharsis for the observers.

Social learning

Main points   Before Bandura, psychologist Julian Rotter had put forth his own theory of social learning. In a 1954 book, titled *Social Learning and Clinical Psychology*, Rotter held that people choose which behaviors to perform based on two factors: reinforcement value and outcome expectancy. Reinforcement value refers to the degree to which an individual values the expected reinforcement, or reward, for an action. Outcome expectancy refers to how strongly the individual expects the action to have a positive result. Clearly, Rotter laid the groundwork for much of Bandura's thinking. He also served as a crucial bridge between behaviorism and Bandura's more modern version of social learning theory.

In his theory, Bandura stressed the importance of observational learning and modeling. However, like Rotter, he also emphasized the role of expected outcomes. Bandura held that, even when people have observed and learned how to perform a behavior, they will only actually do it if they believe their action will lead to a desirable outcome.

Explanation   Bandura believed that the imitation of someone else's behavior was not a passive process. Instead, it was an active choice involving four different mental functions:

- Attention—This factor was affected mainly by characteristics of the person being observed and the situation.

- Retention—This factor was affected mainly by the observer's ability to mentally process the observed behavior and store it in memory.

- Motor reproduction—This factor referred to the observer's ability to turn the stored memory into physical action. It also included the person's capacity for mentally rehearsing the behavior.

- Motivation—This factor referred to the observer's desire or drive to copy the behavior. Of all the factors, this one had the greatest influence on whether an observed behavior was actually imitated.

Bandura believed that people are capable of self-reinforcement. In other words, they can teach themselves to act in a certain way by thinking about the potential consequences of the action. Eventually, Bandura expanded this into a broader concept: self-regulation, or self-control. According to Bandura, self-regulation is the sum of a person's goals, planning, and

self-reinforcement. As part of the self-regulation process, people set their own internal standards of behavior, against which they judge their own success or failure. The standards can be picked up by observational learning, and especially from watching key role models, such as parents and teachers. However, the standards can also be based on the person's own past behavior, which is used as a yardstick against which to measure future actions.

Examples   Bandura studied self-regulation in several ways. For example, along with student Carol Kupers, he conducted research in which children watched either an adult or another child play a bowling game. The models had a supply of candy, from which they rewarded themselves based on either a high performance standard or a low one. Then the children who had been observing were given a chance to play the game. They, too, were provided with candy, and they were allowed to dole out their own rewards according to whatever standards they chose for themselves. Children who had watched a model set a high standard were more likely to adopt a strict standard as well. The reverse was true for children who had watched a model set a low standard.

Bandura has always been interested not only in theory, but also in practice. Based on his research, he developed the use of modeling as a therapeutic tool. Modeling has been used most often in the treatment of phobias, or irrationally intense fears. The client watches a model come into contact with the feared object, then is encouraged to imitate the model's behavior. At first, this is done under relatively nonthreatening conditions. As therapy progresses, though, the threat level is gradually raised. Eventually, the client confronts the feared object on his or her own.

Social learning and aggression

Main points   Aggression is one of the most troubling, yet pervasive, aspects of human existence. It is no wonder, then, that a number of theories about the nature and causes of aggression have been proposed over the years. For example, Sigmund Freud explained aggression as a death wish that is turned outward onto others through a process called displacement. Dollard, Miller, and their colleagues proposed that aggression is a response to the frustration of some goal-directed behavior. And several ethologists who studied animal behavior, such as Konrad Lorenz, have argued that aggression is a natural instinct common to both humans and other animals.

Among these many theories, Bandura's theory of aggression as a socially learned behavior remains one of the most influential. In his early work with Walters, Bandura found that very aggressive teenagers often came from homes where the parents modeled hostile attitudes and aggressive behavior. Even when the parents would not tolerate aggression at home, they often demanded it of their sons when settling disputes with other boys. The parents were hostile toward both the school system, and the students who were blamed for harassing their sons. To Bandura, it seemed clear that the teenagers in these families were imitating the hostility and aggression of the parents.

Bandura explored this idea further in the Bobo doll studies. These studies showed the key role that observational learning plays in aggressive behavior. As Bandura later told Evans:

> If there is any behavior where observational learning is important, it is aggression, because ineffectual aggression can get one disfigured, maimed or killed. One cannot afford to learn through trial and error. So most aggressive patterns are transmitted through modeling.

Examples In the Bobo doll experiments, children watched a short film of an adult behaving violently toward the doll. The adult model not only punched the doll, but also engaged in some unusual aggressive behavior that the children were unlikely to have seen elsewhere. At one point, the model laid the doll on its side, sat on the doll, and punched it repeatedly in the nose. Then the model stood the doll back up and struck it on the head with a mallet. After that, the model threw the doll up into the air aggressively and kicked it around the room. The children were then turned loose in a playroom filled with toys, including the Bobo doll. Many who had watched the film did indeed imitate the aggressive behavior they had observed.

From this finding, it was only a short jump to wondering how media violence might be affecting millions of viewers, especially young ones. The Bobo doll studies attracted the attention of activists and politicians as well as a Presidential Commission on Violence in the Media. Bandura himself testified at congressional hearings on the subject. He also wrote about the widespread influence of media violence in a 1973 book, titled *Aggression: A Social Learning Analysis*. Bandura believed that public hearings and self-regulation by the entertainment industry were of little practical use in curbing media violence. Instead, he championed the cause of viewer demand for less violent alternatives.

In the early years of the twenty-first century, the effect of television has only become more pervasive.

Its global reach has changed the world in many ways—not least of which, by greatly increasing the kinds of behaviors that children have a chance to observe. As Bandura wrote in an article in *European Psychologist*:

> In the past, modeling influences were largely confined to the styles of behavior and social practices in one's immediate community. The advent of television vastly expanded the range of models to which members of society are exposed day in and day out. By drawing on these modeled patterns of thought and behavior, observers transcend the bounds of their customary environment.

Explanation Of course, not everyone who grows up with an aggressive parent or who watches a violent television show goes on to copy what he or she has seen. According to Bandura, there are two major triggers for aggression. One is stress, or frustration, as it is called in Dollard and Miller's theory. However, Bandura notes that stress produces general emotional arousal, not a specific drive to act in a certain way. Some people may express that arousal through aggression, but others may express it by asking for help, becoming withdrawn, or escaping through alcohol or drugs. And still others use the arousal to motivate themselves to take positive steps.

The other major trigger for aggression is the expectation of benefits. This explains why some people behave aggressively even when they are not emotionally aroused. For example, some children learn that, if they act like bullies, the other children will let them have their way. Therefore, aggression can serve many purposes. As Bandura put it:

> Some people will resort to aggression to get material benefits. Others behave aggressively because it gains them status and social approval. Still others rely on aggressive conquests to build their self-esteem and sense of manliness. Some people derive satisfaction from seeing pain inflicted on those they hate. And in many instances, people resort to aggression to terminate mistreatment.

Social-cognitive theory
Main points Bandura's work on self-regulation shed new light on how people understand their own motivations and control their own actions. It also aroused Bandura's interest in how people exercise control over the nature and quality of their own lives—a capacity he refers to as human agency. Writing in the *Annual Review of Psychology*, Bandura explained the concept of agency this way: "To be an agent is to intentionally make things happen by one's actions." This capacity involves not only self-regulatory skills, but also other abilities and

belief systems that play a role in self-directed change. It allows people to adapt to changing circumstances, and it gives them a means of self-development and self-renewal.

In Bandura's view, agency has certain core features that cut to the very heart of what it means to be human:

- Intentionality—Agency refers to acts that are done intentionally, and this implies the ability to make future plans.

- Forethought—In addition to making plans, people think about the future in other ways. They set goals, anticipate the likely consequences of different actions, and choose a course of action that is likely to produce positive consequences and avoid negative ones.

- Self-reactiveness—Once people have formed an intention and created an action plan, they still have to put the plan in motion. Therefore, people also must be able to motivate themselves and regulate their own behavior.

- Self-reflectiveness—People are not only agents of action, but also of thought. They have the ability to reflect on their own thoughts, motivations, and values as well as the meaning of their lives.

Giving an address as honorary president of the Canadian Psychological Association, Bandura explained why human agency holds such an important place in his social-cognitive theory:

> People have the power to influence what they do and to make things happen. They are not just onlooking hosts of brain mechanisms orchestrated by environmental events. The sensory, motor, and cerebral systems are tools people can use to accomplish things that give meaning, direction, and satisfaction to their lives.

Explanation   In the 1980s, Bandura gathered all the diverse strands from his earlier research into a single theory, which he dubbed social-cognitive theory. This theory sees human functioning as the dynamic interplay of personal, environmental, and behavioral factors. (Personal factors include an individual's beliefs, thoughts, feelings, and physical responses.) Each of the three factors influences the others and is influenced by them in turn. Therefore, people are not only products of their environment, but also producers of it.

This broader view of human functioning led Bandura to realize that there might be wider possibilities for promoting change. Within the social-cognitive

view, a change at any point in the three-part system can lead to changes in the other parts. The implication is that a therapy or social program can be aimed at a variety of targets and still succeed. It can be aimed at instilling positive beliefs, thoughts, feelings, and motivations. *Or*, it can be aimed at decreasing undesirable behaviors and increasing desirable ones. *Or*, it can be aimed at changing the social conditions under which people live, work, and go to school. In other words, there is more than one path to the same destination.

Examples   Consider the example of an educational program aimed at improving the academic performance of students. Teachers might address personal factors by encouraging a positive attitude toward school and instilling a realistic sense of confidence in the students. They might address behavioral factors by teaching students the academic skills and good work habits that are needed to do well in school. Or, they might address environmental factors by asking the school board for funds to buy better books and supplies.

In recent years, the trend in psychology has been to shy away from grand, comprehensive theories. Bandura's social-cognitive theroy is a notable exception to the rule. By bucking the trend, Bandura has set himself apart, drawn attention to his ideas, and left his mark on fields ranging from psychology and education to healthcare and business. As he told Evans, "I have tried to analyze human lives from a broader social perspective that transcends the arbitrary boundaries of academic disciplines."

Self-efficacy

Main points   The centerpiece of social-cognitive theory is self-efficacy. Bandura defines perceived self-efficacy as people's beliefs about their capability to produce desired results through their own actions. According to Bandura, people with a high sense of self-efficacy approach difficult tasks as challenges to be met, rather than threats to be avoided. They also set challenging goals for themselves, and they maintain a strong commitment to achieving them. When faced with a setback, they quickly recover their confidence and simply redouble their efforts. Bandura states that this type of outlook leads to personal successes while reducing stress and decreasing the risk of depression.

In contrast, people with a low sense of self-efficacy avoid difficult tasks, which they view as personal threats. They rarely push themselves to excel, and they have a weak commitment to any goals they do decide to pursue. When faced with an obstacle, they dwell on their personal weaknesses and the potential for failure rather than looking for solutions. If a setback occurs, they are quick to give up and slow to recover their confidence afterward. It takes relatively little for such individuals to lose faith in themselves. As a result, they easily fall prey to stress and depression.

In an article in *European Psychologist*, Bandura explained why self-efficacy beliefs are so crucial to his social-cognitive theory:

> Among the mechanisms of self-regulation none is more central or pervasive than beliefs of personal efficacy. This belief system is the foundation of human agency. Unless people believe they can produce desired outcomes and forestall undesired ones by their actions they have little incentive to act or to persevere in the face of difficulties. Whatever other factors serve as guides and motivators, they are rooted in the core belief that one has the power to produce changes by one's actions.

Explanation   According to Bandura, people's motivations, thoughts, feelings, and actions often have more to do with what they believe than with what is really true. He posits that self-efficacy beliefs have such a strong impact because they affect four major psychological processes:

- Cognitive processes—Most courses of action are first organized in thought. Often, they revolve around setting goals. The stronger people's perceived self-efficacy, higher the goals they are apt to set for themselves, and greater their commitment to achieving them. People who think of themselves as having high efficacy also tend to imagine successful outcomes. These imagined scenes of success help them plan and rehearse the steps they need to take in order to succeed in real life. In addition, people with a strong sense of self-efficacy are better equipped than those with low self-efficacy to stay task-oriented in the face of pressures, setbacks, and failures.

- Motivational processes—There are different theories about how people motivate themselves, but all are consistent with Bandura's concept of self-efficacy. For example, in attribution theory, people keep themselves motivated by attributing failures to insufficient effort, rather than low ability. This kind of thinking is typical of people with high perceived self-efficacy. In expectancy-value theory, motivation is based on people's expectation that a given action will lead to a particular result, as well as on the value they attach to that result. People who are high in perceived self-efficacy are more likely to expect that their behavior will lead to a desirable outcome. On the other hand, people who are low in perceived self-efficacy may not go after valued goals, because they do not expect to achieve them.

- Affective processes—Affective states, or feelings, are also closely tied to perceived self-efficacy. In particular, people's beliefs about their ability to cope seem to have a significant effect on how much stress and depression they actually feel in threatening or difficult situations. People who believe they can control their own disturbing thoughts are less likely to be overwhelmed by anxious or depressed thinking. In addition, two common paths to depression are unfulfilled dreams and social isolation. People with a low sense of self-efficacy are less likely to fulfill their dreams and attain their social goals.

- Selection processes—While people can affect their environment, the environment affects them in return. Therefore, one final way in which perceived self-efficacy can help shape people's lives is by influencing the kinds of environments in which they put themselves. In a 1994 article, Bandura gave the example of perceived self-efficacy affecting career choice: "The higher the level of people's perceived self-efficacy the wider the range of career options they seriously consider, the greater their interest in them, and the better they prepare themselves educationally for the occupational pursuits they choose. . ."

Obviously, a strong belief in one's own efficacy has many benefits, based on Bandura's theory. It follows that knowing how to foster this self-belief would be very helpful. Bandura has outlined four ways in which a strong sense of self-efficacy can be developed. The first and most effective way is through mastery experiences. Simply put, past successes strengthen the belief that future success is possible, while past failures undermine it. After people become convinced they have what it takes to succeed, they are more likely to stick with their goals, even when problems arise.

A second way to build strong self-efficacy beliefs is through vicarious experience; in other words, by watching other people perform the behavior. The impact of modeling on perceived self-efficacy depends largely on how much the observer sees himself or herself as being like the model. The more similar the model and observer, greater the effect. When people watch someone similar to themselves accomplish a task through sustained effort, they are more likely to believe that they can do it, too. At the same time, they may learn some of the skills they need to succeed by observing the successful model. On the other hand, when people see someone fail despite great effort, they are more likely to lose faith in their own abilities as well.

A third way to instill self-efficacy beliefs is by social persuasion; that is, by telling people that they can be successful. People who are persuaded by others that they have what it takes to succeed are likely to try harder and be more persistent than those who hold self-doubts. Unfortunately, it is much harder to build up perceived self-efficacy this way than it is to destroy it. Unrealistically positive messages may be quickly disproved, leading to failure and demoralization. On the other hand, overly negative messages may keep people from achieving as much as they could, by persuading them not to attempt a challenging task in the first place or by convincing them to give up at the first sign of difficulty.

A final way that self-efficacy beliefs are reinforced is through emotional and physiological reactions. When people face a stressful or challenging situation, they naturally experience emotional and physiological arousal. Those who are high in perceived self-efficacy may see this arousal as a sign that they are energized. The energetic feeling, in turn, helps them perform their best, which adds to their sense of self-efficacy in the future. In contrast, people who are low in perceived self-efficacy may see arousal as a sign of stress they are helpless to control. The situation can quickly turn into a self-fulfilling prophesy. For example, athletes who view arousal before a game as a sign of fear or weakness are unlikely to play their best. The poor performance, in turn, further lowers their sense of self-efficacy.

In sum, Bandura contends that perceived self-efficacy is critical to success in almost any area. As he wrote in his 1994 article, "the successful, the venturesome, the sociable, the nonanxious, the nondepressed, the social reformers, and the innovators take an optimistic view of their personal capabilities to exercise influence over events that affect their lives. If not unrealistically exaggerated, such self-beliefs foster positive well-being and human accomplishments."

Examples   Everyday life is filled with obstacles and difficulties. Bandura believes that people need a strong sense of self-efficacy in order to take on a challenge or keep plugging away when problems arise. He notes that when people vastly overestimate their own abilities, this can lead to trouble. However, people may need a somewhat optimistic view of themselves in order to achieve great things. As Bandura wrote in a 1994 article: "If efficacy beliefs always reflected only what people can do routinely they would rarely fail but they would not set aspirations beyond their immediate reach nor mount the extra effort needed to surpass their ordinary performances."

High perceived self-efficacy can help people keep trying in the face of setbacks. As an example of this, Bandura cites a number of great authors, artists, musicians, and scientists who met with early rejection,

including James Joyce, Vincent Van Gogh, Igor Stravinsky, and Robert Goddard. Without a strong belief in their own capability to achieve something worthwhile through their actions, these individuals might have given up early in their careers, and the world would have been the poorer for it.

Bandura claims that groups of people can hold beliefs about their collective self-efficacy as well. He says that the strength of organizations and even whole nations lies partly in the members' belief that they can improve their lives through their combined efforts. Without this belief, people may not choose to work as a group, or they may not put much effort into it. They also may not have the determination to stick with their goals if their joint efforts fail to produce fast results.

How do different people come to see themselves as having more or less self-efficacy? According to Bandura, people's experiences at key points in life can affect the development of their perceived self-efficacy. These are not firm stages that everyone must pass through, however. Instead, they are merely typical experiences that help shape many people's views of their own abilities and limitations.

- Infancy—Newborns have no sense of self, according to Bandura. However, as babies grow, they gradually develop an awareness of their ability to produce effects by their own actions. They shake a rattle to make a sound, for instance, or cry to bring Mom into the room. Babies who get reliable results from their actions start to become more and more attuned to their own behavior and its effects. At the same time, babies become increasingly aware of their separateness from other people. Eventually, they form an abstract idea of themselves as a distinct self.

- Childhood and families—Young children continue to test their abilities and learn from the results they get. At this early age, children are adding new physical, mental, social, and language skills almost daily. If they are able to put these new skills to good use, then they develop a sense of self-efficacy. Bandura believes that parents can encourage this process by being responsive to their babies' behavior and providing a safe but rich environment for trying out the new skills. For example, a toddler might learn that every time he says "Momma, look," Mom appears and takes a few minutes to talk to him. Or, a young child might learn that she is able to create fascinating, colorful patterns by moving a crayon across a sheet of paper. From these kinds of daily experiences, children learn that they have the power to control some of the things that occur in their world.

- Childhood and peers—As children grow, they begin to learn from and compare themselves to other children. Older children may serve as role models, while children of the same age provide a standard against which youngsters can compare their own abilities. Because peers serve as important influences, a lack of interaction with siblings and friends can interfere with the development of perceived self-efficacy.

- Childhood and school—As children reach school age, school becomes the main place in which they acquire and test their mental abilities. These abilities are learned not only through formal education, but also from observing how other students use their thinking skills. Several factors affect how children come to see their own abilities. These factors include comparisons to other students, comments from teachers, rewards for progress, and the satisfaction of achieving goals.

- Adolescence—The teen years are a period of rapid change. Teenagers need a strong sense of self-efficacy to handle all the physical, mental, and social changes in their lives. Tricky new issues may arise, such as decisions about drug use and sexual behavior. According to Bandura, teenagers who are overly sheltered from making these kinds of choices may not have a chance to learn good decision-making skills. On the other hand, teenagers with a weak sense of self-efficacy may not be prepared to stand up to peer pressure. During these years, teenagers also must get ready for the challenges of adulthood that lie ahead. This means they need to master a whole new set of skills for living in adult society. In addition, they must make important choices about college and career, and their beliefs about their own abilities are likely to have a big impact on the choices they make.

- Early adulthood—As young adults, people need to cope with many new demands, including marriage, parenthood, and career. A firm sense of self-efficacy can help them master the skills they need. On the other hand, those who see themselves as low in self-efficacy are likely to find that they are plagued by self-doubts and ill-equipped to tackle new challenges. As a result, they may fall victim to stress and depression.

- Middle age—In middle adulthood, people tend to settle into stable routines, which helps them solidify their sense of self-efficacy in key areas of their lives. However, the apparent stability is an illusion. It is always balanced by the need to keep up with changes in society. At work, there is constant pressure from younger competitors. Even in middle age, then, people need to keep growing and learning. A strong belief in their own efficacy helps them accomplish this growth.

- Late adulthood—The major issues of late life often revolve around retirement, illness, and the loss of loved ones. As in earlier years, a firm sense of self-efficacy helps. For example, people with high perceived self-efficacy are better prepared to take up a new hobby or make new friends after retirement. In addition, older adults with a strong sense of self-efficacy are less likely to exaggerate the decline in abilities that occurs with age. In contrast, those with low perceived self-efficacy are apt to see every small problem as a sign that they are going downhill fast. This belief may keep them from fully enjoying the last years of their lives.

A quick survey of any psychology journal from just a few years ago will reveal that many of the studies and theories published in these journals are already outdated. Yet Bandura's work over the span of more than 40 years has remained remarkably fresh and timely. His first important research dealt with modeling and aggression. Much of his more recent work deals with the development and importance of self-efficacy beliefs in a variety of settings. Both lines of research are still very active and relevant areas of study—a tribute to Bandura's skill as both researcher and theorist.

Social-cognitive theory and moral disengagement

Main points   Bandura began his career by studying aggression in children and teenagers. Near the end of his career, the roots of aggression and violence are still of great interest to him. He has extended his research to include all kinds of moral disengagement; in other words, the capacity for all types of antisocial and immoral acts. In social-cognitive theory, the capacity for self-control over moral behavior has two functions. On one hand, it gives people the ability to refrain from acting inhumanely. On the other hand, it gives people the ability to behave in a kind and sensitive manner.

According to Bandura, people set standards for themselves that guide their moral behavior. Most of the time, these standards help people keep themselves in line. People refrain from behaving badly, because that would bring self-blame and guilt. Instead, they usually prefer to act in a way that leaves them with a sense of worth and self-respect. Sometimes, however, people use tricks of thinking to let themselves off the hook for violating their own standards.

Explanation The kinds of thoughts that lead to moral disengagement include:

- Moral justification—To make bad conduct seem more acceptable, people tell themselves that it serves a worthy purpose.
- Euphemistic labeling—When discussing offensive or upsetting behavior, people avoid describing it bluntly and instead substitute harmless-sounding terms.
- Advantageous comparison—To make vile acts seem less reprehensible, people compare them to even worse behavior.
- Displacement of responsibility—To avoid personal responsibility for their actions, people view themselves as just following orders.
- Diffusion of responsibility—To reduce their own responsibility for an act, people share the labor and focus on just their part of it, which seems harmless by itself.
- Disregard or distortion of consequences—When people hurt others, they think about the consequences in ways that ignore or minimize the harm.
- Dehumanization—To justify inhumane behavior, people view the victims as being less than human.
- Attribution of blame—To excuse cruel or violent behavior, people blame it on the victims.

Fortunately, just as people can use their thoughts to justify immorality, they can also use them to motivate moral behavior. As Bandura sees it, moral thinking helps stop immoral actions in part by helping people control their angry feelings. Anger control, in turn, is based partly on people's belief in their ability to handle their emotions; in other words, on their perceived self-efficacy for emotional control.

Social factors also play a big role in moral behavior. Problems can arise when there is a conflict between the moral standards people set for themselves and the standards of society. At times, people may find themselves being pressured by others to follow courses of action that are at odds with their own moral code. The response to this kind of pressure depends on the relative strength of the personal and social forces. In some cases, a moral tug-of-war can produce principled dissent and social activism. In other cases, however, it may lead to moral disengagement.

Examples In recent years, Bandura has studied how people reach the point of moral disengagement. For example, in one study, Bandura and three colleagues from the University of Rome studied 799 Italian students in the sixth through eighth grades. The

students filled out several questionnaires designed to assess their moral disengagement as well as other relevant aspects of their thoughts, feelings, and behaviors. The researchers found that students who reported lots of morally disengaged thinking did indeed tend to commit more aggressive and antisocial acts.

Compared to students with a strong sense of morality, those who were morally disengaged also tended to be easily angered. In addition, they were prone to thinking about revenge for past slights. These feelings and thoughts just added to their propensity for aggression. When the morally disengaged students did act aggressively, they were not much bothered by guilt. They also did not feel the need to make amends for any harm they had caused.

The flip side is that morally oriented thinking can prevent many aggressive and antisocial acts. People who take personal responsibility for their actions are less likely to behave badly, even when provoked. When such people have an aggressive impulse, one way they keep themselves from acting on it is through self-reproof. And if they occasionally fail to keep their behavior in check, such people try to make amends to those they have hurt.

In these dangerous times, exploring ways to promote a more humane society seems like a particularly important use of social-cognitive theory. In Bandura's words, "At the social level, we need to create control mechanisms so that social systems support compassionate behavior rather than inhumane activities."

HISTORICAL CONTEXT

On an Emory University website devoted to Bandura, there is a page that traces Bandura's "professional genealogy" back through six previous generations of psychologists. The line of descent goes like this:

- William James influenced
- James Rowland Angell at Harvard University, who influenced
- John Watson at the University of Chicago, who influenced
- Karl Spencer Lashley at Johns Hopkins University, who influenced
- Carney Landis at the University of Minnesota, who influenced
- Art Benton at Columbia University, who influenced
- Albert Bandura at the University of Iowa

	POSITIVE	NEGATIVE
REINFORCEMENT		
The frequency of a behavior is increased because of the behavior of the subject.	When a person receives reinforcement after engaging in some behavior, the person is likely to repeat that behavior.	When a person experiences a negative state and does something to eliminate the undesired state, the person is likely to repeat that behavior.
PUNISHMENT		
The frequency of a behavior is decreased because of the behavior of the subject.	When a person engages in a behavior and something negative is applied as a result, that behavior is less likely to be repeated.	When a person engages in a behavior and something positive is taken away, that behavior is less likely to be repeated.

(Courtesy Thomson Gale.)

Although this is a lighthearted exercise, it has a serious point: No scientist works in isolation. All scientists, including Bandura, are heavily influenced by the work of those who have gone before. In some cases, Bandura built upon the ideas of his predecessors. In other cases, he reacted against an idea by proposing an alternative.

Hull, Spence, and behaviorism

At the time Bandura was in graduate school, psychology was dominated by behaviorism, a theory that holds that people can be conditioned to respond in specific ways to specific stimuli. According to strict behaviorism, people's personalities are nothing more than the sum total of the behaviors learned through this conditioning process. Thus, with complete understanding of stimuli and responses, it should be possible to predict and control the behavior of individuals and even entire cultures.

One of the central concepts of behaviorism is reinforcement. Simply put, this is an event that strengthens a behavior and makes it more likely to be repeated in the future. Positive reinforcement produces pleasant feelings, while negative reinforcement relieves unpleasant feelings. Either way, the person feels better after performing the behavior. Punishment, on the other hand, is an event that decreases the likelihood that a behavior will be repeated in the future. It produces this effect by making the person feel worse after performing the behavior. Although punishment may make a behavior less likely in the short term, it is usually not a good way to get rid of a behavior permanently. In general, its impact on behavior is not as powerful as that of reinforcement. As the saying goes, you can catch more flies with honey than with vinegar.

In its purest form, behaviorism implies that behavior is nothing more than a function of stimuli, rewards, and punishments. By the 1930s and '40s, however, a number of experimental psychologists were already starting to chafe at this notion. While they still believed that external events were paramount, they also thought it was important to consider internal states. Hull, a professor at Yale University, was one of the most influential of these new-style behaviorists.

Hull did most of his research in white rats, rather than humans. Like other behaviorists, he believed that it was only logical to start by studying the simpler stimuli and responses of lower animals. The information gleaned from these animals could then be used to understand complex human behaviors. Hull believed that animals made responses in order to relieve an internal drive. The responses themselves then became stimuli, leading to more responses. This explained how a rat presented with the stimulus of a maze could make a whole series of responses to find its way to food, which would reduce its hunger drive.

Hull's main contribution, however, was turning attention onto the internal state of the animal while it was learning. Other researchers built on this idea. Among them was Kenneth Spence, who had studied with Hull at Yale University. Spence believed that reinforcement was not absolutely necessary for learning to occur. However, he still thought that reinforcement was a very powerful motivator. Spence became head of the psychology department at the University of Iowa in 1942. When Bandura arrived there, Spence was still the guiding force in the department, and the University of Iowa was a major center of experimental psychology.

Thus, Bandura was immersed in behaviorism as a student. Right from the start, however, he was uncomfortable with some of its tenets. From the beginning of his research career, Bandura argued against conditioning as the main method of learning new behaviors. Instead, he argued for the importance of observational learning and modeling. Of course, Bandura did not deny that conditioning could occur, nor did he claim that rewards and punishments were completely ineffective. He simply suggested that the observation of models was a more efficient way of learning in most situations.

Bandura also stressed that, when reinforcement had an effect, it was not a mindless process. In fact, reinforcement worked by teaching people to expect positive outcomes; in other words, by affecting the way they thought about things. Therefore, while behaviorism focused on outer stimuli and responses, Bandura focused on the inner thinking that connected the two. This was the cognitive part of his social-cognitive theory.

In addition, Bandura disagreed with the behaviorist focus on the control of human behavior through outward rewards and punishments. Early on, he emphasized the power of self-regulation. He believed that people could control their own behavior by setting personal standards and rewarding themselves for meeting these self-imposed goals. Over time, this idea evolved into the broader concept of human agency, which holds that people can exercise some control over the nature and quality of events around them. As Bandura sees it, people are not just passive pawns of their environment. On the contrary, they are active directors of their own lives.

Miller, Dollard, and social learning

Miller and Dollard were also part of the group of psychologists who had gathered at Yale in the 1930s and '40s and were influenced by Hull. Miller and Dollard produced the first scholarly work on social learning. As they saw it, social learning involved habits, which were the associations between particular stimuli and responses. These habits were built up by way of a hierarchy of acquired drives. As an example, say a boy was petting a dog, when the dog suddenly attacked him. The boy would learn to avoid dogs whenever possible in the future. Beyond that, though, the boy would probably feel fear if a dog ran up to him in the park. This learned fear, in turn, would be an acquired drive that could itself lead to new behaviors that reduced the fear. For example, the boy might learn to always carry a stick for protection when walking through the park. Or, the boy might learn to wear headphones and play his favorite music. Of course, the

music would not do anything to protect him from the dog, but it would reduce the acquired drive of fear.

Miller and Dollard tried to use this concept of acquired drives to show how a complex adult personality could be built up out of the simple drives and responses of a baby. For example, if a baby is regularly rewarded for smiling and cooing when being held and fed, the baby may learn to be more socially active. Over time, this could develop into an outgoing personality. Miller and Dollard stressed that children's personalities were formed through social rewards. They also allowed for inner drives and motivations. Yet ultimately, their theory was still firmly rooted in conditioning.

Bandura picked up where Miller and Dollard left off. He, too, emphasized that children learn from social situations. However, he suggested that rewards were not necessary for this to occur. Bandura also moved internal thought processes to center stage. For Miller, Dollard, and the behaviorists before them, the essence of personality was in people's behavior. For Bandura, it was in their thoughts and beliefs.

Rotter and social learning

Rotter was another graduate of the University of Iowa, where he took classes with Lewin. However, he had moved on before Bandura arrived. In 1954, Rotter published *Social Learning and Clinical Psychology*, in which he laid out his own theory of social learning. Where Miller and Dollard's work in this area had been firmly grounded in conditioning and reinforcement, Rotter's work was a step further removed from behaviorism. Of course, this means it was also a step closer to Bandura's theory, which followed. In fact, Rotter's theory is often seen as a bridge between behaviorally based social learning theories and Bandura's cognitively based ideas.

Rotter believed that what we call personality is really an interaction between a person and the environment. Personality does not exist within a person independently of the environment in which that individual lives. By the same token, though, personality also does not consist of just a simple set of responses to stimuli. Instead, the very nature of the environment that a person responds to is affected by that individual's past learning experiences. To continue the earlier example, say the person who had been attacked by a dog in the past is walking with a friend when another dog approaches. The first person will respond with fear. However, if the friend has happy memories of a beloved childhood pet, she will probably have an entirely different response to the same dog. The difference in the two individuals' responses is based on their very different set of expectations.

According to Rotter, the way people ultimately act in a particular situation will be determined by two things: outcome expectancy, or how strongly they expect the behavior to have a positive result, and reinforcement value, or how much they value the expected reward. In the 1960s, Rotter also began looking at people's expectations about whether they could affect the rewards they received. Those who generally expected that they could achieve desired rewards through their own actions were said to have an internal locus of control. Those who believed that rewards were due to fate or luck, and therefore out of their hands, were said to have an external locus of control.

Rotter thought that reinforcement had a big influence on human behavior. However, he also recognized that people had long-lasting personal traits that were quite important as well. He identified locus of control as a trait that affected a whole range of behaviors in a number of settings. Subsequent research has shown that individuals do indeed seem to differ in locus of control, and that this difference is relatively stable over time.

It is easy to see the seeds of many of Bandura's ideas in Rotter's work. Both men stressed that behavior is the result of an interaction between the outer world and the inner thoughts of an individual. In particular, both men emphasized the importance of outcome expectations. In addition, Bandura's concept of perceived self-efficacy bears a notable similarity to Rotter's locus of control. Each of these concepts deals with people's beliefs about their ability to get the results they want through their own actions.

Sears and childhood aggression

At the time that Bandura began his career at Stanford, Robert Sears was chairman of the psychology department there. Sears was yet another member of the group of psychologists who had been heavily influenced by Hull at Yale, and who had gone on to make their own mark in psychology. Sears was especially interested in studying child-rearing patterns. He hoped to find observable behaviors that could be tied to psychoanalytic concepts of personality development. Psychoanalytic theory, originally developed by Sigmund Freud, held that people's behavior is often the result of unconscious mental activity. According to the theory, many adult emotional problems are the result of unconscious conflicts that first arose during critical stages of emotional development in childhood.

In an effort to find the childhood sources of dependency and aggression, Sears compared children's personality traits to their mothers' child-rearing practices. There were some flaws in the way Sears designed his study. For one thing, he relied on the mothers' self-reports of their practices, which may not have been accurate. Nevertheless, Sears found that more use of punishment by the mothers was related to higher levels of both dependency and aggression in the children.

Sears was only one of many psychologists at the time who were looking for a way to reconcile behaviorism, with its total focus on external behavior, and psychoanalytic theory, with its opposite focus on internal experience. For example, Dollard and Miller had also suggested that many emotional disorders might be conditioned responses to parental punishments. This idea received at least partial support in Sears's research.

Like Sears, Bandura was interested in exploring the childhood roots of aggressive behavior. However, Sears believed that parents influenced their children to become more aggressive through the use of punishments. Bandura, on the other hand, stressed that parents were role models for their children, who learned to behave aggressively mainly by imitation.

Television and aggression

In the early 1960s, Bandura was just publishing the results of his Bobo doll experiments. At about the same time, television was in the midst of a great boom. In 1945, there were probably fewer than 10,000 TV sets in the entire United States. By 1960, that figure had soared to almost 60 million. Along with TV's explosive growth in popularity, there was also an increase in criticism of the programs that were offered. Critics accused the TV networks of promoting antisocial and aggressive behavior by bringing a steady stream of violence into American homes.

As public debate began to heat up, researchers started to look for links between televised violence and the real thing. Bandura's research on modeling and aggression in children dovetailed nicely with this trend. As with other behaviors, Bandura stressed that merely observing violence and aggression on TV did not necessarily translate into copying it. Yet sometimes it did, occasionally with tragic consequences. As Bandura told Evans,

> I draw the important distinction between the power of the media to produce learning and its power to affect action. The learning effects are rather uniform. If children watch one hundred ways of killing people hundreds of times they will learn one hundred ways to kill people. But the effects on action are variable. We need to explain the conditions under which people are going to act on what they have learned.

A number of researchers have taken up this challenge. It has been estimated that more than 3,000 studies have now attempted to look for the links between televised and real-life violence. Nevertheless, it is still unclear exactly how TV exerts its effects on vulnerable individuals. In general, though, research has shown that children who are exposed to TV violence are more likely to behave aggressively. In addition, they may become less sensitive to the pain and suffering of others, and they may be more fearful of the outside world.

Humanistic psychology

Around the time that Bandura came on the scene, other psychologists were starting to rebel against the confines of strict behaviorism as well. In particular, many were dissatisfied with behaviorism's focus on observable behavior. Instead, they preferred to focus on inner experience, mental processes, and people's concept of self. In the 1960s, this led to the rise of the humanistic movement in psychology.

Humanists rejected the behaviorist view that people's behavior is nothing more than a set of responses to environmental stimuli. They felt that this took the humanity out of human behavior, reducing people to the level of machines. At the same time, humanists also rejected the psychoanalytic view that a selfish desire for pleasure was at the heart of all human behavior. Rather, the humanists emphasized the innate potential of people and their ability to exercise control over their own destinies.

The self is a central concept in humanistic psychology. Carl Rogers, one of the leaders of the movement, believed that behavior problems were the result of people's failure to trust their own experience, which led to a distorted view of the self. The goal of therapy was to reduce this distortion by helping people gain self-understanding and self-acceptance. Abraham Maslow, another key figure in humanistic psychology, wrote about people's innate drive to achieve self-actualization—a process of inner growth in which they realized their potential.

While not a humanistic psychologist, Bandura is also very interested in the self. He has written about something he calls the self-system—a set of cognitive processes that people use to perceive, evaluate, and control their own behavior. This self-system allows people to adapt their behavior so that it is appropriate for the situation at hand and effective for helping them achieve their goals.

Cognitive psychology

Another movement in psychology undoubtedly played a big role in shaping Bandura's opinions. In the 1950s, cognitive psychology began moving to the forefront of research and theory. This branch of psychology sees human perception and thought processes as being central to the human experience. Cognitive, or thought, processes can involve language, symbols, or imagery. Such processes include perceiving, recognizing, evaluating, imagining, and remembering information. They are essential for attention, reasoning, planning, problem solving, and decision making.

There are several reasons why cognitive psychology became so popular in the mid-twentieth century. One was the growing dissatisfaction with behaviorism. Another was the advent of modern linguistics, which shed new light on how people learn and use language. Yet another was the birth of computer science, which led scientists to ponder the difference between human thought and machine "intelligence." Around the same time, developmental psychologists such as Jean Piaget aroused new interest in the way human mental abilities unfold as children mature. Meanwhile, innovative research on verbal learning and memory gave rise to fresh insights about how memory works.

All of these developments helped focus attention on the crucial role of thought processes. Of course, such processes are at the core of Bandura's ideas about how people learn and function. In fact, he renamed his theory social-*cognitive* theory to emphasize that very point. As Bandura wrote in *Social Foundations of Thought and Action*: "A theory that denies that thoughts can regulate actions does not lend itself readily to the explanation of complex human behavior."

CRITICAL RESPONSE

Bandura's ideas have met with wide acceptance and have been very influential. Like any strong leader, Bandura has inspired many followers. However, he has also attracted his share of challengers and critics. In fact, it is largely through give-and-take with colleagues and competitors that scientific theories such as Bandura's are refined over the years.

Newer cognitive approaches

As its name implies, social-cognitive theory is at its best when it comes to describing social and cognitive factors. It does a particularly good job of explaining the social situations in which complex behaviors are learned and the cognitive processes by which people decide whether or not to imitate those behaviors. Bandura and his followers argue that cognitive processes are especially important to study and understand, because they capture the very essence of what it means to be human.

Social-cognitive theory arose as a reaction to behaviorism and, to a lesser extent, psychoanalytic theory. Bandura was very successful at breaking free from these earlier viewpoints. Yet critics argue that the pendulum may have swung too far in the opposite direction. Some claim that social-cognitive theory goes too far in downplaying the role of reinforcement and conditioning in affecting behavior. Others complain that the theory ignores the emotional and unconscious aspects of personality.

Still other critics fault social-cognitive theory for oversimplifying cognition as well. In recent decades, cognitive psychology has been strongly influenced by technological advances in both computer science and neuroscience. This combination of cognitive psychology and neuroscience has given birth to a brand-new field: cognitive neuroscience. The hybrid field attempts to unite the study of the mind with the study of the brain. It looks at both psychological and physiological aspects of memory, sensation, perception, problem solving, language, motor functions, and thought. There is even a subspecialty called social-cognitive neuroscience, which looks specifically at the mind/brain processes involved in social learning and interpersonal communication.

There are several reasons why cognitive neuroscience has taken off so quickly. One is the development of sophisticated brain imaging techniques, such as position emission tomography (PET) and functional magnetic resonance imaging (fMRI). These techniques allow scientists to peer into the human brain and observe it in action as never before. For the first time, the goal of identifying specific brain pathways linked to particular thoughts, feelings, and behaviors seems more like science than science fiction. It is little wonder that scientists are excited. Today, many are trying to develop psychological models of thought processes that are consistent with what is known about the structure and function of the nervous system.

It could be argued that a cognitive theory without a solid foundation in neuroscience is a bit old-fashioned in this high-tech age. Yet cognitive neuroscience is still in its infancy, and research has a long way to go before it comes close to fully describing how a thought is formed or how memory is stored. Even if it becomes possible someday to break down a single thought into a detailed series of connections within the brain, however, this still would not explain how the overall system of connections works. More importantly, it would not show how that system translates into thought, emotion, or individual personality.

Defining the terms

Another point raised by some critics is that Bandura's concepts are not as precisely defined as they could be. As a result, there is some room for ambiguity. While this might be fine in everyday life, it is a serious problem in science, where the goal is to be as precise and accurate as possible.

In an article in *American Psychologist*, William Powers outlined concerns about Bandura's use of the word "belief" in a variety of contexts:

> Bandura spoke of belief in ways that sometimes seem to mean a kind of goal (as in a belief that one is justified in setting high goals), at other times seem to describe perceptions (beliefs about one's actual effectiveness in achieving a given goal), and at still others suggest imagination (rehearsing or imagining achieving a goal without actually behaving.

Powers noted that the role played by a belief in affecting behavior would be different, depending on which of these meanings was intended.

Critics have also charged that some of Bandura's terms are just new labels given to existing concepts. For example, Bandura's self-efficacy is similar to Rotter's locus of control. Not surprisingly, research has indicated that there is some overlap between the two concepts, based on statistical comparisons of people's scores on tests of both.

However, this does not mean the two concepts are identical. In a 1991 article, Bandura explained the difference this way:

> Perceived self-efficacy is concerned with people's beliefs about their capabilities to organize and execute designated courses of action. Locus of control refers to people's beliefs that outcomes are dependent on their actions or are the result of chance, fate, or luck. Beliefs about whether one can produce certain performances cannot, by any stretch of the imagination, be considered the same as beliefs about whether actions affect outcomes.

Bandura's focus on outcome expectations is also similar to Rotter's outcome expectancy and reinforcement value. In a 2003 article with Edwin Locke, Bandura explained the difference as he sees it:

> In expectancy-value theory, motivation is governed by the expectation that given performances will produce particular outcomes and the value individuals place on the expected outcomes. However, people act on their beliefs about what they can do as well as their beliefs about the likely outcomes of performance.

Bandura notes that people may rule out behaviors on self-efficacy grounds without bothering to think about the expected costs and benefits. For example, a student who sees himself as having low math self-efficacy might rule out signing up for an advanced math class before even considering how much work the class would require or whether it would help him get into college.

Power of self-efficacy

None of Bandura's ideas has had broader appeal than the concept of self-efficacy. A search of PsycINFO database, the APA's bibliographic listing of the psychological literature, found 3,453 journal articles with "self-efficacy" as the subject published from 1974 through 2003. Dozens of questionnaires for assessing specific kinds of self-efficacy have been developed for use in such studies. The particular types of beliefs that researchers have tried to study include self-efficacy for academic achievement, alcohol abstinence, arthritis self-care, chronic disease management, computer use, controlling eating habits, diabetes self-care, dissertation completion, drinking refusal, driving, foreign language learning, exercise, Internet teaching, leisure time skills, mathematics, meeting others' expectations, occupational skills, problem solving, science laboratory skills, self-assertiveness, self-directed learning, social interactions, teaching, and writing, to name just a few.

As with any concept that is so widely used, the results have varied in their nature and quality. However, a substantial literature now exists on the role of self-efficacy beliefs in educational and occupational success. Numerous studies have also looked at the importance of perceived self-efficacy in determining whether people adopt healthy behaviors and how well they manage the symptoms of chronic illness when it occurs. Beyond this, Bandura has also discussed the collective efficacy of groups.

One key question is whether self-efficacy beliefs really have as much impact on behavior as Bandura claims. Bandura makes a strong case that they do. In a 2003 article, he points out that this question has now been addressed using a wide variety of study designs and statistical techniques. Nine large meta-analyses—statistical analyses that combine the results of several studies—have also been done. These meta-analyses looked at diverse topics, including self-efficacy for work performance, social functioning, academic achievement, and sports performance. They involved children, teenagers, and adults. Some included laboratory studies where self-efficacy beliefs were altered experimentally, while others included studies of self-efficacy in real life. Two meta-analyses looked at the perceived efficacy of groups of people working together.

Bandura sums up the findings this way: "The evidence from these meta-analyses is consistent in showing that efficacy beliefs contribute significantly to the level of motivation and performance." Studies have shown that groups of people with different levels of perceived self-efficacy tend to behave differently. In addition, studies have shown that it is often possible to predict behavior changes within individuals as their self-efficacy beliefs change over time. The fact that so many different kinds of studies using different designs have found evidence for the power of self-efficacy makes Bandura's claims that much more convincing.

Of course, not every study has yielded positive results. Also, critics have noted that many of the studies that found a positive link between self-efficacy beliefs and behavior had a correlational design. This type of study can show the degree of association between two variables, but it cannot show whether one caused the other. Some studies with experimental designs, which do indicate a causal effect, have found support for Bandura's theory. However, others have not, and a few have even found that high perceived self-efficacy was related to worse, not better, performance on a task. Overall, however, the research seems to support the usefulness of self-efficacy beliefs.

Accuracy of self-beliefs

Bandura has argued that it may be most helpful if people's judgments of their own efficacy slightly exceed their current ability level. This slight overestimation may push people to increase their effort and ultimately improve their skills. However, it seems likely that there is a point where confidence becomes overconfidence, and it starts to hurt rather than help people's performance. Such overconfidence might push people to keep setting unrealistic goals and attempting tasks for which they are completely unprepared. This kind of mismatch between people's beliefs and their true ability is almost certain to lead to failure. One issue that researchers still need to clarify, then, is the point where high self-efficacy beliefs become *too* high.

This is a real concern for managers, teachers, therapists, and others who are interested in helping people develop useful self-efficacy beliefs. Few experts would suggest devising programs or therapies specifically to lower people's sense of self-efficacy. However, it may be just as bad to try to overinflate people's notions of what they can do. A better alternative may be to help people understand exactly what they do and do not know, so that they can more effectively choose how to approach a particular task.

While some people tend to overestimate their own efficacy, others are prone to underestimation. One well-known example is the difference between male and female students. Girls, on average, perform as well as boys on a variety of academic tasks.

However, girls often see themselves as less academically capable, and this gap just widens the longer they are in school. This belief may translate into choosing less challenging classes, ruling out areas of study without even trying them, putting less effort in excelling, or giving up too quickly when problems arise. Therefore, it is clearly just as important for teachers and others to provide a reality check when self-beliefs are too low as when they are too high.

Self-efficacy and explanatory style

Cognitive psychology continues to evolve. As already noted, one research-oriented branch has merged with neuroscience. Another branch, with closer ties to clinical practice, has turned its attention to the cognitive styles that characterize different people. Explanatory style is the name usually given to the set of cognitive variables that describe how a person habitually interprets the events in his or her life. One example of an explanatory style is optimism versus pessimism. Although optimism is different from high perceived self-efficacy, the two concepts have some features in common.

Martin Seligman has been a leading figure in this area. In the 1960s and '70s, he conducted studies in which he showed how animals could develop learned helplessness. In a classic set of experiments, Seligman gave unpleasant electric shocks to dogs, who were restrained so that they could not avoid or escape the shocks. Later, the restraints were removed, and the dogs were given shocks again. The dogs tended to stay in place and suffer the consequences, even though they could have easily escaped. It was as if the dogs had given up trying to help themselves. Research with people has shown similar results. If people learn that they have no control over their situation, they tend to stop trying to accomplish much, even when it might be within their power. Over time, this can lead to depression, stress, and apathy.

More recently, Seligman has written about learned optimism and pessimism. As Seligman describes them, pessimists tend to believe that bad events will last a long time, undermining whatever they do. They also think that these bad events are their own fault. Optimists, in contrast, have the opposite reaction when faced with the same hard knocks. They tend to see problems as just temporary setbacks with limited effects. They also believe the problems are not their fault. Instead, the problems are blamed on circumstances, bad luck, or other people—not their own lack of capability. When faced with a tough situation, optimists see it as a challenge and redouble their efforts to succeed.

Seligman's is only one of several theories that look at how people explain successes and failures. These theories, like Bandura's theory of self-efficacy, attempt to show what motivates people to act. However, explanatory styles, such as optimism or pessimism, tend to be generalized, affecting all areas of life. Self-efficacy beliefs, on the other hand, tend to be specific. It is quite possible for a person to see herself as high in athletic self-efficacy but low in academic self-efficacy, for instance. Yet that same person may also have a general tendency to be an optimist or pessimist in most situations most of the time.

Self-efficacy at work

A number of studies have looked at the way self-efficacy beliefs influence people's choice of career. This research has shed light on how perceived self-efficacy affect decision-making in general. In a 2003 article with Locke, Bandura summed up the findings this way:

> The findings of this substantial body of research showed that the higher the perceived self-efficacy to fulfill educational requirements and occupational roles is, the wider are the career options people seriously consider pursuing, the greater is the interest they have in them, the better they prepare themselves educationally for different occupational careers, and the greater is their staying power in challenging career pursuits.

Occupational self-efficacy may actually become an issue long before people apply for their first job. That is because students' beliefs about their job capabilities and preferences are formed at an early age, based on studies that have looked at this subject. In one study by Bandura and his colleagues, information was gathered about a group of students when they entered junior high school. The combination of self-efficacy beliefs and social factors at that time predicted the kinds of career goals that the same students had by the end of junior high. This, in turn, might have affected whether the students took the classes they needed in order to reach their goals.

Bandura has noted that the modern workplace is demanding ever-greater self-efficacy of its workers. The highly skilled nature of many jobs today means that people must take the necessary steps to train for their careers. The fast pace of change and the constant flood of new information means that workers must take an active role to keep their skills up-to-date. Rather than settling into one job for life, most workers also need the ability to adapt to various jobs and work settings over the course of their careers.

Bandura says that collective self-efficacy is important for modern companies, too. Companies have to adapt to a rapidly changing global market-place. They need to keep up with the latest technologies as well. A sense of self-efficacy as a group may be a key ingredient of long-term success, if it allows the company to successfully adapt and innovate.

Self-efficacy at school

In a knowledge-based society, school is more important than ever before. According to self-efficacy theory, the beliefs that students hold about themselves are vital factors in their success or failure at school. Such beliefs may influence why students pick some classes and activities and avoid others. Self-efficacy beliefs also may affect whether students make the necessary effort to succeed. In addition, differences in self-efficacy beliefs may explain why some students are enthusiastic and confident, while others who are equally talented are filled with dread and panic whenever they have to give a presentation or take a test.

Several studies have now looked at perceived self-efficacy in math and science. Not surprisingly, the studies have shown that college students tend to choose college majors and career fields in which they feel most competent, and to avoid fields in which they feel less competent. In many cases, young women avoid math and science courses not because they lack competence, but because they underestimate their own capabilities in this area. This is a loss not only for the young women, but also for society as a whole, which needs more math- and science-trained workers.

A second group of studies have shown that teachers' beliefs about their own efficacy affect how and what they teach. This, in turn, affects what students learn in their classes. Teachers with a low sense of self-efficacy also tend to take a dim view of their students' motivation. The teachers focus on rigid control of the students' classroom behavior, and they try to use rewards and punishments to get students to study. In contrast, teachers with a high sense of self-efficacy create opportunities for success. They know that past successes strengthen the belief that future success is possible, which may encourage students to do what it takes to succeed.

A third line of research has shown that academic self-efficacy beliefs are associated with several other aspects of motivation. These include observation learning from role models, explanatory style, goal setting, and self-esteem. Self-efficacy beliefs also seem to be related to actual improvements in school performance. The beliefs may have this effect by influencing the amount of effort students put into their schoolwork and the degree to which they stick with it, even when problems arise.

Self-efficacy and health

A large body of research has also looked at the relationship between self-efficacy beliefs and health. In healthy people, a strong sense of self-efficacy can help them adopt a lifestyle that promotes wellness and prevents disease. In people with a chronic illness, self-efficacy beliefs can help them manage pain and other symptoms, reduce the stress associated with being ill, and improve their overall quality of life.

In a 2002 article, Bandura explained the benefits for health promotion and disease prevention: "By managing their health habits, people can live longer, healthier, and slow the process of aging. To stay healthy, people should exercise, refrain from smoking, reduce the amount of dietary fat, keep blood pressure down, and develop effective ways of coping with stressors." Of course, most people know about the benefits of healthy lifestyle habits. Turning that knowledge into action is not always easy, though. High perceived self-efficacy helps people have the confidence to make needed changes and the determination to stick with them.

One interesting line of research has looked at public health messages that are aimed at getting people to make healthy lifestyle changes. There are several possible approaches: giving people factual information, instilling fear, changing people's perception of the risks involved, or enhancing people's perceived self-efficacy. Research has shown that the most effective messages increase people's belief that they have some control over their own health. Scare tactics, on the other hand, do not seem to work as well.

Self-efficacy beliefs also may affect health by influencing how people respond to potentially stressful situations. When someone is faced with a threat—real or imagined, psychological or physical—the threat sets off an alarm in the person's brain, which reacts by preparing the body for defensive action. The pulse quickens, breathing deepens, the senses become sharper, and the muscles tense as the person prepares to fight or flee. In a real emergency, this physiological stress response can be a literal lifesaver. If the response continues over a long period of time, however, it can take a toll on the body, increasing the risk of depression, heart attack, stroke, various aches and pains, and perhaps even cancer. This kind of chronic stress can occur when people have trouble coping with long-term pressures, such as family conflicts, work or school demands, money problems, and the like.

Social-cognitive theory views stress as the result of a perceived inability to have any control over a threatening situation. If people believe they can deal effectively with a situation, it does not lead to stress. It is only when people believe they cannot control an unpleasant situation that they get stressed out by it. Therefore, the higher people's sense of self-efficacy, the less stress they are likely to feel, and fewer stress-related medical problems they are apt to develop.

For people who are already ill, a strong sense of self-efficacy can help them better manage their symptoms and stick to their treatment plan. Studies have shown benefits from perceived self-efficacy in a wide range of medical situations, such as recovering from a heart attack, coping with cancer, taking medication as prescribed, sticking to a rehabilitation program, reducing cholesterol in the diet, controlling arthritis pain, managing diabetes, and eliminating muscle tension headaches.

Such benefits are particularly relevant today, when the burden of chronic disease is heavier than at any other time in history. People are living longer than ever, but this also means that more people are developing age-related chronic illnesses, such as heart disease, osteoarthritis, type 2 diabetes, and cancer. These illnesses are among the most common and costly—but also most preventable—of all medical conditions.

According to the Centers for Disease Control and Prevention, chronic diseases now cause major limitations in activity for more than one out of every 10 Americans. They also account for more than 75% of all medical care costs in the United States. Anything that can reduce this burden is tremendously helpful to individual patients, their families, and society at large. High perceived self-efficacy is one factor that seems to help, both by promoting health and by giving people the confidence they need to cope with a disease.

Collective self-efficacy

Individuals are not the only people who hold beliefs about their own efficacy. Organizations, companies, and even whole nations have beliefs about what they can and cannot achieve when their members work together. These beliefs can profoundly impact current actions and future success of the groups. As Bandura wrote in *Self-Efficacy in Changing Societies*:

> People's beliefs in their collective efficacy influence the type of social future they seek to achieve, how much effort they put into it, and their endurance when collective efforts fail to produce quick results. The stronger they believe in their capabilities to effect social change the more actively they engage in collective efforts to alter national policies and practices.

Bandura argues that many aspects of modern life serve to undermine people's sense of collective self-efficacy. At the national level, a nation's economic and political welfare are often directly affected by events halfway around the world. Unfortunately, it is hard for people to feel they have much control over events that occur so far away. Closer to home, the social structure of modern society can also frustrate people's efforts to act as a group. Government is organized by bureaucracy, and large corporations are complex mazes of subsidiaries, divisions, and departments. It can be daunting to try to bring about change in such complex social settings, and many people simply give up.

However, even in today's world, it is still possible to make a difference through group effort. According to Bandura:

> People who have a sense of collective efficacy will mobilize their efforts and resources to cope with external obstacles to the changes they seek. But those convinced of their collective powerlessness will cease trying even though changes are attainable through perseverant collective action.

THEORIES IN ACTION

Bandura's social-cognitive theory has inspired a vast body of research as well as a large number of practical applications. More than 40 years after Bandura's work on social-cognitive theory, it is still giving rise to lively debates, active research programs, and innovative treatment approaches.

Research

Bandura first became known for the clever design of his Bobo doll experiments. His theorizing has remained firmly grounded in research ever since. Over the years, Bandura has published more than 240 journal articles and book chapters, many of which describe original research. In addition, Bandura's concepts have attracted hundreds of other researchers as well.

As of 2004, an Emory University website devoted to self-efficacy theory listed 83 researchers in the field of educational self-efficacy alone. Even more impressive, it listed 344 graduate students currently conducting self-efficacy research. Their research projects involved self-efficacy beliefs as they related to a wide range of topics, including academics, career, collective action, computers and technology, creativity, gifted education, language arts and literacy, leisure activities, health, mathematics and science, music, motivation, organizations and business, social and psychological issues, special education, spirituality, sports and exercise, and teaching.

The whole scope of this research would be impossible to cover here. However, a few representative studies are described below. These studies provide a small glimpse of the kinds of studies that are currently being done on self-efficacy and social-cognitive theory.

Study of occupational self-efficacy   Bandura and his followers claim that self-efficacy beliefs have a big effect on how people actually do their jobs. Some of the strongest evidence for this effect comes from studies in which people's opinions of their own abilities are artificially raised or lowered. For example, in a study published in the *Journal of Personality and Social Psychology* in 1991, Bandura and a colleague presented 60 graduate business students with a computer simulation of a furniture-making business. In the simulation, students were asked to play the role of manager and make decisions based on information about the manufacturing process, weekly orders, and available employees. The goal of the activity was to use goal setting, feedback, and social rewards to motivate the "employees" and maximize production.

The students were told that they would get feedback about how well they were doing at certain points in the activity. Their score was displayed on the computer screen along with another score that was supposedly the average earned by other participants in the study. The students' own scores were based on their actual performance, but the comparison scores were bogus. Compared to the students' scores, the comparison scores were preprogrammed to be either consistently similar, consistently lower, gradually lower, or gradually higher. During the simulation, the students were also asked to respond to computerized surveys about their self-beliefs.

When students were led to believe that they had gradually surpassed the comparison group, they reported an increase in their perceived self-efficacy. They also outperformed the students in the other groups. Within the simulation, they showed improvements in using efficient thinking strategies, setting challenging goals, and having positive emotional self-reactions to their own performance. In contrast, when students were led to believe that they had gradually fallen behind the comparison group, their actual performance suffered. Just changing how these students viewed their abilities seemed to alter their behavior in a way that could spell the difference between business success and failure in the real world.

Study of educational self-efficacy   Self-efficacy has also been studied in schools. In one study published in the *Journal of Personality and Social Psychology* in 1999, Bandura and his Italian colleagues looked at 282 children from two middle schools near Rome.

The children were asked to fill out several questionnaires that assessed their perceived self-efficacy, depression, and other factors. Teachers and other students also rated the children's behavior and depression, and the children's academic performance was graded by their teachers. One to two years later, the children's depression was assessed again.

The researchers found that children with a low sense of their own academic and social efficacy were more prone to depression than those with a high sense. This was true at the time depression was first assessed, and it was still true one to two years later. In the short run, the children's depression seemed to be related mainly to their perceived lack of academic ability. In the long run, low perceived self-efficacy seemed to keep the depression going by way of poor academic achievement and behavior problems, such as aggressiveness, hyperactivity, anxiety, and withdrawal. A perceived lack of social skills also had an impact on depression, but the effect was stronger in girls than in boys.

On the other hand, children with a strong belief in their own abilities benefited in several ways. They were able to better manage their schoolwork, which led to higher grades. They also had good social skills and few behavior problems. When it comes to school, Bandura says that a strong sense of self-efficacy can motivate students to do their best and help them bounce back from occasional disappointments. It also seems to help protect them from developing depression.

Study of health self-efficacy   One way in which self-efficacy beliefs are thought to affect physical health is by helping people take good care of themselves. When people with high perceived self-efficacy do become ill, they are better equipped to cope with their symptoms, which can reduce their stress and suffering in the short term. If the disease lasts for the long term, strong self-management skills can also help people feel better, maintain a more active lifestyle, and stick to their treatment plan. Over time, this kind of self-care may also help halt or slow the worsening of their disease and perhaps ward off serious complications.

For the past two decades, Kate Lorig and her colleagues at the Stanford University School of Medicine have been studying the effects of a patient education program for people with arthritis and other chronic illnesses. Lorig's program is based on self-management education. Rather than simply providing people with facts, it teaches them problem-solving skills. The underlying concept is that teaching people to cope with common disease-related problems enhances their sense of self-efficacy. This, in turn, improves their ability to adapt to the disease effectively.

Research has shown that Lorig's self-management program leads to better medical outcomes than ones that simply provide information. For example, Lorig's program has been shown to improve pain control in people with arthritis, enhance blood glucose control in people with diabetes, and reduce disability in people with a range of medical conditions. Some studies have also found that the program can reduce medical costs.

Empowerment programs Thousands of studies have now shown the many benefits of high perceived self-efficacy in a wide range of situations. The studies, in turn, have spurred the development of both individual therapies and group programs aimed at helping people get a more accurate sense of their own abilities. In one way or another, many of these approaches center around empowerment. In other words, the goal is to help participants become aware of their power to have some control over the environment and other people as well as to accomplish what they need to do. Of course, these ideas are also at the heart of Bandura's social-cognitive theory, including his concept of self-efficacy.

Employees can be empowered to take responsibility for their personal work. In the same way, students can be empowered to take charge of their own learning, based on guidance from their teachers. And medical patients can be empowered to accept responsibility for managing their own conditions and solving their own problems, based on information from their doctors. One implication of this approach is that people are active players in their own lives.

Programs designed to increase empowerment help people improve their problem-solving and decision-making skills. However, they also help people develop the sense of self-efficacy they need in order to put these skills to good use. Lorig's chronic disease self-management program is an excellent example of a research-based empowerment program. It is also a prime example of Bandura's ideas about human agency and self-efficacy put into practical use.

Modeling therapy Bandura's theories have also been applied to individual therapy. The best-known example is modeling therapy, in which someone with a psychological disorder is given a chance to observe a model cope with the same issues in a healthy way. In particular, this idea has been used for the treatment of phobias, or irrationally intense fears. With modeling therapy, the client is given a chance to watch a model interact with the feared object.

Bandura's early research in this area involved people with an irrationally strong fear of snakes. The client would look through a window into a laboratory room. In that room, there would be a chair and a table, on which sat a latched cage containing a clearly visible snake. The client would then observe the person who was serving as a model slowly approach the snake. The model would act terrified at first, but then appear to pull himself together and start over. Eventually, the model would reach the point where he could open the cage, remove the snake, sit down in the chair, and drape the snake around his neck. All the while, the model would be giving himself calming instructions.

After the client had observed all this, he would be invited to try it himself. The client would be aware that the model was an actor, not a person with a true phobia. Nevertheless, just seeing someone go through the motions of overcoming a phobia was very powerful. Many clients were able to imitate the whole routine after watching the model.

One drawback to this approach is its complexity. It requires not only a therapist, but also an actor, props, and two rooms with a window between them. To simplify the process, Bandura and his students have tested versions of the therapy using recordings of actors. They have also tried having therapists guide clients through the process in their imagination. These methods proved to be almost as effective as using live models.

Research on media violence Bandura's early work on observational learning helped inspire a host of studies on the influence of media violence. This continues to be a timely topic. Studies have shown that even children's television shows contain about 20 violent acts each hour. It comes as no surprise, then, that children who watch a lot of TV tend to think of the world as a scary and dangerous place.

Research has shown that children tend to behave differently after watching violent programs on television. Specifically, children who have watched violent shows are more likely to strike out at playmates, argue, and disobey authority figures than those who have watched nonviolent programs. Children are also less willing to wait patiently for things after viewing TV violence.

In addition, long-term research by Leonard Eron and his colleagues suggests that the effects of television violence may be quite lasting. The researchers found that children who watched hour after hour of TV violence while in elementary school tended to act more aggressively as teenagers. They also were more likely to be arrested and tried for criminal acts as adults.

Findings such as these helped spur the development of the V-chip, technology that lets parents block television programming they do not want their

CHRONOLOGY

1925: Born on December 4, 1925, in Mundare, Alberta, Canada.

1949: Receives a bachelor's degree from the University of British Columbia.

1952: Receives a PhD in clinical psychology from the University of Iowa. Married Virginia Varns.

1953: Takes a job as a psychology instructor at Stanford University.

1954: Birth of his daughter Mary.

1958: Birth of his daughter Carol.

1959: Publishes his first book, *Adolescent Aggression*, with Richard Walters.

1963: Publishes *Social Learning and Personality Development*, which summarized his research on observational learning and the Bobo doll experiments.

1964: Becomes a full professor at Stanford.

1977: Publishes *Social Learning Theory*, which aroused interest in social learning and modeling.

1974: Serves as president of the American Psychological Association.

1986: Publishes *Social Foundations of Thought and Action: A Social Cognitive Theory*, which described his social-cognitive theory of human functioning.

1997: Publishes *Self-Efficacy: The Exercise of Control*, which set forth his ideas about self-efficacy beliefs.

children to see. Most TV shows are now given a rating, which is encoded into the program. The V-chip technology reads this rating and blocks the TV set from showing programs that do not meet whatever rating standards have been selected by the parents. As of January 1, 2000, the Federal Communications Commission required all new television sets 13 inches (33 cm) or larger that are sold in the United States to contain V-chip technology.

While the V-chip is helpful, it is far from a complete solution to the problem. Not every parent

chooses to use the technology. In addition, violence is also depicted in movies as well as video and computer games. There are still plenty of opportunities for children to learn violent and aggressive behavior by watching role models in the media.

Research on positive media effects If media images are so powerful, why not put them to good use? That is the question asked by other researchers who have tried to use media role models to teach positive behaviors. Using social learning principles, these researchers have developed long-running television and radio series that have aired around the world. The series have been aimed at social goals such as reducing the spread of HIV, slowing population growth, preventing unwanted pregnancies, encouraging literacy, and empowering women.

The programs depict likable characters whose positive actions bring about good results. There are also unsavory villains whose negative actions have the opposite effect. In addition, there are role models who start out behaving badly, but who gradually adopt more positive behavior as the show goes on. The aim is to teach by showing the consequences of positive behavior rather than by lecturing viewers about them. The programs also give viewers information about where to turn for real-world help if they need it.

Research indicates that such "entertainment-education" programs may really make a difference. For example, an organization called Population Communications International airs television and radio programs in countries such as China, India, Kenya, Mexico, and Peru. The organization also conducts controlled studies to track changes in audience behavior. In Mexico and Kenya, dramas revolving around family planning were associated with real-life increases in new users of contraception. In Tanzania, a drama about the spread of HIV was associated with a real-world drop in number of sex partners.

Bandura says that such results should teach psychology a lesson. In a 2002 article in *Monitor on Psychology*, Bandura was quoted as saying, "The problem we have in psychology is that we don't profit from our successes. We construct theories and clarify how they produce their effects, but we lack implementation models for translating theory into effective practice." When people do find creative ways to put theory into practice, however, it is clear that the results are often well worth the effort.

Case studies

Bandura is known mainly as a theorist and researcher. However, he sometimes uses anecdotes to

FURTHER ANALYSIS:
Personality theories

Why does one child who watches a violent cartoon hit a playmate afterward, while another plays peacefully? Why does one teenager abuse drugs and alcohol, while another chooses a healthier lifestyle? Why does one employee stay motivated to succeed, while another falls prey to apathy and self-doubt? These are some of the kinds of questions addressed by personality psychology.

Bandura's social-cognitive theory is one example of a personality theory, which attempts to explain what makes people who they are. This type of theory also explores how and why individuals differ from one another. Over the years, a host of different theories have focused on various aspects of personality, including:

- Social dimension—People's ongoing interaction and communication with other individuals around them.

- Cognitive dimension—The way that people think about and actively interpret events in the outside world.

- Ego forces—The conscious part of personality that embodies a person's sense of identity or self.

- Unconscious forces—The part of personality that is not in moment-to-moment awareness, but is still influential.

- Traits, abilities, and skills—The unique set of predispositions and capabilities that a person possesses.

- Conditioning and learning—The way people's behavior is shaped by their experiences and the world.

- Biological dimension—The unique genetic, anatomical, and physiological makeup of an individual.

- Spiritual dimension—People's inward sense of connection to a higher power or meaning that transcends the individual.

Research in this area ranges from laboratory studies of the genetic and biological bases of individual differences to field studies of the social and cultural bases of thoughts, feelings, and behavior. Other studies use the numerous personality tests that have been developed over the decades. And still others are in-depth case studies of individuals or long-term studies that follow a group of people for many years. This is not only a broad area of psychology, but also a deeply fascinating one. It is hard to imagine any subject with more appeal than trying to figure out what it really means to be a person.

---

illustrate key points in his theories. For example, to illustrate the difference between learning a behavior by observation and actually imitating it, Bandura recalled a boy who took part in the Bobo doll experiments:

> There was this one child who had watched the modeled aggression on film. In the experimental room, where the children were tested for how much aggression they would show spontaneously, he displayed very little aggression. When I was walking back to the nursery school with him, he said, 'You know, I saw a cartoon with Rocky, and Rocky sat on the Bobo doll and he punched it in the nose.' He ran off the entire aggressive repertoire. . .What a striking demonstration of the difference between learning and performance!

Fortunate events and chance encounters   In addition, there is one area of interest in which Bandura has relied more heavily than usual on anecdotal evidence: the relationship between personal behavior and

fortunate life events. Like so many other people, Bandura has noticed that fortunate events and chance encounters—such as signing up for his first psychology class because it fit his schedule or meeting his wife while golfing—have sometimes changed the whole course of his life.

Bandura also told of one incident in which he was delivering an address about the psychology of chance encounters and life paths. A man entering the lecture hall as it was rapidly filling up grabbed an empty seat. He wound up sitting next to the woman he would later marry—a life-altering chance encounter that took place at a lecture devoted to that very topic.

Bandura has suggested that fortunate events are just one more example of the environmental forces that interact with personal and behavioral factors to shape people's lives. As such, he says the influence of

FURTHER ANALYSIS:
Self-esteem

Self-esteem is a concept that is closely related to—and sometimes confused with—Bandura's concept of self-efficacy. Nathaniel Branden, a popular theorist in this area, has suggested that a sense of self-efficacy is actually one of two components that make up self-esteem. The other is self-respect, or having a sense of one's value and right to a happy life. Added together, these two components make up self-esteem, which can be defined as the belief that one is both capable of meeting life's challenges and worthy of enjoying happiness.

Few people would dispute that high self-esteem, defined this way, is a good thing. In recent years, however, self-esteem has gotten a bad rap, partly because some people confused it with simply feeling good about oneself. Others confused it with arrogance or conceit, which many psychologists say are actually ways that people with *low* self-esteem try to bolster their shaky confidence.

Several possible methods of enhancing self-esteem have been suggested. For example, affirmations are brief, positive statements that have special meaning for a person, such as "I accept myself as I am" or "I believe in myself." Individuals are often counseled to repeat these statements to themselves several times a day. A second strategy is to associate with positive people who provide encouragement and support. A third strategy is to make a list of past successes, such as passing a difficult test or scoring a goal in a game. This list can then be reviewed periodically as a reminder of the joy and satisfaction the person felt at the time.

---

fortunate events could be studied in research like any other kind of environmental variable. He believes that psychology will never be able to predict chance events before they happen. However, psychology can provide a theoretical framework for understanding the impact such events have on people's lives once they have occurred.

Similarly, people can learn to make chance work for them. Bandura notes that people who are open-minded, flexible, and venturesome are better able to make the most of unexpected opportunities when they arise. At the same time, those who are able to critically analyze a situation are better equipped to tell a true branch in their life path from a dead end. Therefore, the same kinds of mental abilities that serve people so well at other times can also be quite handy when good fortune comes along.

Relevance to modern readers

Bandura's social-cognitive theory emphasizes that people are capable of self-regulation, or controlling their own behavior. There are three parts to the self-regulation process:

- Self-observation—This involves observing and tracking one's own thoughts, feelings, and behaviors.

- Judgment—This involves comparing oneself to standards. The standards can be set either by oneself or by others.

- Self-response—This involves giving oneself rewards for doing well compared to the standards, or punishments for doing poorly. In general, self-rewards work better than self-punishments.

The three basic principles can be applied to changing almost any undesirable thought or behavior pattern. For example, if a person's problem is an unrealistically low sense of self-efficacy when doing some task, the following steps might help:

- Self-observation—The person should monitor her thoughts, feelings, and behaviors when doing the task in question. For example, if the problem is an unreasonably low sense of self-efficacy for doing math, the person might keep a journal in which she writes down all her negative thoughts, feelings, and physical reactions whenever she is called on in math class, doing math homework, or taking a math test.

- Judgment—The person should make sure her standards for the task are appropriate. If they are too high, she may be setting herself up for failure. If they are too low, on the other hand, she may be shortchanging herself. For example, if the best grade a person has received so far in math class is a C, she might aim for a B on the next test. Aiming for an A+ right off the bat might be too difficult to attain, but aiming for a C+ might be too easy to make much difference.

- Self-response—The person should find ways to celebrate her successes when doing the task, not dwell on her failures. When the person makes a B on the math test, for instance, she should tell herself what a great job she has done. She might also give herself a little treat, such as buying a new CD, going for a bike ride with a friend, or watching her favorite movie again.

For students, a somewhat optimistic view of one's own abilities can make a world of difference. As Bandura wrote in *Self-Efficacy in Changing Societies*: "The higher the students' beliefs in their efficacy to regulate their own motivation and learning activities, the more assured they are in their efficacy to master academic subjects. Perceived academic efficacy, in turn, promotes intellectual achievement both directly and by raising academic aspirations."

Moreover, Bandura says that students "who have a high sense of efficacy to regulate their own learning and to master academic skills behave more prosocially, are more popular, and experience less rejection by their peers than do [students] who believe they lack these forms of academic efficacy." Clearly, self-efficacy beliefs can have wide-ranging effects. Bandura has been the driving force in explaining what these effects are and how they can be changed through self-regulation.

BIBLIOGRAPHY

Sources

Bandura, Albert. "The Changing Face of Psychology at the Dawning of a Globalization Era." *Canadian Psychology* 42 (2001): 12–24.

Albert Bandura. Emory University. [cited April 11, 2004]. http://www.emory.edu/EDUCATION/mfp/Bandura.

Bandura, Albert. "Exercise of Personal and Collective Efficacy in Changing Societies." In *Self-Efficacy in Changing Societies,* edited by Albert Bandura. New York: Cambridge University Press, 1995.

Bandura, Albert. "Exploration of Fortuitous Determinants of Life Paths." *Psychological Inquiry* 9 (1998): 95–99.

Bandura, Albert. "Growing Primacy of Human Agency in Adaptation and Change in the Electronic Era." *European Psychologist* 7 (2002): 2–16.

Bandura, Albert. "Human Agency: The Rhetoric and the Reality." *American Psychologist* 46 (1991): 157–62.

Bandura, Albert. "Selective Moral Disengagement in the Exercise of Moral Agency." *Journal of Moral Education* 31 (2002): 101–19.

Bandura, Albert. "Self-Efficacy." In *Encyclopedia of Human Behavior: Volume 4,* edited by V. S. Ramachaudran. New York: Academic Press, 1994.

Bandura, Albert. "Social Cognitive Theory: An Agentic Perspective." *Annual Review of Psychology* 52 (2001): 1–26.

Bandura, Albert, Claudio Barbaranelli, Gian Vittorio Caprara, and Concetta Pastorelli. "Mechanisms of Moral Disengagement in the Exercise of Moral Agency." *Journal of Personality and Social Psychology* 71 (1996): 364–74.

Bandura, Albert, and Forest J. Jourden. "Self-Regulatory Mechanisms Governing the Impact of Social Comparison on Complex Decision Making." *Journal of Personality and Social Psychology* 60 (1991): 941–51.

Bandura, Albert, and Edwin A. Locke. "Negative Self-Efficacy and Goal Effects Revisited." *Journal of Applied Psychology* 88 (2003): 87–99.

Bandura, Albert, Concetta Pastorelli, Claudio Barbaranelli, and Gian Vittorio Caprara. "Self-Efficacy Pathways to Childhood Depression." *Journal of Personality and Social Psychology* 76 (1999): 258–69.

Bandura, Albert, Dorothea Ross, and Sheila A. Ross. "Transmission of Aggression Through Imitation of Aggressive Models." *Journal of Abnormal and Social Psychology* 63 (1961): 575–82.

Bodenheimer, Thomas, Kate Lorig, Halsted Holman, and Kevin Grumbach. "Patient Self-Management of Chronic Disease in Primary Care." *JAMA* 288 (2002): 2469–475.

Boeree, C. George. *Albert Bandura.* Shippensburg University. 1998 [cited April 28, 2004]. http://www.ship.edu/~cgboeree/bandura.html.

Evans, Richard I. *Albert Bandura: The Man and His Ideas—A Dialogue.* New York: Praeger, 1989.

Haggbloom, Steven J., Renee Warnick, Jason E. Warnick, Vinessa K. Jones, Gary L. Yarbrough, Tenea M. Russell, et al. "The 100 Most Eminent Psychologists of the 20th Century." *Review of General Psychology* 6 (2002): 139–52.

Information on Self-Efficacy: A Community of Scholars. Emory University. January 28, 2004 [cited April 11, 2004]. http://www.emory.edu/EDUCATION/mfp/self-efficacy.html.

Pajares, Frank. *Self-Efficacy Beliefs in Academic Contexts: An Outline.* Emory University. 2002 [cited April 8, 2004]. http://www.emory.edu/EDUCATION/mfp/efftalk.html.

Powers, William T. "Commentary on Bandura's 'Human Agency.'" *American Psychologist* 46 (1991): 151–53.

Smith, Deborah. "The Theory Heard 'Round the World." *Monitor on Psychology* 33 (2002): 30.

Vancouver, Jeffrey B., Charles M. Thompson, E. Casey Tischner, and Dan J. Putka. "Two Studies Examining the Negative Effect of Self-Efficacy on Performance." *Journal of Applied Psychology* 87 (2002): 506–16.

Further readings

Acton, G. Scott. *Great Ideas in Personality.* 2004 [cited April 28, 2004]. http://www.personalityresearch.org.

Boeree, C. George. *Personality Theories.* Shippensburg University. 1998 [cited April 28, 2004]. http://www.ship.edu/~cgboeree/perscontents.html.

Branden, Nathaniel. *The Six Pillars of Self-Esteem.* New York: Bantam, 1994.

Brannon, Linda, and Jess Feist. *Health Psychology: An Introduction to Behavior and Health.* 5th ed. Belmont, CA: Wadsworth, 2003.

Friedman, Howard S., and Miriam W. Schustack. *Personality: Classic Theories and Modern Research.* 2nd ed. Boston: Allyn and Bacon, 2002.

Kids and the Media. American Psychological Association. 2004 [cited April 27, 2004]. http://www.apa.org/topics/topic_ kidsmedia.html.

Media Violence and Children. Adults and Children Together Against Violence. 2004 [cited April 20, 2004]. http://www. actagainstviolence.com/mediaviolence.

National Association for Self-Esteem. 2004 [cited April 20, 2004]. http://www.self-esteem-nase.org.

Population Communications International. 2003 [cited April 26, 2004]. http://www.population.org.

Revelle, William. *The Personality Project.* Northwestern University. 2004 [cited April 28, 2004]. http://www.personality-project.org.

Strickland, Bonnie B., ed. *Gale Encyclopedia of Psychology.* 2nd ed. Farmington Hills, MI: Gale Group, 2000.

Aaron Temkin Beck

1921-

AMERICAN PSYCHIATRIST, RESEARCHER

YALE MEDICAL SCHOOL, MD, 1946

BRIEF OVERVIEW

Aaron Beck is one of the founders of cognitive therapy, a form of talk therapy that incorporates an information-processing model of human psychology rather than one based on instinct, motivation, or biochemistry. As of the early twenty-first century, cognitive therapy has become the reigning model of short-term psychotherapy in the United Kingdom as well as the United States, supplanting both psychoanalytical and behavioral approaches to the study and treatment of mental disorders. Beck has enjoyed widespread success and professional recognition. He was the only person, as of 2004, to have received research awards from both the American Psychological Association and the American Psychiatric Association. His honors include the Sarnat Award from the Institute of Medicine (2003), the Heinz Award for the Human Condition from the Heinz Foundation (2001), and honorary doctorates from Brown University and Assumption College (1995). An article that appeared in a French Canadian psychiatric journal in 2002 named Beck as one of ten individuals who "have changed the face of American psychiatry." He has also been listed as one of the five most influential psychotherapists since Sigmund Freud.

Beck's cognitive therapy may be categorized as a variant of constructivism, a term that has become increasingly popular among academic psychologists since the mid-1970s. Although theorists as otherwise different as William James, Jean Piaget, George Kelly, and Albert Bandura have been grouped together as

Aaron T. Beck. (Photo courtesy of Dr. Aaron Beck. Reproduced by permission.)

constructivists, it is possible to identify several recurrent themes in their work. The psychotherapist M. J. Mahoney has listed five such common themes:

- Humans are active agents with the power to effect changes in their own lives. This theme stands in contrast to the view that humans are passively controlled by larger forces.

- Humans are actively engaged in ordering their experiences through assigning emotional as well as intellectual significance to them.

- These processes of ordering are primarily self-referential; that is, they underlie a person's sense of selfhood or personal identity.

- On the other hand, humans are not isolated individuals; they cannot be understood apart from their relationships to other people, larger communities, and symbol systems.

- Humans continue to grow and develop over the entire course of their lifespan.

These themes are prominent features of Beck's work as well as the writings of other constructivists.

In terms of the history of psychotherapy, Beck's contribution is the development of an effective form of short-term treatment well-suited to the age of managed care, cost containment, and evidence-based medicine. The future of cognitive therapy as a distinctive approach sharply set off from other forms of talk therapy, however, is less certain. As the integrative movement in psychotherapy continues to grow, the theories and techniques of cognitive therapy may simply be appropriated by therapists from a wide variety of backgrounds.

BIOGRAPHY

Early years

Aaron T. Beck was born in Providence, Rhode Island, on July 18, 1921, the youngest of five children. Both of his parents were Russian Jewish immigrants to the United States. Two of Beck's siblings had died before his birth, an older brother in childhood and an older sister in the influenza pandemic of 1919. As a result of these tragedies, Beck's mother was chronically depressed for several years and became overprotective of her youngest son. Beck came to think that he was a replacement for his sister, and that his mother was disappointed that he was not a girl. When Beck was seven years old, he broke an arm in a playground accident. The broken bone became infected, resulting in a generalized septicemia (blood poisoning) that kept him in the hospital long enough to miss promotion into second grade. Beck recalled later that he came to feel "stupid": "I was held back in the first grade and I always felt it was because I was dumb. Many years later I asked my mother and she said it was because I'd been sick a great deal."

Beck missed his friends and didn't like being a grade behind them. With the help of some tutoring from his older brothers, as well as his own determination, Beck not only caught up with his former classmates but ended up being promoted a year ahead of them. He regarded his success as a psychological turning point: ". . . it did show some evidence that I could do things, that if I got into a hole I could dig myself out. I could do it on my own." Beck eventually graduated at the head of his class from Hope High School and entered Brown University in the fall of 1938.

Beck developed several phobias in the course of his childhood. One was a blood/injury phobia, which he related to his experience with surgery for his broken arm at age seven. The surgeon apparently began to make the incision before Beck was fully anesthetized. During Beck's medical training years later, he had to fight anxiety and a tendency to feel dizzy while assisting with operations. He dealt with his blood/injury phobia by exposing himself gradually to the sights and sounds of an operating room, and by keeping busy while he was assisting with surgery.

"I wasn't fazed at all as long as I was . . . doing something. I learned an awful lot from my own experience. As long as you're actively involved in something, anxiety tends to hold back."

A second phobia was fear of suffocation, which was apparently caused by a bad case of whooping cough, chronic childhood asthma, and an older brother who used to tease Beck by putting a pillow over his face. Beck's fear of suffocation also emerged in the form of a tunnel phobia; he would feel tightness in his chest and have difficulty breathing while driving through a tunnel. In addition he developed fears of heights and of public speaking. He maintains that he was able to resolve these fears by working them through cognitively. Beck also drew from his own experiences when writing his first book on depression, which he published in 1967. Beck was mildly depressed while he was writing the book, but regarded the project as a kind of self-treatment.

Beck's childhood and adolescence also included many positive experiences. He recalled during an interview in 2001 that he "was largely interested in nature" when he was growing up, becoming a bird watcher, learning to identify plants and trees, and eventually serving as a camp counselor and naturalist. Beck's parents encouraged his interest in science. He later credited these early explorations with stimulating his interest "in what makes people tick; particularly what makes them happy or sad, and confident or insecure."

Education

Beck was uncertain of his career plans during his undergraduate years; he majored in political science and English literature at Brown rather than chemistry or another premedical major. He also served as associate editor of the campus newspaper, the *Brown Daily Herald*. Because his scholarship did not cover all his expenses, he delivered newspapers, worked in the library, and sold Fuller brushes door-to-door in order to make ends meet. Beck graduated from the university *magna cum laude* in 1942. He won a number of honors and awards as an undergraduate, including the Francis Wayland Scholarship, the Gaston Prize for Oratory, and election to Brown's chapter of Phi Beta Kappa.

Following graduation from Brown, Beck went to medical school at Yale University, where he completed his degree in 1946. He was not interested in psychiatry at that point in his career; after receiving his MD, he served a rotating internship followed by a residency in pathology at Rhode Island Hospital. Beck then decided to specialize in neurology because he was attracted by the degree of precision that the specialty demands of its practitioners. While he was completing a required rotation in psychiatry during his residency at the Cushing

PRINCIPAL PUBLICATIONS

- *Depression: Causes and Treatment.* Philadelphia: University of Pennsylvania Press, 1967.
- *The Diagnosis and Management of Depression.* Philadelphia: University of Pennsylvania Press, 1973.
- *The Prediction of Suicide.* Bowie, MD: The Charles Press, 1974.
- *Cognitive Therapy and the Emotional Disorders.* New York: International Universities Press, 1976.
- *Cognitive Therapy of Depression.* New York: The Guilford Press, 1979.
- *Anxiety Disorders and Phobias: A Cognitive Perspective.* New York: Basic Books, 1985.
- *Love Is Never Enough.* New York: Harper & Row, 1988.
- *Cognitive Therapy in Clinical Practice: An Illustrative Casebook.* London and New York: Routledge, 1989.
- *Cognitive Therapy with Inpatients: Developing a Cognitive Milieu.* New York: Guilford Press, 1992.
- *Cognitive Therapy of Substance Abuse.* New York: Guilford Press, 1993.
- *The Integrative Power of Cognitive Therapy.* New York and London: Guilford Press, 1998.
- *Prisoners of Hate: The Cognitive Basis of Anger, Hostility, and Violence.* New York: HarperCollins Publishers, 1999.
- *Scientific Foundations of Cognitive Theory and Therapy of Depression.* New York: John Wiley, 1999.
- *Cognitive Therapy of Personality Disorders*, 2nd ed. New York: The Guilford Press, 2004.

Veterans Administration Hospital in Framingham, Massachusetts, he became interested in some of the recent developments in the treatment of mental illness. Beck then decided to become a psychotherapist.

Beck was originally trained in the theories and techniques of classical psychoanalysis. After finishing his residency in Framingham, Beck accepted a two-year fellowship at the Austin Riggs Center, a small private psychiatric hospital in Stockbridge, Massachusetts, which had been founded in 1919. The Center provided Beck with extensive experience in treating patients who needed long-term psychotherapy. When the Korean War broke out in 1951, Beck moved to Pennsylvania and accepted the position of assistant chief of neuropsychiatry at the Valley Forge Army Hospital. There he treated soldiers suffering from what is now termed post-traumatic stress disorder, or PTSD. Beck received his board certification in psychiatry in 1953, joined the Department of Psychiatry of the University of Pennsylvania in 1954, and completed his graduate training in psychoanalysis at the Philadelphia Psychoanalytic Institute (which changed its name to the Psychoanalytic Center of Philadelphia in 2001) in 1958. Beck remained at Penn until he retired from active teaching in 1992, when he was appointed University Professor Emeritus of Psychiatry. In addition to his teaching at Penn, he served as an adjunct professor at Temple University and the University of Medicine and Dentistry of New Jersey. He was also a visiting professor at Oxford University in 1986.

Beck has published over 465 books and articles as of early 2004. He has received funding for his various research projects from the University of Pennsylvania, the National Institute of Mental Health (NIMH), and the Centers for Disease Control and Prevention (CDC).

Early depression studies   Beck developed cognitive therapy almost by accident in the course of his growing discontent with Freudian psychoanalysis. As a practicing therapist, Beck was aware that academic psychologists whose work he respected questioned Freud's account of depression because of the lack of supportive evidence from well-conducted studies. In addition, Beck had had difficulty with much of Freudian theory since medical school. His dislike was reinforced by a rebellious streak in his character and a self-acknowledged need for control. Beck told an interviewer in 1990, "I thought [psychoanalysis] was nonsense. I could not see that it really fitted. . . . there was a rebellious aspect [in me] I just couldn't control. . . . Being the youngest son probably had something to do with it." Beck initially dealt with his distrust of mainstream Freudianism by moving in the direction of the so-called neo-Freudians, a group that included Alfred Adler (1870–1937), Karen Horney (1885–1952), Harry Stack Sullivan (1892–1949), and Erik Erikson (1902–1994), who had been one of Beck's supervisors at Riggs. In general, the neo-Freudians placed a greater emphasis on social, interpersonal, and cultural influences in human development, and downplayed the significance of innate biological drives.

Freud had posited in *Mourning and Melancholia* (1917) that depression results from anger turned inward against the self, emerging outwardly as the patient's "need to suffer." Beck decided to set up a series of studies involving depressed patients, partly to collect data to convince psychologists of the soundness of Freud's hypothesis, and partly to design a brief form of psychotherapy that would target the core symptoms of depression. He received a research grant from Penn in 1959, and consulted two colleagues in the psychology department, Seymour Feshbach and Marvin Hurvich, for research methodology and statistical analysis. Beck then analyzed the dreams of 12 patients diagnosed with depression. The patients' dreams did in fact contain such themes as losing something of value, being prevented from achieving a goal, or appearing ugly, damaged, or diseased.

When Beck gave the depressed patients verbal conditioning and card-sorting tests, however, they reacted positively to successful outcomes, gaining self-esteem and performing better on subsequent tests. If Freud's theory of a "need to suffer" had been correct, the patients should have been upset by their successes. This discrepancy between psychoanalytic theory and research findings led Beck to reappraise his theoretical position. He went back to his dream study and began to compare the material in his patients' dreams with the verbal content of their interviews. In Beck's view, the comparison refuted Freud's notion of dreams as representing unconscious motivations and wish fulfillment. He recalled,

> . . . it became clear to me as I went into it that the dream themes were consistent with the waking themes. It seemed to me a simpler notion about the dreams was that they simply incorporated the person's self-concept. Well, if it is just a question of the person's self-concept, you don't have to invoke the notion of the dreams being motivated. . . . If you take motivation and wish fulfillment out of the dream, this undermines the whole motivational model of psychoanalysis.

Following this reevaluation, Beck then constructed his first cognitive model of depression, which incorporated three specific concepts: the so-called cognitive triad; schemas, or stable patterns of thinking; and cognitive errors, or faulty information processing. According to Beck, the cognitive triad encompasses a depressed person's view of himself, his ongoing experiences, and his future, causing him (or her) to regard present experiences or interactions with others as defeats or failures, and to think of the future as one of "unremitting hardship, frustration, and deprivation." This triad of negative cognitive patterns then generates the emotional disturbances and loss of energy or motivation associated with depression. Next, Beck devised an approach to therapy intended to identify a patient's thought distortions, test them against the rules of logic and external reality, and help the patient correct the distorted patterns of thinking.

Extension of cognitive therapy   Beck was cautious in extending his cognitive model of depression to other mental disorders; he has always been a methodical researcher, careful to restrict his claims to demonstrable results. For example, his first book on the treatment of depression recommended limiting cognitive therapy to nonpsychotic patients with unipolar depression who had not responded to or refused to take antidepressant medication. After the 1970s, however, the cognitive model was successfully applied by Beck's followers to a wide range of problems, including anxiety disorders, substance abuse, marital conflict, eating disorders, and anger management. One study reported that the interest in cognitive therapy among mental health care professionals increased 600% in the 16 years between 1973 and 1989. In the 1990s, cognitive therapists published outcome studies that reported success in treating psychotic disturbances and personality disorders—historically regarded as the most difficult mental disorders to treat.

Recent research interests   Since the early 1990s, Beck has expanded his research interests to include such topics as human evolutionary biology and the movement toward psychotherapy integration. With regard to evolution, Beck has studied the works of anthropologists and experts in the biology of nonhuman primates in order to investigate the possible evolutionary roots of depression, anxiety, and personality disorders in humans. Beck's book on anger and aggression, *Prisoners of Hate* (1999), opens with an analysis of chimpanzees and hunter-gatherer societies for an evolutionary basis for empathy and social cooperation among humans. Similarly, the second edition of *Cognitive Therapy of Personality Disorders* (2004) contains a section on the relationship between affective or personality disorders and evolutionary survival "strategies."

The integrative movement in psychotherapy began in the late 1970s as the result of three factors: general dissatisfaction among mental health professionals with single schools of therapy; the failure of any one school to dominate outcome studies for all mental disorders; and demands for greater accountability from health insurers. Some of Beck's students had already begun to use techniques derived from Gestalt therapy in treating depressed patients, and Beck himself had started to acknowledge the importance of unconscious factors as well as the therapeutic relationship in conducting cognitive therapy. Since the early 1990s, Beck has maintained in his publications that cognitive therapy is *the* therapy that can integrate all the others, partly because its emphasis on cognition offers common ground with a range of other approaches, and partly because Beck's research has sought to demonstrate the capacity of cognitive therapy to successfully incorporate techniques from these approaches.

Marriage and family

Beck, who is known to family and friends as Tim (from his middle name), has been married for over half a century and is the father of four children. Beck married Phyllis Whitman in 1950. He had met her when she was an undergraduate at Brown and he was completing his medical internship. Phyllis worked as a newspaper reporter for several years after the marriage, but also completed degrees in social work and law while rearing their four children. She graduated at the head of her class from Temple University School of Law, taught law at both Temple and the University of Pennsylvania, and became the first woman judge appointed to the Superior Court of Pennsylvania in 1981. Beck frequently tried out his ideas on his wife during the years of his discontent with psychoanalysis, and credits her with suggesting the word "schema" to describe cognitive structures. He once paid tribute to Phyllis as "the balance wheel between my self-doubts and my runaway fantasies."

Beck's daughter Judith became a clinical psychologist and presently serves as director of the Beck Institute for Cognitive Therapy and Research in Bala Cynwyd, Pennsylvania, which was founded in 1994. She has published several books of her own on cognitive therapy and oversees training programs for cognitive therapists at the Institute.

THEORIES

Structures of human cognition

Beck defines cognitive therapy as "an active, directive, time-limited, structured approach used to treat a variety of psychiatric disorders . . . . based on an underlying theoretical rationale that an individual's affect and behavior are largely determined by the way in which he structures the world." According to Beck, the cognitive organization of the human mind consists of various levels of verbal or pictorial "events" that vary among themselves in terms of accessibility and resistance to change. Beck has identified four such levels:

- Voluntary thoughts. These are the most readily accessible group of cognitions and appear in the patient's stream of consciousness.

- Automatic thoughts. These cognitions are less accessible, often come to the surface when the patient is under stress, and may be difficult to block.

- Assumptions and values. These cognitions are associated with the meanings that patients attribute to situations and events.

- Schemas. Schemas are cognitive structures based on a network of core beliefs established by a person's early learning experiences. They operate below the level of conscious awareness, and are dormant until they are activated or triggered by specific events. The schemas then serve as filters or screens that determine the person's interpretation of the event.

Driving a car in the city offers a useful example of Beck's layers of cognitions. Someone who is approaching a four-way intersection might notice that a driver on the cross street is going through the stop sign. "That driver isn't even slowing down; I'd better be careful and start applying the brakes" would be a typical set of voluntary thoughts. "People like that are scary" might be the person's automatic thought. "It is important to be a safe and careful driver" would be an example of an assumption. "The world is a dangerous and unfriendly place," would be an example of a core schema that might be triggered by the need for a quick response to the other driver's behavior.

Main points   Schemas, as Beck uses the term, vary in their extensiveness; their flexibility (the degree to which they can be modified in therapy); their density (the extent to which they dominate the person's cognitions); and valence (the degree of their activation at any given moment). For example, the schema of "feeling helpless" may be activated in some people fairly easily, in a wide variety of circumstances, and may be relatively resistant to change. In others, the "feeling helpless" schema may be activated only when the person is depressed, and it may be modified by therapy.

Beck distinguishes several different categories of schemas according to function and content:

- Cognitive schemas. These schemas deal with abstract thinking, interpretation of events, and memory or recall.

- Affective schemas. These schemas govern the emotions that arise from the person's cognitions.

- Motivational schemas. These are concerned with wishes and desires.

- Instrumental schemas. These schemas deal with making plans and preparing to take action.

- Control schemas. These are concerned with self-monitoring and acting or refraining from acting.

Beck regards these schemas as activated in the order of the preceding list. As an illustration, a person out hiking in the woods sees a snake slither across the trail in front of him. His memory tells him that some snakes are dangerous, and that he is not enough of an expert on snakes to know whether the one he just saw is poisonous or not (cognitive schema). He feels afraid (affective schema). He would like to run away (motivational schema). He prepares to turn around and go back (instrumental schema). He decides that the satisfaction he might have from proceeding with his hike is not worth the risk of snakebite, and turns back (control schema). This order is important, in that it reflects the belief of cognitive therapists that emotional responses to situations result from cognitive interpretations, not the other way around.

Schemas form interlocking sets that Beck calls systems. In cognitive therapy, it is a system that governs the sequence of events that begins with the person's reception and interpretation of a stimulus from the environment and ends with the person's behavioral response. In the preceding example, the hiker's perception of a snake and the possibility of injury produced an interpretation ("I'd rather not take the chance that the snake is poisonous"), which in turn led to his decision to return to his camp. Another hiker might interpret the same perceptions differently ("The snake might be poisonous, but I have a snakebite kit in my backpack and I know how to use it") and decide to stay on the trail.

Systems in turn may function as a group to form a mode. A mode, in Beck's usage, represents what he calls a "cognitive shift," which takes place when a person develops an anxiety disorder or depression. To give an example, Beck describes depression as a cognitive shift in which the patient "moves away from normal cognitive processing to a predominance of processing from the negative schemas that constitute the depressive mode." In other words, the "depressive mode" amounts to a systematic negative bias in recalling past events and interpreting present ones. Similarly, general anxiety disorder can be described as a cognitive shift into the "danger mode," in which memories and current events are interpreted in terms of threats to the self.

Explanation   There are several features to note in Beck's descriptions of cognitions and schemas. The first is that he is relatively unconcerned with causality; that is, he does not attempt to explain the ultimate cause or origin of a patient's dysfunctional schemas. With regard to depression in particular, he allows that mood disorders may be related to genetic vulnerabilities, brain injury, or hormonal disturbances as well as dysfunctional thought patterns. In addition, he observes that the dysfunctional schemas may be triggered in adult life by a variety of psychological stressors, biochemical factors, or a combination of both.

Second, Beck's understanding of cognitions and schemas helps to explain his focus on the patient's present situation. In his early writings on depression, Beck explicitly contrasted his approach with the historical concerns of psychoanalysis: "In contrast to psychoanalytic therapy, the content of cognitive therapy is focused on 'here-and-now' problems. Little attention is paid to childhood recollections except to clarify present observations. . . . We do not make interpretations of unconscious factors." Beck did, however, modify his emphasis on the present when he turned from the treatment of Axis I affective disorders (depression and the anxiety disorders) to therapy with patients suffering from Axis II personality disorders. Cognitive therapists who work with this patient population spend more time exploring the patient's childhood memories.

A third point that Beck wished to emphasize is that exploration of the patient's cognitions and schemas lends itself to experimental testing. "[Cognitive therapists] formulate the patient's dysfunctional idea and beliefs about himself, his experiences, and his future into hypotheses and then attempt to test the validity of these hypotheses in a systematic way." This emphasis on empirical testing distinguishes cognitive therapy from psychoanalysis, in which the analyst's interpretations of the patient's dreams or free associations are difficult to either disprove or verify.

Another contrast between Beck's understanding of human cognition and the classical Freudian view is his focus on the accessibility and nonmysterious quality of the patient's thoughts. Whereas psychoanalysis regarded a patient's feeling and behavior as driven by unconscious motivations that the analyst had to uncover and piece together from the material that the patient brought to therapy sessions, Beck attempted to demystify the cognitive distortions that generate emotional distress and behavioral problems. One consequence of Beck's rejection of such Freudian notions as the unconscious or defense mechanisms is that the therapist can approach the patient's dysfunctional beliefs in a direct way, by simple questioning that draws out the patient's full point of view rather than by complex interpretations that may miss the mark entirely.

Examples   Beck listed what he considered the major categories of "faulty information processing" that

"maintain the patient's belief in the validity of his negative concepts despite the presence of contradictory evidence" as early as 1967. An example of each category is given:

- Arbitrary inference. In this pattern of thought distortion, the patient draws a specific conclusion in the absence of evidence to support it. A patient may say, for example, that her husband is going to divorce her because she is depressed in spite of his reassurances to the contrary.

- Selective abstraction. In selective abstraction, the patient takes a small detail out of context, ignoring other features of the situation and interpreting the whole on the basis of the detail. For example, a college student may conclude on the basis of one poor grade on a weekly laboratory report that she will fail the entire course and have to give up her dreams of medical school.

- Overgeneralization. A patient who is overgeneralizing draws a sweeping conclusion from one or a few isolated incidents and applies it across the board even to unrelated situations. A person who has trouble fixing a leaky faucet, for example, may decide that he is completely incompetent at any task involving manual dexterity or mechanical skills.

- Magnification/minimization. This form of thought distortion involves extreme exaggeration of the significance of a situation or event. For example, a patient diagnosed with obsessive-compulsive disorder tells her therapist that it is "absolutely horrible" to be unable to do everything well.

- Personalization. In personalization, the patient tends to interpret external events as relating to him or herself even when there is no logical basis for a connection, or takes more than his or her share of responsibility for a negative outcome. An example would be a professional baseball player who assumes that his fielding errors are the reason his team ended up at the bottom of its league.

- Dichotomous or black-and-white thinking. This form of thought distortion places all experiences in one of two absolute categories. People with borderline personality disorder, for example, typically categorize others in their lives as completely wonderful and loving or as hateful persecutors. Narcissists often assume that if they are not "the best" in some respect, they must be "the worst."

To uncover the cognitive fallacies that are skewing a patient's interpretations of other people and events, the therapist may use a type of questioning that Beck calls "cognitive probing" or the "downward arrow" technique. The patient is asked to recall a recent incident that illustrates one of his or her recurrent difficulties. Cognitive probing allows therapist and patient together to examine the patient's problematic patterns of reasoning as well as identify automatic thoughts and core schemas. The following is an example of the "downward arrow" technique in the treatment of a patient with avoidant personality disorder. The event that the patient brought for discussion concerned a workplace friend who had gotten absorbed in a lunchtime conversation with a third friend.

- Therapist: What went through your mind at lunch?
- Patient: Linda is ignoring me. [arbitrary inference, personalization]
- T: What did that mean?
- P: That I can't get along with people. [overgeneralization]
- T: What does that mean?
- P: That I will never have any friends. [magnification]
- T: What does it mean "not to have friends"?
- P: I am all alone. [core schema]
- T: What does it mean to be "all alone"?
- P: That I will always be unhappy. [core schema]

A case study of a patient diagnosed with obsessive-compulsive disorder provides an example of the way in which cognitive therapists encourage patients to test their assumptions and beliefs by behavioral experimentation in real-life situations. The patient was an engineer in his mid-forties with a history of chronic pain in his back, neck, and shoulders. He had begun to consider the possibility that the pain was at least partly caused by psychological stress. The patient was not only highly critical of himself, but also thought that others were critical and disapproving. The therapist asked the patient at one point what he might do to "find out if these thoughts are accurate or not." The patient replied that he could ask others what they were thinking, but added that they "might not like [his] asking." The therapist then suggested starting with someone who is "pretty honest and nonjudgmental."

- Therapist: Who do you think might fit that description?
- Patient: My boss is a decent guy and I'd really like to not have to worry that he is judging me all the time.
- T: Can you think of a relatively safe way you could ask your boss how he is feeling about you or your work?
- P: I suppose I could say . . . 'Jack, you seem to be concerned about something. Is anything bothering you about the way my project is going?'

- T: That sounds pretty good. Would you be willing to accept that as your homework for next week?

Over the next several weeks the patient kept a record of asking others what they were thinking when he thought they were judging him negatively. He found that with one exception, he had completely misinterpreted their thoughts or opinions.

Beck's continuity hypothesis
Main points   Beck advanced what he calls his "continuity hypothesis" as early as 1976, when he published *Cognitive Therapy and the Emotional Disorders.* What he means by this phrase is that human behaviors can be placed at various points along a continuum instead of being divided sharply into "normal" and "pathological" behaviors. Beck's interest in evolutionary biology allows him to situate the continuity hypothesis within the larger framework of human evolution, and thus to describe dysfunctional attitudes and behaviors as potentially adaptive. He uses the example of a graduate student who fails an examination:

> Although it is important to realize that anger [directed at the examiners] and anxiety are potentially adaptive reactions, they can become maladaptive when we exaggerate the degree of danger or the magnitude of an offense. The student who exaggerates his vulnerability during an oral examination may find that his mind goes blank and he performs just as badly as he feared he would.

The theoretical account of personality disorders in *Cognitive Therapy of Personality Disorders* discusses the origin of these Axis II syndromes in terms of "evolutionary-based strategies" that may have been necessary for survival in prehistoric times but are no longer adaptive in contemporary societies. The diagnosis of a personality disorder may reflect only a "bad fit" between a given individual and our present "highly individualized and technological society," rather than a clear-cut instance of untreatable psychopathology. Or, as Beck puts it in *Prisoners of Hate,* "The most hypersensitive reactors among us are destined to receive a psychiatric diagnosis, which serves as a mandate to receive help in moderating the exaggerated reactions."

Beck applied his continuity hypothesis to consciousness itself as well as to emotions and behaviors. Speaking in a 1991 interview, Beck openly disagreed with Freud's notion of "a thick concrete wall of repression" separating conscious thinking and feeling from unconscious wishes and drives. "Now my own notion is that consciousness is on a continuum. Some things are more conscious than others and some are less conscious. . . . When you drive your car, you're [ordinarily] not conscious of every single move you're making, but if you're focusing on it, then you do become aware of what you're doing." Otherwise stated, for Beck consciousness is not a unitary or either/or condition, but a flexible set of responses to the environment.

Explanation Beck's continuity hypothesis has systematic as well as practical consequences. In terms of his system of thought, the continuity hypothesis provides a bridge between schemas and cognitions on the one hand and what Beck calls automatic thoughts on the other. Beck's concept of automatic thoughts, which he defines as "brief signals at the periphery of consciousness," grew out of his early work with depressed patients. One patient undergoing treatment in 1959, when Beck was still practicing traditional psychoanalysis, reported a secondary succession of thoughts that occurred while he was free-associating and angrily criticizing Beck. The thoughts concerned feelings of guilt for verbally attacking the therapist. Beck was intrigued by the patient's account of his internal monologue and began asking other patients if they had thoughts during therapy sessions that they had not mentioned. On the basis of their replies, he elaborated his notion of automatic thoughts.

In practical terms, Beck's continuity hypothesis is helpful to many patients in that it removes some of the feelings of shame and social stigma that many associate with a psychiatric diagnosis. Instead of being placed on one side of a categorical wall that separates a patient from "normal" people, he or she can think of therapy as helping him or her to move along a continuum from a more to a less extreme position on the continuum. Interestingly, many of the strategies recommended to people in therapy for dealing with the stigma attached to mental disorders are essentially cognitive techniques.

Examples Beck's continuity hypothesis is the basis of a technique that some cognitive therapists refer to as the continuum technique. It is used specifically to challenge all-or-nothing thinking. *Cognitive Therapy of Personality Disorders* includes an example of this technique with a patient diagnosed with paranoid personality disorder. The patient was a radiologist who had an all-or-nothing view of competence; in his own words, a person was either completely "good at what he does" or a total "screw-up." The therapist began by asking the patient to describe a competent person, and then a "screw-up." He made a list of the qualities the patient associated with competence, such as "doing

hard tasks well," "being relaxed while doing them," "catching and correcting mistakes," and "knowing one's limits," and a second list of their opposites. The therapist then drew a linear scale marked from "0" to "10," and asked the patient to rate himself on the continuum for each of the qualities he associated with competency. The radiologist quickly realized that he did not see himself as very relaxed at any time, and that neither he nor anyone else can function at their peak all the time. As the patient's view of competency became less polarized, the therapist then extended the continuum technique to his view of other people as either "completely trustworthy" or "totally malevolent, just like [his] family." Gradually the patient began to recognize that people, like skills, are not all-or-nothing packages, and he began to apply the continuum technique for himself to a range of social as well as occupational situations.

Emotions in cognitive therapy

Main points Beck has been criticized for paying insufficient attention to the role of emotions in treating mental disorders, although he did devote a full chapter in his landmark *Cognitive Therapy of Depression* to "The Role of Emotions in Cognitive Therapy." One important function of emotions in cognitive therapy is that they help patient and therapist to target core symptoms for the work of therapy rather than being distracted by relatively superficial issues. A strong emotional reaction during the initial interview and history-taking is usually evidence that the therapist has touched on a core problem. Beck also recommended the use of several techniques, including imagery work, sensory awareness, and flooding, as ways to identify the patient's core issues. His interest in these techniques goes back to his treatment of depressed Korean War veterans in the 1950s.

A second function served by the patient's expression of emotions during cognitive therapy sessions is stress relief, in that many people feel compelled to hide or suppress their feelings in the workplace or around family members. Beck notes that "Uninhibited crying seems to have some intrinsic therapeutic merit in many cases. . . . [the patient has] a sanctuary for self-expression without being judged." Beck adds that patients who find that they feel better after crying or expressing anger in the therapist's office are also more likely to stay in therapy.

A third aspect of the role of emotions in cognitive therapy is the therapist's utilization of state-dependent memory. State-dependent memory is a term that refers to the fact that people are better able to remember an event in their past if they are in the same emotional state that they were in when the event occurred. In order to help a patient retrieve the automatic thoughts that occur when he or she is anxious, for example, the therapist may try to recreate an anxiety-provoking situation during the therapy session. Other techniques related to state-dependent learning are discussed in *Cognitive Therapy of Depression.* They include scheduling therapy sessions at times when the distressing emotion is most likely to surface; for example, a patient who is bothered by feelings of loneliness might be asked to come in on a weekend or at night. In other situations, the therapist might visit the patient's home or enlist a family member or friend to use certain therapeutic strategies in the home situation.

Cognitive therapists do not, however, encourage the examination and expression of feelings to the extent practiced by experiential, or abreactive, schools of psychotherapy. An example of the experiential approach is the "primal scream" therapy practiced by Arthur Janov in the 1960s. Janov maintained that many physical as well as mental disorders result from early trauma, and can be relieved by expressing the pain and other strong feelings resulting from that trauma. Beck maintained that abreactive therapies encourage "the production of excessive, inappropriate emotional reactions," and do not help patients identify the distorted cognitions that underlie their painful feelings.

Explanation   The role of emotions in human behavior is a major area in which cognitive therapy has evolved since the early 1970s. As cognitive therapy was extended from depression to the treatment of personality disorders, Beck and his colleagues began to recognize the extent to which the dysfunctional cognitive profiles that characterize these disorders are attached to, and perpetuated by, strong emotions. The second edition of *Cognitive Therapy of Personality Disorders* contains extensive discussions of the role of emotions in the therapist/patient relationship and the importance of helping patients cope with painful feelings.

Examples   *Cognitive Therapy of Depression* contains an instructive example of an emotional outburst by a patient. The patient in this case was a depressed, 35-year-old married woman whose complaints included tiring easily and feeling physically weak. She initially described her marriage as "fine," adding, "I don't have any problems in my marriage." When the therapist asked her to describe some specific interactions with her husband, however, the patient began to sob. As she continued to describe her husband's behavior patterns,

she cried uncontrollably. She then said, "You know . . . I think those things bother me more than I realized." She was able to link her sad feelings to such specific cognitions as "My husband always gets his own way," and "He is inconsiderate and doesn't care about what I want." This patient's course of therapy included some work on restructuring her relationship with her spouse as well as learning to identify the cognitions that were maintaining her depression.

An example of eliciting a state-dependent memory during a therapy session concerns a patient diagnosed with avoidant personality disorder. Guided discovery is often used with these patients, because they frequently report that their minds "go blank" when painful feelings are aroused. In this instance, the therapist had been doing an imagery exercise with the patient, asking her to imagine herself going out to eat with a friend. Suddenly, the patient stated that she didn't want to go on with the exercise. When the therapist asked her what she was feeling, she replied, "Depressed . . . and . . . real scared." The therapist continued, "What do you think will happen if you keep feeling this way?" The patient said that she would "freak out," "go crazy," and that the therapist would see her as "a basket case." The therapist reassured her that the feelings she was trying to avoid would "lead to some useful information" if she could stay with them just a little longer. Returning to the image of sharing a restaurant meal with her friend, the patient began to sob, and said she thought the friend would be angry with her. She added, "I'm a rotten person for making him so unhappy." Guided discovery was used for the next several sessions to help the patient develop greater tolerance for painful feelings as well as uncover other automatic thoughts.

Role of the therapist

Main points   Beck describes cognitive therapy as a "collaborative enterprise" or "collaborative empiricism." What he means by these expressions is that the therapist works together with the patient to uncover the specific underlying assumptions that trigger the patient's emotional pain and motivational difficulties. The patient brings what Beck calls "raw data" to the therapeutic relationship, while the therapist offers guidance in collecting appropriate data and using them in therapy. The therapist is not regarded as an "expert" who knows the patient's mind better than she does herself; the patient is asked and expected to correct the therapist if he has misunderstood her. Beck emphasizes that the distorted cognitions involved in mental disorders are often idiosyncratic and cannot be deduced automatically from the event that has brought the patient into therapy.

BIOGRAPHY:

Albert Ellis

Albert Ellis (1913–) is the founder of rational-emotive behavior therapy, or REBT. He did not set out to become a therapist, but majored in business at the City University of New York. Ellis graduated from CUNY in 1934, in the midst of the Great Depression. While supporting himself by managing a gift and novelty firm, Ellis hoped to become a great writer— but had little success in publishing his short stories and plays. He did discover, however, from conversations with friends that he had a flair for counseling. He entered the graduate program in clinical psychology at Columbia, earning his doctorate in 1947.

Ellis thought at the time of his graduation from Columbia that psychoanalysis was the most effective form of therapy. In the late 1940s, the American psychoanalytic institutes refused to accept trainees without MDs, but Ellis found a student of Karen Horney's who agreed to work with him. He practiced classical psychoanalysis for several years while teaching at Rutgers and New York University. Like Beck, however, Ellis found himself losing faith in Freud's ideas, and abandoned psychoanalysis altogether by 1955. Like Beck, Ellis was influenced by the Stoic philosophers and the neo-Freudians, and began to publish his early work on REBT in the 1950s. His landmark books came out earlier than Beck's. *Guide to Rational Living* was published in 1961, and *Reason and Emotion in Psychotherapy* appeared in 1962.

Unlike Beck, Ellis is not a researcher. He promoted his approach to psychotherapy largely through popular self-help books and workshops rather than through publications in professional journals. Some observers believe that Ellis did not have as much of an impact as Beck because he did not work in an academic or medical school setting. Beck credits Ellis, however, with advancing the recognition that thoughts and beliefs are much more accessible to

patients than psychoanalysts had maintained. In addition, Ellis was the first to concentrate the work of therapy on the patient's present-day issues as compared to childhood memories or traumas. Beck has always acknowledged Ellis's influence on his work, beginning with his first major book on depression. In particular he derived his technique of Socratic questioning from Ellis.

REBT and cognitive therapy share several characteristics: the assumption that dysfunctional thinking is a factor in psychological distress; a focus on changing thought processes in order to bring about changes in feelings and behavior; and a time-limited concentration on specific target symptoms in therapy. There are also, however, several important differences between the two approaches: cognitive therapy seeks to correct the systematic biases in a patient's information processing as well as examine the content of specific dysfunctional beliefs; cognitive therapy allows for idiosyncratic beliefs, whereas REBT therapists tend to assume that the same set of "irrational beliefs" operates in everyone; and Beck tends to give greater weight to the role of life experiences in shaping a patient's beliefs while Ellis favors a biological basis for irrational thinking. Finally, Beck and Ellis disagree on what they consider the foundational problem in mental disorders: Beck believes that the ultimate source is fear, whereas Ellis follows Horney in referring to the "tyranny of the 'shoulds'," or in his own memorable phrase, "MUSTerbatory thinking."

Albert Ellis. (Institute for *Rational–Emotive Therapy. Reproduced by permission.*)

Beck's concept of the therapist's role includes several innovations related to his model of collaborative empiricism:

- Testing the patient's beliefs against real-life experience. Along with Albert Ellis, Beck was one of the first therapists to invite patients to reevaluate dysfunctional thoughts or images by conducting

behavioral experiments and considering alternative explanations of other people's actions. An example of this technique was described earlier.

- Socratic questioning. Cognitive therapists ask questions of their patients far more frequently than therapists trained in psychoanalytic techniques. Beck is careful to distinguish, however,

---

between rapid-fire questioning that may come across to the patient as interrogation, and what he terms "Socratic questioning." This approach, which takes its name from the types of questions that the philosopher Socrates asked his friends to guide them to insight, is intended to be a nonjudgmental way for the therapist to model examination of one's cognitive patterns or previously unquestioned assumptions.

• Guided discovery. Guided discovery refers to the general process of teaching patients to discover their own misperceptions and flawed logic, as opposed to the therapist's arguing or disputing with them. Guided discovery is also used to help the patient learn to identify themes that distort his or her interactions in the present and relate these themes to past experiences.

The cognitive therapist takes an active role in the therapy process. Prior to the initial interview with the patient, the cognitive therapist is expected to plan a tentative outline of treatment based on the patient's history and his or her scores on one or more of Beck's diagnostic instruments. As is described in more detail under "Theories in Action," the therapist introduces the patient to the basic concepts and principles of cognitive therapy and gathers information about the patient and his or her dysfunctional thought patterns. In general, however, cognitive therapists are more active at the beginning of treatment than at the end, particularly when working with depressed patients.

Cognitive therapists are also highly directive; that is, they assign the patient tasks ("homework") to be completed before the next session, and may use a range of behavioral techniques to nudge the patient out of passivity. The collaborative aspect of cognitive therapy is very much task-oriented. Beck draws an explicit contrast between cognitive therapy and supportive or "relationship" therapies. ". . . [in cognitive therapy] the therapeutic relationship is used not simply as *the* instrument to alleviate suffering but as a vehicle to facilitate . . . carrying out specific goals." As will be illustrated below, patients in cognitive therapy are asked to think of specific changes they would like to see in their lives that require concrete actions: reducing or eliminating some of the symptoms of their disorder, improving management skills in the workplace or home, pursuing new intellectual or spiritual interests, tackling bad habits, and the like.

Explanation There are several rationales underlying Beck's view of the therapist's role. One is to maximize the benefits of short-term therapy. Homework

assignments, keeping written records of dysfunctional thoughts, and similar tasks are thought to maintain and reinforce the patient's progress between sessions. In addition, the patient's use of logs or written notes provides him or her with a visible "track record" of progress. This record is particularly beneficial if and when the patient has a temporary setback during therapy.

A second rationale for Beck's emphasis on collaborative therapy is to restore the patient's sense of control or mastery. Depressed patients in particular frequently feel helpless or overwhelmed by their situation, and feelings of accomplishment or satisfaction serve to lift morale as well as counteract dysfunctional thoughts. A behavioral technique that cognitive therapists often use with depressed patients is keeping a schedule of activities, and rating each for mastery (completing the task) and pleasure (deriving enjoyment or fun from the activity).

The third rationale for such specific techniques as Socratic questioning and guided discovery is that they enable the patient to become his or her own therapist after formal treatment has ended. Given the high rate of recurrence or relapse among patients diagnosed with major depression (as noted in the 2001 STAR*D protocol, between 20% and 35% experience a chronic course of the disorder), the possibility that cognitive therapy may lower this rate is often used to recommend it.

Examples Beck's 1979 *Cognitive Therapy of Depression* contains an example of Socratic questioning used in treating a depressed graduate student worried about admission to law school by exploring the meaning she attached to it.

• Patient: I get depressed when things go wrong. Like when I fail a test.

• Therapist: How can failing a test make you depressed?

• P: Well, if I fail I'll never get into law school.

• T: So failing the test means a lot to you. But if failing a test could drive people into clinical depression, wouldn't you expect everyone who failed the test to have a depression? . . . .

• P: It depends on how important the test was to the person.

• T: Right, and who decides the importance?

• P: I do.

• T: And so, what we have to examine is the way . . . that you think about the test, and how it affects your chances of getting into law school. Do you agree?

• P: Right.

An example of Beck's use of guided discovery to uncover automatic thoughts as well as to draw connections between thoughts and feelings concerns a young man with an anxiety disorder. Asked to list situations that he found particularly upsetting, the patient had mentioned sports, playing cards with friends, and dating.

- Therapist: What thoughts go through your mind . . . when you don't do so well at swimming?
- Patient: I think that people think much less of me, that I'm not a winner.
- T: And how about if you make a mistake playing cards?
- P: I doubt my own intelligence.
- T: And if a girl rejects you?
- P: It means I'm not special. I lose value as a person.
- T: Do you see any connections here among these thoughts?
- P: Well, I guess my mood depends on what other people think of me. But that's important—I don't want to be lonely.
- T: What would that mean to you, to be lonely?
- P: It would mean there's something wrong with me, that I'm a loser.

HISTORICAL CONTEXT

Cognitive therapy is rooted in philosophical systems dating back two millennia that are part of the high culture of the West as well as in medical and psychological research since Freud.

Classical Western philosophical tradition

Beck's interest in the humanities as an undergraduate led him to situate his approach to psychotherapy within the mainstream of Western philosophy, which has traditionally emphasized the role of human reason as the guide or governor of the emotions. He has explicitly mentioned his indebtedness to Greek and Roman Stoicism, the critical idealism of Immanuel Kant (1724–1804), and the phenomenology of Edmund Husserl (1859–1938) and Martin Heidegger (1889–1976). Stoicism numbered among its adherents such writers as Zeno of Citium (333–264 B.C.), Cicero (106–46 B.C.), Seneca (3 B.C.–65 A.D.), Epictetus (55–135 A.D.), and the Roman emperor Marcus Aurelius Antoninus (121–180 A.D.). One of Epictetus's sayings is: "People are disturbed not by things but by the view which they take of them." Similarly, Marcus Aurelius wrote in his

Meditations that "If you are distressed by anything external, the pain is not due to the thing itself, but to your estimate of it; and this you have the power to revoke at any moment."

Previous dominance of the psychoanalytic model

As the preceding outline of Beck's medical training indicates, classical psychoanalysis was the basic model for practicing psychotherapy in the United States in the 1930s through the 1950s. Its influence was particularly strong in the Northeast, where Beck received his undergraduate as well as his professional education. This influence stemmed in part from the famous series of lectures that Freud had delivered at Clark University in Massachusetts in 1909. The Boston Psychoanalytic Society and Institute (BPSI) was founded in 1928, followed by the Philadelphia Psychoanalytic Institute and Society, where Beck received his training in the 1950s. At the time that Beck joined the University of Pennsylvania faculty in 1954, the only mainstream alternative to psychoanalysis was pharmacotherapy, or treating psychiatric patients with medications. Lithium carbonate had been found to be effective in treating mania by Australian researchers in 1948. Chlorpromazine (thorazine), the first of the effective antipsychotic drugs, had been discovered by a French surgeon named Henri Laborit in 1952. Psychotropic medications, however, proved to have several disadvantages that included the risk of addiction as well as other severe side effects.

Beck's dissatisfaction with the psychoanalytic method and his gradual divergence from Freudian presuppositions resulted in a period of professional isolation and some loss of grant funding. He later remarked, "One colleague [at Penn] told me [cognitive therapy] was like treating malaria with an electric fan." During this period Beck relied primarily on his wife and on Gerald Davison, a psychologist at the State University of New York at Stony Brook, for feedback and support. Another source of encouragement was Albert Ellis, who had also begun his career in therapy as a psychoanalyst, become disenchanted with the Freudian mainstream, and developed his own form of psychotherapy-rational-emotive behavioral therapy or REBT. Ellis first wrote to Beck in 1963 after reading one of his articles in the *Archives of General Psychiatry*. The two men have continued to communicate with each other and exchange ideas ever since. Beck even underwent a session of REBT with Ellis, hoping to cure his lifelong fear of public speaking—but neither felt the session was completely successful.

The cognitive revolution

The growing acceptance of Beck's theories within the therapeutic community during the 1970s was in part the result of the so-called "cognitive revolution" in psychology, in which psychologists began to move away from behaviorism and its model of learning as operant conditioning toward a model of learning as information processing. Jean Piaget's work on the process of childhood learning indicated that children perceive, remember, and learn to think in categories—such structures as number, quantity, volume, and space. Other researchers found that categorization appears to be both innate in humans and cross-cultural. Another structural psychologist whose work influenced Beck was George Kelly, whose two-volume *Psychology of Personal Constructs* (1955) proposed that psychopathology could be understood in terms of faulty information processing. Beck initially used Kelly's term "constructs" to describe his "schemas."

The cognitive revolution also included researchers who applied the information-processing model to social psychology, studying such processes as impression formation, decision-making, problem-solving, self-perception, and self-control. Beck was particularly influenced by the work of Donald Meichenbaum in cognitive behavioral modification and Albert Bandura (1925–) in social modeling and self-regulation theory.

Managed care and evidence-based practice

Cognitive therapy has enjoyed renewed popularity in the early twenty-first century because of its cost-effectiveness and long-term benefits. The rise of managed care and subsequent pressures for cost containment in the treatment of psychiatric disorders have made cognitive therapy the dominant model of psychotherapy in the United States. According to a 2002 article in the *Washington Post*, this dominance has caused resentment among psychoanalysts and practitioners of psychodynamic therapy. The reporter concluded, "Therapists feel they are being railroaded into a single school of therapeutic thinking—the one supported by managed care companies, which care less about patients than about holding costs down."

Similar comments have been made by therapists working in the United Kingdom, where the National Health Service's publication *Treatment Choice in Psychological Therapies and Counselling* is seen as promoting cognitive behavior therapy as the treatment of choice. One British psychiatrist remarked in 2002 that ". . . it is hard to escape the suspicion that cognitive behaviour therapy seems so far ahead of the field in part because of its research and marketing strategy rather than because it is intrinsically superior to other therapies."

Self-help groups and bibliotherapy

Another historical factor that has favored the growth of cognitive therapy since the 1970s is the rapid proliferation of self-help groups and the growing popularity of self-help books. Bibliotherapy, or the use of books to help people solve problems or train themselves in such techniques as those used in cognitive therapy, has become widely used since it was first discussed in the early 1980s. In addition, the Twelve Steps of Alcoholics Anonymous (AA) and similar groups (Al-Anon, Overeaters Anonymous, Gamblers Anonymous, etc.) have been described in the psychiatric literature as a form of cognitive restructuring that helps uncover the distortions of "stinkin' thinkin'" and the emotional problems associated with addictions. Beck has contributed to the self-help movement both theoretically and practically. His theoretical contribution lies in his emphasis on the collaborative aspect of the therapist/patient relationship and the therapist's role in teaching the patient techniques for thought monitoring and belief testing that can be used after the termination of formal therapy.

In practical terms, Beck and some of his students have written self-help guides and other books for the interested nonspecialist. In 1988 Beck published a book called *Love Is Never Enough*, which introduced the concept of couples' therapy as well as cognitive therapy within the framework of a guide written for the general public. David Burns, who completed a residency in psychiatry under Beck in the late 1970s, has published several self-help books based on the principles of cognitive therapy, including *Feeling Good: The New Mood Therapy* (1980), *Intimate Connections* (1985), and *The Feeling Good Handbook* (1990). Burns's books are often recommended as "homework" for patients in cognitive therapy. Lastly, Beck's work on the cognitive distortions underlying anger and violence, called *Prisoners of Hate*, appeared in 1999. While it is not a self-help book in the strict sense, *Prisoners* discusses the cognitive bases of spouse and child abuse, hate crimes, and terrorism in a clear and accessible fashion.

CRITICAL RESPONSE

Behaviorist criticisms

The earliest criticisms of Beck's work came from behaviorist psychologists, particularly Joseph Wolpe and B. F. Skinner, on the grounds that cognitive therapy is a form of mentalism, which may be defined as the belief that mental processes are autonomous and cannot be explained by an organism's behavior.

Behaviorists have also criticized Beck for departing from basic science in his use of self-report paper-and-pencil questionnaires and his inability to demonstrate that cognitions are anything more than conditioned behaviors. Behaviorist critiques of Beck since the 1970s have generally focused on the uneasy relationship between cognitive therapy and behavior therapy. Most criticisms of cognitive therapy, however, have come from practitioners of psychoanalysis and psychodynamic psychotherapy.

Simplistic and technique-oriented

One of the most common criticisms of cognitive therapy is that it is superficial and consists of a "cookbook" or mechanical approach to psychotherapy. This line of criticism gathered force after 1979, when Beck published *Cognitive Therapy of Depression.* The book offered therapists an explicit description of the course of therapy, from a discussion of the structure of the therapeutic interview and a session-by-session outline of the treatment of a depressed patient to explanations of therapeutic homework and ways to focus on target symptoms. Beck's critics, however, used the book to argue that cognitive therapy is too technique-oriented, focuses too narrowly on short-term symptom reduction, underestimates the level of skill required to be a competent therapist, and oversimplifies the complexity of patients' problems. The cost-control emphasis of managed care has intensified this particular criticism of cognitive therapy. Practitioners of psychodynamic therapy in particular have maintained that they would rather treat fewer patients than be constrained by insurance companies who only allow as few as eight sessions of treatment.

Beck's reply to this criticism began to emerge in the 1980s, when the National Institute of Mental Health (NIHM) funded a multi-site outcome study intended to compare the effectiveness of cognitive therapy for depression with short-term interpersonal psychotherapy, which was based on a psychodynamic model. Beck was skeptical of the value of a multi-site study, but he did obtain a small grant to train therapists in cognitive therapy for three months. A major problem was that there was a far larger pool of therapists trained in psychodynamic therapy to draw from, and they quickly mastered the adjustments that were necessary to practice interpersonal psychotherapy. There were very few experienced cognitive therapists, however, and the trainees who completed Beck's three-month "crash program" barely met competency standards. The result was that cognitive therapy did not appear to be as efficacious in comparison to other treatment methods as other outcome studies had indicated. Beck subsequently regarded the NIMH study, which was published in 1989,

as a setback. On the other hand, the fact that three months of training in cognitive therapy was clearly inadequate indicated that cognitive therapy is not just a matter of following an easily mastered set of techniques.

Beck's later publications have been careful to spell out that rote mastery of therapeutic technique is not enough to be a competent practitioner of cognitive therapy. *Cognitive Therapy of Personality Disorders* contains the following admonition:

> . . . methods that are successful with at a particular time with a given patient may be ineffective at another time. Therapists must use their best judgment in designing treatment plans and selecting the most useful techniques . . . or improvising new ones. A certain amount of trial and error may be necessary.

Inadequate account of human emotions

A second common critique of cognitive therapy is that it focuses on cognition to the point of discounting the role of emotions in effecting change during psychotherapy. Other critics maintain that cognitive therapy is rationalistic in the sense of making a detached or common-sense attitude toward life as the implicit goal of therapy. Cognitive therapy does not, however, regard intellectual insight by itself as sufficient to bring about change, nor does it hold that all emotional distress is caused by dysfunctional thinking.

A related objection to cognitive therapy's approach to the emotions is that it encourages people to trivialize painful feelings or reinterpret them in inappropriately positive ways. One commentator refers to David Burns's popular book *Feeling Good* as an example of this reductionism, quoting Burns on the proper way to grieve for someone's death:

> [Burns says] "You validly think 'I lost him (or her), and I will continue to miss the companionship and love we shared.' The feelings such a thought creates are tender, realistic and desirable. Your emotions will enhance your humanity . . . . In this way you *gain* from your loss."

> My first thought on reading this was "Thank God I am not loved by David Burns." What about mourning? . . . . The new rush to "positivize" everything turns even death and mourning into a matter of gain. . . . David Burns' idealized mourner is a narcissist who is incapable of any deep feeling at all, or who has to distort emotion into a "desirable" channel before it can be felt.

Inadequate utilization of the therapist/patient relationship

A frequent criticism of cognitive therapy in its early years was that it neglected the therapeutic relationship as a locus of, or impetus for, change. Most researchers who took this position were either psychoanalysts or practitioners of psychodynamic therapy. Psychodynamic psychotherapy is itself a derivative of classical psychoanalysis and shares many of its presuppositions—specifically, that therapy works by bringing the patient's unconscious motivations into conscious awareness, by achieving insights into one's past, and by resolving emotional conflicts by working them through with the therapist. It is assumed that any relational problem the patient has with others will resurface in the therapeutic relationship, and will provide subject matter for reflection and behavioral change. The emergence and resolution of the so-called transference relationship is the centerpiece of psychoanalytically oriented therapies.

Beck's description of the patient's contribution to therapy as "raw data" has been criticized by followers of the psychoanalytic tradition as simplistic. They maintain that unconscious processes can shape the patient's presentation of the "raw data" of his or her experience. Since the rise of the integrative movement in psychotherapy, however, many cognitive therapists are more open to investigating the role of the unconscious in human experience and information processing.

Another factor that has led to a reappraisal of the therapeutic relationship in cognitive therapy is the extension of cognitive approaches to the treatment of the Axis II personality disorders. In contrast to Beck's straightforward statement in 1979 that cognitive therapists "do not make interpretations of unconscious factors" in therapy, the second edition of *Cognitive Therapy of Personality Disorders* makes explicit reference to the significance of the transference relationship: "The patient's emotional reactions to the process of therapy and the therapist are of central concern. Always alert but not provoking, the therapist is ready to explore these reactions for more information about the patient's system of thoughts and beliefs." It should be noted, however, that the reason given for exploring the transference is to strengthen the collaboration between patient and therapist rather than to provide insight or allow emotional release through the process of "working through" transference issues: "If not explored, possible distorted interpretations will persist and may interfere with collaboration." In addition, the book's extensive discussion of the therapeutic relationship is clearly concerned to avoid terminology associated with the psychoanalytic tradition: "To avoid confusion with psychodynamic assumptions and remain focused within the cognitive model, we refer to [transference and countertransference] simply as emotional reactions within the therapy process."

Reality-based depressions

One objection to Beck's theory of cognition is that people may be depressed without necessarily distorting reality. For example, a person who belongs to a socially marginalized group, or who has been severely disfigured in an accident, or has a physical handicap is not necessarily being illogical or irrational for feeling pessimistic about his or her future. In addition, some well-conducted studies have challenged Beck's hypothesis that depressed people are more prone to cognitive distortions that nondepressed people. In 1979, Lauren Alloy and Lyn Abramson of the State University of New York at Stony Brook performed a series of experiments that indicated that depressed subjects judged themselves and their circumstances more accurately than those who were not depressed. This postulate is sometimes known as depressive realism. Other studies carried out between 1979 and the mid-1990s also found that most people's self-understanding is not only inaccurate but skewed in an overly positive direction. In general, most people assume they have a greater degree of control over their lives than what reality warrants. A British critic of cognitive therapy has said

> Aaron Beck's approach to depression assumes that far more control is possible; his "wrong thinkers" live in delusion as he sees it—and this may be *his* illusion. . . . [but] none of us cares to admit how little control we might really have over our own world. To see things too clearly may be terrifying.

Therapists from other schools argue that Beck tended to overlook the influence of environmental and family-based factors in depression, especially in his earlier work. In particular, therapists influenced by Virginia Satir or Murray Bowen's family systems theory often point out that many depressed people have one or more family members who are either unsympathetic to them, or seem to have a vested interest in maintaining the patient's depression. As the terms "identified patient" or "symptom bearer" suggest, the depressed individual may be carrying the burden of an extended family's collective dysfunction. Therapists who work out of a family systems orientation maintain that cognitive therapy for the identified patient does little long-term good if the patient must interact with others who tend to reinforce his or her distorted cognitions.

Beck began to reformulate his account of depression in the early 1980s to accommodate social factors. On the basis of work with outpatients in his clinic, he posited two major personality types with different vulnerabilities to depression, which he termed "sociotropy" and "autonomy." A sociotropic person, according to Beck, depends on harmonious social relationships for gratification, and is vulnerable to depression when significant relationships are lost or threatened. An autonomous person, on the other hand, has a strong need for achievement, desires freedom from control by others, and prefers solitude. This type of person is more likely to become depressed when he or she is frustrated or thwarted in attaining goals. Beck, however, incorporated this typology into his continuity hypothesis and asserted that these two categories represent the extremes of a continuum; they are not mutually exclusive.

Superficial view of major life changes

The short-term focus of cognitive therapy has led some observers to argue that its practitioners underestimate the hard work and suffering involved in major life changes. An example might be a junior college faculty member who recognizes that she is not going to get tenure in spite of an excellent record of publications and enthusiastic evaluations as a teacher. The external circumstances may include departmental politics, cutbacks in the number of tenured positions, older professors who do not wish to retire at the usual age, and many others. The instructor will have to make cognitive changes in the way she views herself, the world, and her place in it, but these changed cognitions are far more fundamental than correcting misperceptions or recognizing logical fallacies. In sum, major life transitions require more than merely cognitive alterations. As one of Beck's critics has put it, "Courage, endurance, and the acquisition of humility may [also] have something to do with making the needful changes."

In addition, cognitive changes themselves do not appear to be as straightforward and logical as Beck describes them. The creative processes in any human activity are still not amenable to scientific analysis. The junior faculty member in the example just given will have to work out a new way of understanding herself and her future, but she is not likely to arrive at this end by logic alone. Such qualities as imagination and faith are often involved in the complex and roundabout route that leads people to envision new possibilities for their futures. Profound changes in a person's life are not fully controlled by consciousness and rational will, nor are they always comfortable. Major life transitions require courage, as they can be intensely disturbing and frightening. It is commonplace in Twelve-Step group meetings that people often feel worse in early recovery than they did before entering the program. But there is little in the framework of cognitive therapy that allows for creative imagination in the process of change, or for fear and anxiety in the face of making the necessary changes.

Recent discoveries in cognitive science

Some observers note that discoveries about consciousness and the functioning of the human brain

that were made in the 1980s and 1990s do not support Beck's notion of a close relationship between cognitions and emotions. The first such discovery was made in the course of so-called "split-brain" research. Split-brain research refers to studies carried out with epileptic subjects who have had a commissurotomy. In this procedure, the neurosurgeon cuts the corpus callosum, a band of tissue that carries nerve impulses between the two cerebral hemispheres, in order to control the patient's seizures. The researchers discovered that the human mind is not a unified entity, but consists of modules operating independently of one another. The parts of the brain that govern emotional states may have little to do with the parts that process information. What split-brain studies indicate is that consciousness cannot be an exact mirror of what is going on in the brain. Yet consciousness plays a central role in the theories underlying cognitive therapy.

Another area of research that raises questions about cognitive therapy is social psychologists' studies of cognition in relation to decision-making. Numerous experiments have shown that a person's explanation of how he or she came to a conclusion may be quite different from what was actually done. In addition, evidence has accumulated since the 1980s that there is no universal pattern of judgment and reasoning that holds true for all humans; rather, cultures play a role in shaping notions of cognition. These studies imply that cognitive therapy depends on a culturally limited view of reason and logic, and a correspondingly limited understanding of "dysfunctional thinking," rather than being based on a truly universal human characteristic.

THEORIES IN ACTION

Practice of cognitive therapy

Cognitive therapy is a highly structured form of short-term therapy. Practitioners who have been trained at the Beck Institute or have passed the certification examination of the Academy for Cognitive Therapy (ACT) follow a standard format for treatment, which will be outlined below. Standardization is an important feature of cognitive therapy, as Judith Beck explains:

> A major goal of the cognitive therapist is to make the process of therapy understandable to both therapist and patient . . . [and] to do therapy as efficiently as possible. Adhering to a standard format (as well as teaching the tools of therapy to the patient) facilitates these objectives.

It is difficult, however, to estimate the actual number of therapists in North America and the United Kingdom who practice some form of cognitive therapy. As of late 2002 there were about 350 accredited cognitive therapists in the United States. Other practitioners are graduates of doctoral programs approved by the ACT (10 as of early 2004) or have trained at centers for cognitive therapy in New York, Atlanta, Cleveland, Huntington Beach, California, or Oxford, England, but have not yet taken the ACT's certification examination. Many therapists in the United States, however, practice "eclectic" or integrative therapy, using techniques derived from psychodynamic psychotherapy or other orientations as well as cognitive therapy. A survey published in a professional psychology journal in the early 1990s found that 68% of therapists surveyed identified themselves as "eclectic" therapists; 72% of these reported that they used a psychodynamic approach in their work, as compared with only 54% who made use of cognitive therapy. Therapists who described themselves as following one approach exclusively included 17% who practiced psychodynamic therapy and 5% who solely practiced cognitive therapy.

In terms of recognition by the medical specialty of psychiatry, however, cognitive therapy is now a required part of residency training. As of 2003, the Residency Review Committee for Psychiatry of the Accreditation Council on Graduate Medical Education (ACGME) mandated that all psychiatric residents be required to demonstrate competency in the practice of cognitive behavior therapy.

Preparation Practitioners of cognitive therapy are expected to gather as much information about the patient as possible prior to the initial interview, in order to make the most of the available number of sessions. The patient will ordinarily have had a thorough diagnostic examination to determine how the standard format of cognitive therapy should be adjusted for the patient. Most cognitive therapists will also ask the patient to complete the Beck Depression Inventory, revised version (BDI-II), the Beck Anxiety Inventory (BAI), and the Beck Hopelessness Scale (BHS) before the initial interview in order to obtain baseline scores on these instruments. The therapist then studies the patient's history, symptoms, level of current functioning, and presenting complaints in order to draw up a general plan for treatment and make a tentative conceptualization of the patient's problems. This cognitive case conceptualization is regarded as a critical and necessary blueprint for the therapist's interventions.

Initial interview Cognitive therapists cover a great deal of ground in the initial interview with the patient.

Judith Beck lists the following as the therapist's objectives for this session: establishing rapport with the patient and gaining his or her trust; instructing the patient about the purpose and methods of cognitive therapy; teaching the patient about his or her specific disorder from the perspective of the cognitive model; reassuring the patient about the normality of his or her difficulties and "instilling hope"; discussing the patient's expectations of therapy and correcting them if necessary; gathering additional information about the patient's problems; and drawing up a list of goals for the treatment.

To meet these objectives, the cognitive therapist will set an agenda for the session; perform a mood check, which is usually done by administering the BDI; review the presenting problem with the patient and obtain an update covering the time period since the initial evaluation; educate the patient about cognitive therapy and his or her diagnosis; assign homework for the next session; summarize the session; and ask the patient for feedback. If the use of medications and/or substance abuse are issues for the patient, these are also placed on the agenda of the initial session.

Basic components of a cognitive therapy session Later sessions are based on the following structure:

- Brief update. This part of the session allows the patient to discuss significant events and his or her reactions to them since the previous session.

- Bridge from previous session. Here the therapist draws connections between the work of the previous session and the patient's present feelings or thoughts.

- Setting an agenda. Both the therapist and the patient contribute items for discussion during the session. Agenda-setting is done in order to cut down on the amount of unproductive conversation during sessions and help both parties focus on the patient's core issues. A typical agenda might include four or five items, such as "review the patient's activity schedule"; "begin to demonstrate relationship between thinking, behavior and affect by using specific experiences of patient"; "discuss the booklet on depression that was given to the patient to read at home"; and similar items.

- Homework review. As was mentioned earlier, homework is an integral part of cognitive therapy. Patients who associate the term with unpleasant school experiences may prefer to call these activities "self-help work." As with agenda setting, therapist and patient arrive at the list of items jointly. Bibliotherapy, usually a book on cognitive therapy written for the general public; monitoring one's activities; and keeping a record of mood changes and accompanying thoughts or images are common homework assignments. The therapist's primary concern is helping the patient to experience success by choosing activities that will increase his or her sense of mastery or satisfaction. Homework review allows the therapist to monitor and evaluate the patient's successes or failures—including feelings of success or failure, which may or may not be appropriate to the patient's actual accomplishments.

- Discussion of goals or target issue(s). Because cognitive therapy is a time-limited approach, clear focus is an essential aspect of the treatment plan. Therapist and patient together agree on a list of "core" or "target" symptoms that can be addressed over the course of a limited number of sessions. The symptoms that are targeted usually fall into one of two categories: those that the patient considers most distressing, and those that can be effectively treated. The symptoms may be emotional, motivational, physiological, cognitive, or a mixture of these. With regard to goal setting, patients are taught to think in terms of specific changes that can be described in behavioral terms ("keeping up with course work in school" or "planning more outings with my spouse") rather than vague generalities ("feeling better" or "feeling happier").

- New homework.

- Summary and feedback. At the end of each session the therapist summarizes what has happened during the session and asks the patient for feedback. Feedback serves several purposes: it reinforces the patient's role as an active participant in the work of therapy; it strengthens the rapport between the patient and the therapist; and it allows the patient to correct any misunderstandings or misinterpretations on the therapist's part. Some cognitive therapists provide their patients with written forms to fill out in the waiting room after the session.

Number and spacing of treatment sessions   A typical course of cognitive therapy ranges between six weeks and four months in length, although patients with personality disorders or other severe psychological problems may remain in treatment for a year or longer. With the exception of severely depressed or suicidal individuals who need more frequent support, patient and therapist meet on a weekly basis until the patient begins to feel measurably better. At that point, the sessions are spaced further apart, once every two weeks

and then once every three or four weeks toward the end of treatment. Judith Beck gives eight to 14 as an average total number of sessions, although her father's earlier publications mention an average of 20 to 22 sessions. Decisions about the spacing of sessions are made jointly by the therapist and the patient. The rationale behind less frequent sessions is that it provides the patient with more opportunities to solve problems alone and tests the growing ability to be his or her own therapist. After termination, patients are encouraged to return for "booster" sessions two or three times a year.

Medication   A pamphlet published by the Beck Institute notes that some patients improve more rapidly with combination therapy, and that a consultation with a psychopharmacologist is often advisable to make sure that the patient is taking the right type and dosage of medication.

Training in cognitive therapy

Training in cognitive therapy is available to students in graduate programs in social work, clinical psychology, and psychiatric nursing as well as for medical students and practicing psychiatrists. About 20 of the 197 accredited programs in clinical psychology in the United States offer coursework in cognitive therapy.

The Beck Institute   The Beck Institute, which was founded in 1994 and is presently directed by Judith Beck, offers a range of training programs and workshops for mental health professionals, as well as a speakers' bureau and videoconferences. An extramural distance learning program is available for clinicians working outside North America. Books, audiotapes, and other multimedia presentations on cognitive therapy can also be ordered through the Institute.

Professional organizations   The Academy of Cognitive Therapy (ACT) was established in 1999 after a three-year process of consultation that involved the directors of 36 different training programs in cognitive therapy. The establishment of the academy was considered necessary to maintain a distinctive identity for cognitive therapy and to provide certification for qualified practitioners. The ACT's Web site states that

> There has been confusion in the distinction between psychotherapy which incorporates some cognitive techniques, and cognitive therapy which is based on a cognitive conceptualization. Many therapists identify themselves as cognitive therapists when their practice does not reflect such an orientation. Consumers, agencies, insurance companies, and researchers may be misled by this self-appellation.

Research

Effectiveness of cognitive therapy

Beck's research orientation is reflected in the fact that cognitive therapy is commonly regarded as "the most rigorously studied kind of talk therapy," according to one report. As of late 2002, cognitive therapy had been evaluated in at least 325 clinical trials. The Beck Institute conducts ongoing research projects, its most recent being an examination of the effects of stress reactivity and coping style on depressed patients being treated with cognitive therapy.

Judith Beck and one of her associates at the Beck Institute published a study in 2000 of 14 meta-analyses of the effectiveness of cognitive therapy. Their findings may be briefly summarized as follows:

- Comparison of cognitive therapy with antidepressant medications. Cognitive therapy was found to be somewhat superior to medications in the treatment of unipolar depression in adults. Follow-up studies a year after the end of treatment indicated, however, that only 30% of the patients treated with cognitive therapy had suffered relapses, compared to 60% of the patients who had been given antidepressants.

- Comparison with supportive or nondirective talk therapies. This category included two studies of adolescent depression and two of generalized anxiety disorder (GAD). Cognitive therapy was found to be "moderately superior" to supportive psychotherapies.

- Comparison with behavior therapy. Cognitive therapy was found to be equally effective as behavior therapy in treating adult patients diagnosed with depression or obsessive-compulsive disorder (OCD).

- Other studies. Cognitive therapy was found to be "somewhat superior" to other psychotherapies in treating sexual offenders. It was also found to be effective in treating patients with bulimia nervosa.

Critics of cognitive therapy maintain, however, that much of the research regarding the efficacy of cognitive therapy is not of the highest quality. James C. Coyne, a psychologist at the University of Pennsylvania who specializes in studying anxiety disorders and depression in cancer patients, stated as early as 1989 that ". . . in the large body of research that [cognitive therapy] has generated, the measurements that have been made have typically been crude, confounded, and incapable of supporting precise distinctions between possible cognitive concepts." As was mentioned earlier, the NIMH multi-site study done in the 1980s did not find any significant differences in recovery rates among patients treated with a tricyclic antidepressant (imipramine), a placebo, cognitive therapy, or interpersonal psychotherapy—although the findings were attributed in part to site differences.

In addition, some of Beck's early hypotheses have not been borne out by subsequent research. These include the notion that depressive thinking is per se irrational; that there is such a thing as cognitive vulnerability to depression; and the concept of the cognitive triad. With regard to the cognitive triad, Beck initially proposed that the interlocking schemas incorporating negative beliefs about the self, the world, and one's future are stable traits. Research indicates, however, that these schemas fluctuate with the patient's moods. Moreover, some researchers maintain that the notion of a triad is itself somewhat arbitrary, that Beck's model really has only two components—the self in relation to the patient's personal world, rather than the world in general, and the self in relation to the future.

The STAR*D study

The Sequenced Treatment Alternatives to Relieve Depression study, or STAR*D, is a five-year research study of treatment alternatives for depression funded by the NIMH. STAR*D began in October 1999 and will conclude in September 2004. The study's findings are scheduled for publication in 2006. STAR*D has five major objectives:

- Determine the best next step in treating depressed patients who fail to respond to previous therapies.

- Compare the relative effectiveness and patients' acceptance of different treatments.

- Evaluate the long-term benefits of successful treatments.

- Compare the side effects and economic costs of different treatments.

- Determine the predictors of a given patient's response to specific treatments.

The STAR*D protocol published in 2001 noted that research has not yet established the proper place of psychotherapy in the care of patients diagnosed with major depression. Cognitive therapy, however, is the only form of psychotherapy included in the STAR*D study. It will be evaluated as a Level 2 treatment, either as the patient's sole form of treatment or in combination with citalopram (Celexa), a selective serotonin reuptake inhibitor. (All patients enrolled in STAR*D receive citalopram at Level 1 and are then switched to a different antidepressant medication, cognitive therapy, or citalopram plus one of the other therapies at Level 2.) According to the protocol, the study's selection of cognitive therapy as the sole form of psychotherapy to be compared with pharmacotherapy is its "substantial evidence of efficacy in RCTs [randomized controlled trials] for depression." It should be noted that one of STAR*D's principal investigators, A. John Rush, completed a residency in psychiatry at the University of Pennsylvania under Aaron Beck in 1975, and is listed as one of Beck's coauthors for *Cognitive Therapy of Depression.*

Suicidology One major area of research opened up by Beck's work on depression is suicidology. Beck's work has led to a standardization of the terminology for suicidal behavior, and his scales for the assessment of depression, hopelessness, and the risk of suicide (the Beck Scale for Suicide Ideation, or BSS) are widely used in clinical and research settings. In line with his general continuity hypothesis, Beck regards the risk of suicide as existing along a continuum ranging from occasional fleeting thoughts of "ending it all" to openly self-harmful behavior. Beck helped to establish hopelessness as the most important variable in predicting suicidal behavior; a cutoff score of nine on his Hopelessness Scale is considered predictive of the patient's eventual suicide.

Beck presented findings from 30 years of suicide research at a workshop sponsored by the Institute of Medicine (IOM) in 2001, including data from an ongoing prospective study of suicide prevention at the University of Pennsylvania. One significant finding concerned the fact that suicidal behaviors vary markedly across psychiatric diagnoses, particularly in patients diagnosed with Axis II personality disorders. A study of patients admitted to hospital emergency rooms in Philadelphia following a suicide attempt reported that 8.2% of the patients diagnosed with borderline personality disorder (BPD) committed suicide during a five-year period of follow-up, compared with 4.6% in patients diagnosed with major depression without a personality disorder. In addition to Beck's research group at Penn, a team of researchers at Vanderbilt University reported on the effectiveness of cognitive therapy in reducing the risk of suicide at the annual meeting of the American Psychiatric Association in the summer of 2002.

Case studies

The case studies that follow illustrate both the broad application of the principles underlying cognitive therapy and their accommodation to different *DSM-IV* diagnoses.

Cognitive therapy in treating depression Beck's *Cognitive Therapy of Depression* presents a summary of a typical course of cognitive therapy requiring 22 sessions to treat depression in a 36-year-old homemaker, married for 15 years to a sales manager for an automotive supply company. The couple had three children ranging in age from seven to 14. Two previous courses of therapy (marital therapy and treatment with antidepressants) had been ineffective. The patient's initial score on the BDI was 41. Prior to the first meeting, the therapist mailed the patient a copy of the booklet *Coping with Depression*, and asked her to read it before beginning therapy.

The first session was devoted to a review of the patient's specific symptoms of depression, with a focus on motivational and behavioral problems. The patient had mentioned suicide as a way to "unburden" her family, and had described herself as a "total failure" as a wife and mother. The therapist noted, however, that the patient felt the booklet had given her hope, and judged that she was not at great risk for suicide. The patient's initial homework consisted of filling out a life history questionnaire and keeping a log of her activities at home. This schedule was intended to provide the therapist with a baseline measurement of the patient's activity level as well as to give the patient a sense of mastery and accomplishment.

In sessions two and three, the therapist reviewed the patient's activity log with her, checking for indications of omissions or distortions. Since the patient appeared to keep relatively busy during the day, the therapist changed her homework to recording cognitions in sessions four and five, particularly cognitions associated with unpleasant feelings. Many of the patient's feelings of sadness, anger, or guilt were related to the thought, "I am an incompetent mother." The therapist discussed common themes in the patient's cognitions related to her husband in session five. She was convinced at that point that he would eventually abandon her because of her depression. In sessions six through eight, the therapist worked with the patient to focus her expectations of therapy. She had difficulty defining reasonable goals, speaking in vague generalities about being a "better wife and mother." An interview with the husband during these three sessions indicated that he genuinely cared for his wife, which helped the patient to recognize that she was misinterpreting the real situation. Homework for sessions five through eight consisted of an ongoing record of negative, automatic thoughts.

As the patient's symptoms began to lift, the therapist redirected the focus of the sessions toward recognizing and challenging the contents of and patterns in her cognitions. She began to work on her patterns of self-criticism and the assumptions underlying them. She came to recognize that she tended to think in terms of what she "should" do to please others rather than on

CHRONOLOGY

1921: Aaron Beck born in Providence, Rhode Island.

1938: Graduates from high school and enters Brown University.

1946: Graduates with a medical degree from Yale University.

1951: Korean War breaks out. Beck takes a position at Valley Forge Field Hospital and treats soldiers with post-traumatic stress disorder.

1954: Joins the Department of Psychiatry of the University of Pennsylvania.

1974: Publishes *The Prediction of Suicide.*

1988: Publishes *Love is Never Enough.*

1992: Retires from activing teaching at the University of Pennsylvania.

2004: Publishes *Cognitive Therapy of Personal Disorders,* second edition.

what she "wanted" to do. Homework for these sessions included listing her "wants," particularly future goals. By session 14, her score on the BDI had dropped to 17. She started thinking about returning to work on a part-time basis. During session 16, the therapist detected the possibility that the patient might relapse. Her parents had visited, and she had noticed that her mother was quite critical of her father. The patient clearly regarded herself as being responsible for her father's well-being. She wondered whether she should take a job after all and was returning to her old dysfunctional thought patterns. The therapist made two important interventions at this point. One involved a review of the similarities between the patient's reaction to her parents' visit and her past thought patterns. The patient herself was able to see that she was "following the old pattern." The second intervention was another interview with the husband, who stated that he liked his wife's "new self" much better than the old one. This information strengthened the patient's motivation to continue with her new course of action. Her homework consisted of discussing her goals in greater detail with her husband.

Sessions 20 through 22 consisted of consolidating the gains of the previous sessions. The patient did in fact take a part-time job, and began to enjoy it after she worked through some initial anxiety. Follow-up sessions took place one, two, and six months after the termination of therapy. At the six-month follow-up, the patient's score on the BDI had fallen to 2, and she regarded herself as happier and more confident.

Cognitive therapy in treating wife battering Beck discusses the case of R, whom he describes as "a typical wife batterer," in *Prisoners of Hate.* R was abused by his parents in his childhood and teased by other boys in his peer group. He viewed the world as "filled with antagonistic people lying in wait for an opportunity to pounce on him." Although R had a comfortable relationship with his wife most of the time, any criticism from her or pressure to do chores around the house would activate his dysfunctional beliefs—that mild pressure from her meant total domination, and that criticism meant rejection—and he reacted with violence. Beck describes a typical incident. R's wife asked him to fix a leaky faucet. He replied, "Get off my back!" She then said, "I would if you'd act like the man of the house." R retorted, "I'll show you what a man is," and hit her in the mouth. After an attack of this sort, R was puzzled by and ashamed of its intensity. Therapy consisted of helping R recognize the beliefs that triggered his attacks.

Beck's treatment of R included asking him to look at the meanings he attached to his wife's remarks. The specific techniques included applying rules of evidence to the wife's behavior (was she invariably disrespectful of R?), considering other explanations for her behavior (might she be simply losing patience when he procrastinated?), examining his beliefs about the world, and modifying unrealistic expectations of others. In addition, Beck used guided imagery to lower R's distress level. He asked R to visualize his wife when she criticized him. R reported that he saw himself "shrink in size, with a scared look on his face." He saw his wife, on the other hand, grow taller and larger, and become very menacing. Beck then asked R to replace this intimidating image of his wife with a less threatening picture of her. R was then able to "reflect that she was not his enemy but was simply upset by his procrastination."

A third technique that Beck used during R's treatment was to substitute more adaptive beliefs in place of the old dysfunctional thoughts. R had already recognized that hitting his wife was not only a way to punish her, but also improved his mood temporarily by

BIOGRAPHY:

David H. Barlow

As of 2004, David H. Barlow was Professor of Psychology and Research Professor of Psychiatry at Boston University as well as director of the university's Center for Anxiety and Related Disorders. Barlow is best known for his work in applying cognitive behavior therapy to anxiety disorders and sexual dysfunction. He has also published in the field of clinical research methodology. He is presently the editor of the journal *Clinical Psychology: Science and Practice*. Barlow's work in the treatment of anxiety disorders led to his selection as a member of the *DSM-IV* Task Force and co-chair of the working group for revising the anxiety disorders categories.

Barlow describes anxiety as "a unique, coherent cognitive-affective construct within a defensive motivational system." At the core of the cognitive construct is "a sense of uncontrollability focused largely on possible future threat." Barlow bases his definition of anxiety as "loss of control over potentially challenging or threatening events" on his findings from research into sexual dysfunction over the past two decades. Once a person has become anxious, Barlow holds, his or her cognitions change, moving rapidly from appraisal of the threatening situation to assessments of one's ability to deal with the threat. As the anxiety level rises, further changes in the person's cognition become apparent, ranging from a narrowed focus of attention to interpretative bias in evaluating incoming information.

Since 1988, Barlow has worked out a "triple vulnerabilities" model to explain the development of anxiety disorders. The first area of vulnerability is a generalized biological vulnerability. The second is generalized psychological vulnerability related to early learning experiences of uncontrollability and unpredictability. These experiences help to form a cognitive "template" that increases the impact of later stressful events in the person's life. The third factor is a specific psychological vulnerability that focuses the person's anxiety on a specific object or event.

The most controversial part of Barlow's work, however, is not a theoretical but a clinical claim—that he can cure people suffering from anxiety disorders by forcing them to confront their terrors over a 10- to 12-week period. At the Center for Anxiety and Related Disorders, Barlow typically treats patients by not only exposing them to the stimulus that makes them anxious, but increasing the anxiety level until they have proved to themselves that they can survive the emotional experience of terror. His basic hypothesis is that the patient's problem is not the pain itself but his or her relationship to the pain. By accepting and even seeking out anxiety or depression, Barlow holds, the patient disarms his or her problem. One of Barlow's patients was a claustrophobic businessman who was assigned "homework" that involved shutting himself in a small space for as long as he could tolerate the anxiety. The man decided

David Barlow. (AP/Wide World Photos. Reproduced by permission.)

to lock himself in the trunk of his car. The first time, he had to leave after three minutes, but eventually worked up to spending half an hour in the trunk. At that point, he reported that he felt "bored." Although Barlow maintains that 85% of his patients are cured of their anxiety, some critics argue that his treatment is superficial and worse yet, it amounts to emotional torture.

---

bolstering his shaky self-esteem. Beck then discussed "the value of violence as a mood-normalizer" with R. He asked the patient whether he was more of a man by hitting a smaller person, or "by being cool, taking insults without flinching and maintaining control of himself and the problematic situation." The patient was intrigued by this interpretation; he worked at changing his underlying belief from "A man doesn't take any crap from his wife" to "A man can take the crap without allowing it to get to him."

By the time R left therapy, Beck had given him three specific methods he could use to control his violent impulses: the first was to leave the room for a "time out"; the second was to visualize his wife as vulnerable and upset rather than hostile and threatening; and the third was to remind himself that the way to "feel like a man" is to be calm and masterful when provoked.

Relevance to modern readers   People diagnosed with a mental disorder are increasingly likely to be treated with some form of cognitive therapy—whether their specific problem is an eating disorder, substance abuse, an anxiety disorder, or a personality disorder. This likelihood is particularly high if they are diagnosed with depression; as we have seen, cognitive therapy is the only form of nonpharmacological treatment used in the ongoing NIMH STAR*D study of depression. The popular appeal and widespread use of cognitive therapy, however, are due only in part to economic and public policy considerations.

In addition, cognitive therapy has become a part of the intellectual backdrop of popular culture in the early twenty-first century. It is noteworthy that many current talk-show therapists and writers of self-help books put cognitive issues at the center of their work, even though they may differ from one another in other ways. For example, Nathaniel Branden's books on self-esteem all make the basic point that greater self-awareness—what Beck would call uncovering automatic thoughts—is a necessary step in building self-esteem. Phil McGraw's best-sellers are based on the notion that distorted perceptions and internal "filters" of experience require correction if people are to improve their "self-concepts." Much of what McGraw calls "labels" and "tapes" would be called automatic thoughts in Beck's terminology. Lastly, the emergence of philosophical counseling, which is a controversial descendant of Beck and Ellis's work, is associated with the notion that clearer thinking by itself can help people to turn their lives around.

BIBLIOGRAPHY

Sources

American Psychiatric Association. *Diagnostic and Statistical Manual of Mental Disorders,* 4th ed. Washington, DC: American Psychiatric Association, 2000.

Baumeister, Roy F. *Evil: Inside Human Violence and Cruelty.* 2nd ed. Foreword by Aaron T. Beck. New York: W. H. Freeman and Company, 1999.

Beck, Aaron T. *Depression: Causes and Treatment.* Philadelphia: University of Pennsylvania Press, 1967.

Beck, Aaron T. *Prisoners of Hate: The Cognitive Basis of Anger, Hostility, and Violence.* New York: HarperCollins Publishers, 1999.

Beck, Aaron T., Arthur Freeman, Denise D. Davis, et al. *Cognitive Therapy of Personality Disorders,* 2nd ed. New York: The Guilford Press, 2004.

Beck, Aaron T., M. Kovacs, and A. Weissman. "Hopelessness and Suicidal Behavior: An Overview." *Journal of the American Medical Association* 234 (December 1975): 1146–149.

Beck, Aaron T., A. John Rush, Brian F. Shaw, and Gary Emery. *Cognitive Therapy of Depression.* New York: The Guilford Press, 1979.

Beck, Aaron T., and Marjorie E. Weishaar. "Suicide Risk Assessment and Prediction." *Crisis* 11 (November 1990): 22–30.

Beck, Judith S., Ph D *Cognitive Therapy: Basics and Beyond.* New York: Guilford Press, 1995.

Beck, Judith S., and Andrew C. Butler. "Cognitive Therapy Outcomes: A Review of Meta-Analyses." *Journal of the Norwegian Psychological Association* 37 (2000): 1–9.

Bienefeld, David, MD. "Personality Disorders." *eMedicine*, 30 December 2003. <http://www.emedicine.com/med/topic3472.htm>.

Branden, Nathaniel. *How to Raise Your Self-Esteem.* New York: Bantam Books, 1988.

Coyne, James C. "Thinking Postcognitively About Depression." In Arthur Freeman, et al., eds., *Comprehensive Handbook of Cognitive Therapy.* Cambridge, MA: Perseus Publishing, 1989.

Fancher, Robert T. *Cultures of Healing: Correcting the Image of American Mental Health Care.* New York: W. H. Freeman and Company, 1997.

Goldsmith, Sara K. *Suicide Prevention and Intervention: Summary of a Workshop.* Washington, DC: Institute of Medicine and the National Academy Press, 2001.

Hazleton, Lesley. *The Right to Feel Bad: Coming to Terms with Normal Depression.* New York: Ballantine Books, 1984.

Holmes, Jeremy. "All You Need Is Cognitive Behaviour Therapy?" *British Medical Journal* 324 (2 February 2002): 288–94.

Leahy, Robert L., ed. *Practicing Cognitive Therapy: A Guide to Interventions,* 2nd ed. Northvale, NJ: Jason Aronson, 2001.

Mahoney, Michael J. *Constructive Psychotherapy: A Practical Guide.* New York: Guilford Press, 2003.

McGraw, Phillip C. *Self Matters.* New York: Simon & Schuster, Inc., 2001.

National Institute of Mental Health (NIMH). *Challenges in Preventing Relapse in Major Depression.* Bethesda, MD: NIMH, 2001.

National Institute of Mental Health (NIMH). *Sequenced Treatment Alternatives to Relieve Depression (STAR*D) Study Protocol.* Bethesda, MD: NIMH, 2001.

Needleman, Lawrence D. *Cognitive Case Conceptualization: A Guidebook for Practitioners.* New York: Lawrence Erlbaum Associates, 1999.

Plakun, Eric M. "Treatment of Personality Disorders in an Era of Limited Resources." *Psychiatric Services* 47 (February 1996): 128–30.

Rush, John A., Madhukar Trivedi, and Maurizio Fava. "STAR*D Treatment Trial for Depression." *American Journal of Psychiatry* 160 (February 2003): 237.

Scott, Jan, and Edward Watkins. "Brief Psychotherapies for Depression: Current Status." *Current Opinion in Psychiatry* 17 (2004): 3–7.

Seligman, Martin E. P. *Learned Optimism.* New York: Simon & Schuster, Inc., 1990.

Steigerwald, F., and D. Stone. "Cognitive Restructuring and the 12-Step Program of Alcoholics Anonymous." *Journal of Substance Abuse Treatment* 16 (June 1999): 321–27.

Sudak, D. M., J. S. Beck, and J. Wright. "Cognitive Behavioral Therapy: A Blueprint for Attaining and Assessing Psychiatry Resident Competency." *Academic Psychiatry* 27 (Fall 2003): 154–59.

Wahl, Otto F. *Telling Is Risky Business: Mental Health Consumers Confront Stigma.* New Brunswick, NJ: Rutgers University Press, 1999.

Weishaar, Marjorie. *Aaron T. Beck.* Thousand Oaks, CA: Sage Publications, 1993.

White, C. A. "Cognitive Behavior Treatment of Chronic Disease." *Western Journal of Medicine* 175 (November 2001): 338–42.

Further readings

Barlow, David H. "The Nature and Development of Anxiety and Its Disorders: Triple Vulnerability Theory." *Eye on Psi Chi* 7 (Winter 2003): 14–20.

Beck, Aaron T. *Prisoners of Hate: The Cognitive Basis of Anger, Hostility, and Violence.* New York: HarperCollins Publishers, 1999.

Beck, Aaron T. *Love Is Never Enough.* New York: Harper & Row, 1988.

Burns, David D., MD. *Feeling Good: The New Mood Therapy.* Preface by Aaron T. Beck. New York: Signet Books, 1980.

Burns, David D., MD. *The Feeling Good Handbook.* New York: Plume/Penguin Books, 1990.

Duane, Daniel. "The Socratic Shrink." *New York Times Magazine* (21 March 2004): 36–40.

Ellis, Albert. *Reason and Emotion in Psychotherapy.* Secaucus, NJ: Lyle Stuart, 1962.

Simon, Cecilia Capuzzi. "A Change of Mind." *Washington Post* (3 September 2002): HE01.

Slater, Lauren. "The Cruelest Cure." *New York Times Magazine* (2 November 2003): 34–40.

Alfred Binet

1857–1911

FRENCH PSYCHOLOGIST, INTELLIGENCE
RESEARCHER

SORBONNE, DOCTORATE IN NATURAL SCIENCE,
1894

BRIEF OVERVIEW

Alfred Binet is best remembered as the developer of the first useful test for measuring intelligence. Along with Théodore Simon, Binet developed the Binet-Simon Scale, the forerunner of modern IQ tests. Binet's original goal for the scale was relatively modest and very practical. In the early years of the 1900s, the French government had just enacted laws requiring that all children be given a public education. For the first time, mentally "subnormal" children—those who today might be called mentally retarded or developmentally disabled—were to be provided with special classes, rather than simply ignored by the schools. However, this raised the issue of how to identify which children would benefit from special programs. Binet and Simon set out to solve this problem. In the process, they developed a revolutionary approach to testing mental abilities.

Yet intelligence testing was only one small part of Binet's highly productive career. Although his work was cut short when he died at age 54, he still managed to author almost 300 published books, articles, and reviews. His wide-ranging interests included sensitivity to touch, mental associations, hypnosis, child development, personality, memory, eyewitness testimony, and creativity, to name just a few. The breadth of his interests led him to study a wide spectrum of the population, including schoolchildren, experts at chess and mental arithmetic, authors, mentally retarded individuals, and his own two daughters.

Alfred Binet. (Psychology Archives—The University of Akron. Reproduced by permission.)

Nevertheless, Binet is mainly remembered for his groundbreaking intelligence test. It was so useful for predicting school performance that a variation, the Stanford-Binet Intelligence Scales, is still in use today. In a 1930 essay, Lewis Terman, the American psychologist who developed the Stanford-Binet, described his great predecessor this way: "My favorite of all psychologists is Binet; not because of his intelligence test, which was only a by-product of his life work, but because of his originality, insight, and open-mindedness, and because of the rare charm of personality that shines through all his writings."

BIOGRAPHY

Binet's life is notable for both its successes and its failures. On one hand, Binet's intelligence test became one of the most influential tests in the history of psychology. On the other hand, his innovative ideas about child development and memory had a much more limited impact. Both of these results can be traced, at least in part, to the independence that marked Binet's career. Self-taught in psychology, he never held a position as a university professor. This kept him from building alliances with other professors and from training many students to follow in his footsteps. Yet it also gave him free rein to nurture his own tremendous curiosity and creativity.

The early years

Binet was born on July 8, 1857, in Nice, France. He was the only child of a father who was a physician and a mother who dabbled in art. His wealthy parents separated when he was young, leaving his mother, Moïna Binet, with most of the responsibility for raising him. Until age 15, Binet attended school in Nice. He also spent some summers at a boardinghouse in England, where he undoubtedly improved his fluency in English. This paid off later, when he was able to read the English and American psychological literature.

Once Binet turned 15, his mother took him to Paris so that he could attend a renowned school, the Lycée Louis-le-Grand. Binet studied there for three years. Upon graduating, he had trouble deciding what career path he wanted to pursue. He first earned a law license in 1878; however, he seems to have almost immediately concluded that practicing law was not for him. Next came a brief stint studying medicine. There was a strong medical tradition in his family; his father and both of his grandfathers had been physicians. This choice, too, proved short-lived. Binet suffered an emotional breakdown and dropped out of medical school.

False starts and lessons learned

Discouraged and directionless, Binet began spending time in the Bibliothèque Nationale, a great library in Paris. There, he started browsing through books on psychology. He was fascinated by what he found. In particular, his interest was drawn to experiments on the two-point threshold, the smallest distance at which touching the skin at two different points at once is felt as two sensations rather than just one. Previous research had shown that this distance varied from one part of the body to another. For example, the distance was about 30 times greater on the small of the back than on the tip of the index finger. Several theories had been proposed explaining the differences. After trying a few simple experiments on himself and his friends, Binet concluded that these theories contained some errors. In 1880, he published his ideas in a paper titled "On the Fusion of Similar Sensations." He soon learned a lesson about the hazards of rushing into print. Joseph Delboeuf, a Belgian physiologist who had already done much more complex research on the subject, published an article outlining the flaws in Binet's work. Fortunately, Binet's interest in psychology was strong enough to withstand the blow.

Early on, Binet became an avid reader of British philosopher John Stuart Mill. In his theory of associationism, Mill had proposed that the flow of thoughts and ideas through a person's consciousness was controlled by the associations among these ideas. Mill had also outlined the basic laws that he believed determined which ideas would arise from a particular thought. In 1886, Binet published his first book, a fervent defense of associationism. In the book, titled *The Psychology of Reasoning,* Binet argued that the laws of associationism could explain everything that happened in the mind. Yet cracks in this theory had already become apparent. For example, associationism was unable to explain how one starting idea might lead to totally different trains of thought under different circumstances. Binet realized that he was on shaky ground once again. He soon gave up the position that associationism alone could explain all mental phenomena. However, he never stopped believing in the great, although incomplete, power of mental associations. Years later, he would argue that intelligence could not be studied without considering an individual's personal associations, circumstances, and experiences.

Not all of Binet's early ideas about psychology came from books. In 1883, Binet began working as an unpaid researcher for Jean Martin Charcot, director of the Salpêtrière, a famous hospital in Paris. Charcot was one of the most esteemed neurologists in the world. At the time, he was studying hypnosis, a temporary state of altered attention. Charcot noted that, under hypnosis, good subjects often became unable to move, insensitive to pain, or unable to remember what had happened. These were very much like the symptoms seen in patients with hysteria, a mental disorder in which people had physical ailments when no physical cause could be found. In fact, the similarities were so striking that Charcot jumped to some wrong conclusions. He believed that the ability to be hypnotized was actually a sign of hysteria. He also believed that the unusual behavior seen under hypnosis was caused by some underlying feature of the nervous system. In fact, it turned out to be caused by nothing more than the subject's response to suggestions given by the hypnotist.

When Binet first arrived at the Salpêtrière, however, he accepted the older man's theories without question. Binet and a young doctor named Charles Féré spent the next seven years doing research under Charcot's guidance. The two researchers were assigned to study a woman named Blanche Wittmann, called Wit in their writings. Recalling the days when hypnotism was known as "animal magnetism," Binet and Féré found that they could reverse Wit's physical symptoms or emotional state under hypnosis simply by reversing a magnet. One minute, Wit would be laughing. The next minute, with a turn of the magnet, she was sobbing. Not surprisingly,

PRINCIPAL PUBLICATIONS

- *The Psychology of Reasoning.* Paris: Alcan, 1886. Translated by A. G. Whyte. Chicago: Open Court, 1886.
- With Charles Féré. *Animal Magnetism.* Paris: Alcan, 1887. New York: Appleton, 1892.
- *The Experimental Study of Intelligence.* Paris: Schleicher Frères, 1903.
- With Théodore Simon. "New Methods for the Diagnosis of the Intellectual Level of Subnormals." *L'Année psychologique* 12 (1905): 191–244.
- With Théodore Simon. "A method of measuring the development of the intelligence of young children." *Bulletin de la Société Libre pour l'Etude l'sychologique de l'Enfant* 70–1 (1911): 187–248. Translated by C. H. Town. Chicago: Medical Book Co., 1913.
- Translated by E. S. Kite. *The Development of Intelligence in Children.* Vineland, NJ: Publications of the Training School at Vineland, 1916.
- With Théodore Simon. "The Development of Intelligence in Children." *L'Année psychologique* 14 (1908): 1–94. Translated by E. S. Kite. Baltimore: Williams & Wilkins, 1916.
- *Modern Ideas About Children.* Paris: Flammarion, 1909. Translated by Suzanne Heisler. Menlo Park, CA: 1984.

when Binet and Féré published their findings, other scientists reacted with skepticism. One skeptic was Delboeuf, the same physiologist who had debunked Binet's earlier work on the two-point threshold. Delboeuf finally traveled to Paris to observe Wit in person. He immediately saw the obvious: The hypnotist was reversing the large magnet right in front of Wit. It seemed clear that Wit was responding to the hypnotist, rather than the magnet. At first, Binet defended his findings. Slowly, however, the truth dawned. He was forced to admit that he had been blinded by Charcot's reputation.

Binet's career was off to a rocky start. After public missteps in work on the two-point threshold, associationism, and hypnosis, Binet appeared destined for anything but greatness. Yet these setbacks just seemed to strengthen his resolve to move ahead and make his mark on psychology.

The psychologist at home

The years at the Salpêtrière were a time of growth and change in Binet's home life as well. In 1884, Binet married Laure Balbiani, daughter of biologist E. G. Balbiani. Two daughters soon followed: Madeleine, born in 1885, and Alice, born in 1887. Ever the scientist, Binet began coming up with tests and puzzles for his young daughters to solve. He proved to be a keen observer of their developing minds and personalities. In papers about his observations, Binet called the girls Marguerite and Armande.

Many of the first tests Binet tried were based on the ones used by two earlier pioneers in intelligence research, Francis Galton and James McKeen Cattell. Both men had tried to measure mental ability using physiological tests. For example, some tests measured reaction time, the split-second needed for mental processing between the time when an event occurs and the time when the muscles start responding to it. Such tests were thought to measure how efficiently the nervous system worked. Other tests, such as the two-point threshold, measured the sharpness of the senses. The idea was that intelligence requires information, and this information comes from sensations.

When Binet tried reaction-time tests with his daughters and their young friends, he found that their average reaction times were indeed longer than those of adults. However, the children's individual reaction times varied widely. Sometimes, the children reacted just as quickly as adults, but other times, they were much slower. Binet concluded that the real difference between children and adults was not in the speed with which they could react, but in their ability to pay attention to the task. When the children's attention wandered, as it often did, their reaction times suffered. These observations led Binet to doubt that simple physiological tests could ever be useful for sorting out the differences between immature and mature minds. Instead, it seemed that more complex tests, such as those requiring sustained attention, would be needed. This realization probably played a role in shaping the kinds of tasks Binet chose for his intelligence test years later.

In hindsight, many of the ideas that Binet formed about child development seem ahead of their time. Several of them appear to foreshadow the later work of Jean Piaget, the famous Swiss psychologist who described four stages in children's mental development. Like Piaget, Binet believed that the purpose of mental development was to adapt effectively to the demands of the outside world. He also thought that new information was incorporated into existing ways of thinking. In addition, he believed that intelligence played a role in all human activities, from the simple to the complex.

Binet did not believe in distinct stages of development. Yet some of his descriptions of mental differences between children and adults come close to Piaget's descriptions of various stages. For example, Binet noted that a young child might be struck by a detail on an object that an adult would overlook. Yet that same child might be unable to see the object as a whole the way an adult could.

Might the similarities between the ideas of Binet and those of Piaget be more than just coincidence? This question is still unclear. Piaget never acknowledged any such influence. After Binet's death, however, Piaget spent time working in Paris with Simon, coauthor of the Binet-Simon Scale. In this setting, it seems likely that some of Binet's ideas might have rubbed off on Piaget.

Along with watching his daughters' developing mental abilities, Binet also observed their personality differences. Madeleine tended to be thoughtful and cautious in her actions, while Alice tended to be impulsive and easily distracted. This observation convinced Binet that problem-solving was a matter not only of ability level, but also of personal style. It was another theme that would reappear in his later work on intelligence.

A second chance at success

After the split from Charcot, Binet found himself at loose ends. Although his family wealth meant he did not need to work for money, he was still eager to get on with his research. In 1891, Binet happened to meet Henri Beaunis in a railway station at Rouen, France. Beaunis, a physiologist, was director of the new Laboratory of Physiological Psychology at the Sorbonne, a world-famous college in Paris. During the hypnosis controversy, Beaunis had publicly criticized Binet. It must have taken courage and perhaps desperation on Binet's part to ask Beaunis for a job in his lab. Yet that is exactly what Binet did, offering to work without pay. Beaunis, for his part, was struggling to staff the lab with limited funds. He agreed to give Binet a position. It turned out to be an excellent bargain. In 1895, when Beaunis retired, Binet took over as director. This job, which Binet held until his death, lent him legitimacy and gave him freedom to pursue his own research ideas.

Binet flourished at the Sorbonne laboratory. The events during just two years, 1894–95, show how amazingly productive he could be, given the right environment. During this period, Binet published two books. One was an introduction to experimental psychology, and the other described his research on experts at chess and mental calculations. He and Beaunis also founded and edited the first French psychological journal, *L'Année psychologique,* for which Binet himself wrote 85 reviews and four original articles. In addition, Binet was appointed to the board of a new American journal, *Psychological Review.* At the same time, he studied optical illusions and developed a method for making a graphic record of piano playing. With Jacques Passy, he studied dramatic authors. With Victor Henri, he studied memory in schoolchildren.

Somehow, Binet also found time to finish his doctoral degree in 1894. Six years earlier, he had begun studying biology in his father-in-law's laboratory. Over time, he grew fascinated by the behavior, anatomy, and physiology of insects. His thesis, titled "A Contribution to the Study of the Subintestinal Nervous System of Insects," was filled with detailed drawings, most of which he made himself. This detour into natural science just added to Binet's credentials as a well-rounded scientist and skilled observer.

Binet continued to be very interested in child development as well. With the authority of his new job behind him, he was no longer limited to just studying his own daughters. Now, he could gain access to the schools to observe subjects of all ages. During this period, Binet and Henri conducted studies of children's memory that are still surprisingly up-to-date. In experiments on prose memory, the researchers presented schoolchildren with paragraphs, and then asked the children to write down what they remembered. The researchers found that the children tended to remember general ideas better than specific words. The longer the delay between testing and recall, the more pronounced this difference became. Also, the more important an idea was within the overall paragraph, the more likely it was to be recalled. Binet and Henri concluded that memory processes for connected ideas and memory processes for isolated words were totally different. Once again, Binet was ahead of the curve. These findings were eventually borne out by studies on prose memory in the 1970s.

Binet's research also foretold later findings on eyewitness testimony. In one study, Binet presented schoolchildren with a poster depicting several objects and a scene. The children were allowed to look at the poster for just a matter of seconds. Afterward, they were asked about what they remembered. The answers tended to vary depending on how the questions were worded, a result that has been confirmed many times in recent years.

Although Binet had clearly learned the value of testing his ideas in larger groups of subjects, he also continued to conduct in-depth case studies of individuals. By studying a handful of individuals with extraordinary skill at playing chess or doing mental arithmetic, he explored the nature and limits of these mental abilities. By studying the working habits of leading French authors, he explored creativity. Of course, Binet's longest-running case studies were of his own daughters. As they grew older, he continued to test them on everything from number judgment and memory to inkblot interpretation and storytelling. He described the results from 20 of these tests in a 1903 book called *The Experimental Study of Intelligence.* Despite its title, however, the book was less about intelligence than about general mental development and personality.

The stage is set for greatness

In 1896, Binet and his assistant, Henri, published a paper describing what they called "individual psychology." As they explained it, general psychology dealt with broad psychological properties that are common to everyone. Individual psychology, in contrast, dealt with properties that vary from one person to another. Their aim was to study this variation both within and across individuals. In order to do that, however, Binet soon realized that he needed practical tests of psychological functioning. He set an ambitious goal for himself: to devise a series of such tests that could be given in less than two hours and would assess 10 major psychological processes. The processes were memory, imagery, imagination, attention, comprehension, suggestibility, aesthetic sentiment, moral sentiment, muscular strength and willpower, and motor ability and eye-hand coordination.

Unfortunately, the tests Binet and Henri devised were a flop. In one influential study, Stella Sharp, a graduate student at Cornell University, gave the tests to seven of her fellow psychology students. She found little evidence of a meaningful pattern in the scores. There was also a troubling lack of relationship among the scores for subtests that were supposed to measure the same ability. Binet himself found similarly disappointing results. In 1904, after eight years of effort, Binet admitted defeat. Today, the goal of developing a quick yet complete test of psychological functioning remains elusive. Yet Binet's time had not been wasted. It had prepared him well for his next challenge: devising an intelligence test.

Several other events also helped to set the stage for Binet's achievement. In 1899, Simon began to perform doctoral research under Binet's supervision. At the time, Simon was a young doctor working at a large institution for the mentally retarded, and Binet was eager to try out his tests on this new group of subjects. Their collaboration was the most fruitful of Binet's career, and the two researchers became close friends.

The next year, Binet played a key role in organizing the new Free Society for the Psychological Study of the Child. This was a group of psychologists and educators who banded together to seek solutions to problems facing the schools. Binet became a leader of the group and founded its *Bulletin* for publishing members' research. One of the most pressing problems was how to carry out new laws requiring that all French children be provided a public education. This included mentally retarded children, who in earlier years would never have gone to school or would have dropped out early. In 1904, the French government appointed Binet to a commission that was charged with improving the education of this previously overlooked group of children.

Binet soon zeroed in on a critical problem: identifying which children should be considered mentally retarded and placed in special educational programs. Binet and Simon set out to solve this problem by developing a test. Traditionally, mentally retarded individuals had been divided into three categories: profoundly retarded (called *idiots*), moderately retarded (called *imbeciles*), and mildly retarded. Binet called the mildly retarded group *débiles*, or "weak ones." His English translators later substituted the term *moron*, from a Greek word meaning "dull." The test was intended to sort out children who belonged in one of these categories from the children whose intelligence could be considered normal. The first Binet-Simon Scale was introduced in 1905. That same year, Binet opened a research center in the school at Belleville, a working-class neighborhood of Paris. The next several years were spent improving his test. Revisions followed in 1908 and 1911.

Triumphs and disappointments

Binet was busy revising the scale when he died in Paris on October 18, 1911. He was at the height of a remarkable career. Binet's final years, however, were marked by disappointments as well as triumphs. Perhaps the greatest disappointment was his failure to secure a position as a university professor. In 1895, Binet visited the University of Bucharest in Romania as a guest lecturer. His lectures were a hit with the

students, and he was invited to stay on as a professor. He turned down the offer, partly because he hoped to get a similar post in France. As was the custom of the time, he proposed himself for two such positions: one at the College of France, and one at the Sorbonne. He was not chosen for either post, however.

Binet's family life had once been a source of comfort. He and his wife lived in Paris when they were first married, but they later moved to a suburb called Meudon. The Binets stayed there until 1908, when they returned to Paris. Life in Meudon seems to have been quite pleasant for several years. The family shared interests in art and drama. They also enjoyed a lovely home and garden, pets, bicycling, long walks, and summer vacations.

After about 1900, however, Binet's family life took a turn for the worse. His wife became depressed and ill, and the couple rarely went out socially. His daughters had been isolated, too, since they were schooled at home. As the girls grew into young women, Binet worried about their ability to form healthy friendships. He also fretted about Alice's health and Madeleine's marriage, of which he did not approve. The gloomy atmosphere at home may have been reflected in Binet's hobby. In the last years of his life, he wrote plays with dramatist André de Lorde, nicknamed "The Prince of Terror." The plays all dealt with ghoulish themes, such as a released mental patient who committed murder and a scientist who tried to bring his dead daughter back to life.

In the ultimate irony, even Binet's intelligence test was largely ignored and even ridiculed in France during his lifetime. It was already being hailed abroad, however. After Binet's death, his test and those that followed had a profound impact on psychology, education, and society at large. Binet's name became forever linked with intelligence tests.

THEORIES

Although Binet intended his intelligence test to be a practical tool, it became impossible to separate this tool from the theoretical questions it raised: What was intelligence? How can it be tested? And how should researchers use the test results? These questions remain at the heart of a lively debate over intelligence testing.

Main points

Binet's ideas about intelligence were rooted in his earlier theory of individual psychology. He continued to stress variation, both within and across individuals. Based on his previous work, Binet was also convinced that such individual differences could best be detected by studying complex mental processes, such as memory, attention, imagination, and comprehension.

What is intelligence? Binet was always more concerned with measuring intelligence than with defining it. Nevertheless, the test he developed embodied his ideas about the nature of intelligence. Binet believed that intelligence was not a single entity. Instead, he viewed it as a collection of specific processes. Therefore, any general test of intelligence needed to sample the whole range of mental processes, rather than just one or two isolated abilities.

Binet also believed that people's mental abilities differed in quality as well as quantity. His observations of his daughters apparently convinced him of this point. From a very young age, Madeleine seemed to think things through more carefully, while Alice seemed to act more impulsively. When the girls were learning to walk, for example, Binet noticed that Madeleine would go only to objects a short distance away. Alice, on the other hand, would head straight for an empty part of the room, apparently unconcerned about whether or not it contained an object she could grab for support.

Based on such observations, Binet was well aware that two children might arrive at the same overall result on his test by two very different paths. He wrote about the importance of noting the specific errors made by a child on the test, in order to get a more complete picture of how that child's mind worked. Unlike many psychologists who followed, Binet was unwilling to reduce a person's whole intelligence to a single number. In fact, the concept of an IQ score was not introduced until after Binet's death.

Binet also believed that intelligence was changeable within limits, rather than fixed; consequently, an individual's intelligence level could be raised through proper education. Binet acknowledged, however, that each person probably had an upper limit, but he thought that very few people came close to reaching it. Therefore, there was usually room for improvement. This was especially true of the mentally retarded children that Binet's test was designed to identify. In a 1909 book, titled *Modern Ideas About Children,* Binet decried the "brutal pessimism" of psychologists and educators who believed intelligence to be fixed at a set level.

Binet never set forth a rigorous definition of intelligence. In a 1905 paper, however, he and Simon argued that judgment played a central role:

> It seems to us that in intelligence there is a fundamental faculty, the alteration or lack of which, is of the utmost importance for practical life. This faculty is judgment, otherwise called good sense, practical sense, initiative, the faculty of adapting one's self to circumstances. To judge well, to comprehend well, to reason well, these are the essential activities of intelligence.

To Binet, the very essence of intelligence was rooted in practical experience.

How can intelligence be tested? To develop his test, Binet started with groups of children who had been identified by teachers or doctors as mentally retarded or of normal intelligence. Binet then had both groups perform a wide variety of tasks. He hoped to find tasks that would clearly differentiate the groups. He quickly ran into a snag, however. It proved nearly impossible to find tasks that were almost always done successfully by the normal intelligence group, but almost never by the retarded group. There was always some overlap in the results.

Then, Binet had one of the most important insights of his career. He realized that age made a critical difference. Both the retarded children and those with normal intelligence might eventually master the same skill. However, the normal intelligence children did so at a younger age. This idea has become so widely accepted that it seems like common sense today. Before Binet, however, other researchers had missed the crucial connection.

With this insight as a starting point, Binet and Simon came up with 30 tasks of gradually increasing difficulty. The simplest tasks were at the very basic level of intelligence seen in normal infants or in the most profoundly retarded children of any age. The hardest tasks could be passed easily by normal 11- or 12-year-olds, but were beyond the grasp of even the oldest and most capable retarded children. These items, and the others in between, made up the first Binet-Simon Scale of 1905.

A child's score on the total scale revealed his mental level. For example, a seven-year-old child who passed all the tasks normally passed by children of his age would have a mental level of seven. However, if that same child could only pass the tasks normally passed by five-year-olds, he would have a mental level of five. Binet noted that it was common for children to have a mental level that lagged behind their chronological age by a year. Most of these children did fine in a regular classroom. If a child's mental level trailed his chronological age by at least two years, however, *and* if the child came from an ordinary French background and was healthy and alert when he took the test, then a diagnosis of mental retardation could be considered.

Binet wanted his test to be psychological rather than educational. Therefore, he avoided tasks that relied heavily on reading, writing, and other school-related skills. Yet he also believed that the test should assess judgment in lifelike situations. Therefore, he included many tasks that required a basic knowledge of French culture and life. Binet knew this meant that his test would only be valid for children who had grown up in the mainstream French culture, but he reasoned that it would be able to accurately assess most of the French schoolchildren for whom the test was designed.

Although the Binet-Simon Scale of 1905 was a groundbreaking achievement, it had some flaws. For one thing, the mental levels were based on research that had studied only 50 normal-intelligence children and 45 mentally retarded children. Therefore, the levels provided only rough guidelines. In addition, more than half of the tasks were geared to very young or severely retarded children. Yet, in real life, most of the tough decisions that needed to be made involved older children around the borderline between mental retardation and normal intelligence. Binet and Simon attempted to correct these flaws in the 1908 and 1911 revisions of the scale.

To do this, the researchers set out to expand and refine the tasks that made up the test. Starting in 1905, they tested numerous tasks in a larger number of children between the ages of three and 13. For a task to be assigned a mental level of seven, for example, it had to be passed by only a few of the six-year-olds, most of the seven-year-olds, and even more of the eight-year-olds with normal intelligence. Of course, not all tasks broke down neatly this way. By 1908, however, Binet and Simon had found 58 tasks that met their criteria. These refined tasks made up the 1908 revision of the Binet-Simon Scale.

That same year, Simon left Paris to become director of a mental hospital in Rouen. He and Binet continued to work together afterward, but not as closely as before. Meanwhile, Binet expanded the intelligence scale up to a mental level of 15. He also adjusted the test so that there were exactly five items for each age level. In an effort to better standardize and quantify the test, Binet came up with a formula. It calculated the mental level of a child by counting one-fifth of a year for each subtest passed. Binet worried that dividing year levels into fifths implied a misleading degree of precision, however. He warned that the fractions "do not merit absolute confidence." Even for the same person, they could vary noticeably from one test-taking to another. The higher age level and the new formula were included in the 1911 revision of the test.

How should intelligence test results be used? For Binet, there were at least two reasons why intelligence test results should not be considered exact measurements of mental ability. One, the test itself was imperfect, containing sources of error and unreliability. Two, he believed intelligence could change over time. The latter view set Binet apart from some of the psychologists who expanded upon his test in the decades after his death. It also led Binet to recommend frequent retesting.

Before the Binet-Simon Scale, children had been placed in special educational programs based on nothing more than subjective opinions. Binet knew that such opinions were often biased. For example, teachers in regular schools might label troublemakers as mentally retarded to get them out of their classes. Conversely, teachers in special schools might exaggerate their students' achievements to makes themselves look good. Likewise, parents might understate their children's mental ability to escape responsibility for them. Or, they might overstate to avoid embarrassment. Even professional evaluators tended to be quite inconsistent. For example, one principal claimed not to have a single mentally retarded child at his school, while another claimed to have 50 of them. Clearly, a more objective means of assessment was needed.

Binet argued that his test should be adopted for two reasons. First, it avoided the bias and inconsistency that occurred when placement decisions were based strictly on subjective opinions. Instead, the test was rooted in objective data. Second, the test tried to assess mental capability rather than school-based learning. Therefore, a child's performance on the test was thought to be relatively independent of his or her past school experiences.

Binet thought his test could identify which children would be able to succeed in regular classrooms and which would need special educational programs. He also believed, however, that the categories of normal and retarded were not carved in stone. Steps could be taken to raise the intelligence of mentally retarded children, at least to a degree. To this end, he helped design a series of exercises called "mental orthopedics." Binet had noted that retarded children, much like young children of normal intelligence, had trouble paying attention to anything for very long. Therefore, many of the exercises were geared to helping children increase their attention span. For example, one exercise was the game Statue. The teacher would give a signal to freeze, and the children would try to hold their position until they were told to relax.

Explanation

Binet had begun his career by studying mental ability using simple physiological measures, such as the two-point threshold and reaction time. Eventually, however, he concluded that measures of complex mental processes—such as memory, attention, imagination, and comprehension—were needed to sort out individual differences in intelligence. Therefore, his intelligence test included tasks that were intended to assess these complex processes.

Binet-Simon Scale of 1905

The first Binet-Simon Scale included 30 items. They are listed below in order from easiest to most difficult.

- *Le regard.* This item tested a child's ability to follow a lighted match with his or her eyes. The goal was to assess a very basic capacity for attention.

- Prehension provoked by a tactile stimulus. This item tested a child's ability to grasp a small object placed in his or her hand, hold it without letting it fall, and carry it to the mouth.

- Prehension provoked by a visual perception. This item was similar to the previous one; however, it tested a child's ability to reach for and grab an object placed within his or her view.

- Recognition of food. In this task, a piece of chocolate was placed next to a little cube of wood. The aim was to see whether the child could tell by sight alone which of the objects was food.

- Quest of food complicated by a slight mechanical difficulty. In this task, a piece of candy was shown to the child and then wrapped in paper. The aim was to see whether the child would unwrap the candy.

- Execution of simple commands and imitation of simple gestures. This item tested whether the child knew how to shake hands with the examiner and comply with simple spoken or gestured commands. The goal was to assess very basic social and language skills. Children with normal intelligence could pass the first six items on the test by age two. Some of the items, however, were too difficult for the most profoundly retarded children. Therefore, profound retardation came to be defined as a mental level no higher than that of a two-year-old with normal intelligence, including the inability to interact socially and use language.

- Verbal knowledge of objects. In this task, the examiner asked the child to point to various parts of the body. The child was then asked to give the examiner various common objects, such as a cup and a key.

- Verbal knowledge of pictures. In this task, the child was asked to point to familiar objects in a picture, such as a window and a broom.

- Naming of designated objects. This item was the opposite of the previous one. Using another picture, the examiner pointed to familiar objects and asked the child to name them.

- Immediate comparison of two lines of unequal lengths. In this task, the child was shown pieces of paper with pairs of lines on them. One line was always 4 cm long; the other, 3 cm. The child was asked to indicate which line was longer.

- Repetition of three figures. This item tested a child's ability to repeat back a string of three numbers.

- Comparison of two weights. In this task, the child was shown two boxes that looked identical, but were of different weights. The child was asked to decide which box was heavier.

- Suggestibility. In some of the previous tasks, the examiner would make false suggestions to see how the child would respond. For example, after asking the child to point to various common objects, the examiner would ask the child about an object that was not there.

- Verbal definition of known objects. This item tested a child's ability to give simple definitions for familiar things, such as a house and a fork.

- Repetition of sentences of 15 words. This item tested a child's ability to repeat back sentences averaging 15 words long. These last nine items on the test could be passed by children with normal intelligence by age five. The items assessed simple vocabulary and language skills as well as basic judgment and memory. This particular item was considered the cut-off point for moderate retardation. That is, moderately retarded children were thought to operate at the level of a two- to five-year-old with normal intelligence.

- Comparison of known objects from memory. In this task, the child was asked to state the differences between pairs of common objects, such as a piece of wood and a piece of glass.

- Exercise of memory on pictures. In this task, the child was shown several pictures of familiar objects for a brief time. The child was then asked to name the objects from memory.

- Drawing a design from memory. In this task, the child was briefly shown two geometric designs, then asked to draw them from memory.

- Immediate repetition of figures. This item was identical to the earlier one in which the examiner asked the child to repeat back a string of three numbers. Now, however, the examiner gave greater weight to the nature of any errors.

- Resemblances of several known objects given from memory. In this task, the child was asked to state the similarities between sets of objects, such as a fly, an ant, a butterfly, and a flea.

- Comparison of lengths. In this task, the child was shown pieces of paper with pairs of lines on them. The child was asked to indicate which line was longer. While this was similar to an earlier task, the differences in line lengths were smaller this time.

- Five weights to be placed in order. This item required the child to arrange five identical-looking boxes in order of heaviness. The boxes varied in weight from 3 grams to 15 grams.

- Gap in weights. After the previous task, one of the middle boxes was removed while the child closed his or her eyes. The child was then asked to figure out which box was missing by hand-weighing.

- Exercise upon rhymes. This item tested the child's ability to name words that rhymed with the French word *obéissance*.

- Verbal gaps to be filled. This item tested the child's ability to fill in the blanks in simple spoken sentences. For example, one sentence was: "The weather is clear, the sky is (blue)."

- Synthesis of three words in one sentence. In this task, the child was given three words: "Paris," "river," and "fortune." The child was then asked to make up a sentences using all the words.

- Reply to an abstract question. This item tested the child's ability to answer 25 questions dealing with practical problem-solving and social judgment. The questions ranged from very easy to fairly difficult. For example, one medium-difficulty question asked: "When anyone has offended you and asks you to excuse him, what ought you to do?"

- Reversal of the hands of a clock. This item tested the child's ability to figure out in his or her head what time it would be if the large and small hands on a clock were reversed for various times.

- Paper cutting. In front of the child, the examiner folded a paper into quarters, and then cut out a triangle at the edge with a single fold. Without actually unfolding the paper, the child was then asked to draw the design he would see if the paper were opened.

- Definitions of abstract terms. In this task, the child was asked to state the differences between two abstract terms, such as weariness and sadness.

These last 15 items on the test contained the boundary line between mild retardation and normal intelligence. In general, these items could be passed by children of normal intelligence between the ages of 5 and 11. However, some of the most difficult tasks near the end were not always passed by even 11-year-olds with normal intelligence.

Binet-Simon Scale of 1911 The final version of the Binet-Simon Scale included similar items. Some examples are given below. The ages refer to the age at which typical children of normal intelligence were able to perform certain tasks.

- Age three: Pointing as told to the eyes, nose, and mouth; naming common objects in a picture; repeating back a string of two numbers; repeating a six-syllable sentence; knowing their last names.

- Age six: Telling the difference between morning and evening; telling an "attractive" face from an "ugly" one in a picture; copying a diamond-shaped design from memory; counting 13 pennies; giving simple definitions for familiar things, such as a fork and a table.

- Age 10: Copying line drawings from memory; composing a sentence with the words "Paris," "fortune," and "river"; placing five identical-looking boxes in order by weight; answering questions involving social judgment; finding and explaining absurdities in statements. Some of the latter statements showed Binet's fascination with ghoulish themes, similar to the subject matter of the plays he was writing at the time. For example, one item asked children to explain what was wrong with this statement: "The body of an unfortunate girl was found, cut into 18 pieces. It is thought that she killed herself."

- Age 15: Repeating back a string of seven numbers; naming three rhymes for the French word *obéissance*; repeating a 26-syllable sentence; giving appropriate explanations for pictured scenes of people; solving problems such as this one: "My neighbor has just been receiving strange visitors. He has received in turn a doctor, a lawyer, and then a priest. What is taking place?"

Test-giving procedures Binet and Simon provided general instructions on how to give their test. Many of these echo the procedures still used in individual testing today. For example, the test was to be given in a quiet room with no distractions. When the child met the examiner for the first time, a familiar person, such as a relative or the school principal, was to be present. The examiner was to greet the child with "friendly familiarity," to help put the child at ease. Binet realized that the child's emotional state and motivation could affect the results, so he stressed that these factors should not be ignored.

Binet had not forgotten his early mistake made when studying hypnosis; specifically, that the subject's behavior had unintentionally been changed by suggestions from the hypnotist. Binet's research on memory in schoolchildren had also underscored the power of suggestion to affect behavior. Therefore, Binet was well aware that unwitting suggestions by an examiner might affect children's performance on the intelligence test. In a 1905 paper, he and Simon warned: "It is a difficult art to be able to encourage a subject, to hold his attention, to make him do his best without giving aid in any form by an unskillful suggestion."

Examples

In his 1909 book, *Modern Ideas About Children,* Binet noted four mental processes that he thought played a key role in intelligence. He also described how these processes might look in young children of normal intelligence. Of course, these descriptions also fit older children and adults with moderate retardation.

- Comprehension. This term referred to the ability to notice and understand things. Binet wrote that young children experienced the world largely through their senses. They also tended to see parts of things rather than the whole, and they had trouble differentiating unimportant details from important ones. When it came to language, the children used few adjectives and conjunctions. They also tended to use concrete words rather than abstract ones. In short, they had "a comprehension that remains always on the surface."

- Inventiveness. This concept referred to the ability to describe and interpret things. Binet wrote that young children still used words in a very limited and rather dull way. When shown a picture, the children described it in vague terms that could describe any number of pictures.

- Direction. This term referred to the ability to pay attention and stay on task. Binet noted that young children frequently forgot what they were doing. They tended to get carried away by fantasy, losing track of their real-world aims. When speaking, the children jumped from subject to subject, based on chance associations rather than logical connections.

- Criticism. This referred to the ability to make critical judgments. Binet noted that this ability, too, was quite limited in young children. The children naively accepted the most absurd explanations. They also told lies because of their weak ability to tell the difference between reality and fantasy. In addition, young children were highly suggestible.

HISTORICAL CONTEXT

Like everyone else, Binet was shaped by the times in which he lived. In part, his intelligence test was a reaction to earlier efforts by two of his colleagues, British Sir Francis Galton and American James McKeen Cattell, who each had tried to assess mental ability with physiological measures.

Galton and hereditary intelligence

The first person to try to develop a scientific intelligence test was Francis Galton. This British scientist, a half-cousin of English naturalist Charles Darwin, was a polymath, a person who is knowledgeable in many scientific areas. His interests included studying weather, fingerprints, and the peoples of Africa. Galton argued that plants and animals varied in systematic ways, and he devised new statistical methods for studying heredity. When it came to people, Galton proposed a controversial idea: the planned selection of superior parents as a means of improving the human race. To this end, he coined the term "eugenics" for the theoretical science of human breeding.

Before a practical program of eugenics could gain wide support, however, Galton had to show that his ideas were sound. Galton had been greatly influenced by his famous half-cousin's theory of evolution. A basic premise of that theory is that the variation among members of any species is inherited. The differences among parents in one generation are passed down to their offspring in the next generation.

In an 1869 book titled *Hereditary Genius,* Galton set out to show that high mental ability was passed down this way. It is likely that Galton's own family tree inspired this line of thinking, since both he and Darwin were grandsons of Erasmus Darwin, a noted physician and naturalist in his own right.

For the book, Galton picked a sample of people who had achieved great enough success in their careers to be listed in biographical reference works. Galton then researched their family backgrounds and found that about 10% had at least one close relative who was successful enough to be listed, too. Although this was a small percentage, it was still a much higher rate than would have been expected based on chance alone. This finding was consistent with Galton's theory of hereditary ability. It did not settle the issue, however, since most individuals in the same family share not only genes, but also similar lifestyles and experiences. Thus began the great nature-nurture debate, which asks: How much of people's intelligence is due to nature (the genes they inherited from their parents), and how much is due to nurture (the way they were raised and the experiences they have had)? This question continues to be hotly debated today.

In 1865, Galton suggested that a test might be devised to measure inherited differences in mental ability. When it came time to actually develop such a test, however, he was stumped. All he had was a vague notion that the inherited differences must arise from measurable differences within the brain and nervous system. Eventually, Galton developed a series of physiological tests for measuring reaction time, the sharpness of the senses, and physical energy. He hoped these tests would show the efficiency of a person's nervous system and, thus, the basis for his or her hereditary intelligence.

In 1884, Galton set up a laboratory at the South Kensington Museum in London to measure individual differences in mental ability. For a small fee, people could be tested there. Today, Galton's choice of tests seems amusingly misguided. For one test, he used a special whistle to measure the highest pitch people could hear. For another, he tested people's sensitivity to the smell of roses. Perhaps it is not surprising, then, that the tests did not work out as well as Galton had hoped. People with sharp senses and fast reaction times did not, as a group, turn out to especially gifted in other areas. Still, about 9,000 people paid for Galton's services, and scientists took note. If nothing else, Galton's laboratory was very successful at introducing the idea of intelligence testing to scientists and to the public.

Cattell and mental tests

James McKeen Cattell, an American psychologist, soon built upon Galton's physiological method of measuring intelligence. In 1890, he published a set of "mental tests," a catchy term he coined. Cattell suggested 10 mental tests for use with the general public.

- Dynamometer pressure. This test measured the strength of a person's hand grip. Cattell explained that he included this test because "it is impossible to separate bodily from mental energy."

- Rate of hand movement. This test measured how quickly a person could move his or her hand across 50 centimeters.

- Two-point threshold. A researcher touched a pair of rubber-tipped compass points to the back of a person's hand. When the tips were very close together, the subject felt them as a single point. The researcher attempted to find the smallest distance at which the tips were felt by the subject as two separate points.

- Pressure-causing pain. An instrument was pressed against a person's forehead with increasing force. The aim was to find the amount of pressure needed to cause signs of pain.

- Weight differentiation. This test required a person to put a set of identical-looking boxes in order by weight. The boxes, which differed in weight by 1 gram, ranged from 100 to 110 grams.

- Reaction time for sound. This test measured the very brief period that elapsed between the time when a sound was made and the time when a person's muscles started reacting to it.

- Time for naming colors. A set of red, yellow, green, and blue patches, arranged in random order, was shown to a person. The aim was to measure how long it took the person to name the colors.

- Bisection of line. A 50-centimeter strip of wood with a sliding line attached was used. The person was asked to place the line as close as possible to the exact middle of the strip.

- Judgment of time. In this test, the examiner first tapped out a 10-second interval. The examiner then tapped on the table and asked the person to signal when another 10 seconds had passed.

- Number of repeated letters. This test measured how well a person could repeat back lists of random consonants.

A flurry of this kind of mental testing followed in the 1890s. When powerful new statistical methods came into use, however, it soon became clear that the tests were sorely lacking. Earlier, Galton had developed the concept of a correlation, the degree and direction of association between two things. Karl Pearson perfected the method of computing a correlation coefficient, an index of the strength of the relationship between two things when certain conditions are met. This statistic became known as the Pearson *r*. Now, researchers had a more sophisticated way to analyze test results.

In 1901, Clark Wissler, one of Cattell's own graduate students, dealt a death blow to this type of mental testing. Using the new statistical methods, he studied the scores of college students who had taken Cattell's tests. Wissler found virtually no correlation among the tests. In other words, a student who did well on one of the tests was not especially likely to do well on any of the other tests. Even worse, scores on the tests also did not correlate with college grades. This meant Cattell's tests and college grades were measuring different things. Since college grades were thought to reflect intelligence, it seemed Cattell's tests must be measuring something else.

Binet compared to Galton and Cattell

The failure of Galton's and Cattell's intelligence tests opened the door for Binet to develop a more practical alternative. He succeeded where they had failed at devising a test that was related to intelligent behavior in real life. Today, most useful intelligence tests for people of all ages are still based on Binet's model. Such tests require people to use several mental abilities to perform a broad range of complex tasks.

One factor that may have helped Binet succeed was his choice of study population. Galton and his followers had been mainly interested in studying intelligence in adults at the high end of the ability range. Binet, in contrast, was interested in testing the intelligence of children at the low end. Because he worked with children, Binet was able to see the way intelligence developed over time. And because he looked at less advanced mental processes, basic patterns may have been easier to notice.

Binet's own studies of very creative adults, such as dramatists, had found that there was great individuality and complexity in higher-order abilities. When the Binet-Simon Scale was introduced, Binet noted that some children had a mental level that was a year or more ahead of their age in years. Were these children destined to grow up into very bright and talented adults? At first, Binet believed that it might be possible to answer that question by extending his scale upward. By 1908, however, he had developed doubts. The mixture of mental abilities measured by his test had only been shown to be something that prevented

people from being retarded. They had not been shown to be the source of high ability, talent, or genius. Therefore, the very nature of the "intelligence" measured by Binet's test seemed to be rather different from the "intelligence" Galton had had in mind.

Another major difference between Binet and Galton was their position on the nature-nurture debate. Galton mainly focused on the nature side of the equation. He viewed the upper limits of a person's ability as fixed by genetics rather than culture. Binet, in contrast, was more interested in the role of nurture. He believed that cultural factors played a large role in shaping an individual's mental abilities. He also stressed that intelligence was changeable within limits through proper education.

Because Binet saw culture and intelligence as closely related, he had no qualms about including culturally based items on his test. Of course, this meant that the test was only valid for people who came from a certain background. Galton's and Cattell's physiological tests, on the other hand, would have been more applicable to people from many different backgrounds—if only they had worked.

By a twist of fate, both Galton and Binet died in 1911. After the two men's deaths, a strange thing occurred: Binet's scale was immediately taken up by scientists whose views and goals were otherwise much closer to Galton's. Clearly, Binet's test survived because it had practical value. The theory behind the test, however, was not as quickly embraced. In part, this may have been because Binet himself was always more interested in measuring intelligence than in explaining it within a theoretical framework.

It may also have been due, in part, however, to the way the two scientists led their lives. At the time of their deaths, Galton was an old man, long past his active research days, while Binet was still in the prime of his career. Yet Galton held greater sway in scientific circles. During the last years of his life, Galton drummed up considerable support for his eugenics program and the hereditary theory of intelligence. Binet, on the other hand, had gained far fewer followers. As a result, the next generation of intelligence testers tended to use Binet's techniques to advance Galton's ideas.

Spearman and general intelligence

Around the same time that Binet introduced his intelligence test, English psychologist Charles Spearman published his own theory of intelligence. It, too, was at odds with Binet's concepts. Yet in later years, Spearman's ideas, like those of Galton and Cattell, were often promoted using Binet's test.

Spearman's early work was actually inspired by Galton and Cattell. In one experiment, he studied two dozen schoolchildren in three ways. First, he had their teacher rank them on "cleverness in school." Second, he had the two oldest children rank their classmates on "sharpness and common sense out of school." Third, Spearman himself ranked the children's performance on tests designed to measure the sharpness of their senses. Then Spearman calculated the correlations among these measures. He found a modest association between the teacher's and classmates' rankings, on one hand, and the sensory rankings, on the other. These findings differed from Clark Wissler's results, who had found no correlation. Spearman explained the difference, however, by pointing out flaws in Wissler's work. In truth, Spearman's own method was far from perfect. Later researchers have tended to confirm Wissler rather than Spearman, finding very little association between sensory abilities and mental abilities.

Nevertheless, Spearman was encouraged. He went on to study the grades that children had earned in various school subjects. He found that children who did well in one subject tended to do well in the others, too. Likewise, children who did poorly tended to do so across the board. Taken together, Spearman's findings seemed to point to a common thread tying together all these measures of mental ability. Spearman referred to this single, broad capability as general intelligence, or *g*. He first published his theory of general intelligence in an influential 1904 paper.

Spearman viewed general intelligence as a single, broad entity. Binet, in contrast, viewed intelligence as a group of mental processes that were arranged in different patterns within different people. Unlike Spearmen, Binet did not focus on finding a unifying factor for these processes.

Although Spearman disagreed with Binet's theory, he was quite impressed by the Binet-Simon Scale. Even Spearman realized that his own method of measuring intelligence with teacher rankings, classmate rankings, and grades was not ideal. For one thing, it was too closely tied to school performance. Binet's test offered a useful alternative that was not as greatly affected by past classroom experiences.

Of course, Spearman saw Binet's test from his own point of view. When Spearman calculated the correlations among individual items on the test, he found a familiar trend: Children who did well on one item tended to also do well on the others. Spearman took this as evidence that the items were actually measuring general intelligence to a large extent. He argued that Binet's test worked precisely because the

overall result provided a useful estimate of a person's level of general intelligence. In addition, he believed that a person's general intelligence level owed more to heredity than to lifestyle and experiences. This became a popular view, even though Binet himself did not share many of Spearman's ideas.

CRITICAL RESPONSE

When Binet died, he considered his test to be a work in progress. He was still constantly striving to improve it. Yet this imperfect test was itself widely adopted, and it became the model for other tests that have had an enormous impact on society. Since Binet's death, the field of intelligence testing has attracted both ardent supporters and vocal critics. Few other areas of psychology have proven to be such lightning rods for controversy.

Stern and the intelligence quotient

Today, the terms "intelligence test" and "IQ test" are often used interchangeably. Therefore, many people assume incorrectly that Binet came up with the idea of an intelligence quotient (IQ), a single number for expressing the overall result on an intelligence test. This distinction actually goes to German psychologist William Stern. In fact, Binet resisted the idea of reducing a person's intelligence to a single number. When Stern introduced the concept of IQ in 1912, Binet was no longer alive to complain. But his coauthor, Simon, later called the IQ concept a betrayal of their original ideas.

Nevertheless, Stern's concept caught on quickly; it involved some seemingly small but critical changes in the way Binet's test results were used. Binet had talked about the mental level of children who took his test. Stern recast this as mental age, which implied a more precise measurement scale. Then, Stern proposed that mental age could be divided by chronological age to yield a handy numerical score. In 1916, the American psychologist Lewis Terman suggested multiplying this score by 100 to get rid of fractions. For example, consider a seven-year-old child with a mental age of six. To calculate this child's IQ, an examiner would divide six by seven, then multiply the answer by 100. The child's IQ would be 86.

Most people would agree that a five-year-old with a mental age of three has a more serious delay than a 15-year-old with a mental age of 13. Using Binet's method, both children would simply be regarded as being two years behind. Using the IQ method, however, the differences in severity would be more obvious. The 15-year-old would have an IQ of 87 (in the normal intelligence range), while the five-year-old would have an IQ of only 60 (in the mentally retarded range). The 15-year-old would need to have a mental age of nine to get an IQ score that low. As this example shows, the use of IQs helped to equalize the scores for children who had roughly the same degree of mental retardation or normal intelligence, but who were of different ages.

Expressing intelligence as a single number also had other effects however. For one thing, it encouraged people to look at intelligence as a single entity, along the lines of Spearman's General Intelligence. For another thing, it gave researchers a number they could use in correlational studies. A flood of studies followed in which researchers looked at the association between "intelligence" (as measured by IQ tests) and an endless list of other variables. Yet many people had—and still have—grave doubts about whether something as complex as intelligence could really be boiled down into something as simple as a numerical score.

Goddard and negative eugenics

Stern may have come up with the IQ formula, but American psychologist Henry Goddard did the most to popularize the Binet-Simon Scale in the early days. As director of research at the Training School for the Feebleminded in Vineland, New Jersey, Goddard was eager to learn all about the latest advances in the mental retardation field. In 1908, he traveled to Europe to see what was being doing there. Although he visited Paris, he never met Binet. At the time, Binet had yet to earn prestige within his own country, and Goddard got the impression that Binet was making little progress. In fact, Goddard did not even realize that Binet had just published a revision of his scale. As Goddard wrote in his travel diary: "Visited Sorbonne. Binet's lab is largely a myth. Not much being done. . ."

When Goddard reached Belgium, however, he found out just how wrong he had been, learning there about the latest revision of the Binet-Simon Scale. Back in New Jersey, Goddard translated the test. Although skeptical at first, he gave the test to the mentally retarded children at his school. He became an instant convert when he saw how well the test classified the children's degree of retardation. By 1915, Goddard had distributed more than 22,000 copies of the translated test and 88,000 answer blanks around the United States.

Goddard was a fan of Binet's test, but not of his ideas. Instead, Goddard believed firmly in hereditary

intelligence and eugenics. In fact, he took these views to an extreme. Galton, the founder of eugenics, had mainly wanted to *foster* breeding among people at the upper end of the intelligence range. Binet, the opposing voice, had wanted to promote the education and improve the lives of people at the lower end. Goddard, in contrast to both, was determined to *prevent* breeding among people with low intelligence—a policy called negative eugenics. Austrian biologist Gregor Mendel's basic laws of heredity, which had gone unnoticed when he proposed them in the 1860s, had been rediscovered in the early 1900s. Influenced by the excitement over Mendel's laws, Goddard incorrectly believed that mental retardation was caused by a single gene, and he thought it could be wiped out by preventing people with defective intelligence genes from having children.

In 1912, Goddard published a popular book titled *The Kallikak Family: A Study in the Heredity of Feeble-Mindedness.* This book was a sensationalized account of two branches of a family. One branch supposedly had a gene for feeblemindedness, which showed up in all manner of unsavory and immoral behavior among the relatives. The other branch, which supposedly lacked the gene, was filled with upstanding citizens. Goddard's methods of gathering and presenting data for this book were later shown to be quite biased. Yet, even taking his arguments at face value, they failed to prove his hereditary theory. As with Galton's earlier study of genius, it was impossible to separate the effects of nature and nurture.

While Goddard's book may not have been great science, it was certainly effective propaganda. As a result of his book and others like it, several states passed laws requiring the involuntary sterilization of people with mental retardation. Intelligence tests were used to help identify which individuals would be candidates for sterilization.

Tragically, events in Nazi Germany during the 1930s and 1940s would highlight all too clearly the dark side of eugenics. In the early years of Nazism, more than 200,000 "degenerates" of all types, including people with mental retardation, were sterilized in Germany. Later, Germans with mental retardation and physical disabilities were among the millions of people killed alongside the Jews during the Holocaust. Once the extent of these atrocities became known, public revulsion helped turn opinion against negative eugenics, including the practice of involuntary sterilization. Today, some states still have involuntary sterilization laws on the books, but the policy is rarely enforced.

It is sad that it took such a brutal turn of events to make a crucial point: The improvement of the human race depends not only on heredity, but also on providing a better environment and improved education. Modern social policy often focuses on environmental and educational programs. Thus, society has come full circle to embrace the views of Binet and his "mental orthopedics." Yet it is ironic that Binet's test was used by others to justify policies that were so at odds with his personal philosophy.

Terman and the Stanford-Binet intelligence scales

While Goddard introduced Binet's test to the United States, it was Lewis Terman who ensured its lasting popularity. At the same time that Binet and Simon were developing the first version of their scale in France, Terman was working on his doctoral thesis at Clark University in Massachusetts. A former teacher, Terman had noted that some students seemed to sail through all of their classes, while other students always struggled. He wanted to find mental tests that would distinguish one group of students from the other. To do this, he gave a series of tests to 14 schoolboys—seven of whom had been singled out by their teachers as exceptionally bright, and seven of whom had been singled out as exceptionally dull. Although Terman was still unaware of Binet's work, the tests he chose were more similar to those of Binet than to those of Galton or Cattell. The tests involved creative imagination, logic, mathematical ability, language mastery, interpretation of fables, the game of chess, memory, and motor skill.

As Terman had expected, the bright boys did better, on average, than the dull boys on all the tests except those for motor skill. There was some overlap, however. On most of the tests, the best of the "dull" boys outdid the worst of the "bright" boys. As a result, Terman was disappointed by his findings. Yet the results only seemed like a failure because Terman had downplayed a key factor: The dull boys were almost a full year older, on average, than the bright ones. Had the two groups been the same age, the differences in their performance would have been greater. At the time, however, Binet had not yet pointed out the critical need for age standards in intelligence testing. Terman had failed to appreciate just how important age was.

In 1910, Terman accepted a teaching position at Stanford University. Around this time, he also learned about the Binet-Simon Scale. He immediately saw the advantage of using age standards. When age was taken into account, both his test items

and those on the Binet-Simon Scale did a relatively good job of predicting school success. However, Terman also saw that the Binet-Simon Scale needed to be adapted for a U.S. audience. Terman showed that, in its original form, the Binet test seriously overestimated intelligence in young American children, but underestimated it in older children. Clearly, some of the test items and scoring needed to be adjusted.

Terman set out to assess Binet's test items on a large number of American children. Several new items, some of which were based on Terman's doctoral research, were assessed as well. Since Terman used better methods for choosing children on whom to try out the test, his results were more accurate than those of Binet. In 1916, Terman published his Stanford Revision and Extension of the Binet-Simon Scale, an unwieldy name that was quickly shortened to Stanford-Binet. The new test was more than a mere translation of the Binet-Simon Scale, however—it was a big leap forward. Forty new test items had been added, and some of the less reliable original items had been dropped. In addition, Terman had borrowed Stern's idea of expressing results on the test as an IQ score.

The Stanford-Binet was an advance in other ways as well. For example, it was the first published intelligence test to include very specific, detailed instructions on test giving and scoring. It also offered alternate items to be used under certain circumstances; for example, if the examiner made a mistake when giving the regular item.

The Stanford-Binet quickly became the best intelligence test in the world and the gold standard by which future tests would be judged. It included six tasks at each age level. Following are two examples.

- Age four: Saying which of two horizontal lines is longer; matching shapes; counting four pennies; copying a square; repeating a string of four numbers; answering a question such as: "What must you do when you are sleepy?"

- Age nine: Knowing the current day of the week and year; arranging five weights from heaviest to lightest; doing mental arithmetic; repeating a string of four numbers backward; producing a sentence using three specified words; finding rhymes.

In 1926, Terman began working on a revision of the test with his colleague Maude Merrill. The project took them 11 years to complete. The 1937 revision offered two equivalent forms of the test. It also added new types of tasks for preschool and adult test takers.

Another revision of the test was already well under way at the time of Terman's death in 1956. Published in 1960, this third edition of the Stanford-Binet offered only one form of the test, composed of the best items from the two earlier forms. No new items were added. There was one big change, however: the introduction of a new way of calculating IQ. No longer was it simply a matter of dividing mental age by chronological age, then multiplying by 100. Instead, a deviation IQ was used. The deviation IQ was based on a comparison of the performance of an individual with the performance of a group of same-aged people during the test's development phase. Test performance was converted to a score where the average was always 100, and the standard deviation, a measure of variance in the scores, was 16. In the current version of the Stanford-Binet, the standard deviation is 15, but the average is still 100.

To understand how this works, it helps to picture the range of scores fitting neatly into a bell-shaped curve. About two-thirds of all scores fall between the average (at the top of the bell) and one standard deviation on either side. In other words, about two-thirds of all people have IQ scores between 85 and 115. Ninety-five percent of all scores fall between the average and two standard deviations on either side. In other words, only 5% of all people have IQ scores lower than 70 or higher than 130. This type of test, with an average of 100 and a standard deviation of 15, has become the industry standard in intelligence testing.

Binet compared to Terman

Binet's method of intelligence testing was an excellent match for Terman's own interests and background. With Binet's work as a starting point, Terman made great strides in refining the intelligence test. One way he did this was by focusing on standardization, the process of test development in which a test is given to a representative sample of individuals under clearly specified conditions, and the results are scored and interpreted according to set criteria. The goal is to spell out a standardized method of giving, scoring, and interpreting the test in the future. This approach helps to ensure that as much as possible of the variance in scores is caused by true differences in individual ability, and not by differences in the testing situation.

A key part of this process is the selection of the standardization sample: the group of people on whom the test is tried out during the development phase. The underlying assumption is that this group is representative of the whole population of people who will eventually take the test. Terman's sample was much larger than Binet's, and he went to what were then

unprecedented lengths to select his standardization sample. By modern standards, however, Terman's sample still fell short. It was not representative of the full spectrum of people living in the United States.

It is not just the standardization sample that needs to reflect the whole test population, however. The test materials need to do so as well. Otherwise, the test may be biased against those who find the materials less familiar or relevant. Binet recognized that his own test was valid only for children with a a knowledge of mainstream French culture. Terman's Stanford-Binet also tended to focus heavily on the majority culture in the United States. For example, the pictures in the test kit depicted mainly white people and middle-class situations. Critics argued that the test was biased against members of certain racial, ethnic, and social groups.

In addition, the test seemed to reward conformity. For example, Terman added this item to the test: "An Indian who had come to town for the first time in his life saw a white man riding along the street. As the white man rode by, the Indian said—'The white man is lazy; he walks sitting down.' What was the white man riding on that caused the Indian to say, 'He walks sitting down.'" The only answer accepted as correct was bicycle. Cars and other vehicles were considered incorrect, because legs don't go up and down on them. A horse was considered incorrect, because it was assumed that the Indian would know a horse if he saw one. Creative responses, such as a person riding on someone else's back, were also marked wrong. Critics noted that the test seemed to measure conventional, rather than creative, thinking.

Both Terman and Binet were interested in educational uses for their tests. Binet was concerned primarily with identifying mentally retarded children who might need special educational programs. Terman, on the other hand, was fascinated by gifted children. In fact, he is remembered as much today for his research on the gifted as for his intelligence test. In the early 1900s, many people believed the popular catchphrase "early ripe, early rot." In other words, they thought that child prodigies often burned out at an early age. Terman suspected that the reverse was actually true, but he needed evidence. Binet's testing method seemed tailor-made for such research.

One of the first hurdles Terman faced was showing that high IQ scores in childhood really were good predictors of high achievement in adulthood. One way he tried to address this was by having a graduate student, Catherine Cox, study the childhood biographies of some 300 people rated to be among history's greatest geniuses. The goal was to estimate their childhood IQs based on reports of the ages at which they had reached various landmarks in mental development. Obviously, this method left a lot to be desired. In many cases, little was known about the childhoods of these geniuses, and the information that was available was clearly not objective. Nevertheless, Terman and Cox believed that the study confirmed their basic point: These geniuses had "ripened" early, but they had certainly not gone to rot as adults.

Encouraged, Terman undertook a more ambitious project. In the early 1920s, his assistants tested more than 250,000 California schoolchildren. From this sample, Terman identified nearly 1,500 children with high IQs of 135 or above. Extensive background information was gathered on these children, nicknamed Terman's Termites. In what turned out to be the longest-running study ever done, the children have been followed ever since. This study showed that most of the children were normal, happy, and healthy. As the Termites grew up, they continued to thrive as a group. Most of them were also relatively healthy, successful, and content with their lives as adults. Although the study had its flaws, it went a long way toward disproving the "early rot" myth.

When it came to people with less exalted IQs, however, Terman's views could be less benign. Binet had wanted to identify children with below-normal intelligence so that they could be helped to learn and improve their lot in life. Terman, on the other hand, often seemed more concerned with putting a ceiling on what people could hope to achieve. He believed that, in an ideal world, everyone would be tested and then channeled into a job deemed appropriate for his or her intelligence. In general, he thought, jobs offering much in the way of status or money should be reserved for people with IQs over 100.

On the surface, this might seem logical enough. Yet there were at least two dangerous flaws in Terman's logic. First, Terman's IQ test was not a perfect predictor of true ability. Therefore, a low score might have kept someone from getting a good job that he or she would have been quite capable of doing. Second, the test had been criticized as being unfair to members of certain racial, ethnic, and social groups. If the test were indeed biased against individuals from these groups, then they would be likely to get lower-than-average scores for reasons unrelated to their actual intelligence. Yet those same scores could then be used to limit opportunities for advancement. Thus, it had become all too easy to turn IQ scores into a means of perpetuating social inequality. Binet himself would surely have been dismayed by this misuse of his creation.

Yerkes, Brigham, and group intelligence tests

Terman and Goddard had introduced intelligence testing to America. Soon, world events would turn it into a national priority. In 1917, the year after Terman first published the Stanford-Binet, the United States entered World War I. Like many other Americans, psychologist Robert Yerkes was eager to serve his country. As president of the American Psychological Association, he also wanted show the value of the young science he represented. Yerkes set up committees to explore the military uses of psychology. He made himself chairman of a committee that was charged with developing an intelligence test for matching military recruits to the right jobs. Terman and Goddard were included among the other psychologists named to the committee.

The task Yerkes had taken on was extremely difficult, however. First, given the sheer number of recruits, the individual testing method developed by Binet and refined by Terman would not have been practical. A whole new kind of group intelligence test, which could be given to several people at once, would need to be developed. Second, the test would have to not only screen out those with low ability, but also identify those with high ability who might be officer material. Third, the test would have to be designed specifically for adults, rather than for children. Fourth, the test development would have to be accomplished very quickly, since results were needed right away.

Yerkes' committee promptly put together two prototype tests: one for recruits who could read English, and another for those who could not. A trial on 80,000 men impressed the Army enough that it authorized the testing of all new recruits by the beginning of 1918. The tests were revised and renamed Army Alpha (for literate recruits) and Beta (for illiterate recruits). Soon, the tests were being given to some 200,000 men per month. By the time war ended in November 1918, about 1,750,000 men had taken one of the tests. This prodigious feat brought intelligence testing to the attention of the public. It introduced the idea of nearly universal testing, and it opened up a huge market for group tests after the war. In addition, the massive amount of data collected on the Army tests became the subject of intense study and led to much public debate about the state of intelligence in American society.

In 1921, Yerkes published *Psychological Examining in the United States Army,* an 800-page book analyzing the Army test data. Two years later, one of his junior colleagues named Carl Brigham published *A Study of American Intelligence,* which explored the same topic. The books made several questionable claims. For one thing, they claimed that the average mental age for all Army recruits was about 13 years. At the time, the mental age for an average adult was thought to be 16, and a mental age of 12 in an adult was considered the upper borderline for mild retardation. Therefore, the supposed mental age of the recruits was shockingly low. It might have been logical to conclude that the hastily thrown-together tests had been less than accurate. Yerkes, however, concluded that the results indicated a distressingly low level of intelligence in society at large.

Some of Yerkes' and Brigham's other conclusions were even more controversial. For example, the psychologists noted that, compared to native-born whites, immigrants and blacks tended to score lower on the tests. Once again, it might have been sensible to conclude that the tests had been biased toward members of the majority American culture. On the Alpha test, for example, individuals were expected to know that Overland cars were made in Toledo and that Crisco was a food product. On the Beta test, individuals were expected to be familiar with pictures of middle-class objects, such as a tennis court or a phonograph. Yet Yerkes and Brigham instead took the position that the lower scores obtained by immigrants and blacks indicated lower levels of natural mental ability in those groups.

At the time, racial segregation and discrimination were the norms in much of American society. Public sentiment had also turned sharply against immigration. In fact, in 1924, Congress passed a bill that set strict immigration quotas for each national group. This social climate helped to support Yerkes' and Brigham's conclusions. Yet, even at the time, there were opposing voices. One belonged to Franz Boas, a German immigrant himself and a leading American anthropologist of the early 1900s. Boas argued that many racial and ethnic characteristics were passed from generation to generation not by heredity, but by culture, through such mechanisms as shared values, language, and child-rearing customs.

American Otto Klineberg, a graduate student in psychology, was one of the first researchers to apply Boas' ideas to group differences in intelligence test scores. While studying Yakima Indian children in the state of Washington, he noticed that they seemed indifferent to time limits. They took their time, no matter how much they were urged to hurry, but they also made relatively few mistakes. Klineberg noted that, in Yakima culture, speed was not considered a sign of intelligence. On the contrary, it was thought to reflect carelessness. This was clearly a cultural

rather than a genetic difference. Yet it put the Yakima children at a disadvantage on timed intelligence tests. Similar observations in other cultures soon added up to a convincing case. By the 1930s, all but the most diehard eugenicists had conceded that culture played an important role in causing group differences in IQ scores.

In 1926, Brigham made his mark on group intelligence testing in another way. He introduced a brand-new kind of standardized test of mental ability. IQ tests looked at general thinking ability. This new type of test, however, looked more specifically at the kinds of word and number skills that were used in school. Brigham's test became the forerunner of the SAT, a test that is still very familiar to high-school students.

Thurstone and the structure of intelligence

Meanwhile, research on the structure of intelligence was moving ahead as well. One of the most important figures in this field was American psychologist Louis Thurstone. He challenged Spearman's ideas and, in the process, changed the way many psychologists viewed intelligence.

Spearman had proposed the existence of a unifying factor called general intelligence. He believed that all of the variation in intelligence test scores could be explained by the pervasive influence of general intelligence, combined with specific effects that were unique to the particular test activity at hand. Thurstone developed new statistical methods, and when he applied them to intelligence test scores, he noted that mental abilities tended to cluster into several groups rather than just one. In 1938, Thurstone published a book titled *Primary Mental Abilities,* in which he proposed that there were actually seven clusters of mental abilities. He called the clusters verbal comprehension, word fluency, number facility, spatial visualization, associative memory, perceptual speed, and reasoning.

When originally introduced, Spearman's and Thurstone's findings seemed to be directly opposed to each other. One currently popular view of intelligence, however, combines the two theories. Intelligence is often seen as having a three-level, hierarchical structure. General intelligence is on the top. Clusters of mental abilities make up the second level. Although separate from each other, in combination they all form general intelligence. A host of specific mental abilities make up the various clusters on the third level. Even psychologists who accept this structure, however, have different opinions about which level to emphasize. Some still see general intelligence as the

Boy taking a Wechsler Intelligence Scales for Children (WISC) test, a common intelligence test. (Copyright Lew Merrim/Science Source/Photo Researchers, Inc. Reproduced by permission.)

most crucial consideration. Others, however, think it is more worthwhile to focus on each person's distinctive pattern of strengths and weaknesses at the second level. The latter viewpoint echoes the view of intelligence put forth by Binet many decades before.

The Stanford-Binet after Terman

Terman died in 1956, but his legacy lives on. The fourth edition of the Stanford-Binet was introduced in 1972, 16 years after Terman's death. This version contained major changes. Previous versions of the Stanford-Binet had included age scales, in which test items were grouped together by the age at which most individuals could pass them. The fourth edition, in contrast, introduced a point scale, in which all the test items of a particular type were grouped together. The test was then evaluated in terms of how many items of each type were answered correctly, rather than in terms of an age level. By the 1970s, this was a very common test structure. It was also the type of structure used for the Wechsler Intelligence Scales, which had by then eclipsed the Stanford-Binet as the most widely used intelligence tests.

Previous editions of the Stanford-Binet had yielded an overall IQ score, considered to be a measure of general intelligence. The fourth edition, however, went beyond just providing a general IQ. It contained 15 subtests that also yielded scores on four clusters of mental abilities: verbal reasoning, abstract/visual reasoning, quantitative reasoning, and short-term memory.

Verbal reasoning:

- Vocabulary. In this subtest, individuals are asked to identify pictured objects and define words.

- Comprehension. These items range from identifying parts of the body to answering more complex questions using social judgment; for example, "Why should people be quiet in a hospital?"

- Absurdities. Individuals are asked to identify what is wrong or silly about a picture.

- Verbal relations. Individuals are given four words; for example, "newspaper," "magazine," "book," "television." They are asked to state what is similar about the first three things, but different about the fourth.

Abstract/visual reasoning:

- Pattern analysis. These tasks, which must be completed within a set time limit, range from putting cutout forms into a form-board to copying complex designs with blocks.

BIOGRAPHY:

David Wechsler

Alfred Binet may have invented intelligence testing, but the distinction of developing the most popular IQ test used today goes to David Wechsler. Wechsler was born in Romania in 1896. He moved with his family to the United States when he was six years old. By the time the United States entered World War I, Wechsler was a young graduate student studying psychology at Columbia University. At the start of the war, Wechsler served for a time as a volunteer scorer of the Army Alpha test. Once he became a junior officer, he was assigned to give the Stanford-Binet test to recruits who had been referred for extra testing. This experience gave Wechsler a firsthand glimpse of the strengths and weaknesses of the leading intelligence tests of the day. In particular, he became aware that the Stanford-Binet test did not always work well for assessing intelligence in adults.

After the war, Wechsler completed his Ph.D. and continued to conduct intelligence testing in the course of his work as a psychologist. In 1932, he became chief psychologist at Bellevue Hospital in New York, where he oversaw the testing of thousands of mentally ill patients. More convinced than ever that existing intelligence tests were insufficient, Wechsler set out to develop an alternative. First, he wanted his test to be tailored to the needs of adults rather than children.

Second, he wanted it to be suitable for people from diverse ethnic, linguistic, and social backgrounds. Third, he wanted it to include a point scale, rather than an age scale, that would yield a deviation IQ. The latter method of calculating IQs converted test performance to a score where the average was always 100 and the standard deviation was 15. This method became so successful that it was soon adopted by almost all intelligence test developers, including those researchers who developed later revisions of the Stanford-Binet.

The test created by Wechsler gave equal weight to verbal items, similar to those on the Stanford-Binet and Army Alpha tests, and nonverbal performance items, similar to those on the Army Beta test. It yielded a Verbal Scale IQ and Performance Scale IQ as well as a Full Scale IQ. Wechsler introduced his Wechsler Bellevue Scale for adults in 1939. This was replaced by the Wechsler Adult Intelligence Scale (WAIS) in 1955. The test was so well received that Wechsler also developed two versions for children: the Wechsler Intelligence Scale for Children (WISC) for those of school age, and the Wechsler Preschool and Primary Scale of Intelligence (WPPSI) for preschoolers. Wechsler died in 1981, but the latest versions of his tests are still widely used.

- Copying. Individuals are asked to copy designs with blocks or by drawing.
- Matrices. Individuals are shown an incomplete matrix—a systematic arrangement of geometric symbols, letters, or common objects. They are then asked to pick the object that is needed to complete the matrix.
- Paper folding and cutting. In these multiple-choice items, individuals are asked to decide how a folded and cut piece of paper will look when unfolded.

Quantitative reasoning:

- Quantitative subtest. These items range from simple counting to knowledge of arithmetic concepts and operations.
- Number series. Individuals are asked to complete a sequence of numbers with the number that would come next.

- Equation building. Individuals are asked to rearrange a scrambled arithmetic equation so that it makes sense.

Short-term memory:

- Bead memory. In this subtest, individuals study a picture of a bead sequence for five seconds. They are then asked to reproduce the sequence using actual beads of varying color and shape.
- Memory for sentences. Individuals are asked to repeat sentences ranging in length from two to 22 words.
- Memory for digits. Individuals are asked to repeat strings of numbers.
- Memory for objects. In this subtest, familiar objects are presented at one-second intervals. Individuals are then asked to recall the objects in the correct order.

The fifth and latest edition of the Stanford-Binet was published in 2003. It is the most recent attempt to wed the rich tradition of this test with the newest research on mental abilities and intelligence testing. In the fifth edition, the traditional age scale has been brought back. Like the fourth edition, however, the test now yields scores on several clusters of mental abilities as well as on general intelligence.

In recent versions of the Stanford-Binet, developers have tried to weed out any systematic bias against members of particular racial, ethnic, or social groups. For example, the test kit now contains pictures showing children of different races and with disabilities, and the word "brunette" has been cut from the vocabulary test because it was not as meaningful to black children as to whites. A broader standardization sample has been chosen to better reflect the entire population of the nation. And psychologists from various racial and ethnic backgrounds have reviewed the materials for potential problems. Nevertheless, the test remains a product of its culture, and it may well be impossible to eliminate all bias.

A common criticism of previous versions of the Stanford-Binet test was that they relied too heavily on verbal abilities. The test was often unfavorably compared in this regard to the popular Wechsler Intelligence Scales, which David Wechsler first introduced in 1939. The Wechsler tests have two parts: Verbal and Performance. While the Verbal tasks are heavy on word skills, the Performance tasks rely less on language abilities. Instead, they involve nonverbal activities, such as completing pictures, making block designs, solving mazes, and using abstract symbols. This kind of test may be better suited to people for whom language is a barrier, as well as to those who have higher nonverbal abilities. The fifth edition of the Stanford-Binet, for the first time, tries to offer a better balance of verbal and nonverbal items.

One advantage of the Stanford-Binet is that it is an adaptive test, which means it is tailored to each test taker's individual needs. The examiner uses information about a person to decide where to begin testing. This approach reduces the frustration that the person might feel if he or she was asked to complete tasks that were much too hard or too easy. It also cuts down on wasted time. Nevertheless, the Stanford-Binet is still an individual test, which means it is given by a trained examiner to only one person at a time, rather than to a group. The test usually takes about 45 to 60 minutes to give. As a result, it would usually not be feasible to give it to every student in a school, for example. Like the Wechsler scales and other individ-

ual tests, the Stanford-Binet typically is given only to individuals who have already been singled out as needing extra testing.

THEORIES IN ACTION

Today, psychologists can choose from among many different individual and group intelligence tests. These tests are used for a wide variety of purposes. Indeed, intelligence testing has become one of the most widespread uses of psychology in everyday life. Research using intelligence tests has also helped fuel the ongoing debate over the very nature of intelligence.

Research on the nature of intelligence

What is intelligence? Binet struggled with this question in his day, and modern scientists are still grappling with it. In the 1920s, one of the more infamous answers was offered by American psychologist Edwin Boring, who pronounced that "intelligence is what the tests test." This kind of circular reasoning may be amusing, but it is not very instructive for scientists seeking serious answers.

Whatever it is that intelligence tests measure, though, the tests seem to work best for predicting academic success. In study after study, intelligence test scores have been found to have a correlation of 0.4 to 0.6 (on a 0 to 1 scale) with school grades. Statistically speaking, this is considered a moderate to large correlation. But even a test that predicts school grades with a correlation of 0.5, however, still accounts for only 25% of the variation in school performance among individual students. This means that 75% of the variation is due to other factors. Clearly, the kind of intelligence that is measured on IQ tests is not the only predictor of academic performance. Other factors, such as good schools and high individual motivation, also seem to count for a lot.

Once researchers moved beyond the classroom and into the workplace, the predictive power of intelligence tests grew even weaker. In general, studies have found correlations between IQ scores and work performance of about 0.3. This means that the tests accounted for just 10% of the variation in performance among individual workers; therefore, 90% of the variation must be explained by other factors. In 1990, American psychologists Peter Salovey and John Mayer coined the term "emotional intelligence" to describe the emotional abilities and interpersonal skills that may play a critical role in workplace success.

This idea raises a related question: Is intelligence really just one thing or is it many? Some modern theorists have suggested that there may actually be several types of intelligence, some of which are not assessed by standard intelligence tests at all. One of these theorists is Howard Gardner, a professor of education at Harvard University. In 1983, Gardner published a book called *Frames of Mind,* in which he introduced his theory of multiple intelligences. Gardner thinks there are several different "intelligences" that are separate but equal in the mind. Some people learn more easily by using one kind of intelligence; others, by using another. So far, Gardner has described eight intelligences: linguistic, logical-mathematical, spatial, musical, bodily-kinesthetic, naturalist, interpersonal, and intrapersonal. Of these, linguistic and logical-mathematical are most similar to the kinds of word and number skills used in school and assessed on IQ tests.

Fresh ideas such as Salovey and Mayer's emotional intelligence and Gardner's multiple intelligences are intriguing. Yet research on these alternate intelligences has been hampered by the lack of well-validated tests to measure them. Only time will tell whether these new concepts will hold up to rigorous testing as well as General Intelligence has.

Research on the nature-nurture debate

Another research question remains as relevant today as it was in Galton's time: Is intelligence mainly the result of nature or nurture? Modern research methods are shedding some new light on this old puzzle. Some of the most interesting findings have come from the Minnesota Study of Twins Reared Apart. For this study, the researchers brought together from all over the world sets of twins who had been separated during childhood and, in most cases, have lived apart ever since. The twins were then put through a week of intense psychological and medical testing, including intelligence tests.

Since Galton's time, scientists have realized that twin studies presented a unique opportunity for exploring the genetic basis of intelligence. Identical twins share exactly the same genetic makeup. Therefore, their inherited intelligence should theoretically be the same. When identical twins are reared apart, the resulting differences in their intelligence should be largely due to differences in their separate environments. Of course, this is not perfectly true. For one thing, twins do share at least one crucial part of their lives: the prenatal part in the womb. For another thing, even when twins have been reared apart, they may have been placed in similar homes.

CHRONOLOGY

1857: Born on July 8 in Nice, France.

1878: Receives a license in law, a career he chose not to pursue.

1879 or 1880: Began reading about psychology in a Paris library.

1880: Publishes his first article, "On the Fusion of Similar Sensations."

1884: Marries Laure Balbiani, daughter of biologist E. G. Balbiani.

1885: Birth of his daughter, Madeleine.

1886: Publishes his first book, *The Psychology of Reasoning.*

1887: Birth of his daughter, Alice.

1894: Receives a doctoral degree in natural science from the Sorbonne.

1895: Helps found the first French psychological journal.

1896: Publishes a paper outlining "individual psychology" with Victor Henri.

1899: Began working with Théodore Simon.

1900: Helps organize the Free Society for the Psychological Study of the Child.

1905: Along with Simon, introduces the first version of the Binet-Simon Scale.

1911: Makes the last revision of the Binet-Simon Scale. Dies on October 18.

Nevertheless, twin studies are one of the best tools psychologists have for separating the effects of nature and nurture.

The Minnesota study showed that identical twins who had been raised apart grew up to be almost as similar in intelligence as identical twins who had been raised together. The degree of similarity was impressive. For example, one test the twins took was the Wechsler Adult Intelligence Scale, currently the most widely used IQ test for adults. The scores of identical twins reared apart correlated at 0.69, a high correlation that was not much different from the 0.88 correlation in the scores of identical twins reared together.

On some other tests of mental ability, the correlations were even closer. For example, on a test called Raven's Progressive Matrices, the correlation for the reared apart identical twins was 0.78. For the reared-together identical twins, it was 0.76.

Overall, the Minnesota study and others like it have found that about half of the differences in intelligence within a group of people may be due to differences in genes. Of course, this also means that half of the differences are due to other things. In addition, what is true for a group of people is not always true for a particular individual. In the Minnesota study, for example, one pair of twins scored almost 30 points apart in IQ.

Case studies

Studies of extreme cases are another way of exploring the nature and limits of intelligence. The nearly 1,500 high-IQ children who took part in Lewis Terman's long-running study of giftedness have become one of the best-researched groups in history. Over the years, some participants have chosen to reveal their identities, and reports have been published documenting their personal triumphs and tribulations. The life stories of Terman's Termites, as the study's participants came to be called, reveal a lot about the benefits and limitations of having a high IQ.

As a group, the Termites have fared relatively well. Although no world-class geniuses emerged from the group, some members achieved success and even a measure of fame as adults. For example, Jess Oppenheimer became the creator, producer, and head writer of *I Love Lucy,* one of the best-loved television shows of all time. Ancel Keys discovered the link between cholesterol and heart disease. Others in the group included Norris Bradbury, former director of the Los Alamos National Laboratory, and Shelley Smith Mydans, a one-time journalist for *Life* magazine. Yet none of the Termites ever won a Nobel or Pulitzer Prize. It is an interesting footnote that two of children who were tested for the study but whose IQs failed to make the cut did go on to win the Nobel Prize in Physics: William Shockley in 1956 and Luis Alvarez in 1968.

Another Termite who eventually made a name for himself was Edward Dmytryk. At age 14, Edward was picked up by the authorities as a runaway. He had reportedly left home to escape an abusive father, who was said to have torn up his schoolbooks and clubbed him with a board. The father wanted Edward returned, although a caseworker suspected that this might have been only because Edward brought home income. Terman wrote a letter to the authorities on Edward's

behalf, and the boy wound up being placed in a good foster home instead. This kind of meddling by a researcher in his subject's lives was typical of Terman. It may have affected the results of his study, thereby undermining the data from a scientific perspective, but it also demonstrated the deep interest that Terman took in the children. As an adult, Dmytryk went on to direct 23 movies, including *The Caine Mutiny,* a classic 1954 film starring Humphrey Bogart.

Of course, not all of Terman's Termites achieved happiness and success as adults. For example, the study included two half-sisters raised by the same mother, both of whom went to college at Stanford University. One became well-known as a freelance writer. The other died of alcoholism. Terman's study showed that high IQ was helpful in adulthood, but, by itself, it was clearly no guarantee of the good life. Among the personal traits that seemed to be associated with adult success were the ability to set goals and the perseverance to achieve them. In addition, a stable marriage and a satisfying job also were related to happiness as an adult. If nothing else, then, the study underscored the fact that people with high IQs have basically the same needs and desires as everyone else. At best, they may just have a running start at fulfilling those needs.

Relevance to modern readers

Until recently, two-thirds of school districts in the United States used group intelligence tests on a routine basis to screen 90% of their students. The remaining 10% were given individual tests. Over the last few decades, though, concerns over the potential for error and bias have curtailed the routine use of group tests. Many states have passed laws banning the use of group test scores alone for placing children in different educational tracks. Nevertheless, group intelligence test scores are still sometimes used by school districts for educational planning. The scores can also identify children who might need more detailed assessment with individual tests.

Such children include not only those with developmental and learning disabilities but also those with special gifts. Thanks to Terman, the idea of IQ as an index of giftedness is firmly rooted in American society. Yet Binet himself had doubts about the ability of intelligence tests to identify gifted or talented individuals, and some modern psychologists share his concerns. It seems that highly creative thinking might, by its very nature, defy conventional testing. In addition, there are many kinds of valuable abilities—including musical, artistic, athletic, and leadership skills—only a few of which are tapped by

BIOGRAPHY:

Robert Sternberg

Today, Robert Sternberg is one of the world's leading authorities on intelligence. His relationship with intelligence tests got off to an unpromising start, however. Born in 1949 in New Jersey, Sternberg struggled with IQ tests as a youngster. As he later recalled in his 1996 book *Successful Intelligence*, "I was incredibly test-anxious. Just the sight of the school psychologist coming into the classroom to give a group IQ test sent me into a wild panic attack."

Fortunately, Sternberg overcame his test phobia. He went on to earn a Ph.D. in psychology from Stanford University in 1975. That same year, he took a position at Yale University, where he has taught psychology ever since. In 1985, Sternberg published an influential book titled *Beyond IQ: A Triarchic Theory of Human Intelligence,* in which he outlined a three-part structure for intelligence. This view was later expanded into his theory of successful intelligence, which refers to the capacity to achieve real-world success in everyday life.

According to Sternberg,

> successfully intelligent individuals succeed in part because they achieve a functional balance among a

'triarchy' of abilities: analytical abilities, which are used to analyze, evaluate, judge, compare and contrast; creative abilities, which are used to create, invent, discover, imagine; practical abilities, which are used to apply, utilize, implement, and activate.

Sternberg believes that while successful people do not necessarily possess high aptitude in all three ability areas, they do find a way to effectively use their particular pattern of abilities. Of the three types of talents described by Sternberg, only analytical abilities are tapped by conventional intelligence tests. As a result, one of the basic premises of his work is that ordinary IQ tests often miss important kinds of mental talent. Sternberg also believes that all three kinds of abilities can be improved through training and practice.

Robert Sternberg. (AP/Wide World Photos. Reproduced by permission)

---

standard IQ tests. Today, various states and school districts use a wide range of methods for identifying gifted students. Many use standardized tests. Along with intelligence tests, however, assessment for gifted programs may involve tests for creative thinking, artistic ability, leadership, or motivation. In addition, screening might involve non-test measures, such as teacher checklists, teacher or parent recommendations, or the student's work in a portfolio.

Another common use for group tests is to help predict which high school students are likely to do well in college. The SAT is one familiar example of this kind of scholastic aptitude test. The scores from such tests tend to be highly correlated with IQ, and many psychologists regard scholastic aptitude tests as just another kind of intelligence test. Along with high school grades, SAT scores often play a big role in deciding who gets into a particular college and who does not. In 2003, 1.4 million high-school students took the SAT. Once those students are in college,

similar tests are often used to help determine which of them will be admitted to graduate, medical, law, or business school.

The use of the SAT and similar tests to make educational decisions has long been the subject of controversy. The main advantage of the tests is that they make it easier to compare people coming from different schools and backgrounds. Grades are less comparable, since they reflect not only a student's ability, but also the difficulty of the courses the student has taken and the standards of the school. On the other hand, SAT scores show nothing about factors such as a student's motivation and work habits. Most psychologists now agree that, even when SAT scores are used, grades and other evidence of past performance also need to be considered.

Individual tests, such as the Stanford-Binet and Wechsler Intelligence Scales, are still widely used as well. They are often used for diagnosing specific educational or developmental problems. Public Law

---

94-142, the Education for All Handicapped Children Act of 1975, helped solidify this role in the United States for intelligence tests. This law, and others that followed it, required the development of individualized educational plans for children with learning, mental, and physical disabilities. A key step in developing such plans is evaluating each disabled child's level of mental functioning.

Interestingly, the latter use for intelligence testing is very close to the one originally envisioned by Binet. In his critically acclaimed 1981 book *The Mismeasure of Man,* American paleontologist and author Stephen Jay Gould commented:

> Ironically, many American school boards have come full cycle, and now use IQ tests only as Binet originally recommended: as instruments for assessing children with specific learning problems. Speaking personally, I feel that tests of the IQ type were helpful in the proper diagnosis of my own learning-disabled son. His average score, the IQ itself, meant nothing, for it was only an amalgam of some very high and very low scores; but the pattern of low values indicated his areas of deficit.

Indeed, many of Binet's ideas still seem timely today, a century after he first stated them. Binet stressed that intelligence test results should never be used to label people as innately incapable. Instead, the results should be used to help people make the most of their inborn mental abilities. Some of Binet's earliest followers failed to heed this part of his message. Over the years, however, society has learned from its mistakes. Most modern psychologists have come to appreciate the wisdom of Binet's views.

BIBLIOGRAPHY

Sources

Becker, Kirk A. "History of the Stanford-Binet Intelligence Scales: Content and Psychometrics." *Stanford-Binet Intelligence Scales, Fifth Edition: Assessment Service Bulletin* 1 (2003) 1–14.

Fancher, Raymond E. *The Intelligence Men: Makers of the IQ Controversy.* New York: W. W. Norton, 1985.

Gould, Stephen Jay. *The Mismeasure of Man.* Rev. ed. New York: W. W. Norton, 1996.

Minton, Henry L. "Introduction to 'New Methods for the Diagnosis of the Intellectual Levels of Subnormals.' Alfred Binet & Theodore Simon (1905)." In Christopher D. Green, ed.

Classics in the History of Psychology. York University, 1998 [cited March 9, 2004]. http://psychclassics.yorku.ca/Binet/intro.htm.

Nicolas, Serge, and Ludovic Ferrand. "Alfred Binet and Higher Education." *History of Psychology* 5 (2002) 264–83.

Pollack, Robert H., and Margaret W. Brenner, eds. *The Experimental Psychology of Alfred Binet: Selected Papers.* New York: Springer Publishing Company, 1969.

Siegler, Robert S. "The Other Alfred Binet." *Developmental Psychology* 28 (1992) 179–90.

Terman, Lewis M. "Autobiography of Lewis M. Terman." In Carl Murchison, ed. *History of Psychology in Autobiography, Volume 2.* Worcester, MA: Clark University Press, 1930, 297–331. Republished by Christopher D. Green, ed. *Classics in the History of Psychology.* York University, 1998 [cited March 9, 2004]. http://psychclassics.yorku.ca/Terman/murchison.htm.

Wolf, Theta H. *Alfred Binet.* Chicago: University of Chicago Press, 1973.

Zazzo, René. "Alfred Binet." *Prospects: The Quarterly Review of Comparative Education* 23 (1993): 101–12.

Further readings

American Educational Research Association, American Psychological Association, and National Council on Measurement in Education. *Standards for Educational and Psychological Testing.* Washington, DC: American Educational Research Association, 1999.

Deary, Ian J. *Intelligence: A Very Short Introduction.* New York: Oxford University Press, 2001.

Green, Christopher D., ed. *Classics in the History of Psychology.* York University [cited March 9, 2004]. http://psychclassics.yorku.ca.

Kline, Paul. *Intelligence: The Psychometric View.* New York: Routledge, 1991.

Mackintosh, N. J. *IQ and Human Intelligence.* New York: Oxford University Press, 1998.

Shurkin, Joel N. *Terman's Kids: The Groundbreaking Study of How the Gifted Grow Up.* Boston: Little, Brown and Company, 1992.

Stanford-Binet Intelligence Scales: Fifth Edition. Riverside Publishing [cited March 26, 2004]. http://www.riverpub.com/products/clinical/sbis/home.html.

Sternberg, Robert J., ed. *Handbook of Intelligence.* New York: Cambridge University Press, 2000.

Sternberg, Robert J. "How Intelligent Is Intelligence Testing?" *Scientific American Presents: Exploring Intelligence* 9 (1998) 12–17.

Sternberg, Robert J. *Successful Intelligence: How Practical and Creative Intelligence Determine Success in Life.* New York: Plume, 1996.

Kenneth Bancroft Clark

1914-

AMERICAN EDUCATOR, SOCIAL PSYCHOLOGIST, HUMAN RIGHTS ACTIVIST

HOWARD UNIVERSITY, B.A. 1935, M.S. 1936; COLUMBIA UNIVERSITY, Ph.D. 1940

BRIEF OVERVIEW

Kenneth Bancroft Clark (1914–), an eminent American social psychologist, educator, and human rights activist, is well known for his expert testimony in the consolidated school desegregation cases known as *Brown v. Board of Education*. The landmark case, argued by the NAACP legal team before the Supreme Court in 1954, declared school segregation a violation of the Fourteenth Amendment of the U.S. Constitution. The social science testimony of Kenneth Clark was a significant factor in the Court's decision, and secured his place in the historical record among social psychologists whose research has influenced significant social change in the twentieth century.

Kenneth Clark was born in the Panama Canal Zone on July 24, 1914, and lived there until he was five years of age. His Jamaican-born mother, Miriam Hanson Clark, moved to Harlem with Kenneth and his two-year-old sister, Beulah, in 1919. Kenneth's father, Arthur Bancroft Clark, a native of the West Indies, would not relinquish his employment with the United Fruit Company in Panama to accompany his family to New York. Miriam Clark supported her two children working as a seamstress in New York's garment district. Kenneth came of age in Harlem during its political and cultural zenith in the 1920s.

Kenneth was educated in the desegregated public elementary and junior high schools of Harlem. His mother encouraged the intellectual pursuits and academic education of her son, and advocated for his

Kenneth Bancroft Clark. (*Archive Photos, Inc. Reproduced by permission.*)

admission to George Washington High School, where he graduated in 1931. That same year he became a naturalized U.S. citizen. Clark received his B.A. (1935) and M.S. (1936) degrees from Howard University in Washington, D.C., where he became a leader in demonstrations opposing racial segregation. While a graduate student and teaching assistant in the psychology department at Howard University, Clark met and married Mamie Phipps, from Little Rock, Arkansas. The two went on to become the first and second African-American students to earn doctorate degrees in psychology from Columbia University in New York.

It was Mamie Phipps-Clark's 1939 master's thesis at Howard University, titled "The Development of Consciousness of Self in Negro Pre-School Children," that initiated the couple's extensive intellectual collaboration throughout their professional careers. They studied how young children's race affects their self-concept and self-esteem. Between 1939 and 1950, the Clarks published their innovative research in the *Journal of Social Psychology* and other scientific journals. This led to an award of a Rosenwald Fellowship in 1939 that supported their continued investigations on self esteem in black children.

Dr. Clark taught at City College in New York City from 1942 until his retirement in 1975. He authored and collaborated on more than 16 books, and

published numerous research papers and journal articles. He served as president of the American Psychological Association from 1970 to 1971, where he promoted an ethic of social responsibility within the profession and confronted the institutional racism within the organization. In 1994, he received APA's Lifetime Achievement Award. Clark believed that the prime goal of serious and relevant social science should be to help society "move toward humanity and justice with minimum irrationality, instability, and cruelty." His legacy of integrity and compassion distinguish Clark as one of the leading social psychologists of the twentieth century.

BIOGRAPHY

Harlem: The early years

New York's Harlem village was a thriving African-American community on the threshold of a Renaissance in 1919 when Kenneth Bancroft Clark arrived on a passenger boat from the Panama Canal Zone. Kenneth's mother, Miriam Hanson Clark, left her husband and home in Panama to bring her children, Kenneth, almost five, and two-year-old Beulah, to live in a country she believed would offer her children more opportunity. Within the decade, the black population of Harlem had increased by 100,000. The

Clarks made their home in a series of tenement apartments in integrated neighborhoods, living side by side in the crowded city with Irish and Jewish immigrants.

"My family moved from house to house, and from neighborhood to neighborhood within the walls of the ghetto in a desperate attempt to escape its creeping blight," Clark later wrote, recalling his early years in Harlem. Soon after the Clarks emigrated from Panama, Congress began to pass laws setting immigration quotas favoring Anglo-Saxons. A revived Ku Klux Klan had spread into the North, and by 1924 had nearly five million members.

Clark's mother was a skilled seamstress and soon found work in the garment district in New York City to support her children. She became an early shop steward with the International Ladies' Garment Workers Union, and maintained high hopes for her children. Kenneth's father, Arthur Bancroft Clark, a native of the West Indies, did not share her optimism. He remained in Panama to keep his employment with the United Fruit Company.

Black pride and black literary voices were strong influences in the Harlem of Clark's boyhood. It was a time of tremendous creativity and growth of social and political movements. Harlem nurtured black intellectuals such as Arthur Schomburg, curator of the 135th Street Branch of the New York Public Library, a center of intellectual and cultural activity in Harlem, and home to his extensive collection of black literature and historical documents. Black poets and writers including Countee Cullen, who taught at Kenneth Clark's junior high school; Langston Hughes, Harlem's Poet Laureate, and Zora Neale Hurston were among the prominent cultural lights of Harlem during Kenneth Clark's childhood years.

Another lively presence in the 1920s was Marcus Garvey, a Jamaican-born charismatic black leader. Garvey gathered tremendous support for his black nationalist movement in Harlem and by the time the Clarks arrived, Garvey claimed a huge following of African Americans who responded to his call for black pride and economic independence. In 1920, Garvey led a parade of 50,000 people from throughout the United States, the Caribbean, Central America, and Africa through the streets of Harlem with their banners, uniforms, and colorfully decorated cars. Harlem was a vibrant and vital community in the 1920s, and a place that remained close to Clark's heart throughout his life.

"I first learned about people, about love, about cruelty, about sacrifice, about cowardice, about courage, about bombast in Harlem," Clark later wrote

PRINCIPAL PUBLICATIONS

- *Prejudice and Your Child.* Boston: Beacon Press, 1955; 1957.
- *The Negro Protest: James Baldwin, Malcolm X, Martin Luther King talk with Kenneth B. Clark.* Boston: Beacon Press, 1963.
- With Jeannette Hopkins. *A Relevant War Against Poverty.* New York: Harper and Row, 1970.
- *A Possible Reality: A Design for the Attainment of High Academic Achievement for Inner-City Students.* New York: Emerson Hall, 1972.
- *The Educationally Deprived: The Potential for Change.* Metropolitan Applied Research Center, 1972.
- *Pathos of Power.* New York: Harper and Row, 1974.
- *How to Protect Children Against Prejudice.* Child Study Association of America, New York: 1983.
- *Dark Ghetto: Dilemmas of Social Power.* Middletown, Connecticut: Wesleyan University Press, 1989.
- *Intelligence, the University, and Society.* United Chapters of Phi Beta Kappa; Washington DC: 1992.

in his 1965 book, *Dark Ghetto*. He introduced the book as "a summation of my personal experiences and observations as a prisoner within the ghetto long before I was aware that I was really a prisoner."

Young Kenneth attended desegregated elementary and junior high schools in Harlem and excelled as a student. When it came time for high school, though, the school counselors who were long accustomed to tracking black youth into vocational education programs were surprised when Miriam Clark arrived at the doorstep with her strong objections to vocational school. She intervened with the counselors to ensure that her bright young son would have a place in the academically focused George Washington High School.

It was his education that helped lead Kenneth Clark out of the prison of the ghetto, and it was his chosen profession as a social psychologist that led him back to Harlem as an "involved observer" using, as he wrote, "the real community, the market place, the arena of politics and power" as his laboratory to "confront and seek to understand the dynamics of social action and social change."

The Depression of 1929 hit Harlem hard. The numbers of unemployed applying for relief quadrupled within two years. Clark showed an interest in the problems of economics during his high school years, and he might have sustained that interest, but one of his teachers refused to give Kenneth an economics award he had earned for outstanding performance in the class. Despite the sting of discrimination, Clark excelled in his studies and graduated from George Washington High School in 1931. That same year he became a naturalized U.S. citizen.

Howard University: A mecca for black intellectuals

Intent on the study of medicine, Clark left Harlem for Washington, D.C., to enroll in the historic Howard University, an integrated, co-educational school from its founding days in 1867. Howard was established to train teachers and ministers who would then go out to teach the four million freed slaves and 25,000 free-born blacks in the years following the Civil War. The university became known as a "black intellectual mecca," attracting talented and distinguished African-American scholars to the faculty and student body, including Alain Locke, professor of philosophy; Ralph Bunche, professor of political science; sociologist E. Franklin Frazier; and Francis Cecil Sumner, chair of the psychology department.

By his sophomore year, Clark had switched his major to psychology. He was influenced by Professor Sumner, the first black American psychologist. Sumner was an Arkansas born scholar and World War I infantry veteran. He began his teaching career at Howard in 1928 and built the psychology department there into the foremost program for the training of African-American psychologists.

"Professor Sumner had rigorous standards for his students," Clark later said. "And he didn't just teach psychology. He taught integrity." Professor Sumner "was a model for me. In fact, he has always been my standard when I evaluate myself." Clark explained his change in career plans from medicine to psychology in a 1982 *New Yorker* interview. The method of psychological study that he learned from Professor Sumner, Clark said, provided insight into "the seemingly intractable nature of racism." Clark would

spend much of his professional life investigating the damaging effects of this social problem on the lives of those facing discrimination and of those imposing it upon others.

Another distinguished Howard professor during Clark's time there was Ralph Bunche. In 1950, he became the first black American to win the Nobel Peace prize. Professor Bunche held the view that segregation and democracy were incompatible. He encouraged Clark's leadership in opposing Jim Crow legislation. Later, Clark worked with professor Bunche on a research project initiated by the Swedish economist Gunnar Myrdal. The work was later published as the 1944 book, *An American Dilemma: The Negro Problem and Modern Democracy*.

While at Howard, Clark also served as editor of the student newspaper *The Hilltop,* writing incisive editorials opposing militarism, capitalism, and fascism. He led other students in off-campus demonstrations opposing segregation in public spaces in Washington, D.C. For these civil rights actions, Clark and other students were arrested and booked, then released when an Irish-American officer applauded their courage and had the charges dropped. Clark's willingness to take his concerns as a social scientist into the arena of real-life problems was to become a guiding philosophy in his professional career. Clark graduated from Howard with a B.A. in 1935 and an M.S. degree in 1936.

Mixing romance and intellectual collaboration

Clark stayed on at Howard to teach psychology during the 1937–38 academic year. Mamie Phipps, a physics and mathematics major from Hot Springs, Arkansas, was one of his students. At Clark's suggestion, she switched her major field of study to psychology, in part because of the lack of support she experienced in her pursuit of mathematics. It proved to be a fortuitous choice.

At the advice of Professor Sumner, Clark returned to New York in 1939 to enroll in a Ph.D. program in Psychology at Columbia. Mamie continued with her studies at Howard. The friendship, by now, had turned to romance and they became engaged. Kenneth wrote to Mamie's father with a formal introduction. The reply he received was not warm. "Our objective with regard to Mamie is to have her complete her education and to be equipped to earn her own living if that should ever become necessary," Dr. Phipps declared. He warned Kenneth that he "would not countenance anything that would interrupt that course."

Despite the disapproval of her parents, Kenneth and Mamie remained engaged. They corresponded regularly during their separation and visited from time to time. Mamie's father wrote to her telling her she had "contracted a marriage that I cannot approve." His dreams for his daughter, he wrote, were for "a brilliant scholastic career; equal brilliance in your chosen field of endeavor." She would not disappoint him.

In the spring of 1938, the two young psychologists eloped. They kept the marriage a secret from Mamie's parents and the school authorities while Mamie worked to complete her B.S. degree. Mamie Phipps-Clark graduated magna cum laude from Howard University in 1938.

During the summer following her graduation, Phipps-Clark worked in the law office of William Houston, a civil rights attorney in Washington, D.C., and also made the acquaintance of the civil rights attorney and later Supreme Court Justice, Thurgood Marshall, a man who would play a significant part in Clark's career in subsequent years.

Phipps-Clark also worked in a segregated nursery for black children. Following on the research into "self-identification" of Ruth and Gene Horowitz, Phipps-Clark tested the children's development of racial identity using a coloring test and two pairs of white and brown dolls. These studies were the basis of her master's thesis, "The Development of Consciousness of Self in Negro Pre-School Children."

Clark recognized the importance of his wife's work and the two began collaborative research on children's race recognition and self-esteem. They jointly published their findings in professional journals. This led to an award of a Rosenwald Fellowship in 1939, renewed for Phipps-Clark for two subsequent years. The funds supported their continued investigations on self-esteem in black children and Phipps-Clark's pursuit of a doctorate degree at Columbia University. During these years the Clarks' first child, a daughter named Kate, was born. In 1940, Clark completed his studies at Columbia University with a Ph.D. in experimental psychology. In 1943, Phipps-Clark became the first woman and the second African American to receive a Ph.D. in psychology from Columbia. By this time the busy young couple were parents of their second child, a son named Hilton, born in 1943.

Social justice and social responsibility: A career ethic

Clark taught psychology for one semester at Hampton Institute in Virginia, but resigned due to disagreements with the administration. He then worked as a research psychologist with the Office of War Information for the federal government studying morale among black civilians. In 1942 he became a professor of psychology at City College, City University of New York, a position he held until his retirement in 1975. Clark was the first black full professor at City College.

In 1946 the Clarks founded the Northside Child Development Center in Harlem. They received financial assistance from Phipps-Clark's parents, and volunteer commitments from psychologists and social workers. The center was the first full-time child guidance center in Harlem to offer psychiatric, psychological, and casework services to children and families. One particular contribution was the Center's intelligence testing services, which provided evidence to counter the public schools' misplacement of minority children in programs for the mentally retarded. Phipps-Clark served as Center Director until her retirement in 1979.

Expert testimony at the Supreme Court

In 1950 Clark prepared the report "Effect of Prejudice and Discrimination on Personality Development" for the Mid-Century White House Conference on Children and Youth, summarizing his and his wife's work, and reviewing available literature from other researchers on the psychological effects of segregation. The material became the basis for his first book, *Prejudice and Your Child*. The Clarks were soon recognized as experts in the field, and were called upon by the NAACP Legal Defense and Education Fund to testify in several court cases challenging segregation in public schools.

Clark and others prepared a paper titled "The Effects of Segregation and the Consequences of Desegregation: A social science statement," used by NAACP attorney Thurgood Marshall in 1954 in his arguments before the Supreme Court in the consolidated desegregation cases collectively known as *Brown v. Board of Education*. Marshall's strategy was to prove to the court that actual harm was being done to schoolchildren who were subjected to legal segregation. The court cited Clark's study as the "modern scientific authority" and concluded that segregation "generates a feeling of inferiority as to their status in the community that may affect the children's hearts and minds in a way unlikely ever to be undone." It was a decision that changed the lives of African-American students for generations, and propelled Clark into a wider community of influence.

Clark was appointed by the Kennedy administration to head the Harlem Youth Opportunities project, a forerunner of the War on Poverty program. His planning document, "Youth in the Ghetto: A Study of the Consequences of Powerlessness and a Blueprint for Change," received national press attention. But political complications in funding that usurped control of the project led Clark to resign in disappointment. His two years of work on the project, however, also led to his 1965 book, *Dark Ghetto*, which Clark called "a study of the total phenomena of the ghetto."

In 1966 Clark served as the only black member of the New York State Education Department Board of Regents, where he continued as a member until 1986, working to assure equal educational opportunities for all children. He was founder and president of the Metropolitan Applied Research Center, an organization that served as an "advocate for the poor and powerless in American cities."

Clark was a prominent activist in the Civil Rights movement and helped to bring Martin Luther King, Jr. to speak at the annual meeting of the American Psychological Association in 1967. Many in the leadership of the APA strongly opposed the idea, but equivocation on issues of racial equality were not long to be tolerated. In 1970 Clark was elected President of the Association, and during his year tenure he helped to move the APA toward more social relevance in every facet of its work. At the December 1970 meeting of the Board of Directors, Clark urged the members to give highest priority to determining "ways in which psychologists and psychology can integrate the imperative for social responsibility as a dominant theme of this science and profession." His concerns led to the creation of the Board of Social and Ethical Responsibility for Psychology, the forerunner of the Board for The Advancement of Psychology in the Public Interest.

Clark has received numerous awards, including the APA Gold Medal Award, The Franklin D. Roosevelt Four Freedom Award, the NAACP Spingarn Medal, and honorary degrees from nine colleges and universities, including a 2004 honorary degree from Earlham College awarded to both Phipps-Clark and Clark to mark the 50th anniversary of their "historic contributions to the cause of equal rights for all Americans."

In April 2000, The Kenneth B. Clark Center, dedicated to "using social research to help poor communities share in the benefits of the new information economy," opened at the University of Illinois, Chicago. At the opening celebration, John Hagedorn, Associate Professor in the Department of Criminal Justice, read Clark's challenging words that illustrate the passion and ethical commitment that have been the touchstones of his life.

> It is argued that detachment and objectivity are required for the discovery of truth. But what is the value of a soulless truth? Does not truth require meaning? And does not meaning require a context of values? Is there any meaning or relevant truth without commitment? How is it possible to study a slum objectively? What kind of human being can remain detached as he watches the dehumanization of other human beings? Why should one want to study a sick child except to make him well?

THEORIES

Civil rights and social science

Main points   Kenneth Bancroft Clark, the "antiracist psychologist-activist" emerged as a prominent social scientist in the mid-twentieth century largely as a result of his role in the 1954 *Brown v. Board of Education* Supreme Court case. Clark remained a politically engaged intellectual throughout his career and boldly articulated the democratic ideal of equal rights during decades of legitimized racism and de facto segregation. Clark applied social psychology to leverage democratic social change, and followed the lead of such notable scholars as U.N. diplomat Ralph Bunche, social psychologist Otto Klineberg, and Supreme Court Justice Thurgood Marshall, with whom he shared early educational and professional relationships.

More than a decade prior to his selection as an expert witness in the Supreme Court case outlawing school segregation, Clark worked with Gunnar Myrdal, the Swedish economist commissioned in 1938 by the Carnegie Corporation to direct a two-year study of the condition of African Americans. Myrdal employed 48 writers and researchers including Ralph Bunche and Kenneth B. Clark. The resulting book, *An American Dilemma*, published in 1944, became a classic in the study of American racism and was included in the social science research supporting public school integration. Clark agreed with Myrdal about the gulf between the American ideals of democracy and brotherhood on the one hand, and the existence of racial prejudice, discrimination, and segregation on the other.

The relevant research Clark provided to the NAACP legal team was cited by the Court in a footnote to its published decision. In 1954 the Supreme Court ruled that "in the field of public education the doctrine of 'separate but equal' has no place."

The landmark decision is considered by many Constitutional lawyers and historians to be the most important U.S. Supreme Court decision of the twentieth century. It "was humane, among the most humane moments in all our history," according to federal circuit court Judge J. Harvie Wilkinson, III, author of *From Brown to Bakke: the Supreme Court and school integration, 1954–1978.*

It can also be said that Clark is among the most humane social psychologists of the twentieth century. This is evident in his articulation of a guiding philosophy of his professional life. "The appropriate technology of serious and relevant social science," Clark contends, "would have as its prime goal helping society move toward humanity and justice with a minimum irrationality, instability, and cruelty."

Early research   Clark's keen sense of justice is reflected in his lifelong activism for educational reform, and more particularly in his early work demonstrating the psychological damages inflicted on children when forced by law into separate but very unequal educational settings. His early psychological research, in collaboration with his wife, Mamie Phipps-Clark, was concerned with the nature and development of the self and the problems of ego and racial identification.

In a series of five studies, from 1939 to 1950, the two psychologists systematically examined factors relating to the racial identity of black children:

- "The Development of Consciousness of Self and the Emergence of Racial Identification in Negro Preschool Children," *Journal of Social Psychology* (1939)
- "Segregation as a Factor in the Racial Identification of Negro Pre-school Children," *Journal of Experimental Education* (1939)
- "Skin Color as a Factor in Racial Identification of Negro Pre-School Children," *Journal of Social Psychology* (1940)
- "Racial Identification and Preference in Negro Children," *Readings in Social Psychology* (1947)
- "Emotional Factors in Racial Identification and Preference in Negro Children," *Journal of Negro Education* (1950)

The Clarks developed three primary investigative methods for use in their studies of racial self-concept, following on the earlier work of psychologist R. E. Horowitz, whose study "Racial Aspects of Self-Identification in Nursery School Children" was published in 1939. The methods the Clarks used were especially suited to the very young age (three to seven

years) of the children they tested. The Clarks considered such factors as the child's racial identity, age, gender, geographic region, and educational circumstances (segregated or mixed classrooms) in the analysis of their findings.

The research methods the Clarks developed or modified include line drawings, the doll study, and the coloring test.

Line drawings   The line drawing test was a modification of the picture technique used in an earlier study by R. E. Horowitz (1939). The Clarks used three sets of line drawings in an attempt to investigate early levels in the development of consciousness of self in preschool children. Set A depicted one white boy, one colored boy, a lion, and a dog; Set B depicted one white boy, two colored boys, and a clown; Set C depicted two white boys, one colored boy, and a hen. The only differences in the line drawings of the boys was skin color.

The Clarks' subjects in the 1939 study were 150 black children, 75 each of male and female, and 50 each of three-, four-, and five-year-olds from segregated Washington, D.C. nursery schools. When asked to identify themselves or others from the drawings, the majority of children tested identified with the "colored" boy, the Clarks found. The choice of the "colored" boy increased with age while choices of the lion, dog, clown, and hen dropped off in participants by four years of age. The Clarks interpreted this result to indicate "a level of development in consciousness of self where identification of one's self is in terms of a distinct person rather than in terms of animals or other characters." The finding that the sharpest increase in identifications with the "colored" boy occurred between the three- and four-year level indicated to the Clarks that "the picture technique might not be as sensitive a device when used with five-year-olds," or that these five-year-olds "had reached a stage of self-awareness approaching a concept of self in terms of a concrete intrinsic self, less capable of abstractions or external representations."

The coloring test   The coloring test consisted of drawings of an apple, a leaf, an orange, a mouse, a boy, and a girl. In an attempt to determine the influence of skin color as another factor in racial identification of Negro preschool children, The Clarks offered children a box with 24 crayons, including the colors brown, black, yellow, white, pink, and tan. The children were divided into three groups, those with light, medium, and dark skin. Each was asked to pretend that the little girl or boy in the drawing was him- or herself, and to color the picture the same color as they were. The child was then asked to color the opposite gendered picture the color they wanted it to be. The Clarks found that the children with very light skin would choose a color similar to their own light skin, but most of the darker skinned children would color the picture with yellow or white crayons. Some children even used red or green. The Clarks concluded that the children's choice of inappropriate colors indicated some level of emotional anxiety regarding their own skin color. The dark-skinned children frequently colored the line drawing of the child a shade lighter than their own skin. The Clarks were disturbed to discover that the children's choice seemed to indicate a trend among light-skinned children "to make identifications contrary to the objective clue of their own skin color." This was evidence, the Clarks believed, of a further stage of development in self-concept where "characteristics of perceived self become modified by social factors."

In a later study the Clarks compared the test results of black children in the segregated schools of Washington, D.C. with the responses of children in racially mixed schools in New York City. The evidence indicated that the children in Washington, D.C.'s segregated schools were more aware of color than Negro children in the racially mixed schools in New York. The Clarks discovered significant differences in the color choices between northern and southern children. "Nearly 80% of southern children colored their preferences brown, whereas only 36% of the northern children did," Clark wrote.

Example   With the coloring test, children not only had to choose a crayon of a certain color, but also had to use the crayon long enough to color the drawing. Clark observed that many children spent a very long time looking at all the different colors before making a choice. Some of them, he noticed, would pick out one crayon, look at it, put it back, and then choose another one, usually of a lighter color. Clark interpreted this behavior to indicate "how deeply embedded in their personality is the conflict about what color they are and what color they want to be."

The dolls' test   The most famous of the Clarks' methods of investigation is the dolls test. The Clarks presented preschool children with four identical dolls, two brown and two white. They asked the children to identify the doll that best represented certain positive statements: "Give me the doll you like best; Give me the doll that is a nice doll; Give me the doll that looks bad"; and "Give me the doll that is a nice color." The majority of the children tested, some as young as three

years old, and living in communities as diverse as Philadelphia, Boston, Springfield, Massachusetts, and Pine Bluff, Hot Springs, and Little Rock, Arkansas, demonstrated "an unmistakable preference for the white doll and a rejection of the brown doll." The Clarks discovered that at an early age "Negro children are affected by the prejudices, discrimination, and segregation to which the larger society subjects them."

Example   Clark reported that some children, when asked to choose between white and brown dolls, reacted with such intense emotions that they became unable to finish the task. "One little girl who had shown a clear preference for the white doll and who described the brown doll as 'ugly' and 'dirty' broke into a torrent of tears when she was asked to identify herself with one of the dolls." This extreme emotional reaction, Clark noted, only occurred with northern children. When southern children were presented with a choice of dolls, they were matter of fact in making the choice. Some giggled self-consciously when choosing the brown doll as representing themselves, Clark reported. Other children merely stated flatly: "This one. It's a nigger. I'm a nigger."

Clark later recalled, as reported in the 1977 book *Simple Justice*:

> We were really disturbed by our findings, and we sat on them for a number of years. What was surprising was the degree to which the children suffered from self rejection with its truncating effect on their personalities, and the earliness of the corrosive awareness of color. I don't think we had quite realized the extent of the cruelty of racism and how hard it hit.

Clark summarized the findings of the early research on black children's self concept in the 1950 report "Effect of Prejudice and Discrimination on Personality Development" that he prepared for the Mid-Century White House Conference on Children and Youth. This report caught the attention of the NAACP legal team, who were attempting to prove that segregated schooling caused psychological damage to children.

Lining up with the majority view   Clark's further investigations into the development of racial awareness, racial identification, and racial preference in both black and white children revealed that children's racial ideas are less rigid and more easily changed than the racial ideas of adults. Clark found that children are more influenced in their opinions by the expressed opinions of the majority of their classmates, than they are by the opinion of a teacher or other person in authority.

Example   Clark studied 173 children in New York City between the ages of seven and 13. Using a simple method of drawing different lengths of lines, Clark asked the children "to estimate the length of lines, to compare one line with a standard line, and to match lines with lines of different lengths." The experimenter pitted small groups of children against other groups, an individual child against a number of other children, and a child against his teacher. Without the knowledge of the child being observed, Clark instructed one of the groups or the teacher to give obviously incorrect answers to the test. When an individual child realized that the majority of his own classmates were unanimous in making an incorrect judgment, he tended to modify his own judgments according to the opinion of the rest. When it was a teacher who tried to influence the child's judgment with an incorrect answer, however, not one of the children followed the teacher's judgment completely. Clark concluded that the study, though not concerned directly with racial attitudes, suggests that "children of this age group are more likely to be influenced by friends of their own age than by adults."

Social science and the rule of law: Desegregation

Clark strove to protect the psychological well-being of all children. Working through the summer of 1953, he gathered all the information he could find on desegregation, completing a comprehensive review of the scientific literature on the subject. He published the results of this research in an article entitled "Desegregation: An Appraisal of the Evidence" in the *Journal of Social Issues* in 1953.

Clark served on a committee of the Society for the Psychological Study of Social Issues (SPSSI), charged with preparing a social-science appendix for an NAACP legal brief to be submitted to the Supreme Court in the 1954 case of *Brown v. Board of Education*. Clark had earlier testified with other social scientists as an expert witness in several cases in the lower courts that were combined for argument before the Supreme Court in the challenge to racial integration of public schools.

The Supreme Court held in the *Brown* decision that "separate educational facilities are inherently unequal," and thus declared public school segregation a violation of the equal protection clause of the 14th Amendment of the Constitution:

No State shall make or enforce any law which shall abridge the privileges or immunities of citizens of the United States; nor shall any State deprive any person of life, liberty, or property, without due process of

law; nor deny to any person within its jurisdiction the equal protection of the laws.

"The Supreme Court, in effect, challenged boards of education, public officials, parents, educators, and all citizens who believe in democracy to re-examine American social practices in order to determine whether they damage or enhance the human potentialities of children," Clark wrote of the Court's decision. His compilation of research, including as many as 60 references, formed the basis of the social science brief that was pivotal in the Court's decision.

The social psychologists put forward two arguments in the final social science statement, according to historian John P. Jackson, Jr.:

* Segregation is psychologically damaging both to minority and majority group children.

* Desegregation will proceed smoothly and without trouble if it is done quickly and firmly.

Explanation   The status as a "rejected minority," Clark proposed, "has an unquestioned detrimental effect upon the personality of black children." In his report to the Mid-Century White House Conference on Children and Youth, Clark noted that black children subjected to segregation "often react with feelings of inferiority and a sense of personal humiliation. Many of them become confused about their own personal worth." The effect of segregation on minority group children, Clark wrote, is a "generally defeatist attitude and a lowering of personal ambitions."

Clark understood that white children also suffer significant psychological damage from the social disease of racial prejudice and segregation. In his book *Prejudice And Your Child*, he wrote that "Those children who learn the prejudices of our society are also being taught to gain personal status in an unrealistic and non-adaptive way." White children are "insidiously and negatively disturbed by these contradictions in the American democratic creed." Healthy forms of self-esteem, built on solid and realistic personal achievement, are subverted by racist attitudes. White children who establish their identity as persons and members of a group through hatred and rejection of others become blocked in the full creativity inherent in their personalities, Clark believed.

Social-science research demonstrated that "the mold of racial prejudice with its fixed social expectations was set at an appallingly early age," according to historian Richard Kluger in his book *Simple Justice*. "If anything was to be done about the problem it had to be done very early before despair and self hatred took their fatal toll."

The Supreme Court decision striking down school segregation was of vast significance for constitutional law and civil-rights litigation, and it changed the lives of generations of school children. The ruling displaced the 1896 *Plessy v. Ferguson* "separate but equal" doctrine, concluding that "whatever may have been the extent of psychological knowledge at the time of *Plessy v. Ferguson*, this finding is amply supported by modern authority." The "modern authority" the Court cited was the expert testimony of social psychologists who, "translated their political and ethical beliefs into social science, and their social science into social action," according to John P. Jackson, Jr., writing about the case in the Spring, 1998 *Journal of Social Issues*.

Yet despite the Court's findings outlawing segregation, desegregation of public schools was painfully slow in implementation. The court postponed until 1955 the specific implementation decrees, and in a separate decision, known as *Brown II*, set guidelines without deadlines for desegregation of the nation's schools.

Clark provided the court with a compilation of social scientists' perspectives on the smoothest way to desegregate the schools, but the Court, using the phrase, "with all deliberate speed," provided the means of delay in the long-overdue process of desegregation.

Clark suggested to the Court several criteria necessary for the most effective method of desegregation:

- The abolition of all segregated facilities which are so inadequate that it would be economically and otherwise inefficient to attempt to use them.

- The assignment of all remaining facilities to all individuals without regard to such arbitrary distinctions as race.

- The restriction of the time allowed for this transition to the minimum required for the necessary administrative adjustments to insure effectiveness and impartiality.

- The specification of an inflexible deadline, based on the particulars (not necessarily determined by the court) of the administrative adjustments which will take place during the interval.

Despite the social scientists' warnings, the doctrine of "separate but equal" was replaced with a doctrine of "gradualism," at a pace Clark considered "contrary to the recommendations presented by the social scientists on the strength of their findings." Throughout the South, white reaction to the Court's decision ranged from "defiance, tokenism, and gradualism, to very incremental change," according to political scientist Dr. Dwight Mullen, in his opening

remarks for the program, "Mountain Reflections on Brown vs. Board of Education: 50 Years Later," held in Asheville, North Carolina in April 2004. Resistance included "Delayed action, white flight, tracking systems, racial gerrymandering, and racial cross over," Mullen explained.

"The Asheville City School system was the first in the south to integrate the whole system at one time," according to Dr. John Holt, who served on the Asheville School Board during the period of public school desegregation. "It was not a popular decision. Not popular with anyone," Holt said.

Resistance to the desegregation order was widespread and virulent throughout the south. Nineteen senators, representing 11 States, and 77 members of the House of Representatives signed "The Southern Manifesto." The statement condemned the *Brown* decision.

> This unwarranted exercise of power by the Court, contrary to the Constitution, is creating chaos and confusion in the States principally affected. It is destroying the amicable relations between the white and Negro races that have been created through 90 years of patient effort by the good people of both races. It has planted hatred and suspicion where there has been heretofore friendship and understanding.

White segregationists began a massive campaign of resistance. The media participated with publication of IQ studies in a resurgence of the race and intelligence debates. The *Brown* decision politicized the entire decade.

In the essay "The Desegregation Cases: Criticism of the Social Scientist's Role," Clark offered an explanation for the reaction: "Those who attempt to use the methods of social science in dealing with problems which threaten the status quo must realistically expect retaliatory attacks." He predicted that some social scientists would continue to play a role in the legal and judicial process despite criticism because "they see the valid goals of the law, government, social institutions, religion, and science as identical; namely to secure for man personal fulfillment in a just, stable and viable society."

Clark's fame and stature increased dramatically in the wake of the Supreme Court decision. He was widely considered to be a social science expert on the issues of race and the process of desegregation, a status he held well into the next decade. Yet the controversy over the role social science should have played in the Supreme Court's decision on segregation continues to generate debate more than half a century following the historic Court ruling, and de facto segregation persists in the nation's schools.

Clark's 1972 book, *A Possible Reality, A Design for the Attainment of High Academic Achievement for Inner-City Students*, grew out of his work with the Metropolitan Applied Research Center, Inc. in Washington, D.C. and reflected Clark's continued concern with the educational achievements of minority and black children. "Urban public school systems," Clark wrote, have "produced hundreds of thousands of functional illiterates who are unable to compete with educationally more privileged youth on a single competitive standard."

Racial segregation continues to be "the American way of life," Clark wrote of the Washington, D.C. public schools that at the time were more than 90% black. "Whites have fled to the surrounding suburbs, and return to the city only to exercise their rights and prerogatives as controllers of the instruments of government, otherwise abandoning the city to its black minorities." This fact, according to Clark, has led to the abandonment of the "goal of attaining high-quality education through the democratic process of realistic and administratively feasible forms of desegregation."

"If we continue to frustrate these students educationally, they will be, in fact, the ingredients of the 'social dynamite' which threatens the stability of our cities, our economy, and the democratic form of government."

Articulating the principles of democracy

During his long tenure as a professor of psychology at City College, City University of New York, Clark continued to articulate his theories and to work to counter the negative effects of prejudice and discrimination. His book *Prejudice and Your Child*, published in 1955, was an attempt to provide parents with "a clear understanding of the nature of racial prejudices and the effects of these prejudices upon American society in general and upon the personality development of children."

Clark wrote in the introduction to this first book:

> The "American Creed" which emphasizes the essential dignity of the human personality, the fundamental equality of man, and the inalienable rights to freedom, justice, and equal opportunity, is clearly contradicted by the denial of these to certain human beings because of their race, religion, or nationality background.

Prejudice and Your Child has been called a "how-to" manual for parents concerned about raising children who will grow up freed from the damages of racist thinking and behavior.

In a chapter titled "What Can Parents Do?" Clark listed some requirements for white parents who wish to model and teach more positive racial attitudes:

- Parents should exercise control over expressions of his own racial feelings.

- They should face their own prejudice and recognize its manifestations.

- Parents should establish the same standards for their children's black friends as for their white friends.

- They should recognize the wide range of differences in all people and choose interracial friendships based on common interests, compatibility of personality, and other criteria relevant to friendships with members of the same race.

Dark Ghetto: *The involved observer*

In 1962 Clark was called upon by the Kennedy administration to serve as chairman of the Harlem Youth Opportunities project, a forerunner of the War on Poverty program. His planning document for the project, titled "Youth in the Ghetto: A Study of the Consequences of Powerlessness and a Blueprint for Change," received national press attention. The document was published at a time when little or nothing could be found in the social science literature to help a student understand the realities and complexities of the ghetto, Clark said. His two years of work on the project became a starting point for his 1965 book, *Dark Ghetto*, a work he described as "a study of the total phenomena of the ghetto," and "the cry of a social psychologist." To write the book, Clark returned to Harlem as an "involved observer" using "the real community, the market place, the arena of politics and power" as his laboratory to "confront and seek to understand the dynamics of social action and social change."

Explanations Clark's social science activist methodology took many forms, according to Layli Phillips, writing about Clark in the book *Defining Difference, Race, and Racism in the History of Psychology*. "Black activism has historically derived its distinctiveness from its singular focus on contesting and subverting the dehumanization and external social control of black people," Phillips contends. Characterizing the civil rights activism of the mid-twentieth century as a "decolonial struggle," Phillips points to Clark's activist methodology beginning with his days as editor of the Howard University student newspaper *Hilltop*, which he transformed "from a social register to a political organ," to his media sophistication as host of the highly rated 1963 Public Broadcasting Service series *Negro Protest*. In the program Clark hosted conversations with Malcolm X, Martin Luther King, Jr., and James Baldwin, helping to bring the ideas and challenges of these social activists to the mainstream consciousness. Clark also used his training as a social scientist to turn the dominant racist ideology and its spokespersons against the dominant power structure, according to Phillips. He did this through the use of traditional social-scientific research methodology that challenged the academic racism of other social science researchers.

In his systematic approach to the study of the Harlem ghetto, Clark used many traditional social science methods, including observation, tape recordings, and individual and group interviews. Clark sought to discover what the personal and social consequences of ghetto life were, not only for those who lacked the power to change their status, but for those who have the power but are unable or unwilling to use it for social change.

Writing in *Pathos of Power*, Clark addressed his fellow social scientists: "I ask of them that they share with me the belief that their choice in this use of their intelligence and their training brings with it an obligation to develop the behavioral sciences with that clarity, precision, and sensitivity required for an effective moral technology." Clark challenged social scientists to engage in a "disciplined human intelligence" that includes moral and ethical concerns in their approach to social psychology. This, Clark contends, is "absolutely necessary for the ultimate practicality—the survival of the human species."

Responsibilities of the social scientist

Clark described the social sciences as "the sciences of human morality." His understanding of the role of a social psychologist was influenced, among others, by psychologist Kurt Lewin, whose field theory proposed that human behavior is the function of both the person and the environment. Clark responded particularly to what he called Lewin's "insistence upon action research as an indispensable tool of verification in the social sciences."

Social scientists have a responsibility to contribute their knowledge, insights, and approach toward an effective and democratic resolution of the complex problems of society, Clark wrote in his 1974 book *Pathos of Power*. The goal of science itself is "a total concern for truth wherever it may lead, whatever it may threaten."

"I believe that it is the business of the psychologist, as it is the business of all social scientists, to be concerned with the totality of man and with the health, the stability, and the effectiveness of the human society as a whole."

Kenneth Bancroft Clark, the antiracist social scientist-activist has demonstrated in his life and his career his unapologetic advocacy and bias "in favor of respect for the life and positive potentials of the individual human being; and a bias against any form of destruction, rejection, dehumanization, and cruelty which impairs the capacity of a human being to live and love and contribute to the welfare of other human beings."

HISTORICAL CONTEXT

Racism permeated every aspect of American life throughout Clark's educational and career years. His theoretical research reflected a deep concern for the psychological damage racism inflicts on the entire community, particularly young children. He came of age during a time of entrenched racial apartheid, enforced by law and sustained by custom. As a self described "social critic and diagnostician," Clark was powerfully influenced during his years at Howard University, a center for black intellectuals and a laboratory for human rights activism. He began his psychology career energized by his concerns for social justice, social morality, and social responsibility.

"Militant dissatisfaction with the plight of blacks is what drove the place," historian Richard Kluger wrote of Howard University in his book, *Simple Justice*. "The whole atmosphere of the place was heady," Kevin Clark recalled, "and every scholar was eager to relate classroom work to social action." During the 1930s the radical activism at Howard was sufficient to raise fears of "Communist" activities, bringing calls for Congressional investigations.

Clark turned to the study of psychology with the hope that the scientific discipline might shed some light on the "intractable nature of racism," a social illness that he believed "had rotted the roots of American life North and South." However, the very discipline he embraced in his attempt to understand racism had long been used by others to justify segregation and to curtail educational and employment opportunities for people of color. G. O. Ferguson's 1916 study, *The Psychology of the Negro: An Experimental Study* found that "the Negro is yet very capable in the sensory and motor powers which are involved in manual work," and concluded that "training should be concentrated upon these capacities" for the "best return for the educative effort."

In 1917–18, psychologists administered IQ tests to tens of thousands of World War I military conscripts and concluded that white Anglo Saxons were of superior intelligence compared with other ethnic and racial groups. Princeton professor and eugenicist Carl C. Brigham, in a 1923 paper, "A Study of American Intelligence," published a racial analysis of the findings of the IQ tests. He concluded that racial mixing had contributed to a decline in American education. Such studies were used to enforce racist immigration quotas with the intent of protecting white Americans from "degeneration."

After World War I, the former military testing psychologists, now called psychometric psychologists, began testing students at all levels in the educational system. These examiners were white, and whites supplied the standards by which all Americans were measured, according to Robert V. Guthrie, in his book, *Even the Rat was White*. "Significant numbers of psychological studies during the 1920s and 1930s purported to show a relationship between white ancestry and IQ test scores of black children," Guthrie reported. The conclusion drew fire from black educators, including W. E. B. Dubois, who said he had "too often seen science made the slave of caste and race hate." Dr. Horace Mann Bond, in a 1927 article, with tongue-in-cheek parody, characterized the testing of black children as a major indoor sport among white psychologists.

Clark's early research on racial identity and self esteem was inspired by the work of his wife, Mamie Phipps-Clark. The two psychologists collaborated on several studies and published their findings as "The Development of Consciousness of Self and the Emergence of Racial Identification in Negro Preschool Children," and "Skin Color as a Factor in Racial Identification of Negro Preschool Children," in the *Journal of Social Psychology* in 1939 and 1940. "Segregation as a Factor in the Racial Identification of Negro Pre-School Children" was published in the *Journal of Experimental Education* in 1939.

In 1935, the perspective in social science regarding innate intellectual inferiority began to shift with the publication of *Race Differences* by Columbia University Social Psychologist Otto Klineberg, who concluded that "there is no adequate proof of fundamental race differences in mentality, and those differences which are found are in all probability due to culture and social environment." Klineberg was Kenneth Clark's academic advisor at Columbia University.

The economic and political crisis brought on by the Great Depression of 1929 resulted in further shifts in thinking within the field of psychology. In 1936 the Society for the Psychological Study of Social Issues (SPSSI) was established. The formal goal of the organization was the analysis of "contemporary psychological problems." Psychologists who joined the ranks of the SPSSI were deeply concerned with the social inequalities of the times and sought solutions through scientific study and action programs. The organization also served its members as a clearinghouse for employment opportunities. In 1937, Gardner Murphy and others published *Experimental Social Psychology*, helping to define the emerging new field.

Prior to World War II, Clark and many other psychologists, found work with the Office of War Information. He traveled the country to study the morale of Negro civilians. Historian Howard Zinn, in his *A People's History of the United States*, recounts the perspective of one student in a Negro college during the war years: "The Army jim crows us. The Navy lets us serve only as mess men. The Red Cross refuses our blood. Employers and labor unions shut us out. Lynchings continue. We are disenfranchised, jim-crowed, spat upon. What more could Hitler do than that?" Such was the climate of the times when Clark began his professional career as one of a very few Negro psychologists in the United States in the mid-twentieth century.

In 1945, the annihilation of the civilian population of Hiroshima, Japan, by the U.S. atomic bomb deeply troubled Clark. Writing in his 1974 book, *Pathos of Power*, he said:

> I found myself re-examining my ideas about the characteristics of human beings; the problems of justice and injustices; possible safeguards against human cruelties; the role of religion, philosophy, and science as realistic, moral, and practical barriers to human chaos and ultimate destructiveness.

It was the early research of Mamie and Kenneth Clark, published 14 years before, that provided the crucial social science evidence in the landmark 1954 civil rights victory of *Brown v. Board of Education*. As recently as the 1950s, 21 states and the District of Columbia still required or permitted racial segregation in public schools. The Clarks' research provided persuasive evidence to the Supreme Court that segregation itself means inequality. The victory was not without backlash, however.

One of the fiercest opponents to the desegregation ruling was Dr. Henry E. Garrett, a Columbia University professor and the academic advisor of Mamie Clark. Professor Garrett believed that black and white differences could not be changed by any environmental intervention.

"The field of psychology was itself a microcosm of the larger world in terms of its contending progressive and conservative factions and its various supports for and impediments to activism and social change," Dr. Layli Phillips wrote in the book *Defining Difference, Race and Racism in the History of Psychology*. And throughout Clark's career, there continued to be those psychologists who used their scientific research and expertise to bring an end to discrimination, and those others who turned their studies to the support of racist beliefs. As Andrew S. Winston wrote in his introduction to *Defining Difference: Race and Racism in the History of Psychology*, "Hatred and support for oppression could be wrapped in a value neutral cloak."

Clark served as chief project consultant for the planning stage of Harlem Youth Opportunities Unlimited for two years, beginning in 1962. He began a systematic approach to the study of the ghetto as an "involved observer" of the conditions of Harlem youth. These observations and experiences in Harlem became the starting point for his 1965 book *Dark Ghetto*. The summer of 1964 brought violent protests to American ghettos, and Clark's book provided a relevant social psychologist's view of the dynamics of ghetto life. Even after passage of the Civil Rights Act of 1964, the revolts continued. "It was so long in coming," Clark wrote, "it served merely to remind many Negroes of their continued rejection and second class status."

Clark's influence with the young black activists began to wane with the rise of the black nationalist movement in the mid 1960s. His integrationist approach was viewed with skepticism. Clark, in turn, called the separatist movement "sick, regressive, and tyrannical." He considered it a manifestation of "racial self hatred," and "a ritualized denial of anguished despair and resentment of the failure of society to keep its promises." For the social scientist and scholar Clark, the black Nationalist movement was "anti-intellectual. Its main source of energy is emotionalism rather that thought," he charged.

Clark's life and work spanned the most turbulent and violent century in human history, through years of crisis, rebellion, and "shamefully inadequate" progress in civil rights. Through it all, this remarkable social psychologist called for the "trained intellect" to be applied to the "ultimate moral question of human survival" as its highest and best use. Progress with social change is not linear, Clark contended, and many of the same racist challenges he spent a lifetime seeking to understand and eradicate are again surfacing.

"We have not yet made education a process whereby students are taught to respect the inalienable dignity of other human beings," he wrote in a 1993 article, "Unfinished Business: The Toll of Psychic Violence." Clark believes that when empathetic behavior is encouraged and rewarded, we will protect all our children from ignorance and cruelty, and by helping them to understand the commonality of being human, "we will be educating them."

CRITICAL RESPONSE

Kenneth and Mamie Phipps-Clark's primary research on racial identification and preference in black school children, published from 1939 to 1950, was replicated and extended by the work of various social scientists in the 1940s and early 1950s. The Clarks' conclusion that segregated schools cause psychological damage to black children was a view shared by 90% of social scientists surveyed in a 1948 study by M. Deutscher and Isador Chein, titled "The Psychological Effects of Enforced Segregation: A Survey of Social Science Opinion." The study also revealed that 83% of social scientists surveyed believed that racial segregation also has detrimental psychological effects on members of the privileged group.

The same year as the *Brown v. Board of Education* decision in 1954, Gordon Allport published *The Nature of Prejudice*. Allport observed that contact between groups is a necessary component to reducing prejudice. He proposed that when such contact results in a "true acquaintanceship," it is more likely to lessen bias and dispel prejudice. When the sustained contact is genuine and occurs among individuals who regard themselves as being of equal status, the prejudice is further reduced. Allport's view, known as the "contact hypothesis," became a principal argument in support of racial integration.

"To be maximally effective," Allport wrote, "contact and acquaintanceship programs should lead to a sense of equality in social status, should occur in ordinary purposeful pursuits, avoid artificiality, and if possible enjoy the sanction of the community in which they occur."

In an effort to provide empirical evidence to the NAACP about the psychological harm to black children of racial segregation, Kenneth Clark, Isador Chein, and Stuart Cook drafted the social science statement from an impressive list of 60 research references that became part of the NAACP legal brief presented to the Supreme Court. Thirty-two social scientists signed the document, agreeing in principle with the premise that legally imposed segregation is psychologically damaging to the personalities of young children.

BIOGRAPHY:

Gordon W. Allport

Gordon W. Allport (1897–1967), one of 100 Eminent Psychologists of the Twentieth Century, according to *The Review of General Psychology*, was a Harvard-educated humanist and psychologist concerned both with science and social action. His theoretical research included the study of personality and the investigation of prejudice and group conflict in both American and foreign societies. Allport believed in the uniqueness of individual personalities and promoted what he called "idiographic" methods, using interviews and observation, as well as analysis of letters and diaries, to study one person at a time.

Allport's 1937 publication, *Personality: A Psychological Interpretation*, became a bestseller among social-psychological texts. He described three types of personality traits: cardinal, reflecting the true nature of the person; central, reflecting the general nature of a person's behavior; and secondary, reflecting attitudes or behaviors inconsistent with the true nature of the individual.

His now classic text, *The Nature of Prejudice*, was published in 1954, the same year of the *Brown v. Board of Education* Supreme Court decision that declared segregated schools unconstitutional. Allport defined prejudice as "an antipathy based upon a faulty and inflexible generalization." He believed that such stereotyping and prejudgment is a regrettable, but all too human, tendency fueled by feelings of hate, envy, fear, and threat.

Allport observed that sustained contact with others is necessary to dispel prejudice, and that the opportunity to form a "true acquaintanceship" is more likely to lessen bias than mere "casual contact." Sustained contact between individuals who consider themselves to be of similar social status, and among those engaged in teamwork, provides the most likely climate to undo prejudice, Allport suggested.

"The deeper and more genuine the association," he wrote, "the greater its effect to reduce prejudice." Allport extended his study of prejudice to religion. He defined two kinds of religiosity: extrinsic, or institutionalized; and intrinsic, interiorized religious values. The institutionalized religious types, his studies show, are more likely to reveal traits of prejudice and bigotry, regardless of their religious persuasion, than individuals with a deeply interiorized religion. Allport also demonstrated a correlation between prejudice and authoritarian personalities.

Allport received his Ph.D. from Harvard University in 1922. After travel and study in Germany and England, he returned to teach at Harvard in 1924. His course, titled "Personality: Its Psychological and Social Aspects," was one of the first offered on personality theory. After a few intervening years teaching at Dartmouth, Allport returned to Harvard in 1930, where he remained until his death in 1967. He chaired the Psychology Department from 1936-1946, served as President of the Society for the Psychological Study of Social Issues (SPSSI) in 1944, and edited the *Journal of Abnormal and Social Psychology*.

Gordon W. Allport.

(Archives of the History of American Psychology. Reproduced by permission.)

Allport assisted the American Psychological Association in the late 1930s and throughout the Second World War as head of an Emergency Committee working with European refugee-scholars. He was President of the American Psychological Association in 1939, and in 1964 received the APA's Distinguished Scientific Contribution to Psychology award.

Social science activism and scrutiny

It was Clark's move into the arena of social change as an expert witness in the *Brown v. Board of Education* decision that exposed both his research findings, and the fact of their use in the Supreme Court decision, to widespread scrutiny. The debate has continued into the twenty-first century as the role of social scientists' opinions in legal and public policy issues continues to be a subject of debate and commentary in the professional journals.

Dr. Bruno Bettelheim of the University of Chicago, writing a 1956 review of Clark's book *Prejudice and*

Your Child, charged that there was "no scientific evidence that racial segregation damages the human personality." Other social scientists shared the concern, including strident voices of those scientists who promoted theories of race differences in intelligence (RDI) as grounds for segregation. Dissenting opinions also came from the legal profession, whose members were unaccustomed to social science evidence bearing so much weight in the legal decisions of the Court system.

New York University professor of law Edmond Cahn responded promptly to the *Brown* decision with a 1955 *New York University Law Review* article. With reference to the Social Science legal brief, Cahn charged that the constitutional rights upheld in the *Brown* decision should not "rest on any such flimsy foundation as some of the scientific demonstrations in these records." Cahn felt that the significance of the contribution of social science experts to the desegregation cases was exaggerated; and that the social science research conveyed little or no information beyond what he called "literary psychology."

Herbert Wechsler, writing in his 1959 book *Toward Neutral Principles of Constitutional Law*, pointed out that while *Brown v. Board of Education* ruled that racial segregation was a "denial of equality for the minorities against whom it is directed," it failed to consider the "associational rights of segregationist whites." According to law professor John C. Brittain, "Wechsler theorized that *Brown* had created a conflict between the whites' freedom of association, which presumably included the right not to associate with blacks, and certain principles of equality with respect to blacks." Wechsler sought a "neutral principle," one that could reconcile the two constitutional maxims, but concluded that this "was not likely and that there probably was a principle that would elevate racial equality over the free-association rights of segregationists," according to Brittain.

But the "most intense and specific criticism," Clark said, came from Ernest van den Haag, professor of social philosophy at New York University. He published a critical rejection of the *Brown* decision in the *Villanova Law Review*. In the 1960 article, "Social Science Testimony in the Desegregation Cases," van den Haag questioned the validity of the Clarks' findings, specifically the study results obtained from black children in segregated schools in Pine Bluff, Arkansas, compared with the same tests administered to children in the non-segregated schools of Springfield, Massachusetts. Van den Haag disagreed with the Clarks' findings that racial segregation is psychologically damaging to children. He suggested that a more accurate analysis of the comparative data would "demonstrate that the damage is less with segregation and greater with congregation." Van den Haag also objected to what he called "compulsory congregation." He proposed maintenance of separate schools for both whites and blacks and creation of additional schools open to both races.

Segregationist psychologists

"Psychology's scientific racists fought hard to provide statistical evidence to prevent racial integration in the public schools," according to Robert V. Guthrie, writing in the book *Even the Rat Was White*. One of the most prominent of the segregationist psychologists was Henry E. Garrett, a militant opponent of the 1954 Supreme Court decision. According to the Institute for the Study of Academic Racism, Garrett "used his credentials as a psychologist—and as a past president of the APA—to legitimize his opinion." Garrett was Chair of the Department of Psychology at Columbia University from 1941 to 1955, during the time Kenneth and Mamie Phipps-Clark desegregated Columbia's Ph.D. psychology program.

According to Professor Andrew S. Winston, author of "Science in the Service of the Far Right: Henry E. Garrett, the IAAEE, and the Liberty Lobby," published in the Spring 1998 *Journal of Social Issues*:

> In the 1950s Garrett helped organize an international group of scholars [the International Association for the Advancement of Ethnology and Eugenics (IAAEE)] dedicated to preventing race mixing, preserving segregation, and promoting the principles of early twentieth century eugenics and "race hygiene."

Henry Garrett persisted in his efforts to find a scientific basis for segregation throughout his career. In his tract "How Classroom Desegregation Will Work," distributed during the 1960s, Garrett "supplied weak comparative IQ test data between whites and blacks and cranial capacities to argue for the end of compensatory education programs such as Head Start."

Other anti-segregationist critics followed Garrett. Audrey Shuey, chair of the psychology department at Randolph-Macon Women's College in Lynchburg, Virginia, published a 1958 compilation of several hundred studies comparing intelligence test results for black and white Americans. In her article "The Testing of Negro Intelligence," Shuey's conclusion that the mass of data indicated racial differences in intelligence was right in line with the racist thinking of her academic advisor at Columbia, Henry E. Garrett.

A measure of self-esteem

"Racial preference behavior is not synonymous with self esteem, particularly for young children," according to Vinay Harpalani, in an essay "Simple Justice or Complex Injustice?: The Ironic Legacies of *Brown v. Board of Education*." Harpalani cites the work of several researchers, including that of Margaret Beale Spencer in the early 1980s, who found that most black children who demonstrate a preference for the white doll still score high on self-esteem measures. Harpalani contends that the Clarks' interpretation of data "was affected by an ethos of black pathology."

In a 1970 replication of the Clarks' doll study by Hraba and Grant, the researchers found that similar results to those of the Clarks' when measuring racial awareness and self identification. But when measuring for racial preference, Hraba and Grant found that black children and white children both preferred the doll of their own race. The researchers attributed this change in results to an enhanced sense of racial pride in the children.

Clinical psychologist Darlene Powell-Hopson replicated the Clarks' early findings in the doll tests. In a 1985 study, Powell-Hopson found that nearly two-thirds of black children tested preferred white dolls. Three out of four of the black children said that these black dolls looked "bad." Powell-Hopson believes that the children's preferences for the white dolls is less about self esteem than it is a reflection of a race awareness absorbed from the denigrating racial attitudes of the surrounding white culture. In another doll study in 1988, Powell-Hopson and Hopson added an element of positive reinforcement to the classic test. Whenever a child chose the black doll, the researchers encouraged the children to hold up the black doll while repeating positive statements about the doll, such as "pretty," "nice," "handsome," and "smart." When all the children were again asked which doll they preferred, both black and white children were more likely than before to choose the black doll. The opinions of others weighed significantly in their own changed opinions.

Roy L. Brooks, law professor at the University of San Diego, argues in his 1996 book *Integration or Separation: A Strategy for Racial Equality* that the Clarks' misinterpreted the dolls test when they concluded that segregation harmed the self esteem of black children. Like other earlier critics, notably Ernest van den Haag, Brooks argues that the dolls studies, if correctly interpreted, would indicate that black children in segregated schools demonstrated higher self esteem than northern children in non-segregated schools.

Brooks maintains that racial integration has failed in that it neither strengthened black identity, nor improved or equalized scholastic performance. Brooks cites what he calls "dignity harms," present in integrated schools, and the power and persistence of "white racism" as reasons for his call for a policy of limited, voluntary separation that "neither subordinates nor stigmatizes."

Sociologist Dr. Doris Y. Wilkinson, the first African-American woman to be hired as a full-time regular faculty member at the University of Kentucky, also disagrees with the Clarks' conclusion that segregated schools are psychologically damaging to black children. In a 1996 article "Integration Dilemmas in a Racist Culture," Wilkinson contends that "public school integration and the associated demolition of the black school has had a devastating impact on African-American children." Forced public school integration has impacted "their self esteem, motivation to succeed, conceptions of heroes or role models, respect for adults, and academic performance," Wilkinson says. She warns that unless rational alternatives are developed that take into account "the uniqueness of the African-American heritage," the situation will become even more destructive to the health of the children and to the nation as a whole.

Wilkinson asks, as others have, if "the constitutionality of segregation could have been questioned on grounds other than its psychological effects." She refutes the Supreme Court finding that segregated schools were "inherently unequal." The decision that declared the black school fundamentally deficient, she says, "did not apply to the dedication and capabilities of teachers, the unbiased learning environment, or the opportunities for developing healthy self-attitudes." Wilkinson also criticizes busing, a hardship borne primarily by poor and working-class children. "What could be more harmful than taking children away from familiar environments for the purposes of implementing a dominant-sector philosophy?"

Howard University psychologist W. Curtis Banks, author of the 1992 book *African American Psychology Theory, Research, and Practice*, reviewed the findings in the Clarks' doll studies. He concluded that the results could have been attributed to chance and that the children under study may not have fully understood what they were being asked to do.

In the article "Even Their Soul is Defective," published in *The Psychologist* in March 1999, social scientists Dr. Kwame Owusu-Bempah and Dr. Dennis Howitt write that "racism is undeniably harmful to black children (and adults), but it is not their self-worth that is damaged by it. Rather, it is their life chances which are restricted by racism, especially institutional racism." The British social scientists argue that psychology perpetuates racism. They contend:

> Biological racism—a belief in the hereditary inferiority of the black "race"—has been replaced within the discipline by cultural and professional racism. Black people's plight is now attributed to either their "defective culture" or psychological make-up, or both. Characterizing the Clarks' "let's pretend studies," and others like them, as "seriously flawed," Owusu-Bempah and Howitt charge that the notion of black self-hatred "is a myth that persists in theory, policy, and practice." They propose that the racist system itself must be the target for change rather than the psychology of individual children.

"I am not convinced that there has ever been strong evidence of dramatically lower self-esteem among blacks," Psychologist Bernadette Gray-Little of the University of North Carolina at Chapel Hill says. Using a technique called meta-analysis, she reanalyzed data from 261 studies assessing black self-esteem and concluded that black youth exhibited self-esteem that was at least as healthy as that of their white counterparts.

"Many people confuse self-esteem with the status a racial group occupies in society," Gray-Little said in a March 26, 2000, *Washington Post* article. "Frequently, doll tests and other devices intended to measure self-esteem instead capture participants' sense of how their racial groups are viewed by the wider society." Gray-Little also offers the hypothesis that black self-esteem may be linked to group pride, and the sense of satisfaction blacks derive from their ethnic identification.

The persistence of racism

In the more than five decades since the desegregation of American public schools, and the Civil Rights victories eliminating the Jim Crow era of racial segregation, the problems of racial inequity persist. James M. Jones, in the *Journal of Social Issues* in 1998, writes about "The New American Dilemma." Jones proposes what he calls a psychological critical race theory to explain "the gap between apparent positive racial attitudes and interracial behaviors and persistent racial inequalities." According to Jones, "Something happened on the way to racial equality."

In a 1998 PBS Frontline interview Henry Louis Gates, Jr., chair of Harvard University's Afro-American study program, recalled that

> Thurgood Marshall told his associates the day of *Brown v. Board*, "it's all over now, boys, in five years we won't even need the NAACP, we won't even need advocacy groups, we will all be members of the American mainstream." And as we know all too painfully that didn't take place.

"There are now nine times as many African Americans in prison or jail as on the day of the *Brown* decision. An estimated 98,000 blacks were incarcerated in 1954, a figure that has risen to 884,500 today," according to the Washington, D.C. advocacy group The Sentencing Project in the 2004 report, "Schools And Prisons: 50 Years After *Brown v. Board of Education*." This and other harsh realities faced by the black community help to explain an undeniable racial achievement gap in education. "When placed within the broader context of race relations in American society, Harvard Professor Pedro A. Noguera contends:

> [T]he gap is merely another reflection of the disparities in experience and life chances for individuals from different racial groups. In fact, given the history of racism in the United States, and the ongoing reality of racial discrimination, it would be even more surprising if an achievement gap did not exist. If the children of those who are most likely to be incarcerated, denied housing and employment, passed over for promotions, or harassed by the police did just as well in school as those whose lives are largely free of such encumbrances, this would truly be remarkable news. But this is not the case, and if we recognize that educational patterns generally mimic other social patterns, we should not be surprised.

The controversy continues

Criticisms of the validity of the Clarks' findings and the role of social scientists in the *Brown* decision seem to emerge on every celebrated anniversary of the historic Supreme Court decision, and numerous books and essays have been published on the issue. The book *What Brown V. Board of Education Should Have Said: The Nation's Top Legal Experts Rewrite America's Landmark Civil Rights Decision*, published in 2001, consists of essays by nine of America's top constitutional and civil rights experts writing about how they might have argued the case.

Another book, *The Inseparability of Law and Morality: The Constitution, Natural Law, and the Rule of Law* by legal scholar Ellis Washington, objects to both the validity of the Clarks' social science research and the use of social science research as evidence in the Supreme Court decision. Writing in the journal *Issues & Views* in 2003, Washington stated that the *Brown* decision "was based on the false social science of racial relativism," and the "flawed scientific research of Dr. Kenneth Clark and Dr. Mamie Phipps-Clark." Professor Washington objects to what he calls the "public policy fiction" that "black children must be allowed to attend public school with white children in order to get equally educated." He also contends that the decision of the Court should have been based on "explicit Constitutional guarantees," for which legal precedent already exists, rather than what he calls "pop psychology."

In his book *Forced Justice*, sociologist David Armor examines the impact and effectiveness of court-ordered desegregation. Armor questions the social science research, particularly the Clarks' doll studies, and the finding that low self-esteem in black children is a result of segregated classrooms. Armor contends that the court-ordered desegregation was based on questionable interpretations of the Clarks' studies.

Howard H. Kendler, in a 2002 article in the journal *History of Psychology*, questions the social activism of Kenneth Clark and other social scientists who drafted the social science statement used in the Supreme Court desegregation case. Kendler asks if the social scientists operated as "detached scientists or political advocates." John P. Jackson, Jr., author of the 2001 book *Social Scientists for Social Justice*, takes issue with Kendler's position that Clark and the other social scientists "allowed their political and social agenda to warp their scientific findings." Jackson contends that Clark and others were not making "value claims on the desirability of a given social situation," but rather, based on the available social science research, were "offering empirical evidence on the psychological impact of the social situation."

Historian James T. Patterson, in his 2001 book *Brown v. Board of Education: A Civil Rights Milestone and its Troubled Legacy*, acknowledges that the expectations for the success of integration were unrealistically high in 1954, but Patterson contends that the Supreme Court decision helped to bring substantial improvements in race relations. According to book reviewer Timothy N. Thurber, Patterson credits the Warren Supreme Court for helping to "set the stage for other branches of government to act more forcefully on behalf of racial equality."

Much of Kenneth Bancroft Clark's work was shadowed by his role in the Supreme Court desegregation cases, and the subsequent and ongoing criticisms of his research conclusions about the psychological damages to young persons brought about through legal segregation. However, his life and work was always focused on the well-being of all children, and on the elimination of racism in America. Clark worked to promote a "morally and socially responsible science." He believed that "Psychology and psychologists, together with other behavioral scientists, must dare to assume the new and difficult responsibility of serving as ombudsmen for society," and that "Psychology must

now assume its proper role of enhancing and conserving human resources without apology and with full scientific integrity."

THEORIES IN ACTION

The volatile issues of racism, racial identity, and equal protection of the law came dramatically to the forefront in the second half of the twentieth century. These issues continue to be the subject of research and public debate in the twenty-first century. The pioneering work of early social psychologists such as Kenneth Bancroft Clark and Mamie Phipps-Clark remains relevant today. It provides a starting point for continued investigations into how children develop a healthy personal and social identity and self-esteem in an increasingly multicultural environment; and what the proper role of social science is in helping to inform effective public policy change that will bring about social justice and harmony in a diverse and endangered world.

Research

"Were efforts to desegregate the public schools worthwhile?" Researchers from Teachers College, Columbia University, and the University of California, Los Angeles, interviewed 242 graduates from six racially diverse high schools across the country. The five-year study, "How Desegregation Changed Us: The Effects of Racially Mixed Schools on Students and Society," was published in 2004. Researchers asked the question of students in the class of 1980; 75% of the participants were white and 60% were non-white graduates.

"Our central finding is that school desegregation fundamentally changed the people who lived through it, yet had a more limited impact on the larger society," the researchers concluded.

> The vast majority of graduates across racial and ethnic lines greatly valued the daily cross-racial interaction in their high schools. They found it to be one of the most meaningful experiences of their lives, the best—and sometimes the only—opportunity to meet and interact regularly with people of different backgrounds.

"The Race Connection," a study by Thomas Dee of Swarthmore College, analyzed data from a "randomized field trial of the effects of class size on student performance." Dee found that both white and black students perform better on the Stanford Achievement Test when they have a teacher of the same racial background as they are. "Black students learn more from black teachers and white students from white teachers," Dee concluded. Only 8% of public school teachers nationwide are black, Dee notes, though 17% of the students are African American. This may account for the "persistent racial gap in student performance," Dee suggests.

In the commentary "The Impact of 'Brown'; Fifty Years Later, Still More Rhetoric Than Commitment," in *The Post Standard* of Syracuse, New York, Linda Carty, and Paula C. Johnson write that "The societal context of the Brown decision in 1954 parallels Reconstruction in that despite grand legal pronouncements on racial equality, both eras suffered from lack of political, institutional, and individual will to enforce rights and opportunities for people of color." Carty, chair of the African-American Studies Department at Syracuse University, and Johnson, professor of law at Syracuse, cite the Harvard Civil Rights Project report indicating that children of color, particularly African Americans and Latinos, "attend substantially segregated and poorly funded primary and secondary schools." For Brown to have worked, the writers contend, would have "necessitated government policy addressing inequality in housing, employment, social welfare, health care, the legal system, and many other realms of society."

Professor Pedro A. Noguera of Harvard University, and Antwi Akom, a doctoral student in Sociology at the University of Pennsylvania, in 2000 studied "The Significance of Race in the Racial Gap in Academic Achievement," an issue, they say, that has historically generated "controversy and paralysis for those charged with figuring out what should be done." It is at the level of policy and practice, the researchers contend, that lack of clarity on these issues is most apparent. The researchers put forth many explanations for the disparities in achievement that have been found in almost every school in the nation. They cite the close correspondence between test scores and broader patterns of social inequality within American society, particularly manifest in "woefully inadequate" inner-city schools. But the racial achievement gap is evident also in the scores of middle-class African-American and Latino students.

Noguera and Akom suggest that the explanation may be found in understanding "the ways in which children come to perceive the relationship between their racial identities and what they believe they can do academically. Racial images rooted in stereotypes, which diminish the importance of intellectual pursuits," the researchers believe, "limit the aspirations of young African-American and Latino students." Noguera and

Akom believe that if racial inequities are ever to be eliminated, "it is more likely to occur in education than in any other sector." Public education, they contend, "remains the most democratic and accessible institution in the country," and "all that remains of the social safety net for poor children."

The evolution of identity

Psychologist Dr. Eun Rhee, of the University of Delaware, received a five-year grant in 2002 to study the development of racial identity in children and its impact on their well-being. The project, "Racial Identity and Psychosocial Consequence," is funded by the National Institute of Mental Health. Rhee is concerned with the "development of social identities, particularly racial identity, in African-American, Asian-American, and European-American children." Rhee's research focuses on the "role of social factors, such as perceptions of group status; on the development of racial identity; and the impact of this identity on mental health, social behavior, and development of inter-group attitudes." She is investigating how racial identity evolves and how children of color learn to cope with perceived discrimination as they grow older. Her methods also include interviews with parents to discover what ideas and support they offer their children, and what degree of preparation they offer to help their children cope with discrimination.

Raising unbiased kids is an outcome of diversity education that begins in the home, according to Derek S. Hopson and Darlene Powell Hopson. The Hopsons are authors of the book *Teaching Your Children to be Successful in a Multicultural Society*. They suggest that positive and realistic interactions with others are a necessary part of preventing racial distrust, conflict, aggression, and violence.

"Segregation is damaging to the individual, damaging to the society's claim to justice, and damaging to whites as well as blacks," Clark said in a 1995 *Washington Post* interview. However, de facto segregation persists throughout the country and at all levels of society, perpetuating racial tensions.

In a 2003 study published in the *Journal of Social Psychology*, K. Kowalski assessed preschool-aged children's attitudes toward their own group and two different ethnic or racial groups: Japanese and Mexican. The study was done in the Southwest United States with 70 children (32 girls and 38 boys) from three to five years of age. The authors used dolls and asked the children to assign positive and negative traits to the dolls that represented their own racial or ethnic group and that of two other groups. When forced to choose between their own group and an ethnically or racially different group, the researcher discovered, the children clearly favored their own group. Kowalski concludes that "young children's positive own-group feelings do not necessarily entail negative out-group attitudes."

Thandeka, author of *Learning to be White: Money, Race, and God in America*, believes that racism is not innate, but something we are taught through custom and beliefs that are passed from one generation to the next. Thandeka is a minister and teacher at Meadville-Lombard Theological School in Chicago. Like Clark, Thandeka believes that whites, too, are harmed by racism "The first racial victim of the white community is its own child," she said in a 2004 interview in the Dallas Morning News. Children are forced to adapt to the way of life of the community or risk being ostracized, she says. Thandeka, whose name was given her by Archbishop Desmond Tutu, believes that much of the racial division in America is due to social and family pressures to declare a racial identity at an early age. The chosen racial identity becomes a marker that divides us, she said. Thandeka suggests that an obsession with problems of race can divert us from the realities of class in our society. Many whites are as much victims of an unjust economic order as blacks, she notes.

Debra Dickerson, author of the book *The End of Blackness: Returning the Souls of Black Folk to Their Rightful Owners*, believes that it is "everybody's responsibility to fight injustice. This is America," she says. "We pride ourselves on being the land of the free. It's not just black people's job to fight against injustice. It's America's job because it hurts America." Dickerson discussed her book on National Public Radio with host Tavis Smiley in January 2004. Dickerson proposes:

> I think we ought to have a moratorium on mentioning white folk. And that's really, really hard to do, and again it's not because racism is not a problem. Racism is a problem. But the answer is not to constantly be trying to fix other people's hearts and minds. All we need for them to do is leave us alone. They don't have to learn to love us. We have to learn to love and believe in ourselves.

"Americans are choosing to opt out of any racial classifications on the Census, college applications, and the SAT," according to Eric Wang writing in *The Cavalier Daily*, the online publication of the University of Virginia. "We cannot talk about racial progress without using the language of race and collective identities," he says. Given the growing diversity and multicultural face of America, the five commonly used racial categories, according to Wang, "fail to capture the full array of diversity in our society."

CHRONOLOGY

1914: Clark born in Panama.

1919: Comes to America with mother and sister.

1931: Graduates from high school in New York City.

1934: Earns his bachelor's degree from Howard University. Gains his master's the following year.

1950: Publishes "Effect of Prejudice and Discrimination on Personality Development" for the Mid-Century White House Conference on Children and Youth.

1954: *Brown v. Board of Education* uses Clark's studies as a basis for school desegregation.

1955: First edition of Kenneth Clark's book *Prejudice and Your Child* published as Clark's first public scientific commentary.

1959: Elected president of the Society for the Psychological Study of Social Issues.

1961: Awarded the Spingarn Medal by the NAACP.

1965: Publishes *Dark Ghetto*.

1971: Elected president of the American Psychological Association. Clark has been the only black to serve in that capacity.

1974: Publishes *Pathos of Power*.

1975–1995: Serves on the New York Board of Regents.

1994: Receives the APA Award for Outstanding Lifetime Contribution to Psychology.

2004: 50th anniversary of *Brown v. Board of Education*. Kenneth Bancroft Clark and Mamie Phipps-Clark awarded honorary degrees from Earlham College to mark their "historic contributions to the cause of equal rights for all Americans."

Relevance to modern readers

Discussions about the issue of race and identity, and debates about who is harmed and who benefits from segregation, continue, even as the demographics of America change to reflect a diversity of racial and ethnic blending that defies easy classification. For Census 2000, 63 possible combinations of the six basic racial categories exist, including six categories for those who report exactly one race, and 57 categories for those

BIOGRAPHY:
Claude Steele

Claude Steele, Professor and Chair of the Department of Psychology at Stanford University, has focused his theoretical research for decades on the social psychology of race and race relations. Steele's interest in the processes of self-evaluation, and the coping mechanisms that come into play when self-image is threatened, has led to his general theory of self-affirmation and the concept he calls "stereotype threat." This threat, according to Steele, "characterizes the daily experiences of black students on predominantly white campuses and in a predominantly white society."

Stereotype threat is a very general effect, Steele's studies reveal, and "one that is undoubtedly capable of undermining the standardized test performance of any group negatively stereotyped in the area of achievement tested by the test." This detrimental effect is magnified in those students most invested in succeeding on the particular test. "Relying on these tests too extensively in the admissions process will preempt the admission of a significant portion of highly qualified minority students," Steele contends.

Stereotype threat occurs when an individual expects that he or she is being perceived through the lens of a negative stereotype and becomes anxious about being judged on that misperception, or fears that he or she may somehow do something that might confirm the stereotype. Steele's studies indicate that "when this threat occurs in the midst of taking a high-stakes standardized test, it directly interferes with performance." Steele has found that the deleterious effects of stereotypes goes beyond any effects of socioeconomic disadvantage that individuals may be burdened with, and affects "even the best prepared, most invested students," many from middle-class backgrounds.

Steele's study, "Stereotype threat and the intellectual test performance of African Americans," was published in 1995 in the *Journal of Personality and Social Psychology.* "A Threat in the Air: How Stereotypes Shape the Intellectual Identities and Performance of Women and African Americans," was published in 1997 in the *American Psychologist.* He has published in a variety of professional journals and collaborated on books and articles on the subjects of race, stereotype, and the testing and schooling of black Americans.

As a result of his considerable research, Steele was called on to provide expert testimony in affirmative action cases brought against the University of Michigan, where he concluded that

> Standardized admissions tests such as the SAT, the ACT, and the LSAT are of limited value in evaluating "merit" or determining admissions qualifications of all students, but particularly for African-American, Hispanic, and American-Indian applicants for whom systematic influences make these tests even less diagnostic of their scholastic potential.

Claude Steele received his Ph.D. in social psychology from Ohio State University in 1971. He has served as President of the Western Psychological Association, on the board of directors of the American Psychological Society, and on the executive committee of the Society of Experimental Social Psychologists. He is a recipient of numerous awards including the 1996 Gordon Allport Intergroup Relations Prize and the William James Fellow Award of the American Psychological Society, for "brilliant research" that "exemplifies the very best of problem-based theoretical work."

Claude Steele. (Stanford University. Reproduced by permission.)

---

who report two or more races. Clearly the issue of identity is still in flux. Perhaps Kenneth and Mamie Clark's brown and white dolls will need multi-hued companions to reflect the changing face of America.

New ways of understanding black identity and community are emerging, according to psychologist Layli Phillips, and black Americans are finding ways to articulate their sometimes very profound differences. Yet the persistence of racism and discrimination still provides a foundation for common cause.

The relevance of the life and work of Kenneth Clark is perhaps less in the doll study experiments, for

Kenneth Bancroft Clark working with colleagues. (AP/Wide World Photos Reproduced by permission.)

which he is most famous, but more in his consistent call for a social psychology that is relevant and responsive to the problems of society, and capable of informing public policy that will bring about a more just and humane society.

BIBLIOGRAPHY

Sources

Andersen, Margaret L., and Howard F. Taylor. "Socialization and Self Esteem." *Sociology: Understanding a diverse Society.*, 3rd ed [cited April 26, 2004]. http://164.78.63.75/Samples/0450203AndersenTaylorUDS3Ch3.pdf.

Andrews, Louis. "Why not Limited Separation?" *Stalking the Wild Taboo.* A review of *Integration or Separation: A Strategy for Racial Equality,* by Roy L. Brooks [cited April 17, 2004] http://www.1rainc.com/swtaboo/library/lra_si.html.

"Back to neighborhood schools, 'with all deliberate speed.'" *Issues&Views* January 2003. [cited April 24, 2004] http://www.issues-views.com/index.php/sect/22000/article/22052.

Beggs, Gordon. "Novel Expert Evidence in Federal Civil Rights Litigation." *The American University Law Review* 45, 1995 [cited April 11, 2004] http://varenne.tc.columbia.edu/class/common/dolls_in_brown_vs_board.html.

Benjamin, Ludy T., Jr., and Ellen M. Crouse. "The American Psychological Association's Response to *Brown v. Board of Education.* The Case of Kenneth B. Clark." *American Psychologist* 57, no. 1 (January 2002): 38–50.

Bornstein, David. "Attacking the Cancer of Ethnic Bias: Schools as Laboratories." *Changemakers.net Journal* December 1999. [cited April 25, 2004] http://www.changemakers.net/journal/99december/bornstein.cfm.

Brittain, John C. "Direct Democracy By The Majority Can Jeopardize the Civil Rights of Minority or Other Powerless Groups." *New York University School of Law.* [cited April 26, 2004]. http://www.law.nyu.edu/journals/legislation/articles/vol1num1/brittain.pdf.

"Brown v. Board of Education." *Africana: Gateway to the Black World.* [cited April 12, 2004] http://www.africana.com/research/encarta/tt_100.asp.

"Brown v. Board of Education." *Civnet.* [cited April 20, 2004] http://www.civnet.org/resources/tach/basic/part6/36.htm.

Carty, Linda, and Paula C. Johnson. "The Impact of 'Brown'; Fifty Years Later, Still More Rhetoric Than Commitment." *The Post-Standard.* April 15, 2004 [cited April 27, 2004] http://0-web.lexis-nexis.com.wnclnwncln.org/universe/document?_m=cb4f494l3lb755f71f7257f3157e9.

"Clark Center Opening, Focus on Social Responsibility in Research." [cited April 11, 2004] http://gangresearch.net/Archives/documents/field/Soul.html.

Clark, Kenneth B. *Dark Ghetto.* New York: Harper & Row Publishers, 1965.

Clark, Kenneth B. *Pathos of Power.* New York: Harper & Row Publishers, 1974.

Clark, Kenneth B. *Prejudice and Your Child.* New York: Beacon Press, 1963. Wesleyan University Press, 1988.

Clark, Kenneth B. "Unfinished Business: The Toll of Psychic Violence." *Newsweek* 121, no. 2 (Jan. 11, 1993): 38.

Clark, Kenneth B., and Mamie K. Clark (1939). "The development of consciousness of self and the emergence of racial identification in Negro preschool children." *Journal of Social Psychology, S.P.S.S.I. Bulletin* (10) 591–599. *Classics in the History of Psychology.* [cited April 11, 2004] http://psychclassics.yorku.ca/Clark/Self-cons.

Clark, Kenneth B., and Mamie K. Clark (1940). "Skin Color as a Factor in Racial Identification of Negro Preschool Children." *Journal of Social Psychology, S.P.S.S.I. Bulletin* (11)159–169. *Classics in the History of Psychology.* [cited April 13, 2004] http://psychclassics.yorku.ca/Clark/Self-cons.

Clark, Kenneth Bancroft, and MARC staff. *A Possible Reality: A Design for the Attainment of High Academic Achievement for Inner-City Students.* New York: Emerson Hall, 1972.

"Claude Steele has Scores to Settle." *NY Times Magazine.* September 17, 1995 [cited April 15, 2004] http://www.cs.appstate.edu/`sjg/class/1010/we/stats/stereotype.html.

"Consensus Panel on Improving Race Relations in the Nation's Schools, College, and Universities." *RE:AERA.* [cited April 15, 2004]. http://www.aera.net/about/whoswho/racere100.htm.

Cross, June. "Interview Henry Louis Gates, Jr." *Frontline: The Two Nations of Black America.* [cited April 26, 2004] http://www.pbs.org/wbh/pages/frontline/shows/race/interviews/gates.html.

Dee, Thomas S. "Study Finds That Students Score Higher on Tests, if They Have Teachers Who Share Their Racial Background." *Business Wire.* February 17, 2004. [cited April 27, 2004] http://0-web.lexis-nexis.com.wncln.wncln.org/universe/document?_m=3d08ac866aa020a253e94d63222d.

Guthrie, Robert V. *Even the Rat was White: Historical View of Psychology,* 2nd ed. Boston: Allyn&Bacon, 1998, 1976.

Hamilton, Kendra. "Fresh takes on law, IQ and race. (Book Review)." *Black Issues in Higher Education.* Nov. 21, 2002 [cited April 23, 2004] http://www.findarticles.com/cf_0/m0DxK/20_19/95148368/pl/article.jhtml?term.

"Harlem 1900–1940, Exhibition: Marcus Mosiah Garvey." *The Schomburg Center for Research in Black Culture.* [cited April 13, 2004] http://www.si.umich.edu/CHICO/Harlem/text/garvey.html.

Harpalani, Vinay. "Simple Justice or Complex Injustice?: The Ironic Legacies of *Brown v. Board of Education.*" [cited April 17, 2004] http://convention.allacademic.com/aera2004/AERA_papers/AERA_3095_13774a.PDF.

Hendrie, Caroline. "'Doll man' secured the role of social scientists." *Education Week* 18, no, 28 (March 24, 1999): 34.

"Henry Garrett and the APA." *Biographies: Institute for the Study of Academic Racism.* [cited April 25, 2004] http://www.ferris.edu/isar/bios/Cattell/garrett.htm.

"Honorary Degrees to Clarks Recognize Crucial Work, *Brown* Anniversary." *Earlham College, News from Public Affairs.* April

7, 2004. [cited April 16, 2004] http://www.earlham.edu/`publicaf/clarks040704.html.

Hopson, Derek S., Ph.D., and Darlene Powell Hopson, Ph.D. "Raising Unbiased Kids: How parents and schools can teach diversity." *FamilyFun.com.* http://jas.family.go.com.

"How Desegregation Changed Us: The Effects of Racially Mixed Schools on Students and Society." *Teachers College, Columbia University..* [cited April 27, 2004] http://www.tc.edu/newsbureau/features/wells033004.htm.

"The Hraba and Grant Page." *AS Psychology..* [cited April 27, 2004] http://www.holah.karoo.net/hraba.htm.

"Human Intelligence: Arthur Jensen." *Human Intelligence.* [cited April 20, 2004] http://www.indiana.edu/~intell/jensen.shtml.

Jeffers, Jr., Gromer. "Howard University is steeped in a history of activism." *The Dallas Morning News.* April 17, 2004 [cited April 18, 2004]. http://www.dallasnews.com/sharedcontent/dws/fea/texasliving/stories/041804dnlivcampuscrawl.d4b18.ht.

Jackson, Jr., John P. "Creating a consensus: psychologists, the Supreme Court, and school desegregation, 1952–1955." *Journal of Social Issues* (Spring 1998).

Jackson, Jr., John P. "Facts, Values, And Policies: A Comment on Howard H. Kendler (2002)." *History of Psychology* 6, no. 2 (2003): 195–202. [cited April 13, 2004] http://comm.colorado.edu/jjackson/research/kendler.pdf.

Jackson, Thomas, reviewer. "The Children's Crusade." *American Renaissance* 6, no. 12, December 1995. [cited April 20, 2004]. http://www.commonsenseclub.com/Childrens.html.

Jones, James M. "Psychological knowledge and the new American dilemma of race. (race-neutral vs. race-conscious social policies)." *Journal of Social Issues* (Winter 1998).

"Kenneth B. Clark, activist, psychologist and author." *The African American Registry.* [cited April 8, 2004] http://www.aaregistry.com/african_american_history/283/Kennth_B_Clark_activist_psychologist_and_author.

"Kenneth B. Clark and Mamie Phipps-Clark." *Columbia 250, C250 Celebrates Columbians Ahead of Their Time.* [cited April 8,2004] http://c250.columbia.edu/c250_celebrates/remarkable_columbians/kenneth_mamie_clark.html.

Kluger, Richard. *Simple Justice, The History of Brown v. Board of Education and Black America's Struggle for Equality.* New York: Vintage Books, 1977.

Kowalski, K. "The emergence of ethnic and racial attitudes in preschool-aged children." *Journal of Social Psychology* 143, no. 6 (Dec. 2003): 677–90. [cited April 28,2004] http://0-web.lexis-nexis.com.wncln.wncln.lrg/universe/document?m=660f53ec8ee0cd84f2d35bf5a4982.

Lagemann, Ellen Condliffe, and Lamar P. Miller, editors. *Brown v. Board of Education, The Challenge for Today's Schools.* New York: Teachers College Press, Columbia University, 1996.

Louis, Debbie. *And We Are Not Saved.* 25th Anniversary Edition. Columbia, Maryland: The Press at Water's Edge, 1970, 1997.

Lowery, Charles D., and John F Marszalek. "Clark, Kenneth Bancroft." *LexisNexis.* [cited April 8, 2004] http://0-cisweb. lexis-nexis.com.wncln.wncln.org/histuniv/DocListDocument.asp?_rsrch=%3cD%3a_srch.

"Mamie Clark, a supporter of the black child!" *The African American Registry*. [cited April 11, 2004] http://www.aaregistry.com/african_american_history/2196/Mamie_Clark_a_supporter_of_the_Black_child.

"Mamie Phipps-Clark (1917–1983)" [cited April 14, 2004] http://www.arches.uga.edu/˜acrobert/home.html.

Mendelsohn, Jim. "Harlem, New York." *Africana: Gateway to the Black World*. [cited April 12, 2004] http://www.africana.com/research/encarta/tt_020.asp.

"NABSE Hall of Fame to Spotlight Distinguished African-American Educators." *National Alliance of Black School Educators and Simon&Schuster Honor Living Legends Kenneth B. Clark, Willie W. Herenton, and Marva N. Collins*. PR Newswire Association, Inc. 1995. [cited April 8, 2004] Info Trac Web.

Noguera, Pedro A., and Antwi Akom. "The Significance of Race in the Racial Gap in Academic Achievement." *In Motion Magazine*. [cited April 26, 2004] http://www.inmotionmagazine.com/pnaa.html.

Owusu-Bempah, Kwame, and Dennis Howitt. "Even their soul is defective." *The Psychologist Online* 12, no. 3 (March 1999). British Psychological Society. [cited April 24, 2002]. http://www.bps.org.uk/publications/thepsychologistdet.cfm?ID=90.

Parsons, Talcott, and Kenneth B. Clark, editors. *The Negro American*. Boston: Houghton Mifflin Company, 1966.

Pettigrew, Thomas F. "Gordon Willard Allport: A Tribute. *Journal of Social Issues* 55, no. 3 (Fall 1999): 415.

Pickren, Wade E., and Henry Tomes. "The Legacy of Kenneth B. Clark to the APA, The Board of Social and Ethical Responsibility for Psychology." *American Psychologist*. January 2002. [cited April 11, 2004] http://www.apa.org/journals/amp/amp5751.pdf.

Plucker, J. A., editor (2003). "Arthur Jensen." *Human intelligence: Historical influences, current controversies, teaching resources*. [cited April 20, 2004] http://www.indiana.edu/~intell.

"Professional Profile, Claude Steele." *Social Psychology Network*. [cited April 15, 2004] http://steele.socialpsychology.org.

"Professor researches the effect of racial identity on children." *UDAILY*. University of Delaware. [cited April 24, 2004] http://www.udel.edu/PR/UDaily/01-02/rhee112202.html.

Ragland, James. "If Racism Is Learned, Can We Unlearn It?" *The Dallas Morning News*. March 30, 2004 [cited April 27, 2004] http://0-web.lexis-nexis.com.wncln.wncln.org/universe/document?_m=d410fd0e4a227d0c4f571a608b28d.

"Segregation Ruled Unequal, and Therefore Unconstitutional." *Psychology Matters. American Psychological Association*. [cited April 11, 2004] http://www.psychology matters.org//clark.html.

"Schools and Prisons: 50 Years After *Brown v. Board of Education*." *The Sentencing Project*. [cited April 24, 2004] http://www.sentencingproject.org.

Shea, Christopher. "I am Somebody!" *Salon*. [cited April 11, 2004] http://archive.salon.com/health/feature/2000/06/02/black_self_esteem/print.html.

"The Southern Manifesto." *Congressional Record*. 84th Congress Second Session. Vol. 102, part 4, (March 12, 1956). Washington, D.C.: Governmental Printing Office, 1956. 4459–4460. [cited April 20, 2004] http://www.people.fas.harvard.edu/~bnjohns/Southern Manifesto.htm.

Spangler, Michael, et al. "Kenneth Bancroft Clark. A Register of His Papers in the Library of Congress." *The Library of Congress*. [cited April 12, 2004] http://lcweb2.loc.gov/cgi-bin/faidfrequery/r?faid/faidfr:@field(DOCID=ms998002000.

"The Spingarn Medal, 1915–2002." *World Almanac & Book of Facts* 2003, p. 295.

Thurber, Timothy N. "Review of James T. Patterson, Brown v. Board of Education: A Civil Rights Milestone and its Troubled Legacy," H-Pol, H-Net Reviews, October, 2001. [cited April 19, 2004] http://www.h-net.msu.edu/reviews/showrev.cgi?path=177111003348185.

Steele, Claude. "Expert Report of Claude M. Steele, Gratz, et al. v. Bollinger, et al., No 97-75321 (E.D. Mich.); Grutter, et al. v. Bollinger, et al., No. 97-75928 (E.D. Mich.)." [cited April 16, 2004] http://www.umich.edu/˜urel/admissions/legal/expert/steele.html.

Steele, Claude M. "Race and the Schooling of Black Americans." *The Atlantic Monthly* 259 (April 1992): 67–78. [cited April 15, 2004] http://www.theatlantic.com/politics/race/steelel.htm.

Talmadge, William Tracy. "Francis Cecil Sumner." *Project for History of Psychology*. [cited April 13, 2004] http://www.arches.uga.edu/~tmoney/index.html.

Teslik, Lee Hudson. "Equal but Separate: Cities face persistent racial self-segregation." *Harvard Political Review* January 1, 2004. [cited April 17, 304] http://www.hpronline.org/news/2002/05/14/Cover/Equal.But.Separate-251828.shtml.

Tomes, Dr. Henry. "In the public interest, Recognizing Kenneth B. Clark's legacy." *APA ONLINE, Monitor on Psychology* V. 33, No. 11, December 2002. [cited April 8, 2004] http://www.apa.org/monitor/dec02/itpi.html.

Tavis Smiley. "Debra Dickerson discusses her book, *The End of Blackness*." *National Public Radio*. January 22, 2004 [cited April 27, 2004] http://0-web.lexis-nexis.com.wncln.wncln.org/universe/document?_m=2bcce4e402b1068871fac95a81840.

"UNCA Sponsors Program on Asheville's Segregation, Desegregation; Dwight Mullen to Give Talk on Brown vs. Board of Education." *The University of North Carolina Asheville*. [cited April 21, 2004] http://www.unca.edu/news/releases/2004/brown.html.

Wang, Eric. "Rejecting Race." *The Cavalier Daily Online*. April 14, 2004 [cited April 16, 2004] http://www.cavalier-daily.com.

Washington, Ellis. "The Brown v. Board of Education Fraud: Pop psychology masquerading as legal reasoning." *Issues & Views*. July 15, 2003 [cited April 17, 2004] http://www.issues-views.com.

Weiss, Adrian. "Mamie Phipps-Clark 1917–1983." *Women's Intellectual Contributions to the Study of Mind and Society*. [cited April 11, 2004] http://www.webser.edu/~woolflm/mamieclark.html.

Whiteley, John M. "Intelligence In The Service of Love and Kindness. Kenneth B. Clark." *Quest for Peace Video Series.* 1985 [cited April 8, 2004] http://sun3.lib.uci.edu/racyberlib/ Quest/interview-kenneth_b_clark.html.

Wilkinson, Doris Y. "Are School Integration Efforts Doomed to Failure?" *Issue.* from "Integration Dilemmas in a Racist Culture." *Society.* March/April 1996 [cited April 24, 2004] http://www.mhhe.com/socscience/english/allwrite3/seyler/ssite /seyler/se04/race.pdf.

"William James Fellow Award: Claude Steele." *American Psychological Society.* [cited April 15, 2004] http://www. psychologicalscience.org/awards/james/citations/steele.cfm.

Winston, Andrew S., ed. *Defining difference: Race and racism in the history of psychology.* Washington, D.C.: American Psychological Association, 2004.

Zinn, Howard. *A People's History of the United States.* New York: Harper Perennial, Harper Collins Publishers, 1980.

Further readings

Armor, David. *Forced Justice: School Desegregation and the Law.* Oxford University Press, 1995.

Clark, Kenneth Bancroft. *Dark Ghetto: Dilemmas of Social Power.* Middletown, Connecticut: Wesleyan University Press, 1989.

Clark, Kenneth Bancroft. *The Negro Protest: James Baldwin, Malcolm X, Martin Luther King talk with Kenneth B. Clark.* Boston: Beacon Press, 1963.

Clark, Kenneth Bancroft. *Pathos of Power.* New York: Harper and Row, 1974.

Clark, Kenneth Bancroft. *Prejudice and Your Child.* Boston: Beacon Press, 1957.

Clark, Kenneth B., and Mamie K. Clark (1939). "The development of consciousness of self and the emergence of racial identification in Negro preschool children." *Journal of Social Psychology, S.P.S.S.I. Bulletin* 10: 591–599. *Classics in the History of Psychology.* http://psychclassics.yorku.ca/Clark/Self-cons.

Clark, Kenneth B., and Mamie P. Clark (1947). "Racial identification and preference in Negro children," Reprinted E. M. Maccoby, T. M. Newcomb, and E. L. Hartley, editors, (1958). *Readings in social psychology,* 3rd ed.

Clark, Kenneth B., and Mamie K. Clark (1940). "Skin Color as a Factor in Racial Identification of Negro Preschool Children." *Journal of Social Psychology, S.P.S.S.I. Bulletin* 11 :159–169. *Classics in the History of Psychology.* http://psychclassics. yorku.ca/Clark/Self-cons.

Guthrie, Robert V. *Even the Rat was White: A Historical View of Psychology.* Boston: Allyn & Bacon, 1998, 1976.

I. Bulletin e consistento, and Jackson, Jr., J. P. *Social Scientists for Social Justice: Making the Case Against Segregation.* New York: New York University Press, 2001.

Kluger, Richard. *Simple Justice, The History of Brown v. Board of Education and Black America's Struggle for Equality.* New York: Vintage Books, 1977.

Spangler, Michael, et. al. "Kenneth Bancroft Clark. A Register of His Papers in the Library of Congress." *The Library of Congress.* [cited April 12, 2004] http://lcweb2.loc.gov/cgi-bin/faidfre-query/r?faid/faidfr:@field(DOCID=ms998002000.

Valdes, Francisco, Jerome McCristal Culp, and Angela P. Harris, eds. *Crossroads, Directions, and a New Critical Race Theory.* Temple University Press, 2002.

Winston, Andrew S., ed. *Defining Difference: Race and Racism in the History of Psychology.* Washington, D.C.: American Psychological Association, 2004.

Sigmund Schlomo Freud

1856–1939

AUSTRIAN PHYSICIAN, PSYCHIATRIST

VIENNA UNIVERSITY, M.D., 1881

BRIEF OVERVIEW

Although Sigmund Freud was not the first person to formally study psychology, many consider him the most pivotal figure in the development of the field as we know it today. Freud changed the way society has come to think about and treat mental illness. Before Freud, mental illness was thought to result from deterioration or disease of the brain. Freud changed all of this by explicitly rejecting the purely organic or physical explanations of his predecessors. Instead he believed that unconscious motives and drives controlled most behavior.

During a career that spanned 58 years, beginning with an earned medical degree in 1881 and continuing to his death in 1939, he developed and repeatedly revised his theory of psychoanalysis. Most of Freud's theory was developed from contact he had with patients seen in his private practice in Vienna. This type of "clinical" work was a radical departure from the laboratory research that was practiced by most leading psychologists of the day.

When Freud first presented his ideas in the 1890s, many of his contemporaries reacted with hostility. In fact, throughout his career, Freud faced enormous opposition to many of his ideas. Those especially controversial included notions about the role of the unconscious in behavior, childhood sexuality, and how the mind was governed (id, ego, and superego). But despite the opposition, Freud eventually attracted a group of followers that included well-known theorists

Sigmund Freud. (Copyright Hulton–Deutsch Collection/Corbis. Reproduced by permission.)

Alfred Adler and Carl Jung. Over time though, Adler and Jung distanced themselves from Freud and those loyal to him, due to theoretical disagreements with some of the core principles of psychoanalysis. Jung and Adler went on to develop their own theories of psychology.

Freud was a prolific writer and published many books and articles during his lifetime. Among the most influential books were *The Interpretation of Dreams* (1900), *Three Essays on the Theory of Sexuality* (1905), *The Ego and the Id* (1923), and *Civilization and Its Discontents* (1930). His combined writing fills 24 volumes in the standard American edition of his complete works.

Despite much controversy over his theories and psychoanalysis as a form of treatment, Freud's is considered to be one of the most influential thinkers in history. His theories on sexual development, although dismissed now by many, at the time led to open discussion and treatment of sexual matters and problems previously ignored. His stress on childhood development helped establish the importance of an emotionally nurturing environment for children. In addition, Freud's insights paved the way for other disciplines such as anthropology and sociology. Most social scientists accept his concept that an adult's social relationships are patterned after his or her early family relationships.

BIOGRAPHY

Early years

Sigmund Schlomo Freud was born on May 6, 1856, in a small town in Freiberg, Moravia, located in what is now the Czech Republic. Freud's father Jacob was 40 when Freud was born, 20 years older than Freud's mother Amalie. The patriarch of a large family, Freud's father had already been married twice, with two grown boys from his first marriage that were now older than Amalie. The dynamics of his extended family left their impression on Freud in his first years of life. In 1860 the family settled in Vienna where Sigmund, as he came to call himself, received an education emphasizing classical literature and philosophy. Little did he know that this education would eventually serve him well in developing his theories and conveying them to a wide audience.

Sigmund was the first child of Jacob and Amalie Freud. About a year and a half after Sigmund's birth another son, Julius, was born. Years later, Freud recounted memories of being extremely jealous of Julius after his arrival and admitted to having a secret wish that he could somehow rid himself of this other child who monopolized his mother's love and attention. A number of critics have proposed that Freud's early jealously of Julius played significantly in the development of his later theories on sibling rivalry. Tragically, Julius died less than a year later, on April 15, 1858. Freud later admitted that his childhood wish to be rid of his brother caused him lingering guilt throughout his life.

In December of the same year that Julius died, another child was born: Anna, the Freuds' first daughter. During the next six years, five more children, four girls and one boy, would round out the Freud family. Despite the many children his parents were responsible for, Sigmund was aware that he was the favored child.

Almost all of the details of Freud's early years stem from his own recollections. Most of the events were recounted and recorded during his pivotal time of self-analysis, following the death of his father. His self-analysis was also described in letters he had written to his colleague Wilhelm Fliess, which have since been published.

Jacob and Amalie Freud had both been raised as Orthodox Jews, but they gave their children a relatively nonreligious upbringing. At an early age, Sigmund began to distance himself from any hint of formal religion. As an adult he was firmly atheistic and at times, antagonistic regarding religion. He associated religion with superstition and was uncompromisingly committed to science as a means of measuring the cause and effect of behavior. But though he rejected formal religion, he did not reject his Jewish roots. In fact, he was proud of his Jewish identity and did not attempt to hide his Jewish heritage, though his relationship to it was purely secular.

Freud's early schooling, like that of his siblings, took place at home under his mother's direction. His father, Jacob, contributed to his education as Freud grew older. At the age of nine Freud passed the examination that allowed him to enter the Sperl Gymnasium, a German equivalent of a combined grammar and high school, with a strong emphasis on Latin and Greek. He also learned French and English and in his spare time taught himself the rudiments of Spanish and Italian. He had a keen interest in science at a young age that may have been sparked by a copy of *History of Animal Life* awarded as a school prize when he was eleven. He would frequently bring home plant and flower specimens collected during solitary walks in the nearby woods.

Despite comments in his later years that suggested his childhood was an unhappy one, he seemed to enjoy the Gymnasium. Freud, always very serious and studious, was first in his class for seven years until he graduated at age 17. His parents recognized his exceptional intellect at an early age and strongly encouraged him to pursue a scholarly career. In their quest to see him succeed, they showed obvious favoritism by giving him his own room and the privilege of using a gas light instead of candles to accomplish his schoolwork. From this point forward, Freud's singular focus was on scholarship.

In 1873, at the early age of 17, Freud entered the University of Vienna as a medical student. He had briefly considered a career in law, but found the allure of science too compelling to ignore. Although he was content to be engaged in work that might benefit humanity through working as a physician, research and the search for knowledge held a deep fascination for him.

University years

It took Freud eight years—an unusually long time—before he finally received his medical degree in 1881. Reports from friends who knew him during that time, as well as information from Freud's own letters,

suggest that he was less diligent about his medical studies than he might have been. He focused instead on scientific research. In the spring of 1876 he obtained a coveted grant to perform research at a nearby research center maintained by Vienna University. Although it wasn't necessarily the most compelling subject—studying the sexual organs of eels—Freud was nonetheless enthused by the prospect of engaging in a long-held dream to conduct research. Freud performed his assigned task satisfactorily, but without brilliant results. In 1877, disappointed at his results and perhaps less than thrilled at the prospect of dissecting more eels, Freud moved to the laboratory of Ernst Brücke, the man who was to become his first and most important role model in science.

Freud's move to Brücke's laboratory was one he never regretted. Brücke was a celebrated physiologist teaching at the University of Vienna and was regarded by Freud as the greatest authority he had ever met. According to his own account, he spent some of his happiest years in Brücke's lab. As a physiologist, Brücke was concerned with the function of particular cells and organs, not just with their structure. Brücke's work thus focused on the attempt to discover basic physical laws that governed the processes that took place in living systems.

In Brücke's laboratory, Freud worked on the anatomy of the brain and other tissues. His most important project was determining whether a certain kind of nerve cell in frogs was the same kind found in humans. In other words, did the brain cells in humans reflect a commonality with those found in "lower animals?" This project had relevance to an ongoing debate that had been sparked by Charles Darwin's *Origin of the Species*, published some 20 years earlier. Freud's work in Brücke's laboratory showed that the human and frog spinal neurons cells were of the same type. So, in a small way, Freud furthered Darwin's theory by showing that humans were genetically and historically linked to other animals. Throughout his life, Freud viewed Darwin's work as the precursor for many of his own discoveries in the development of psychoanalysis.

It was also in Brücke's laboratory that Freud first met Josef Breuer, the doctor whom Freud would later claim "brought psychoanalysis into being." Breuer was fourteen years older than Freud and had built a thriving private practice in Vienna by the time of their meeting. It was Breuer who first realized that symptoms of hysteria completely disappeared when the patient recalled and relived past emotional circumstances brought forth from the unconscious. Much of Breuer's insight along these lines was gleaned from his clinical work with a young hysterical woman he

PRINCIPAL
PUBLICATIONS

- *The Standard Edition of the Complete Psychological Works of Sigmund Freud.* 24 vols. Edited by J. Strachey with Anna Freud. London: 1953–1964.

- *Standard Edition Vol. I. Pre-Psycho-Analytic Publications and Unpublished Drafts.* 1886–1899.

- *Standard Edition Vol. II. Studies in Hysteria.* With Josef Breuer. 1893–95.

- *Standard Edition Vol. III. Early Psycho-Analytic Publications.* 1893–99

- *Standard Edition Vol. IV. The Interpretation of Dreams (I).* 1900.

- *Standard Edition Vol. V. The Interpretation of Dreams (II) and On Dreams.* 1900–01.

- *Standard Edition Vol. VI. The Psychopatholgoy of Everyday Life.* 1901.

- *Standard Edition Vol. XII. Case History of Schreber, Papers on Technique, and Other Works.* 1911–13.

- *Standard Edition Vol. VIII. Jokes and their Relation to the Unconscious.* 1905.

- *Standard Edition Vol. IX. Jensen's 'Gradiva,' and Other Works.* 1906–09.

- *Standard Edition Vol. X. The Cases of 'Little Hans' and the 'Rat Man.'* 1909.

- *Standard Edition Vol. XI. Five Lectures on Psycho-Analysis, Leonardo, and Other Works.* 1910.

- *Standard Edition Vol. XII. Case History of Schreber, Papers on Technique, and Other Works.* 1911–13.

- *Standard Edition Vol. XIII. Totem and Taboo and Other Works.* 1913–14.

- *Standard Edition Vol. XIV. On the History of the Psycho-Analytic Movement, Papers on Metapsychology and Other Works.* 1914–16.

- *Standard Edition Vol. XV. Introductory Lectures on Psycho-Analysis (Parts I and II).* 1915–16.

- *Standard Edition Vol. XVI. Introductory Lectures on Psycho-Analysis (Part III).* 1916–17.

- *Standard Edition Vol. XVII. An Infantile Neurosis and Other Works.* 1917–19.

- *Standard Edition Vol. XVIII. Beyond the Pleasure Principle, Group Psychology and Other Works.* 1920–22.

- *Standard Edition Vol. XIX. The Ego and the Id and Other Works.* 1923–25.

- *Standard Edition Vol. XX. An Autobiographical Study, Inhibitions, Symptoms and Anxiety, Lay Analysis, and Other Works.* 1925–26.

- *Standard Edition Vol. XXI. The Future of an Illusion, Civilization and its Discontents and Other Works.* 1927–31.

- *Standard Edition Vol. XXII. New Introductory Lectures on Psycho-Analysis and Other Works.* 1932–36.

- *Standard Edition Vol. XXIII. Moses and Monotheism, An Outline of Psycho-Analysis and Other Works.* 1937–39.

- *Standard Edition Vol. XXIV. Indexes and Bibliographies.* Compiled by Angela Richards, 1974. London: Hogarth Press and the Institute of Psycho-Analysis, 1953–74.

---

worked with named Anna O. According to Freud, these insights were the birth of what he later called catharsis. Freud and Breuer's professional collaboration also developed into a friendship that was nurtured by their mutual interest in music, painting, and literature and lasted for over 15 years.

In 1875, early in Freud's university career, he took his first of three trips to England. There, he visited his half-brother Emmanuel and his family in Manchester. Freud adored the English language and culture, and greatly enjoyed his visit. He returned only twice more during his lifetime. His second trip in

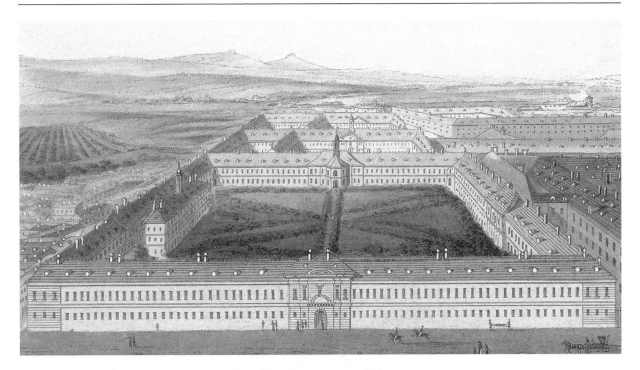

General Hospital in Vienna, Austria, where Freud spent most of his career. (Copyright Austrian Archives/Corbis. Reproduced by permission.)

1908 was also to visit his brother in Manchester. His final trip in 1938, 63 years after his first visit, occurred when the Nazi takeover of Austria in World War II forced him to flee Vienna.

Amid the years Freud worked in Brücke's laboratory, there was an unwelcome interruption to his research. In 1879 and 1880, he was forced to take a year away from his research to fulfill compulsory military service. This obligation meant that he was to be "on duty" as a doctor to attend to sick or injured soldiers as the need arose. Though he found the military service tedious due to long stretches of idle time, he struck up a relationship with a German publisher who commissioned him to translate four essays from John Stuart Mill's collected works. This allowed Freud to at least partially exercise his intellect during this hiatus from the work with Brücke.

On his return from military service to university life, Freud decided at last to sit for his medical degree. Despite an earnest desire to help people, he had previously shown no particular enthusiasm for a doctor's life. By this time he had probed into several areas of medical research without committing himself to any one field. And from evidence that has survived, it appears that his aim was not so much to make his mark in some chosen area as much as turn an opportunity into a profitable venture. He didn't doubt that he had a mission in life, but at this point he wasn't what it was.

It wasn't until the summer of 1882 that he left Brucke's laboratory, at Brücke's suggestion, to take a post at Vienna's General Hospital. While laboratory research was stimulating to Freud, he was always on the verge of poverty. Had he not been living at home during these years, it would have been very difficult for him to have supported himself on the meager wages he earned. His motivation for earning more money was not simply to build a financial reserve for its own sake, he began thinking about the possibility of marrying.

Marriage and family

In 1881 Freud made the acquaintance of Martha Bernays, the sister of one of Freud's university friends. Martha was slim and self-assured, with long dark hair and a narrow face. It seems to have been love at first sight. Martha was five years his junior and only two months after their first meeting they were secretly engaged. But both were too poor to marry and continued a long-distance relationship for another five years before marrying.

With no real prospect of ever earning a livelihood from his scientific work and desperate to marry

Martha, Freud made a painful decision. Just six months after he met her, Freud sacrificed his scientific ambitions for the woman he loved: he decided to become a doctor. At Brücke's suggestion, Freud left laboratory work and spent the next three years at Vienna General Hospital, trying his hand at surgery, internal medicine, and psychiatry, not knowing which might become his specialty.

During their engagement Freud rarely saw Martha. By some estimates, they spent four and a half of those five years apart. She had moved with her family to Hamburg in northern Germany, far from Vienna. He continued working by day, and at night he read incessantly. He also wrote long, romantic letters to Martha every day.

Martha was Freud's first love, and he conveyed a passion for her that was reciprocated by her for him. However, money became increasingly important as he contemplated how to support a partner and the children that would follow after their marriage. Seeking financial support from Freud's father was out of the question. His father had been out of work for some time and was barely supporting his own family. In fact, Freud increasingly felt the burden of needing to help support his parents and sisters in addition to his own family as time passed.

On September 14, 1886, after five years of waiting, 30-year old Sigmund Freud married Martha Bernays. And even though Freud had been trying to save money after leaving laboratory work to pay for the marriage, their celebration was largely funded by generous friends.

They quickly settled into married life by setting up a home, and soon after began a family. Freud and Martha went on to have six children over the next nine years: Mathilde, Jean Martin, Oliver, Ernst, Sophie, and finally Anna. Anna would be the only child to follow in her father's work. Martha quickly became the kind of wife for whom Freud had hoped. She raised their children and managed their household while Freud attended to his medical practice and researched his theories.

Martha also had her own convictions that emerged as their children grew and the theory of psychoanalysis took shape, however. Martha had been raised in a religious family; her grandfather had been chief rabbi of Hamsburg, Germany. Her religious upbringing formed in her a steadfast commitment to her faith that she did not relinquish. Of course, this turned out to be a life-long point of contention in her marriage with Freud, whose atheistic orientation undoubtedly created distance between them. In addition, Martha disagreed

with a number of aspects of psychoanalysis as the theory emerged. What those disagreements were in detail is not precisely known.

It was known to Freud, Martha, and others, however, that their relationship was slowly disintegrating. As Freud delved deeper into his research and explored the mysteries of behavior that still eluded him, the passion once evident in his relationship with Martha faded. Although he remained married to Martha throughout his life, his work became his mistress.

Only one question has been raised regarding Freud's faithfulness to his wife. It concerns his sister-in-law Minna, who originally came in 1895 to live with them for several months, but ended up staying for the rest of her life. Freud had stated at one point that it was Minna Bernays along with his long-time friend Wilhelm Fliess who sustained his faith in himself when he was developing psychoanalysis in the face of much opposition. Freud occasionally went on summer holidays with his sister-in-law while Martha joined them later. Some observers found it difficult to believe that their relationship was entirely platonic.

After 10 years of marriage, Freud had firmly established himself as the patriarch of his own large family. His exhaustive work to find a cure for hysteria, however, had not brought him the fame, success, and happiness he longed for. Fears of poverty from his childhood resurfaced to haunt him.

Early days as a neurologist

In the spring of 1886, in a small office in the heart of Vienna, Freud began to practice medicine. His specialty was neurology and involved treating patients with both physical and so-called "nervous disorders." The majority of his work though focused on the causes and treatment for hysteria. Conventional treatment at the time consisted of measured electric shock and hypnosis, both of which Freud used in the early years of his practice.

But Freud eventually abandoned both of these treatments. He found hypnosis, despite its increasing popularity, to be of little help in working with neurotic disorders. He began experimenting with a number of methods to elicit the retrieval of memories from the unconscious. Eventually he hit upon a technique that seemed to work. He simply asked his patients to begin talking freely, verbally following their thoughts in any direction they were inclined to go. He called this technique "free association," and it eventually became the cornerstone of his treatment for hysteria.

FURTHER ANALYSIS
Hypnosis

The application of hypnosis to the treatment of emotional disturbances was introduced by Franz Anton Mesmer, a Viennese physician who was part scientist, part showman. Mesmer believed that the human body contained a magnetic force that operated like the magnets used by physicists. This magnetism was capable of penetrating objects and acting on them from a distance. Mesmer also believed that magnetism could cure nervous disorders by restoring equilibrium between a patient's magnetic levels and the levels present in the environment. Not surprisingly, Vienna's medical community considered him a quack. Yet, Mesmer became very successful in Paris and attracted quite a following. That is, until an investigative commission reported unfavorably on his so-called "cures," and he fled to Switzerland. But, despite this, the practice of using magnetism to cure, which eventually came to be known as mesmerism, spread to many other geographic areas including England and the United States.

Hypnosis gained more legitimacy and professional recognition in medical circles with the work of French physician Jean Martin Charcot, head of a neurological clinic in Paris for insane women. Charcot had some success treating hysterical patients by using hypnosis. More important, he described the symptoms of hysteria and the use of hypnosis in medical terminology, making them more acceptable to the French Academy of Science. But Charcot's work was primarily neurological, emphasizing physical disturbances such as paralysis.

One of Charcot's students, Pierre Janet, took hypnosis one step further. He was a strong proponent of viewing hysteria as a mental disorder caused by memory impairment and unconscious forces. He chose hypnosis as his preferred method of treatment. Thus, during the early years of Freud's career, the medical establishment was paying increasing attention to hypnosis and the psychological causes of mental illness.

Most of Freud's patients at this time were young, middle-class, Jewish women who suffered from a host of "neurological" symptoms such as paralysis, partial blindness, hallucinations, and loss of motor control; these symptoms, however, appeared to have no real neurological cause. For most of the 1880s and well into the 1890s, Freud treated these kinds of patients with a combination of massage, rest therapy, and hypnosis.

Freud was thus eager to find a more effective technique, and his partnership with Breuer was about to provide him with one. About this time, Freud visited France and was impressed by the therapeutic potential of hypnosis for neurotic disorders. On his return to Vienna he used hypnosis to help his neurotic patients recall disturbing events that they had apparently forgotten. Soon thereafter, however, he became disillusioned with hypnosis because he was not obtaining the results for which he had hoped.

The case of Anna O. that Breuer conducted, and to which Freud was privy through innumerable conversations with Breuer, was the beginning of what Breuer called "the talking cure," a conversational style of interaction that seemed capable of unlocking material in the unconscious.

As Freud began to develop his system of psychoanalysis, theoretical considerations, as well as the difficulty he encountered in hypnotizing some patients, led him to eventually discard hypnosis in favor of what he would later call free association. Free association was characterized by spontaneous disclosure of thoughts and emotion as it would arise without censorship.

It was this new technique of talking through the patient's hidden memories that would become the center of Freud's technique. Freud believed that the hidden, or "repressed," memories that lay behind hysterical symptoms were always of a sexual nature. Breuer did not hold with this belief, which led to a split between the two men soon after the publication of the studies.

Despite Freud's influential adoption and then rejection of hypnosis, some use was made of the technique in the psychoanalytic treatment of soldiers with combat neuroses during World Wars I and II. Hypnosis subsequently acquired various other limited uses in medicine. Various researchers have put forth differing theories of what hypnosis is and how it could be understood, but there is currently still no generally accepted explanatory theory for the phenomenon.

MYTHS ABOUT HYPNOSIS	
Myth	**Scientific response**
Hypnosis places the subject in someone else's control.	Magicians and other entertainers use the illusion of power to control their subjects' behavior. In reality, people who act silly or respond to instructions to do foolish things do so because they want to. The hypnotist creates a setting where the subject will follow suggestions—but the subject must be willing to cooperate.
A subject can become "stuck" in a trance.	Subjects can come out of a hypnotic state any time they wish. The subject has control of the process of hypnosis, with the hypnotist simply guiding him or her.
The hypnotist can plant a suggestion in the subject's mind—even for something to be done in the future.	It is impossible for anyone to be implanted with suggestions to do anything against his or her will.
Hypnosis may be used to improve accuracy of the subject's memory.	Memories recovered under hypnosis are no more reliable than others.

(Courtesy Thomson Gale.)

Freud considered everything a patient said to be important—even their dreams. Though other physicians of the day discounted dreams, Freud examined their role in the unconscious mind and eventually interpreted the meaning of dreams. These and other techniques enabled Freud to create the theory of psychoanalysis bit by bit, layer upon layer.

Research on cocaine

One of Freud's most promising areas of research, which he conducted on his own time, had to do with a drug that had only recently been made available in Europe—cocaine. Although the effects of the coca plant had been known for quite some time, it was only in the 1880s that refined cocaine—the active ingredient in the coca leaf—became widely available in Europe. Freud was one of the first researchers to study the effects of cocaine on the mind and body. He used himself as the prime subject. The results of his earliest experiments—mostly subjective reports on how cocaine affected his own mood, wakefulness, and somatic symptoms—were published in July of 1884 in a paper called "Über Coca" ("On Coca"). His general assessment of the drug was that it might be useful not only in treating low mood but also in treating morphine addiction.

What Freud failed to emphasize sufficiently, however, was the anesthetic effect of cocaine on mucous membranes such as the nose and mouth. A colleague of his, Dr. Carl Koller, performed experiments that showed it could also be used to anesthetize the eye for the purposes of eye surgery. Since there was no other effective way to do this at the time, Kohler's discovery was a major one, and Freud deeply regretted not making the discovery himself.

After this disappointment, Freud continued his research with cocaine, eventually publishing two more papers. The first one was slightly more subdued in its praise than "Über Coca" had been, and the third one was even more skeptical. Freud frequently used cocaine himself to deal with minor aches and pains, and he recommended it enthusiastically to friends and acquaintances, even going as far as sending it to his fiancé, Martha Bernays, for her own use.

His enthusiasm for cocaine was sharply curtailed, however, by an ugly incident in 1885 in which he tried to treat a friend's morphine addiction by giving him cocaine. The friend, Ernst von Fleischl-Marxow, who had been one of Brücke's assistants while Freud was working in the same laboratory, abruptly gave up his morphine addiction and replaced it with a voracious appetite for cocaine. The incessant use of cocaine contributed to Fleischl-Marxow's death in 1891. The episode affected Freud deeply and soured him permanently on cocaine. Nonetheless, it appears from his correspondence with Wilhelm Fliess, a nose and throat specialist from Berlin and Freud's best friend and confidant during the 1890s, that Freud used cocaine occasionally, and sometimes heavily, through the mid-90s. After that time, however, he seems to have stopped using it entirely.

Self-analysis

The years between 1896, when Freud's father died, and 1899, when *The Interpretation of Dreams* was completed and published, were some of the most difficult but productive years of Freud's life. During this time, he formulated the basic techniques and theoretical framework of psychoanalysis. Aside from his patients, Freud's primary source of data was himself. He analyzed his dreams, his slips of the tongue, and the childhood memories he was able to dredge up from his unconscious. Freud called this process of interpreting himself his "self-analysis" and it proved to have a significant effect on his theories. Ongoing self-analysis was a routine that he more or less practiced the rest of his life. We know about this period only because of letters written to and saved by Marie Bonaparte, a princess of Greece and Denmark who was one of Freud's most loyal patients. She was also instrumental in his escape from Austria in 1938.

On October 23, 1896, after an illness of four months, Freud's father, 80-year-old Jacob Freud, died in Vienna. Freud was deeply shaken. Freud's feelings about his father's death were complex and confusing to him. He felt in some way he had distanced himself from his father in his pursuit of his mother's affections during childhood. In an effort to understand the nature of hysteria, he had wrongly imagined that his father had abused him and some of his siblings.

The suspicions about his father, he now realized, were no more than a figment of Freud's own imagination. It caused him a great deal of emotional consternation to admit this error. He wondered that his own mistake in assuming his father's alleged perversion might also mean that he had misinterpreted the many seduction stories heard by his patients. But years later, he would conclude that he had not done so, and that his practice simply had a disproportionate number of patients with seduction in their background. To the charge of "suggesting" to his patients that they might have been sexually traumatized, he both admitted to the possibility and also denied it at various times in his professional career.

Through self-analysis, Freud was able to see the truth about his relationship with his parents. Freud came to realize that his father was innocent, and that as a boy he had wanted to marry his mother. He saw his father as a rival for her love. Freud interpreted his own wishes as that which is common to all young boys in all cultures. He called this newly discovered phenomenon the Oedipus complex, and it would

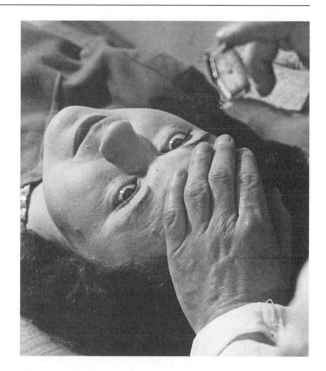

Hypnosis being used on a woman in London in 1947. (Hulton Archive/Getty Images. Reproduced by permission.)

become one of his most important ideas. He later formed a parallel concept he called the Electra complex that pertained to girls and their fathers, although he did not develop this concept as thoroughly as the Oedipus complex.

After his father's death, Freud began to work on a book based on the self-analysis of his own dreams. The *Interpretation of Dreams* was published in November 1899, with the title page dated 1900. During the next six years, the book sold only 351 copies. It took two decades before Freud achieved the fame he had always imagined. But *The Interpretation of Dreams* would be the book that would establish Freud as a seminal thinker in his time. The book eventually brought him more wealth and fame than his father could have imagined. In his latter years, Freud still viewed this book as his most important.

Psychoanalysis taking shape

With the publication of *The Interpretation of Dreams* and another of Freud's books, *The Psychopathology of Everyday Life*, his writings gained a much wider audience. This presented lecture opportunities and gained him a substantial following. It was at this time that Freud began hosting a weekly discussion group at his home on Wednesday evenings called the "Wednesday Psychological Society." After several years and a significant increase in membership, the group became formally known as the Viennese Psychological Society.

Among notable participants in the society were Carl G. Jung, Sandor Ferenczi, and Alfred Adler. Although membership in the society included many brilliant men, Freud considered himself the residing expert on all matters pertaining to psychoanalytic thought. He was not tolerant of disagreements, especially those that challenged core concepts of his theories. Such rigid expectations for adherence to his ideas inevitably caused sharp divisions among members. A number found aspects of Freud's theory to be weak or unhelpful as they employed the theories in their clinical practices. Others wanted to refine the ideas, but Freud would not waver from his own observations.

Sharp disagreements arose between Freud and key members of the Society in 1911. This was significant regarding Jung, because Jung had been Freud's intended heir to lead the Psychoanalytic Society to the next plateau. By 1914, however, the theoretical differences between Freud and several esteemed members had frayed to the breaking point. As a result, a number of leading members resigned from the society, including Adler and Jung. Freud was unforgiving in his separation from these and other resigning members and had little contact with them from that time onward.

The society resignations were quickly overshadowed by the beginning of the First World War in 1914, which was a major setback for the movement and its members. Freud was too old to fight, but his three sons, Martin, Oliver, and Ernst were all drafted. They eventually returned without loss of life or major injury.

Despite Freud's new position as a well-respected, if not world-famous, psychologist, the 1920s were not pleasant ones. Freud's daughter Sophie died of influenza in 1920. Her son, Heinz, who had been Freud's favorite grandchild, died of tuberculosis in June of 1923. Freud took the death of Heinz particularly hard. He seems to have invested much of his hope for the future in his grandson, and Heinz's death was a crushing blow. Josef Breuer, a man from whom Freud had been estranged for many years but whom he still respected, also died in June of 1925. During this decade, Freud also saw his close, inner circle of supporters, named the Committee, begin to unravel.

Also during this tumultuous period of time, Freud suffered from a personal illness. Freud had, for his entire adult life, been a vigorous and unrepentant cigar smoker. It is reported that he smoked an average of 20 cigars a day. As evidence of his habit, most photo-

graphs show him holding a cigar. In 1923, undoubtedly as a result of this habit, a cancerous growth appeared in his mouth on the inside of his right cheek. Drastic surgical measures were necessary to prevent the spread of the cancer. Surgery was performed in two separate sessions in the beginning of October of that year to remove Freud's upper right jaw and hard palate. For the next 16 years, until his death in 1938, Freud wore an uncomfortable prosthesis that resembled a large set of dentures. Talking and eating were difficult. Over the course of these 16 years, 33 different operations were performed to remove cancerous or pre-cancerous growths in Freud's mouth. Yet remarkably, he never stopped smoking.

The final years

From 1930 to 1938, Freud continued to live and work in Vienna. The international psychoanalytic movement was now well established. Freud had become famous and most of the turbulence within the movement during the 1920s had calmed down. Yet, due to his increasingly poor health, Freud was slowly becoming less involved in the inner workings of the psychoanalytic movement. In fact, in the mid-1920s he stopped attending meetings of the International Psychoanalytic Association.

For the last 15 to 20 years of Freud's life, beginning from the time he was diagnosed with mouth cancer in 1923, his daughter, Anna, was his nurse and constant companion. In 1923 she became a member of the Viennese Psychoanalytic Society and remained an important figure in psychoanalysis after her father's death. She gradually took over increasing amounts of responsibility from her father as it pertained to his work in the Association. Anna Freud became best known for her work on defense mechanisms and the analysis of children.

The early 1930s represented a time of political unrest and the eventual outbreak of war in Europe. On March 12, 1938, Hitler's forces invaded Austria and quickly took over the country. Although he initially resisted, his need to leave the country became apparent after numerous threats. On March 13, the Vienna Psychoanalytic Society voted to dissolve and recommended that all of its members flee Austria and reconvene, if possible, wherever Freud took up residence. Over the next week, Freud's home was raided several times, and on March 22, his daughter Anna Freud was arrested and questioned by the Gestapo. Fortunately, no one was hurt. Although money and valuables were stolen from Freud's home, his private study was left untouched. The property of the psychoanalytic publishing house, on the other hand, which was located a few doors down from Freud's home and office, was confiscated in its entirety.

Freud moved to England on July 6, 1938, with his wife and daughter Anna. They settled into his last home, a house that Anna Freud kept until her death 40 years later. Surprisingly, Freud's joy at the pleasures of their new home, including freedom from Nazi persecution, was tempered by a surprising homesickness for Vienna. He had always claimed that he hated Vienna. Now that he was gone, however, he longed for the familiarity of the city.

This homesickness was no doubt accentuated by the need for another surgical procedure to treat his ongoing mouth cancer in September of that year. Since Freud's first operations for mouth cancer in 1923, numerous pre-cancerous growths had appeared and been removed. In 1936, however, a cancerous growth had reappeared. Now, in 1938, the cancer had returned once more. Removing it this time required a significant procedure that left Freud very weakened.

In February of 1939, despite the drastic surgery that had been performed only five months earlier, Freud's cancer returned. This time the doctors deemed the tumor inaccessible and inoperable. Freud would have to live with it until he died. Over the course of the next eight months, Freud grew increasingly weak, and the tumor increased in size. By September, it had eaten through to the outside of his cheek, creating a large, unpleasant open sore.

On September 21, Freud, in severe pain, asked his doctor to administer a dose of morphine large enough to ease him out of life. His doctor complied, giving him several large injections of morphine over the course of the next few days. Freud died near midnight on September 23, 1939. He was cremated three days later on September 26. Ernest Jones, who became his first and most authoritative biographer, gave the funeral oration.

THEORIES

Freud's psychoanalytic system evolved over nearly 60 years of professional work. He himself was constantly revising aspects of his theory to better reflect what he was learning on a continual basis. There are a number of concepts that are essential for understanding psychoanalytic theory.

The psyche
Main points Freud's theory of the unconscious is the foundation upon which much of his psychoanalytic

theory is built. Freud hypothesized that the mind is divided into three main parts: the unconscious, the conscious, and the preconscious. The unconscious is by far the larger and most important part of the mind according to Freud. It includes all the things that are not easily available to awareness. Freud suggested that the unconscious mind acts like a repository for those thoughts, memories, experiences, and feelings that can't or won't easily move into the conscious mind. Items may come to this repository because of trauma or for any number of reasons for which a person might protect him or herself from unpleasant emotion. The unconscious also includes drives or instincts that cause humans to behave the way they do.

The conscious mind also plays a key role. Freud believed that everything we are aware of is stored in our conscious mind. At any given time, a person is only aware of a very small part of what makes up his or her personality; the rest is buried in the unconscious and is inaccessible. Though small in comparison to the unconscious, the conscious mind is still essential and important for adaptive functioning.

The final part is the preconscious or subconscious. This is the part of mind that can be accessed if prompted, but is not in our active conscious. The preconscious exists just below the surface, and is buried until needed. Common information such as one's telephone number, childhood memories, or one's home address is stored in the preconscious.

Conflict between conscious and unconscious impulses are said to give rise to anxiety, which Freud believed to be common to all people. The most common way to counteract anxiety, according to Freud, was to employ the use of what he called defense mechanisms. To tap the unconscious, Freud used a variety of techniques, including hypnosis, free association, and dream interpretation. Carl G. Jung expanded on the Freudian concept, adding the idea of an inherited unconscious, known as the collective unconscious.

Also residing in the unconscious are the instincts or drives. The instincts, for Freud, are the principal motivating forces that "energize" the mind in all of its functions. There are, he held, an indefinite number of such instincts, but these can be reduced to a small number of basic ones, which he grouped into two broad generic categories: Eros (the life instinct), which covers all self-preserving and erotic instincts, and Thanatos (the death instinct), which covers all the instincts towards aggression, self-destruction, and cruelty.

Explanation Although Freud didn't invent the idea of the unconscious mind, he certainly was the one who made it popular. Given the work by other theorists in the nineteenth century, it is not surprising that Freud's concept of mind, especially the unconscious, grew to prominence. He took the principles that dominated the thought of those working with the physiology of the body and applied them systematically to the sphere of the mind. Thus Freud's conception of the unconscious explained behavioral patterns set in motion by unconscious instincts and drives, which were previously unexplained.

The unconscious material of a person's life drives behavior in both positive and negative ways. But when unconscious experience or emotion creates maladaptive living, the unconscious material cannot simply be brought into consciousness at will. It must be coaxed out using the proper techniques. Freud created the techniques of psychoanalysis as the means of bringing material from the unconscious into the conscious mind, so that it could be investigated and possibly changed. The analogy of an iceberg has been often used to help visualize the role of the conscious as compared to the unconscious mind. The bulk of the iceberg, the unconscious mind, lies below the surface, exerting a dynamic and determining influence over the direction of the mass. The visible part, the conscious mind, is small in comparison and is subject to the weight of the portion below the surface.

Regarding instincts and drives, Freud is often referenced as having said that all human actions spring from motivations which are sexual in origin. This assertion is not completely accurate. Freud did state that sexual drives play an important and central role in human life, actions, and behavior. This was the subject of much controversy for the sexually repressed time period in which he lived. He went also took it further by saying that sexual drives exist and can be discerned in children from birth, and that sexual energy (libido) is the single most important motivating force in adult life. However, even here a crucial qualification has to be added. Freud effectively redefined the term sexuality to include any form of pleasure that is or can be derived from the body. Thus his theory of the instincts or drives is essentially that the human being is energized or driven from birth by the desire to acquire and enhance bodily pleasure.

Examples   One of Freud's patients once described to him a repeating dream that involved her chasing a man she worked with up several flights of stairs. The woman claimed that even though she ran faster and faster, she never caught the man nor reached the top of the stairway, which caused her immense frustration. Freud interpreted such dreams as the unconscious mind representing a desire or drive for sexual contact

with the person she was chasing. Freud would say that the dream expressed itself through the unconscious because it might be too threatening, psychologically speaking, for the patient to admit this to herself. It might threaten her self-concept or sense of morality to admit to such lustful urges. So instead, her unconscious mind turned the urges into a non-threatening symbol—running up flights of stairs.

Structure of the mind (id, ego, superego)

Main points   Freud further divided the conscious and unconscious mind into three structures or systems that performed different roles. These systems he named the id, ego, and superego. Freud viewed human beings as energy systems, where only one system can be in control at any given time, while the other two systems give themselves over to the psychic energy of the one in control.

The id is the original system of personality and the dominant one at birth. In German, the word was literally translated as the "it." The id is primarily the source of psychic energy and the core of all instincts. It is infantile in the way it manifests and functions on the unconscious level. It lacks organization and is demanding, insistent, and impulsive. The id cannot tolerate tension and works to discharge tension as quickly as possible and return to a balanced state. Therefore the id operates according to the demands of what Freud called the pleasure principle. That is, it wants to satisfy its desires so as to relieve the tension.

The ego, in contrast, works not by the pleasure principle but rather by the reality principle. In other words, there is a real world out there that must be reckoned with. The ego (literally "I") is the personality structure that develops to deal with the real world and solve the problems of life. It acts as the "executive" branch of the personality that governs, controls, and regulates matters of life. The ego functions as part of the conscious mind.

The superego is the judicial branch of the personality. It imposes a moral code, concerning itself with whether a particular action is good or bad; right or wrong. It represents the ideal, rather than a reflection of reality, and strives for perfection instead of pleasure. The superego represents the ideals of society as they are passed from one generation to another. The superego can be represented by both the unconscious and conscious mind depending on the particular function it is serving.

Explanation   The id never matures, remaining infantile in its impulses and urges while seeking pleasure and avoiding tension at all costs. If it had its way it would forever seek indulgence, the same way a young child seeks only to get his or her selfish needs met. If left to its own appetite, the id would be unable to function in the world.

To temper the id's urges, the ego steps in to acknowledge an objective reality that must be dealt with. Other people, for instance, also have needs that must be considered. While it is the job of the ego to help satisfy the id's inclinations, it also must mediate how serving those needs will affect one's reality. Over time, the ego's efforts create a "dialogue" of sorts with the real world that transforms into actual skills, competencies, and memories. These resources are then internalized into what Freud referred to as the "self," an emerging sense of personhood, instead of a bundle of urges and needs.

The superego works to inhibit the id's impulses while persuading the ego to substitute moralistic goals for realistic ones and to strive for perfection. The superego works off the basis of psychological rewards and punishments. If a person responds in the "right" manner, the reward might be a feeling of pride or self-love. If the individual deems their action as immoral or "wrong," the resulting punishment might be guilt or feelings of inferiority.

Example   Freud conceived the mind as being in constant conflict with itself. He understood this conflict as the primary cause of human anxiety and unhappiness. His classic example is the patient Anna O., who displayed a rash of psychological and physiological symptoms: assorted paralyses, hysterical squints, coughs, and speech disorders, among others. Under hypnosis, Josef Breuer, a fellow physician and close friend of Freud, traced many of these symptoms to memories of a period when she cared for her dying father. One symptom, a nervous cough, they related to a particular event at her father's bedside. Upon hearing dance music that was drifting from a neighbor's house, she felt an urge to be there, gone from her father's bedside. Immediately, she was struck with guilt and self-reproach for having the desire to leave him. She covered this internal conflict with a nervous cough, and from that day on, coughed reflexively at the sound of rhythmic music. Freud's investigations into internal conflicts such as this led him to eventually construct the divisions of the mind now known as id, ego, and superego.

Defense mechanisms

Main points   Because the ego is the great equalizer between the id and superego, conflict is inevitable. This conflict, according to Freud, brings anxiety and serves as a signal to the ego that its survival may be in jeopardy. Freud further divided anxiety into three kinds: realistic anxiety (fear of real situations), moral anxiety (fear that stems from the internalized ideal world of the superego), and neurotic anxiety (fear that results from impulses originating in the id). It is the unconscious neurotic anxiety that most intrigued Freud and formed the basis for his research. Psychoanalytic therapy was developed to treat the various neuroses that were largely unconscious. Freud postulated that the ego aids this process of repressing the anxiety through use of what he called defense mechanisms.

The ego deals with the demands of reality, the urges of the id, and the perfectionist tendencies of the superego as best as it can. But when the anxiety becomes overwhelming, the ego must defend itself. It does so by unconsciously blocking the impulses or distorting them into a more acceptable, less threatening form. The techniques for doing this are called the ego defense mechanisms. Freud, his daughter Anna, and other disciples have discovered a number of defense mechanisms that accomplish this purpose.

Explanation: Repression   Repression is one of the most important Freudian processes, and it is the basis for other ego defenses and neurotic disorders. It is a means of defense through which threatening or painful thoughts or feelings are excluded from awareness. Freud explained repression as an involuntary removal of something from consciousness. Anna Freud called it "motivated forgetting."

Examples   Victims of war or other trauma sometimes face experiences that are too overwhelming for them to assimilate into their conscious mind. In order to cope, they must protect themselves from letting the painful experience incapacitate them. The result is that they unconsciously repress the emotion. This emotion may resurface unexpectedly if a similar life event such as an accident or other victimization triggers the repressed memories.

Explanation: Denial   Denial involves blocking external events from awareness. For example, if a particular situation is too much for a person to handle, he or she simply refuses to allow the experience to become reality for them, despite the fact that it happened. The use of denial is a primitive and dangerous defense because eventually the individual must face reality. The longer one attempts to deny the objective reality, the greater may be the consequences. Denial can operate by itself or, more commonly, in combination with other, more subtle defense mechanisms that support it.

Examples   Denial can be unconscious as when a dying person refuses to admit that their life will soon end or when a person with a heart condition denies that their overeating or smoking is of any consequence. It can also take a semi-conscious state where the individual accepts a portion of the situation but denies another. For instance, a person may acknowledge that they were in an automobile accident but they will not accept the fact that a loved one who was critically injured might die.

Explanation: Displacement   Displacement is the redirection of anxiety onto a substitute or "safer" target. The redirected energy, often anger, cannot be discharged in the most logical way, so it must find another way to be released.

Examples   The classic example is the frustrated worker who feels victimized by his boss but cannot express his anger directly at his supervisor. Instead, he finds a safer target and yells at his family when he arrives home. According to Freud, the man does not intentionally displace his anger and frustration on his family, but unconsciously does so because he finds the relationships of his family "safer." Venting his frustration at home will minimize consequences arising from his actions, were he to express his anger on the job.

Explanation: Projection   Projection takes one's own anxiety-arousing impulses and attributes them to someone else.

Examples   A husband finds himself attracted to a charming and flirtatious woman at work. Instead of acknowledging his attraction, he becomes increasingly jealous of his wife and worried about her faithfulness to the marriage. Freud would say that the jealous husband is simply projecting his own feelings onto his wife in an effort to reduce the anxiety he feels about his own unacceptable feelings.

Explanation: Reaction formation   Reaction formation helps protect against threatening impulses by overemphasizing the opposite of one's actual thoughts and actions.

Examples   A pastor who is involved in a secret extramarital affair unconsciously attempts to push away threatening impulses related to his behavior by preaching vehemently against sexual impurity. The pastor, according to psychoanalytic theory, is attempting to reduce his own feelings of guilt and almost atone for his secretive behavior by taking the opposite or morally "right" stance.

Explanation: Regression   Regression involves going back to an earlier phase of development when there were fewer demands. In the face of severe stress, individuals may attempt to cope with anxiety by clinging to immature behaviors.

Examples   Children who are frightened in school may indulge in infantile behavior such as weeping, excessive dependency, thumb-sucking, and clinging to the teacher. Again, this is perceived by psychoanalytic theory as an unconscious wish on the part of the child to obtain nurturing, attention, or some type of consolation to cope with stressors they feel unable to handle. So, regression to an earlier, more helpless state can either provide them with the safety they feel they need or exempt them from responsibilities they perceive are beyond their capabilities.

Explanation: Rationalization   Rationalization helps a person justify specific behaviors or decisions that may not be acceptable to the conscious mind.

Examples   A woman interviews for a job that she really wants, but after the interview is over and she is not offered the position, she claims that she really did not want the job anyway. Rather than admitting to herself that she may not have conducted the interview in an appropriate manner or did not have the necessary skills or experience the employer was seeking, she portrays the situation as one where she is the decision-maker. This distortion of the situation helps her minimize potential feelings of failure, inadequacy, or inferiority.

Explanation: Sublimation   Sublimation, according to a psychoanalytic perspective, involves diverting sexual or aggressive energy into other channels that are often socially acceptable and even admirable.

Examples   A male with aggressive impulses becomes an all-state linebacker on the school football team. Were these same aggressive impulses acted out in common social situations, it would be considered inappropriate and possibly abusive to those on the receiving end. But given that "hitting" is inherent in a contact sport, the student can legitimately channel his aggressive tendencies toward a socially acceptable "performance." Not only does this give the student a release for the unconscious aggression, but it may also provide social approval for reinforcing the aggressive behavior in that context.

Interior of Sigmund Freud's study. (Archive Photos, Inc. Reproduced by permission.)

Psychosexual development

Main points Freud's theory of psychosexual development had its origins in, and was a generalization of, Josef Breuer's earlier discovery that traumatic childhood events could have devastating negative effects upon the adult. This view assumed that early childhood sexual experiences were the crucial factors in the determination of the adult personality. Freud's believed that from the moment of birth, the infant is driven in his actions by the desire for bodily/sexual pleasure. Initially, infants gain such release, and derive such pleasure, through the act of sucking. Freud termed this period the oral stage of development. This is followed by a stage in which the locus of pleasure or energy release is the anus, particularly in the act of defecation, and this he termed the anal stage. Then the young child develops an interest in its sexual organs as a site of pleasure and an accompanying sexual attraction for the parent of the opposite sex, while developing a subtle hatred for the parent of the same sex. This, Freud called the phallic stage of development. Following this the child then enters what Freud called the latency period, in which sexual motivations become much less pronounced. This lasts until puberty, when the mature genital stage of development begins, and the pleasure drive refocuses around the genital area.

This developmental sequence best described the progression of normal human development, according to Freud. A child at a given stage of development has certain needs and demands, such as the need of the infant to nurse. Frustration occurs when these needs are not met. Freud called these frustrations conflicts, and the child encounters them as part of the developmental process. Successful resolution of the conflict is crucial to adjustment and eventual adult mental health. According to Freud, when a child experiences a significant degree of frustration or overindulgence around these conflicts, the child's sexual urges become stuck to some extent in that stage of development. He called this inability to resolve the conflict a fixation. The child then continues to repeat the maladaptive behaviors that are indicative of that unresolved conflict. In contrast, if the child progresses normally through the stages, resolving each conflict and moving on, then the sexual urges do not become fixated and will progress normally.

In Freud's view, many mental illnesses, particularly hysteria, can be traced back to unresolved conflicts experienced at one of these developmental stages or to events which otherwise disrupt the normal pattern of infant development. For example, homosexuality is seen by some Freudians as resulting from a failure to resolve the conflicts inherent in the phallic stage, particularly a failure to identify with the parent of the same sex. The obsessive concern with washing one's hands and personal hygiene, which characterizes the behavior of some neurotics, is seen as resulting from unresolved conflicts/repressions occurring at the anal stage.

Explanation: Oral stage   The oral stage of psychosexual development begins at birth when the oral cavity is the primary focus of psychosexual energy (libido). The child, of course, preoccupies himself with nursing and receives the pleasure of sucking and accepting things into the mouth. The child who is frustrated at this stage and unable to get his needs met adequately, because his mother refuses to nurse him on demand or who ends nursing sessions early, is characterized by pessimism, envy, suspicion, and sarcasm. The overindulged infant, whose nursing urges were often excessively satisfied, is optimistic, gullible, and is full of admiration for others around him. This stage culminates in the primary conflict of weaning, which both deprives the child of the sensory pleasures of nursing and of the psychological pleasure of being cared for, mothered, and held. This stage lasts approximately one and one-half years.

Examples   A child fixated at the oral stage of development may become very dependent on his or her mother, clinging to her and becoming fearful of being away from her. This, according to Freud, results because the child was unable to adequately resolve the dependency needs in the oral stage of development.

Explanation: Anal stage   At approximately 18 months of age, the child enters the anal stage of psychosexual development. With the advent of toilet training comes the child's obsession with the anus and with the retention or expulsion of the feces. This represents a classic conflict between the id, which derives pleasure from expulsion of bodily wastes, and the ego and superego, which represent the practical and societal pressures to control the bodily functions. The child meets the conflict between physical desires and the parent's demands in one of two ways: Either he puts up a fight or he simply refuses to go. The child who wants to fight takes pleasure in excreting maliciously, perhaps just before or just after being placed on the toilet. If the parents are too lenient and the child manages to derive pleasure and success from this expulsion, it will result in the formation of what Freud called the "anal expulsive character." This characterizes adults who are generally messy, disorganized, reckless, careless, and defiant. In contrast, a child may opt to retain feces, thereby spiting his parents while

enjoying the pleasurable pressure of the built-up feces in his intestine. If this tactic succeeds and the child is overindulged, he will develop into an "anal retentive character." This type of person is stereotypically viewed as neat, precise, orderly, careful, stingy, withholding, obstinate, meticulous, and passive-aggressive. The resolution of the anal stage, which includes proper toilet training, permanently affects the individual's inclinations to possess and their attitudes toward authority. This stage lasts from ages one and one-half to two years.

Examples   According to psychoanalytic theory, if a child becomes fixated at the anal stage, it carries over into the rest of the person's life. For instance, an adult who has anal expulsive traits may like crude or inappropriate bathroom humor or exhibit passive-aggressive behavior toward others. Those characterized by the anal retentive trait may be overly concerned with order, cleanliness, or organization. This behavior is sometimes diagnosed as obsessive-compulsive disorder and may pose significant problems for the person as he or she attempts to carry on normal activities of living.

Explanation: Phallic stage   The phallic stage is the setting for the most crucial sexual conflict in Freud's psychosexual model of development. In this stage, the child's genital region becomes the focus. As the child becomes more interested in his or her genitals and in the genitals of others, conflict arises. This conflict, which Freud labeled the "Oedipus complex" for boys and the "Electra complex" for girls, involves the child's unconscious desire to possess the opposite-sexed parent and to eliminate the same-sexed one.

In the young male, the Oedipus conflict stems from his natural love for his mother, a love which becomes sexual as his libidinal energy transfers from the anal region to his genitals. Unfortunately for the boy, his father stands in the way of possessing his mother. The boy therefore feels aggression and envy towards this rival, his father, and also feels fear that the father will strike back at him. The boy, by this time, has undoubtedly noticed that women, his mother in particular, do not have penises. Although he understands that this is a male-only fixture, he fears that his father will do something to take away his penis. Freud called this fear "castration anxiety," which helps the boy to repress his desire for his mother. Moreover, while the boy recognizes now that he cannot possess his mother, because his father does, he can possess her vicariously by identifying with his father and becoming as much like him as possible. This identification indoctrinates the boy into his appropriate sexual role in life.

While the Oedipal conflict was developed in great detail, Freud did not provide as much clarity on the Electra complex. The Electra complex has its roots in a young girl's discovery that she, along with her mother and all other women, lack the penis that her father and other men possess. Her love for her father then becomes both erotic and envious, as she yearns for a penis of her own. She comes to blame her mother for her perceived castration, and is struck by "penis envy," the apparent counterpart to the boy's castration anxiety. The resolution of the Electra complex is far less clear-cut than the resolution of the Oedipus complex is in males. Freud stated that the resolution comes much later and is never truly complete. Just as the boy learned his sexual role by identifying with his father, so the girl learns her role by identifying with her mother in an attempt to possess her father vicariously. At the eventual resolution of the conflict, the girl passes into the latency period, though Freud implies that she always remains slightly fixated at the phallic stage.

Fixation at the phallic stage develops a phallic character who is reckless, resolute, self-assured, and narcissistic. The failure to resolve the conflict can also cause a person to be afraid of or incapable of close love. Freud also postulated that fixation could be a root cause of homosexuality.

Examples   Freud believed that adults may unconsciously replay unresolved conflicts from their childhoods if fixated at that stage. Perhaps the best example is young adults who seek the company of the opposite sex, and may eventually marry someone like their own mother or father. Freud would say that this not only represents familiarity, but an unconscious effort to resolve the fixated conflict from the phallic stage of psychosexual development. The young person may try to "win" the affection of the desired one in an effort to finally achieve the maternal or paternal closeness for which they have longed.

Explanation: Latency   The resolution of the phallic stage leads to the latency period, which is not a psychosexual stage of development, but a period in which the sexual drive lies dormant. Freud saw latency as a period of unparalleled repression of sexual desires and impulses. During the latency period, children pour this repressed libidinal energy into asexual pursuits such as school, athletics, and same-sex friendships. But soon puberty strikes, and the genitals once again become a central focus of libidinal energy. The latency stage extends approximately from ages six to 12. Critics claim that Freud's assumption of a latency period of sexual development,

especially at this stage of growth, represents a significant weakness in his theory.

Examples   Boys and girls in the latency stage, for the most part, have same-sex playmates and show little interest in being in the company of peers of the opposite sex. During this period, boys and girls typically begin evidencing their sex roles through play. Boys gravitate to those activities characterized as masculine, participating in more aggressive play. Girls tend to favor more feminine activities such as playing with dolls or dressing up.

Explanation: Genital stage   In the genital stage, as the child's energy once again focuses on his or her genitals, interest turns to heterosexual relationships. The less energy the child has fixated in unresolved psychosexual development, the greater the capacity will be to develop normal relationships with the opposite sex. Freud thought that if a person did not get trapped in any of sequential psychosexual stages, then adolescence would mark the beginning of an adult life and normal sexual relations, marriage, and child-rearing. If, however, the person remained fixated, particularly in the phallic stage, development would be troubled as he or she struggled to resolve the points of contention. Unfortunately, the person will often resort to repression and other defense mechanisms because he or she does not know how to truly resolve the unconscious issues. Freud, unlike Erik Erikson who expanded his stages to cover the full span of life, believed that the crucial conflict of the genital stage occurred between the ages of 12 and 18, but left the impression that the genital stage continues indefinitely.

Examples   The genital stage primarily comprises adolescents who are intensely interested in the opposite sex, dating, and sexual experimentation. If young people have resolved the previous conflicts in earlier psychosexual stages, they should be able to contain their genital urges in an appropriate manner. If not, they will, according to Freud, act out their unresolved conflicts in aberrant ways. For instance, a male who has not resolved the phallic stage conflict may become possessive and jealous of his girlfriend, attempting to restrict her social life and thereby demanding loyalty to him exclusively.

HISTORICAL CONTEXT

There were three major sources of influence on the psychoanalytic movement: previous assumptions about the unconscious, early notions about psycho-pathology, and evolutionary theory.

Assumptions of the unconscious

As early as the eighteenth century, German philosopher and mathematician Gottfried Wilhelm Leibnitz developed the notion that there were degrees of consciousness ranging from completely unconscious to fully conscious. A century later, German philosopher Johann Friedrich Herbart refined Leibnitz's concept of the unconscious by stating that only conscious ideas are perceived in awareness. Gustav Theodore Fechner, who preceded Freud but had contact with him in the later part of the nineteenth century, also speculated about the unconscious. Fechner conceived the classic illustration of an iceberg to visualize the contrast between the conscious and unconscious mind.

Discussion of the unconscious was very much a part of the European intellectual community during the 1880s when Freud was beginning his clinical practice. But the unconscious was not only of interest to professionals. It had become a fashionable topic of conversation among the educated public. A book entitled *Philosophy of the Unconscious* became so popular that it appeared in nine editions. In the 1870s, at least a half dozen other books published in Germany included the word "unconscious" in their titles.

So, although Freud is often credited with "discovering" the unconscious, his genius was more accurately stated as having taken the preexisting notions of the unconscious that were popular in his day and fashioning them into a coherent and tangible system.

Early ideas about psychopathology

History is replete with examples of misconceptions about mental illness. In the Middle Ages people who were mentally ill were perceived as being possessed by the devil. It was believed that only severe punishment of these individuals could yield a cure. Those who would not publicly repent of their "sins" were often executed. Over time this view softened. By the eighteenth century, mental illness came to be viewed more as irrational behavior. Mentally ill persons were confined in institutions similar to jails. Although they were no longer put to death, they were offered no treatment.

In the early 1880s, a French physician by the name of Philippe Pinel recognized the need for treating those suffering from mental illness and began attempting to make sense of a patient's problems by listening to them. Under Pinel's direction, a number of patients previously thought to be hopelessly disturbed began to be cured.

This concept of a "talking cure" began to spread rapidly throughout Europe and then to the United States.

During the nineteenth century, psychiatrists were divided into two camps, the somatic and the psychic. The somatic approach held that abnormal behavior had physical causes such as brain lesions, or understimulated or overly tight nerves. The psychic school subscribed to emotional or psychological explanations for abnormal behavior. In general, the somatic viewpoint dominated, supported by the ideas of the German philosopher Immanuel Kant, who ridiculed the view that emotional problems somehow led to mental illness.

The discipline of psychoanalysis developed as a revolt against the somatic orientation. It was against this backdrop that Freud later adopted his "talking therapy" techniques, which he used extensively with his neurotic patients.

Evolutionary theory

Freud's thinking was greatly influenced by the writings of Charles Darwin. Freud read all of Darwin's works and made notations in the margins of each book. He regularly praised the works to colleagues and in his own publications. Some have claimed that Darwin's writings exerted more influence on Freud's thinking, and therefore on the development of psychoanalytic theory, than any other single source. As almost a confirmation of this, Freud insisted later in life that the study of Darwin's theory of evolution should be an essential part of the training program for psychoanalysts.

Darwin discussed several ideas that Freud later emphasized in psychoanalysis, including unconscious mental processes and conflicts, significance of dreams, hidden symbolism of certain behaviors, and importance of sexual arousal. On the whole, Darwin focused, as Freud did later, on the nonrational aspects of thought and behavior. Darwin's theories also affected Freud's ideas about childhood development and the notion that humans were driven by the biological forces of love and hunger.

Rise of the sciences

The sciences also experienced a boom during Freud's first few decades in Vienna. In addition to Darwin's writings, most notably *The Origin of Species*, published between the years 1859 and 1880, there were numerous other avenues of innovation. Alfred Noble invented dynamite. Alexander Graham Bell invented the telephone. Vienna was eager to join the ranks of Europe's leading cities and showcased its latest innovations during the Vienna World's Fair in 1873, which Freud eagerly attended.

Revolt against Jews

With Vienna's prosperity also came a growing prejudice against the newly arrived Jews of eastern Europe. And when the populist, anti-Semitic Karl Lueger was elected as the city's new mayor in 1897, Freud and his fellow liberal, middle-class Jews were revolted.

World War I, 1914–1918

The First World War created a significant uproar in Europe as it was sparked by the assassination of the Archduke Ferdinand in Serbia. The Austro-Hungarian attempt to punish the Serbs for the assassination instigated a series of threats and counter-threats by the European powers. Eventually almost all of Europe became involved in a war that lasted far longer than anyone had expected and resulted in the defeat of the Central Powers and the destruction of the Austro-Hungarian Empire.

During this four-year period when the war was being waged, the psychoanalytic movement slowed its prewar growth but survived. During the war years, all international congresses were canceled, since half of the nations represented at the International Psychoanalytic Association's were at war with nations represented by the other half. Communications between members were restricted for the same reason. In 1918, with the war winding down, the fifth International Psychoanalytic Congress met in Budapest, Hungary, and attracted a number of government officials from Austria, Germany, and Hungary. This was a direct result of interest sparked by the application of psychoanalysis to war neuroses.

World War II, 1939–1945

By the time World War II started, Freud was famous, and the psychoanalytic movement was well established. Internal conflict between Freud and key members of the Psychoanalytic Society had resulted in the resignation of several important figures, including Jung and Adler. The society had resettled by the beginning of the Second World War. The most significant event for Freud and the psychoanalytic movement during this time occurred in March 1938, when the German Nazis invaded Austria. The event forced Freud to flee to England and fragmented the Psychoanalytic Society for several years. It also marked a turning point for Freud as he began to recede into the background of the movement and allowed others, his daughter Anna in particular, to assume greater leadership over the direction the movement would take.

CRITICAL RESPONSE

Freudian psychoanalytic theory did not long remain the only method of explaining the human personality. Even during Freud's lifetime, alternatives were offered by a number of other theorists, resulting in a splintering of psychological thought.

Freud's early disciples

Freud's theory of psychoanalysis was built on the assumption that human beings have an unconscious mind. This unconscious mind, with its hidden drives and instincts, is what drives behavior. And since the unconscious is so pervasive and directive, it determines behavior, or to say it more philosophically, is deterministic. Psychoanalysis is a highly deterministic approach to human behavior because it assumes that behavioral patterns established in youth determine one's behavior later in life. This deterministic presupposition is in large part what made Freud's theory so intriguing and controversial.

Yet despite the controversy, psychoanalysis spread rapidly within professional circles and attracted some of the brightest physicians of the day. This included both Alfred Adler and Carl Jung, two names that would become synonymous with Freud as much for their alliance as for their eventual split.

Alfred Adler, a medical doctor with a deep interest in psychology and human nature, met Freud in their native Vienna in 1900 at a medical conference where Freud presented his new ideas about dreams and the unconscious. Freud's radical ideas were met with scorn and open hostility, as they often were during these early years of the psychoanalytic movement. Adler, one of the few who had recognized the brilliance of Freud's first major work, *The Interpretation of Dreams*, was dismayed by the proceedings and came to Freud's defense in an article he wrote for a medical journal. In the article, he demanded that Freud's views be given the respect and attention they deserved. Adler soon joined the circle of psychologists who gathered at Freud's home on Wednesday evenings for animated discussion, debate, and collaboration about emerging psychoanalytic theory. Buttressed by his loyal supporters, many of them insightful psychologists and original thinkers in their own right, Freud's movement grew as his seminal ideas gradually captured the imagination of intellectuals throughout Europe, England, and America. Adler was for a time the president of the Vienna Psychoanalytic Association and the editor of its journal. Yet there had always been differences between Adler's views and Freud's, and over the years, these differences became increasingly apparent and problematic. First,

A group of prominent psychologists at Clark University, Massachusetts, in 1909. In the front row are (left to right) Sigmund Freud, G. Stanley Hall, and Carl Jung. (Copyright Bettmann/Corbis. Reproduced by permission.)

Adler never accepted Freud's views about the overarching significance of infantile sexual trauma. Freud was typically intolerant of disagreement, though, and in a dramatic and politically charged break, Adler resigned his posts in 1911, leaving Freud's circle along with a group of eight colleagues to found his own school of psychology. He and Freud never met again.

Individual psychology   Adler then took his ideas and his followers and began what he called individual psychology, which was based on the idea of the indivisibility of the personality. His most significant divergence from Freud's theory was his belief that the human being is a whole person, not a conglomeration of mechanisms, drives, or dynamic parts. And in contrast to most psychological thinking of the time, Adler believed that human beings are fundamentally

self-determined. Central to his therapeutic approach, and in direct conflict with Freud's views, was his belief that people always have control over their lives; their choices are what shape them. "Individual Psychology breaks through the theory of determinism," Jung wrote. "No experience is a cause of success or failure. We do not suffer from the shock of our experiences—the so-called trauma—but we make out of them just what suits our purposes. We are self-determined by the meaning we give to our experiences." Adler's emphasis on the wholeness of the person and the fact that our values inevitably shape our experience led to his conviction that, in the end, there is only one true meaning to human life: care and love for our fellow humans. "There have always been men who understood this fact; who knew that the meaning of life is to be interested in the whole of mankind and who tried to develop social interest and love. In all religions we find this concern for the salvation of man." For Adler, it is only this meaning, this interpretation of our experience as it pertains to the whole of humankind that leads to the genuine mental health and happiness of the individual.

Analytical psychology   Carl Jung met Freud in 1907, after he sent Freud a report on some of his early research in the psychotherapeutic technique of word association, to which Freud responded with an invitation to meet him in Vienna. Jung lived in Zurich, where he was practicing psychiatry and teaching at Zurich University. At that first meeting in Freud's home, the two men talked "virtually without a pause for thirteen hours." Each was captivated by the other's genius and passionate interest in psychology, and they began a close correspondence in which they exchanged letters as often as three times a week. Jung quickly stepped into a leading role in the psychoanalytic movement, becoming a staunch defender and chief disseminator of Freud's ideas. Freud confided to Jung that he saw him as his "successor and crown prince," and Jung became, for all concerned, Freud's heir apparent. From the beginning, Jung found Freud's theories about repression and the unconscious to be ingenious explanations of much of what he was finding in his work with his own patients. But, as Adler did, he struggled with Freud's insistence on the primacy of the sexual drive.

There was another significant tension between Freud and Jung, however. Jung had a burgeoning interest in world religions, mythology, and alchemy, interests with which Freud had little patience. In fact, Freud was by this time openly atheistic and viewed religion as inferior to science. In contrast, religious imagery and occultism had in fact been a recurring fascination for Jung, and he had had several "paranormal" experiences and encounters with psychic mediums during his youth.

A major turning point in Jung's intellectual career was his book *Symbols of Transformation*, researched and written between 1909 and 1912, while he was still Freud's champion spokesman and organizer. Jung immersed himself in a world of mythology, fantasy, and preverbal imagery. "The whole thing came upon me like a landslide that cannot be stopped," he wrote of his work during this period. "It was the explosion of all those psychic contents which could find no room, no breathing space, in the constricting atmosphere of Freudian psychology and its narrow outlook."

In 1914 Jung broke with Freud to develop his own school of psychology. His analytical psychology emphasized the interpretation of the psyche's symbols from a universal mythological perspective rather than a personal biographical one. Jung believed that the psyche has a collective ancestry that goes back millions of years. He argued that the psyche was made up of what he termed archetypes, which are primordial images inherited from our ancestors. As support for such a theory, he spoke of the immediate attachment infants have for their mother, the inevitable fear of the dark seen in young children, and how images such as the sun, moon, wise old man, angels, and evil all seem to be predominant themes throughout history. The aim of life, according to Jung, is to know oneself. He thought the best way to do that is to explore both the personal unconscious and the collective unconscious.

Other schools of thought

Freud and his theory of psychoanalysis were so pivotal in the establishment of modern psychology that a strong argument can be made that virtually every major psychological theory of the twentieth century was either a hybrid of or a reaction to psychoanalysis. Even staunch behaviorists such as John Watson, and later B. F. Skinner, used psychoanalysis as a reference point to develop radically different theories of the personality that had little or no resemblance to Freud's ideas.

Object relations   Freud used the word "object" to refer to any person, object, or activity that can satisfy an instinctive desire. In his view, the first object in an infant's life that can gratify such a desire is the mother's breast. As the child grows, other people become desire-gratifying objects in a variety of different ways.

Object relations theory owes its roots to Freud but diverged on a different path. Its core principles focus on interpersonal relationships with these objects, whereas Freud emphasized the instinctual drives themselves with little attention given to a child's actual relationship to the object. Object relations theorists see the social and environmental influences on personality, particularly between the mother and child, as crucial to the development of personality and the child's sense of self or ego. Object relations is closely aligned with what is also known in professional circles as ego psychology. Two well-known pioneers in object relations theory are Melanie Klein and Heinz Kohut. Klein's early career overlapped Freud's later years, and Kohut's began around the time of Freud's death.

Karen Horney   Karen Horney was trained as a Freudian psychoanalyst in Berlin and is considered one of the first modern feminists. From 1914 to 1918 she underwent psychoanalytic training at the Berlin Psychoanalytic Institute and later became a faculty member there. Though initially devoted to Freud's systematic paradigm of psychoanalysis, she eventually disputed several of his key concepts. In particular she took issue with his view on unchanging biological forces as the determining factors for personality development. She denied the high status of sexual factors in his theory, including the Oedipal complex, the concepts of libido, and the three-part structure of the personality (id, ego, and superego). In fact, she left Freud's psychoanalytic circle over his views that women have poorly developed superegos and inferiority feelings about their bodies because they lack a penis. She countered Freud's view by saying that men have "womb envy," an unconscious desire for a womb.

Other criticisms of Freud and psychoanalysis

As more has been learned about child development since Freud's theories were first launched, there has been an increasing lack of support for some of his assumptions about the human personality. Perhaps none of his ideas have met with as much criticism as his psychosexual stages of development. While many modern-day clinicians still find aspects of his stages helpful, most do not adhere to the presupposition of sexual conflict being the central task of developmental maturity. Thus, concepts like Oedipal and Electra complexes are held by a very small minority of professionals overall.

Another criticism of Freud concerns his training as a physician and his extensive reliance on a medical model to develop his theory of psychoanalysis. His strong emphasis on pathology causes him to label behavior as "problematic" or "inappropriate" that most in contemporary times would classify as normative or common to the human condition. In other words, he is accused by some of "creating" psychopathology when it may not be anything out of the ordinary human experience.

Example: Data collection and report Freud's
methods of collecting data from his patients have also drawn much criticism by scholars. The following represent some of the most prominent concerns:

Freud did not make verbatim transcripts of his conversations with patients. If he made notes at all it was typically hours after the interaction. Critics claim that important data would inevitably be lost because recall of specific details would fade the longer the interval between analysis and recording. This opened up the possibility that there were important omissions and distortions of the original data.

Because a central component of Freud's theory involved interpretation of a patient's disclosures, some critics claim that Freud could have easily recalled and recorded only what he wanted to hear or selectively chosen those aspects that would support his assumptions.

Freud claimed that a high percentage of his female clients had experienced sexual abuse as children, often by their fathers. Some have suggested that Freud used suggestive or even coercive procedures to elicit or plant memories of child sexual abuse in his patients. Freud himself later acknowledged that some recollections by his patients may have been fantasies they imagined. He even left the door open to the possibility, though he did not explicitly state it as fact, that he may have influenced their recollection in a coercive way.

Researchers have found discrepancies between Freud's notes and those cases histories on which those notes were supposedly based. This is a difficult problem to trace because Freud destroyed most of his patient files. Freud only published six case histories, and none are considered to be compelling evidence for the soundness of psychoanalysis. One of the cases he published was not even one of his patient, but that of another physician.

Even if Freud's recollections of events discussed in therapy were completely accurate, the reports given to him by patients may not have matched reality. Freud is known to have spent little time verifying accounts about patient's childhood experiences, especially those accusing family members of sexual abuse. Critics argue that he should have questioned family members to determine the accuracy of patient reports.

Critics have also pointed out that Freud's theories are based upon a very small homogenous sample group made up almost exclusively of upper-class Austrian women. Not only is it limited in gender and geographical location, but it is also influenced by a late nineteenth century society that was Victorian in manner, which manifested as sexually repressed. Such a sample, many contend, made Freud's focus on sex simply a reflection of the time period more than a determinant of personality.

Example: Is psychoanalysis science? Some
psychologists claim that psychoanalysis is good science, others that it is bad science, and still others that it is not science at all. Those who believe psychoanalysis is good science are no doubt the minority based on findings in the latter half of the twentieth century. Surprisingly, not all psychoanalysts fall into this group. Rather, a fair number of psychoanalysts are

willing to concede that psychoanalysis is not science and that it was never meant to be science. Instead, they claim that it is more like a worldview that helps people see connections that they otherwise would miss.

It is questionable whether Freud himself thought of his theory of psychoanalysis as science. Despite the growing popularity of psychoanalysis for therapy during his lifetime and beyond, Freud admittedly had little personal interest in the potential treatment value of his system. His primary concern was not to cure his patients but rather to explain the dynamics of human behavior. Though he thought of himself as a scientist more than a therapist, he did not apply scientific methods to how he gathered or analyzed the work upon which his theory was built.

THEORIES IN ACTION

Freud's laboratory did not consist of various apparatus like beakers, scales, or microscopes. Instead, his lab consisted of essentially one piece of furniture: the couch. Most who told their stories on his couch did so as if they were speaking to themselves, since Freud traditionally sat at the head of the couch, out of sight. Some say this therapeutic remoteness was necessary for objectivity; others claim it is evidence of his lack of warmth. Freud admitted to having less interest in treating patients and more passion for understanding the workings of the human personality. His patients were simply his subjects or the means by which to gather the data toward that end.

Despite the many critics Freud has garnered in the last several decades, he did create a number of important techniques that were repeatedly used with his patients and that were adopted by large numbers of followers in subsequent years. Traditional psychoanalysts still use some of these techniques in treatment, much in the same way Freud attempted them. Many others use modified versions that faintly resemble Freud's original work. The fact remains, however, that the discipline of psychology owes a large debt to this pioneer for how he challenged and contributed to our treatment of mental disorders.

The techniques of psychoanalytic therapy are designed to increase awareness, foster insights into the patient's behavior, and shed light on the meaning of one's symptoms. Following are some of the most important techniques that are associated with psychoanalysis.

Free association

Free association plays a central role in analytic treatment. In using free association, patients are encouraged to say whatever comes to mind, regardless of how painful or irrelevant it may seem. The aim of this unchecked verbalization is to open the door of the unconscious so that thoughts, wishes, fantasies, conflicts, and motivations held in the unconscious mind can flow into consciousness without censorship. Free association often leads the patient to remember past experiences that may have been repressed and can result in an intense expression of emotion, called catharsis.

During the free-association process, the therapist's task is to identify the repressed material that is locked in the unconscious. If there is any disruption in the flow, this usually indicates the presence of anxiety, which the therapist attempts to identify and interpret.

Dream analysis

Dream analysis is also an important procedure for uncovering unconscious material and giving the patient insight into areas of unresolved problems. During sleep, defenses are lowered and repressed feelings surface. Freud called dreams the "royal road to consciousness," because in them unconscious wishes, needs, and fears are expressed. Some motivations and fears are so unacceptable to the person that they are expressed in disguised or symbolic form through dreams rather than being directly revealed in some other way.

Dreams have two levels of content: latent content and manifest content. Latent content consists of hidden, symbolic, and unconscious motives, wishes, and fears. But latent content, if revealed directly, can be very painful for the person to experience. So to make it less threatening, it transforms into what is called manifest content, which is the dream as it appears to the dreamer. This manifest content is often disguised in symbols. The therapist's task in dream analysis is to identify the symbols in dreams and provide guidance to the patient as to the dream's meaning.

As part of dream analysis, the therapist may ask the patient to free associate some aspect of the manifest content to help him or her understand latent meanings. As the meaning of the dreams are recognized, it helps the patient unlock the repression that has kept the material hidden and allows the patient new potential to deal effectively with the material.

Analysis and interpretation of transference

Transference is the unconscious shifting of feelings from someone in the patient's personal life to the therapist. Transference allows the patient to understand and resolve previously "unfinished business" from past relationships. As therapy progresses, childhood feelings and conflicts begin to surface from the unconscious. A patient may unconsciously transfer feelings of love, sexuality, hostility, or any number of other emotions onto the therapist during the process of therapy. If the therapy is to produce real change, the transference relationship must be worked through.

The transference situation is considered valuable because it allows the patient an opportunity to re-experience a variety of feelings that would not other-wise be accessible to them. By using the therapist as a safe or neutral object to express these wishes, beliefs, and desires, patients are able to change some of their long-standing patterns of behavior.

The analysis of transference is an important technique in psychoanalytic therapy because it allows the patient to achieve present-moment insight into past relational issues. As the therapist interprets the transference process for the patient, he or she can work with the insights to make changes in desired areas.

Analysis and interpretation of resistance

Resistance in a psychoanalytic context is anything that works against the progress of therapy and prevents the patient from accessing unconscious material. Resistance then is any idea, attitude, feeling, or action that gets in the way of potential change. During free association, a patient may show an unwillingness to relate to certain thoughts or experiences. Freud views resistance as an unconscious process that people use to protect themselves against intolerable anxiety and pain that might result if they became aware of the repressed feelings.

In therapy, resistance blocks both the patient and therapist from gaining insight into the processes of the unconscious. The analytic therapist's role is to point out resistance when it is observed in hopes that the patient will acknowledge the block and deal with the conflict.

Resistance in psychoanalytic therapy is not something to be rid of, but something that must be dealt with. The anxiety that causes the resistance will not lessen unless the resistance is faced. Having said this, it is important that the analytic therapist respects the resistances of clients and assists them in working therapeutically with their defenses. When handled properly, resistance can be one of the most valuable tools in understanding the patient.

Research

It appears that the current status of psychoanalytic theory is going through an identity crisis of its own and has been since the mid-1980s. Some in the psychoanalytic community believe that the theory and practice of psychoanalysis are declining due to several key factors.

Terms long used in psychoanalysis are familiar to many but remain vague and imprecise. This makes continuity of use across the professional landscape difficult and open to various interpretations, some of which may be contradictory. Second, many terms in psychoanalytic theory refer to abstractions, such as drives or instincts, yet are often treated as if they refer to substantial entities. Yet, without more concrete ways of describing these abstractions, some fear that psychoanalysis will never be subjected to the rigorous empirical testing that would enhance its credibility in a therapeutic environment that increasingly values measurable therapeutic outcomes. Another problem within psychoanalytic theory surrounds the multiple layering of concepts and terms, often making it redundant and more complicated than it needs to be.

On the issue of empirical testing, those in the psychoanalytic community differ widely. Some believe that the theories are not empirically verifiable, while others believe they already have been extensively tested. Proponents cite two important facts. First, they claim that a large body of experimental evidence already exists on psychoanalytic ideas, some confirming the theory and others not. Second, while psychoanalysis does not seek to validate their concepts using empirical methods, it does use a holistic method of viewing the entire person as a single organism. This procedure is widely used with validity in both the social sciences and the "hard" sciences. Recognizing the holistic nature of psychoanalytic ideas and therapy suggests that some kinds of interpretation are more valid than others. In the minds of some psychoanalysts, the use of a holistic method nullifies the debate about whether psychoanalysis is a science or merely a means of interpretation.

Some general propositions have been set forth that most of today's practitioners would agree form core foundational ideas of modern psychoanalysis:

- Humans have many thoughts, emotions, and motives that are unconscious. Neurological studies supply ample evidence that unconscious processes of cognition exist. Defense mechanisms like repression and denial against emotions that are unpleasant are well documented as real responses.

- Personality patterns form in childhood and shape later relationships. Observational and longitudinal studies have shown that adult personality traits have parallels that begin in childhood.

- Mental representations of the self, others, and relationships guide our social patterns. Considerable

CHRONOLOGY

1856: Sigismund Freud is born (changes his name to Sigmund at age 22).

1873: Receives a summa cum laude award on graduation from the Gymnasium. He is already able to read in several languages.

1877: Joins Brücke's laboratory.

1880: A year of military service. Breuer provides treatment to Bertha Pappenheim (Anna O.).

1881: Awarded a delayed doctor's degree in medicine.

1882: Meets Martha Bernays and becomes secretly engaged to her.

1884: Discovers the analgesic properties of cocaine.

1886: Starts private practice. Marries Martha in September.

1887: Starts using hypnosis. The birth of daughter Mathilda.

1889: Birth of son Martin.

1891: Birth of son Olivier.

1892: Birth of son Ernst.

1893: Birth of daughter Sophie.

1895: Birth of daughter Anna.

1896: Freud for the first time uses the term "psychoanalysis." Death of Jacob Freud.

1897: Postulates Oedipus complex.

1899: *The Interpretation of Dreams* is published on November 4.

1902: Begins the Wednesday Psychological Society meetings at his home.

1906: C. G. Jung starts his correspondence with Sigmund Freud.

1909: Publication of *Analysis of a Phobia in a Five-Year-Old Boy (Little Hans)*.

1911: Adler's resignation.

1913: Break from Jung. Publication of *Totem and Taboo*.

1920: Publishes *Beyond the Pleasure Principle*.

1921: Publishes *Group Psychology and the Analysis of the Ego*.

1923: Diagnosed with cancer of the jaw. Publication of *The Ego and the Id*.

1930: Freud's mother dies.

1933: Sigmund Freud has a letter exchange with Albert Einstein on the topic Why the War? The Nazis publicly burn Freud's work in Berlin.

1938: March 13th: Austria's annexation (Anschluss). Freud's house and the headquarters of the Vienna Association of Psychoanalysis are searched. Anna Freud is arrested and interrogated by the Gestapo. In June, Freud and his family emigrate to Great Britain.

1939: September 23rd, Freud's death. *Moses and Monotheism* is published.

---

research on attachment behaviors both in animals and humans confirm this.

- Personality development is more than simply working through sexual conflict (Freud's theory). It also involves learning to move from dependency to interdependency.

Not all of the research on Freud's ideas supports psychoanalytic theory. Studies on personality development do not confirm the suggestion that personality is formed by age five and changes little after that, as Freud thought. Most psychologists accept that personality continues to develop over time and can change dramatically after childhood. Contemporary research on instincts as the driving force of personality shows

that Freud's conception of these ideas is no longer a useful model for human motivation. But the most important finding is that some psychoanalytic concepts can be reduced to propositions testable by the methods of science.

Case studies

Each of Freud's five major case histories was written for colleagues and was intended as an explanation of the meaning of the patient's symptoms along with his observations and analysis. All of his case histories are relevant to the development of his theory and practice of psychoanalysis, but three are of particular importance because they demonstrate how his theory

BIOGRAPHY:

Anna Freud

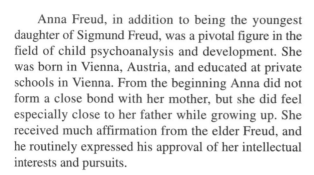

Anna Freud, in addition to being the youngest daughter of Sigmund Freud, was a pivotal figure in the field of child psychoanalysis and development. She was born in Vienna, Austria, and educated at private schools in Vienna. From the beginning Anna did not form a close bond with her mother, but she did feel especially close to her father while growing up. She received much affirmation from the elder Freud, and he routinely expressed his approval of her intellectual interests and pursuits.

As a student she was bored and restless with formal education and openly complained about attending school. She claims to have learned less in her formal education than from guests that her father had at their home. This is where she supposedly learned several languages such as Hebrew, German, English, French, and Italian. At age of 19, Anna began two years of study to become a teacher, and in the summer of 1915 she successfully passed her teacher's examination.

When Anna Freud was 23 years old, she underwent psychoanalysis with her father as analyst, which was unusual, even at that time. This analysis continued for several years, and Anna seemed to form a dependence on her father from which she never broke free until his later years. In 1923, when her father had the first of many operations on his jaw to remove cancer growths, Anna felt it was her duty to care for him because he was ill. She remained his constant companion and primary caregiver until his death many years later.

Shortly after this, in 1924, Anna Freud began taking more responsibility over her father's professional career and performing active service in the psychoanalytic community. That same year she became a member of the Committee of her father's closest advisors. In 1925, she was on the executive board of the Vienna Psychoanalytic Institute and started work as a training analyst. In addition, she also took over all the aspects of production of the *Verlag*, a psychoanalytic publication similar to a journal that her father created.

Anna Freud's long-time interest had been children. Though she never married nor had her own, she devoted her professional career, first a teacher and then as a psychoanalyst, to working with children. She was undoubtedly influenced profoundly by her father's psychoanalytic theories. She used these theories as a framework to understand the experiences of children and the stages of their normal psychological development.

In 1927 Freud and two of her closest friends, Eva Rosenfeld and Dorothy Burlingham, organized a nursery school for local children. Within this school Freud and her colleagues (the most famous of which was Erik Erikson) taught alternate teaching methods while taking careful notes of the process. Anna would increasingly use her work with children as a means to study the developing ego of children. She eventually published, *The Ego and the Mechanisms of Defense* in 1936 in honor of her father's 80th birthday.

World War II brought dramatic changes in the structure of the psychoanalytic movement. After the Nazis took control of Austria in 1938, Anna and her father emigrated to London, England, where Sigmund Freud died a year later.

In 1947, Freud and Burlingham established the Hampstead Child Therapy Course and Clinic in London, which provided training opportunities for individuals interested in the psychological and emotional development of children. From the 1950s until her death, psychoanalysts, child psychologists, and teachers worldwide sought opportunities to hear Freud lecture, and to benefit from the insights she developed from a lifetime of working with children.

After her father's death, Anna Freud's career flourished. She published several books of her own, adhering mostly to the psychoanalytic principles her father had set, but expanding or refining in places that set her apart from him. Among her important written works are: *The Psychoanalytical Treatment of Children* (1946), *Normality and Pathology in Childhood* (1965), and the seven-volume *Writings of Anna Freud* (1973).

and methods evolved. The first, the case of Anna O., was conducted by Dr. Joseph Breuer, Freud's mentor. The remaining two, the "Rat Man" and "Dora," were conducted and recorded by Freud.

Anna O.: free association Joseph Breuer was a famous physician that had befriended the young Freud as he was just beginning his practice. The two men frequently discussed Breuer's patients at length. One in particular, a 21-year-old Anna O., would become a pivotal case in the development of psychoanalysis.

An intelligent and attractive woman, Anna O. suffered from severe hysterical complaints including paralysis, memory loss, mental deterioration, nausea, and disturbances of vision and speech. The symptoms first appeared when she was nursing her dying father, who had always pampered her.

Breuer began Anna's treatment by using hypnosis. He found that while hypnotized she would recall specific experiences that seemed to have given rise to certain symptoms. Talking about the experiences under hypnosis often relieved the symptoms. For more than a year Breuer saw Anna every day. She would recount the day's disturbing incidents and after they talked she sometimes reported that her symptoms had been eased. She referred to their conversations as the "talking cure."

Freud's interest in what lay beyond conscious life and in hypnotism and hysteria led him to study with the famous neurologist Jean-Martin Charcot in Paris. When Freud returned to Vienna, he began using hypnosis, massage, and pressure on the head to get patients to dredge up thoughts related to their symptoms. Only later did he ask them to say whatever crossed their minds. This he called free association, what the patient called Anna O. had already labeled as the "talking cure." Freud's investigations into internal conflicts such as this case also led him to determine that the mind was divided into three conflicting, now known as id, ego, and superego. So, in a very real sense, Anna O. was the first psychoanalytic patient even though Freud did not administer the treatment.

"Rat Man" One of Freud's best known cases involved a young lawyer he assigned the name "Rat Man." The young man's case was thus named by Freud because he had obsessive thoughts concerning rats, torture, and punishment. Treatment included having the man talk about the first things that came to mind as he considered his disturbing thoughts. Freud used this technique, which he called free association, to probe the man's unconscious conflicts that resist direct expres-

Anna Freud with her dog. (AP/Wide World Photos. Reproduced by permission.)

sion. Freud then interpreted the man's symptoms and found them rooted in ambivalence about sexuality and about his hostile feelings toward his father. For Freud, interpretation was necessary to give meaning to the apparently random thoughts of free association. In the case of "Rat Man," Freud wove together elaborate stories, explanations, and speculations to make sense out of constellations of symptoms that seemed impossibly puzzling.

"Dora": Transference The famous and controversial case of "Dora," an 18-year old female, would become the first of Freud's major case histories. "Dora," as Freud called her, worked intensely with him in analysis initially but abruptly ended her work with him after just 11 weeks. Through the process of analysis, Dora had "transferred" on Freud some very passionate feelings ranging from love to fury during their work together. Freud initially did not recognize the significance of these emotions. Also embedded in her disclosures was a homosexual theme which Freud failed to fully appreciate, in large part because he had not yet discovered how homosexual urges manifested in neuroses.

Upon completion of the analysis, Freud had originally intended this case to be an exposition on dream interpretation but after reflection, considered it a failure in this regard. Instead he chose to evaluate the transfer of emotion that was a prominent dynamic of "Dora's" analysis. Freud used the concept of transference to refer to the strong emotions that are projected by the patient onto the therapist. This case, perhaps more than any other, helped formalize his concept of transference and its essential role in effective psychoanalysis.

Relevance to the modern reader

Freud and his theory of psychoanalysis have had a great impact on Western society and specifically on American popular culture. Perhaps one of the most obvious ways psychoanalysis has affected popular culture is the legitimization it gave to sexuality in the early part of the twentieth century. Sexual restraints were already starting to loosen around the time that Freud began espousing his ideas publicly, but the popularity of psychoanalysis was a great boost to public openness toward sexual issues.

Freud's psychoanalysis, though dated, can still provide students of psychology a number of helpful insights into the human condition. Nearly every person can benefit from understanding basic aspects of psychoanalytic thought like transference, resistance, ego-defense mechanisms, etc. Whether in a professional context or lay context, these and other psychoanalytic concepts provide a conceptual framework for looking at and understanding the origins and manifestations of behavior. This is something nearly everyone is curious about.

It is feasible for someone to not accept the orthodox Freudian position and still benefit from the many psychoanalytic concepts that shed light on inner conflicts and human relationships. From a broader perspective, psychoanalysis shows us that there are patterns to life and relationships, patterns that are often established in the early phases of development. This has significant implications for many areas of human interaction, such as intimate relationships, the family and child rearing, and therapeutic relationships.

As newer psychoanalytic theorists refine classical analytic techniques, it opens the possibility that psychoanalytic theory will regain some of the influence it has lost over the years. Current directions in psychoanalytic therapy are focusing on building collaborative working relationships with patients, instead of giving the therapist control over the therapeutic relationship. Also, there is a push in some circles to incorporate briefer forms of psychoanalytic therapy due to societal pressure for accountability and cost-effectiveness. This is also a trend that uses psychoanalytic theory as the basis for group therapy, which has been well received.

BIBLIOGRAPHY

Sources

AllPsych Online. *Psychology 101*. March 21, 2004. [cited March 28, 2004]. http://allpsych.com/psychology101/sexual_development.html.

AllPsych Online. *Psychology 101*. March 21, 2004. [cited March 28, 2004]. http://allpsych.com/psychology101/ego.html.

AllPsych Online. *Psychology 101*. March 21, 2004. [cited March 28, 2004]. http://allpsych.com/psychology101/defenses.html.

Clark, Ronald. *Freud: The Man and the Cause*. New York: Random House, 1980.

Freud, Sigmund. *Standard Edition: Two Case Studies*. Vol. 10. Translated by James Strachey. London: The Hogarth Press, 1955. [cited March 30, 2004]. http://www.clas.ufl.edu/users/gthursby/fonda/freud10.html.

Gay, Peter. *The Freud Reader*. London: Vintage, 1995.

Gay, Peter. *Freud: A Life for Our Time*. New York: W.W. Norton, 1998.

Hale, Nathan G. *The Rise and Crisis of Psychoanalysis in the United States*. New York: Oxford University Press, 1995.

Holland, Norman. *Psychoanalysis as a Holistic Science*. University of Florida. January 2, 2004. [cited April 3, 2004]. http://www.clas.ufl.edu/users/nnh/psas&sci.htm.

Holt, Robert. *Freud Reappraised*. New York: Guilford Press, 1989.

"Hypnosis." *Encyclopedia Britannica Online*. [cited April 2, 2004]. http://www.britannica.com/eb/article?eu=42754&tocid=0&query=freud&ct=eb.

Hypnotherapy and Brief Therapy Resource Pages. [cited April 4, 2004]. http://www.geocities.com/Athens/Agora/1380/page5.html.

Library of Congress. *Freud: Conflict and Culture*. November 7, 2001. [cited March 24, 2004]. http://www.loc.gov/exhibits/freud/freud01.html.

Library of Congress. *Freud: Conflict and Culture*. November 7, 2001. [cited March 24, 2004]. http://www.loc.gov/exhibits/freud/freud02.html.

Library of Congress. *Freud: Conflict and Culture*. November 7, 2001. [cited March 24, 2004]. http://www.loc.gov/exhibits/freud/freud03.html.

Schultz, Duane P., and Sydney E. Schultz. *A History of Modern Psychology*. 8th ed. Belmont, CA: Wadsworth/Thompsom, 2004.

Schur, Max. *Freud: Living and Dying*. New York: International University Press, 1972.

Sparknotes. *Barnes and Noble*. [cited March 26, 2004]. http://www.sparknotes.com/biography/freud/section1.html.

Webster University. *Women's Intellectual Contributions to the Study of Mind and Society*. [cited April 4, 2004]. http://www.webster.edu/~woolflm/annafreud.html.

Young-Bruehl, Elisabeth. *Anna Freud: A Biography*. New York: Summit Books, 1988.

Further readings

Breger, Louis. *Freud: Darkness in the Midst of Vision*. New York: John Wiley & Sons, 2000.

Breuer, Joseph, and Sigmund Freud. *Studies in Hysteria*. Boston: Beacon Hill Press, 1950.

Clark, Ronald. *Freud: The Man and the Cause*. New York: Random House, 1980.

Ferris, Paul. *Dr. Freud: A Life*. London: Pimlico, 1997.

Freud, Ernst. *The Letters of Sigmund Freud*. New York: Basic Books, 1975.

Freud, Ernst, Lucie Freud, and Ilse Grubich-Simitis, eds. *Sigmund Freud: His Life in Pictures and Words*. New York: New York: W.W. Norton & Co., Inc., 1998.

Freud, Sigmund. *An Autobiographical Study*. London: Hogarth Press and The Institute of Psycho-Ananlysis, 1946.

Freud, Sigmund. *The Interpretation of Dreams*. New York, Avon Books, 1965.

Gay, Peter. *Freud: A Life for Our Time*. New York: W.W. Norton, 1998.

Freud, Sigmund. *An Autobiographical Study*. London: Hogarth Press and The Institute of Psycho-Ananlysis, 1946.

Gay, Peter. *The Freud Reader*. London: Vintage, 1995.

Freud, Sigmund. *An Autobiographical Study*. London: Hogarth Press and The Institute of Psycho-Ananlysis, 1946.

Jones, Ernest. *The Life and Work of Sigmund Freud*. New York: Basic Books, Inc., 1953.

Krull, Marianne. *Freud and His Father*. London: Hutchinson, 1986.Masson, Jeffrey, ed. *The Complete Letters of Sigmund Freud to Wilhelm Fliess*. Cambridge, MA: Belnap Press, 1985.

Rieff, Phillip, ed. *Freud: Early Psychoanalytic Writings*. New York, Collier Books, 1963.

Trilling, Lionel, and Steven Marcus, eds. *The Life and Work of Sigmund Freud*. New York: Basic Books, 1961.

Young-Bruehl, Elisabeth. *Anna Freud: A Biography*. New York: W.W. Norton, 1994.

Karen Clementine Horney

BRIEF OVERVIEW

The study of mental health and the feminist movement are deeply indebted to Karen Horney for offering the world innovative and alternative views of psychodynamic theories. She influenced society and the treatment of the mentally ill in the late nineteenth and early twentieth centuries. Ironically, Horney never perceived herself as a feminist, and many aspects of her lifestyle—especially her dependence on having a man in her life—appear to make that label problem atic. In Europe, where Horney was born and began her career, the study of the mind was completely male-dominated, and came to be firmly under the sway of three men that were her contemporaries: Sigmund Freud, Carl Jung, and Alfred Adler. Yet despite these three disparate voices, Karen Horney was also able to make her voice heard.

Horney is often described as a neo-Freudian, but her view of neurosis is markedly different from Freud's. She became convinced that neurosis was much more a normal component of life than it was in Freud's universe. Where Freud perceived neurotics made sick by forces beyond their control in the subconscious, Horney saw people termed neurotic attempting to make their lives bearable. She called their symptoms a means of "interpersonal and intrapsychic control and coping." Where Freud viewed culture as the necessary bulwark for survival pitted against the primitive desires of the id, Horney saw culture as the problem. Culture provided bad environments that caused frustration of people's

1885–1952

GERMAN PSYCHIATRIST, PSYCHOANALYST, PROFESSOR

UNIVERSITY OF FREIBURG; UNIVERSITY OF BERLIN

Karen Horney. (Corbis–Bettmann. Reproduced by permission.)

emotional needs and created hostility, fear, and insecurity, leading to neurosis.

Freud believed that sick patients could be saved by healthy doctors. Horney, however, came to believe something that was anathema to Freud and the rest of the psychological community of her time: People suffering from mental illness could take responsibility for the illness and help themselves. The concept that people dealing with minor problems caused by neurosis could be their own psychiatrists was far from a popular view among the providers of psychiatric care. Though the concept of self-help is not consistently given credence by mental health professionals today, self-help programs for a wide variety of emotional, social, and physical problems have become a standard facet of treatment. Karen Horney was far ahead of her time when, in 1942, she published *Self-Analysis*, one of the earliest self-help books ever written. Much of her work was based upon her own terribly personal and painful experiences, and yet from that pain she gave birth to optimism. Karen Horney was, in herself, living proof that human beings, even neurotic, depressed human beings, can do great things. Her honesty and unflinching ability to look inward and use that vision became the tools that she used to help others. Sadly, for most of her life, she was unable to help herself.

Horney's unique vision of the treatment of mental illness didn't stop with self-help. One of the leading feminist thinkers in the psychological world of her time, Horney was an early critic of Freud's penis envy and Oedipus complex hypotheses. One of her earliest published works, a collection of essays titled *Feminine Psychology*, went into print in 1936. Though she agreed that such a phenomena as penis envy could and did exist among little girls, she was convinced that it was far less significant an issue among adult women than Freud and his followers believed. Horney could accept that it was possible for penis envy to be a component of some neurotic females' psyches, but adamantly disputed that it was as universal as Freud believed. Much of her early writings suggest that what Freud called penis envy may instead be the justified resentment that women feel as they attempt to survive as second-class citizens of a male-dominated world.

It is unclear if Horney was thumbing her nose at Freud when she developed a premise that indeed there may be a male version of penis envy. Horney called this "womb envy." Womb envy, she stated, was the unexpressed inadequacy some men felt because they could not bear children. She suggested that womb envy manifests itself in two ways: men trying to dominate women, and in over-achievement and the drive to succeed.

In reviewing Horney's theories over the span of her life, there are marked changes in those beliefs. It could be said that she was inconsistent—at first espousing Freud's theories regarding childhood sexual conflict and transference and later attacking them. But this change demonstrates one of Horney's great abilities: to hold nothing sacrosanct. Horney seems to have received this gift from living with a fanatically religious father and a sanctimonious mother. It gave her a unique aptitude to critically look at her own ideas as well as the viewpoints of others, and to revise her own tenets as they needed changing, due her life experiences. This open-mindedness—this refusal to become rigidly orthodox—it appears, was for Horney the reason her beliefs and approach to psychoanalysis have remained a part of mental health treatment decades after her death.

Horney's critics also called her politically incorrect. There is some evidence to support that criticism. Surely her ongoing attacks against Freud within months after his death might have been avoided by a more circumspect person. Her statements about the "pious Jew thanking his God. . .that he was not created a woman," made in Germany in the years that the Nazis were fighting to gain control of the country, sound anti-Semitic and inflammatory. Yet early on, Horney equally expressed anger at her family's discrimination against (the first of several) Jewish lovers. In her decades-long battle with Freud and his followers, Horney certainly wore no velvet gloves. Neither did her critics. However, for all the evidence of political incorrectness, there is at least as much substantiation that Horney was among the most courageous, honest, and forthright of the analysts of her time.

BIOGRAPHY

Horney's family of origin and early years

Eilbek was a bustling small town on the outskirts of the port of Hamburg, Germany, when Karen Clementine Danielsen was born there on September 15th, 1885. She was the second (and last) child born to Berndt (Wackels) Danielsen, a Norwegian sea captain and his young wife, Sonni. Captain Danielsen had been married before, and had four grown children before he fell in love with this woman 20 years his junior. Clothilde Sonni Van Ronzelen Danielsen was an unusual woman for her time. Described as beautiful, well-educated, sophisticated, and liberal, Sonni was the daughter of a well-known Amsterdam architect. Sonni came to the marriage an independent woman in an era when men were the unquestioned masters of their homes. From early childhood, Karen's mother confided the unhappy details of her married life to her children. As a young girl Karen already knew that her mother had married Wackels Danielsen in 1880 less because of love than the fear that she might not marry at all. She also came to know that her mother wished Captain Danielsen dead. In 1881, their first child, a son also named Berndt had been born, but it did little to stop the already-looming battle between the poorly educated, overly religious Wackels Danielsen and his freethinking, urbane wife. Karen's birth four years later was equally ineffective in uniting the unhappy couple. Throughout their marriage, Wackels Danielsen would continue to go into frequent angry tirades. Equally, Sonni would persist in looking in disdain upon him, considering him far beneath her in life-station.

Horney wrote of her father,

> He delivers conversion sermons, says endless, rather stupid prayers every morning. . . . I cannot listen to his sensuous, materialistic, illogical, intolerant views of everything high and holy. He is simply a low, ordinary, stupid character who cannot rise to higher things.

This excerpt from Horney's diary that she began to keep at age 13 is quite telling. Karen and young Berndt Danielsen called their father "the Bible thrower." Apparently Wackels Danielsen's interactions

PRINCIPAL PUBLICATIONS

- *Feminine Psychology*. New York: W. W. Norton Co., Inc. 1936.
- *The Neurotic Personality of Our Time*. New York: W. W. Norton Co., Inc. 1937.
- "New Ways in Psychoanalysis." *Psychological Review*. New York: W. W. Norton Co., Inc., 1939.
- "Self-Analysis." *Psychological Review*. New York: W. W. Norton Co., Inc., 1942.
- "Our Inner Conflicts." *Psychological Review*. New York: W. W. Norton Co., Inc., 1945.
- "Are You Considering Psychoanalysis?" *Psychological Review*. New York: W. W. Norton Co., Inc., 1946.
- "Neurosis and Human Growth." *Psychological Review*. New York: W. W. Norton Co., Inc., 1950.

with the family when he was not at sea fluctuated between brief periods of quiet interspersed with terrible arguments with Sonni and severe punitive measures aimed at his children. He was given to rages during which it was not uncommon for him to throw his ever-present Bible across the room. Karen alternately feared and hated her father both for his religious hypocrisy and harsh, authoritarian ways. But perhaps his greatest sin, in her eyes, sprang from her belief that he favored her older brother over her simply because she was a girl.

Captain Danielsen, for all the negatives attributed to him, is also described as having brought young Karen on three of his voyages, something rarely done by sea captains in the late 1800s. He also reportedly brought her presents from all over the world. Those trips with her father remained some of Karen's better childhood memories. Even as an adult, she still remembered hearing the Norwegian sailors read aloud on these journeys. In her writings and lectures, she quoted passages from Kierkegaard and other Norwegian writers that they had read. Despite the sea voyages and the gifts, Karen viewed her father as a hypocrite fixated on religion, and invariably sided with her mother in the frequent battles that disrupted the Danielsen household. Even with the healing passage of time, Karen's recollections of her early years were conflicted and painful, replete with conflict of a cold, uncaring father battling with a mother she came to view as smothering.

Despite her overwhelming possessiveness, Sonni seemed to truly love Karen and in childhood often referred to her as "my little lamb." Yet she often gave the appearance of being closer to, and confiding more in, her son Berndt. That closeness between mother and son, along with Sonni's beauty and grace, seem to have made Karen feel alienated and to view herself as an ugly duckling. The resultant bitter, rebellious, and angry little girl seems to have tried to gain her brother Berndt's affection in lieu of her parents' love. There apparently was some sexual play between them as children, and Karen, with characteristic candor, describes childhood incestuous feelings toward her older brother. When young Berndt reached adolescence and turned his back on her, Karen was for some time devastated by his rejection.

"If I couldn't be pretty, I decided I would be smart." A childhood picture of Karen Danielsen shows a blonde-haired little girl that clearly is at least attractive. Yet it seems that Karen never perceived herself that way. Much of her memories suggest that instead she felt awkward, unwanted, and valued less than her brother because she was a girl. Despite emotional problems that were already clearly in evidence (Karen's first depression, she states, was at the age of nine), she found an escape from her unhappiness in her studies. By the time she was 13, she already was determined to become a doctor. When she decided that she wanted to transfer from the church-run school that she had been attending to a newly opened gymnasium in Hamburg to prepare girls for university, the struggle between her parents reached new heights. Captain Danielsen, tight-fisted and not a believer in higher education for girls, as might be expected saw the move as foolish and a waste of money. He apparently wanted Karen to stay at home and help out, making it possible for the family to dispense with the services of their maid. But Sonni prevailed, and in 1901, Karen, then 16, began high school in preparation for attending the university, paid for by her father.

Schooling and marriage

In those high school years, Karen expanded her education in more than academics. She was a gifted student, but while still in her teens, she began a series of affairs with an unending parade of men. Such liaisons would characterize most of her life. In the diary she began to keep at age 13, Karen noted,

"Being in love displaced all other worries: for if he is my thought day and night, how then should others have room?" Her first love was an unnamed actor, followed by an equally anonymous friend of her older brother's in 1903, but these liaisons were brief. A longer affair with a Jewish musician named Rolf soon followed. It was during this relationship with Rolf that Karen discovered and railed against her mother's and brother Berndt's condescension and anti-Semitism. In 1904, a momentous event happened that would change many things for Karen Horney. She was still involved with Rolf when nearly a quarter century of marital discord between Sonni and Berndt Danielsen came to an end. Sonni separated from her husband, moved out of the Danielsen home, and joined Karen in Hamburg.

Sonni's departure also signaled the end of financial support for both she and Karen. It is at least arguable that in addition to fears of being left on the shelf, Sonni had married Berndt Danielsen for his money. It is clear that at least at the end of her marriage, she had no financial resources of her own. To make ends meet after Sonni left her husband, she began to take in boarders and Karen began to tutor. Her parent's separation made Karen increasingly conscious that the mother she had defended all of her life might not be a model of perfection after all. Earlier, Karen had made cutting remarks about her father, saying that "mother is our greatest happiness" and "we are so unspeakably happy when you are not here." Karen now began to describe Sonni as "depressed, irritable, and domineering." Karen quickly became involved with one of her mother's boarders, a man only referred to as "Ernst." With equal speed, Sonni made it known to her daughter that she did not approve. This led to even more tension between mother and daughter.

In 1906, at the age of 21, Karen began medical school at Freiburg University. Once more she was free of her parents, who had caused so many conflicting feelings in her young life. Inevitably, she met and began a liaison with a fellow medical student named Louis Grote Losch. For once, Sonni approved of the relationship and in what was beginning to be a pattern, moved to Freiburg to be near Karen. Sonni even took in Losch and another of his friends as lodgers. By then, Karen was beginning to see her relationship with Sonni as too close, overwhelming. She described feeling "as if I would suffocate under all the love and care surrounding me." In the autumn of 1906, in a move rampant with rebellion and reminiscent of a Freudian case study in which a woman "marries her father," Karen began an affair with one of Losch's friends, a young law student named Oskar Horney. Passing her medical examinations the next year, Karen moved to Gottingen to begin her medical internship. But the affair with Oskar Horney continued unabated.

"In Oskar," she said in a letter at the time, "I found everything I consciously wished for." By all accounts, Oskar Horney's political beliefs could minimally be called right wing while Karen, though never overly involved in politics, was rather liberal. But in October of 1909 these two opposites were married and moved to Berlin. It would soon be evident that she had indeed "married her father." Oskar Horney was every bit as harsh a disciplinarian and as unfeeling a man as her father had been. In Berlin her new husband quickly found employment with a man named Stinnes. Stinnes owned a giant German industrial conglomerate most noted at the time for its cruel squashing of a strike in the Stinnes coalmines the year before. The newlyweds initially lived in a boarding house, but soon, thanks to Oskar's early and frequent promotions, they were able to upgrade their living accommodations to their own apartment in a middle-class section of Lankwitz, a suburb of Berlin. They quickly began to lead an upper-class lifestyle. She and Oskar almost immediately became part of the freewheeling culture that pervaded Berlin just prior to the onset of World War I. That milieu was replete with sexual abandon, and by 1912 their marriage was what is commonly today called an open marriage, with both partners blatantly having affairs outside of their marriage.

Karen continued her studies at the Berlin Medical School during this time, affiliating at the school's neuropsychiatric clinic. Sometime during this period of time, Karen became depressed once more. The reason given was discouragement at being excluded from dissection classes as medical school because she was female. It was also during this time that she first met Berlin's premier psychoanalyst, Karl Abraham, a rigid adherent of Sigmund Freud.

In a pattern that would emerge over and over in her life, things did not continue to go well for Karen. The next year, she continued to become even more depressed, experiencing something new with her feelings of hopelessness—sexual difficulties. In 1910 she began psychoanalysis with Karl Abraham. Her melancholy was compounded that same year in May when her father, the source of much of her internal conflict, died. Even more depressed by summer, and now also pregnant, she stopped psychoanalysis. She would later try psychoanalysis again with Hans Sachs in the 1920s, but it would never help her to any appreciable degree. In *Mothers of Psychoanalysis*, Janet Sayers describes Horney's reaction to the pregnancy. It was

remarkable for both its uniqueness and honesty: She feared it would "interfere with her affairs and vagabonding." Yet the thought of becoming a mother made her "happy and proud." In February of 1911, Karen's mother Sonni suffered a stroke and died, missing by one month the arrival of her first granddaughter, Brigitte.

In 1911 with her depression once more on the wane, Horney began to attend meetings of the Berlin Psychoanalytic Society. The next year, she presented there a paper on the sexual education of children. Horney was still, at that point, sufficiently a Freudian that Karl Abraham wrote to Freud in Vienna recommending Horney's paper as "showing a real understanding." In 1915, with so many men away at war, she was elected secretary of the Berlin Society. Oskar's continued affiliation with the Stinnes businesses became even more profitable with the inception of World War I. In 1913 the Horneys' second daughter, Marianne had been born, followed in 1916 by a third daughter, Renate. They bought a home in a wealthy town, Zehlendorf, and vacationed along the Baltic coast and in the mountains around Berchtesgaden, where Adolph Hitler would later locate his vacation home.

Horney seems to have been determined not to suffocate her children as her mother had once smothered her. Early in life, her first-born, Brigitte, contracted tuberculosis, an illness common even in developed countries in the early part of the twentieth century. Karen promptly shipped Brigitte, then six years old, and her younger sister, four-year-old Marianne, off to Switzerland. They were sent without her and stayed for several months, Karen said, because she wanted them to become independent. Her children—especially her middle daughter Marianne—would experience Karen as both benignly neglectful and often unavailable. She impulsively sent them to a number of experimental schools and began sending all three of her daughters to fellow analyst Melanie Klein for therapy in 1923 when the eldest, Brigitte was 11. Apparently neither the stay in Switzerland nor therapy with Melanie Klein was designed to protect her children. Though the girls would remember their father as playing with them more than their mother did, he would also be remembered as a harsh disciplinarian. In an ironic replay of her own childhood, Karen Horney was already allowing her husband Oskar to inflict the same type of verbal and physical abuse of her daughters that she and her brother had once endured. With characteristic honesty, she would later say that at the time she had believed that she should not interfere, that the discipline was good for her children, and that it would foster their independence. It was a belief that she would later come to see as incorrect.

In 1920, the prestigious Berlin Psychoanalytic Clinic and Institute, the first clinic that made psychoanalysis available to the public, opened its doors. Its ahead-of-its-time mindset would give Horney her first feminist victories: She would become both the Institute's first female member and its first female instructor. Once more she attempted psychoanalysis, this time with Vienna-born Hans Sachs. Her mothering experience in the previous decade had led Horney to insights regarding feminine sexuality and psychology that were beginning to clash with Freud's theories. Adding insult to injury, her first therapist, Karl Abraham, at a conference in The Hague that year opined that women really wanted to be men. He based this belief upon Freud's penis envy theory. That same year, for the first time, Horney wrote a paper expressing psychoanalytical criticism of Freud's male-domination philosophy. It was not destined to be her last.

Though many of her male, Freudian colleagues soon began to openly disagree with her increasingly antagonistic perception of Freud's psychosexual theories, especially those involving women, Horney did encounter some triumphs in her work. Her 1922 appearance at the Berlin Psychoanalytic Congress in which she dismissed Freud and Abraham's beliefs as nothing more than "masculine narcissism" drew a larger audience than any other speaker. She lectured on female sexuality, drawing large crowds, and even was covered in Berlin newspapers. But the price for this success was high. More and more the members of the Institute saw her as a heretic from orthodox Freudian psychology, and in another parody of her childhood, Horney felt increasingly alone and estranged from everyone around her. Increasingly she expanded on thinking begun in the prior decade, in the times of her own pregnancies, about the unexplored importance of motherhood. In a letter to another therapist she noted, "I consider it rather one-sided that the (Freudian) emphasis is always on the attitude toward the father. . .always explaining that for simplicity's sake only the attitude toward the father is mentioned but it would also apply to the attitude toward the mother. But it does not."

World War I's end left a vanquished Germany awash in economic chaos. Even a man as ruthless as Stinnes was not able to avoid financial collapse, and Oskar lost his job. In 1923, Oskar also came down with meningitis, which was soon followed by his own financial failure and bankruptcy. Never a particularly pleasant man, Oskar became progressively more depressed and aggressive after his illness and business failures. In 1926 the Horneys had to sell their home in Zehlendorf. The straw that broke the camel's back occurred that same year when Karen's 42-year-old brother Berndt developed pneumonia and died. After Berndt's death, she felt unable to cope. While on vacation at the Baltic seashore that summer, she contemplated suicide by drowning, but did not. She continued work at an increasingly hostile Berlin Institute and remained in an increasingly unhappy marriage with Oskar. Three years later, in 1927, 42-year old Horney and her three children moved out of that house, never again to return. They relocated to a Berlin apartment, and like her mother, Horney took in lodgers. In 1936, Horney returned to Nazi Germany on one of her many visits and began divorce proceedings against Oskar. He would eventually marry his secretary, with whom he had become romantically involved.

There were those who said Horney only married Oskar Horney for his money. The same suspicion had been raised regarding Horney's mother Sonni years before. There is no way of knowing. What is known is that despite her reduced financial status, Karen Horney seemed to blossom after she left her marriage. Though she had written and lectured on feminist themes even in the early twenties, in 1932 she published two essays that clearly set forth her views on men, women, and Freud: "The Problems of Marriage," and "The Dread of Women." Adolph Hitler and his National Socialist Party were rapidly replacing Germany's anarchy and turmoil, and clearly would soon be in power. Horney, though apolitical, was never an admirer of the Nazis. When a former student, Hungarian analyst Franz Alexander offered her a position in the United States as Assistant Director of the Chicago Psychoanalytic Institute in 1932. Horney jumped at the chance to leave Germany. Now 47 years old, she and her youngest daughter Renate moved to the United States. They arrived in Chicago on September 22nd of that year, leaving behind in Germany Brigitte, now 21 and already an up-and-coming movie actress, and Marianne, studying to be a doctor.

The early years in the United States

Horney passed her U.S. medical board examinations the next year and applied for U.S. citizenship. She also began her practice in the Chicago area and an affair with a younger man she was supervising in analysis, Leon Saul. Horney's experience treating American neurotics increased an already burgeoning belief that Freud's tenets had depended too heavily on constitutional factors and not enough on the social.

The next year, when Erich Fromm came to lecture at the Chicago Institute, Horney renewed an acquaintance that was to change her life. Fromm, a 34-year-old psychoanalyst from Frankfurt, Germany, and recent escapee from Nazi Germany, had, like Franz Alexander, previously been one of her students at the German Psychoanalytic Institute. Though he was 15 years her junior, Horney and Fromm began an affair that would go on for several years.

If Freud's theories could be broken down to a belief that biology shaped us, it was Fromm's conviction that society made us who we are. Fromm's ideas would validate and enhance the theories Horney was already developing, as her ideas would nourish and enhance Fromm's work. Fromm is often described as a melding of Marx and Freud, and indeed, both men were his mentors. Fromm was born in Frankfurt, Germany, of Orthodox Jewish parents. Like Horney, his childhood memories were less than idyllic, containing a moody, business-obsessed father and a depressed mother. The suicide of a beautiful woman, a friend of the Fromm family, and the insanity he perceived in Germany related to World War I were the motivations for Erich to become interested in the workings of the human mind. By 1922, he, like Horney, was working as a psychotherapist. But by 1934, Fromm could see what lay ahead for Germany as well as both Jews and Communists, the two identities he shared. He came to the United States as a refugee, as did so many other intellectuals from Germany and Central Europe.

In 1934, Horney resigned from the Chicago Psychoanalytic Institute and took a teaching position at the Washington-Baltimore Society for Psychoanalysis. The main motivation for this job change seems to have been her desire to be closer to Erich Fromm. When Fromm moved to Brooklyn, New York, then a cultural center for Europe's earliest refugees from the Nazis, Horney followed him there, requiring her to commute from New York to Washington and Baltimore to teach. Marianne had completed her studies, left Germany, and begun an internship in Chicago. In 1935, Renate, now 19, chose to drop out of school and return to Nazi Germany to marry her childhood sweetheart rather than remaining in the United States with her mother. Yet for all these changes within her family, this was a happy and prolific time for Horney. She was elected a member of the New York Psychoanalytic Society and began to teach at the New School for Social Research, part of the University of Exile, a school developed by the vast number of intellectuals being driven out of Europe. She published the first of her many books, the collection of her essays and lectures entitled *Feminine Psychology* in

1936. She eventually published seven major works on neurosis, psychotherapy and self-help, as well as more layman-oriented, "pop" versions of these books.

Karen Horney and the Nazis

Horney made several trips back and forth to Germany in the 1930s, both to see her daughters and to lecture. As an expatriate, she was more welcome than one might have expected, perhaps due to her anti-Freud stance over the years. A full-scale Nazi attack on Freudian thought, calling it "Jewish Science," was underway in Germany at the time. (Ironically, Carl Jung, who had been Freud's collaborator and later, like Horney, one of those that disagreed with his psychosexual theories, was also welcomed by the Nazis. Though he was said to disagree privately with the Nazis, Jung never offered any audible disagreement with the Nazis' anti-Freud stance. Jung in fact served as the head of the German Medical Society for Psychotherapy, an early breakaway group defecting from Freud's tenets. Horney was a member and supporter of the group.) While attending one of Brigitte's plays one evening, Horney was even mistaken for a Nazi party official. Her trips to Germany invariably included giving lectures. On a bittersweet note, one of these lectures was at her alma mater, the Berlin Institute, now commonly called the Goering Institute, after the relative of Hermann Goering, Deputy Führer, who was now in charge there, and where discussion of Freudian principles was no longer allowed. This cousin of Goering's so enjoyed Horney's address (which apparently complied with the ban on mentioning Freud) that he requested a copy of one of her books, which she later sent him.

Horney was never involved to any degree in politics, and unlike other intellectuals of that time who constantly spoke out during World War II, she kept her thoughts her own. Her only known reference to the war concerned mothers and mothering, and how such an event as World War II caused stress to mothers. Horney knew something of that stress: she, too, had the added concern of still having two daughters living in Germany in the 1930s. But on the eve of World War II, in 1939, she did relate her long-held theories to the rise of fascism in Europe. She stated that on an individual level, her parental lack of approval for any kind of dissent on her part was instrumental in keeping her from becoming politically active. On a larger scale, she speculated that this early fear of losing acceptance conditioned people to "uncritically adore one parent. . .or become subservient to the demands of a self-sacrificing mother." Horney believed that this early conditioning made people ready targets for fascism, easily agreeing to blindly obey in return for "promises to fulfill all their needs." She saw Adolph Hitler as the consummate patriarchal figure, ready to dispense whatever was needed by the German people in return for their absolute obedience. The only defense against dictators, she believed, was for people to "become stronger in their self-resolve and individual capacity for forming judgments and making decisions."

In 1941, there were marriages on both sides of the Atlantic for Horney's family. Marianne, in analysis with Fromm for some time, married in New York while Brigitte married in Germany, in Berlin. Brigitte was growing increasingly unhappy with life in Nazi Germany, however. When a close friend of hers, Joachim Gottschalk, committed suicide along with his (Jewish) wife and child rather than be arrested by the Gestapo, Brigitte desperately wanted to leave her native land. However before that could happen, she had a recurrence of the tuberculosis that had plagued her in her childhood. She spent most of the war in a sanitarium in Switzerland.

Later years

Horney and Fromm's affair had been at its height during the 1930s. They lived well and seemed to be good for each other. Their love affair was far more than physical attraction. It was a meeting of the minds, a sharing of Horney's view of psychoanalysis and Fromm's of both sociology and psychotherapy that was mutually beneficial. Despite Fromm's socialist views, they hosted lavish parties replete with the finest gourmet dining, roulette parties, or even being serenaded by Erich Fromm and Hasidic choruses. These affairs were attended by most of the luminaries of the time. Among the regular attendees were Karl Menninger, Harry Stack Sullivan, and Margaret Mead. Up until the onset of World War II, Horney and Fromm took frequent vacations to France and Switzerland. Karen Horney had arrived. Thanks to her psychoanalytic practice, her books, and her lectures, money was no longer a problem. She enjoyed the good life, and bought several homes, including a vacation home at Croton-on-Hudson. The last of Horney's homes were located on Fire Island and Wildwood Hills, Long Island.

It was a basic tenet of Horney's life, however, that things never went well for any great length of time. She had always, dating back to her years in Berlin, been tremendously popular with her students, and this adoration continued at the New York Institute. In June of that year, though, New York Institute students submitted a petition to the school asking that Horney's work be included in the school's curriculum, a request

met with hostility by the institute's administration. In September of 1939, as World War II was beginning, Sigmund Freud died in London. His death did nothing to diminish Horney's continuing outspoken, anti-Freud stance. Once more it would make her a lightning-rod for her colleagues' censure. Her teaching position was downgraded to sporadic lecturing and a senior year elective course. An October 1939 address, one month after Freud's death, added insult to injury. Once more Horney assailed the prominence Freud had given childhood psychosexual experience in creating neurosis. This time Horney's anti-Freud message was greeted with stony silence or derision. Mystified by the response and in tears, Horney asked, "Why can't we have different opinions and still be friends?"

The next year, the school required several of her students' papers to be revised, causing these students to feel that attending Horney's classes doomed them to unfair grading and prejudice. A special inquiry into this incident, including a student questionnaire the next year supported their belief, but it made no difference to the New York Institute. In April of 1941, Horney's teaching status was further downgraded to infrequent lecturer. At that point, Horney and several of her supporters (including the 14 students who believed themselves discriminated against) resigned from the New York Institute. She, together with Fromm, Harry Stack Sullivan, William Silverberg, Clara Thompson, and others, soon formed the Association for the Advancement of Psychoanalysis (AAP) in late 1941. The association seemed to get off to a good start, initiating its own training program and a publication, *The American Journal of Psychoanalysis*.

During this stressful time, Horney's relationship with Erich Fromm had been deteriorating as well. *Self Analysis*, her work advocating that neurotic people could aid in their own therapy, was published in 1942. It received lukewarm reviews at best from the psychoanalytic community, and for the most part, was completely ignored. Fromm, too, had published a book the previous year: the landmark *Escape From Freedom*, which had been far better received. A summer vacation at Monhegan the previous year proved to be their last as a couple. It was Fromm that left the relationship, but it is believed that their breakup was mostly related to her jealousy over the recognition his book received. The fact that he continued to teach at the New York Institute after the institute's treatment of her and that Fromm, too, was a highly popular teacher, apparently added to her resentment. Always the survivor, Horney threw herself into her work. Her private practice was thriving, and she remained actively involved in the AAP. At least in some ways, the AAP proved a freewheeling group. (At its first annual conference, the association began a tradition: the toasting of "luxurious and lecherous living.") Karen had also become editor of the group's journal, *The American Journal of Psychoanalysis*.

During her years of analysis with Fromm, Horney's daughter Marianne had come to realize the hostility she felt toward her mother. In spite of this, she, now also a psychoanalyst, joined Horney's new psychoanalytic association. As this antagonism surfaced, Horney seems to have blamed her former lover for Marianne's feelings. This quickly became another cause of the rift between them. Horney and Fromm managed to put aside their differences, and both remained in the new organization for several months. In 1943, in a parody of the situation Horney had just put behind her at the New York Institute, a request by students for Fromm to teach both clinical and theoretical subjects was blocked by Horney. Soon after, his teaching privileges were revoked. The reason given was Fromm's lack of a medical degree, but most saw it as the vengeful reaction of a rejected and bitter woman. When Fromm resigned from the AAP in April of 1943, several others, including Harry Stack Sullivan and Clara Thompson, followed. One of the most painful defections for Horney was her daughter, Marianne. Six further defectors later that year, including William Silverberg, assured that Horney's AAP would not receive the acceptance of recognized psychoanalytic organizations.

Following these bitter disappointments, she once more looked to another younger man, her trainee Harold Kelman, to become her lover. Kelman would not be the last. She never remarried, though there were several relationships, often with admiring younger men, over the ensuing years. There continued to be turbulence in her life due to her outspoken disagreement with Freudian teachings, her poor relationships with many of her colleagues, and her penchant for getting into relationships with the wrong men. She was described by many as "imperious" in her management style. Yet she remained the dean of the American Institute for Psychoanalysis for another decade. Her private life remained replete with dinner parties and social activities with artists and existentialist philosophers from both sides of the Atlantic. Among her friends was a wealthy manufacturer, Cornelius Crane, who introduced her to a Zen Buddhist scholar named Suzuki. That meeting would lead to a later fascination with Zen Buddhism.

In those later years, when Horney was in her late 60s, it seems that she finally began to make some personal progress toward the self-realization she had sought for others for most of her life. Though she continued to work hard, seeing patients from early morning until late in the day, she also seemed to find more enjoyment in her private life. She took up painting, traveled a good deal, and the bond with her daughters improved as she visited Brigitte in Switzerland and Renate in Mexico. They accompanied her on trips and spent pleasant summers vacationing together. She published her last book, *Neurosis and Human Growth*, in 1950. Her earlier contact with Suzuki led to an expanding interest in Zen philosophy. In pursuit of that interest, she traveled to Japan with Suzuki and her daughter Brigitte, now divorced, in 1952. Shortly after she returned from Japan, she was diagnosed with stomach cancer, already quite advanced. She died on December 4th of that year.

THEORIES

Horney's Freudian beginnings

No discussion of the philosophy of Horney is possible without first elaborating on the ideas that initially formed her theories—the work of Sigmund Freud. More than Alfred Adler and Carl Jung, whose breaks with Freud in the early twentieth century were well documented and publicized, Horney initially seemed to agree with Freud. It is for this reason that she is so often characterized as being a neo-Freudian, and why Horney would always, even after tremendous differences developed between them, express great appreciation for Freud's ground-breaking discoveries. It was the material that Horney would build on.

Freud discovered that he could bring relief to patients suffering from neurosis by encouraging them to talk with him about their feelings. This free-talking method, called free association by Freud, gave rise to the treatment modality Sigmund Freud is famous for: psychoanalysis. The famed Viennese psychiatrist and his disciple Carl Jung introduced this concept in the United States in 1909. Freud's work with patients using free association and dream analysis created experience that helped him to map what soon became known as the unconscious. Freud defined portions of the human mind as the id (the primitive, undisciplined part of the mind), the superego (the conscience), and the ego (the self-concept that regulates and integrates all the rest). Freud hypothesized that unconscious processes and their relationship to early childhood experiences were the primary factors in determining personality adjustment or maladjustment in adulthood. He also came to believe that sexual conflict was the principal reason for neurosis.

Freud's ideas were the first and most famous theories in psychology. Most of the leading mental health professionals of his time began to follow him. At certain junctures after that early acceptance, opinions would split, and at each of these divisions, some of Freud's followers took different paths. Carl Jung, along with another follower, Alfred Adler, were the first separate from Freud's road and begin the journey on their own paths. Horney would soon fill one of the vacancies in the Freudian ranks—but only for a brief time.

Horney spent three decades bringing the world innovative psychiatric and psychological theories that have led the way for many schools of psychological thought and are still considered to hold great relevance today. Her contributions in many ways match the decades of her life as a psychiatrist, with each decade highlighting a separate portion of her theory development:

- Early essays on feminist psychology in the 1920s. These are said to be the actual beginnings of Horney's break from standard Freudian thought. Because of her feminist stance in those years, she is often credited with being the founder of feminine psychology, creating its original political and theoretical philosophy. She saw penis envy, Oedipal complexes, and the lack of focus on motherhood and mothering as the flaws in Freud's patriarchal-based beliefs, and set out to remedy these deficiencies.

- Psychoanalytic experience supported her growing belief that the society people live in and relationships that they experience are far more important in the development of neurosis than Freud's predetermined instinctual and biological causation. The development of these convictions by Horney make her one of the founders of humanist psychology.

- Her work in the last decade of her life culminated in the development of what she termed interpersonal defenses and intrapsychic defenses, and her hypothesis of how these defenses develop as a means of dealing with anxiety.

Horney and feminist thought
Explanation

She is said to be at home only in the realm of Eros. Spiritual matters are alien to her innermost being, and she is at odds with cultural trends. She therefore is, as Asians frankly state, a second-rate being. She is prevented from real accomplishments by the deplorable, bloody tragedies of menstruation and childbirth. And so every man silently thanks his God, just as the pious Jew does in his prayers, that he was not created a woman.

These words, from Horney's first book, *Feminine Psychology* published in 1936, are echoes of earlier essays written in the 1920s, soon after Freud first published his theories of female sexuality. Horney believed that classic Freudian psychoanalysis (which she had then recently undergone with Freud disciple Karl Abraham) inherently perceived women as imperfect because it was the work of a male (Freud) in a male-dominated society. Horney saw Freud's hypotheses regarding female sexuality were nothing more than an attempt to curb the "power struggle between the sexes." Horney made every effort to stimulate debate on this difference between Freud and feminists during her years at the Berlin Psychoanalytic Institute, but was unsuccessful. Both Freud in Vienna and her male colleagues at the Institute in Berlin allowed the issue to die a natural death by simply ignoring it. For Horney, though, it did not die.

Horney's disagreement with Freud's penis envy theory

When Freud disciple Karl Abraham in 1920 posited that women, because of penis envy, actually wanted to be men, he went on to state that he believed that this desire to be men led to lesbianism, women with masculine ambition, and feminists. Horney, who was from all reports not a lesbian, and did not consider herself a feminist (but may have possessed what Abraham called masculine ambition), was offended. Horney, who had already witnessed decades of male sexism, was put off by this theory not because of feminism but because of its illogical nature. Horney was feminist in her beliefs, but too much of an individual to join any organized feminist movement for any period of time. One of Horney's responses to Karl Abraham's idea was, "that one half of the human race is discontented with the sex assigned to it. . .is decidedly unsatisfying, not only to feminine narcissism but to biological science."

Perhaps because of her own childhood experiences, Horney was fascinated by how men view women and the reasons for their perceptions. What she concluded seems based, as is typical of Horney, in her own experience. Her feminist theories seem to have developed during her childbearing years, a time when she described being pregnant as, "It is just the expectation and joy in it that are now so indescribably beautiful. And the feeling of carrying in me a small, becoming human being invests one with higher dignity and importance that makes me very happy and proud." In her disagreements with Freud over penis envy, Horney came to believe that there was an even more common phenomenon—womb envy. Men unconsciously devalued women out of long-suppressed jealousy of the female reproduction capacity, the male lack of a uterus for childbearing and breasts for nurturing. She further noted that apparently womb envy was evidently more prominent a problem than penis envy, as men appear to have a far stronger urge to degrade women than women have to denigrate men.

Examples From infancy onward, Horney believed, men perceive their mothers as "nurturing, selfless, and self-sacrificing. . .the ideal embodiment of the woman who could fulfill all of his expectations and longings." This leads to envy of not being able to become this nurturing person themselves. As compensation for this, men have created a society where women are considered inferior to men, motherhood is cheapened, and male sexuality is over-esteemed.

A lecture given by Horney in 1930 in Dresden noted that the (then) male-dominated specialty of obstetrics was the theft of a power that women had traditionally held (as midwives)—the ability to facilitate childbirth. She saw it as an unconscious wish on the part of men to divest women of the capacity to be mothers.

In "The Dread of Women," one of her early papers written in 1920 rebutting Karl Abraham's statements regarding all females desiring to be males, Horney expressed the belief that male children had an innate dread of females, fearing that their reproductive organ was inadequate when compared with the reproductive organs of women. This dismissed Freud's supposition that men fear castration by women, replacing it with what Horney saw as the real fear: humiliation and devaluation of the boy's masculine self-image.

The symbolic manifestation of this fear, Horney states, is expressed in dreams of "a motorcar is rushing along and suddenly falls into a pit and is dashed to pieces," or "a boat is sailing in a narrow channel and is suddenly sucked into a whirlpool." In Horney's experience, dread of being rejected or humiliated was a component of analysis with every male patient, no matter what his mental status was or the structure of his neurosis.

In place of Freud's Oedipus complex, wherein sons identified with fathers in wanting sexual relationship with mothers and daughters equally desired their fathers, Horney believed that female babies from birth identify with their mothers. The reason for Oedipal feelings in girls is not based upon desire to have sex with their fathers, but rather in their perception that this is what their mothers do. In Freud's patriarchal theoretical realm, this was not possible. Horney was joined in her promotion of mothers and mothering as

essential in the development of the psyche by Melanie Klein, a contemporary female psychoanalyst. (Klein was also the person who analyzed Horney's children.)

Horney often superimposed the tremendous power of mothering over the fear of the father that Freud posited so much. This feminine power could be used in varying ways, some leading to neurosis: the demanding mother who requires total devotion, constant attention, and sacrifices from her children simply "because she is the mother and she has borne them in pain," "making her offspring feel guilty if they do not constantly meet her needs" is one example.

The obvious irony in this discussion of Horney's early years in the psychoanalytic field is that Horney did not see herself as a feminist. For her, the issues expressed were simply matters of attitudinal and intellectual difference that she perceived as creating psychiatric difficulties. She found it entirely possible that little girls wished for penises like their little brothers, but felt that it was irrelevant to the larger discussion. What women really wanted, Horney believed, was not penises, but rather the opportunity to develop their own unlimited potential in a fair and unbiased society. Initially she focused strongly on a feminine persona, motherhood, and young girls' identification with their mothers. But as time went on, she developed equal difficulty with the concept of a feminine mystique. Though convinced that there were male and female personality traits, she believed that male-dominated society had so obscured and modified whatever personality qualities were distinctly feminine that it was no longer possible to determine what these traits are. Therefore Horney came to favor gender neutrality. In a 1935 lecture in Paris, France entitled "Women's Fear of Action," she summed it up in this way:

> We should stop bothering about what is feminine. Standards of masculinity and femininity are artificial standards. . . . Differences between the two sexes certainly exist, but we shall never be able to discover what they are until we have first developed our potentialities as human beings. Paradoxical as it may sound, we shall find out about these differences only if we forget about them.

Perhaps the greatest reason Horney did not consider herself a feminist springs forth, as so many other things in her theories, from her own life experience. From her teens on, as her ex-therapist Karl Abraham had noted, Horney seems to have wandered from one heterosexual relationship to another. Her one marriage to Oskar Horney could not be termed a success, and in the long run, neither were most of her affairs. Her essay, "The Overvaluation of Love," published in 1934, looks at this behavior as one of her neurotic symptoms. It is actually the case studies of seven women possessing a compulsive need for having a man in their lives yet never being able to form a fulfilling and loving relationship. It is widely believed that one of these case studies is indeed a self-description by Horney. Her examination of these self-described neurotic needs is an early span in the bridge between her feminist years and those in which she more closely looked at society's role in creating neurosis.

One classic example of how valid feminine personality traits can be altered by a male-dominated society's expectations that Horney cites is the Victorian woman. Because it was expected of her by the society she lived in, women of Victorian times were so delicate that they frequently fainted, and could do very little. There is no scientific reason why these women would faint or be so weak and unable to do any sort of physical work. Therefore, the only possible explanation for their delicacy and weakness is the programming of the society in which they lived.

Horney also speaks of a woman clearly "more gifted than her husband," and of this woman's total inability to do anything for herself. This problem can be overlooked, Horney states, in a society where females are expected to be passive and not be achievers. This would then, in such a society, be considered "a normal feminine attitude."

Main points   Horney's feminist theories as opposed to classic Freudian thought of her time:

- More focus on the pride and fulfillment of being a mother and mothering, rather than wishing to be male and have a penis as Freudians believed.
- Replacement of Freud's castration theory with the belief that the fear in young boys is of male inadequacy and the loss of self esteem.
- Society's perception of women: Horney's belief was that feminine psychological traits were impossible to determine because the male-dominated society she lived in had so completely obscured them. Freud's view was that women were both definable and treatable as a group because of these personality traits. Horney believed that it was preferable to look at the person's experience with and interaction with his or her environment rather than at sexuality.
- Freud's Oedipus and penis envy theories: Horney's basic tenet is that women do not experience penis envy as much as they experience the desire for equal status living in a just and fair society instead of a patriarchal one.

- However she also felt that if indeed penis envy did exist, it was equally possible for men to experience womb envy. She reasoned that womb envy was the precursor, in male-dominated societies, of men trying to subjugate women.

Horney's middle-decade theories: "Basic anxiety" and neurosis

No doubt because of her own life experience, Horney put great emphasis on childhood hostility developed toward rejecting parents. Because this hostility could not be safely expressed for fear of parental retaliation or abandonment, the child learns to avoid any kind of friction with the parent. This creates a psychic situation that makes it impossible for the child to stand up for his or her rights, and requires that he or she tolerate parental injustice. Desires and needs become submerged, and much of the child's energy is depleted in fighting these internal, dangerous impulses. The final result of this struggle is the crippling of personality development leading to neurosis or other psychopathological conditions. For Horney, the object of psychoanalysis was to assist her patients in being able to give up their defenses. These defenses, she believed, barred them from their real selves—from being aware of the things they innately loved, hated, feared, or wanted. This notion of self-realization would become one of the tenets of humanistic psychology. Her early espousal of, and emphasis on, self-realization as mental health makes her one of this movement's founders.

Examples   Horney uses one of her patients as an example of this submersion of needs and desires. The patient's initial anxiety occurred when she wanted something for herself simply because she wanted it— not because it was necessary to her health or education. She felt rage, but suppressed it when people did not do what she wanted them to, or when she wasn't first in competitions. The unexpressed rage resulted for her in a feeling of exhaustion.

Horney cites her own lack of involvement in politics as an example of this. She states that because she was not expected to have her own opinions as a child, she did not grow up considering what opinion she should have. This is actually rather remarkable, considering that her life encompassed World War I, the Weimar Republic, and the rise of Nazism.

Basic anxiety

As noted previously, Horney came to perceive neurosis as one major type of maladaptive personality development, not nearly as abnormal as psychiatric thinkers prior to her had believed. Like Freud, she was convinced that it developed out of childhood experience. Surprisingly, she did not believe that parental abuse or neglect necessarily caused children to grow into neurotics. However she was convinced that what she termed "the basic evil," the lack of warmth or caring, the indifference of parents, did create neurotic personalities. Most significant about her observations is that she viewed this totally from the viewpoint of the patient. The parent may not have even actually been cold and uncaring, but if the child perceives the parent in this way, it becomes a reality for that child. Even those considered good parents may show a preference for one sibling over another; humiliate, shame, or unjustly blame a child; or alternate between being loving and rejecting behaviors. These parental actions, so tellingly similar to those of Horney's childhood, became for her the great underpinning of all neurotic psychic activity.

Generally children are thought of as defenseless and submissive, but Horney describes the earliest and primary response to parental indifference as "basic hostility," feelings of rage and aggression. If the child experiences victory from this reaction, belligerent behavior may become the method of choice for coping with life situations. But Horney notes that aggression is not the usual reaction that sustains the neurotic person through life. Instead "basic hostility" is typically followed by "basic anxiety," the fear of being helpless and abandoned as punishment for having had these angry feelings. In order to survive, the "basic hostility" felt must then be concealed, and every effort made to convince the indifferent parents that the child is worthy of their love. This is, according to Horney, the progression for the majority of these children. Despite their rage, if they experience success through making themselves pleasing and lovable, then this will be the façade they will present to the world throughout their lives. However, Horney also describes a third group. These children simply withdraw and make every attempt to make themselves self-sufficient in the belief that if no one can get close to them, no one can hurt them.

Horney said that children can only express this anger in dreams or fantasy. These include fears of being attacked and torn apart by wild animals, or ghosts or burglars chasing them. As long as this basic anger against indifferent or shaming parents is held in check, Horney states, the neurosis is held in check. When the angry child grows up and an event the person's life brings up the issues of love and rejection, the person may exhibit neurotic behaviors.

Example In analyzing the reasons for what she perceived to be Adolph Hitler's sado-masochistic

perversions and nightmares, Horney posits that his mother was too afraid of her cruel and domineering husband to protect her son (Adolph) from him, and too obsessed with deifying his older, dead siblings to really love him for himself.

Horney spoke of a patient who told her that he disliked his mother intensely yet was able to live in the same house with her. They came to "a fine understanding" between them, but there were times when he suddenly and inexplicably broke out into an unprovoked rage.

Neurosis

As stated, the basis for all of Horney's theories was her personal experience. She considered herself neurotic, and all of her work relates to the treatment of neurosis. She also considered herself and the neurotic patients she saw to be victims. The psychic pain she had experienced from her earliest years convinced her that the events of her childhood had colored all of the rest of her life. In this belief—the notion that neurosis has its basis in childhood experiences—she and Freud concurred completely. Over the years though, Horney began to believe that these childhood experiences, while truly the basis of the neurosis, needed to put into their proper perspective. Dealing with the patient's current array of coping devices and inner conflicts became more important for Horney, because these could be treated. The ability to exchange ineffective defense mechanisms for those behaviors that led to self-realization became the emphasis of Horney's psychoanalytic practice.

Example Horney's path to self-realization required a patient to focus on the present. It would be impossible to change or repair the original causes of the neurosis as the person is no longer the same as they were when the basic hostility and basic anxiety first emerged. She used the example of the man who considered himself to be very gifted at times, and then considered himself stupid. He showed virtually no emotion most of the time, but was at times given to becoming very upset and angry. Horney chose to ignore interpreting the similarity between his interaction with Horney, as his analyst, and with his mother. She focused instead on getting him to see the connection between his attempts at being rational and unemotional and his fear of being disliked and humiliated.

Differences with Freud about neurosis After the divergence regarding feminine psychology, probably the next basic difference Horney encountered between her beliefs and Freudian thought regarded the definition of neurosis. Freud viewed neurotic behavior as biological, driven by instincts, the inevitable consequence of the clash between a necessary and orderly society and an equally necessary but disorderly id. Horney's early observations, though, convinced her that neurosis was far more common than previously thought. In fact, it was a method people use to cope with problems and feel like they have control over their lives. Of the two ideas, hers was clearly the more optimistic perception. Freud further had viewed the behaviors he studied as being universal, common to all humans, while Horney was convinced that cultural factors contributed heavily to the neurotic adaptation to life. She also believed that neurosis could not even be diagnosed without a careful examination of the society from which the person originated. Probably most important of all, Freud's vision of humans increasingly was one of pessimism. He thought the human race was condemned to repeat a pattern of destruction and suffering. Horney saw it differently. In *Our Inner Conflicts*, she said in this affirmation of hope: "Man can change, and go on changing, as long as he lives."

Horney's unsuccessful attempts at psychoanalysis as a young adult with both Freudian analyst Karl Abraham and Hans Sachs led her to try self-analysis. This was a concept few if any of her colleagues viewed as viable or useful. For Horney self-analysis proved to have value, but only because she had a remarkable and unusual gift: an ability to dispassionately pursue her own truth without rationalization or excuse. The knowledge she gleaned from that self-analysis became the information she imparted to mental health professionals through her books and to her patients in therapy. She addressed only neurosis, but many mental health professionals believe that her theory of neurosis is the best in existence. Horney defines neurosis as "psychic disturbance brought by fears and defenses against these fears, and by attempts to find compromise solutions for conflicting tendencies." Put more simply, neurosis is an attempt by the person to make life bearable.

Horney's approach to psychoanalysis was also different from Freud's. Freud saw analysts leading their patients through a complex maze of transference (falling in love with the analyst), repression, and denial. She saw the role of the therapist as a much more a humanistic one, helping the person to change the perceptions of him or herself and life—"striving toward a clearer and deeper experiencing" of the direction of life. Mental health, Horney felt, involved having an accurate understanding of who you are—self-realization. When that understanding is present, it

is quite possible for a person to reach a mentally healthy potential. In *Self-Analysis*, Horney describes psychoanalysis as helping people toward their best possible further development. Freud's insistence of universal transference, too, seemed invalid in Horney's view—the patient in analysis "is not prompted by love for the analyst," she argues in *Self-Analysis*. She speculated instead that what Freud considered transference may actually be more related to the person's fear of others and the inadequate methods neurotics use in their attempt to cope with life.

Examples   In psychotherapy, Horney from her earliest days was perceived by her patients and her students as an Earth mother. She describes one of her patients that clearly was extremely dependent on Horney and constantly craved her affection. When the patient was offered an extra therapy session because she was upset, the patient began to feel humiliated. This was because the offer made her perceive her own greed for both the therapist's time and for Horney's unconditional love.

Main points
- Neurosis, according to Horney, is an attempt to make life bearable.

- It includes the use of an array of defenses that a person develops against what Horney terms "basic anxiety."

- The initial reaction to parental indifference is anger. Ordinarily this anger creates fear ("basic anxiety") in the child over the possibility that he or she will be abandoned or punished because of having these angry feelings.

- These defense mechanisms are ultimately self-defeating and conflicted, and must be recognized by the person and then changed.

- It is necessary to move beyond this realization of the childhood "basic anxiety" to focus on the self-defeating coping devices currently in use. Only in recognizing and changing these methods of coping can the person reach self-realization.

Horney's later years: Self-realization, neurotic needs, and coping mechanisms

Like Carl Jung, Horney preferred the term "self" to the Freudian term ego. Horney's self is not a fixed entity. She believed that it was composed of both hereditary factors, including temperament, predisposition, talents, and abilities; and environmental factors such as the family of origin and area of residence. In a further expansion of discoveries of the 1930s, Horney began to

Karen Horney with her pet dog. (Copyright Bettmann/Corbis. Reproduced by permission.)

see that in mentally healthy people, self-realization is necessary to allow people to see who they are and what they are capable of. This realization of self is what endows them with the ability to be spontaneous, enjoy life, and reach life goals. Neurotics, created by the "greatest evil," parental indifference, lack the capacity to view themselves in this way. Instead, the neurotic self is divided into two parts: the despised self and the ideal self. The neurotic person is in perpetual conflict, wavering each day between the despised and the ideal. Horney calls this conflict "the tyranny of the shoulds." The person finds the despised self to be unbearable; but equally, the ideal part is impossible to attain.

Horney's ten neurotic needs

In Horney's practice, she began to see patterns of needs in the neurotic patients she treated. She noted in *The Neurotic Personality of Our Time* in 1942 that neurotics utilize extreme and unrealistic measures to meet these needs, and will not even be aware that they are doing it.

She categorized these need patterns as the following:

- The need for acceptance and affection: All human beings need acceptance and affection, but in people with healthier selves, the need is balanced by an understanding of what is possible and what is not. This need in neurotics can be manifested by an obsessive need to please others and be liked by them, or an unreasonable belief that others will meet every need. As these techniques are unrealistic and doomed to failure, anxiety is constantly generated when this need, as perceived by the neurotic, is not met.

- The need for love: Obviously all people want and need to be loved, but again, the neurotic's perception of what this means is unrealistic. Loved ones are expected to completely take over the neurotic's life, and solve all difficulties and conflicts for them.

- The need to simplify what is seen as the complexity of life: This is clearly a need that is tempting to all people at times, but again the neurotic takes this need to a problematic level. He or she may desire a very small number of material possessions, or wish to have no laws or schedule to follow. The neurotic seeks to be able to virtually become invisible when stress-increasing confrontation occurs. This invisibility is aimed at making them safer and decreasing their stress.

- The need for having power: We all desire to be empowered, but the neurotic feels a desperate need to control and have power over others.

- The need to manipulate others: Generated in a basic belief that others are simply there to be used, the neurotic, who perceives him- or herself as having been manipulated and used, tries to carry out a preemptory attack against others. The primary rationale for this behavior is to avoid looking stupid or being used by others.

- The need for social recognition: Again, it is the outer limit of a desire that is considered normal, our innate need for prestige and recognition. The neurotic takes this to another level with overwhelming fear of not looking good, being popular, or considered "in the loop." No matter how difficult it may be, the neurotic tries to be sociable.

- The need for the admiring recognition of others: Among the greatest fears of the neurotic is that the people they interact with every day will see them as being less than important, or as worthless or irrelevant.

- The need for achievement: Clearly setting goals and reaching them are important facets of all people. But the neurotic becomes obsessed with succeeding at meeting goals and being the best in whatever they attempt to do. Failure to achieve their unachievable goals results in more mental

pain and/or the devaluation of whatever it is that they try to do.

- The need for independence: Autonomy is important to all people, but the neurotic takes this to the extreme. The illusion of self-sufficiency becomes more important than seeking help when it is needed. At some level neurotics truly believe that they can handle the situation by themselves, but there is also the self-centered portion of their psyche that does not want another person to help them and be recognized for an achievement. This would take away from the individual attention they feel should belong only to them.

- The need for perfection: Neurotics have an innately immature view of the world in which they live. There should be happy endings for everything, and the neurotic should be in control of all situations at all times. There is a terror of being flawed, of others seeing the mistakes the neurotic makes.

Horney's coping strategies

In the course of Horney's experience in analysis with her patients, she began to see that these neurotic needs correlated with the psychic personality development she had observed and documented earlier. She called meshing of these neurotic personality types, and the needs addressed by each behavior, "coping strategies." Her coping strategies are broken down into three types: compliance, aggression, and withdrawal.

Compliance According to Horney, compliance, or the "basic anxiety" that overcomes "basic hostility" has its origin in fears of abandonment or punishment. This abandonment or punishment would be in retaliation for the feelings of rage experienced by the child in the early years of life. It is found, she believes, in neurotic needs number one, two, and three. If in fact "basic hostility" must be hidden and the victim of parental indifference must become more loveable in order to survive, then clearly the need for acceptance and affection, even to the point of people pleasing, becomes critical. So, too, is the need for all-encompassing love. Number three—the need for simplification, the rejection of schedules and laws—initially seems the antithesis of compliance. But when this is viewed as part of the need to avoid confrontation by becoming unnoticeable, it becomes more clear. That avoidance of confrontation is yet another means of not allowing the "basic hostility" to be witnessed by others, resulting in rejection and the desertion of loved ones. Horney sometimes referred to this strategy as the "moving toward" or the "self-effacing solution."

Aggression   Aggression, also called the "moving against" or the "expansive solution," is the second coping strategy and deals with neurotic needs four through eight. The requirements of having complete power over others; the ability to exploit others; and to have total (unrealistic) social recognition, admiration, and fame are obvious. The need to be fiercely competitive and always to be number one in accomplishments is equally self-evident and easily seen as aggressive behavior in this light.

Withdrawal   What Horney calls withdrawal is represented, she states, by neurotic needs three, nine, and ten: To be self-sufficient and perfect clearly correlate with a retreat from being a member of the human race. The totally independent person requires no one else, never needs to ask for help from anyone, and is completely unfettered from any type of committed relationship. The perfect person, it is immediately evident, is also divorced from the rest of the human race as none of the rest of those on Earth are perfect. Interestingly, Horney added number three neurotic need because of her belief that the total independence and perfection were not possible in the neurotic's view unless limitations were put on the dimensions and complexity of life. Withdrawal is also referred to in Horney's writings as the "moving away," or "resigning solution."

In Horney's lexicon, the defensive strategies people use for dealing with the outside world are termed interpersonal strategies, while those used for dealing with the inner selves are called Horney intrapsychic processes.

Example   In *Our Inner Conflicts*, Horney paraphrases Franz Wittels' description of the neurotic's pursuit of love: "Love becomes a phantom that is chased to the exclusion of everything else." This need for love, she asserts, is the only way that the neurotic needs to be liked and to dominate someone else can both be simultaneously fulfilled. Horney often discussed this neurotic pursuit of love in thinly disguised references to herself and a lifetime of affairs.

Main points   Self-realization is the goal of psychotherapy and the benchmark of mental health. It can be defined as the restoration of the person to their "center of gravity," making it possible for them to spontaneously achieve their goals. Without gaining self-realization, people cannot attain either spontaneous enjoyment of life or accomplish their dreams and goals. The self is fluid and ever changing; it is composed of all of our genetic features—temperament, predisposition, talents, and abilities—as well as the environment in which we live. The neurotic person lacks the innate capacity to recognize self accurately, instead dividing self into "the despised self" and the ideal self.

Horney recognizes three basic coping strategies linked to the ten neurotic needs in the following ways:

- Compliance is the first of these strategies. It is related to neurotic needs for (1) acceptance and affection, (2) all-encompassing love, and (3) avoiding confrontation and having no rules or regulations.

- Aggression is the next coping strategy and is associated with the needs to (4) have control over others, (5) manipulate others, (6) to be recognized socially, (7) have others admire them, and to (8) obsessively achieve.

- Withdrawal is the last of these. It is demonstrated in the needs for (3) avoiding confrontation and having no rules or regulations, (9) having complete independence including never asking for help, and (10) the need for perfection.

HISTORICAL CONTEXT

It is important to note that psychoanalysis was not a creation of Sigmund Freud. Islamic (Sufi) literature frequently discusses psychological insight and what we would consider psychotherapy. Afghanistan's Jalaludal Rumi and El Ghazali from Persia are two of the known psychotherapists of ancient times. Writings from over three millennia ago mention "healing through words" used in both Ancient Egypt and Greece. But if the era often referred to in the Western World as *The Golden Age of Psychotherapy* was birthed by Freud, Adler, Jung, Horney, and the other luminaries of psychoanalysis from the late nineteenth and early twentieth centuries, then it follows that a disgraced charlatan was the midwife. Franz Anton Mesmer graduated from the University of Vienna, then one of the foremost schools in Europe, in 1766. In 1773, one of his patients, a Miss Oesterlin came to him complaining of a multiplicity of somatic ailments. Mesmer's doctoral dissertation had been on the influence of the planets on human illness. He quickly began to explore the possibility that the woman's recurring symptoms were based on tidal variations related to such cosmic phenomena. He concocted a tonic containing iron that he had her drink. He attached magnets to her body, and remarkably, her symptoms improved. With repeated treatment, her symptoms totally disappeared. Such a remarkable cure quickly made Franz Anton Mesmer among the most famed men in Vienna medical circles.

BIOGRAPHY:

Women of Freudian psychology

"If it had been a son I should have sent you the news by telegram, but as it is a little girl. . .you get the news later."

Sigmund Freud's words, written to his friend Wilhelm Fleiss (also his cocaine-supplier) in 1895 upon the birth of his daughter Anna show the bias encountered by early female psychologists. From birth, Anna had a poor relationship with her mother and siblings, describing herself as "not part of them," but not her famous father. Early in life, Anna became her father's favored child and showed herself to be brilliant. She was self-taught for the most part as she hated school, but availed herself of the many members of the intelligentsia that frequented the Freud household. (In her teens she spoke five languages.) At 14, she wrote to her father: "I have read some of your books, but you should not be horrified by that, for I am already grown up and so it is no surprise that I am interested." Her father's possessiveness and her total loyalty to him kept her tied to him, and she never strayed very far from his rigid beliefs. Anna taught in England, wrote several books, and together with Melanie Klein, she co-founded the discipline of child psychology and became one of its foremost thinkers. The Freuds escaped Vienna in 1938 just as the Nazis were coming to power in Austria. They settled in London, England, where her famous father died the next year, but Anna continued an illustrious career. (Among her many claims to fame are the fact that she was famed American movie-actress Marilyn Monroe's analyst.) Anna Freud died in 1982 at the age of 87.

Born in 1882, Melanie (Reizes) Klein apparently always resented her domineering mother. Melanie's Jewish, middle-class parents strongly encouraged education and enrolled her in a gymnasium in preparation for university. But family financial reverses made higher education for Melanie an impossibility. Like Horney, she married, had three children, and suffered from depression. Her husband Arthur's career

as an industrial chemist brought them to Budapest, where she was analyzed by Sandor Ferenczi. Psychotherapy for children was then unknown, and Ferenczi encouraged her to learn by analyzing her own children. A pioneer of child psychotherapy, she developed the play technique and what is known as object relations theory—the belief that the mother-infant relationship is the hub of personality development. She moved to Berlin and then to London in 1927 after her marriage failed and her second analyst Karl Abraham (Karen Horney's old nemesis) died. Despite her work, Klein's relationship with her own children was poor. Her son Hans apparently committed suicide while mountain climbing, and her therapist daughter remained her implacable enemy. Klein died of cancer in London at the age of 78.

In some ways, Helene (Rosenbach) Deutsch's life paralleled Horney's. Born in Galacia, a Polish-speaking Austro-Hungarian province, her childhood was conflicted. Unlike Horney, it was Deutsch's mother that considered her "poison" because she was female. She would win the battle for her liberal attorney father's affection because of her rejection of her mother's bourgeois values and her own social activism. (Deutsch was an early feminist and protestor for social reform. Her protests even included the Vietnam War.) Following an affair with a married man and an abortion while at medical school, she met and married fellow-physician Felix Deutsch in 1912. Freud's *Interpretation of Dreams* made her a disciple, and she eventually worked in Freud's clinic. She unwaveringly supported her mentor (though she sometimes felt Freud focused on fathers too much to the exclusion of mothers) and reported at one point feeling that she was in love with Freud. She and her husband came to the United States in 1935. They lived in Cambridge, Massachusetts, and Deutsch practiced psychiatry at Massachusetts General and wrote extensively. She died in 1982 at the age of 91.

But Mesmer's early and dramatic success was speedily followed by marked skepticism among his scientific colleagues. Under a shroud of suspicion, he left Vienna for Paris. In Paris, once again Mesmer enjoyed early triumphs and a bustling practice. In

large treatment sessions, he used lighting and music with his magnetic therapies. Eventually, he came under scrutiny for his failed cures, and an investigation came to the conclusion that there simply was no scientific evidence supporting Mesmer's ideas.

Disgraced, Mesmer left Paris and returned to his birth-place in Germany. He died there in obscurity in 1815.

However, those in the scientific community began to question what had actually happened to produce successful outcomes in some of Mesmer's patients. After a prolonged study of the subject, an English physician named James Braid concluded that mesmerists induced "a peculiar condition of the nervous system, induced by fixed and abstracted attention. . .not through the mediation of any special agency passing through the body." Due to Mesmer's sullied reputation, Braid called the subject of his research "hypnotism." This is the treatment tool that was being used by Joseph Breuer in Vienna when Sigmund Freud began to work with him in 1893.

When Horney grew up, Germany was a place noted for fine education and intellectual pursuit. Art, philosophy, and medicine all flourished there. Yet when she graduated from medical school, married, and had her children, Horney did not have the right to vote. Women's suffrage came to Germany and Austria in 1918, only two years before the beginning of her feminist disputes with the Freudians. At that, both Germany and Austria were still ahead of the United States, where a woman's right to vote was not granted nation-wide until two years later, in 1920.

The start of Horney's career and her child-rearing years were contemporary with World War I, an era when the dreadfulness of modern warfare first saturated Western humankind's consciousness. It was the first time that cavalry units, little changed from the days of Napoleon, went into battle against tanks, airplanes, and machine guns. It was the first wide-spread use of chemical warfare. These horrors would add a new term to our vocabulary: "shell-shock." Shell-shock and the breakdown of Victorian society as the barbarism of World War I continued would prove good for business in the realm of mental health treatment. Certainly, witnessing the return of World War I soldiers with obvious emotional difficulties helped to assure that the theories of Freud, Horney, and others would not be discounted.

The other tragedy of the second decade of the twentieth century was less influenced by the actions of humans. The influenza pandemic of 1918 was mind-boggling in its severity and its ability to travel worldwide. It has been estimated that more people died of what came to be known as "the Spanish flu" than had died in the Black Death bubonic plague epidemic of 1347 to 1351. Admittedly spread to some degree by the movement of troops and refugees during World War I, this influenza pandemic moved rapidly across Europe, the United States, and eventually even

to Asia, Africa, Brazil, and the South Pacific. No accurate figures exist for the death toll worldwide, but a paper entitled "The Influenza Pandemic of 1918" by Molly Billings of Stanford University estimates that the figure is between 20 and 40 million people. The uncertainty generated by the war and influenza added greatly to the stress and need for mental health treatment in both Europe and the United States.

The 1920s, a time of financial collapse and political chaos in post-war Germany, became the building block for the beginnings of the National Socialist Party (Nazis) under Adolph Hitler. It was a time of absurd inflation (it took over four billion German Marks to equal one American dollar) and abject poverty for many Germans. Gangs of armed Nazis and Communists fought each other openly in the streets. Though Horney does not appear to have ever been terribly involved in politics, she does seem to have early realized that the total annihilation of creativity and individuality was fast approaching in Germany as the Nazis gained members, support, and power. It apparently was a large factor in her reason for leaving for the United States just prior to Hitler's takeover in 1933. Since her daughter Brigitte, a movie actress, remained in Germany and another daughter Renate returned there to live prior to World War II, Horney had more than one occasion to visit Nazi Germany. As noted, she made these visits without problem and even lectured there. She never made her feelings public as her adopted country, the United States, and her childhood home, Germany, fought to the death. She did mention that the war created stress for women and mothers.

CRITICAL RESPONSE

Feminist theory arguments

From Horney's earliest (feminist) arguments against Freudian thought and through the development of her own theories, she was embroiled in controversy. In many ways, this controversy was a product of Horney's interpersonal style. She took on, at one time or another throughout her career, nearly every other luminary of psychotherapy that shared her time in history. Obviously the disagreements she became involved in with Freud and his disciple Karl Abraham from 1920 on were the first shots fired in what would come to be for Horney a long, long war. In 1926, she was asked to write an essay as part of a book honoring Sigmund Freud on his 70th birthday. Horney started with a brief complimentary recognition of his penis envy theory, but quickly went on the attack. She quoted Simmel's observation that men manage, in a male-dominated society, to invalidly fashion their subjective experience into what they term objective truth. It is said that Freud once characterized her as "malicious-mean."

Her lectures and papers expressing disbelief in Freud's Oedipus complex premise prompted Abraham to note her personal penchant for becoming involved with what he termed "forceful men," men similar to her own father. Karl Abraham's 1920 lecture at The Hague seems aimed at discrediting Horney. He cited his female patients' transference, making him a father figure, as evidence that women really wished to be men. He specifically mentioned a Horney theme—that this desire is based on being denigrated by a male-dominated society. But Abraham adamantly insisted that this female desire to be a man is not based upon any social factor, but rather on the little girl's lack of, and desire to have a penis. He went on to add, based upon his recent analysis of his own daughter, that female children believe, "I had a penis once, as boys have. But it was taken from me." He described women as carrying an unconscious sense that they had been wounded in their genital area (where the penis had once been), and that this sense of injury was re-stimulated by the onset of menses, sexual intercourse, and childbirth.

Karl Abraham took penis envy even further to insist that young daughters initially expect or hope that their father, who is responsible for providing for their wants and needs, will restore their penises to them. When they are disappointed in this wish, they then, as a second choice, hope to be given a baby. This patriarchal assertion clearly is in conflict with Horney's early conviction that feminine identity is innate in female children and derived from their identification with their mothers. In what almost appears a personal attack on Horney recounted by Janet Sayers in *Mothers of Psychoanalysis*, Abraham went on to state that this early sense of being wounded and deprived of their penis creates what Abraham perceived as "women's sense of vengeance against men." This, he states, accounts for two alternative behaviors in women: being frigid or (as was the case for Horney) a "defensive belittling of men by taking a succession of lovers."

In *The Neurotic Personality of Our Time*, Horney again disputed Freud's paper on "Some Psychological Consequences of the Anatomical Distinction Between the Sexes." This time she used quotations from Ruth Benedict's *Patterns of Culture* as an argument, thereby stressing another of her basic differences with the Freudians, her belief that the culture a person lives in plays a huge role in determining neurosis. Horney states: "In making statements like these (regarding

penis envy), Freud is yielding to the temptation of his time: to make generalizations about human nature for the whole of mankind, though his generalization grows from the observation of only one culture zone." She goes on to question if Freud's hypothesis remains true in other societies where men are customarily more jealous than women, or cultures where there is no observable jealousy at all.

> Is not the tremendous strength in men of the impulse to creative work in every field precisely due to their feeling of playing a relatively small part in the creation of living beings, which constantly impels them to an overcompensation in achievement?

Horney's belief that men tried to overcompensate (because of their inability to experience motherhood) caused both arguments from some male psychologists and affirmation from some female ones. Freud, too, felt compelled to argue against Horney's stance on maternal identification. In 1925 he once more insisted that female heterosexuality is not the result of early association with the mother, as Horney contended. He argued that if this were the case, as he felt could not be assumed, then it was necessary to explain how the young girl makes the transition from this affinity with the mother to a heterosexual wish for sexual intercourse (in Freud's belief, a desire for intercourse with the father). Freud referred to the work of Helene Deutsch, a contemporary of both Horney and Freud, who completely supported Freudian theory. Invited as a speaker to the International Congress of Mental Hygiene in Washington in 1930, newspapers described Deutsch as "a lady-in-waiting at the Freudian court," and "the master's foremost feminine disciple." Deutsch then became the target of Horney's assaults. Deutsch had stated that childbirth concerned both loss of the phallus and orgasm, claims that Horney, based upon her own child-bearing experience, quickly ridiculed as "patently absurd."

It seems that Melanie Klein must have been in agreement with Horney in some area, since Horney trusted her enough to send her three daughters for analysis with Klein when they were still very young. That point of agreement may have been Klein's development of play therapy for children, in which games are analyzed in much the same way dreams are probed in Freudian (adult) psychoanalysis. Klein's psychoanalytic theory modified one area that had been in dispute between Freud and Horney: she believed that sexual envy occurred in both sexes. However, there is determinism in Klein's work that seems at odds with Horney's optimistic belief that people can modify defense mechanisms and change. For Klein, one of the earliest and most basic of desires in infants is to experience the pleasure derived from the "good breast." Frustration of these pleasurable experiences, especially in the first year of life, created a schizoid, paranoid personality manifested by isolationism and suspiciousness. She believed in the presence of a primitive super-ego in infants, and posited that if the frustration was too severe, it would lead to depression later in life. Klein's death instinct theory was similar to beliefs held by Freud in his later years after experiencing the world wars and the rise of Nazism.

It was the death instinct theory that finally put Horney on the attack against Klein. Klein believed this death instinct to be the cause of childhood fantasies about harming their mothers. Horney countered that in her experience, these fantasies were not instinctual but rather the result of children being humiliated, abused, or rejected.

Neurosis arguments

Horney wrote extensively, disputing Freud's assumption that the Oedipus complex is a purely biological phenomenon. In her 1937 book *The Neurotic Personality of Our Time*, she cites several other analysts and writers of her time—Bronislaw Malinowski, Felix Boehm, Erich Fromm, and Wilhelm Reich—as asserting that this force is culturally driven, not biological. She went on to note that in her experience she knew of no case where "it was not neurotic parents who by terror and tenderness forced the child into these passionate attachments, with all the implications of possessiveness and jealousy described by Freud."

Franz Alexander, Horney's former student from the Berlin Psychoanalytic Institute and responsible for bringing her to the United States, came to believe in what he termed "corrective emotional experience," psychoanalytic therapy in which the patient gets the opportunity to alter the effects of past traumatic events from their early years. He believed that with a compassionate and affirmative therapist, these patients can change the way these childhood psychic injuries affect them and that they can grow from these experiences. In one way, Alexander's theory is contrary to the conclusions that Horney had reached. She had come to believe that the issues of early childhood were significant only as reference points. The neurotic coping mechanisms in use in the present time were what needed to be looked at. However, she and Alexander shared an optimism common among the humanist psychoanalysts—that people are capable of change.

By 1935, about the same time that she was elected a member of the New York Psychoanalytic

Society, Horney began propounding an expansion of earlier (feminist) theories that she had espoused. She argued that the cause of neurosis was not the result of the conflict between masculinity and femininity; nor was it related to an Oedipus complex or conflict around perceived castration. Neurosis, she argued, was the direct effect of another conflict—between character trends that are sadistic and masochistic. These character trends, Horney believed, were the result of resentment and the desire for love generated in infancy by cold, unloving mothers. This belief would ultimately cost Horney her teaching position at the New York Institute.

She also differed from Alfred Adler's belief that an "inferiority complex" is the basis for neurosis. Neurotic strivings toward power, prestige, and possessing things, for both Adler and Horney, can be manifestations of neurosis. Adler's view was that efforts to gain power, prestige, and possession of things are a normal component of human nature, and that the more intense, out-of-balance forms of these seen in neurotics were a product of either an inferiority complex or physical handicap. Horney's perception was markedly more complex. For her, the goal of power is a bulwark against helplessness. It expresses itself in overbearing, bossy behavior. The aim of obtaining prestige is to prevent humiliation, and is manifested by a tendency to shame others. The importance of possessing things is to be protected against destitution. In neurotics, its manifestation is a penchant for depriving others of these things.

Despite these differences, Horney's three coping mechanisms seem related to Adler's three personality types. Horney's second mechanism, aggression, is quite similar to Adler's first type: the "ruling type," a person noteworthy for being aggressive and requiring domination over others. (In Adler's description, bullies and sadists are good examples.) Horney's first mechanism, compliance, seems like the very methods used by Adler's "leaning type." He describes them as sensitive and dependent on other people to aid them in surviving life problems. When overwhelmed, they develop classic neurotic symptoms quite similar to those described by Horney. The third coping mechanism in Horney's scheme is withdrawal, which certainly appears to coincide with Adler's third personality type, the "avoiding type," who only make it through life by avoiding life. They manifest this avoidance by shunning other people. Adler sees them as fragile. If pressed too hard, he believed, avoiding-type people would become psychotic, making the final withdrawal into their own inner world. Adler actually has a fourth personality type, the "socially useful type." "Socially useful" people appear to be Horney's individual who has reached self-realization.

Ultimately, it seems clear that Horney indeed was the victim of criticism and even ostracizing by other members of the psychoanalytic community for her disagreements with Freud and classic Freudian tenets. Her colleagues at the Berlin Institute in the 1920s surely made her a pariah because of her feminist and self-help beliefs, as well as her arguments against Freud's Oedipus complex and penis envy theories. When her book *Self-Analysis* was published in 1942, it was largely ignored or considered "simple-minded cultural determinism" by many of her peers, according to Janet Sayers in *Mothers of Analysis*. Horney's status downgrade at the New York Institute two decades later seems equally related to her failure to follow orthodox Freudian thought. However, she is hardly the only one to have disagreed with Freud.

There is much evidence to suggest that many of Horney's difficulties with others in her field were more related to her personal communication style than her professional beliefs. In fact, Horney's communication style seems as conflicted as any of the neurotic people she treated or wrote about. There are volumes of evidence to suggest that Horney, as a teacher, had students who literally lined up to take her courses. Described as "no beauty," and the flow of her lectures "interrupted by endless smoking," she was yet described by one of her students as "a little coy. . .a little of the actress in her. And everybody was just hanging on what she had to say." After her demotion at the New York Institute and her creation of the American Psychoanalytic Institute, well-known peers, including Harry Stack Sullivan, Clara Thompson, and Erich Fromm, flocked to join her newly formed organization. Within a year, however, they had left to form their own institute. If Erich Fromm could be taken out of the equation because of his personal relationship with Horney, there is still the question of why Sullivan and Thompson left. The most commonly given answer to this question is that Horney, for all the punishment inflicted on her for not following Freud's dogma, would not allow others to stray from her own tenets.

Horney's self-help stance

Probably no one will ever know if two transplanted Vermont Yankees that first met in Akron, Ohio, in April of 1935, had read the works of Horney. But Bill Wilson and Dr. Bob Smith, the co-founders of Alcoholics Anonymous, surely came to concur with Horney's ideas of self-help. Neither Wilson nor Smith were strangers to psychoanalytic theory. One of the earliest members of the Oxford Group, a spiritual assemblage that was the predecessor of Alcoholics Anonymous, had been in therapy with Carl Jung. When Wilson joined the Oxford Group, Smith shared his insights. In fact, Wilson and Jung continued a dialogue via letters over a period of many years. More interesting, perhaps, is the group that developed as an off-shoot of Alcoholics Anonymous—Al-Anon. It was begun by the loved ones of early members of AA who often accompanied their alcoholic family members or friends to meetings. As they talked over cups of coffee and snacks, they discovered that quite often they had a great deal in common. *Al-Anon faces Alcoholism*, a sharing of members' experience, strength, and hope first published in 1965, discusses many of the subjects Horney dealt with in her therapy sessions—anxiety, frustration, low self-esteem, and dependence on others for happiness.

THEORIES IN ACTION

Horney's greatest contribution to psychoanalytic thought clearly was her inability to accept the theories of her contemporaries as unquestionable. That ability to doubt was born in listening to her dogmatic, Bible-throwing father preach his "truth." Once Freud's work had gained acceptance in Europe during Horney's time, it became the ultimate reality. It did not become reality for Horney and a few other free-thinkers, however. Like Jung and Adler, Horney for the most part was able to dispassionately consider what parts of Freud's theories had validity and what parts did not. This led to the germination of a rich variety of psychoanalytic schools of thought. (There are an estimated 400 of them today.) Varied psychoanalytic thought ultimately makes it possible for patients to choose from abundant resources to find what will be helpful to them. Without Horney's (and others') voices, the Western world would have been condemned to only Freudian treatment with its (at least perceived) denigration of women and hopeless outlook. When Horney published *The Neurotic Personality of Our Time* in 1937, for the first time the mental health community and laypeople were offered a glimpse of therapy that was neither cold and distant nor all-knowing, as Freudian analysis tended to be. It was instead motherly, warm, and supportive. It would lead into treatment modes totally divorced from Freud's. *The Neurotic Personality of Our Time* would prove so immensely popular that it would be reprinted 12 more times.

Horney's earliest work was related to the feminist movement, and it certainly has influenced women's rights worldwide since. She was hardly the mother of feminism, however. Many other more deserving candidates for that position exist in the annals of history. Horney and Erich Fromm, though, certainly do deserve the credit for founding the "culturist school" of psychotherapy. Their shared notion, that the outer world in which people exist is at least as important as their inner world, would greatly influence social scientists and even social programs in every Western nation. As noted in the statistics below, under Research, it appears that the Culturist School of Psychoanalysis—the insistence upon seeing poverty, domestic abuse, and other social evils as relating to mental illness—has become even more significant. Its beginnings are very much a part of both Horney's and Fromm's work, which has grown and remains viable.

Horney's impact on the world in the years since her death and the legacy she left behind can be measured by the organizations and treatment centers that still further the work Horney began, now more than 50 years after her death. Three years after her death, the Karen Horney Institute came into being. This New York-based foundation runs the Karen Horney Clinic, self-described as a nonprofit center serving a diverse socioeconomic group and providing affordable mental health treatment on a sliding scale payment basis.

In looking at Horney's life, it seems appropriate that among the services offered are:

• programs for people in the arts
• adult treatment programs
• child and adolescent programs
• foster care program
• therapeutic nursery
• victim treatment center
• treatment center for incest and abuse
• eating disorders treatment
• HIV and AIDS clinical services

The American Institute for Psychoanalysis begun by Horney in 1941 is yet another part of the Karen Horney Institute, along with the Association for the Advancement of Psychoanalysis. Both of these associations work closely with the clinic, providing training opportunities for advanced mental health professionals and an internship in social work.

The prevalence of mental health practitioners of the humanistic school of psychoanalysis today is further evidence of the validity of Horney's beliefs.

CHRONOLOGY

1885: Horney is born outside Hamburg, Germany.

1904: After a tumultuous marriage, her parents divorce.

1909: Marries Oskar Horney.

1911: First child, daughter Brigitte, is born.

1927: After an increasingly unhappy marriage, Horney leaves her husband, taking her three daughters.

1932: Moves to United States with her youngest daughter, Renate.

1933: Begins psychiatric practice in United States.

1934: Takes teaching position at Washington-Baltimore Society for Psychoanalysis.

1936: Publishes *Feminine Psychology*.

1942: Publishes *Self-Analysis*.

1952: Dies of stomach cancer at age 67.

As noted by Elizabeth Capelle in *The Readers Companion to American History*, "Horney was a thinker of undeniable originality, and many of the issues she raised can now be seen to be crucial to the psychoanalytic enterprise. Her questions, if not in every case her answers, have been vindicated."

Research

Psychoanalysis is far too nebulous an undertaking to be quantified into a numerical breakdown of cures from one form of therapy or another. There is even some question as to whether psychoanalysis—the talking therapy—is an art, rather than a science. This further muddies the waters of the efficacy of treatments. Patrick Kavanaugh of the Academy for the Study of the Psychoanalytic Arts has described mental health treatment in this era of the brain and of managed care as "conceptual understandings of human behavior based upon a biologized-medicalized-chemicalized-pathologized reductive metaphysical position." Put simply, nearly all psychoanalytic and biological theories propounded over the decades of the twentieth century have had some validity and have

BIOGRAPHY:

Mary Whiton Calkins

In 1863, when Mary Whiton Calkins was born, the United States was a broken and bloody place, in the full throes of a terrible and fratricidal Civil War. Born in Hartford, Connecticut but living a good part of her life in Buffalo, New York, Calkins came from a family that could best be described as eccentric. Her Welsh father and American (Puritan) mother spoke German, and were opposed to the American education system, believing their five children could be better educated by having them board with German and French families. Both parents actively encouraged all of their children to receive good educations. If there were any neurosis-producing issues in Mary Whiton Calkins' childhood, she kept them to herself. She began studies at Smith College in 1882, entering as a sophomore. The illness and subsequent death of her younger sister caused her to leave school for a while, but she returned and graduated in 1885.

The family traveled to Europe the next year and it is believed that Mary furthered her studies at the University of Leipzig. She had planned to tutor upon her return from Europe, but was soon invited to fill a vacancy at Wellesley College in the Greek department. When Wellesley expanded their philosophy department to include the newly added field of psychology the next year, Calkins was invited to take the position of professor of psychology, providing she studied psychology for a year. In 1890, Harvard, Yale, and even Clark University were not enthusiastic about a female student in their psychology programs. Calkins took courses at the Harvard Annex (not officially part of Harvard), but was soon encouraged to

press for attending the university by Josiah Royce, her professor, who quickly had perceived her great promise. With petitions from Royce and her father, Mary was allowed to attend classes, but still not as a regular student. She went on to work in the psychology lab at Clark University and began teaching at Wellesley in 1891. She continued to attempt to complete graduate studies at Harvard, but was again refused. She finally was given an informal examination at Harvard, which she passed, but was still not given a degree.

In 1905 she became the first woman president of the American Psychological Association, and in 1918, the first woman president of the American Philosophical Association. She taught at Wellesley until 1927, when she retired. She was a prolific writer, advocating self-based psychology. She created a

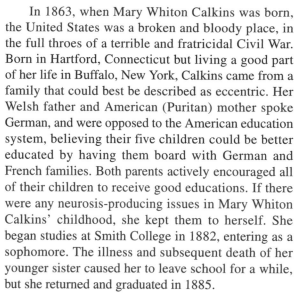

Mary Whiton Calkins.
(Archives of the History of American Psychology. Reproduced by permission.)

method of improving memory called "The Right Associates Method," and wrote extensively on a variety of subjects, including dream research, memorization, animal consciousness, and many others. She was the author of one of the earliest textbooks used in teaching psychology, *Introduction to Psychology*. She never married, and died in 1930 of cancer.

---

been effective in helping some people. As noted by Mark Tyrell in *Uncommon Knowledge, Ltd.*,

> So, what works in psychotherapy? What research tells us is effective is brief (that is to say time-limited and not endless) therapy which includes behavioral, cognitive, and hypnotic therapy and, if necessary, interpersonal (communication) training and practical support and help. Seeing someone as part of a wider system such as their family, community, and work environment is also essential to truly help them.

However, there is an area of statistical research that supports one of Horney's most basic premises: that society is a primary factor of much of our mental

ills. The most recent (worldwide) statistics released by the World Health Organization (WHO), Mental Health and Substance Dependence Division, look at mental illness in a way that Horney, Erich Fromm, and other culturist psychoanalysts would favor. These figures are unequivocal in their support of the premise that social factors influence mental health.

These figures, as reported by Dr. Benedetto Sarancenoe, Director of WHO, Mental Health and Substance Dependence, in September of 2003 show that:

- 450 million people on this planet suffer from mental health problems.

- At minimum one member of each four families worldwide has a mental disorder.

- Though no sector of any society is free of mental illness, the possibility of having a mental illness looms larger among children and adolescents living in poverty, the unemployed, poorly educated people, refugees, minority populations, abused women, other victims of violence, and neglected elderly persons.

- Though most mental illnesses are not fatal, they do account for 31% of all disability, worldwide.

- It is estimated that depression is emerging as among the most common mental health problems in the world, and by the year 2020, will be the second most common cause of disability.

Case studies

The classic case study in any discussion of Horney is the story of "Clare." It is believed to be autobiographical, or at least a melding of her life and some of her patients, as it clearly traces a woman's life that is markedly similar to the life of Horney. Clare is the second and unwanted daughter of parents involved in an unhappy marriage. The parents wanted no more children after their first child, a son. The father is a physician who is seldom home, and the mother is rather pompous and insists upon absolute loyalty and veneration from her children. Clare initially tries to win the love of the father, but soon discovers that her father is not interested in her or her brother. He is far too obsessed by his beautiful and clever wife to even notice the children. However his wife totally detests him and makes no secret of wishing him dead. Clare soon begins to see her mother as the much more powerful of the two parents, and allies herself with her mother.

This alliance with her mother does not give Clare the love she so desperately wants, but it does make her "the wonderful daughter of a wonderful mother." Totally divorced from her own feelings, Clare relies on her mother and others for her self-esteem, depending upon their admiration of qualities in herself that she actually detests. This early pattern of behavior leads to denial or lack of awareness of her own wishes, excessive need for and dependence on other people, and fierce competitiveness arising from the need to be better than others in order to replenish her self-esteem. Horney states that analysis for someone like Clare involves uncovering the reasons for these behavior patterns, how they manifest themselves in her life, and what effects they cause in her life.

Clare has, while in her 20s, separated from her husband. In self-analysis, Clare discovers why she felt unable to ask her estranged lover to return. It has to do with an unconscious fear from childhood of asking her mother for anything. The source of the fear was the possibility that her mother would reject her. Clare obsessively sought out men she could idealize—that would protect her and care for her. When these men didn't meet her obsessive needs, she hid her resentful feelings behind being a martyr and desperately sought attention and solace. Horney's belief was that human beings had an innate ability to overcome denial—the resistance to knowing themselves. Only when individuals were too much divorced from their "real selves" would they be unable to successfully enter into self-analysis. For Horney, Clare was a suitable candidate for self-analysis because she is not yet too alienated from her real self.

Horney also describes a patient referred to only as "a French girl" that she treated while in Germany in the 1920s. This girl was one of the several Horney saw during this time whose parents had believed her to be "feeble-minded" (cognitively impaired, what we commonly call mental retardation). No further description of the parents is ever given. After seeing the girl for several weeks, Horney began to question whether this patient was not, indeed, cognitively limited. Though the girl understood German perfectly, according to Horney, she seemed to understand nothing that was said to her, even when Horney used simpler language. In the process of their sessions, however, the French girl did begin to speak of dreams she was having that had to do with Horney's office. The girl was dreaming that the office was a jail or that it was the office of a physician who had examined her physically, something she hated.

These dreams, Horney states, were indicative of the girl's fear of being found out. Horney obtained further evidence that she was far from "feeble-minded" when the young woman spoke of an incident during which she was legally required to present her passport, but forgot to do so. She laughed as she explained how she had finally gone to the appropriate official with her passport, but had feigned not being able to speak German in hopes that this would keep her from getting in trouble. As she described the incident, the girl realized that this behavior was identical to how she had been dealing with Horney. This insight helped her to realize that this behavior was a pattern in her life: in order to avoid punishment or accusation, she pretended to be stupid and not able to understand. Horney states, "From this time on she proved to be a very intelligent girl."

BIBLIOGRAPHY

Sources

Billings, Molly. *The Influenza Pandemic of 1918.* 1997. http://www.stanford.edu/group/virus/uda.

Boeree, C. George. *Personality Theories/Erich Fromm.* 2000. http://www.ship.edu/~cgboeree/fromm.html.

Capelle, Elizabeth, Eric Foner, and John Garraty. *The Reader's Companion to American History.* Houghton Mifflin Co., 1991.

Coleman, James. *Abnormal Psychology and Modern Life.* Chicago: Scott, Foresman and Co., 1956.

4000 Years of Women in Science. *Mary Whiton Calkins.* 1999. http://www.astr.ua.edu.

Hoffman, Dassie. 2000. *Sandor Ferenczi and the Humanistic Psychologists.* http://www.sonoma.edu/psychology.

Horney, Karen, M.D. *The Neurotic Personality of Our Time.* New York: W. W. Norton and Co. Inc., 1937.

Horney, Karen, M.D. *New Ways in Psychoanalysis.* New York: W. W. Norton and Co. Inc., 1939.

Horney, Karen, M.D. *Our Inner Conflicts.* New York: W. W. Norton and Co. Inc., 1945.

Inter-parliamentary Union, England. "Women's Suffrage." *Serendipity.* http://www.ipu.org.

Kaplan, Harold I., M.D., and Benjamin J. Sadock, M.D. *Synopsis of Psychiatry, Behavioral Sciences, and Clinical Psychiatry.* Baltimore: William and Wilkins, 1991.

Marcus, Paul, and Alan Rosenberg. *Psychoanalytic Versions of the Human Condition: Philosophies of Life and Their Impact on Practice.* New York University Press, 1998.

"Press Release." *World Health Report, 2001, Mental Health: New Understanding, New Horizons.* 2001. http://www.who.int/whr.

"Trance and Trauma: Functional Nervous Disorders and the Subconscious Mind." *Serendipity.* http://www.serendip.brynmawr.edu.

Sayers, Janet. *Mothers of Psychoanalysis.* New York: W. W. Norton and Co. Inc., 1991.

Tyrrel, Mark, and Roger Elliot. *The Mad, Mad World of Psychotherapy.* Uncommon Knowledge, Ltd., 2003.

Further readings

Paris, Bernard. *Karen Horney: A Psychoanalyst's Search for Self-Understanding.* New Haven, Ct: Yale University Press, 1994.

Rubins, Jack L. *Karen Horney: Gentle Rebel of Psychoanalysis.* New York: Dial Press, 1978.

Quinn, S. *A Mind of her Own: The Life of Karen Horney.* New York: Summit Books, 1987.

Carl Gustaf Jung

1875–1961

SWISS PHYSICIAN, PSYCHIATRIST

UNIVERSITY OF BASEL, M.D., 1900

BRIEF OVERVIEW

Carl Gustaf Jung (1875–1961) is considered to be, together with Sigmund Freud and Alfred Adler, one of the three outstanding figures in the first generation of the psychoanalytic movement. Jung was the son of a Swiss Reformed pastor and spent all of his childhood and adolescence in Switzerland. He was trained as a medical doctor at the University of Basel. Originally intending to become a surgeon or internist, Jung decided to specialize in psychiatry within a year of the publication of Freud's groundbreaking book, *The Interpretation of Dreams.* Jung quickly put Freud's theories to work during his residency at the Burghölzli, a mental hospital for schizophrenics in the city of Zurich. Jung's early defense of Freud's findings led to a friendship that ended with Jung's publication of *Symbols of Transformation,* a work that indicated how far Jung's thinking had departed from Freud's.

Jung's break with Freud was one of the most critical events in the history of psychology in the early twentieth century. In 1913 Jung began a period of intense self-analysis and withdrawal from outside activities. After 1917, he emerged from his personal encounter with the unconscious with new theories about the existence of archetypes, the collective unconscious, the structures of the human psyche, the different types of human personality, and the individuation process. He combined these theories with an interest in comparative mythology and dream interpretation to construct an approach to therapy that he

Carl Jung. *(Courtesy of the Library of Congress.)*

BIOGRAPHY

BIOGRAPHY

Early years

Carl Gustaf Jung was born on July 26, 1875, at Kesswil in Switzerland. Jung's father, Johannes Paul Jung, was a pastor in the Swiss Reformed Church and a scholar with an interest in the Greek and Roman classics and Oriental languages. Paul Jung had originally hoped to become a professor of classical languages, but he settled for theology, on the grounds that the ministry offered a better chance of employment than university teaching. In addition, several other men in the extended family served as clergy. Jung's mother, Emilie Preiswerk, was a warmhearted woman with an unpredictable side that Jung found rather frightening. In spite of this aspect of her personality, however, Jung felt closer to her than he did to his father.

Jung was an only child for the first nine years of his life, which may partly account for his lifelong tendency to feel "different" and isolated from most of his age mates. Even in his eighties, he remarked on his isolation: "As a child, I felt myself to be alone, and I am still, because I know things . . . which others apparently know nothing of, and for the most part do not want to know." In addition to being so much older than his sister, Jung was an intellectually precocious youngster. His father began to teach him Latin and other ancient languages when he was only six years old, which also set him apart from other children. While Jung's father was a kind and gentle man, his mother had a more forceful character. Emilie was hospitalized when he was three years old for an illness that Jung later attributed to stresses in the marriage. Jung came to regard his father as weak, and his mother as the source of his lifelong distrust of women. "I was deeply troubled by my mother's being away. . . . The feeling I associated with 'woman' was for a long time that of innate unreliability. 'Father,' on the other hand, meant reliability and—powerlessness."

Because Jung's parents were not well-off financially, he was educated in a country school until he was eleven, when he was sent to a school in the city of Basel. This period of his education was stressful for him. "Then, for the first time, I became aware [of] how poor we were . . . I began to see my parents with different eyes, and to understand their cares and worries." Although Jung disliked mathematics—"sheer terror and torture"—and physical education, he was a gifted student who rose quickly to the top of his class. His success provoked the envy of his classmates, however, and he settled for second place in the class in order to avoid their hostility. Jung's anxiety about drawing attention to himself and his tendency to pull back from

called analytical psychology. The keynotes of analytical psychology are its emphasis on the human psyche's drive toward balance and wholeness, on the importance of bringing material from the unconscious into consciousness, and on the patient's significance as the best guide to his or her own maturation and individuation.

Jung continued to refine and rework his theories throughout his mature career. His published works fill 20 volumes in the standard American edition. In addition to his private practice, he lectured throughout Europe and supervised the next generation of analytical trainees. Although Jung was reluctant at first to set up a training institute devoted solely to analytical psychology, he helped to establish and direct the first Jung Institute in Zurich in 1948. As of 2001, there were Jung Institutes and study groups located throughout the world, and at least a dozen scholarly periodicals existed in the field of Jungian theory and practice. Jungian theories have had an extensive influence outside the fields of psychology and psychotherapy; they are widely used in literary and film criticism, religious studies, comparative literature, and cultural commentary. In recent years they have also been applied in political science and sociology.

competition remained with him throughout his life; among other symptoms, he developed a tendency to faint under stress. He remained in Basel, however, for his university education. Although Jung's father could not afford the full cost of tuition, the university awarded Jung a scholarship to cover the remainder. He originally wanted to become an archaeologist, but since the University of Basel did not have a department of archaeology, Jung entered medical school instead. Although Jung's father died in 1896, during his first year at the university, he completed the requirements for his M.D. in 1900. He had thought of specializing in surgery or internal medicine, but decided toward the end of his last year in medical school to seek further training in psychiatry. This decision was prompted by his reading a psychiatry textbook, combined with his own fascination with religious and philosophical questions. Psychiatry appeared to be a specialty that would allow him to combine his interest in natural science with his equally strong search for meaning and value in life.

Jung had first become interested as a child with the notion that different personalities can exist within the same human being. He thought of his mother's changes in behavior as the result of two different personalities inside her. When Jung was 12, he began to think of himself as also possessing two personalities, one a shy and awkward schoolboy, and the other a wise old man, respected and powerful. "It occurred to me that I was actually two different persons. One of them was the schoolboy who could not grasp algebra . . . the other was important, a high authority, a man not to be trifled with." In addition, Jung developed an interest in paranormal phenomena and the occult that led him to do extensive reading in comparative religion and mythology. As a boy growing up in a rural area, he was reassured to discover that the peasants in the countryside were also fascinated by the occult and by inexplicable events. Jung wrote his thesis for his M.D. degree on his 15-year-old female cousin, who claimed to receive messages from the dead when she went into trances. Jung noted that the girl spoke only High German when she was in a trance state, whereas she spoke only Swiss German in her normal waking condition. He published his thesis in 1902.

Jung's postgraduate training in psychiatry reinforced his interest in the internal division, or even disintegration, of a human personality. In December 1900, he took a position as a clinical assistant at the Burghölzli, a mental hospital in Zurich. He began to do research on schizophrenia, a mental disorder in which the patient loses touch with the real world, as reflected in illogical thinking, delusions, hallucinations, and other behavioral or emotional disturbances.

PRINCIPAL PUBLICATIONS

- *On the Psychology and Pathology of So-Called Occult Phenomena.* Basel, 1902.
- *Studies in Word Association.* Zurich, 1904, 1910; New York, 1919.
- *Symbols of Transformation.* Leipzig and Vienna, 1912; London, 1916.
- "The Association Method [in three parts]." *American Journal of Psychology* 31 (1910): 219–69.
- *Collected Papers on Analytical Psychology.* New York, 1919.
- *Psychological Types.* Zurich, 1921; New York and London, 1925.
- *Analytical Psychology, Its Theory and Practice: The Tavistock Lectures, 1935.* New York: Pantheon Books, 1968.
- *Psychology and Religion (The Terry Lectures, 1937).* New Haven, CT, and London, UK: Yale University Press, 1938.
- *Essays on Contemporary Events.* London, 1947.
- *Essays on a Science of Mythology (with C. Kerényi).* New York, 1949.
- *Answer to Job.* London, 1954.
- *The Undiscovered Self.* Boston and London, 1958.
- *Flying Saucers: A Modern Myth of Things Seen in the Skies.* New York and London, 1959.
- *Memories, Dreams, Reflections.* Recorded and edited by Aniela Jaffé; translated by Richard and Clara Winston. Rev. ed. New York: Random House, 1965.

Schizophrenia is classified as a psychosis or psychotic disorder; that is, it is a severe mental illness that is not only characterized by loss of contact with reality, but also damages the patient's ability to function in society. At the Burghölzli, Jung worked under the supervision of Eugen Bleuler, a world-renowned expert on schizophrenia. Although schizophrenia was then considered to be incurable, Jung came to believe that ". . . much of what we had hitherto regarded as senseless was not as crazy as it seems . . . even with such patients there remains in the background a personality which must be called normal . . . looking on, so to speak."

Another important aspect of Jung's work during his psychiatric residency was his research in word-association testing. Originally designed as a test of a subject's basic intelligence, word-association testing has also been used to probe into a subject's unconscious preoccupations. In this evaluation, the examiner reads a list of stimulus words and the subject responds to each. The interval between the stimulus word and the response is timed with a stopwatch. Most subjects respond immediately to words that have no emotional significance, but will stutter, hesitate, or prolong the reaction time if the stimulus word is disturbing to them. In one case, Jung deduced that a patient he was testing had gotten into a fight when he was drunk, based on the man's responses to the words knife, bottle, beat, and pointed. Jung was invited along with Freud to give lectures in the United States in 1909 on the basis of his word-association research.

Marriage and private life

In 1903, Jung married Emma Rauschenbach. The marriage produced five children—four daughters and one son—but it did not satisfy all of Jung's emotional needs. Even though Jung credited his wife and children with keeping him sane during his psychological crisis in 1913–14, he had a succession of lovers. The first was a Russian patient of his named Sabina Spielrein, who had come to Switzerland to attend medical school and had had a nervous breakdown. The affair began in 1904, when Spielrein was living temporarily in Jung's house. Spielrein later became a psychoanalyst herself. After Spielrein moved to Vienna in 1911 to study with Freud, Jung became involved with Antonia (Toni) Wolff, another patient who became a professional colleague. Jung maintained a triangular relationship with his wife and Toni until the latter died of a heart attack in 1953. Jung's wife, who also became an analyst, died two years later, in 1955. In addition to Sabina Spielrein and Toni Wolff, Jung had an affair with Christiana Morgan, an American patient of his who later returned to Boston and, with Henry Murray, developed the thematic apperception test (TAT).

Jung worked at the Burghölzli for nine years, until 1909. In 1905 he was appointed to a lectureship in psychiatry at the University of Zurich, which he held until 1913. His clinical experience in the treatment of schizophrenics influenced his later thought in

several important respects. First of all, he continued to study mythology and comparative religion, and he noticed that the fantasies and delusions reported by his patients often contained themes or images found in ancient myths or religious writings. Since his patients could hardly have read these books, Jung began to consider the possibility that all human minds contain a layer that represents a general unconscious, distinct from the individual's personal unconscious. Jung later called this psychic layer the "collective unconscious," which he defined as containing "the whole spiritual heritage of mankind's evolution, born anew in the brain structure of every individual."

Secondly, Jung's work with schizophrenics stimulated his interest in dream interpretation as an approach to psychotherapy. He recognized that his patients' waking fantasies had a dreamlike quality, and he concluded that the dreams of less disturbed individuals might still reveal important aspects of their personalities or their current life situations. One example that he gave in a later essay called "Dream-Analysis in Its Practical Application" came from his treatment of a patient who dreamed of climbing a mountain but had to stop short of the summit due to altitude sickness. Jung interpreted the dream as a symbolic picture of the man's career dilemma. The patient had risen to a position of relative success from very humble origins, but wanted to advance even higher even though he lacked the necessary talents to get to the very top in his field. Jung viewed the altitude sickness in the dream as a warning to the patient to stop his striving and learn to be content with what he had already attained.

The development of Jung's analytical psychology

Jung's mature contributions to psychology grew out of two important developments: the first was his relationship with Sigmund Freud (1856–1939), the founder of psychoanalysis; and the second was the mental crisis that overtook him in 1913 and provoked him to analyze his own inner workings.

Jung and Freud   Jung had acquainted himself in medical school with Freud's ideas, and he had read Freud's *Interpretation of Dreams* when it was published in 1900. Jung began to correspond with Freud in 1904 about Jung's work with the schizophrenics at the Burghölzli. He also began to apply Freud's method of psychoanalytic treatment to his own patients, and he delivered a course of lectures on Freud's method as part of his university lectureship. In 1906 Freud invited Jung to Vienna, and Jung went to visit him in February 1907. Jung's interest in meeting Freud required a certain amount of courage, because Freud's publications had stirred up considerable controversy in the medical community. Jung was, in fact, warned that his career might suffer if he continued to defend Freud, as he had for several years. For the next six years, Jung collaborated with Freud through letters and occasional meetings, and accompanied Freud on his trip to the United States in 1909. Freud thought of Jung at this point as his potential successor as the leader of the psychoanalytic movement, helping to secure Jung's appointment as permanent president of the Association of Psychoanalysis in 1910. By 1911, however, Jung began to recognize that his thinking was moving in a direction that was increasingly difficult to reconcile with Freud's approach. When Jung published his *Psychology of the Unconscious* (later republished under the title *Symbols of Transformation*) in 1913, the break between the two men was complete. Freud felt personally betrayed by Jung's rejection of his theories. In 1914 Jung resigned his membership in the Association of Psychoanalysis.

The break between Jung and Freud was the end result of a combination of factors. One factor was the difference in their family backgrounds and postgraduate training. Even though both were products of the university system of German-speaking Europe and were trained as medical doctors, Freud remained an outsider to the medical "establishment" of the nineteenth century because he was a Jew, whereas Jung was not a target of anti-Semitic prejudice. In addition, Jung had longer and more intensive experience working in a mental hospital than Freud. This difference in clinical experience was reflected in their psychological theories—Freud's concept of repression and the role of the unconscious was shaped by his treatment of neurotic patients suffering from obsessions and what was then termed hysteria, while Jung's concept of the unconscious grew out of his work with psychotic patients.

Another factor was the generational difference between the two men. Freud, who was nineteen years older than Jung, was born before the American Civil War and died before the outbreak of World War II. At the end of World War I, which proved to be a major turning point in Western intellectual and cultural history, Freud was close to retirement age, while Jung was still in his early forties. Jung noted in his autobiography that in the early years of their friendship, he had regarded Freud as a father-like "superior personality"; only gradually did Jung feel the need to declare his intellectual independence from this "father."

The difference between Freud's and Jung's concepts of the unconscious helps to explain some of their other differences. Freud originally regarded the unconscious as a part of the psyche that came into

being through repression (the unconscious exclusion of unacceptable thoughts or desires from the conscious mind). Jung, on the other hand, saw the unconscious as an innate layer of the psyche acting as a reservoir of images and symbols that emerged in human art and creativity, as well as in emotional disturbances. It was Jung's emphasis in his 1913 publication on the role of symbolism in the functioning of the unconscious that had antagonized Freud. Moreover, Freud attempted to be "scientific" and "objective" in his approach to psychotherapy; while he recognized the distinction between reason and fantasy, he considered fantasy an inferior mode of thought. Jung, by contrast, regarded rational thought and fantasy as equally valuable and equally important to human well-being. Where Freud's medical model of psychotherapy stressed the distinction between the "healthy" therapist and the "sick" patient, Jung regarded all human beings as possessing divided souls. Therapist and patient stand at different points along a continuum of mental health, rather than being sharply separated by the categories of the medical model. In addition, where Freud attributed mental disorders to distortions of the sexual impulse, Jung regarded sexuality as only one among several sources of emotional energy. He noted that "Freud never asked himself why he was compelled to talk continually of sex, why this idea had taken such possession of him." Jung had come to the conclusion that the fundamental problems of his patients were religious rather than sexual in nature. Lastly, Freud's approach to psychotherapy was basically retrospective; that is, he asked his patients to look backward into their infancy and childhood years for the origin of their problems. Jung, on the other hand, emphasized the prospective dimension of therapy, which is to say that a patient's dreams and fantasies could be viewed as attempts at self-healing in the present with the hope of improvement in the future. On the whole, Jung's understanding of human psychology gave a much smaller place to childhood experiences than Freud's. He preferred to focus on adult issues, particularly those related to the second half of life.

The final factor that led to Jung's break with Freud was a personal rather than a theoretical disagreement—namely, Jung's relationship with Sabina Spielrein. Author John Kerr's analysis of Spielrein's diary and the correspondence between Freud and Jung indicates that the affair changed Freud's mind about his Swiss colleague and dissolved what was left of their friendship.

Crisis and self-analysis Toward the end of 1913, Jung underwent a period of uncertainty and inner

A group of prominent psychologists at Clark University, Massachusetts, in 1909. In the front row are (left to right) Sigmund Freud, G. Stanley Hall, and Carl Jung. (Copyright Bettmann/Corbis. Reproduced by permission.)

distress, which he described in his autobiography as "a state of disorientation." He began to have dreams and visions of the end of the world, or of world destruction. At one point he saw a "monstrous flood" engulfing most of Europe. "When it came up to Switzerland I saw that the mountains grew higher and higher to protect our country." Thousands of people were drowning in the flood and entire civilizations were collapsing into it. "Then the sea turned to blood." This vision was followed, in the next few weeks, by dreams of an everlasting winter: ". . . in the middle of summer an Arctic cold wave descended and froze the land to ice. . . . the whole of Lorraine and its canals frozen and the entire region totally deserted by human beings." Nightmares of this sort often precede a psychotic episode and Jung himself later admitted that he was "menaced by a psychosis" during this period.

His apocalyptic visions persisted through the spring and early summer of 1914; but when World War I broke out in August of that year, Jung reinterpreted his doomsday visions as a prophetic anticipation of the war. As a result, he decided to analyze his own psyche. "An incessant stream of fantasies had been released, and I did my best not to lose my head but to find some way to understand these strange things."

To outside observers, Jung's turmoil was at least partly related to his break with Freud and to the nature of his clinical practice. While Freud himself was genuinely pained by Jung's "defection," Jung experienced the loss of Freud's friendship as a shattering blow. In addition, Jung's work with schizophrenic patients placed him at some risk of developing a disturbance of his own. Some therapists believe that certain mental disorders are contagious, in the sense that the patient's intense emotions or disordered thinking can affect the therapist's psychological equilibrium. For example, therapists who treat survivors of extreme trauma (severe childhood abuse, military combat, terrorist attacks, and similar experiences) frequently have nightmares or mood swings that reflect the survivor's trauma. Similarly, therapists who treat psychotics sometimes find themselves pulled into the patient's delusions and fantasies.

But although Jung recognized that he was not far removed from the condition of the patients he was treating in 1913, he also saw himself as an exceptionally creative and gifted individual. For this reason, he thought that his self-analysis would benefit others. Although this probing into his own psyche was potentially dangerous, it laid the foundation of his mature theorizing, and it also affected his techniques of psychotherapy. During this period of self-analysis, which lasted until 1918, Jung discovered the usefulness of painting as a way for patients to understand their dreams and fantasies. As he explained in an article on "The Aims of Psychotherapy,"

> . . . something invaluable is won, namely . . . a step toward psychological maturity. The patient can make himself creatively independent by this method. . . . He is no longer dependent on his dreams or on his doctor's knowledge, but can give form to his own inner experience by painting it.

The most important type of painting that Jung recommended to his patients is the mandala. Mandalas are ritualistic geometric designs that originated in Hinduism and Buddhism as aids to meditation. They are thought to symbolize the structure of the universe. Jung regarded mandalas—particularly mandalas with a quaternary or fourfold design—as symbolic images that could help his patients to draw out the fantasies and other material in their unconscious minds.

Jung gave up his academic lectureship and withdrew from public speaking during his self-analysis. He maintained a connection to the outside world through his wife and children on the one hand, and his relationship with Toni Wolff on the other. He also turned to yoga as a form of physical exercise that would help to calm and stabilize his emotions.

Later career

From an external perspective, Jung's later years were relatively quiet. He maintained a private psychiatric practice in Küsnacht, a suburb of Zurich, until his death in 1961. He continued to publish essays and articles that reflected his wide-ranging reading and reflection.

Jung's reading in the period following his crisis, between 1918 and 1926, included the writings of the Gnostics, a group of pre-Christian and early Christian sects. The Gnostic cults taught that human beings are redeemed from the world through initiation into secret knowledge. In addition to Gnostic works, Jung studied the writings of the medieval alchemists, which he came to regard as symbolic descriptions of the process of psychological transformation. "I had stumbled upon the historical counterpart of my psychology of the unconscious." He also continued to paint mandalas as expressions of his self-development. "It became increasingly plain to me that the mandala . . . is the path to the center [of the self], to individuation." In early 1928, Jung drew a mandala that struck him as Chinese in its form and choice of colors. That same year, an expert on China named Richard Wilhelm sent Jung a copy of a Taoist text called "The Secret of the Golden Flower," which also could be read as an account of the process of psychological development. Jung later said that he "devoured the manuscript at once, for the text gave [him] undreamed-of confirmation of [his] ideas about the mandala." The close connection in time between Jung's "Chinese" drawing and the arrival of Wilhelm's gift was one of the coincidences that eventually led Jung to his theory of synchronicity.

Jung combined his extensive reading with occasional trips abroad to study non-Western cultures. His self-analysis had caused him to wonder whether there was a part of his personality that had not been influenced by Western culture and education. "In traveling to Africa . . . I unconsciously wanted to find that part of my personality which had become invisible under the influence and pressure of being European." In 1920 he traveled to North Africa. This journey was followed by a visit to the Pueblo Indians of New Mexico, a second trip to Africa in 1925, and a journey to India and Ceylon in 1938. Jung's encounter with Indian forms of Buddhism led him to new insights about the historical Buddha: "I grasped the life of the Buddha as the reality of the self . . . which represents the essence of human existence and of the world as a whole. . . . Buddha became, as it were, the image of the development of the self."

Jung began to publish his studies of medieval European alchemy in the 1930s. During this period he resumed lecturing and was awarded a number of honorary degrees, including honorary doctorates from Harvard, Oxford, and two Swiss universities. In 1944 he suffered a foot fracture followed by a severe heart attack; these medical mishaps caused him to give up his public lectures, but they also provided him with another opportunity for creative work. While he was recuperating from the heart attack, he had a series of dreams and visions that led him to some new formulations. Some of these insights concerned the completion of the

"Queen Katharine Dream" by artist William Blake. Dream symbolism is frequently referenced in literature and the arts. (National Gallery of Art. Reproduced by permission.)

process of individuation, which Jung came to associate with objectivity and detachment from emotional ties. Another insight that Jung derived from his illness was an attitude of acceptance: ". . . an affirmation of things as they are; an unconditional 'yes' to that which is . . . acceptance of the conditions of existence as I see them and understand them, acceptance of my own nature, as I happen to be." He died in June 1961 after a brief illness.

THEORIES

Jung's theories are not easy to explain or understand, whether in the original German or in English translation, because he did not express himself clearly. As Anthony Storr, one of Jung's biographers, has written, "I know of no creative person who was more hamstrung by his inability to write." In addition, Jung sometimes defined the same concept in several different ways in his various writings, which complicates the matter further. Readers who are interested in specific topics may want to start with Jung's autobiography, or with one of the collections of his essays that

are available in inexpensive paperback editions, and then move on to other sections of the *Collected Works* that address those topics.

The structure of the psyche
Main points   To Jung, the human psyche represented the totality of all mental processes, unconscious as well as conscious. Although Jung used some of Freud's terminology to describe the various structures of the human psyche, he did not use the words in the same way. For Freud, the term ego referred to a part of the psyche that acts as a mediator between the internalized demands of parents and society (the superego) and the person's instinctual drives (the id). The ego could also be defined in Freudian terms as the part of the psyche that is conscious, is in immediate control of thinking processes, and is most fully in touch with the external world. For Jung, in contrast, the ego is one example among many of a complex, which is an emotionally charged group of images or ideas. Jung wrote that ". . . the ego is how one sees oneself, along with the conscious and unconscious feelings that accompany that view." The goal of psychotherapy is not the development of the ego as such, but rather a fuller experience of the Self. The Self in Jungian therapy is the central organizing principle of the psyche, but at the same time it is a transpersonal force or power that goes beyond the conscious ego. Jung believed that experiences of the Self have a revelatory or religious quality; in one of his early writings, he even referred to the Self as "the God within us."

Two other important parts of the psyche are the shadow and the persona. The shadow contains the hidden or unconscious aspects of the personality, good as well as bad, which the ego has never recognized or has repressed. In most cases, these aspects have been shut out of the conscious ego because of parental or societal disapproval. For this reason, the shadow may contain positive qualities that the individual has been forbidden or unable to acknowledge, as well as primitive or childlike impulses. The psyche tends to project the shadow onto other people or groups. In dreams, the shadow usually appears as a person of the same sex as the dreamer, embodying traits or qualities that the dreamer rejects. For example, the shadow of a man who is a committed pacifist may appear in dreams as a soldier, a street bully, or something similar. Jung once recorded a dream in which he was with "an unknown, brown-skinned man, a savage." He identified this "primitive" figure as his personal shadow, the embodiment of all the qualities that a highly educated European would want to root out in himself.

The persona, in contrast, is the psyche's public face, the set of traits and characteristics in conformity

FURTHER ANALYSIS:

Dream symbolism in Jung

Jung regarded dream symbols in general as having two primary functions—to give expression to parts of the patient's personality that have been frustrated or underdeveloped, and to give form or shape to an archetype. The first function refers to a person's past and present, while the second concerns the dreamer's future. Jung thought that dream symbolism often predicted the outlines of a patient's future personality development, particularly the striving for wholeness or completion. Unlike Freud, Jung did not regard dreams as disguised clues to unacceptable parts of the patient's past that the patient could not confront directly, or as wish fulfillments. Instead, he interpreted symbols that appeared in dreams as either reflections of the patient's present situation—which he called "little dreams,"or as archetypal images pointing in the direction that the patient must take for healing—which he called "big dreams."

Jung used three different techniques in analyzing symbols in his patients' dreams. The first, the method of active imagination, has been described earlier. Jung called his second method the "method of amplification." In this technique, after the patient described the dream symbol, he or she was asked to give the analyst a variety of different meanings that he or she associated with the symbol. Jung maintained that amplification is different from free association in that the patient is expected to talk about the symbol itself rather than following a line of associations that may begin with the symbol but lead away from it. Jung considered amplification necessary because he held that symbols are multifaceted and are never completely knowable on the intellectual level.

In addition to the patient's own associations, the Jungian analyst might help to amplify the symbol by contributing his or her own knowledge of its meanings in folklore, mythology, occult texts, religious writings, or histories of language. For example, a patient who dreamed of a dove might associate it with pacifism, a soap brand, a shade of gray, an interest in biology, a concern for the environment, and many other possibilities. The analyst might then contribute such information as the role of the dove in the story of Noah and the ark in the book of Genesis, the significance of the dove as the sacred bird of the goddess Venus in classical mythology, the dove as the symbol of the Holy Spirit in Christian theology, the roots of the English word "dove" in old Anglo-Saxon, or other items that might help the patient amplify the dream symbol.

The third method that Jung used in analyzing dream symbolism was to write down a series of the patient's dreams and apply the principle of internal consistency to their interpretation. Jung's volume on *Psychology and Alchemy* contains over a hundred pages of analysis of just one patient's series of dreams. Jung said of the dream series method,

> [the dreams] form a coherent series in the course of which the meaning gradually unfolds more or less of its own accord. The series is the context which the dreamer himself supplies. It is as if not one text but many lay before us, throwing light from all sides on the unknown terms . . . . the interpretation of each individual passage is bound to be largely conjecture, but the series as a whole gives us all the clues we need to correct any possible errors.

---

with social expectations that the individual shows to others. In Jung's words, "The persona . . . is a compromise between the individual and society as to what a man should appear to be." The word "persona" is derived from the Greek term for the mask that an actor wears on stage. The persona often includes certain aspects of a person's class position or professional role; for example, if one is a physician, one's persona is likely to include traits related to "how a doctor should act." The persona can serve as a protective cover for one's inner self; it becomes problematic only when someone identifies with their public face to the point of neglecting their inner life. A recent example

of an overly rigid persona is Princess Margaret, the younger sister of Queen Elizabeth. The princess demanded that even her closest friends address her by her royal titles at all times—even in private.

Still another important aspect of the psyche is the so-called contrasexual part, the anima, or inner woman, in a man and the animus, or inner man, in a woman. In a male, the anima is both a complex and an archetypal image of the feminine. In Jung's own words, "Every mother and every beloved is forced to become the carrier and embodiment of this omnipresent and ageless image, which corresponds to the deepest reality in a man." In a woman, the animus ". . . is the deposit, as it were, of all woman's ancestral experiences of man—and not only that, he is also a creative and procreative being, not in the sense of masculine creativity, but in the sense that he brings forth something we might call . . . the spermatic word." Jung, like most psychiatrists of his generation, believed that men and women are fundamentally different, not only in their reproductive organs but in their psyches as well. Moreover, he thought that the animus in women is more powerful than the anima in men because of the tendency of Western culture to overvalue the masculine. The anima (in males) or animus (in females) appears as a member or members of the other sex. In terms of outward behavior, a man who is "possessed by his anima" in Jung's terms is likely to act in moody or overly emotional ways; similarly, a woman "possessed by her animus" becomes opinionated and critical.

Explanation   Jung tended to personify psychic structures. His early belief that there were at least two personalities in both his mother and himself developed in his later work into the notion that the various complexes in the psyche appear as persons in one's dreams and fantasies, and that they influence behavior when they temporarily take over the ego. During Jung's period of self-analysis, he encountered a figure from his unconscious that he called Philemon.

> Philemon represented a force which was not myself. . . . I held conversations with him, and he said things which I had not consciously thought. . . . At times he seemed to me quite real, as if he were a living personality . . . to me he was what the Indians call a guru.

Furthermore, Jung regarded the conscious part of the psyche and the unconscious as compensatory; that is, they provide checks and balances on one another. This notion of compensation reflected Jung's understanding of psychic health as a product of the conjunction of opposites. For Jung, compensation is a natural process intended to keep the psyche in balance. Dreams, for example, are a way for the unconscious to balance or supplement the person's conscious activity. Someone who is overly identified with their persona (socially acceptable outward personality) may find their dreams filled with characters representing their shadow or their anima/animus. Similarly, a person who has devoted most of their conscious energies to intellectual development and has ignored or suppressed feelings will find their emotions emerging in dream material.

In addition, Jung's concept of compensation is related to his understanding of the psyche as self-regulating. In his words, "The psyche does not merely react, it gives its own specific answer to the influences at work upon it." Thus dreams, fantasies, and even neurotic symptoms may be regarded, not as proof of mental illness or cause for worry, but as an indication that material from the unconscious is surfacing in order to bring about a better balance in the conscious mind.

Examples   Jung's autobiography contains an interesting example from his psychiatric practice of dreaming as a compensation for conscious attitudes. The patient in this case was "a highly intelligent woman" whose analysis was not going well; in Jung's opinion, it was becoming increasingly shallow and superficial. Jung then had a dream in which he was walking through a valley with a steep hill on his right. On the top of the hill was a castle, with a woman sitting on its highest tower. In order to see the woman, whom Jung recognized as his patient, he had to tilt his head far backward.

> The interpretation was immediately apparent to me. If in the dream I had to look up at the patient in this fashion, in reality I had probably been looking down on her. . . . I told her of the dream and my interpretation . . . and the treatment once more began to move forward.

Archetypes

The concept of the archetype has been described as Jung's most distinctive contribution to psychology. In Jung's system, an archetype is a symbol or "typical mode of expression" drawn from the collective unconscious. Jung derived his notion of the collective unconscious from his work with the schizophrenic patients at the Burghölzli hospital. Noticing the similarities between some of the images in their fantasies and those found in myths and legends from a wide variety of cultures and historical periods, Jung concluded that there is a substratum, or layer, in the psyche found in all people that is the source of mythology, visions, and certain types of dreams. He called this layer the collective unconscious, and he believed that it underlies each individual's personal unconscious.

In Jungian psychology, the archetypes are basic psychic patterns that arise from the collective unconscious and allow people to organize their experiences into connected patterns. In Jung's earlier usage, archetypes are not themselves ideas or concepts, but innate predispositions to create myths or stories out of ordinary human experience. In Jung's words, "Archetypes are, by definition, factors and motifs that arrange the psychic elements into certain images." After 1944, Jung began to link his concept of archetypes with emotion, by describing them as predispositions to form images under highly charged emotional conditions. Toward the end of his life, Jung strengthened the connection between emotions and archetypes by redefining the archetypes as innate releasing mechanisms linked to universal human emotions, such as hunger, anger, neediness, etc. These universal emotions emerge in the form of images that are remarkably similar across cultures—good or terrible larger-than-life-sized parents, angels and demons, heroes, monsters, magicians, and so forth. Other archetypes that Jung frequently mentions include the Maiden, the Child, the Wise Old Man, the Anthropos (the original or primordial human being), and the Trickster.

Main points The reader will note that Jung personifies his archetypes (represents them as persons) in the same way that he personifies the complexes of the psyche. In a discussion that Jung had with an English clergyman in 1957, he insisted that the archetypes are not "concepts." "In reality it [sic] is a living thing. The archetypes all have a life of their own which follows a biological pattern."

In addition to the roles they play in the individual psyche, Jung also thought that archetypes could function on a national or collective level. To use a historical example, one could understand the witch hunts of medieval Europe as mass projections of a negative mother archetype (the evil destructive mother, or witch) onto thousands of innocent women. In a contemporary context, archetypes can be said to shape the "peculiarities" of each nation. Jung once commented that a person can understand his or her own country only from the standpoint of a "foreign collective psyche." "It has always seemed to me that there can be nothing more useful for a European than some time or another to look out at Europe from the top of an American skyscraper." On both the individual and the collective level, the archetypes carry a heavy emotional charge; consequently, they are typically activated by stressful or extreme situations.

Jung also thought the archetypes helped to restore a sense of meaning and significance to his patients' lives. He believed that the widespread loss of traditional religious faith among educated Europeans had resulted in a sense of futility and purposelessness in daily life. In his opinion, reconnecting with the mythological and archetypal dimension of human experience could help people to recognize a larger-than-life or even cosmic significance in the events of their lives. Jung's conversation with an elderly Pueblo Indian about tribal religion and sun worship during his trip to New Mexico led him to contrast the "dignity" and "tranquil composure" of Native Americans with the "impoverished" mind-set of Western intellectuals. The Native American is

> a son of the sun; his life is cosmologically meaningful, for he helps the father and preserver of all life in his

daily rise and descent. If we set against this our own self-justifications . . . we cannot help but see our poverty. . . . Knowledge does not enrich us; it removes us more and more from the mythic world in which we were once at home by right of birth.

Explanation Jung never concerned himself with trying to develop a clear explanation of the origin of the archetypes. As a result, some of his critics have assumed that he believed that people can inherit ideas or concepts, as well as their physical characteristics, from their parents or remote ancestors. As we have seen, however, Jung specifically stated that the archetypes are not concepts; rather they are templates or patterns with which a person organizes his or her perception of the world. In his 1937 Terry Lectures, Jung described

> . . . a certain unconscious condition carried on by biological inheritance. By this assumption I naturally do not mean an inheritance of representations, which would be difficult if not impossible to prove. The inherited quality . . . must rather be something like a possibility of regenerating the same or at least similar ideas. I have called the possibility 'archetype,' which means a mental precondition. . . .

Later Jungians have frequently debated the nature of the archetypes. Some theorists have argued that they are only cultural symbolic forms, without any biological basis in human nature. Others maintain, on the basis of recent research in the processes of perception and learning in human infants, that the archetypes are "image schemas" that are produced by innate cognitive mechanisms in the brain that have developed through natural selection. These brain processes are activated by certain features in the baby's environment that are essential to survival—such as the faces of other human beings. The cognitive pathways allow the baby to form very basic notions, or image schemas, of space and other aspects of the environment. Another way of describing the results of these findings is that later Jungians ascribe the archetypes to certain universal features of early childhood experience that are combined with inborn emotional "hard-wiring," rather than to a mysterious entity outside human experience.

Examples Specific examples of archetypes and their interpretation are described in the case studies below.

Psychological types

Another important contribution that Jung made to psychology was his categorization of psychological personality types. Jung was not the first theorist to attempt to classify human beings according to differences in temperament—the ancient Greeks, for example, classified people according to their "humors" (bodily fluids that were thought to determine a person's basic disposition). Jung was, however, the first to define extraversion and introversion as descriptions of a person's fundamental psychic orientation. Later psychologists continue to find "extravert" (now commonly spelled "extrovert") and "introvert" useful terms in evaluating people.

Jung was led to make the distinction between these two personality types from his clinical experiences with hysterical patients as well as with schizophrenics. Hysteria in the early years of the twentieth century was defined as a neurosis in which the patient suffered from a variety of physical ailments that were produced by strong but unverbalized emotions. Jung noticed, however, that patients diagnosed with hysteria tended to remain in contact with external reality and to develop a working relationship with the therapist, whereas the schizophrenics withdrew into their own internal fantasies and from human contact. In other words, the hysterics found emotional significance in people and objects in the external world, whereas the schizophrenics found meaning only in their internal landscape. Jung began to describe hysteria as an "extraverted," or "turned outward" disorder, and schizophrenia as an "introverted" or "turned inward" disorder.

Several years later, Jung recognized that extraversion and introversion were useful categories for classifying personality differences among "normal" people. In an essay on "The Psychology of the Unconscious," Jung defined extraverted people as having ". . . an outgoing, candid, and accommodating nature that adapts easily to a given situation, quickly forms attachments, and . . . will often venture forth with careless confidence into unknown situations." By contrast, introverts have ". . . a hesitant, reflective, retiring nature that keeps itself to itself, shrinks from objects, is always slightly on the defensive and prefers to hide behind mistrustful scrutiny." Significantly, Jung classified himself as an introvert.

In Jung's later years, after his travels to Africa and Asia, he found his categorization of personality types to be a useful summary of the large-scale differences between Western and Eastern cultures. "Western man seems predominantly extraverted, Eastern man predominantly introverted. The former projects the meaning and considers that it exists in objects; the latter feels the meaning in himself. But the meaning is both without and within."

Main points Jung's notion of psychological types is closely related to his theory of psychic self-regulation.

We have already seen that Jung thought of the various complexes in the psyche—particularly the shadow, the persona, and the anima or animus—as helping to maintain a balance between the conscious and unconscious layers of the psyche. Similarly, he regarded the extraversion/introversion distinction as another aspect of psychic self-regulation, in that a person's dreams, fantasies, and other products of the unconscious would reflect the opposite of the dreamer's conscious orientation. Thus the dream material of extraverted persons has an introverted quality, and vice versa.

Beyond the introvert/extravert distinction, Jung also thought that people could be subdivided into four additional groups according to their dominant mental function. Jung identified four such functions: sensation, intuition, thinking, and feeling. Sensation to Jung is the mental function that allows a person to recognize that a thing exists. Intuition refers to a capacity to form hunches or to see the possibilities in something. Thinking gives names to things and forms judgments about them. Feeling is concerned with questions of value, whether something is pleasant or unpleasant. Any of these functions could be dominant in either extraverts or introverts, which yields a total of eight possible psychological types. Moreover, reflecting Jung's interest in the reconciliation of opposites, he maintained that thinking is the opposite of feeling, and sensation is the opposite of intuition.

Examples As of 2002, Jung's typing of personality is most often encountered in the field of personality testing. His classification scheme is the basis of a frequently-used American personality test, the Myers-Briggs Type Inventory, or MBTI. The MBTI, which has become widely known through the work of American psychologists David Keirsey and Marilyn Bates, scores subjects on four scales: extraversion/introversion (E/I); intuition/sensation (N/S); thinking/feeling (T/F); and judgment/perception (J/P). There are sixteen possible combinations; thus, a person who is an extraverted-intuitive-thinking-judging type according to the Myers-Briggs test would be classified as an ENTJ. The MBTI also reflects Jung's nonjudgmental view of personality development in that none of the 16 types are considered "good" or "bad"; the profile descriptions of each type are intended to help test subjects understand themselves better and to gain insight into problems or misunderstandings with other personality types.

The process of individuation

Jung regarded the process of individuation as the core of his psychology. "The goal of psychological, as of biological, development is self-realization, or individuation." In contrast to Freud, Jung was more interested in an individual patient's inner development than in his or her interpersonal relationships. Jung's own experience of a mental and emotional crisis in his forties influenced his understanding of the process of individuation in several respects.

Main points   One of the most interesting features of Jung's concept of individuation is that he regarded it as the central task of the second half of a person's life. Modern youth-obsessed culture does not place much value on midlife and the post-retirement years, but Jung saw this phase of life as an opportunity to achieve personal integration and wholeness. For him, the first half of life is a relatively uninteresting preparation for the individuation process. In the first half of a person's life, he or she "fulfills one's obligations," in Jung's words; separates from one's family of origin, completes one's schooling, finds a mate, and starts a new family. But after these external goals have been reached, a person must look inward and confront the parts of the self that have been neglected or suppressed. Jung's study of personality types had convinced him that people develop in a one-sided fashion during the first half of life. In order to accomplish their goals, they typically overuse their dominant mental function while remaining unconscious of the others. Thus, a scholar who has relied primarily on the thinking function is likely to be troubled by outbursts of primitive or childish emotion; or a corporate executive who has succeeded in the business world because of a well-developed sensation function has problems in family relationships because the function of intuition has never been cultivated. Jung believed that midlife is the point at which most people on the path toward individuation recognize that their lives are "stuck" or incomplete, often because a personal crisis of some kind claims their attention.

Another important aspect of Jung's concept of individuation is that he did not regard it as equally possible or appropriate for everyone. "It would . . . be a great mistake to suppose that this is the path every neurotic must travel. . . . It is appropriate only in those cases where consciousness has reached an abnormal degree of development." In other words, Jung's understanding of the individuation process is frankly elitist. After his early psychiatric residency, he had relatively little contact with patients from working-class or rural backgrounds.

Jung thought that there were two actions that a person must take in the second half of life if he or she is to achieve individuation. The first is to open oneself to the unconscious as it expresses itself in dreams and fantasies, and to try to understand these expressions. This activity requires the help of a partner or therapist. Jung believed that Westerners, particularly intellectuals, had overemphasized rational consciousness to the point that they could not investigate the unconscious without running the risk of being overwhelmed by it. The therapist's task is in part that of a guide, to assist the patient in integrating material from the unconscious into his or her personality rather than being pulled apart by it. Jung's own brush with psychosis during his self-analysis left him with a lifelong sensitivity to the dangers as well as the potential benefits of exploring the unconscious.

The second action that is a necessary part of the individuation process is to sacrifice some of the worldly gains that have been achieved through overuse of one's superior function. In order to gain access to the less developed functions in one's personality, one must be prepared to minimize the function that served one so well during the first half of life. Jung had a dream in December 1913, during his own period of crisis, in which he shot and killed Siegfried, a classic hero figure from Germanic mythology. "The dream showed that the attitude embodied by Siegfried, the hero, no longer suited me. Therefore it had to be killed." In Jung's case, his sacrifice took the form of giving up his university lectureship in order to follow "the laws of [his] inner personality."

Lastly, Jung's notion of individuation has a definite quality of detachment and isolation from other people. Several of his biographers and critics have observed that he rarely refers to the effects of analysis on his patients' close relationships or their later careers. His case studies focus almost entirely on their dreams and fantasies; the reader is not given a sense of them as real three-dimensional people. Similarly, Jung has very little to say in his autobiography about his relationship with his wife Emma, his daughters, or the other women in his life. In fact, his description of a dream he had about Emma shortly after her death emphasizes the quality of emotional detachment that Jung regarded as essential to individuation.

> I saw her in a dream which was like a vision. . . . Her expression was neither joyful nor sad, but rather objectively wise and understanding, without the slightest emotional reaction, as though she were beyond the mist of affects. . . . Face to face with such wholeness one remains speechless. . . . The objectivity which I experienced in this dream . . . is part of a completed individuation. It signifies detachment from valuations and from what we call emotional ties.

Explanation   Jung's conception of the process of individuation was affected by the fact that most of the patients he saw in his private practice were exceptionally successful people; they were not like the schizophrenics he had treated in his early years or the neurotics that fill the office schedules of most psychiatrists. In his essay on "The Aims of Psychotherapy," Jung described the people he treated: "Most of my patients are socially well-adapted individuals, often of outstanding ability, to whom normalization means nothing. . . . About a third of my cases are not suffering from any clinically definable neurosis, but from the senselessness and aimlessness of their lives." Yet it was this small and unusually sophisticated group of people that gave Jung the basic material for his definition of individuation. It is difficult to avoid an impression of self-absorption or self-centeredness in Jung's view of "self-realization."

Religion, art, and creativity

Jung has had a greater impact than have most psychologists outside the field of psychology, largely because of the way his approach incorporated art, literature, and religion. Jung's discussions of the archetypes, the process of individuation, the Self, and other subjects assume that the reader is familiar with the Greek and Roman classics, with the Hebrew and Christian Scriptures, and with the major works of European literature. With regard to art, we have seen that Jung encouraged his patients to draw or paint mandalas in order to draw out the contents of their unconscious. Jung's notion of religion has been especially influential in fields such as pastoral counseling and spiritual direction.

Main points   One of Jung's most frequently quoted remarks is a statement from his essay "Psychotherapists or the Clergy": "Among all my patients in the second half of life . . . there has not been one whose problem in the last resort was not that of finding a religious outlook on life." Unlike Freud, who was openly antagonistic to religious faith, Jung seemed to open the way for a reconciliation between religion and psychology.

It is important, however, to recognize that what Jung meant by "a religious outlook on life" has no specific content. He is not recommending any given religion, Western or Eastern, as the answer to the spiritual hungers of his patients, but rather what might be called a general religious attitude toward the problems of existence. For Jung, this religious attitude requires an acceptance of the mysterious dimension of reality—not the concrete doctrines of either historic Judaism or historic Christianity. Jung did state, however, in his autobiography, "Not only do I leave the door open for the Christian message, but I consider it of central importance for Western man." He goes on, however, to describe his reinterpretation of Christianity "in accordance with the changes wrought by the contemporary spirit." In essence, Jung translated Christian doctrine into psychological categories: the Trinity becomes the Christian version of the three stages of human psychological maturation; Jesus becomes an archetype of the Self; and the ritual actions of the Mass become reenactments of the process of individuation.

Jung's most controversial notion, however, is his concept of God's dark side, or shadow. Just as he believed people needed to recognize and wrestle with the contents of their personal shadows, Jung thought that God also must unite opposites—including good and evil—within his being. Jung frequently refers to "the incompleteness of the Christian God-image," by which he means the traditional Christian understanding of God as pure goodness. "Without the integration of evil there can be no totality." Jung was convinced that the concept of the devil became necessary in Christian theology as the dark counterpart to Jesus' sinlessness, and that much of the psychic distress of Westerners stems from the one-sided emphasis on "being and doing good" in the Christian ethical tradition. Jung maintained that people should "beware of thinking of good and evil as absolute opposites. . . . Recognition of the reality of evil necessarily relativizes the good, and the evil likewise, converting both into halves of a paradoxical whole." In sum, Jung's concept of individuation as the reconciliation of opposites within the psyche meant that he replaced the traditional Western ideal of holiness with "wholeness."

Jung had a two-fold approach to art and literature. On the first level, the visual arts and literary productions could become useful forms of therapy; patients who were struggling with their unconscious could come to a better understanding of what was happening to them by "getting it down on paper," whether in verbal or visual form. On the second level, great works of art or literature might also help a person on the path to individuation by stimulating him or her to see parallels between the archetypes activated by the masterpiece and his or her present situation. For example, many people have read the opening passage of Dante's *Divine Comedy*, in which the poet speaks of being in his forties and "lost in a dark wood," as a symbolically powerful description of the midlife crisis. Jung himself spoke of Goethe's *Faust* as answering some of his adolescent questions about the reality of evil and encouraging his desires to investigate "forbidden knowledge."

Explanation   Jung's lifelong interest in religion, combined with his equally strong refusal to identify himself with any particular creed, may reflect his ambivalent relationship with his clergyman father.

While Jung was genuinely fond of his father and recalled a number of pleasant childhood experiences with him, he also saw him as a weak and inadequate role model. Several of Jung's biographers have interpreted his early idealization of Freud, in fact, as an expression of a longing for a strong father figure. A dream that Jung had about his father in 1922 is revealing. Jung dreamed that he was in his library when his father appeared "as if he had returned from a distant journey." Jung was looking forward to telling his father about his newly published book "and what [he] had become," but sensed that his father "wanted something" from him. What his father wanted was expert advice from a psychologist about "the newest insights and information about marital problems." It is almost as if the father-son relationship is reversed, with Jung as the wise teacher enlightening an intellectually inferior parent.

Synchronicity

One of Jung's more unusual contributions to psychology is his notion of synchronicity. Synchronicity can be defined as a coincidence in time of events that seem to be related in a meaningful fashion. A fairly commonplace example of synchronicity occurs when one thinks of a specific acquaintance or friend for no apparent reason and then receives a telephone call from that person in the next few minutes; or hums a certain tune and then hears it played on a radio or television program. Jung conceived of synchronicity as a mysterious principle of explanation that was just as important as causality, and regarded it as another instance of the combination of opposites—in this case, the coincidental timing of movements within the psyche and events in the outside world. He believed that, in the last analysis, a person's psyche and the material universe are simply different forms of energy. In Jung's own words,

> . . .It is not only possible but fairly probable, even, that psyche and matter are two different aspects of one and the same thing. The synchronicity phenomena point, it seems to me, in this direction, for they show that the nonpsychic can behave like the psychic, and vice versa, without there being any causal connection between them.

Jung's understanding of synchronicity reflects his interest in and study of East Asian thought, particularly Taoism.

Main points Jung's concept of synchronicity was influenced by his contacts with J. B. Rhine, the founder of parapsychology and director of the Parapsychology Laboratory at Duke University. Parapsychology is the study of psychological phenomena, such as telepathy, clairvoyance, and extrasensory perception (ESP), that cannot be explained by current scientific knowledge.

Jung corresponded with Rhine for some years about his work, and Rhine apparently persuaded Jung to publish his own thoughts about synchronicity.

In Jung's later years, he linked synchronicity phenomena to his concept of the archetypes. His earlier writings about archetypes had treated them chiefly as organizing principles of the human psyche. But his study of Rhine's work led him to the conclusion that the archetypes might be organizing principles of events in the material world as well. This enlarged understanding of the archetypes fit Rhine's observations that parapsychological events are more likely to occur at times of great personal crisis. For Jung, the archetypes were typically constellated, or activated, precisely by these crises. Jung described the process of constellation as

> . . . simply express[ing] the fact that the outward situation releases a psychic process in which certain contents gather together and prepare for action. When we say that a person is 'constellated' we mean that he has taken up a position from which he can be expected to react in a quite definite way.

Explanation Jung at one point attempted to explain synchronistic phenomena as resulting from the activation of archetypes in the personal as well as the collective unconscious. Speaking of a specific event in his life that he attributed to synchronicity, Jung stated,

> By means of a relativization of time and space in the unconscious it could well be that I had perceived something which in reality was taking place elsewhere. The collective unconscious is common to all; it is the foundation of what the ancients called 'the sympathy of all things.'

Examples Jung's favorite clinical illustration of synchronicity concerned a patient who had been resistant to some of his psychological theories. One afternoon the patient related a dream that she had had about a scarab beetle, which in Egyptian mythology is a symbol of renewal or rebirth. Jung was in the process of explaining the ancient symbolism to his skeptical patient when he noticed a scarab-type beetle tapping at the window of his consulting room. He opened the window and gently carried the beetle on his hand to the startled patient, commenting, "Here is your scarab." This incident apparently overcame the patient's intellectual resistance, and she entered into therapy on a deeper emotional level.

Jung apparently connected synchronicity most frequently with death, the most threatening "archetypal situation." His earliest example of it occurred during his years as a university lecturer in psychiatry.

Jung was treating a man with a history of depression who had gotten married and then developed a new depression. One night Jung was staying in a hotel in a city where he was a visiting lecturer. He awoke in the early hours of the morning with "a feeling of dull pain, as though something had struck my forehead and then the back of my skull." The next day Jung received a telegram informing him that his patient had shot himself. Jung learned later that the bullet had come to rest in the back wall of the patient's skull. Another instance concerned the death of one of Emma Jung's cousins. Jung dreamed that his wife's bed was a deep pit with stone walls resembling a grave. He heard a deep sigh and saw a figure resembling his wife floating upward, wearing a white gown decorated with black symbols. Jung awoke and noticed that it was three o'clock in the morning. Four hours later, he heard that his wife's cousin had died at 3 A.M.

HISTORICAL CONTEXT

Jung's thinking, like Freud's, was shaped by the time and place of his upbringing. Many of Jung's attitudes, such as his views of women and his fascination with the occult, reflect the intellectual and cultural currents of his time.

The disintegration of Western culture in the nineteenth century

One of the intellectual developments that affected most educated Europeans in the nineteenth century was a loss of cultural unity. This fragmentation resulted from several broad social and technological developments. One was the sheer accumulation of information in all fields of human knowledge, requiring people to specialize in relatively small areas of expertise rather than sharing a common body of knowledge. The second was the steady movement of population from the countryside into the cities. As people moved into increasingly large and impersonal urban areas, they lost a sense of connection to institutions that had formerly given them a sense of belonging and identity, such as the village, the church or synagogue, the extended family, or the craft guild. The industrial revolution served to further separate people from their historic ties to family or craft traditions, as work in factories replaced farming and small workshops.

A third factor in the loss of cultural unity in the West was much closer contact with Eastern cultures, brought about by trade and the political expansion of the British, Russian, and Dutch empires. Many Westerners who visited the East as explorers, missionaries, or diplomats became fascinated by Eastern attitudes toward questions of good and evil, human consciousness, and personality. Chinese expert Richard Wilhelm, for example, had gone to China originally as a missionary and instead became a student of Chinese philosophy. Western interest in Asian culture, however, meant that the culture of the West was no longer dominant; it had been relativized, and its "superiority" could no longer be assumed.

The religious crisis of the West

Many of Jung's writings assume that all his educated patients had been alienated from traditional Christian or Jewish faith and practice. "So much of what Christian symbolism taught has gone by the board for large numbers of people, without their ever having understood what they have lost." At the same time, Jung felt that these same patients were disturbed, if only on the unconscious level, by their loss of faith. Crises of religious faith were a major issue for numerous artists, writers, and intellectuals in the late nineteenth century. The autobiographical writings of people as otherwise different as George Eliot, Cardinal Newman, Herman Melville, and Clara Barton indicate that the loss or alteration of religious belief marked a significant turning point in their lives.

People in this period dealt with their religious crises in different ways. Some adopted science or the scientific method as their central value. Freud took this particular route, regarding religion as no more than a childish desire for parental protection. The new discipline of sociology, led by such thinkers as George Sorel and Herbert Spencer, appeared to offer hope that human beings could make themselves and their societies perfect. Spencer wrote in 1892 that ". . . progress is not an accident but a necessity. Surely must evil and immorality disappear; surely must men become perfect." This optimistic line of thought encouraged some writers, such as William Morris and George Bernard Shaw, to substitute political activism for traditional religion. A third reaction to loss of religious faith was an interest in spiritualism, theosophy (a movement influenced by Buddhist and Hindu thought), and the occult. Jung responded this way, reading books on spiritualism and attending spiritualist seances during his years in medical school.

Jung's personal history made religious issues especially troubling for him, primarily because his father and several uncles were Swiss Reformed pastors. One uncle in particular hoped that Jung would follow his father into the ministry, and he invited his nephew to lunch on a regular basis during his high school years. Jung, however, began to have serious doubts about the teaching of the Church during his adolescence. He tried to discuss them with his father, but he was continually frustrated. Although Paul Jung never reproached his son for refusing to take Communion and avoiding church services "as often as possible," he also never answered his son's questions directly. Jung had a series of arguments with his father in 1892–94; his father seemed to be struggling with his faith and gradually sinking into a depression. Jung attributed his father's eventual collapse and death to the emotional suffering he experienced while trying to reconcile the contradiction between the official theology of the Church and his actual experience of God. Unfortunately, Jung's rigid theoretical separation of religious experience from formal doctrine complicated his later attempts to form friendships with theologians and members of the clergy.

The effects of World War I

A third cultural factor that helped to shape Jung's psychology was the widespread feeling of disillusionment and betrayal that followed World War I (1914–18). People who had committed themselves to scientific research instead of religion were forced to recognize that the technological and theoretical advances that had taken place toward the end of the nineteenth century had been exploited for military purposes. People who had trusted the political ideals of socialism and Communism felt betrayed by the events of the postwar period: the dictatorship of Stalin in the Soviet Union, the collapse of democracy in Germany and the rise of the Nazi party, the worldwide Great Depression of the 1930s, and the Spanish Civil War (1936–39). The substitutes for religious faith had not lived up to their promises.

Cultural currents in German-speaking Europe

Jung's psychology must also be considered in the context of early twentieth-century German culture, with its interest in nature-mysticism and pre-Christian mythology. Several publications in recent years have raised the issue of Jung's relationship to the Nazi Party and its teachings about race and ethnic identity. The Nazis borrowed heavily from the themes and imagery of Germanic mythology, and Jung's writings also frequently mention the old Germanic gods as archetypal figures. In one example, Jung attributed Germany's headlong rush to war in 1914 with the activation of "the god of ecstasy, Wotan." When Jung's mother died, he had a dream in which Wotan came to carry her soul away. "Thus the dream says that the soul of my mother was taken into that greater territory of the self which lies beyond the segment of Christian

morality . . . in which conflicts and contradictions are resolved." In addition to Jung's habit of interpreting the behavior of the German nation in terms of its "possession" by the Wotan archetype, he also accepted in 1933 the presidency of a professional society that included Nazi sympathizers in its membership,including Matthias Göring, the cousin of Hitler's Reichsmarshall, Hermann Göring. Although Jung's Swiss nationality and citizenship kept him from being caught up in German politics, his identification with German culture is obvious to readers of his works. In fact, Jung as a young man had felt his Swiss background made him a provincial outsider to the "higher glories" of "the great land of Germany."

CRITICAL RESPONSE

Jung's body of work has provoked more intense controversy than that of most psychologists, partly because of his historic break with Freud, partly because of his unwise professional involvements in the 1930s, and partly because of his ideas themselves.

The 'unscientific' nature of Jung's psychology

One of the earliest criticisms of Jung's work is that it is anti-scientific in its intentions as well as its content. This accusation surfaced as early as Jung's break with Freud in 1913. Jung's view of the functions of symbolism in dreams led to his isolation from the mainstream psychiatric community. As he put it, ". . . all my friends and acquaintances dropped away. My book was declared to be rubbish; I was a mystic, and that settled the matter." The insecure position of the social sciences in the academic pecking order of the early twentieth century might be one reason why other psychiatrists would have felt threatened by some of Jung's ideas. Psychology and sociology have been accepted as legitimate fields of scholarly inquiry only recently; back then, Jung's view of symbolism appeared to undermine the "scientific" status of psychology.

To be more specific, Jung's psychology has been characterized as "unscientific" on the following grounds:

- that some Jungian concepts, such as archetypes and synchronicity, cannot be proven by the scientific method
- that Jung subscribed to a nineteenth-century notion of evolution that has since been discredited
- that Jung's valuation of the mental functions of feeling and intuition on the same level as thinking weakens the attitude of rational objectivity that is essential in scientific research

- that Jung's interest in occult traditions, including the pre-scientific European past (third-century Gnosticism and medieval alchemy) and contemporary Asian cultures (Taoism and Tibetan Buddhism) amounts to a glorification of mysticism and irrationality

- that Jung's clinical specialization in the treatment of schizophrenia and his own brush with psychosis made him an untrustworthy guide to "ordinary" reality

The charge that Jung's psychology is based on an outdated understanding of evolution concerns his concept of the archetypes and the collective unconscious. Jung thought of the archetypes as primordial images within the basic structure of the human psyche that have appeared repeatedly in myths, symbols, and personified forms throughout human history. The similarity of the motifs and themes in the myths and symbols of many different cultures suggests the existence of a collective unconscious shared by all human beings. Some critics have regarded Jung's various attempts to define the archetypes and their manifestations as proof that he accepted an obsolete notion of evolution known as Lamarckianism. This notion takes its name from Jean Baptiste Lamarck (1744–1829), a French biologist who thought that individuals could transmit acquired characteristics to their offspring—for example, that the children of a gifted pianist would inherit the flexibility and strength of the highly trained muscles in their parent's hands. But Jung did not maintain that human beings "inherit" archetypal images from their ancestors in the same way that they inherit such physical characteristics as eye color or height. It is true that Jung was influenced by the evolutionary theories of a German scientist named Ernst Haeckel (1834–1919), who taught zoology at the University of Jena. Haeckel is best known for his theory that "ontogeny recapitulates phylogeny"—that is, that the development of an individual organism follows or repeats the pattern of the development of the species to which it belongs. For example, the fact that the human embryo has gills at one point in its development was thought to echo the evolution of mammals from certain groups of prehistoric fishes. Similarly, Jung thought that the pattern of psychological development over the course of a person's lifetime repeated the development of human culture from primitive societies to the sophisticated cultures of the contemporary West. While Haeckel and Jung were wrong about this specific "law" of evolution, modern evolutionary psychology supports the notion that human psychology as well as physical anatomy has a basis in evolutionary biology.

Jung's interest in pre-scientific, Asian, and occult systems of thought has been a target of much criticism; these beliefs have frequently been dismissed by rational-minded scholars as historical curiosities or primitive superstitions. Those who believe that the scientific and technological achievements of the West prove the superiority of Western culture to all others are understandably offended by Jung's notion that the West's one-sided emphasis on progress needed balance or compensation from Eastern modes of thought. It is not necessary, however, to pass judgment on Gnostic or Asian mythology as such in order to observe that Jung failed to ask how these systems functioned in their specific historical and social contexts. In other words, Jung remains open to criticism as "unscientific" because he tended to assign all of them equal value and relevance. One French scholar has described Jung's work as "a soup, a fish-rearing pond in which all fishes are given a chance."

The argument that Jung's personal emotional problems call his theories into question has no simple answer. Some of Jung's writings certainly convey the impression that he was not always in contact with ordinary reality. For example, at one point in his autobiography, Jung maintains that his mother's house was haunted after his father's death by some force or spirit that was able to split a solid wooden table top and shatter the blade of a bread knife kept inside a cupboard. To give another example, toward the end of his life, Jung became interested in flying saucers. In 1958 he had a dream in which he saw two UFOs flying over his house. He interpreted the widespread interest in UFOs during the Cold War era in terms of his psychological theories, as proof of a movement toward psychic wholeness stirring within the collective unconscious. The round shape of the flying saucers represented a mandala, so that the UFOs were

> circular symbols of unity which represent a synthesis of the opposites within the psyche. . . . Since this process takes place in the collective unconscious, it manifests itself everywhere. The worldwide stories of the UFOs . . . are the symptom of a universally present psychic disposition.

Some of Jung's biographers, such as Paul Stern, have in fact described his work as an example of "the creative uses of incipient madness." On the other hand, many of Jung's patients felt that he had been genuinely helpful to them. Moreover, Jung's ability to maintain a private psychiatric practice alongside a steady stream of writings and publications after 1920 indicates a level of productivity that is not usually found in people with serious mental disturbances.

Prejudices against women and gay people

Jung's view of women is problematic for many contemporary feminists. On the one hand, Jung was relatively untroubled about accepting women as academic colleagues and trainees. He collaborated with Toni Wolff, Emma Jung, and M. Esther Harding, and trained such well-known analysts as Jolande Jacobi and Aniela Jaffé. On the other hand, some of Jung's attitudes toward women are tinged with misogyny. As noted earlier, Jung had an uneasy relationship with his mother. Jung commented that his younger sister "was always a stranger" to him, even though he respected her for her orderly and composed nature. Many of Jung's comments about the contrasexual part of the human psyche—the anima in men and the animus in women—reflect gender stereotypes that are no longer accepted without question. Jung tended to emphasize the negative aspects of the animus in women, stating that it made them quarrelsome and opinionated. As for the anima in men, Jung once remarked that it is inclined to "everything that is unconscious, dark, equivocal, and unrelated in woman, and also for her vanity, frigidity, and helplessness." Most contemporary Jungian analysts have modified Jung's concepts of gender roles, usually by observing that they are historically conditioned rather than timeless and unalterable.

Another aspect of Jung's view of women that troubles contemporary feminists is the tangled connection between the development of his concepts and his extramarital relationships with his patients and trainees. The discovery of Sabina Spielrein's diary in 1977 revealed that Jung's characterization of the anima as "seductive," as well as his accounts of some of his conversations with the anima, derived from his relationship with Spielrein. Likewise, his discussion of the sudden eruption of archetypes in *Symbols of Transformation* is a veiled description of the impact of the affair on his consciousness. Jung appears to have made similar use of his relationship with Toni Wolff in his exploration of his own unconscious in 1913–14. In his published works, however, he speaks of the development of his thinking as if it took place purely within his own mind, without any mention of his interpersonal involvements. The ethical implications of these relationships will be discussed below.

Jung's attitude toward homosexuality is much more of a concern than his views of women for contemporary Jungians, because many of his basic concepts depend on a conception of heterosexuality as normative. His notion of psychic wholeness as the product of the reconciliation of opposites, and his definition of the contrasexual part of the psyche, are based on the notion that masculinity and femininity represent a pair of opposites. In addition, Jung regarded homosexuality itself as a sign of immaturity associated with mental disturbance. At one point in his autobiography, he noted that during his student years, only two of his friends were open admirers of the philosopher

Nietzsche. "Both were homosexual; one of them ended by committing suicide, the other ran to seed as a misunderstood genius." In another passage, he remarked that "the role homosexuality plays in modern society is enormous." Jung attributed this prominence to a combination of "the mother-complex" and a desire to limit human reproduction. One of the most lively debates among contemporary Jungian therapists concerns the possibility of modifying Jungian theory to include homosexuality. Some maintain that it cannot be done without taking apart the entire system of analytic psychology; others are more hopeful.

Jung's "guru" mentality and professional misconduct

Jung's reputation has suffered in recent years from new findings regarding his associations with Nazi ideology and the Nazi Party, as well as from revelations of his sexual relationships with female patients. Both of these aspects of his behavior were rooted in his perception of himself as a prophetic leader. In Jung's autobiography, he frequently spoke of himself in terms usually reserved for mythological heroes or demigods. For example, he recounted a dream that he had when he was three or four years old as his "initiation into the realm of darkness" and "original revelation." In discussing the emotional turmoil of his self-analysis in 1914, Jung described himself as a kind of psychological superman:

> One thunderstorm followed another. My enduring these storms was a question of brute strength. Others have been shattered by them. . . . But there was a demonic strength in me. . . . When I endured these assaults of the unconscious, I had an unswerving conviction that I was obeying a higher will.

Reflecting on his life's work, Jung frequently spoke of himself as possessed by a daimon (in the original Greek sense of an indwelling spirit) of creativity. He felt that this distinction exempted him from normal standards of consideration for other people:

> There was a daimon in me, and in the end its presence proved decisive. It overpowered me, and if I was at times ruthless, it was because I was in the grip of the daimon. . . . I was able to become intensely interested in many people, but as soon as I had seen through them the magic was gone. In this way I made many enemies. A creative person has little power over his own life. He is not free. He is captive and driven by his daimon.

This language of possession, however, is common to many gurus or self-appointed prophets. In the 1950s and 1960s, authors Erich Fromm and Philipp Rieff, respectively, spoke of Jung as "a worshipper of evil gods and goddesses" and a "posthumous prophet of a private religion." In 1994, writer Richard Noll published a book entitled *The Jung Cult,* in which he described Jung as a "pseudo-charismatic figure" who established a "secret church" with himself as chief priest. In 1998, Peter Kramer, the psychiatrist-author of *Listening to Prozac,* said in an interview that Jung was very comfortable in the role of "an idol," even as a secular religious leader. "Jung was much more invested in his own omniscience than Freud." Kramer went on to say that people in the early years of the twentieth century were much more likely to attribute unusual mental powers to intellectual pioneers than they are now, and they were more likely to believe that such "geniuses" were entitled to special privileges.

While it is true that Jung was not the only psychologist of his time to sexualize his relationships with patients, contemporary therapists have been sensitized to the damage that can be done. It appears that Jung's involvement with Sabina Spielrein, for example, encouraged her to remain emotionally dependent on others and damaged her ability to form healthy adult relationships. Other historians of psychology, however, maintain that the damage he inflicted had more to do with Jung's inflated self-importance than with the sexual dimension of the relationship.

Insufficient attention to childhood issues in human development

As was noted earlier, the majority of Jung's private patients after 1920 were adults in the second half of life. Jung's interest in individuation, which he regarded as the central psychic task of this phase of life, left him relatively unconcerned with psychological development in children. As some of Jung's critics have noted, however, certain mental disorders—such as phobias and eating disorders—are more likely explained by a history of upsetting childhood experiences or early family relationships than by Jung's theories of archetypes and psychic self-regulation. Most contemporary Jungian analysts, however, take childhood developmental issues as well as current concerns into account in their treatment of patients, and the so-called "developmental" Jungians emphasize the importance of analytical training in childhood psychology. This emphasis is particularly strong among British Jungians.

Anti-Semitism and involvement with the Nazis

Jung's relationship to National Socialism in Germany in the 1930s is a source of considerable embarrassment to contemporary Jungian analysts. Andrew Samuels, a British Jungian, reported in 1998 that informal interviews with British university students indicated that they associated Jung's name with "Hitler," "Nazis," or "anti-Semites" far more often than with any other word except "Freud." On the one hand, Jung's acceptance of the presidency of a professional group associated with Nazi sympathizers, and his clear fascination with events in Germany in the early 1930s—which he interpreted as the activation of the Wotan archetype—have been attributed to his political naiveté, his misplaced optimism, and his training as a physician to adopt a wait-and-see attitude. Other writers have regarded Jung's failure to perceive what was really happening in Germany as a side-effect of his lingering bitterness toward Freud, combined with his tendency to construe contemporary events in mythic rather than in political or social terms.

On the other hand, other critics have noted that Jung never issued any clear public statement of opposition to Nazi anti-Semitism or Nazi atrocities. Although some of Jung's close friends and colleagues maintained that he disagreed with the position of the Party, all of his objections were made in private. Austrian Otto Rank, another psychoanalyst and a contemporary of Jung's, pointed to Jung's fascination with the Wotan archetype—Jung described it in 1936 as "the god of storm and frenzy, the unleasher of passions and the lust of battle . . . a superlative magician and artist in illusion who is versed in all secrets of an occult nature"—as the outcome of his early work with psychotics, who withdraw from the real world to create their own parallel universes. Rank regarded Jung's fundamental error as undervaluing the healing potential of the patient's return to reality and overvaluing the workings of the patient's unconscious. Jung's 1936 description of the Germans as possessed by "a fundamental attribute of the German psyche" assumes that there is little the individual can do when a nation is gripped by mass hysteria. "We who stand outside judge the Germans far too much as if they were responsible agents, but perhaps it would be nearer the truth to regard them also as victims [of Wotan]." An essay that Jung published in 1946, after the defeat of Germany in World War II, is as disturbing as the 1936 essay. Here he discusses the need for "collective guilt" in a way that also absolves individuals of moral responsibility. At the very least, it is ironic that a psychologist who centered his approach to treatment around the concept of individuation never questioned the appropriateness of submission to group madness.

Inadequate understanding of religion

Although Jungian theory has been attractive to some schools of pastoral counseling, other theologians and historians question the adequacy of Jung's view of religion. Jung's definition of a "religious attitude toward life" led him in the direction of privatizing belief, so that each patient could in effect construct his or her own religion out of the set of symbols that were most meaningful to him or her. Secondly, Jung's concept of individuation produces, in the mind of some critics, a tendency to make one's own process of maturation into a god, to become the object of worship as well as the worshiper. In trying to translate religious symbols into psychological categories, Jung can be said to have made psychology into a religion. Thirdly, Jung's approach to religion has been criticized for detaching educated people from communities of faith and the rituals that sustain them. The major communities of faith in the West, Christianity and Judaism, have for centuries kept people together through corporate prayer and worship, as well as through abstract symbol systems. In the process, these two religions have reminded educated believers that religious faith brings together people from a wide variety of economic backgrounds and intellectual capacities, and is not reserved exclusively for a sophisticated elite.

Two additional criticisms must be mentioned. Jung's notion of God as incorporating a dark or "underground" side within his being, and thus being beyond conventional concepts of good and evil, has obvious dangers for people who are attracted to charismatic leaders. It is not difficult for a leader with a sufficiently forceful or attractive personality to convince troubled or insecure people to accept the leader's redefinitions of "goodness." The revelation of the extent of sexual abuse of parishioners by clergy in mainstream religious bodies over the last two decades, as well as the abuse of members of smaller groups by cult leaders, has led to the drafting of much stricter codes of ethics for clergy, as well as for psychiatrists and psychotherapists. Buddhist groups in the United States have also put in place institutional safeguards against misunderstandings or abuses of teacher/disciple relationships.

Lastly, Jung seems never to have understood the historical nature and doctrinal structure of orthodox Christianity because of his early separation of religious experience from corporate worship and academic theology. He formed several friendships with British as well as German clergy, hoping to persuade Roman Catholics as well as Protestants of the merits of his psychology. Perhaps the most important of these friendships was Jung's relationship with Father Victor White, an English Dominican. The relationship was hindered by Jung's inability to take theology seriously as a form of knowledge in its own right, even though its methods are not the same as those of the natural sciences. In addition, Jung's insistence that the process of individuation is the final stage of human development, whereas Christianity is a transitional and defective stage, was unacceptable to the Catholic priest.

THEORIES IN ACTION

Jung's private practice

Jung's actual practice of psychotherapy differed from Freud's in several respects. First, Jung did not follow the Freudian pattern of scheduling patients for five weekly sessions of analysis. Jung usually saw patients only once or twice a week, depending on the stage of their work with him. He also encouraged his patients to take frequent vacations or "holidays" from analysis. Lastly, Jung felt that Freud's custom of having patients lie on a couch positioned so that they could not see the analyst was a hindrance to the therapeutic relationship; he preferred to work with his patients face-to-face.

Moreover, Jung thought it best to approach each patient as a unique individual, with a minimum of presuppositions. "I am often asked about my psychotherapeutic or analytic method. . . . Therapy is different in every case. . . . Psychotherapy and analysis are as varied as are human individuals. . . . A solution which would be out of the question for me may be just the right one for someone else." For this reason, he preferred to regard therapy more as a process of clearing a path for the patient's progress than as a form of re-education or instruction:

> [Analysis] is only a means for removing the stones from the path of development, and not a method . . . of putting things into the patient that were not there before. It is better to renounce any attempt to give direction, and simply try to throw into relief everything that the analysis brings to light, so that the patient can see it clearly and be able to draw suitable conclusions. Anything he has not acquired himself he will not believe in the long run, and what he takes over from authority merely keeps him infantile. He should rather be put in a position to take his own life in hand. The art of analysis lies in following the patient on all his erring ways and so gathering his strayed sheep together.

The goals of Jungian analysis

Jung referred to his method of treatment as analytical psychology, in order to distinguish it from Freudian psychoanalysis. The distinctive features of analytical psychology are its concern with bringing the contents of the patient's unconscious into consciousness and its interest in furthering the patient's movement toward wholeness and integration (the process of individuation). The contents of the unconscious reveal themselves in dreams, in material produced through the method of active imagination, and in the interactions between the therapist and patient (sometimes referred to as the transference/countertransference relationship).

Active imagination

Active imagination is a method that Jung employed to help patients "digest" the content of their dreams and fantasies through art or a similar form of self-expression. The purpose of this method is to draw out the aspects of an individual's personality that are normally not heard directly—particularly the anima/animus and the shadow—and to open a channel of communication between the conscious mind and the unconscious. Over a period of time, the relationship between the patient and his or her artistic creations leads to a transformation of the patient's consciousness.

Jung distinguished two stages in the use of active imagination. The first stage can occur spontaneously or be deliberately induced. As Jung describes this stage,

> . . . you choose a dream, or some other fantasy-image, and concentrate on it by simply catching hold of it and looking at it. You can also use a bad mood as a starting-point, and then try to find out what sort of fantasy-image it will produce, or what image expresses this mood. You then fix this image in the mind by concentrating your attention. Usually it will alter, as the mere fact of contemplating it animates it. The alterations must be carefully noted down all the time, for they reflect the psychic processes in the unconscious background, which appear in the form of images consisting of conscious memory material. In this way conscious and unconscious are united, just as a waterfall connects above and below.

In the second stage, the patient progresses beyond observing and contemplating the images to participating in them. What Jung meant by participation included a frank acceptance of what the images reveal about the patient, and a commitment to act on the insights received. In Jung's words,

> Although, to a certain extent, [the patient] looks on from outside, impartially, he is also an acting and suffering figure in the drama of the psyche. This recognition is absolutely necessary and marks an important advance. . . . But if you recognize your own involvement you yourself must enter into the process with your personal reactions, just as if you were one of the fantasy figures, or rather, as if the drama being enacted before your eyes were real.

It is important to note that Jung avoided imposing his own interpretations on the material that his patients brought to him in their use of active imagination. As in his practice of analytic psychology in general, Jung assumed that the therapist should stimulate the patient's

interest in his or her inner development rather than "instruct or convince" the patient. In his essay on "The Aims of Psychotherapy," Jung states,

> . . . it seems to me that in psychotherapy especially it is advisable for the physician not to have too fixed a goal. He can scarcely know what is wanted better than do nature and the will-to-live of the sick person. . . . Here we must follow nature as a guide, and the course the physician then adopts is less a question of treatment than of developing the creative possibilities that lie in the patient himself.

Jungian training institutes

Jung was the first major figure in the history of psychology to insist that analysts should themselves undergo analysis.

> We have learned to place in the foreground the personality of the doctor himself as a curative or harmful factor; . . . what is now demanded is his own transformation—the self-education of the educator. . . . The doctor can no longer evade his own difficulty by treating the difficulties of others: the man who suffers from a running abscess is not fit to perform a surgical operation.

Although Jung initially resisted suggestions to launch a training institute specifically based on his ideas, the first center designed to train Jungian analysts and conduct further research in analytical psychology was established in Zurich, Switzerland, in 1948. Jung himself drew up the first set of regulations for the Institute and supervised its activities until his death in 1961. The Jung Institute offers a diploma in analytical psychology upon the successful completion of its training program. The average amount of time required to complete the program is four-and-a-half to five years. Trainees may choose to work with adults only; children and adolescents only; or with both age groups. Lectures are given in both German and English; however, native speakers of English are encouraged to learn German in order to improve their learning opportunities when they begin the clinical part of their instruction. The training program has three major components: a personal analysis of the trainee, academic instruction, and clinical work with clients under the supervision of control analysts.

In the United States, clinical training in Jungian analysis can be obtained at the C. G. Jung Institute in New York or the C. G. Jung Institute in Boston. The New York Institute was formed in 1962 and accredited by the American Board for Accreditation in Psychoanalysis in 1975. Applicants must hold a graduate degree in a mental health field such as psychiatry, social work, psychiatric nursing, or pastoral counseling. In addition to undergoing a personal analysis, candidates for the diploma engage in clinical practice under supervision from the beginning of the program. A minimum of six years of classroom instruction is required; courses and seminars include mythology, anthropology, psychopathology, and the clinical applications of dream interpretation. The Institute divides the training program into three stages: candidacy, examinations, and control. In the first phase, the trainee studies Jung's major works and the management of a private practice. The second stage consists of theoretical studies completed by a midterm examination. The third stage includes independent study, supervised control cases, a final thesis presentation, and a case write-up.

The program of the Boston Institute is divided into two stages and takes a minimum of five years to complete. The course work, clinical practica, and personal analysis requirements are roughly similar to those of the New York Institute; the Boston Institute, however, requires candidates for the diploma to complete a course in professional ethics.

Research

Contemporary Jungian analysis is difficult to summarize briefly because Jung's successors have moved in a number of different directions. Some focus on the functions of human imagination, while others are doing research in the field of evolutionary psychology as a way of grounding Jung's concept of archetypes in recent findings about human learning. As of 2002, there is probably no single classification that will cover all therapists and researchers who consider themselves Jungians. In 1985, a British professor named Andrew Samuels published a book entitled *Jung and the Post-Jungians* that grouped most mainstream practitioners into one of three large groups or schools: the so-called "classical" Jungians, who focus on self and individuation issues; the developmental Jungians, mostly British, who have been influenced by the work of Donald Winnicott, John Bowlby, and other researchers in childhood development; and the archetypal Jungians. This third group, whose best-known writer is James Hillman, is critical of classical Jungianism and less interested in self or ego issues; it emphasizes the exploration of images in therapy.

More recently, Samuels has proposed a fourfold categorization of contemporary Jungians. He regards the classical and developmental schools to have remained largely as they were in 1985, while the archetypal school has been replaced by two new groups, both of which are extreme versions of the classical and developmental schools respectively. Samuels defines the right-wing version of classical Jungianism as "Jungian fundamentalism," and describes it as hostile to intellectual women, ignorant of other schools of thought, and inclined to regard Jung himself as a cult figure. At the other extreme, some of the developmental Jungians—particularly in Germany, the United Kingdom, and the United States—are attempting to merge Jungian psychology with the methods and framework of Freudian psychoanalysis.

Another attempt at categorizing the post-Jungians was made by Adolph Guggenbuhl-Craig, president of the Jung Institute in Zurich in the 1980s. Beginning from the observation that Jung himself was a multifaceted person who combined the roles of clinical psychologist, religious person, and shaman, Guggenbuhl-Craig suggested that post-Jungian practitioners have identified with one or another of these roles. The clinical psychologist Jungians staff most of the training institutes and consider themselves academic psychologists or psychotherapists. The religious Jungians are found among the clergy or among psychologists who once served in the clergy. The shamanistic Jungians do most of their publishing in the Jungian "underground," and may well be the largest of the three groups. They often work with Tarot cards, the *I Ching*, or investigations of paranormal phenomena. Shamanistic Jungians are also often involved in various types of New Age movements, including rebirthing and channeling.

In addition to the long-standing study groups of Jungians in Europe and North America, Jungian psychology has been enriched in recent years by researchers and practitioners from East Asia, the countries of the former Soviet Union, Latin America, and Australia—parts of the world that have been underrepresented in Jungian studies. In the United States, the most recent challenge to the "classical" Jungian tradition has come from gay and lesbian Jungians.

In spite of this variety and vitality, however, some eminent Jungians are concerned about the future of Jungian psychology. One reason for concern is the bad reputation that Jungian psychology as a whole acquired over the past two decades due to revelations about Jung's sexual relationships with patients and his compromises with the Nazis. The controversies that were generated by historical research into Jung and his associates have split contemporary Jungians into a minority that continues to idealize Jung and a larger group that feels burdened by certain aspects of his legacy.

On the wider cultural level, Jungian psychology has become unpopular because of its theoretical commitment to a belief in universal truths or characteristics of the human psyche, such as the Self, the collective unconscious, and the archetypes. The rise of multiculturalism and the intellectual movement known broadly as postmodernism have challenged claims to universal truths. Where Jung was trained in an intellectual setting that focused on the universal and then moved to the study of the individual, contemporary cultural trends assume that only the individual or local can be a serious object of study.

An additional cause for concern in the United States has been the social as well as economic impact of managed care. While the reluctance of managed care organizations to pay for extended courses of psychotherapy has affected all schools of therapy, not just analytical psychology, it has definitely lowered the number of trainees entering the field.

The most hopeful sign for the future of Jungian psychology is the increased interest in it on the part of university researchers and teachers. One possibility that has been suggested is outcome studies of the efficacy of Jungian therapy compared to other approaches. One outcome study was undertaken in Germany in 1997; others are presently underway. A second proposal involves research into clinical process—that is, how the therapist uses the theoretical model in which he or she has been trained in actual interactions with patients. In other fields, studies of the application of analytical psychology to political science, sociology, anthropology, and law are under consideration.

Case studies

Given the variety of fields in which Jungian analysis is presently used, the case studies that follow are taken from private practice, social commentary, and pastoral counseling.

Jungian analysis in psychotherapy "Medusa Appears" is the case study of a 27-year-old art history major who entered therapy after a breakup with a boyfriend. Abby could not understand why she was having trouble recovering from the breakup but thought it might have something to do with fear of abandonment. Although she appeared outwardly competent, controlled, and cheerful, her outward appearance masked inner feelings of shame and emptiness. Abby's family history revealed that she was an adopted child, and that her parents had divorced when she was seven years old. She had never attempted to find her birth parents. Although Abby described her family as "close," the therapist discovered that family members were disturbed by open expressions of strong feelings, and that the emotional boundaries between family members were not well defined. Abby found her first year of college difficult; she flunked out and returned to live with her mother for the next two years. After working for several years, she then resumed her education.

The therapist became aware that Abby had two very different pictures of herself; sometimes she experienced herself as a "fun," interesting, and intelligent person that any man should want as a lifetime companion; at other times she saw herself as an unlovable and unattractive "reject" unworthy of a lasting relationship. Abby came to the sixth therapy session upset by a dream in which a terrifying "Medusa-like creature" came out of her basement. It threatened to "take her over" if she did not meet its basic needs for food and shelter. The therapist interpreted the dream in light of the Medusa myth, in which Medusa is one of three Gorgons, hideous female creatures with snakes for hair. Medusa was so frightening to look at that those who saw her were turned to stone. Medusa had once been a beautiful young maiden, but she had been turned into a monster by the jealous goddess Athena when Athena had found her having sexual intercourse in her own temple. Eventually, the hero Perseus was able to kill Medusa while looking at her face indirectly, reflected on his shield. Athena then placed the Gorgon's head on her own breastplate. In Jungian categories, Medusa represents the negative aspects of femininity cut off from its opposite, nurturing qualities. She is destructive because her positive qualities have been cut off and the negativity that remains is not restrained. On the other hand, Medusa also symbolizes protection. Athena used Medusa's head as a symbol of her own power, and Perseus used it to disarm his enemies.

From the therapist's perspective, the Medusa archetype offered several possibilities for interpretation. Its emergence in the dream could be interpreted as Abby's recognition that parts of her personality—her strong emotions—had been split off in her family of origin because her parents found them unacceptable. She now needed to integrate these parts of herself in order to become a mature adult. Another possibility is that Medusa represented Abby's anxiety about relationships—she seemed to be afraid of being annihilated within relationships with men, but she was also fearful of being without one. A third possibility is that Medusa represented the general existential fear that Abby would have to confront and overcome on her path toward individuation.

Jungian analysis in interpretation of current events Many Jungian therapists and researchers believe that analytical psychology can help to shed light on major historical events. "The Archetypal Dimension of the New York Terrorist Tragedies" is particularly interesting because its analysis makes use of Hindu rather than classical Greek mythology.

The writer regards the tragedy of September 11, 2001, as an archetypal activation of the Hindu trinity:

Shiva, the destroyer of an old world order; Brahma, the creator of a new order; and Vishnu, the upholder of a just order in keeping with the spiritual wisdom of the universe. Each of these gods has female counterparts or consorts: Shiva's two consorts are Parvati, who represents domesticity, and Kali, a martial goddess. Brahma's consort is Sarasvati, the goddess of knowledge, and Vishnu's is Lakshmi, the goddess of peace and prosperity. Whenever there is chaos or disorder in the human psyche or in the wider civilization, these archetypes are activated to restore a just order.

The events of September 11 reflected an imbalance toward darkness in the collective human consciousness. Thus the myth of Shiva, Parvati, and Kali was activated to redress the balance. In this interpretation, Saudi-born terrorist leader Osama bin Laden is seen as an abandoned child filled with narcissistic rage, who seeks attention from parental figures by acting out of the dark side of the human psyche and seeking negative attention. The American president, George W. Bush, has been entrusted with the task of Shiva, to destroy the corrupt structures of terrorism. First Lady Laura Bush is Parvati, who carries her husband's feeling function and supports him and the nation with her comforting presence. She helps to bring the youthful side of his masculinity into greater maturity. U. S. National Security Advisor Condoleeza Rice represents Kali, the strategic ally of Shiva in the destruction of evil. Because Kali has diplomatic as well as warrior-like roles in Hindu mythology, the writer thinks it likely that Dr. Rice will play a decisive role in the resolution of the present conflict.

Jungian analysis in pastoral counseling "The Virgin Mary and the Statue of Artemis" is an example of explicitly religious imagery from different traditions within the same dream. The patient, a middle-aged woman, had had a difficult and painful relationship with her mother while she was growing up. She had had many years of group as well as individual psychotherapy, but was still troubled by what a Jungian analyst would call a negative mother-complex. She could not establish a stable and affectionate relationship with her mother.

Soon after entering analysis with a Jungian pastoral counselor, the patient reported a dream in which she was on her grandfather's estate, looking at a swimming pool that stood behind his house. The face of the Greek goddess Artemis appeared on the floor of the pool. A voice then said: "You should see the statue of Artemis at Ephesus!" The scene then changes to the ground floor of a two-story shack. The patient is standing on this floor while the Virgin Mary

CHRONOLOGY

1875: Born in a country parsonage at Kesswil in Canton Thurgau, Switzerland.

1884: Birth of Jung's younger sister.

1896: Death of Jung's father.

1900: After finishing medical school at the University of Basel, Jung travels to Zurich to study psychiatry under Eugen Bleuler, a world-famous expert on schizophrenia.

1900–09: Works as a psychiatric resident at the Burghölzli, a famous mental hospital in Zurich.

1903: Marriage to Emma Rauschenbach.

1905: Becomes a lecturer in psychiatry at the University of Zurich.

1906: Publishes a book on schizophrenia that applies Freud's psychoanalytic approach to the study of psychosis.

1907: Travels to Vienna to meet Freud in person.

1909: Travels with Freud to the United States to give lectures at Clark University in Massachusetts.

1913: Breaks with Freud. Publishes *Psychology of the Unconscious,* the first account of his analytical psychology as an approach to therapy distinct from psychoanalysis.

1913–14: Experiences a midlife crisis or period of psychological turmoil that resolves with the outbreak of World War I in July 1914.

1921: Publishes *Psychological Types,* a major work that secures his reputation as an original thinker.

1922: Death of Jung's mother.

1937: Invited by Yale University to deliver the Terry Lectures on psychology and religion.

1937–61: Continues to practice medicine in Küssnacht, a suburb of Zurich, until his death in 1961.

is weeping on the floor above. Her tears pass through the ceiling, changing to blood as they form a pool on the ground floor where the patient is standing. The patient dips her hand into the pool of blood and is then able to see the spirit of her dead husband. He walks and talks with her.

BIOGRAPHY:

Marie-Louise von Franz

Marie-Louise von Franz (1915–98) was regarded at the time of her death as Jung's closest colleague and the leading interpreter of his thought. Von Franz was the daughter of an Austrian nobleman. Born and reared in Munich, Germany, she was a shy and socially awkward 18-year-old university student when she first met Jung in 1933. Ironically, the meeting took place because Toni Wolff had invited a group of undergraduates to Jung's home hoping that they would distract him from his growing interest in alchemy. Wolff feared that Jung's fascination with the subject would lead to the loss of his academic reputation. Von Franz was the only woman in the student group, and she was immediately captivated by Jung. Jung advised von Franz to study ancient languages; when she later asked him to accept her as a patient, he offered to treat her without charge if she would agree to translate Greek and Latin alchemy texts in exchange. Von Franz later told one of Jung's biographers that this agreement allowed her to replace Wolff in Jung's life. "[Toni's] big mistake was in not being enthusiastic about alchemy. It was unfortunate that she refused to follow him there, because otherwise he would not have thrown her over to collaborate with me."

Von Franz worked with Jung from 1933 until his death in 1961. She is credited with having done most of the research for the volume of Jung's collected works that appeared in English as *Mysterium Coniunctionis* (1963). Von Franz was also instrumental in the founding of the Jung Institute in Zurich, and had a psychotherapy practice of her own in nearby Kusnacht. She is said to have interpreted over 65,000 of her patients' dreams. In addition to her therapy practice, von Franz published over 20 volumes on analytical psychology, many of them on alchemy, the practice of active imagination, or Jungian archetypes as they appear in fairy tales. Her best-known titles include *Archetypal Patterns in Fairy Tales, The Cat: A Tale of Feminine Redemption, The Interpretation of Fairy Tales, On Dreams and Death: A Jungian Interpretation,* and *Alchemy: An Introduction to the Symbolism and the Psychology.* Von Franz published an admiring biography of Jung in 1998 entitled *C. G. Jung: His Myth in Our Time.* In addition, she coauthored a book about the Holy Grail legend with Emma Jung, who had had to accept her as yet another rival for Jung's attention.

Von Franz was diagnosed with Parkinson's disease in 1984, but she continued to write and publish with the help of a secretary until her death in 1998. Her books are published in both English and German by the Stiftung für Jung'sche Psychologie (Foundation for Jungian Psychology) in Switzerland. Von Franz established the foundation in 1974 with the assistance of several of her students. As of the early 2000s, the foundation organized conferences for Jungian therapists, underwrote research in Jungian psychology, reissued out-of-print books by Jung and von Franz, and prepared von Franz's unpublished manuscripts for eventual publication.

The counselor interpreted the dream as an example of the way in which a patient's personal parents can restrict or limit the expression of archetypes in the patient's life. The patient's personal mother was an inadequate "carrier" of the Great Mother archetype, such that some of the potentials of this archetype remained in the patient's unconscious. They emerged from her unconscious through a series of dreams and one waking vision. In this particular dream, both Artemis and the Virgin Mary represent positive aspects of the maternal archetype. In Christian tradition, Mary is a stable symbol of the nurturing, faithful mother, from her acceptance of the archangel Gabriel's message at the Annunciation to her standing by her dying son Jesus at the foot of the Cross. Artemis has a wider range of mythical meanings. On one hand, she was the protector of women in childbirth and the "Lady of the Beasts," an earth mother who nourished animals as well as human beings. In other legends, Artemis was a virgin huntress who punished men who pursued her. The pool in the patient's dream might have been a reference to the story of Artemis' killing of a hunter named Actaeon, who had surprised her as she was bathing in a pool.

The counselor decided, however, that the voice telling the patient to look at the statue of Artemis at Ephesus narrowed the meaning of the dream to the positive and caring aspects of the mother archetype. Ephesus is a city associated with both Artemis and the Virgin Mary. There was a cult statue of Artemis at Ephesus in which the goddess is shown with many breasts, symbolizing her nurturing qualities. This statue is probably the one referred to in the account of St. Paul's confrontation with the citizens of Ephesus in the New Testament (Acts 19). With respect to the Virgin Mary, post-Biblical tradition held that Christ's "beloved disciple," St. John, took Mary to Ephesus to live with him after Christ's ascension into heaven, and that she "fell asleep" there. This tradition was the basis of the later Roman Catholic doctrine that Mary was assumed directly into heaven at the end of her earthly life. In any event, the double imaging of the positive mother archetype in the dream was interpreted as a compensation for the limitations of the patient's personal mother.

Relevance to modern readers

In spite of Jung's undoubted importance in the history of psychology and psychiatry, contemporary students are far more likely to read his works in such other fields as literary criticism, religion, comparative mythology, or art history than in psychology itself. This loss of influence is partly the result of economic pressures on the practice of psychotherapy. Therapists pressured by managed care favor short-term approaches over long-term types of treatment, and those who practice evidence-based medicine have little patience with the lack of scientific confirmation of Jung's theories, not to mention the mystical and mythological elements in his thought. The majority of therapists practicing in the United States and Canada in the early 2000s described themselves as eclectic— that is, they do not follow any one school of thought exclusively—which means that they usually combined dream analysis or other Jungian practices with cognitive-behavioral therapy, psychodynamic psychotherapy, or similar approaches.

Jung is, however, the intellectual forebear of a grassroots dream work movement in Europe and the United States that encourages people to record and analyze their dreams as a form of self-treatment. Henry Reed, a psychotherapist who worked in Virginia in the 1960s, is usually credited with starting the dream work movement. Other recent leaders include Jeremy Taylor, who conducts therapy groups in which participants share their dreams with one another, and Ann Faraday, an Australian psychologist. The movement has spawned a journal, *Dream Network*, and an international professional group, the Association for the Study of Dreams (ASD). Although some research in dream psychology is being conducted by neurologists and clinical psychologists, popular books and Web sites on dreams and their interpretations indicate that Jung's works are read more often in the new millennium by New Age writers than by mainstream psychologists or psychiatrists.

BIBLIOGRAPHY

Sources

Arraj, James. "Jungian Spirituality: The Question of Victor White." *Spirituality Today* 40 (Autumn 1988): 249–61.

Bedi, Ashok, MD. *The Archetypal Dimension of the New York Terrorist Tragedies of 9/11.* Unpublished paper, C. G. Jung Institute of New York, 2001.

Bjorklund, Pamela. "Medusa Appears: A Case Study of a Narcissistic Disturbance." *Perspectives in Psychiatric Care* 36 (2000): 86–8.

Graf-Nold, A. "The Zürich School of Psychiatry in Theory and Practice: Sabina Spielrein's Treatment at the Burghölzli Clinic in Zürich. *Journal of Analytical Psychology* 46 (2001): 73–104.

Granrose, John. *The Archetype of the Magician.* Unpublished diploma thesis, C. G. Jung Institute, Zurich, 1996.

Hall, James A., MD. *The Unconscious Christian: Images of God in Dreams.* Edited by Daniel J. Meckel. New York and Mahwah, NY: Paulist Press, 1993.

Haule, John Ryan. "Freud and Jung: A Failure of Eros." *Harvest* 39 (1993): 147–58.

Jacobi, Jolande. *The Psychology of C. G. Jung: An Introduction with Illustrations.* Translated by Ralph Manheim. 8th English ed. New Haven, CT and London, UK: Yale University Press, 1973.

Jung, C. G. *Aspects of the Feminine.* Translated by R. F. C. Hull. Princeton, NJ: Princeton University Press, 1982. [articles and extracts from the *Collected Works.*]

Jung, C. G. *Collected Works of C. G. Jung*, 20 vols. Edited by Gerhard Adler et al., translated by R. F. C. Hull (Bollingen Series). Princeton, NJ: Princeton University Press, 1954–79.

Jung, C. G. *Memories, Dreams, Reflections.* Recorded and edited by Aniela Jaffé; translated by Richard and Clara Winston. Rev. ed. New York: Random House, 1965.

Jung, C. G. *Modern Man in Search of a Soul.* Translated by W. S. Dell and Cary F. Baynes. New York: Harcourt, Brace World, 1933.

Jung, C. G. *Psychology and Religion (The Terry Lectures, 1937).* New Haven, CT, and London, UK: Yale University Press, 1938.

Jung, C. G. *Psychology and Western Religion.* Translated by R. F. C. Hull. Princeton, NJ: Princeton University Press, 1984. [articles and extracts from the *Collected Works.*]

Jung, C. G., and C. Kerényi. *Essays on a Science of Mythology: The Myth of the Divine Child and the Mysteries of Eleusis.* Translated by R. F. C. Hull. Princeton, NJ: Princeton University Press, 1969.

Keirsey, David and Marilyn Bates. *Please Understand Me: Character, Temperament and Types.* Del Mar, CA: Prometheus Nemesis Book Company, 1984.

Keller, W., G. Westhoff, et al. *Efficacy and Cost-Effectiveness Aspects of Outpatient Jungian Psychoanalysis and Psychotherapy: A Catamnestic Study.* Free University of Berlin: Department of Psychosomatics and Psychotherapy, University Medical Center, 1997.

Knox, Jean M. "Memories, Fantasies, Archetypes: An Exploration of Some Connections Between Cognitive Science and Analytical Psychology." *Journal of Analytical Psychology* 46 (2001): 613–35.

Samuels, Andrew. *Will the Post-Jungians Survive?* Lecture given to the Irish Analytical Psychology Association in Dublin, November 22, 1997.

Schoener, Gary R. *Assessment and Rehabilitation of Psychotherapists Who Violate Boundaries With Clients.* Paper presented to the Norwegian Psychological Association in Oslo, Norway, September 4, 1997.

Sedgwick, David. "Freud Reconsidered: The Technique of Analysis." *San Francisco Jung Institute Library Journal* 16 (1997): 5–25.

Sharp, Daryl. *The Jung Lexicon: A Primer of Terms & Concepts.* Toronto, ONT: Inner City Books, 1991.

Young-Eisendrath, Polly. *Myth and Body: Pandora's Legacy in a Post-Modern World.* Paper presented at the 1995 International Congress of Analytical Psychology.

Further readings

Briggs-Myers, Isabel, with Peter Myers. *Gifts Differing.* Palo Alto, CA: Consulting Psychologists Press, 1980.

Carotenuto, Aldo. *A Secret Symmetry: Sabina Spielrein Between Jung and Freud.* New York: Pantheon, 1984.

Eranos yearbooks. Princeton, NJ: Princeton University Press, 1996.

Harvest: A Journal for Jungian Studies. Published by the C. G. Jung Analytical Psychology Club of London.

Hayman, Ronald. *A Life of Jung.* London, UK: Bloomsbury, 1999.

Hillman, James. *Re-Visioning Psychology.* New York: Harper Colophon Books, 1977.

Journal of Analytical Psychology. Published by the Society for Analytical Psychology, London, UK.

Kerr, John. *A Most Dangerous Method: The Story of Jung, Freud, and Sabina Spielrein.* New York: Knopf, 1993.

Noll, Richard. *The Aryan Christ: The Secret Life of Carl Jung.* New York: Random House, 1997.

Noll, Richard. *The Jung Cult: Origins of a Charismatic Movement.* Princeton, NJ: Princeton University Press, 1994.

Psychological Perspectives. Published by the C. G. Jung Institute of Los Angeles.

Rieff, Philip. *The Triumph of the Therapeutic: Uses of Faith After Freud.* New York: Harper Torchbooks, 1968.

Samuels, Andrew. *Jung and the Post-Jungians.* London, UK: Routledge and Kegan Paul, 1985.

Schorske, Carl. *Fin-de-Siécle Vienna: Politics and Culture.* New York: Vintage Books, 1981.

Stern, Paul J. *C. G. Jung—The Haunted Prophet.* New York: G. Braziller, 1976.

Storr, Anthony. *C. G. Jung.* New York: Viking Press, 1973.

Taylor, Charles. *Sources of the Self: The Making of the Modern Identity.* Cambridge, MA: Harvard University Press, 1989.

White, Victor. *God and the Unconscious.* London, UK: Harvill Press, 1952.

George Alexander Kelly

BRIEF OVERVIEW

George Alexander Kelly (1905–1967) spent the early years of his career focused on the issue of providing clinical psychologists for schools. He founded and developed the traveling psychological clinic while teaching at the Fort Hays campus of Kansas State College. During the years of the Depression up to the time the United States joined World War II, Kelly and his team—many of them graduate students who learned their trade through this experience—traveled all over Kansas treating teachers, parents, and children. His work at the time included the practical issues of clinical diagnosis, clinical psychology for school settings, and the use of diagnostic testing, in addition to other aspects of dealing with the developmental concerns of students, teachers, and parents. His discoveries during these years formed the basis of his psychology of personal constructs.

Kelly noted an important similarity among the people he treated in the public schools of Kansas. He determined that the problems teachers identified in students were often reflective of themselves more than the personality of the students. The next step that followed for him was a simple one. He concluded that there was no objectivity, or absolute truth, in determining the reality of a situation—specifically, that the meaning of all that happens in a person's life emerges from the way in which that person interprets it. This idea of individual interpretation represented a view known as "constructive alternativism." He argued that the individual acted as a scientist. Kelly contended

1905–1967

AMERICAN CLINICAL PSYCHOLOGIST, UNIVERSITY PROFESSOR

UNIVERSITY OF IOWA, Ph.D., 1931

George Alexander Kelly. (Photo courtesy of the Ohio State University Archives. Reproduced by permission.)

that a person interpreted a situation or environment a particular way, and thus acted deliberately with those interpretations in mind. Also, verbal or nonverbal modifications of an action were usually a result of whatever outcome the person had come to expect through experience. Thus, the person used his or her interpretation as scientific hypothesis, with the resulting actions similar to scientific research and experiments.

By the 1950s when Kelly published his two-volume work, behaviorists and professionals using the psychodynamic approaches in psychology dominated the field. Kelly's approach was regarded as radical. Behaviorists believed that an individual was virtually a passive entity. How a person turned out was due to the environmental forces or influences on the person, rather than the actions a person decided to take. The psychodynamic theory also involved interpreting the individual as passive—but as one who reacted to internal unconscious motivations rather than outer influences. According to Fay Fransella and Robert A. Neimeyer writing about Kelly in the *International Handbook of Personal Construct Psychology* in 2003,

PRINCIPAL PUBLICATIONS

- *The Psychology of Personal Constructs.* Two volumes. New York: W. W. Norton & Company, 1955.

- "The Theory and Technique of Assessment." *Annual Review of Psychology.* 9 (1958): 323–52.

- "Suicide: The Personal Construct Point of View," edited by N. L. Farberow and E. S. Schneidman. *The Cry for Help.* McGraw-Hill, 1961.

- "Europe's Matrix of Decision," edited by M. R. Jones. *Nebraska Symposium on Motivation.* University of Nebraska Press, 1962.

- "Nonparametric factor analysis of personality theories." *Journal of Individual Psychology* 19 (1963): 115–47.

- "The language of hypothesis: Man's psychological instrument." *Journal of Individual Psychology* 20 (1964): 137–52.

- "The strategy of psychological research." *Bulletin of the BPS* 18 (1965): 1–15.

- *Clinical Psychology and Personality: Selected Papers of George Kelly* (published posthumously), edited by B. A. Maher. Wiley, 1969.

- "A brief introduction to personal construct theory." *Perspectives in Personal Construct Theory.* (published posthumously) Bannister, D., Academic Press, 1970.

- "Behavior is an experiment." Bannister, D. *Perspectives in Personal Construct Theory.* (published posthumously) Academic Press, 1970.

- "The psychology of the unknown." Bannister, D. *New Perspectives in Personal Construct Theory.* (published posthumously) Academic Press, 1977.

"For Kelly, we are forms of motion and we propel ourselves—no one or no thing does it 'to' us."

Kelly practiced and published in the midst of others who were also committed to unlocking the mysteries of human behavior and development. Kelly provided a respectful but determined opposition to the psychology his contemporaries espoused. His research had a philosophical approach, and he was influenced by philosophers such as John Dewey, a pragmatist and religious thinker; as well as Alfred Korzybski, a linguistic philosopher. Others who helped form Kelly's psychology included Hans Vaihinger, whose philosophy was one of *as if* in his own version of constructive alternativism; and Jakob Moreno, whose use of psychodrama and its role-playing approach held a place of prominence in personal construct therapy.

Personal construct psychology as first presented by Kelly, and as it has developed over the 50 years since his work was published, has been seen as a complete psychology, not simply a theory. At its basis is the repertory grid, which provides a basic table for an individual to answer questions and analyze what they reveal about that person's cognitive processes. In essence, this method of psychological testing is one that requires the use of the rational mind. Kelly's psychology provides tools to a rational human being for planning future actions, based on knowledge of past and present actions.

BIOGRAPHY

George Alexander Kelly was born outside of Perth, Kansas, on April 28, 1905. He was the only child of a Presbyterian minister, Theodore Vincent Kelly, and Elfreda Merriam Kelly—who was, according to Fay Fransella quoting Kelly in a biographical sketch for the *International Handbook of Personal Construct Psychology,* "the daughter of a Nova Scotian captain of a sailing ship who was driven off the North Atlantic Trade routes by the arrival of steamships." His grandfather had gone then to trade in the Caribbean, settling in Barbados where Kelly's mother was born. Fransella noted that it was "interesting that the 'spirit of adventure' symbolized by this maternal grandfather," later "seeped into the spirit of Kelly's later psychological theorizing."

Kelly's father left the ministry when his son was very young in order to pursue a life of farming. In 1909 the family moved by covered wagon to eastern Colorado to stake a claim on what would be the last of the free land offered to settlers. When the scarcity of water made farming there too difficult, the family returned to Kansas. Both of his parents took part in Kelly's education. The evidence suggested that until he went away to boarding school in Wichita at the age of 13, he had virtually no formal schooling outside of his home. He stayed in Wichita from late 1918 until 1921, when he entered Friends' University academy and took college and academy courses. Kelly enjoyed telling people that he had no high school diploma, having gone to college early. While still at Friends', Kelly was awarded first place in the Peace Oratorical Contest held there in 1924. His speech was titled "The Sincere Motive" and was on the subject of war. He left Friends' and in 1926 completed his bachelor's degree from Parks College in Missouri, where he majored in physics and mathematics. These two subjects would guide his direction and help him formulate his psychology. Any disadvantage he might have had as a student was due to the fact that he was interested in everything but had no specific career plans for the future. He had given some thought to a career in engineering, but changed his mind.

After Parks, he returned to Kansas, where he studied educational psychology at the University of Kansas for a master's degree. He did not receive that degree until 1928, after he took a few more detours for a year. In 1927 with his thesis not completed, Kelly moved to Minneapolis with the intention of enrolling in the University of Minnesota. While there he taught various classes, such as public speaking to labor organizers and bankers through the American Bankers Association, and citizenship classes to immigrants. By the winter of that year he realized he could not afford the school's fees, and left to take a job teaching psychology and speech, and coaching drama at Sheldon Junior college in Sheldon, Iowa. Kelly met his future wife, Gladys Thompson, while there. Perhaps without realizing what it meant for his future in psychology, he also began to build his base of using drama in psychotherapy, or what would commonly come to be known as role-playing. He was able to complete his master's thesis—a study of the leisure-time activities of workers—and received his degree from Kansas in 1928. In addition to the courses necessary for completion of this degree, Kelly also studied labor relations and sociology as his minors. Following a few other short-term jobs, Kelly received a fellowship for an educational exchange in order to attend the University of Edinburgh, Scotland. By 1930 he completed a bachelor of education degree there with a graduating thesis that addressed the issue of predicting teaching success. Kelly knew by then that he wanted to pursue a doctorate in psychology. While at the University of Iowa where he studied under Carl Seashore, Kelly focused his dissertation work on the common factors in reading and speech disabilities. In just one year, Kelly had a Ph.D. America was in the midst of the Depression years as he finally left school in search of a job.

In an essay he wrote in 1963, "Autobiography of a Theory," Kelly recounted his very first course in psychology as a student. Kelly noted that:

> In the very first course in psychology that I took I sat in the back row of a very large class, tilted my chair

against the wall, made myself as comfortable as possible, and kept one ear cocked for anything interesting that might turn up. One day the professor, a very nice person who seemed to be trying hard to convince himself that psychology was something to be taken seriously, turned to the blackboard and wrote an 'S,' an arrow, and an 'R.' Thereupon I straightened up my chair and listened, thinking to myself that now, after two or three weeks of preliminaries, we might be getting to the meat of the matter.

Kelly never did find out what this exercise meant, but went on in the same essay to say that:

> Out of all this I have gradually developed the notion that psychology is pretty much confined to the paradigms it employs and, while you can take off in a great many directions and travel a considerable distance in any of them—as indeed we have with stimulus-response psychology—there is no harm in consorting with a strange paradigm now and then. Indeed the notion has occurred to me that psychology may best be regarded as a collection of paradigms wooed by ex-physicists, ex-physiologists, and ex-preachers, as well as a lot of other intellectual renegades. Even more recently it has struck me that this is the nature of man; he is an inveterate collector of paradigms.

Even Kelly found it interesting that of all the years of his education, and through his various degrees, that his Ph.D. would be in psychology, a subject in which he majored for a total of nine months. He said that he would not recommend such a plan for his students.

In his profession

Kelly's first job that fall of 1931 was at Fort Hays Kansas State College. With his new bride, he traveled into the heart of what would become forever known as the "Dust Bowl," almost a euphemism for the hardship of the Depression itself. In Kelly's own words:

> It did not take many weeks in those depression times to reach the decision to pursue something more humanitarian than physiological psychology. Too many young people were wondering what, if anything, to do with their lives. The schools, only recently established at a secondary level in that part of the state, were only barely functioning as educational institutions, and there were many who thought public education should be abandoned altogether. It was a time for a teacher to talk of courage and adventure in the midst of despair. It was not a time for the 'S,' the arrow, and the 'R'!

He would stay at Fort Hays for 12 years, until the beginning of World War II. As Fransella noted, "Faced with a sea of human suffering aggravated by bank foreclosures and economic hardship," Kelly could no longer find any purpose except for the practical. He decided to put his efforts toward school children, whom he saw as needing his services. To that purpose he founded a clinic for diagnosing psychological problems and offering remedial services. The clinic traveled throughout rural western Kansas. Kelly headed a group of undergraduate and graduate students—the only staff. Even in the economically challenged days of the Depression, the state of Kansas decided the clinic was so worthwhile that the state eventually took over the role of sole funding source. When he published *The Psychology of Personal Constructs,* and throughout the rest of his career, Kelly would reiterate the fact that it was those early days of work with his traveling clinic that set the groundwork for the development of his new psychology.

Kelly took something very simple from his earliest observations during his days with the clinic. He decided that the way that people deal with the issues of living has nothing to do with how they partake of any absolute truth or any objective way that all people see themselves or others. It was what they brought themselves to the interpretation of what they saw that determined an outcome, for instance. At first Kelly had turned to Freud in order to help him solve the students' problems. He was virtually alone in a field that he saw as crucial to the future of the discipline and more certainly, as crucial to the lives of the children he was attempting to treat. Kelly would eventually reject Freud and his notion that only the therapist would bring positive change to the client. Kelly believed that the client could not improve unless clients determined their own interpretations and make decisions based on those. Again, his work seemed to continue to confirm for him that individuals were masters of their own fate.

Kelly wrote his first textbook in 1932, titled *Understanding Psychology,* though it remained unpublished. Another book he wrote with W. G. Warnock, titled *Inductive Trigonometry* in 1935, remained in manuscript draft form. Although it would be another 20 years before he would publish his first major work, Kelly did publish a series of six papers. Their focus was the practical work of clinical diagnosis, the operation of clinical psychology in school settings, and the use of diagnostic testing and similar matters for school children. Kelly's attention to the practical problems in clinical settings remained an interest throughout his career, in addition to his renowned work on personality theory.

During the last couple of years before America entered World War II, Kelly was in charge of a flight-training program at Fort Hays for local civilian pilots. In 1943 he was commissioned in the Naval Reserve and spent some of the war years serving as a Navy aviation psychologist. Kelly moved to the Bureau of Medicine and Surgery of the Navy in Washington, where he was involved in research on instrument panel design and other problems of applied and clinical psychology. In 1945 he was appointed Associate Professor at the University of Maryland. In 1946, Kelly accepted a position at Ohio State University as Professor and Director of Clinical Psychology. It was the year after another famed psychologist, Carl Rogers, left Ohio State.

Kelly devoted his first several years at Ohio State to organizing the graduate program in clinical psychology. That work paid off for the school, which quickly gained recognition as one of the top-ranking graduate training programs in the United States. According to the biographical notes of Brendan Maher in his introduction to *Clinical Psychology and Personality, The Selected Papers of George Kelly,* Kelly "managed to achieve an atmosphere in which clinical interest and perceptiveness were combined with firm commitment to the methods and standards of science in a blend that was, unfortunately, rarely found in other similar programs."

Publication brings fame   All this work was prelude to the events of 1955, when Kelly published what would be recognized as his contribution to the psychology of personality—the book *The Psychology of Personal Constructs.* Kelly's book, based on a substantial body of research and clinical expertise, brought him immediately to the attention of professionals and scholars throughout the United States and the world. The invitations to teach and give guest lectures were numerous. Included among the many universities where Kelly held visiting appointments were the University of Chicago, University of Nebraska, University of Southern California, Northwestern, Brigham Young, Stanford, and the University of New Hampshire. He lectured throughout the United States and around the world in Europe, the Soviet Union, South America, the Caribbean, and Asia.

Kelly not only brought fame to himself, but also to his work. His book provoked extensive research by other professionals into his theories—both the implications of them, and possible applications. He played a key role with the American Psychological Association (APA) as the field of clinical psychology reached a new and important status. Among his many leadership positions, Kelly served the APA in the elected position of President of its Clinical and Consulting Division. In 1965, the year he left Ohio State to accept the Riklis Chair of Behavioral Science at Brandeis University in Waltham, Massachusetts, Kelly was honored by the APA with its Award for Distinguished Contribution to the Science and Profession of Clinical Psychology. He accepted his position at Brandeis through the invitation of Abraham Maslow, another distinguished psychologist.

Kelly was holding the chair when he died on March 6, 1967, less than two months before his sixty-second birthday.

Personal life

Kelly married Gladys Thompson in 1931, who remained devoted to him throughout many moves. The year following his death, Kelly's wife assisted in locating many of his manuscripts and encouraged their publication. The couple had two children: a daughter, Jacqueline; and a son, Joseph Vincent. At the time of his death, his daughter was married to George Edward Sharples. In his introduction to his book, Maher closed his biography of Kelly noting that, "More than most psychologists, perhaps, George Kelly's papers are themselves an autobiography of the man. In them, the reader will find the warmth, humor, and tolerance that characterized him so well to those who knew him best."

Perhaps Kelly was best characterized by his own words, his reflections on the human condition. Kelly recalled his experience in western Kansas during the Depression and how his psychology emerged.

> So I listened to people in trouble and I tried to help them figure out what they could do about it. None of the things I had studied or pursued in the years before seemed to have any very specific bearing on what confronted us, though at one time or another through this period I probably attempted to make some use of everything I knew.

His approach to life was his approach to his work, and to helping people in a simple, straightforward manner.

> In western Kansas when a person came to me, we were pretty much stuck with each other. Our job was to figure out what the two of us could do ourselves. Now that I look back on it this was an open invitation to approach psychology from an unconventional angle. And that is what I am afraid I did.

Kelly died unexpectedly while in the process of completing a new book, in addition to organizing the many papers he had delivered throughout the last decade of his career.

THEORIES

Kelly developed not merely a theory of psychology. He developed an entire psychology based on 20 years of practical clinical experience and the theories he derived from that experience. As he offered in his preface for the book, the structure by which it was organized was essentially the manifestation of the psychology itself. Kelly knew that he not only wanted to let the reader or student know the *how* of the procedures handling a clinician's client base. He would have to present the *why* behind the procedures and techniques. That motivation was the beginning of his written works. Explaining the process through which the book was produced, Kelly also noted what others would quickly see upon reading his work that, "In the years of relatively isolated clinical practice we had wandered far off the beaten paths of psychology, much farther than we had ever suspected." Over the period of the three years that it took him to write the book, Kelly presented first drafts of the manuscript—from one page to as many as 30 pages at a time, as they were completed—in a weekly Thursday night seminar and lecture open to all interested. "That either the writer or the manuscript survived at all is entirely due to the psychological perceptiveness of colleagues who, somehow, always found a way to strike a gentle balance between pity and realism," Kelly recalled.

The theory of constructive alternativism provided Kelly with a solid base for his new psychology, as well as an important point of reference in his discussion of psychotherapeutic techniques. This personality theory began with two basic premises: 1) that an understanding of individual humans is better when derived from a "perspective of the centuries," as Kelly wrote, than "in the flicker of passing moments"; and, 2) that individuals see the context of life in a very personal manner, by the way events and the role in which they find themselves are played out. In other words, the theory involves individuals examining the way in which they interpret and react to their environment.

Kelly wrote that people view their worlds "through transparent patterns or templets," which they themselves create, and utilize them in order to "fit over the realities of which the world is composed." According to him, these patterns were not always a perfect fit, but still helpful. He submitted the term *constructs* to be used for such patterns. These patterns are enlarged or improved as a person matures. They become pieces of a larger construction system through which people live, communicate, and interpret the world around them. These constructs might be explained in more detail by the manner in which an individual uses them. Kelly emphasized that the one crucial assumption for testing or using these systems is that people must assume that all of the present interpretations of the universe were subject to revision or replacement. As he pointed out, "No one needs to paint [himself] into a corner; no one needs to be completely hemmed in by circumstances; no one needs to be the victim of [his] biography." Basically, this philosophy is what has been defined as constructive alternativism.

Kelly authored a 1966 essay that was to be an introduction to a book in personal construct theory. The piece was not completed due to his death, but was published by a student and colleague, Don Bannister, in 1970 as "Perspectives in Personal Construct Theory." Kelly began with a philosophical inquiry, writing,

> Who can say what nature is? Is it what now exits about us, including all the tiny hidden things that wait so patiently to be discovered? Or is it the vista of all that is destined to occur, whether tomorrow or in some distant eon of time? Or is nature infinitely more varied than this, the myriad trains of events that might ensue if we were to be so bold, ingenious, and irreverent as to take a hand in its management? . . . Personal construct theory is a notion about how [man] may launch out from a position of admitted ignorance, and how he may aspire from one day to the next to transcend his own dogmatisms. It is then, a theory of man's personal inquiry—a psychology of human quest. It does not say what has been or will be found, but proposes rather how we might go about looking for it.

Main points

From the ancient Greek mathematician Euclid who formulated the basis for both Greek and modern logic with his book, *Elements*, Kelly found the logical basis for his own system. What Kelly termed the psychology of personal constructs was laid out as a fundamental postulate (or hypothesis statement), which he used 11 corollaries to explain—in much the same way that Euclid laid out his own work. The fundamental postulate was: "A person's processes are psychologically channelized by the ways in which [he] anticipates events." This is a statement to be used for purpose of examination and hypothesis, and not as an absolute truth. Kelly was proposing a new way of looking at human beings and their actions. He stated that he wanted to provide different ways of examining the unconscious mind, and along with that the typical human behaviors such as anxiety, guilt, creativity, aggression, and depression, among others. With the use of his primary diagnostic tool, known as the repertory grid, Kelly built an entire scientific system by which to evaluate human beings and consequently through which they could evaluate themselves.

His marked departure from the school of behaviorism, again, was approaching the issue as one that meant people were not passive beings who merely reacted to either their outer or inner environment. They were scientists who systematically created ways to make an impact in the world by their actions. The underlying theme in Kelly's theory was that of change—the world is continually changing, and therefore humans are continually changing their constructs of the world.

Explanation: Corollaries

Kelly's system is basically a simple one. It is one postulate with 11 corollaries that provide the various directions in which that postulate might go. A person might act in a certain way but due to the whole system of living, inquiry, and discovery a person has established, there are many different parts of it, in a clinical setting, that the individual and therapist must know about and also examine. If a client is seeking treatment for a problem, for instance, the client and the therapist both need to know who this person is by the deliberations they make. Kelly noted that in order for people to anticipate future events, they must create or construct some way that permits them to think of two of them in a similar way.

Examples

Understanding the implications of the corollaries is an important key to understanding the psychology itself. The corollaries were stated by Kelly as:

1. Construction corollary—A person anticipates events by construing their replications.

2. Individual corollary—Persons differ from each other in their constructions of events.

3. Organization corollary—Each person characteristically evolves, for convenience in anticipating events, a construction system embracing ordinal relationships between constructs.

4. Dichotomy corollary—A person's construction system is composed of a finite number of dichotomous constructs.

5. Choice corollary—A person chooses for him- or herself that alternative in dichotomized construct through which is anticipated the greater possibility for extension and definition of the individual's system.

6. Range corollary—A construct is convenient for anticipation of a finite range of events only.

7. Experience corollary—A person's construction system varies as that person successively construes the replications of events.

8. Modulation corollary—The variation in a person's construction system is limited by the permeability of the constructs within whose ranges of convenience the variants lie.

9. Fragmentation corollary—A person may successively imply a variety of construction subsystems

which are inferentially incompatible with each other.

10. Commonality corollary—To the extent that one person employs a construction of experience which is similar to that employed by another, that person's psychological processes are similar to those of the other person.

11. Sociality corollary—To the extent that one person construes the construction processes of another, that person may play a role in a social process involving the other person.

The corollaries can be understood by examining their content as Kelly did.

Construction corollary   How does a person anticipate an event by "construing" the replications of events? Each event that occurs is unique; but some events can be viewed by their similarities. This construction must include both the way to identify the events as similar, as well as how they are different. If a person does not see distinctions between occurrences, then the entire world is perceived to be the same, or homogeneous. If only the differences are realized, the result is a world of events and actions that are totally unrelated. This would create a sort of chaos offering no hope of understanding or communication—specifically, the communication people have with themselves in order to determine the action they will find necessary to perform. This corollary has implications in mathematics, as well. In order to calculate probability and predictability of events, it is necessary to take into account the concept of the replication of events.

Individuality corollary   Each person is unique and constructs events in his or her own way. Because of such individuality in their natures, people are not likely to create identical systems. In later years, Kelly went even further to explain that it would also be unlikely that particular constructions represent identical events. Just as important to recognize is the fact that it is highly improbable that any two people would have joined together their construction systems by the same logical relationships, he noted.

Organization corollary   What does it mean to say that each person anticipates events by evolving "a construction system embracing ordinal relationships between constructs?" A person creates a system that will provide a way to function within it. There must be a way to move comfortably in order to examine in a way that provides solutions to problems and contradictions that are sure to arise. All such difficulties

cannot be solved at once. That is not usually necessary for a person to continue. Some personal issues can remain unsolved indefinitely. The person can continue to imagine the outcome of either of two choices, for example, while figuring out what the future has in store.

Dichotomy corollary   This concept is made up of the reality that a construct is a what might be termed as "black or white," and never gray. A dichotomy always represents a division into two sections. The construct is born out of the contrast between two different groups. When the construct goes up, it distinguishes between its elements and groups them as well. This refers to the nature of such a crucial distinction.

Choice corollary   When people create their constructs, it is most likely that they will choose the one that might provide for expansion, or greater possibilities of their system. A choice implies that a person will desire a system that could also provide for a way to develop its usefulness. According to Kelly, when individuals make choices, they are aligning themselves in terms of their constructs. This does not mean that they will avoid or reach what their object is. It means simply that people choose how it is they want to proceed. Sometimes success in reaching or avoiding an event depends on what a person is willing to do to alter the construct—especially, for instance, when maintaining it might otherwise be psychologically catastrophic.

Range corollary   This corollary refers to the fact that any construct is created only for a limited range of events and is not useful on a universal basis. Any one person cannot anticipate all the world's events. In fact, people do not create the constructs needed to cover the whole scale of events they might encounter. As Kelly explains it, "the geometry of the mind is never a complete system." It is virtually impossible to write a formula that could apply universally. A construct is something created for convenience, and for the set of objects with which it can successfully operate.

Experience corollary   Experience represents a series of events due to the construction people create for the events that occur around them. If the construct is not altered as a person meets with different events, then there is no psychological impact on that person. In essence, change does not occur. If a person does invest energy enough to recognize that what was anticipated turns out to be different from what occurred, then an important connection has been made. When personal investments continue to meet with a movement that forces change from the original expectation, human experience is the result.

Modulation corollary In addition to expanding constructs due to events, sometimes it is necessary to realize an event presents limitations, as well. A construct system must be prepared to meet with this possibility. Otherwise the cycle of experience will fail. The systems that individuals devise must be able to admit revision at the end of this cycle. Unless a system has a permeability to accept new subordinate constructions—represented by new ideas, for instance—anything that does not fit into that system already will have no likelihood of ever fitting into it.

Fragmentation corollary People can make use of various construction subsystems that might not infer compatibility with one another when moving from point A to point B to point C. That is, what they saw when they were at point A might not be the reality when the person finally reaches point C; it might not have been anticipated logically in any way. That is not always an unfortunate consequence of human behavior. It can surpass a person's logic or rational thought, but the result can be the piece of a person's construction that actually brings about greatness.

Commonality corollary The major assumption of personal construct psychology is that people's behavior is governed by their constructs. In that way one person can be said to be psychologically similar to another person—that is what they have in common. Holding to this principle, it can be deduced that though two people who have experienced very different events, and who seem to have gone through the experiential cycle very differently, could emerge with similar constructions of their experiences, and continue to explore further using similar psychological processes. According to Kelly, it is this aspect of the theory that can release psychology "from assumptions about the identity of events" and how people depend on them. Here Kelly made the distinction of his psychology from that of the behaviorists and phenomenologists. His method provided a way to see people who might have to cope with familiar events in new ways, and cooperate with others in order to create a different world in a positive way.

Sociality corollary Kelly considered this corollary as his most far-reaching idea. With this, a person could create an environment in which to understand "role" as a psychological term, and provide for the vision of a psychological basis for society. This corollary would indicate that once a person actually attempts to construe the construction processes of another person, then the first person might not be able to anticipate the actions of that other person. It provides an opportunity for that person to take a guess, anticipate a deeper meaning to the other person's behavior, and attempt to figure out what that person's course of action will be. This implies that people treat each other as people, rather than as simple automatons whose behavior represents something other than a complex human being.

Explanation: Constructs

Kelly's use of the word "construed" rather than "constructed" is important when he is discussing exactly what constructs are. A construct implies the dual nature of something—the relationship between two things or events immediately indicates that the individual has determined their similarity. But simultaneously the differences between the two are also recognized. In the case that a person might construe a situation in terms of a "black vs. white" construct, then even if that construct is misapplied or inappropriate—such as a person seeing only the color of another person's skin rather than the deeper character issues that might be relevant—the individual has applied that construct to matters that are seen only as black or white. In other matters of daily life, whether it is the time of day, the cost of bus fare, or the caloric intake of a fast-food meal, such a construct would not be relevant.

The dual, or "bipolar nature," of constructs, as Kelly termed it, does not precisely follow traditional logic. While it can be deemed that such concepts as "black" and "white" are to be treated as separate concepts, or that the way to view things is that they are either naturally alike or very different, Kelly thought differently. He proposed that while the nature of things might be considered real and unchangeable, that reality exists more clearly in the eyes of the person interpreting it.

Pertinent to his explanation of the nature of constructs, Kelly also outlined and offered 21 additional questions and issues when discussing the matter. Those in the category of *personal usage of constructs*, in addition to the question regarding the basic nature of a personal construct as discussed in the previous paragraph, were:

- Do people mean what they say?
- Implied linkages in the interpretation of personal constructs.
- Constructs and anticipations.

- Constructs as controls.
- The personal construction of one's role.
- The real nature of constructs.

Under the category of *formal aspects of constructs,* Kelly presented the main categories for that aspect of defining his psychology, also with detailed explanation:

- terminology
- symbolism
- communication
- scales of constructs
- scanning by means of constructs
- personal security within the context of a construct
- dimensions of constructs

In the next category, *changing construction,* Kelly adds the following issues for determination:

- validation
- conditions favorable to the formation of new constructs
- conditions unfavorable to the formation of new constructs

The final section of Kelly's outline of explanation deals with *the meaning of experience,* a crucial piece of the puzzle of understanding human constructs, particularly in a clinical setting. The issues under consideration are:

- the construed nature of experience
- the interpretation of experience
- the historical approach
- group expectancies as validators of personal constructs
- gaining access to personal constructs through the study of the culture in which they have grown

Examples   Kelly elaborates each step in his process of unfolding the philosophy behind his psychology. He examined and explained the nature of personal constructs by detailing examples of how to understand each category when considering that question. Focusing on the issue of the therapist in treating clients, Kelly offered the discussion of the final category, that of understanding a person's culture in order to treat them. This matter is a relevant one given the modern-day concept of "political correctness"—in the sense that people are seen within the context of their group or culture. Kelly warned the therapist against stereotyping individuals, and grouping them together simply because they were of a certain culture. He offered the example that:

The Gentile therapist who comes in contact with a series of Jewish clients for the first time may also be baffled by the similarities he sees by way of contrast with his other clients. If he is to understand them as persons, rather than to stereotype them as Jews, he must neither ignore the cultural expectations under which they have validated their constructs—expectation of both Jewish and Gentile groups—nor make the mistake of focusing on the group constructs to the exclusion of the personal constructs of each client.

The responsible therapist using the psychology of personal constructs must be clear in the distinctions and definitions, just as any other scientist would.

Explanation: Repertory grid

The primary tool, or diagnostic instrument, for Kelly's psychology is known as the repertory grid. The original test devised by Kelly was meant to be used in a clinical, or pre-clinical setting. His idea was that the test, role construct repertory test (Rep test), as administered through his "grid" would serve five functions: 1) to define the client's problem in a way that it could most easily be addressed; 2) to uncover the client's own personal constructs, or manner in which the person functions moves and will move for the purpose of the examination; 3) to provide hypotheses in the clinical setting which can be carefully observed, monitored, and utilized; 4) to search and discover what resources the client has available that might not be obvious to a therapist except through such a tool; and 5) to uncover and accent the problems of the client that also might have been overlooked by the therapist.

Examples   The test focuses on role constructs for the purpose of seeking an understanding of a person's personal social behavior. As created by Kelly, it was an application of a psychological test procedure already in use, known as the concept-formation. As the administration of the test developed, it became a simple grid. The grid itself is a table divided into columns, and essentially sorts people. There are two outer columns that list human characteristics. The remaining columns are filled with the names of people or objects that fit into a list of categories. For instance, in addition to places for each parent, siblings, and employer, and other similar categories. There are also places for such listings as a teacher that you liked, and one you disliked; a spouse or significant other; a person of the same sex you disliked in high school; and several other categories of people with whom you've interacted. Kelly's traditional test provided for up to 21 of those columns. Each person is listed with a designated number. The names are also written on cards. The tester shows the subject these cards in groups of three, and always asks the same question: "How are two of these similar and the third one different?" Each answer the subject gives represents a construct of the subject. Individual names rather than generalized concepts such as "male" or "female" are considered preferable because they are more personal to the subject, and provide the first inroads into the gathering of information necessary to analysis. The examiner sorts through these responses and recorded.

Kelly noted six constructs the subject might construe that could create the need for a follow-up to the test in order to make finer distinctions. Such constructs and their explanation are: 1) situational constructs—when a subject might answer, for instance, that two people are alike because they are from the same town; 2) excessively permeable constructs—when a subject would indicate that two people were alike simply because they are both men; 3) excessively impermeable constructs—a subject might answer that two people are alike because they are each firefighters, but the third is different because he or she is a law enforcement officer; 4) superficial constructs—when a subject might find a similarity simply because two people wear the same size of shoes; 5) vague constructs—when the subject indicates that both objects share a similar characteristic by saying something such as, "Oh, I don't like either of them"; and, 6) constructs which are a direct product of the role title—the subject responds to the question of similarity between two people, in the example Kelly offers, by saying that, "Both are hard to understand."

From the beginning, Kelly allowed for the possibility of variations of the rep test. He offered various elaborations through which a therapist might administer the test according to determining both personal and public construct systems. What he did proscribe was that certain assumptions should be accepted as premise to the test. Those he indicated were that: 1) of the "permeability of the constructs elicited"; 2) "preexisting constructs are elicited by the test"; 3) the test must be representative of all the people with whom the subject creates the construed role; 4) the subject must demonstrate an understanding of the constructs of others in order to understand the social interaction, even if that understanding is inadequate; 5) the subject must have clear role association in relation to the object, with constructs regarding that person clearly defined; and, 6) the subject must adequately communicate the constructs created and their explanation to the examiner.

Fixed-role therapy

Central to Kelly's psychology of personal constructs is the way in which that theory is utilized in treating clients. Of the many methods a therapist might employ, one that stands out is fixed-role therapy—creating a new self-characterization for the client based on one the client already provided. The therapy involves focusing around what is considered the primary moral argument of personal construct psychology. Bannister presents the issue in his essay entitled "Kelly versus clockwork psychology" in the *International Handbook of Personal Construct Psychology*. He noted that central to the argument were a couple of questions. The first was, "Is it possible that your personality is an invention?" Questions that follow that initial one would include, "Is it possible that laboriously through your life, step by step, you have been building a personality?" And, "Is it possible that you did not inherit your personality from your parents, that it is not fixed in you genetically or constitutionally or simply taught to you by your environment?" Kelly did not explore this brand of therapy by himself. He noted that in 1939 a group including other psychologists he identified as Edwards, McKenna, Older, along with him, had examined what they termed at the time only as "role therapy."

Explanation The procedure of this therapy employs the use of a sympathetic friend of the client writing the self-characterization, always written in the third person. Then, the therapist produces a fixed-role sketch based on the self-character sketch. This is primarily a character portrait of an imaginary person. The client then becomes that imaginary character for a certain period of time—perhaps for several weeks. What this does is put the client into a new role in order to begin to examine how people might act differently toward that person. Consequently, the client gathers new evidence about the surrounding world—specifically the personal responses and other people's relationships of the people he encounters.

Examples Kelly introduced this practice of fixed-role therapy in his book by introducing readers to a university student he called Ronald Barrett, described as someone who had requested psychological services due to complaints of his difficulties in academic, vocational, and social adjustments. By the time that fixed-role therapy was set for trial, Barrett had been through about nine psychotherapeutic interviews. The therapist could not see much change or promise that his problems would be solved. The school term was ending, and the client had decided to leave that university for another one a thousand miles away.

Kelly reproduced the sketch complete with the original misspellings and grammatical errors. It began with the sentence, "An overall appearance of Ronald Barrett would give one the impression that he had a rather quiet and calm personality." He was portrayed as a young man who was cautious about drawing any attention to himself in an unfavorable light in public. Even if he was only one in a group with someone who was causing a disturbance, he did not like the idea of being seen as a member of such a group. While there were occasions when he did get angry or frustrated and demonstrated those feelings, though not in public, he would rarely target his friends when showing such emotions. Barrett appeared to be a person who was disdainful of his own stupid mistakes, as well as those of others, even when it was a matter considered minor by everyone else. As the sketch went on, it was revealed that he did show great mood extremes. He was also someone who continually tried to impress people, especially those who were older, by relaying his knowledge, maturity, and sincerity. In fact, it seemed that one of his biggest issues was inconsideration on the part of anyone at all, including himself. As someone who embodied a certain morality and set of ethics, Barrett was thus subject to guilt feelings when he felt he did not measure up to the compassion he held as a high priority. He was most critical of his family, correcting them relentlessly when he believed they were wrong on a matter, and went to great lengths to prove he was right. In the same matter, Barrett had often been gullible when believing something too easily and then arguing its correctness even when it turned out not to be. The sketch did note that he seemed to have that characteristic under better control. At that point, he was not as quick to give way to this inclination.

In other matters, Barrett's personality portrait presented someone who was rigid in his beliefs, particularly religious beliefs. He suffered from a lack of confidence especially with members of the opposite sex, creating serious awkwardness when it came to dating—the sketch noted that he put too much thought into kissing a girl on a date, or calling again even if he had already been out with her two or three times. Barrett was described as someone with both positive qualities and negative, especially in certain inconsistencies between his stated beliefs and his actions.

As a part of the therapy for Barrett, the fixed-role sketch gave the subject a different name, that of "Kenneth Norton." The sketch was one that focused on his positive qualities, providing as well for a positive spin on what were originally stated as negative habits. He was portrayed as a person who connected in an intimately cordial way very quickly to all he met. Norton was characterized as a good listener who was not dismissive of anyone else's ideas. He gave attention to the details of views of other people as being something important. Women found him attractive largely because he was so willing to listen to their point of view. He gave even his parents the opportunity to listen to his ideas and share his enthusiasm and his accomplishments. As Kelly pointed out about the sketch, its theme was essentially one that found, "the seeking of answers in the subtle feelings of other people rather than in literalistic dispute with them."

Both of the sketches provide only the beginnings of the fixed-role therapy. The therapist as well as the client has to evaluate the situation and help decide where to proceed. This involves the client's reactions as well as other types of situations the new role might not have included. He and other have explained the whole process in greater detail. What he did emphasize was that he believed that in order for the therapy to be successful, six sessions in a two-week period that included the presentation session was the minimum required in order for the therapist to achieve any positive results. Kelly related the end of his final interview with his client Barrett, telling him that "We did not want to throw Ronald Barrett in the ash can. Rather, Kenneth Norton was in a sense supposed to be another Ronald Barrett, a different version of him. I used the analogy of the onion skin where one layer comes off revealing another layer." Barrett indicated that he understood well, that Norton was just another facet of his personality. Kelly determined that Barrett had made great progress in the sessions through this use of fixed-role therapy.

HISTORICAL CONTEXT

Kelly's life and work followed almost exactly through the first half of the twentieth century—from the time of his birth in 1905 until the time of his death in 1967. This man who was born in the early days of the automobile, only two years after the Wright Brothers' attempt at flying, was already four years old when he went with his parents by covered wagon to settle land in eastern Colorado. He was someone whose place in history might be difficult to fathom for anyone who came of age by the turn of the next century. He was truly a child of the period of time that would come to be known as the "American century."

Kelly grew up through World War I, in which modern warfare technology began to change the face of war. The methods used to wage war using gas as a weapon brought a new horror to the future. Kelly came of age during the 1920s, when technological inventions were transforming industry and society at a rate previously unseen. The beginning of his professional career in western Kansas during the darkest days of the Depression, in an area that suffered perhaps more intensely due to years of drought, was directly affected by the cases he handled. He wrote that during that the 12 years he spent at Fort Hays that he head "several more priceless opportunities to revise my outlook." He recalled that "It was a time for a teacher to talk of courage and adventure in the midst of despair." Still, Kelly would be the first to say that it was not really the circumstances, or that he felt any calling to do what he did. And by that time, he decided that if it was he who initiated his own actions, why would others not do the same?

Even if he wanted to talk more about what he did with how he was raised, Kelly's childhood clearly provided a fascinating historical context for the person he would become as an adult, and ultimately as a psychologist. He emerged from the sort of rugged individualism for which a young country was still known. Kelly understood the principles of self-determination from his father, who gave up a career in the Presbyterian ministry to follow the life of a farmer. His mother was the daughter of an adventurer. She chose to be a Midwestern farmer's wife at a time when America's increasing urbanization might have provided her with a world of culture and society instead of rural isolation. Kelly's early education was an example of determination to learn without the early formality of schooling. His university life would unearth so many matters of interest that it was almost enough to cause concern that he would settle into a stable way to earn a living.

Yet the education he chose did lead to the psychology he would create. As an engineering student who majored in mathematics and physics, it was the scientist in him that would direct his future and provide the motivation for a new way to look at human behavior. As a mathematician, Kelly would find inspiration in the straightforward system of the ancient Greek scholar Euclid who had published a simple book on geometry centuries earlier. The way in which he prepared his 1,000 page manuscript was presented as postulate and corollaries—the same structure Euclid used. In the essay on Kelly for the *International Handbook,* Fransella and Neimeyer did point out that Kelly's reliance on mathematical theory

was such that he pointed out that "Johann Herbart's work on education and particularly mathematical psychology influenced me. I think mathematics is the pure instance of construct functioning—the model of human behavior."

The more positive influences on Kelly did come from various areas of philosophy, as well. He was known to cite John Dewey, the religious thinker and follower of pragmatism. He was also influenced by his study of phenomenonology. Another influence was the linguistic philosopher, Alfred Korzybski, who suggested the idea of "constructs" as interpretations that reveal as much of the humans who utilize them, as about the objects they describe. Hans Vaihinger was a philosopher who proposed the "as if" proposition as he built his own brand of constructive alternativism—already noted as the philosophy on which Kelly began to build his own psychology.

What perhaps influenced Kelly in a negative way was the contemporary popularity of behaviorism and the psychodynamic approach to psychology. He reacted so strongly against that notion that he felt compelled to pursue his own idea that humans were more in charge of themselves than either of those two methods implied. When Kelly published his work on April 15, 1955, America had already entered the age of the atomic and nuclear bombs. The country was also in the midst of the "Red scare" during the Cold War against the Soviet Union and the other Communist countries. School children were practicing air raid drills, people were building bomb shelters, and anxiety over the possibility of nuclear holocaust loomed. It was the era of the "Beatnik," and the gradual evolution of a new kind of individualism. The rumblings of the Civil Rights movement had begun in earnest among black Americans—a time when an oppressed people were speaking up, marching, boycotting, and saying they were no longer going to be victims of a two-tiered justice or social system. The world was in the early dawn of the computer age, as well.

Kelly's work was well received for the most part though it was clearly seen as a major departure from the behaviorism so widely practiced. Indeed, with all of the work he and other psychologists were doing to establish the right of clinical psychologists to separate from the medical profession, and to receive acceptance as scientific practitioners, his work began to pave the way into an age of information technology when even the average person was called on to partake of science. Kelly's system was an obvious beginning to a whole new direction in research of the human psyche and the behavior it produced.

CRITICAL RESPONSE

While Kelly met with praise from the reviews of psychologists such as Carl Rogers and Jerome Bruner, he certainly met with criticism as well. According to the *Biographical Dictionary of Psychology,* the major objections of the time of publication and into a new century centered around three major arguments, as directly quoted:

- The theory had relatively little to offer on the issues of growth and development.

- It is not specific about the motivational basis for many people's decisions (i.e., the connections between construct systems and motivational forces are obscure).

- In dispensing with the distinction between cognition and emotion, his theory underemphasizes the role played by emotional and affective factors.

The third argument was one to which Kelly particularly took exception. He emphasized that any such perceived neglect of emotional issues was not a part of a clinical setting.

Regarding the criticism that Kelly did not address the issue of human development, Fransella has argued that the omission was deliberate. The entire personal construct theory was about development, she noted. "Human beings are seen as forms of motion," Fransella pointed out, no matter what age they are. Another reason for omission was Kelly's reluctance to categorize people, which is what he thought such traditional models (of stages of growth through particular ages) do. While Piaget was known to share some of his affinity for constructivism, Kelly did not subscribe to such theories of his either. Kelly certainly had years of experience with children during his traveling clinic days in Kansas. He believed more that "becoming"—as humans developed into the people they were to become—was a process that was individualized to the extent that both children and adults are constantly changing and not simply staying at one stage or another. Fransella and Neimeyer offered this factor as another possibility for the "neglect" for this part of his theory. Others have since developed this part of his theory more extensively, which will be explained in the next section on research and modern-day relevance.

A crucial issue has been mentioned but should be viewed is the profound contribution Kelly made to scientific research. Kelly was one of the key psychologists who helped alter the way research was conducted. Italian psychologists Gabriele Chiari, of the Centro Studi in Psicoterapia Cognitiva, in Florence, and Maria Laura Nuzzo, of the Centro di Psicologia e Psicoterapia Costruttivista, in Rome, provided a chapter for the *International Handbook* entitled, "Kelly's Philosophy of Constructive Alternativism." In 2003, as an introductory paragraph to their essay, they wrote that:

> Many psychologists prefer to regard psychology as a science that has become one and for all separated from philosophy, its ancestral roots. Science, they think, uses the scientific method, that is, a method that allows its followers to gain access to the ultimate reality, while the speculations of philosophers have no validity as to the knowledge of reality and the verification of the truth. These psychologists fail to consider that the dependence of their inquiries, and of the very scientific method they hold so dear, are based on a definite set of assumptions—usually unspoken—whose questioning and analysis are exactly the prerogative of philosophy.

Kelly, they explained, "was aware that philosophical speculation is inescapable, for any scientific investigation." Chiari and Nuzzo, as did others, pointed out the significance of the two terms Kelly coined—*accumulative fragmentalism,* as opposed to *constructive alternativism.* The former can best be defined as the idea that knowledge is based on the accumulation of fragmented thoughts. According to Kelly, the authors noted "Science proceeds by way of conjectures and refutation: any person, as a scientist, does the same."

Among the names of many well-known scientists and scholars whose ideas penetrate the discussion of Kelly is the name of one philosopher of science, Thomas Kuhn (1922–1996). He appears on the horizon of those theories that are either directly or indirectly connected to Kelly's work. While he cannot be categorized among the followers of Kelly, his work as introduced in his 1962 book, *The Structure of Scientific Revolution,* embodies much of the focus of the constructivists. For further study and research on Kuhn, information is available through the Society for Constructivism in the Human Sciences. His theories on scientific method can provide an enhancement and variation to Kelly's work.

Perhaps a major reason for criticism of Kelly emerged from the fact that he actually created a whole new psychology. There was an initial burst of interest when he published his work, though that interest quickly faded. Most of those who immediately pursued research based on personal construct psychology were clinicians rather than the academicians who would represent the links necessary to further such a groundbreaking direction. Kelly himself tended to avoid being labeled, or linking himself easily to other theories in psychology. He did not receive notice in the United States because of those factors. In 1997,

Dr. C. George Boeree of the psychology department of Shippensburg University in Pennsylvania noted:

> The reasons for this lack of attention are not hard to fathom. The 'science' branch of psychology was at that time still rather mired in a behaviorist approach to psychology that had little patience with the subjective side of things. And the clinical side of psychology found people like Carl Rogers much easier to follow. . . Kelly was a good 20 years ahead of his time. Only recently, with the so-called "cognitive revolution," are people really ready to understand him.

Apparently it was Kelly himself who suggested that if his theory were still around in 10 or 20 years (Kelly died less than 12 years after publishing the psychology), in a form too close to the original, that might not be a good thing. As a true constructive alternativist, Kelly believed that individual views of reality must change. Because he built not only a whole new psychology but a whole new language, Kelly's critics often had a difficult time with their criticism of his work. Again, many critics abandoned him altogether. Yet his base of followers grew, even if the fact remained that he was embraced more readily outside of the United States than inside. Particularly in England he gained quite a modicum of notoriety. Industrial psychologists found his new methods translated efficiently to labor or employment environments. As of 2004, the centers for personal construct psychology and journals are concentrated in England, Australia, Germany, and Canada.

Vincent Kenny is one proponent of Kelly's work who has written extensively about it He is the director of the Institute of Constructivist Psychology in Dublin, Ireland. He has quoted Kelly's comments regarding the hazards of categorizing the psychology. Kelly had said that he had been

> so puzzled over the early labeling of personal construct theory as "cognitive" that several years ago I set out to write another short book to make it clear that I wanted no part of cognitive theory. The manuscript was about a third completed when I gave a lecture at Harvard University with the title, "Personal Construct Theory as a Line of Inference." Following the lecture, Professor Gordon Allport explained to the students that my theory was not a "cognitive" theory but an "emotional" theory. Later the same afternoon, Dr. Henry Murray called me aside and said, "You know, don't you, that you are really an existentialist?"

Kenny further points out that Kelly and his psychology had been categorized in a number of other ways including, a learning theory; psychoanalytic theory—Freudian, Adlerian, Jungian; typically American theory; Marxist Theory; humanistic theory; logical positivistic theory; a Zen Buddhistic theory; a Thomistic theory; a

behavioristic theory; an Apollonian theory; a pragmatistic theory; a reflective theory; and, no theory at all. Kenny added the observation that:

> From these comments it is clear that Kelly's theory has been treated somewhat like a Rorschach inkblot, wherein people can find what they expect to see, by reading in the light of their own theories and therefore not being able to discern the radically different nature of the theory.

In summarizing Kelly's theory, Kenny has provided an interesting perspective. He said that "Personal construct theory is very difficult to grasp largely because it emphasizes organization and structure as opposed to content. It tells us not what to think but rather how to go about understanding what we do think." An important question that remains after the 50 years since Kelly published his work would be: Why did it take so long for Americans to see in the theory what people from countries throughout the world saw almost immediately?

Kelly's legacy

One quick search through the worldwide web of the early twenty-first century can provide an extensive view into the revolution that Kelly brought into being with one book, as well as the many branches of disciplines using constructive philosophy as their basis. Kelly did something more complex than simply giving birth to other psychological trends or theories. His basic system spawned a far-reaching network of other construct theoreticians and practicing clinicians. It was as if he created the design of a building that set a standard for numerous variations of that architecture—possibly for generations to come. Centers throughout the world are dedicated to personal construct psychology. As of 2004, the major centers and organizations around the world that were dedicated to personal construct psychology in the United States and abroad included, North American Personal Construct Network (NAPCN); European Personal Construct Association (EPCA)—yet another testimony to the fact that perhaps Kelly was ahead of his time is that this association was founded in 1990; Australian Personal Construct Group (APCG); Centre for Personal Construct Psychology, in England; Society for Constructivism in the Human Sciences, based in Denton, Texas, devoted to constructivism; Houston Galveston Institute; Institute for the Study of Psychotherapeutic Change; Taos Institute (social constructionism); Constructivism and Discourse Processes Research Group; and the International Network on Personal Meaning.

The *International Handbook* provides a large sampling of all of the theories and research being done by Kelly's disciples—many of whom were born after his death. It is the key reference for the subject. By no means can it cover all of the work being done, or all of the people who are doing it. The use of Kelly's system has spread to such varied areas as business, family therapy, nursing education, and sports. In addition to that book, hundreds of others books, essays, and lectures regarding one of the many aspects of personal construct psychology have been published. Journals focused on the subject include *Journal of Constructivist Psychology, Constructivism in the Human Sciences, Constructivist Chronicle,* the newsletter of the NAPCN, *The International Personal Construct Psychology Newsletter, Narrative Psychology Internet and Resource Guide,* and *Postmodern Therapies NEWS.*

Radical constructivism One of the important offshoots of personal construct psychology is the theory of radical constructivism. The phrase and idea were coined in 1974 by Ernst von Glaserfeld. According to the Web site devoted to the discipline, von Glaserfeld was concerned with compromising constructivism. Unless constructivism is "complete" or "radical," according to him, it could easily relapse into what he called "some kind of fancy realism." Radical constructivism is defined as "an unconventional approach to the problem of knowledge and knowing." It is based on the premise that however knowledge is defined, it "is in the heads of persons." Consequently, the thinking subjects have no other way to act but to construct what they know drawn from their experience. What humans interpret of their experience, much in line with Kelly's original assumption, is the reality of the world for each person, the only realm of consciousness for each individual. The theory also includes the contention that nonetheless, all experiences are basically subjective. People can imagine that the experience of others might be similar to theirs, but have no way of confirming that. For the radical constructivists, this includes the experience and interpretation of language. In that regard, Kelly was only one in a line of scholars who embraced the notion of constructivism, and was by no means the first.

The names of six people emerge as significant in the field of radical constructivism. In addition to Kelly himself, they are Heinz von Foerster (born November 13, 1911); Humberto Maturana, known by the phrase, "Everything said is said by an observer"; Ernst von Glaserfeld; Gordon Pask (died 2003), who developed a conversation theory; and, Jakob von Uexküll, who published his main theories first in 1928 in *Theoretische Biologie.* Von Foerster ran the Biological Computer Laboratory (BCL) at the University of Illinois at Urbana-Champaign (Illinois) from the late

1950s until the middle of the 1970s. The BCL brought together scholars and scientists whose thinking was similar to his. In addition to Maturana and Pask, two other prominent members of the BCL were Francisco Varela, known for developing the ideas of circularity and considered an innovator in cognition; as well as W. Ross Ashby, one of the main figures in the cybernetics movement.

The decade of the 1980s, particularly in Germany, was a time of prolific publication of translations of the work of others in the field, including Siegfried J. Schmidt, Hans-Rudi Fischer, Gerhard Roth, and, Gebhard Rusch. It was during that period also that the work of von Uexküll's work from the 1920s and 1930s was also made more widely available through reissues and translation.

Social constructivism Another theory based on constructivist notions is that of social constructivism. Its premise is that reality or truth is made, not discovered. In Kelly's world that railed against absolute truths and supported an ever-changing reality, this extension seems to find its logical place. Max Hocutt, a professor of philosophy at the University of Alabama, noted in a criticism of the doctrine for the Spring 1999 issue of *Behavior and Philosophy* that the doctrine had achieved followers for a couple of reasons. "First," he wrote, "it is flattering. People like to be told that their opinions are as good as other people's. Second, when taken in a certain way—as the belief that different beliefs might both be true—social constructivism is unobjectionable." In fairness to social constructivists, however, the designation of the word, "truth" or "reality" is crucial to understanding the distinction between beliefs held between two or more people. Hocutt criticizes the use of the word "truth" when belief would be better utilized.

Social psychology is a field that began to gain prominence at a time coinciding with Kelly's publication. It is a field that has been significantly affected by his theories—even those that might transgress from his original principles. Two prominent modern social psychologists, Susan T. Fiske and Elizabeth F. Loftus, who are profiled in this chapter, are further examples of Kelly's legacy. Fiske is a member of the faculty of Princeton University who has become known for her work in defining social relationships, particularly those regarding race, gender, and age. Loftus has achieved fame as a memory specialist best known for her work in the field of exposing repressed memory syndrome. Her 1994 book with Katherine Ketham, *The Myth of Repressed Memory: False Memories and Allegations of Sexual Abuse,* created a public explosion of an increas-

BIOGRAPHY:

Susan T. Fiske

Susan T. Fiske is a prominent social psychologist and professor of psychology at Princeton University. She was born on August 19, 1952, to Donald W. Fiske and Barbara Page Fiske. Fiske has one brother, Alan Page Fiske, a professor of anthropology at UCLA. Her father was a psychologist and psychology professor, as well. His career spanned nearly five decades. He retired from the University of Chicago (UC) and died at the age of 86 in April 2003. Fiske was the first recipient of the Donald W. Fiske Distinguished Lecture series that was established in his honor in 1999 at UC. With her father at UC throughout her childhood, Fiske was raised in the racially integrated, stable university neighborhood of Hyde Park on Chicago's south side. She has mentioned that growing up in such an environment had an impact on her interest in race relations.

Fiske graduated magna cum laude from Radcliffe College, Harvard University, in 1973, with an A.B. in Social Relations. She completed her Ph.D. at Harvard in 1978 in Social Psychology. In 1995 she was honored with a Docteur Honoris Causa, Ph.D. from the Universit Catholique de Louvain, Louvain-la-Neuve, Belgium.

Fiske has authored over 100 journal articles and book chapters; edited seven books and journal special issues. It was her graduate text with Shelley Taylor, *Social Cognition,* first published in 1984, with a second edition in 1991, that provided definition for the sub-field of the way people think about and make sense of other people, according to the UC department of social psychology press release when Fiske received the Fiske Distinguished Lecture honor.

Her research focus has addressed how stereotyping, prejudice, and discrimination are both promoted and discouraged through social relationships. Her work in social cognition also brought her the distinguished honor of being an expert witness for a case before the United States Supreme Court in what was

considered a landmark case in 1984. Addressing similar issues, Fiske was also asked to testify in front of President Clinton's Race Initiative Advisory Board in 1998. Among her many honors, Fiske received the 1991 American Psychological Association Award for Distinguished Contributions to Psychology in the Public Interest, Early Career, partly as a result of her Supreme Court testimony.

As a psychologist specializing in social cognition, Fiske gives witness to the strength of Kelly's personal construct psychology. In "A Conversation with Susan Fiske," for *Psychology is Social, Readings and Conversations in Social Psychology,* Third Edition, Fiske told interviewer Edward Krupat that social cognition

> deals with how people think about other people and themselves and how they come to some kind of coherent understanding of each other. Sometimes what I tell people on airplanes is it's about how people form first impressions of strangers. That's not quite right, but on airplanes it's an effective conversation-stopper when necessary.

In that same interview, Fiske provided an insight to the progress that social cognition and its ancestral theory, had evolved in the last 50 years. She offered the information that the notion of "person as information processor" and the computer metaphor had faded, and fallen out of favor to a degree. She noted that "people are finding it too narrow and too oriented towards sequential, A-leads-to-B-leads-to-C kinds of processes." She explained that, "There are too many things that happen simultaneously, too many things related to emotions, feelings, and behavior."

Fiske published *Social Beings: A Core Motives approach to social psychology* through Wiley, New York, in 2004. In 2004, she was also named to the American Psychological Association Master Lecture award.

---

ingly accepted premise of therapy. At a time when sexual abuse of minors, particularly the major issues of parental abuse, and those regarding accusations against the officials of the Roman Catholic church in the United States, the theory created controversy and continued to do so even 10 years after its publication.

The computer age

Kelly's distaste for labels and the attempts to categorize him has not discouraged the association of his ideas with the explosion of the information-technology age, and the expansion of the computer even in the lives of average people. One e-publication made available through the University of Calgary's Center of Personal Construct Psychology (Alberta, Canada) is entitled "Knowledge Acquisition Tools based on Personal Construct Psychology." Written by Brian R. Gaines and Mildred L. G. Shaw of the Knowledge Science Institute at Calgary, the document chronicles their research into the direct correlation between personal construct psychology and its support of modern-day technology's development. The abstract of their work specified that

> Personal construct psychology is a theory of individual and group psychological and social processes that has been used extensively in knowledge acquisition research to model the cognitive processes of human experts. The psychology takes a constructivist position appropriate to the modeling of human knowledge processes but develops this through the characterization of human conceptual structures in axiomatic terms that translate directly to computational form.

Gaines and Shaw went on to show the close relationship of personal construct psychology to the foundation for artificial intelligence. These researchers have also published further discussion of research that Kelly's work has been significant in cognitive and computational knowledge representation, as "Kelly's 'Geometry of Psychological Space' and its Significance for Cognitive Modeling."

Another major outgrowth of Kelly's repertory grid has been its use for the World Wide Web. Now evolved into WebGrid III, WebGrid is a port of RepGrid/KSS0 used to operate as a service over the World Wide Web. According to its official web site through the University of Calgary, WebGrid requires its users to "define a domain of interest, a context or purpose, and some elements or entities that are a part of the domain and relevant" to the users' purpose. It then gets constructs from users that indicate how they distinguish the elements of their domains that are relevant to their purposes. The system employs a variety of methods for this task, and provides the means for users to compare constructs with other users.

Another example of the inspiration Kelly has been to scientists is the work of two faculty members from the University of the West Indies. S. Haque-Copilah of the department of physics, and S. Rollocks of the department of behavioral sciences, combined in research to determine the parallels between Kelly's theory and Einstein's theory of special relativity.

In his 1966 paper "Ontological Acceleration," Kelly offered yet another challenge for his psychology, as well as that of any. He explained that

> It will not be easy for a psychology modeled on nineteenth century science—and a science that believed that evolution had leveled off, at that—to participate in the accelerated behavioral innovations that promise to change the shape of the human affairs that confront it. Did I say, "not be easy?" I should have said, "be incredible!" Yet I think it should be possible for psychologists, who are less self-conscious about being scientists, to participate in the quickening human enterprise, once they appreciate the creative role of behavior in the affairs of man.

THEORIES IN ACTION

Beginning almost immediately after Kelly published his work, someone began to do research using personal construct psychology as a basis. Kelly was not known to show much interest in acquiring research to support his theories. He found more value in using them abstractly—using them to re-evaluate what people already knew to be true. From that point, experiments could begin with subjects in collaboration with researchers or therapists, continuing to explore the destinations to which all might be headed. Nonetheless, research has been conducted on virtually every aspect of his theory and psychology, in various settings throughout the world. Many examples can be provided. The following represent only a few of them. Modern-day therapists and researchers continue to explore the usefulness of personal construct psychology in a variety of clinical areas that include weight issues, stuttering, post-traumatic stress, substance abuse, grieving and loss, psychotherapy, and, of course, various forms of role therapy. True to Kelly's early work with children, there are many approaches as well in dealing with children—problems with parents, teachers, and the adults' problems with children. In a previously unpublished lecture Kelly had given at the Faculty of General Studies at the University of Puerto Rico in 1958, he even offered direction in how to handle teacher-student relations at a university using his psychology.

Research

According to Jack Adams-Webber of Brock University in Canada, as of 2003, research based on Kelly's psychology only continued to grow. He has noted that certain corollaries have been the subject of extensive research throughout the years. Of those on which he has elaborated are the following: the individuality corollary, the commonality corollary, the sociality corollary, and the range corollary.

Regarding the individuality corollary, following a significant amount of research, Adams-Webber reported that "it has been shown repeatedly that individuals manifest highly stable personal preferences for using particular constructs to interpret events" (noted in Higgins et al., 1982). People were usually found to rate themselves and others more clearly in their own constructs than from any constructs that might have been provided them. Such research has indicated that individuals' own constructs carry more weight due to the personal nature of the viewpoint provided. In another set of research cited by Adams-Webber (Hinkle, 1965; Fransella, 1972; Fransella & Bannister, 1977), there also emerges evidence that each person's constructs are "embedded in a personal context of meaning defined in part by its relationship of implications with other constructs." The basic thrust of this research was that people do not tend to evaluate only the information presented to them. They tend to infer more meaning in the information, also based on previous constructs (Delia et al., 1971). In other research based on the corollary (McDonagh, 1987), the more a person values a particular construction in relation to understanding people, it holds a greater "implication potential"—or proved to increase the number of inferences.

In various findings that spanned from 1971 to 1972, people were shown to be more responsive in social situations among people whose constructs proved to be similar. A series of research studies by Duck (1973), as reported by Adams-Webber, showed that similarity was also significant in forming, developing, and maintaining role relationships. Duck was able to adequately verify that friends as a rule demonstrated "more similarity in terms of elicited personal constructs than pairs of individuals who are not friends." Simply put, a further finding of this research has shown that it is this similarity of construction that usually precedes a friendship, perhaps encouraging it, rather than something that emerges as a result of the friendship. Of the other significant findings, it was found that agreement is greater regarding the pattern of interrelationships among the positive poles of constructs such as "happy" rather than among the negative opposites such as "sad." In findings from research conducted in 1979, Adams-Webber that this "normal usage of the former tends to conform more closely to their standard lexical definitions."

In research focused on the sociality corollary, Niemeyer and Hudson in 1985 suggested that spouses might encourage each other to develop by "validating and extending their systems of understanding." In utilizing a tool known as Crockett's Role Category Questionnaire, (RCQ) Adams-Webber found there was a definite correlation between spouses. People

who fill out the RCQ first nominate a list of acquaintances on the basis of a predetermined set of role categories, such as "a person of the opposite gender whom you like." They then describe that person in detail within a three-minute time limit. The score, known as the cognitive complexity score, represents the number of different personal constructs the person has used across all descriptions. Crockett notes that "if such samples are obtained in a standard manner for a set of people, then the differences in the number of constructs those people employ may be assumed to reflect differences in the total number of constructs that are available to them."

Case studies

In a post-9/11 world and in the midst of terrorist threats—to name only a few traumas of a modern world—utilizing Kelly's psychology to deal with post-traumatic stress is something that could prove to be particularly desirable. In an examination of that, Kenneth W. Sewell of the University of North Texas has provided an approach that he has outlined for the *International Handbook.* He explained that

> the essential feature of Kelly's theory from a post-traumatic stress point of view is found in his fundamental postulate. . .Our psychological processes are channelized by the ways in which we anticipate events. That emphasis makes personal construct theory particularly useful in conceptualizing and helping those who have experienced some trauma.

Sewell offered several case examples from therapy, and in the context of what was necessary in the process for that individual. In order to illustrate certain desired outcomes, Sewell has identified each case under that particular heading.

Symptom management A client identified as an adult male, "Gary," was known to have a very clear memory of the sexual abuse he suffered as a child. Still, when he began therapy he was only able to express his issues in a very vague way. It was early in therapy that Gary realized that overeating was how he sheltered himself from those painful memories. With the help of the therapist, he was able to begin to distinguish between his emotions and his physical hunger. The therapist utilized several techniques including scripted self-talk, "feeling" journal, and relaxation training. These techniques helped Gary handle his disconcerting flashbacks, the sleeplessness his anxiety over the issue had caused him, and his anger, which he was not always able to control, and which would result in sudden outbursts. It was this new way of dealing with his pain that helped him learn what Sewell called "the process of overt introspection."

CHRONOLOGY

1905: Born on a farm near Perth, Kansas, as the only child to Theodore and Elfreda Kelly.

1926: Graduates with a bachelor's degree from Park College, Kansas.

1928: Receives a master's degree from the University of Kansas.

1930: Studies through a fellowship, received a bachelor's degree in education from the University of Edinburgh.

1931: Receives his Ph.D. from the University of Iowa. Married Gladys Thompson on June 3 of that same year.

1941–45: Serves during World War II as a Navy aviation psychologist, and teaches at the University of Maryland.

1946: Accepts the position as director of clinical programs for the school of psychology at the Ohio State University, following Carl Rogers.

1955: W. W. Norton & Company publishes Kelly's groundbreaking, two-volume work, *The Psychology of Personal Constructs*.

1965: Begins research position at Brandeis University where Abraham Maslow was also working at the time.

1967: Dies on March 6.

What resulted for the client was a new role relationship that began his process of reconstructing with the help of a therapist.

Life review   A woman known as Michelle could not assuage the self-blame she felt after she had gotten into a car with a stranger who eventually assaulted her. In the therapy, she was asked to talk about her life before the assault. She expressed the fact that she had experienced abandonment by her parents, and had been street-wise at an early age. Though she was known to be tough as a young child, a trait she developed for survival, Michelle also recounted times of exceptional vulnerability, especially when she was shown kindness by someone. As Sewell noted, "Reconciling what for Michelle were experienced as opposite self-constructions would prove to be a substantial task requisite to readjusting after the trauma." Using the life review or the calling upon a previous metaconstruction, described as "exploring the rear view mirror," Michelle would be able to identify those parts of her past, as well as what of her evaluation needed reconstruction. She would have to risk vulnerability again if she wanted to deal with the therapist successfully enough to enter her world.

Trauma reliving   Tom was a veteran of Vietnam. Every time he even began to approach the details of combat memories, he found a reason to escape the task of going very deeply into the trauma he remembered. He would get what he could from the therapy, but at the same time would act to protect the therapist from the intense pain he had experienced. That resulted in Tom's frustration that he therapist did not understand him very well. Even though the therapist would continue to gently encourage him to relive his memories, offering the safe shelter of time and distance of the therapist's office, the process was difficult. Finally the two of them went together back to war, staying hidden as the enemy disembarked a gunboat searching through the tall grass and eventually finding several of Tom's comrades, according to Sewell. Both Tom and his therapist listened to the screaming of the soldiers and the gunfire that ensued. What was revealed that when the boat was gone, both of them experienced the situation of finding Tom's battalion members tied to trees and skinned alive before they were shot. By reliving this experience together, Tom and his therapist were able to talk from the same place of the painful experience. It would prove to be only the beginning of reconstruction, but the process had finally begun.

Constructive bridging   The client Darla had been both verbally and physically assaulted by a delivery man who had come to her home. She was taking the blame for letting the man into her home, and for not doing more to stop his behavior and protect herself. At first she was not able to look at the situation clearly and examine the sequence of events. When she began to write and talk about the trauma, and then read her account and process it with the previous accounts she had related to the therapist, she was able to also remember what she had done to thwart the attack. As she was able to examine each aspect of her experience, even those she had first viewed as meaningless, she was able to reconstrue herself as someone who acted rather than simply serving as a victim.

Relevance to modern readers

As has already been emphasized, Kelly's psychology has become more widely accepted as an important tool for humans than it was when he introduced it in 1955. America and its people have been through a lot of experiences since that spring day nearly 50 years ago. The national consciousness has had the opportunity to experience its life virtually on a television screen, and through a journey into cyberspace. Though the misconception of the 1950s as simply an ethereal era of stay-at-home mothers and idyllic lives in the suburbs has long been addressed as a misconception, one factor remains true. The presumably "golden age" when Kelly published his new psychology was not only blasted out of range by President Kennedy's assassination, the Vietnam war, and the new age of sexual freedom—as well as the diseases such as AIDS that ultimately came with it. It was, as Kelly would note, altered by years of experience. That being said, why it took so long for so many of his ideas to take hold might be debated for decades to come. In an era when people throughout the world stand against such vivid threats as terrorism or nuclear holocaust, there might be an emerging sense that taking control of life is what is required. At a time when people have so many choices for their lives, when technology offers both caution and promise for the thresholds of new careers, perhaps individuals are ready to face reconstructing their world in order to better partake of the larger one around them.

Kelly once commented that, "To construe is to invent, pure and simple. As far as discovery is concerned, all that one ever discovers is whether or not the predictions, to which his invention has led him, pan out." In the early years of the twenty-first century, the opportunities to find meaning in his theories seem unbounded. Among them, Fransella discussed the several aspects of life that could be explained through the use of personal construct psychology—from music to literary criticism to construing historic decisions.

Franscila wrote in 2003 in her essay, "New Avenues to Explore and Questions to Ask," for the *International Handbook,* that, "One of the few accounts of Kelly's ideas being applied to the world of music comes from Kelly himself in his description of the construction corollary." She noted that every time a person listens to a familiar piece of music, the melody is still recognizable whether it has changed key or rhythm or volume. "Construing is about prediction and anticipation," wrote Fransella, "and a piece of music can only be recognized by our being able to predict those notes that are about to follow."

She has cited a study from Davies (1976) wherein the account of how brass and string players in an orchestra construed each other. Based on the idea that string plays determined that brass players were not as smart, who liked to be in the spotlight, and were often the clowns of the group. The string players were construed by the brass players to be "like a flock of sheep," overly sensitive, and considering themselves to be the true blessings of the musical world. Music exists in the context of movement. Whether it is the experimental jazz of a musician like Sun Ra, or the studied perfection of a classic of Mozart, no piece of music is totally predictable. Numerous studies have been conducted and will continue to be conducted on music and its effects. Should those studies include construing, the revelations about this medium might continue to stun, as well.

With its many implications for an endless range of disciplines and subject, personal construct psychology remains a fascinating tool of exploration. In the political world of a shrinking globe, the way in which the theory could affect insight into history-making decisions was explored by David Gillard in 2002. He said that society "can assume that foreign policy consists of the construing by a small number of identifiable individuals of the behavior of their counterparts in other states," according to Fransella, who went on to explain that, "This they do through identifying their opponents' personal constructs and trying to change of reinforce them by a wide choice of methods, which can range from intimate discussion to total war." The world has witnessed throughout history the way in which some leaders are able to join forces and others are not. Political dispositions, or "constructs," also play a role in the way wars are fought, and laws are made. Gillard's book to be published after 2003, *Why Guarantee Poland?* explores the decision of Britain's Prime Minister in World War II: if Germany attacked Poland, Britain would go to Poland's aid. The controversial matter has long been a subject for discussion of those early war years. Hitler quickly invaded Poland before Britain was ready to join the war—though join the war they did—so such a decision was moot. It was Gillard's opinion that if any approach to understanding international history is valid, it is the theory of personal constructs. Such a notion opens up another possible venue for the future of personal construct psychology. To imagine such a possibility is to imagine that perhaps world diplomacy could be improved through a mutual understanding that leaders would hold for their own constructs as well as those of the others.

BIOGRAPHY:

Elizabeth F. Loftus

Elizabeth F. Loftus, known as the quintessential experimental psychologist, specialized for two decades in the verbal learning field. As a psychologist, Loftus has also specialized in the areas of cognition, law, learning, memory, and psychological statistics. But she gained her greatest notoriety when she became known for her challenge of repressed memory syndrome. With Katherine Ketcham, Loftus published *The Myth of Repressed Memory* in 1994. The dedication at the front of her book would have given George Kelly reason to smile. "Dedicated to the principles of science, which demand that any claim to 'truth' be accompanied by proof."

Elizabeth Fishman was born in Los Angeles in 1944. She grew up in the Bel Air section of the city. When she was 14 her mother drowned. By her own admission, that tragic incident had a profound effect on her life. She attended University of California Los Angeles (UCLA) and received a B.A. in 1966, intending originally to be a high school math teacher. Once her interest turned to psychology after a class she enjoyed at UCLA, her future path was redefined. She received her Ph.D. from Stanford University in 1970. While attending Stanford she met Geoffrey Loftus, whom she married in 1968. It was at Stanford that she first became interested in long-term memory. Both she and her husband received positions at the University of Washington in 1972. They divorced in 1991. Loftus continues to hold an affiliate professorship at the University of Washington, while holding a professorship at the University of California at Irvine. There she is a Distinguished Professor for the Department of Criminology, Law, and Society; and with the Department of Cognitive Sciences. She is also a Fellow of the Center for the Neurobiology of Learning and Memory.

In the early 1970s Loftus first began her research in remembering and misremembering of episodes that came from watching "interactions between different kinds of information, e.g., linguistic, memorial and visual." according to the *Biographical Dictionary of Psychology.* This biography also noted that her research in this field eventually gained her "legendary status," with its research the most heavily cited from any to come from experimental psychology. Her "eyewitness paradigm" presented the eyewitness with photographic slides that chronicled an incident such as an automobile accident. She provided a series of questions about it, some misleading. Her research showed that a "blending" occurs with the eyewitness, and appears to be irreversible. These blendings do not result in false recollection of minor details, she found. What inevitably resulted whether inside or outside the courtroom, was far more dramatic, and could lead to crucial mistakes in determining the truth of an event. Her findings also showed that memory could be manipulated—a damaging trend especially when deciding someone's guilt or innocence.

Her research in memory eventually extended to traumatic events, and those that might include

Elizabeth Loftus. (Photo courtesy of Dr. Elizabeth Loftus. Reproduced by permission.)

"repressed" memories. Such memories of sexual, physical, or psychological abuse could be enhanced, Loftus found, by various methods, including hypnosis, imagination exercises, and guided visualization—even sodium amytal, or other "truth" serums. Loftus has questioned the value of such questionable memory, especially regarding its acceptability in court.

Even the human relations as demonstrated on the television reality shows of the early twenty-first century might be examined through the lens of constructs, especially when the "survival" of a group member be dependent on an individual's stamina—whether it is winning a spot in a Fortune 500 corporation or winning the heart of an attractive person. Indeed, what these reality shows have to say about people and how they construe their universe could possibly become a whole new area of study by the next decade.

The system offered by Kelly's grid has already proven to be a practical tool for the computer age. The promise of what it could offer to further human understanding of artificial intelligence remains to be seen. All of the advances possible have by no means yet been exhausted.

Each few years new trends reveal the manners and fashion of entire cultures. In 2004, globalization continues to redefine the workplace as well as leisure activities. It thus creates opportunities for study from which personal construct psychology and the self-determination it represents will likely benefit.

An appropriate quote from Kelly offers true light into the future possibilities from his work.

> What we know as the body of science, (is) in itself, an amazing display. But this is not the most exciting part of the story that history has to tell us. . . . Infinitely more exciting is what potentiality these audacious feats suggest is locked up in the unrealized future of the [human]. While the [human] of yesterday was developing a physicalistic science that tested itself by experiments and its ability to predict their outcomes, [the human] was, without intending to do so, stating the basic postulates of a psychology for the [human] of tomorrow. Slowly [he] demonstrated not merely that events could be predicted, but, what was vastly more important, that [he] was a predictor. It was not only that hypotheses could be generated, experiments controlled, anticipation checked against realizations, and theories revised, but that [he] [human] was a hypothesizer, an experimenter, an anticipator, a critical observer, and an artful composer of new systems of thought. What [he] did, physically, portrayed what he was psychologically.

BIBLIOGRAPHY

Sources

American Psychological Society. March 2004. http://www.psychologicalscience.org.

Atherton, J. S. *Learning and Teaching: Personal Construct Psychology.* United Kingdom. 2003 [cited March 14, 2004]. http://www.dmu.ac.uk/~jamesa/learning/personal.htm.

Baron, Reuben M., and William G. Graziano, with Charles Stangor. *Social Psychology.* The Society for the Psychological Study of Social Issues (SPSII), Fort Worth, Texas: Holt, Rinehart and Winston, Inc., 1991.

Boeree, C. George. *Personality Theories.* e-text, Shippensburg, Pennsylvania: Shippensburg University, 1997. http://www.ship.edu/~cgboeree/perscontents.html.

Clinical Psychology and Personality: Selected Papers of George Kelly (published posthumously), edited by B. A. Maher. Wiley, 1969.

Fiske, Susan T. *Social Beings: A Core Motives Approach to Social Psychology.* 1st ed. New York: Wiley, 2003.

Fransella, Fay. *Centre for Personal Construct Psychology.* [cited March 3, 2004] http://www.centrepcp.ndirect.co.uk.

Fransella, Fay, ed. *International Handbook of Personal Construct Psychology.* Chichester, England: John Wiley & Sons, LTD, 2003.

Kelly, George A. *The Psychology of Personal Constructs.* Two volumes. New York: W. W. Norton & Company, 1955.

Kenny, Vincent. "An Introduction to the Personal Construct Psychology of George A. Kelly." *Irish Journal of Psychotherapy* 3, no. 1 (March 1984).

Krupat, Edward. *Psychology is Social, Readings and Conversations in Social Psychology.* Harper Collins College Publishers.

Levy-Leboyer, Claude. "Personality: Theories and Applications." *Personnel Psychology* (book review), 56, no. 2 (Summer 2003): 507.

Loftus, Elizabeth, and Katherine Ketcham. *The Myth of Repressed Memory.* New York: St. Martin's Press, 1994.

Shaw, Mildred L. G., and Brian R. Gaines. "Kelly's 'Geometry of Psychological Space,' and its Significance for Cognitive Modeling." *The New Psychologist* October 1992, 23–31.

Sheehy, Noel, Antony J. Chapman, and Wendy A Conroy, editor. *Biographical Dictionary of Psychology.* London and New York: Routledge, 1997.

Warren, Bill. "The problem of religion for constructivist psychology." *Journal of Psychology* 127, no. 5 (Sept. 1993): 481.

Further readings

Neimark, Jill. "The diva of disclosure, memory researcher Elizabeth Loftus." *Psychology Today* January 1996.

Peplau, Letitia Anne, David O. Sears, Shelley E. Taylor, and Jonathan L. Freedman. *Readings in Social Psychology, Classic and Contemporary Contributions.* 2nd ed. Englewood Cliffs, New Jersey: Prentice Hall, 1988.

The Personal Construct Psychology Information Centre, Hamburg, Germany. *Personal Construct Psychology Information Centre.* March 2004. http://www.pcp-net.de.

Westmeyer, Hans. "On the constructive alternativism of George A. Kelly." *PSYCHOLOGISCHE BEITRÄGE* 3, no. 44, 2002.

Lawrence Kohlberg

BRIEF OVERVIEW

Lawrence Kohlberg was regarded for many years as a leader in the field of moral education and development. Trained in an institution identified with the progressive education ideals of American philosopher John Dewey, Kohlberg came to be regarded by his colleagues as more of an educator than a psychologist. Dissatisfied with the traditional character formation, behaviorist, and psychoanalytic models of moral behavior that were available to educators in the 1960s, Kohlberg worked out an approach to moral development known as cognitive structuralism, or cognitive developmentalism. This approach focuses on the growing child's processes of moral reasoning and the changes that take place in the structures of a person's thinking as he or she matures from childhood into adult life. Cognitive developmentalists regard children as independent agents capable of thinking for themselves about moral issues, as contrasted with the Freudian view of children as passive recipients of moral values imposed on them by adults. Kohlberg is best known for his stage theory, which postulated that human moral development progresses through a series of cognitive stages defined as total ways of thinking about moral issues rather than as attitudes toward specific situations.

Kohlberg regarded his work as interdisciplinary, insofar as he believed that moral education must combine psychological research with the insights of moral philosophy. He named John Dewey and Émile Durkheim as his predecessors in the "grand tradition"

1927–1987

AMERICAN PSYCHOLOGIST, EDUCATOR

UNIVERSITY OF CHICAGO, PhD, 1958

Lawrence H. Kohlberg. *(Harvard Office of News and Public Affairs. Reproduced by permission.)*

of unifying these two disciplines. Kohlberg believed that he had succeeded in meeting four requirements that he considered essential to a satisfactory system of moral education:

- It should be based on "the psychological and sociological facts of moral development."

- It should make use of educational methods that stimulate moral change.

- It should be based on a "philosophically defensible" definition of morality.

- It should be compatible with a system of government that guarantees freedom of religious belief.

Although cognitive developmentalists dominated moral education programs for a number of years—Kohlberg's stage theory has been outlined in every college-level psychology textbook published in the past three decades—their approach has been partially supplanted since the early 1980s by character education models. Because of Kohlberg's interest in the practical application of his educational theories as well as their relationship to other disciplines, he did not have extensive influence within the field of psychology itself. In addition, he did not leave behind a large collection of writings or major institutional foundations. Kohlberg's publications were almost entirely in the form of journal articles or book chapters, many coauthored with colleagues, rather than book-length, single-author manuscripts. And although he founded the Center for Moral Education at Harvard shortly after he came to the university, the Center survives as of the early 2000s only in the form of the Risk and Prevention program within the Harvard Graduate School of Education. Moreover, Kohlberg's theories drew considerable criticism from psychologists as well as educators, even during his lifetime. He was, however, widely admired as a teacher, and it may well be that his most important legacy to psychology is the number of former students that he inspired to enter the field.

BIOGRAPHY

Early years

Lawrence Kohlberg was born on October 25, 1927, in Bronxville, New York, an affluent suburb of New York City. His family was well-to-do. Kohlberg's father, Alfred Kohlberg, was an importer of Asian merchandise, while his mother, Charlotte Albrecht, was an amateur chemist. She was his father's second wife. Kohlberg was the youngest of four children; he had two older sisters and one older brother. His parents separated while Kohlberg was still a child. The family's religious background was Jewish, which influenced Kohlberg's later emphasis on justice as well as his commitment to putting his theories into practice.

Kohlberg completed his secondary education at Phillips Academy in Andover, Massachusetts, a private boarding school. Although the school has always been known for its rigorous academic standards, Kohlberg was not particularly interested in intellectual matters during his high school years. A recent appreciation of his life noted that his classmates remembered him "far more for his sense of mischief and forays to nearby girls' schools than for his interest in academic theories." Kohlberg was placed on probation at one point for violating the school's regulations. He later recalled that he had tried to compete in that regard with the school's most famous alumnus—Humphrey Bogart—who had been expelled from Phillips Academy for disciplinary reasons. Kohlberg added that if anyone had predicted at that time that he would specialize in moral education, he would not have believed them.

Kohlberg graduated from Phillips in 1945, but he did not go on to college until the fall of 1948. Although he was too young to serve in the armed forces, he became committed to Zionism—the establishment of the state of Israel. After World War II ended in August 1945 with the surrender of Japan, Kohlberg took advantage of the end of hostilities to go to Europe, where he interviewed survivors of the Holocaust. He then joined the merchant marine and served as second engineer on a South American freighter. The connection between this employment and the Zionist cause was that the freighter smuggled European Jews into Palestine past the British block-ade. Kohlberg's participation in this smuggling was a dangerous activity in the late 1940s, as it was consid-ered an international crime. He maintained a well-developed sense of humor, however; he recalled with glee in later years that he and his shipmates fooled government inspectors by telling them that the ship's improvised beds for its passengers were really containers for storing bananas. When the freighter's true operation was discovered, Kohlberg was arrested and imprisoned for a time in a British internment camp on the island of Cyprus. After his release, he lived as a refugee on an Israeli kibbutz, or agricultural collective. His experience led him to ponder the moral dimensions of disobeying authority, a question he phrased to himself as "When is it permissible to be involved with violent means for supposedly just ends?" Kohlberg eventually returned to Israel in 1969 to study the moral development of young people living in a left-wing kibbutz. This visit proved to be a critical turning point in his later professional career.

Kohlberg returned to the United States in 1948 and applied for entrance to the University of Chicago. His scores on the admissions examinations were so high that he was exempted from most of the univer-sity's course requirements. As a result, he was able to complete his bachelor's degree in one year. Although his first interest had been philosophy, he remained at Chicago to do graduate work in psychology. Kohlberg's explorations of such philosophers as Plato, John Locke, John Stuart Mill, and John Dewey did, however, exert an ongoing influence on his thinking about moral education.

Doctoral research and early teaching career

Kohlberg had the good fortune to study under some of the most outstanding American psychologists of the 1950s during his graduate school years, including such well-regarded researchers as Bruno Bettelheim (1903–1990), Robert Havighurst (1900–1991), Carl Rogers (1902–1987), and Anselm Strauss (1916–1996). When Kohlberg began his graduate work, he initially assumed he would become a clinical psychologist

PRINCIPAL PUBLICATIONS

- *Essays on Moral Development.* Vol. 1, *The Philosophy of Moral Development.* San Francisco: Harper & Row, 1981.
- *Essays on Moral Development.* Vol. 2, *The Psychology of Moral Development.* San Francisco: Harper & Row, 1984.
- With Anne Colby. *The Measurement of Moral Judgment.* Cambridge, UK: Cambridge University Press, 1987.
- With F. C. Power and Ann Higgins. *Lawrence Kohlberg's Approach to Moral Education.* New York: Columbia University Press, 1989.

rather than a researcher, but he was captivated by the writings of the Swiss child psychologist Jean Piaget (1896–1980)—particularly Piaget's account of the moral development of children. Piaget maintained that children's processes of moral reasoning changed as they grew older. In 1955 Kohlberg began a research project for his doctoral dissertation that involved inter-viewing 72 male children and adolescents about moral issues. Kohlberg used the now-famous dilemma of "Heinz," reprinted in the accompanying sidebar, to draw out his subjects' patterns of moral reasoning, as well as to elicit their specific answers to the dilemma. Kohlberg discerned six stages of moral development, divided into three levels, in the material that he outlined in his dissertation. These stages ranged from a preconventional stage, characterized by self-interest, to higher stages associated with subscription to conventional moral standards for the good of society, as well as a specific stage that Kohlberg defined as "postconventional morality." Kohlberg identified postconventional morality with moral reasoning based on the principles underlying ethical rules and norms, rather than on uniform applications of rules. When the dissertation was published in 1958, Kohlberg received his choice of job offers from several prestigious institutions.

Kohlberg first accepted an assistant professorship in the psychology department at Yale University in

FURTHER ANALYSIS:
The Case of Heinz

The first version of Heinz' dilemma that is given here is taken from "Continuities in Childhood and Adult Moral Development Revisited," a chapter that Kohlberg contributed in 1973 to a collection of essays on the cognitive developmental approach to moral education.

Story III. In Europe, a lady was dying because she was very sick. There was one drug that the doctors said might save her. This medicine was discovered by a man living in the same town. It cost him $200 to make it but he charged $2,000 for just a little of it. The sick lady's husband, Heinz, tried to borrow enough money to buy the drug. He went to everyone he knew to borrow the money. But he could borrow only half of what he needed. He told the man who made the drug that his wife was dying, and asked him to sell the medicine cheaper [sic] or let him pay later. But the man said, "No, I made the drug and I'm going to make money from it." So Heinz broke into the store and stole the drug.

The second version, called "Heinz and the Drug," is taken from the 1979 edition of James Rest's Defining Issues Test (DIT).

In Europe, a woman was near death from a special kind of cancer. There was one drug that doctors thought might save her. It was a form of radium that a druggist in the same town had recently discovered. The drug was expensive to make, but the druggist was charging ten times what the drug cost to make. He paid $200 for the radium and charged $2,000 for a small dose of the drug. The sick woman's husband, Heinz, went to everyone he knew to borrow the money, but he could get together about $1,000, which is half of what it cost. He told the druggist that his wife was dying, and asked him to sell it cheaper [sic] or let him pay later. But the druggist said, "No, I discovered the drug and I'm going to make money from it." So Heinz got desperate and began to think about breaking into the store and stealing the drug for his wife.

Should Heinz steal the drug? ___ should steal ___ can't decide ___ should not steal

Please rate the following statements in terms of their importance, on a scale of 1 = great importance to 5 = no importance.

1. Whether a community's laws are going to be upheld.
2. Isn't it only natural for a loving husband to care so much for his wife that he'd steal?
3. Is Heinz willing to risk getting shot as a burglar or going to jail for the chance that stealing the drug might help?
4. Whether Heinz is a professional wrestler, or has considerable influence with professional wrestlers.
5. Whether Heinz is stealing for himself or doing this solely to help someone else.
6. Whether the druggist's rights to his invention have to be respected.
7. Whether the essence of living is more encompassing than the termination of dying, socially and individually.
8. What values are going to be the basis for governing how people act toward each other.
9. Whether the druggist is going to be allowed to hide behind a worthless law which only protects the rich anyhow.
10. Whether the law in this case is getting in the way of the most basic claim of any member of society.
11. Whether the druggist deserves to be robbed for being so greedy and cruel.
12. Would stealing in such a case bring about more total good for the whole society or not?

From the list of questions above, select the four most important:

___ Most important

___ Second most important

___ Third most important

___ Fourth most important

1959, but he returned to teach at the University of Chicago in 1962. In 1968 he moved back to the Northeast as a full professor of education and social psychology at Harvard's Graduate School of Education, where he remained until his death in 1987. Kohlberg left Chicago in part because his developmental approach to the psychology of moral education was not well received by some of his colleagues. After his arrival at Harvard, Kohlberg founded the Center for Moral Development and Education, which, however, did not long survive his death. The establishment of the center, however, indicated that Kohlberg was increasingly concentrating his research and writing on psychology in relation to education, rather than on so-called "pure" psychology. In addition, he published several of his most frequently cited articles during his early years at Harvard, particularly "Stage and Sequence: The Cognitive Developmental Approach to Education," which appeared in 1969, and "Development as the Aim of Education," which was published in 1972.

Starting in the late 1960s, some of Kohlberg's students began to put his concepts of moral education into practice. They started with discussions of moral dilemmas among high-school students in order to find out whether the students matured more rapidly as a result of the conversations. One of these studies was published as the author's doctoral dissertation at the University of Chicago in 1973. In 1971, another group of Kohlberg's students started a similar discussion program at the women's prison in Niantic, Connecticut. Kohlberg was intrigued by these projects and became involved with the establishment of alternative schools and what he called "just communities" or "cluster schools" elsewhere. Most of these were located in Massachusetts or New York, but one was set up inside a high school in France. Kohlberg's expectation was that these "just communities" would serve the moral development of their members by allowing everyone, students as well as teachers, to have a voice in articulating and deciding the community's moral norms. Many of these schools, unfortunately, dissolved within a few years of Kohlberg's death. One exception is the Scarsdale Alternative School, described as one of the case studies below. Another just-community school that was founded after Kohlberg's death is the Shalhevet High School in Los Angeles, a private Jewish day school that was founded in 1992 by one of Kohlberg's former students. The school's Web site states explicitly that its approach to education "is based on the Harvard model of moral development, pioneered by Professor L. Kohlberg and supplemented by Carol Gilligan's emphasis on relationships and carings [sic]."

Controversy with Carol Gilligan

In the years since Kohlberg's death, he has become better known in some quarters as the educator who provoked Carol Gilligan's challenge to his theories and method rather than as a major figure in his own right. One of Kohlberg's colleagues has estimated that Gilligan has had a greater impact on moral education than Kohlberg himself. Gilligan did not feel free to discuss publicly her personal friendship as well as her professional relationship with Kohlberg until 1997, when she delivered the Kohlberg Memorial Lecture at the annual meeting of the Association for Moral Education. While Gilligan had never been one of Kohlberg's students or postdoctoral fellows, having completed her own doctorate in 1963, she agreed to teach a section of an undergraduate course that he offered in 1970 on moral and political choice. She then coauthored a paper with Kohlberg that appeared in *Daedalus* in 1971 as "The Adolescent as a Philosopher," an article that is still regarded as a classic statement of Kohlberg's approach to moral education.

Gilligan's experience in teaching the 1970 course, however, was a turning point for her in that she was struck by the reluctance of the young men in the class "to talk about the draft, aware that there was no room in Larry's theory for them to talk about what they were feeling without sounding morally undeveloped. . . finding no room for uncertainty and indecision, they chose silence over hypocrisy." Gilligan had initially planned to follow these students to their graduation to study their choices regarding military service, but she chose instead to study women considering abortion as an example of a real-life dilemma. At that point she was confronted by what she termed a "dissociation," or a split in consciousness, between women's sense of self and their concern for their relationships. Although Gilligan continued to teach courses with Kohlberg, over time their views grew further and further apart. In her words, "It became very hard to have a conversation, and I felt that I was not being heard." To some extent, their professional disagreement reflected differences in their educational backgrounds; Kohlberg had come to psychology through the study of philosophy, while Gilligan had majored in English literature as an undergraduate. Whereas Kohlberg was committed to an ideal of an objective moral good, Gilligan began to introduce the methods of literary analysis into what she has called "a voice-centered relational method of research." She has described her methodological innovations in detail in a book she coauthored with Lyn Mikel Brown, *Meeting at the Crossroads,* which was published in 1992.

In spite of the intellectual friction between Gilligan and Kohlberg, she as well as others who worked with him remarked on his genuine interest in views that differed from his own. Far from being an intellectual dictator, Kohlberg encouraged the School of Education to hire faculty who represented a variety of different positions on human development. One of his postdoctoral students later remarked, "The people that [Kohlberg] brought in did not necessarily agree with him. He would bring in critics. You never felt an 'us/them' or 'either/or' approach with him." Gilligan remarked in her 1997 lecture that ". . . it is extremely important to remember that [Kohlberg] would invite in people who differed from him to talk with him in the public space of his class about these differences." Gilligan went on to state, however, that while Kohlberg thought that her position could be contained within his basic moral paradigm, she was convinced that the paradigm itself was defective.

Marriage and family

Kohlberg married Lucille Stigberg in 1955, while he was still in graduate school. The couple had two sons, David and Steven. The marriage was not a happy one, and the Kohlbergs separated in the mid-1970s. They were finally divorced in 1985. Kohlberg began a relationship with Ann Higgins, a developmental psychologist, during his separation. They became engaged after Kohlberg's divorce, but were not married at the time of his death.

Some of Kohlberg's associates remarked after his death that his family life as well as his health was affected by his unusual degree of openness and availability—to visitors as well as to his students. According to one of his Harvard colleagues, Kohlberg was in the habit of inviting people to visit his home on Cape Cod at any time. The colleague recalled "digging in the sand for oysters and clams with Kohlberg on the Cape, talking about ideas all the while." Another remarked that Kohlberg "got used by people," but added, "I think he knew this went on, but he was so impassioned about his work that he didn't mind."

Last years and death

Kohlberg's work deteriorated after the mid-1970s, in part because of a parasitic illness that he contracted during a research trip in 1971 to Belize in Central America. The infection was eventually diagnosed as giardiasis, which is caused by an intestinal parasite, *Giardia lamblia*. Giardiasis is not a rare disease; it is a common cause of diarrhea throughout the world, often resulting from drinking contaminated

water, and its causative organism is the most frequently identified intestinal parasite in the United States. Most adults recover completely after a few weeks of treatment with antimicrobial and antibiotic medications; however, a minority of patients develop chronic giardiasis. Kohlberg was unable to build up immunity to the parasite, and suffered from intermittent episodes of diarrhea, nausea, and fatigue for the next sixteen years. His physical symptoms were accompanied by emotional depression, which necessitated turning over most of his teaching and research projects to younger associates. In addition, his frequent need to excuse himself during classroom lectures gave him a reputation for "flakiness" and unpredictability.

In addition to his physical illness, Kohlberg experienced professional setbacks in his later years. His six-stage theory of moral development included the premise, described more fully below, that moral development is unidirectional; that is, that people do not move backward to earlier stages of moral maturity once they have attained higher levels. This premise, however, could be tested only by conducting long-term studies of Kohlberg's subjects. He had planned from the outset to retest the subjects he had interviewed for his dissertation every three or four years. A follow-up study of the boys at the 12-year point, however, produced some data that conflicted with Kohlberg's notion that people do not regress to lower stages of moral development after they have moved to higher levels. Specifically, the 12-year follow-up study indicated that some of the subjects had moved from stage four, characterized by adherence to social norms of morality, to stage two, which Kohlberg had defined as essentially self-centered. Kohlberg and his associates responded to these findings by reworking their coding of subjects' responses during interviews. In the revised coding manual, which did not appear until 1987, Kohlberg explicitly defined each stage of moral development as higher than its predecessor.

In the last several years of his life, Kohlberg experimented out of desperation with a variety of alternative treatments for his disease; some of his friends thought that these therapies might have also damaged his health. In early January 1987 he had a major depressive episode, during which he attempted suicide and was taken to Mount Auburn Hospital in Cambridge. On January 17, he obtained a day pass from the psychiatric unit of the hospital. He then drove his car to nearby Winthrop, parked on a dead-end street, and walked into the ocean. His body was not discovered until April 6, when it washed up on the shore of Boston Harbor near Logan Airport.

THEORIES

Nature of virtue

Main points Kohlberg's approach to human moral development was shaped by his studies of the classical Western philosophers as an undergraduate; his remarks on the nature of virtue and the goals of moral education often took the form of a dialogue with the tradition that began with Plato and Aristotle. The English words "virtue" and "morals" are derived from classical Latin rather than Greek: "virtue" from *virtus*, which originally meant "manliness" in the sense of adult moral excellence, and "morals" from *mores*, which is a plural noun meaning "customs" or "usages." Kohlberg was swimming against the current of mainstream academic psychology by beginning with Plato rather than Freud or Skinner as his "most relevant source," as he put it in a book chapter that was published in 1970. He continued, " . . . as I have tried to trace the stages of development of morality and to use these stages as the basis of a moral education program, I have realized more and more that its implication was the reassertion of the Platonic faith in the power of the rational good."

Kohlberg's reference to "good" in the singular was not accidental, as one of his objections to moral education as it had been traditionally practiced was the "bag of virtues," his term for the notion that personality can be divided up into "cognitive abilities, passions or motives, and traits of character. Moral character [in the older view] consists of a bag of virtues and vices." Kohlberg then went on to point out that a major problem with the traditional account of virtue is that no two observers agreed on the contents of the bag. He began with Hartshorne and May, the authors of a landmark study of American character in the 1920s.

> Their bag of virtues included honesty, service, and self-control. . . . Havighurst and Taba added responsibility, friendliness, and moral courage to the Hartshorne and May bag. Aristotle's original bag included temperance, liberality, pride, good temper, truthfulness, and justice. The Boy Scout bag is well known, a Scout should be honest, loyal, reverent, clean, brave.

Kohlberg did not, however, suggest throwing out the concept of virtue along with the bag metaphor. He argued instead, "like Plato, that virtue is not many, but one, and its name is justice." Kohlberg then proceeded to point out that justice is neither a character trait nor a concrete rule of action. He described justice in words that echo German philosopher Immanuel Kant's categorical imperative: "Justice is not a rule or a set of rules, it is a moral principle. By a moral principle we mean a mode of choosing which is universal, a rule of choosing which we want all people to adopt always in all situations. . . . Because morally mature men [sic] are governed by the principle of justice rather than by a set of rules, there are not many moral virtues but one."

Explanation Kohlberg's search for a unitary definition of virtue was intended to address several concerns. First, it was a protest against so-called "value-free" psychology, or the notion that virtues and vices are no more than "labels by which people award praise or blame to others." Kohlberg did not want the history of disagreements over the content of the "bag of virtues" to end in the establishment of value neutrality, which he defined as "the view that all value systems are equally sound," in public education.

> The school is no more committed to value neutrality than is the government or the law. The school . . . is an institution with a basic function of maintaining and transmitting some, but not all, of the consensual values of society. The most fundamental values of a society are termed moral, and the major moral values in our society are the values of justice.

Second, Kohlberg maintained that his concept of justice as a moral principle was applicable across the full range of human societies, thus answering the question of moral relativism raised by some cultural anthropologists. He referred to research carried out by his students on adult as well as child subjects in Mexico, Turkey, Taiwan, and the United Kingdom, as well as the United States, as proof that "in all cultures we find the same forms of moral thinking . . . concepts of the good are culturally universal." In a later article on religious education, he repeated his contention that ". . . liberty and justice are not the particular values of the American culture but culturally universal moral values which develop regardless of religious membership, education, or belief."

Third, Kohlberg's emphasis on a foundational moral principle, identified as justice, rather than on sets of rules to be followed or character traits to be cultivated, was inseparable from his method of moral education. What is important to state at this point, however, is that Kohlberg saw moral education as a process in which the ethical formation of individuals leads to a higher level of justice in the society as a whole. ". . . while the bag of virtues [approach] encapsulated the need for moral improvement in the child, a genuine concern about the growth of justice in the child implies a similar concern for the growth of justice in the society." Otherwise put, Kohlberg maintained that his concept of virtue had a corporate as well as a personal or individual dimension.

Fourth, Kohlberg's emphasis on justice reflected his belief that moral standards and principles are independent of other fields of thought, and cannot be reduced to purely religious (or political) attitudes or principles. He stated in 1981,

> The starting point of rational discourse about the relation of morality and religion, then, is the recognition in some degree of the autonomy of morality and moral discourse from any other form of discourse, whether religious, scientific, or political.

One consequence of his notion that morality is independent of religious beliefs is that he considered moral education to be the province of the schools rather than of churches or synagogues. Kohlberg based his position on the claim that his cross-cultural research showed that "a morality of justice evolves in every society or religious group . . . [and] cannot be said to represent the beliefs of a religious sect . . . or even to represent the 'Judeo-Christian tradition.'" He concluded that religious education has at best a "very limited influence" on moral development.

> I am not attempting to argue that that religious education may not be capable of playing a role in moral development. I am arguing that religious education has no specifically important or unique role to play in moral development as opposed to the role of the public school and the family. . . . the mark of success of [religious] teaching is that it helps the child to make his religious and his moral beliefs and sentiments an integrated whole, not that it leads to the formulation of basic moral values not found elsewhere.

Nature of human moral development

Main points   Consistent with Kohlberg's emphasis on justice as the foundational moral principle, he regarded moral development as largely a cognitive process. In this regard he was a follower of Jean Piaget, whose studies of children focused as early as 1932 on questions of moral development. As has already been mentioned, Kohlberg's selection of a topic for his doctoral dissertation research was prompted by his interest in the Swiss psychologist's work. Kohlberg's high regard for Piaget was reflected in the fact that he devoted three full pages of an 11-page encyclopedia article that he wrote in 1968 on moral education to Piaget's research and theories. Piaget had concluded from his observations of children playing games that they underwent a process of moral as well as intellectual development. He maintained that young children begin with a heteronomous stage of moral reasoning—that is, they accept rules laid down by others (i.e., adults) as well as the duty of strict obedience to authority. Piaget saw the heteronomous stage as the product of two factors: the limitations of the young child's cognitive structure,

which is fundamentally egocentric; and his or her relative powerlessness compared to adults.

Piaget thought that children made the transition to what he called autonomous moral reasoning through their interactions with the environment—specifically, their peer group. As older children play, they sometimes find strict interpretation of the rules of their games problematic. They learn through working out these problems to regard rules more critically, and to selectively apply the rules in the interest of cooperation and mutual respect. Piaget believed that this transition from heteronomy to autonomy was associated with changes in children's cognitive structures that allow them to look at situations from the perspectives of other people as well as from their own. In sum, Piaget thought that moral development among the members of a group arises from interactions that lead to outcomes considered to be fair by all members. He therefore urged educators to encourage cooperative decision-making and problem-solving among schoolchildren that would lead to rules for the whole group based on fairness. This approach transformed the teacher's role in moral education from one of indoctrinating students with social norms to one of fostering children's personal growth through undertaking cooperative tasks with others.

Kohlberg's 1968 article took issue with Piaget in two major respects. First, Kohlberg argued that cross-cultural research did not support Piaget's assumption, taken from French sociologist Émile Durkheim, that children in the heteronomous stage regard rules as having a "sacral" character that can never be changed; rather, he maintained, the children's acceptance of rules is based "on a more or less pragmatic concern for consequences," i.e., punishment. Second, Kohlberg thought that Piaget was wrong in predicating a general movement from an authoritarian stage of moral development based on submission to adults to a more democratic ethic based on membership in a peer group. "Postulated general age shifts from obedience to authority to peer loyalty, from justice based on conformity to justice based on equality, have not been generally found."

Where Kohlberg agreed with Piaget is telling, though, as he believed his dissertation research supported his position. ". . . however, Piaget is correct in assuming a culturally universal age development of a sense of justice, involving progressive concern for the needs and feelings of others and elaborated conceptions of reciprocity and equality." Kohlberg moved beyond Piaget in carrying his research into older age groups than those that Piaget had studied, concluding that "adult institutions [as well as children's peer groups] have underpinnings of reciprocity, equality of treatment, service to human needs, etc. The last-mentioned conclusion is derived primarily from cross-cultural research by this writer and his colleagues. . . ." The implication of Kohlberg's extension of the age groups under consideration to include adolescents and young adults was that moral development is both a longer and more complex process than Piaget had described.

Explanation It is useful to contrast Piaget's and Kohlberg's cognitive developmental perspective on moral maturation with other models that were being used by American educators in the 1960s. Three of these were the traditional character formation model, the Freudian psychoanalytic model, and the social altruism model. They all emphasized the non-rational dimension of human moral development, coupled with an absence of a definitive pattern or schedule of moral development. In traditional character education, the child's parents or teachers acquaint the child with the contents of their particular "bag of virtues," in Kohlberg's phrase, and impart these virtues to the child through direct discussion of them and by exemplifying them in their own conduct. The child is then given opportunities to practice these virtues and is rewarded for so doing. Kohlberg quotes an example of this approach from one of American author Jonathan Kozol's books in his article "Education for Justice." Kozol was describing a curriculum guide for character education published by the Boston public school system:

> The section on self-control begins by [mention of] the necessity for self-control by all people. The teacher is then advised to give examples of self-disciplined people, Abraham Lincoln, Charles Lindbergh, Robinson Crusoe, Florence Nightingale, Dwight D. Eisenhower.

Presumably the teacher underscores the content of the lesson by maintaining his or her self-control in dealing with disruptive classroom behavior.

According to the psychoanalytic model, however, moral development is in essence a process of internalization, in which the child acquires the culture's norms and values through identification with the parents and other adult authorities. Freud referred to the part of the personality that represented the conscience as the superego, or *über-ich* in the original German. The superego is formed through the resolution of the child's Oedipal complex, in which the child gives up his or her infantile wish to possess the parent of the opposite sex, and identifies through fear of retaliation with the parent of the same sex. The superego thus functions as a kind of inner censor that regulates external behavior through the arousal of guilty feelings. The essence of moral conduct in the Freudian view is that people follow their consciences in order to avoid guilt. An example of a psychoanalytic account of problem behavior in children is one psychiatrist's explanation of schoolyard bullying. Bullying, according to Freudian theory, represents a combination of rage at having to renounce one's mother, fear of the mother's all-pervasive influence, and revenge against the mother for putting the child in this predicament. Although Freud did identify five stages in childhood development (oral, anal, phallic, latency, and genital), related to specific age groups, these stages refer to psychosexual maturation rather than to growth in moral reasoning.

The third model is usually identified with the French sociologist Émile Durkheim (1858–1917), who regarded moral rules as social products rather than the pronouncements or convictions of individuals. The mere fact that a moral rule exists lends it a sacral quality, according to Durkheim. The "group mind" thus logically as well as chronologically precedes the individual's development. The psychological roots of a person's moral attitudes lie in his or her respect for the group, the convictions held in common by the group, and the leaders or authority figures of the group. An individual's core values will then be those that are most widely shared by other members of the group and serve to bind the group most closely together. In other words, people behave morally because they have internalized their society's collective conscience, not because they are afraid of external social restraints or sanctions. Durkheim's position has sometimes been described as moral collectivism; he not only regarded society as the sole determinant of moral rules, but he also believed that society has a moral reality of its own apart from the existence of its individual members. Kohlberg acknowledged his intellectual debt to Durkheim regarding the social origins of moral norms, but disagreed with the French scholar's tendency to think of moral education as "the promotion of collective national discipline" instead of the development of individuals guided by principled morality.

Examples The examples of moral development that will be given in this section are taken from Piaget's *Moral Judgment of the Child,* first published in 1932, to give the reader a basis for comparison with Kohlberg's six stages.

Piaget maintained that younger children do not take a person's intention into account in evaluating a situation, but only the objective outcome. In one example, the interviewer tells two anecdotes about the breakage of household items and asks the child to compare the behavior of the children in the anecdotes. "... I am going to tell you two more stories. A little girl was wiping the cups. She was putting them away, wiping them with the cloth, and she broke five cups. Another little girl is playing with some plates. She breaks a plate. Which of them is the naughtiest [sic]?" The child answers, "The one who broke the five cups."

Piaget used a more complex story to illustrate the difference between younger and older children in placing loyalty to the peer group over unquestioning submission to adult authority. The story is as follows:

> Once, long ago ... there was a father who had two sons. One was very good and obedient. The other was a good sort, but he often did silly things. One day the father goes off on a journey and says to the first son: "You must watch carefully to see what your brother does, and when I come back you shall tell me." The father goes away and the brother goes and does something silly. When the father comes back he asks the first boy to tell him everything. What ought the boy to do?

Piaget found that younger children (between the ages of six and seven) almost always said that the father should be told everything. Children over the age of eight, however, usually replied that "nothing should be told, and some even [went] so far as to prefer a lie to the betrayal of a brother."

Stages of moral development

Main points   Kohlberg divided his six stages of moral development across three levels, with two stages at each level. His descriptions of each stage changed somewhat over the three decades of his teaching career. The descriptions that follow are taken from the second volume of his *Essays on Moral Development,* published in 1984.

Level I: Preconventional morality:

- Stage 1: Heteronomous morality, or the punishment-and-obedience orientation. *What is right*: Avoidance of breaking rules backed by punishment and obedience for its own sake. *Reasons for doing right*: Fear of punishment and the superior power of authorities. *Social perspective*: Egocentric; actions considered from a physical rather than a psychological point of view; cannot take viewpoints of others into account.

- Stage 2: Individualism and instrumental purpose, or the instrumental-relativist orientation. *What is right*: Acting to meet one's own interests or needs and allowing others to do the same; right defined as "what's fair" or "what's expedient." Kohlberg sometimes summarized the morality of Stage 2 as

"You scratch my back and I'll scratch yours." *Reasons for doing right*: To serve one's own needs in a world in which one is forced to recognize that others also have needs. *Social perspective*: Concrete individualism, defined as the awareness that people's interests and needs sometimes conflict.

Level II: Conventional morality:

- Stage 3. Interpersonal expectations and conformity, or the "good boy, good girl" orientation. *What is right*: Living up to what is expected by people close to oneself; "being good" is important and implies trust, loyalty, and gratitude in interpersonal relations. *Reasons for doing right*: The need to be a good person in one's own eyes and those of others; the Golden Rule. *Social perspective*: Centered on relationships with specific other individuals.

- Stage 4. Social system and conscience, or the "law-and-order" orientation. *What is right*: Fulfilling duties to which one has agreed; doing "what is right" includes upholding the laws and contributing to one's group or to society as a whole. *Reasons for doing right*: To meet the demands of one's conscience, and to keep society going. *Social perspective*: Takes account of society as a whole and understands personal relationships as situated within the larger social system.

Level III: Postconventional or principled morality:

- Stage 5. Social contract or legalistic orientation. *What is right*: Awareness of the variety of perspectives and opinions within the larger society; duty defined as general avoidance of arbitrary violations of the rights of others. *Reasons for doing right*: A sense of obligation to laws that uphold the social contract; concern for the protection of all people's rights. *Social perspective*: Considers rights and values as entities that exist prior to social contracts and relationships.

- Stage 6. Universal ethical principle orientation. *What is right*: Following self-chosen ethical principles and obeying specific laws only insofar as they rest on such principles. *Reasons for doing right*: Belief as a rational person in the existence and validity of universal moral principles, and personal commitment to them. *Social perspective*: Based on a moral principle from which particular social arrangements are derived.

Explanation   In addition to defining the stages themselves, Kohlberg had clear-cut views about the trajectory of moral development through the six stages. To begin with, he assumed that while moral development is age-related in a broad sense, it is not age-dependent; in other words, in any group of children or adolescents of the same age, some will have achieved higher levels of moral maturity than others. Kohlberg thought that the two stages of preconventional morality are most commonly seen in children younger than nine, although some adolescents and many criminal offenders remain at this level. Conventional morality he regarded as characteristic of most adolescents and adults in Western societies. By contrast, postconventional or autonomous morality is found only among a minority of adults, and is usually attained only after the age of 20.

Second, Kohlberg argued that moral development is unidirectional; that is, people do not fall backward to lower levels of moral development after they have progressed to higher ones. He also maintained that people usually prefer to solve their moral dilemmas at the highest level of moral development that they have reached. Moreover, Kohlberg did not believe that it is possible for people to skip stages, although he sometimes allowed that they might be able to gain a purely intellectual understanding of moral reasoning two stages above their current level of development.

Kohlberg did, however, remain open to the possibility that his stages might require redefinition or renumbering. Although he was convinced that empirical research proved the existence of his first five stages, he allowed in his later years, following intense criticism of his research, that his sixth stage might be more hypothetical than real. He removed it from the scoring manual he had compiled for his moral development test, but retained it as "a theoretical construct in the realm of philosophical speculation." In addition to his original six stages, he and some of his associates postulated that there might be "a high seventh stage," which would include individuals whose moral reasoning transcended the principle of justice, deriving its meaning from a cosmic perspective that might be explicitly religious, pantheistic, or agnostic. Kohlberg spoke in 1983 of some older adults whose post-postconventional moral principles were "in harmony with the evolution of human nature and the cosmic order." In sum, his seventh stage was an attempt to explain more precisely the relationship between morality and religion.

Examples   Stage 1. Kohlberg cited the following statements of Nazi criminal Adolf Eichmann at his trial for crimes against humanity in 1961–62 as examples of Stage 1 morality.

In actual fact, I was merely a little cog in the machinery that carried out the directives of the German Reich. . . . Where would we have been if everyone had thought things out in those days? You can do that in the 'new' German army. But with us an order was an order. . . . If I had sabotaged the order of the one-time Führer of the German Reich, Adolf Hitler, I would have been not only a scoundrel but a despicable pig like those who . . . join[ed] the ranks of the anti-Hitler criminals in the conspiracy of July 20, 1944.

Stage 2. Kohlberg once used his own son as an example of Stage 2 moral development, as well as proof that the children of moral educators are not necessarily models of virtue at an early age.

. . . my son moved to an expedient Stage 2 orientation when he was six. He told me . . . "You know the reason people don't steal is because they're afraid of the police. If there were no police around everyone would steal." Of course I told him that I and most people didn't steal because we thought it wrong. . . . My son's reply was, "I just don't see it, it's sort of crazy not to steal if there are no police."

Stage 3. Kohlberg cites an Israeli boy's response to the Heinz dilemma as an instance of Stage 3 conventional morality focused on interpersonal relationships.

In one way, if everyone were to break in [to a store] when we need something, where would we get to? But [Heinz] wants to save [his wife] and his feelings would make him do it. He should do it for his wife, after all he wants to save her. Maybe he won't get caught and everything will go all right. This little [bit of] radium wouldn't make such a big difference for the druggist and it would save his wife's life.

Stage 4. Kohlberg gives a sixteen-year-old child's response to a moral dilemma regarding euthanasia— whether a physician should administer a lethal dose of a drug to a woman in extreme pain who wants to die— as an instance of Stage 4 moral development.

I don't know. In one way, it's murder, it's not a right or privilege of man to decide who shall live and who should die. God put life into everybody on earth and you're taking away something from that person that came directly from God. . . . it's in a way part of God and it's almost destroying a part of God when you kill a person. There's something of God in everyone.

Stage 5. An example of Stage 5 morality is the statement of a Vietnam veteran with a doctorate in chemical engineering who was interviewed when he was thirty.

Morality is a series of value judgments. For me to say something is morally right means that in my own conscience, based on my experience and feelings, I would judge it right. But it is up to the individual . . .

to determine if something is right, it need not be right all the time. I guess what I am saying is, I don't think I have a moral right to impose my moral standards on anyone else. Society . . . gets together in groups primarily for the good of themselves in general, but at the same time they then recognize that there is a certain benefit to do things for the good of society, according to a certain set of standards.

Stage 6. Kohlberg regarded one of Martin Luther King Jr.'s statements about civil disobedience as proof that King had progressed to Stage 6:

> One may well ask, "How can you advocate breaking some laws and obeying others?" The answer lies in the fact that there are two types of laws, just and unjust. One has not only a legal but a moral responsibility to obey just laws. One has a moral responsibility to disobey unjust laws. Any law that uplifts human personality is just, any law that degrades human personality is unjust.

Methods of moral education

Main points Kohlberg's cognitive developmental approach to moral education was focused on the child or adolescent's processes of moral reasoning rather than on his or her mastery of abstract concepts, emotional self-control, or outward behavioral conformity to moral norms. As a result, Kohlberg regarded progress from one moral stage to the next as a transformation in the person's overall pattern of moral reasoning. According to Kohlberg, at any given stage in the sequence a person can make moral decisions only within the cognitive limits of that stage. He or she then acts according to his or her understanding of the social environment. At some point, however, the child or adolescent encounters a new situation that does not fit into their present picture of the social world. The young person must then adjust their view to account for the new information. Kohlberg called this cognitive readjustment "equilibration," and he saw it as a necessary stimulus to moral development. He and his students then sought to assist children's progress to higher stages by three specific means: presentation and discussion of moral dilemmas; the establishment of alternative schools or "just communities"; and what Kohlberg described as "exposure to moral reasoning above one's own stage of reasoning." While exploration of moral dilemmas might facilitate the maturation of individual students, Kohlberg maintained that participation in a democratic school community was also necessary for moral growth because it allowed students to "learn by doing." In addition, Kohlberg remarked that "because democratic [school] meetings deal with real-life problems and resolutions, they may more effectively promote moral development than discussions of hypothetical dilemmas."

One should note, however, that Kohlberg's work with just communities was not built into his early research; rather, it emerged from his recognition in the late 1960s and early 1970s that his stage theory of moral development had definite limitations. This recognition was forced on him partly by researchers in educational sociology (as distinct from educational psychology), and partly by his own experiences with actual communities. The specific observation that unsettled Kohlberg was the catchphrase "hidden" or "unstudied curriculum," coined by Philip Jackson, at that time chair of the Elementary Education Council of the Association for Supervision and Curriculum Development. Jackson's 1968 book, entitled *Life in Classrooms*, defined "90 percent of what goes on in classrooms" as a form of social education unrelated to the subject supposedly being taught in class. Jackson thought of the school's hidden curriculum as a "way station" between a child's experience of personal relationships in his or her family and the impersonal achievement orientation of adult life. Jackson summarized the three chief "lessons" of the hidden curriculum as "the crowds, the praise, and the power." "Crowds" refers to the fact that the school-age child must adjust to living and learning among a "crowd" of others of the same age and status. "Praise" and "power" refer to the child's learning to accept the power of and take orders from an impersonal authority figure rather than parents.

Kohlberg's addition to Jackson's sociological analysis was the claim he made in an article on "The Moral Atmosphere of the School" that ". . . the only integrated way of thinking about the hidden curriculum is to think of it as moral education." One of the implications of the hidden curriculum is that children often develop a split between their moral thinking and their actual conduct; for example, they may say what they think the teacher wants to hear during a classroom discussion of justice, for example, yet act as if the competitive practices needed to succeed in school are the real "rules of the game." Kohlberg concluded, however, that the task of the moral educator was not to do away with "the crowds, the praise, and the power," but rather to incorporate the principle of justice within the hidden curriculum itself. "The teaching of justice requires just schools. The crowds, the praise, and the power are neither just nor unjust in themselves. . . . The problem is not to get rid of [them], but to establish a more basic context of justice which gives them meaning."

The next event that stimulated Kohlberg's thinking about just communities was his visit to an Israeli kibbutz. In 1969, a year after the publication of

Jackson's book, Kohlberg accepted an invitation from the Youth Aliyah organization to observe and conduct interviews on a left-wing kibbutz that had attracted his interest. This particular collective farm was unusual in that it educated some lower-class urban adolescents alongside teenagers who had grown up on the kibbutz. Kohlberg conducted a study of these youth in order to test the effectiveness of the kibbutz's educational program in fostering moral development; he found that the young people from the kibbutz scored significantly higher on his tests than a sample of Israeli urban youth. Kohlberg was particularly impressed by the way the Madrich, or educator in charge of the high school program, dealt with the tension between the kibbutz's commitment to the values of justice and equality, and the need for strong cohesion among the members of the group. Kohlberg regarded the kibbutz's educational program as having a dual focus: to maintain collective discipline while doing so in a way that respects democratic process and individual differences or dissent.

Kohlberg did not return from his visit to Israel with a fully worked-out model of group educational practice. Over the next few years, however, he put together a list of characteristics that he considered essential to a model program of moral education through group membership:

- The student's social identity should be defined by the group, and the group should define normative standards of appropriate behavior.

- The group should discipline its members—informally at first, and then by the group as a whole if necessary.

- The members should become emotionally attached to the group, and to other members of the group, both as individuals and because they share a common social identity.

- Group members should be expected to develop a sense of collective responsibility, such that each member recognizes that he or she is in a sense responsible for the behavior of the others.

- Discussions of values and value conflicts should be conducted to promote the group's improvement as a social unit as well as serve the moral development of individual members.

- The educator's role should include introducing the group to the values of the larger society as well as facilitating moral discussions and decisions within the group.

Interestingly, Kohlberg's first experiment with forming a just community in the United States did not take place in a high school or other educational setting but in a prison. This turn of events came about in part as a result of prison riots at Attica and elsewhere in the late 1960s, which made correctional officers more open to new approaches to prison reform. Kohlberg had two colleagues who were interested in prison work. The three researchers obtained a two-year grant and began conducting discussion groups inside a state prison for men located in Cheshire, Connecticut. They quickly discovered that any positive influences they had on the inmates' levels of moral reasoning could not be put into action within the prison environment. Kohlberg's group then looked for a setting in which they could set up a small model community that would embody the kind of group cohesion that Kohlberg had seen in the Israeli kibbutz. They discovered that the women's prison at Niantic, Connecticut, was organized into small group cottages housing 20–30 women apiece. In 1971 Kohlberg's team received permission to set up a model just community in one of the cottages. The Niantic prison project is described in further detail in the section on case studies; its significance here is that it encouraged Kohlberg to try out his educational theories in schools outside prison walls.

Explanation   Kohlberg's approach to moral education was intended at least in part to account for two phenomena that have confronted researchers in the field of moral education since the 1920s. The first is the gap between what people say about their moral standards and the way they actually behave in various situations. The pioneering study by Hartshorne and May in the 1920s was a landmark because of its finding that moral behavior could not be attributed to permanent character traits that shaped the person's conduct in all circumstances; rather, it was influenced by situational factors that included the likelihood of punishment or reward, pressure from the peer group, and the values held by other members of the child's social class. Hartshorne and May found that there was surprisingly little correlation between what children had learned about the virtue of honesty, for example, and the likelihood of their cheating during experimental tests of their moral conduct. Philip Jackson's sociological analysis of the hidden curriculum also touched on this disjunction between children's professed moral values and their actual behavior.

The second phenomenon that Kohlberg hoped to account for is the fact that two individuals at the same stage of moral development may take different positions regarding the proper course of action when a real-life dilemma presents itself. During Kohlberg's teaching career at Harvard, the military draft was the moral dilemma that most frequently preoccupied his students, but their responses took a number of different forms. Kohlberg maintained that his emphasis on the process of moral reasoning itself allowed for a variety of responses without having to exclude some decisions as automatically "immoral."

With specific regard to the use of forced-choice moral dilemmas as an educational technique, one should note that it did not originate with Kohlberg; Piaget is usually credited with its introduction. One important addition that Kohlberg made to Piaget's use of dilemmas in investigating the moral reasoning of children was the development of a scoring system and coding manual for evaluating subjects' responses. A second difference in the two psychologists' use of dilemmas is Kohlberg's emphasis on interpersonal conflict in his stories. Whereas many of Piaget's examples simply involve comparisons of two hypothetical situations, all of Kohlberg's dilemmas involve conflicts between different people's perspectives, needs, and wishes.

Examples   Kohlberg's "Heinz" dilemma is reproduced in the accompanying sidebar. Two of the just communities that he served as a consultant are described in more detail under "Theories in Action."

HISTORICAL CONTEXT

Loss of a universal moral framework

Kohlberg and other twentieth-century educational theorists had to work out notions of moral development against a dark backdrop, namely the loss of a universally agreed-upon framework for posing and answering ethical questions. Although the dissolution of what had been the Western moral consensus was noticeable enough to disturb some observers as early as the eighteenth century, the process accelerated with increasing rapidity in the nineteenth and early twentieth centuries. Charles Taylor has described this sense of loss as follows:

> What Weber called "disenchantment," the dissipation of our sense of the cosmos as a meaningful order, has allegedly destroyed the horizons in which people previously lived their spiritual lives. . . . What is common [at present] is the sense that no framework is shared by everyone . . .

Taylor goes on to say that the defining moral predicament for contemporary people is not a sense of guilt based on failing to meet an unchallengeable set of moral demands, but rather a feeling of meaninglessness resulting from the sheer variety of competing religious as well as nonreligious traditions and philosophies.

Kohlberg's theories about moral education can be regarded from Taylor's perspective as a search for a method of moral education that would maintain a core of objective ethical principles while excluding traditional methods of moral education that relied on indoctrination. This search was particularly important to Kohlberg because of interviews he conducted with survivors of the Holocaust in 1945. Carol Gilligan remarked that much of Kohlberg's resistance to her questioning of the universal adequacy of his stage theory was rooted in his fear of the consequences of widespread moral collapse. ". . . to him, to let go of the notion that there was a universal, objective moral truth was to fall into a stance of moral relativism, or even worse, moral nihilism, and therefore to have no place to stand against moral outrages such as genocide, the Holocaust, slavery."

John Dewey's educational theories

Another important historical factor underlying Kohlberg's theory of moral development was the influence of the American philosopher and educator John Dewey (1859–1952). Dewey favored educational reform that would allow schools to be "major agencies for the development of free personalities." Since Dewey regarded truth as an instrument that human beings use to solve problems rather than an unchanging reality, he thought that schools should teach students how to exercise judgment rather than imparting rote knowledge of facts, so that the children would learn "to pass judgments pertinently and discriminatingly on the problems of human living." Thus he regarded the teacher's role as not "to impose certain ideas or to form certain habits in the child, but . . . to select the influences which shall affect the child and to assist him [sic] in properly responding to those influences."

Dewey considered democracy by itself to be a primary moral value, and the schools to be the necessary foundation of a democratic society. He stated in 1897, "I believe that education is the fundamental method of social progress and reform. . . . I believe . . . that the teacher is engaged, not simply in the training of individuals, but in the formation of the proper social life." Since Dewey maintained that the school "is primarily a social institution" and that education is "a social process," he argued that it is the proper locus of moral as well as academic instruction.

> I believe that the moral education centers upon this conception of the school as a mode of social life, that the best and deepest moral training is precisely that which one gets through having to enter into proper relations with others in a unity of work and thought.

BIOGRAPHY:

Carol Gilligan

Carol Gilligan (1936–) was born in New York City on November 28, 1936. She was educated at Swarthmore College, where she majored in English literature and graduated with highest honors in 1958. She then earned a master's degree in clinical psychology from Radcliffe College in 1961, followed by a Ph.D. in social psychology from Harvard in 1964, shortly after the birth of her second son. Gilligan was disillusioned with psychology at that time, finding its clinical language "abrasive"; as she put it, "It did not resonate with my experience of the human world." She then became involved with the performing arts, becoming a member of a modern dance group, and with local politics. In 1967 she began teaching at Harvard with Erik Erikson, who inspired her to return to the field of psychology. She later credited Erikson for exemplifying "the possibility of speaking [within academic psychology] in a first-person voice. He showed that you cannot take a life out of history, that life history can only be understood in history, and that statement stayed with me for a long time."

Following her work with Erikson, Gilligan became Kohlberg's research assistant in 1970. The course of her friendship as well as her professional relationship with Kohlberg has already been described. Gilligan published her best-known book, *In a Different Voice: Psychological Theory and Women's Development* in 1982. In its pages she took issue with Kohlberg's definition of the stages of moral development on the grounds that its emphasis on justice and rationality was implicitly androcentric.

> Kohlberg defines the highest stages of moral development as deriving from a reflective understanding of human rights. . . . [with an] emphasis on separation rather than connection . . . [and] consideration of the individual rather than the relationship as primary.

Gilligan's position as articulated in this book has been described as "difference feminism," meaning that she maintains that men and women in Western societies undergo different processes of moral as well as psychological development.

> The elusive mystery of women's development lies in its recognition of the continuing importance of attachment in the human life cycle. Woman's place

in man's life cycle is to protect this recognition while [Kohlberg's] developmental litany intones the celebration of separation, autonomy, individuation, and natural rights.

Following the publication of *In a Different Voice,* Gilligan undertook several research projects involving interviews with adolescent girls in a variety of settings. In 1986 Gilligan became a tenured full professor at the Harvard Graduate School of Education. She was a visiting professor of American History and Institutions at Cambridge University in England from 1992 through 1994. Named by *Time* magazine in 1996 as one of the 25 most influential people in the United States, Gilligan was appointed to Harvard's first endowed chair of gender studies in 1997. In 2002 Gilligan left Harvard to join the faculty of New York University as a professor in the School of Law as well as the Graduate School of Education.

Gilligan's research in the development of adolescent girls led her to develop what she calls the listening guide method. The method is intended to evaluate persons' discussions of psychologically difficult or taboo topics through analysis of the latent meanings as well as explicit wording or phrases. The latent meanings are probed through study of the subject's pauses, hesitations, changes in the thread of an argument, and self-descriptions. The interviewer is expected to build a trusting relationship with the subject, in contrast to the attitude of "objectivity" that is taken for granted in most research interviews. In

Carol Gilligan. (Photo *courtesy of Jerry Bauer. Reproduced by permission.)*

addition, each interview transcript is read four times. In the first reading, the interviewer analyzes the content and records her or his inner reaction to it. In the second reading, the interviewer focuses on the subject's self-descriptions. The third and fourth readings highlight specific words, phrases, and repeating themes in the interview, such as "care" or "justice."

He sometimes referred to this principle as "learning by doing."

Dewey first taught at the University of Michigan (1884–1894); later, he joined the faculty at the University of Chicago (1894–1904) and Columbia University (1904–1952). Dewey's most influential publications include *School and Society* (1889), "My Pedagogic Creed" (1897), and *Democracy and Education* (1916). In addition to his writings, however, Dewey led the movement for progressive education in the United States through his influence on actual educational practice. The Laboratory School of the University of Chicago was founded in 1896 in response to Dewey's ideas; it expanded over the years to include four schools (nursery/kindergarten, lower, middle, and high) that had enrolled a total of 1,600 pupils annually as of the early 2000s. Thus, Kohlberg performed his undergraduate and doctoral work in the institution that was identified with both the theory and the practical application of Dewey's ideas.

Kohlberg himself was quite explicit about his indebtedness to Dewey's concept of education. In his early essay on the Platonic roots of his concept of justice, he was careful to note that he had ". . . discussed [his] views within John Dewey's framework. In speaking of a Platonic view [of justice], [he was] not discarding [his] basic Deweyism." In a well known article that Kohlberg coauthored with Rochelle Mayer, he echoed Dewey's insistence on the importance of democratic values:

> In regard to ethical values, the progressive ideology adds the postulates of development and democracy to the postulates of liberalism. The notion of educational democracy is one in which justice between teacher and child means joining in a community in which value decisions are made on a shared and equitable basis.

Social climate of the 1960s and 1970s

Kohlberg's rise to a kind of academic stardom in the early 1970s had much to do with the political and social upheavals in the United States toward the end of the 1960s. The civil rights movement, the Vietnam War, and the political scandal of the Watergate hearings brought moral issues to the forefront of public attention; these conflicts gave the question of moral education in the schools a new urgency. In addition, Kohlberg's emphasis on the importance of bridging academic theory and educational practice led a number of psychologists and educators to become political activists. Most of the just communities and cluster schools studied by Kohlberg's graduate students were founded during this period.

Some historians of American education have suggested that the general atmosphere of social unrest and disruption in the 1970s favored widespread acceptance of Kohlberg's ideas because he was regarded as a protestor against the academic status quo. His notion of conventional morality as a lower stage of moral development also attracted those who wished to see themselves as morally justified as well as intellectually sophisticated opponents of the current social and political system. Kohlberg's popularity was in part a matter of being in the right place at the right time. Many of his critics complained that his tendency to ascribe higher ratings on his scale of moral maturity to student protestors amounted to implicit endorsement of their left-wing political views. An example of the political bias that these critics perceived in Kohlberg's ratings occurs in a book chapter that he coauthored in 1971. Discussing the 1964 free speech sit-ins at Berkeley, Kohlberg maintained that

> . . . willingness to violate authority for civil rights required Stage-6 principled thinking. . . . a Stage-5 social-contract interpretation of justice (which was held by the university administration) did not lead to a clear decision [on the part of students at that level]. . . . about half of the Stage-5 subjects sat in, while eighty percent of the Stage-6 subjects sat in. For students at the conventional levels—Stages 3 and 4—such civil disobedience was viewed as a violation of authority and only ten percent of them sat in.

It should be added that some graduates of Kohlberg's high school programs did not perceive him as a neutral figure. The phrase "moral intimidation" was used by a graduate of the Scarsdale Alternative School described below, who published an article in 1980 regarding Kohlberg's work as a consultant at the school. The student argued that Kohlberg's emphasis on the form rather than the content of moral reasoning did not exclude the potential for teachers to pressure students in their applications of moral education theory.

> The feeling of being pushed toward "higher stages" was very intimidating to many students. They perceived that every issue was presented with a "right" side and a "wrong" side and that there was tremendous pressure to choose the "right" side, despite what they really thought. . . . This I saw happening in our school especially with a big shot Harvard professor in addition to the entire staff supporting certain ideas which they called better. With the notion that there exists a hierarchy of reasoning and values in the air . . . discussions [turn] into battles of who's right and who is wrong based on stages.

CRITICAL RESPONSE

Critiques of Kohlberg's stage theory

Many of Kohlberg's critics have pointed to what they regard as weaknesses in his stage theory of moral development. Some of these concern the number of stages. As was noted earlier, the existence of Kohlberg's sixth stage was questioned by researchers who could not find subjects who seemed to have attained it. In addition, Kohlberg's eventual hypothesis of a seventh stage of moral development, which he called a "soft stage," represented a later modification of his original position.

Other critics question the interrelationship among the stages. Kohlberg's early work described the stages as "hard," in the sense that the stages were not only sequential but relatively separate from one another; that is, people would generally function in all areas of moral decision-making at the highest level of development that they had attained. In 1979, James Rest, one of Kohlberg's associates, proposed a so-called "mixed stage" or "layer cake" model of moral development, according to which a person might use an earlier and less complex level of moral reasoning in certain specific situations. For example, a person who scores at Stage 5, which is considered "postconventional," might well reason at Stage 3 or 4 when dealing with such commonplace obligations of citizenship as registering to vote or serving on a jury. In other words, Rest's "mixed stage" model allows for the simultaneous coexistence of higher and lower stages within a person's cognitive repertoire.

Related to Rest's modification of Kohlberg's stages is domain theory, usually identified with the work of Elliott Turiel. Turiel came to distinguish between children's moral development and other domains of social knowledge in order to account for anomalies in the data from Kohlberg's long-term follow-up studies of the subjects from his dissertation research. Turiel's domain theory holds that children's conceptions of morality and social conventions develop as a result of different social experiences associated with these two domains. Actions in the moral domain have certain effects on other people that occur without regard to social rules that may or may not be associated with the action. An example would be striking another person for no apparent reason. The moral domain is structured around the concepts of fairness, harm caused to others, and the welfare of others. Conventions, by contrast, are agreed-upon rules that smooth social interactions within a group; they are structured to meet the needs of social organization rather than considering the

members' harm or well-being. An example might be the convention of addressing a physician in public as "Doctor" rather than using his or her first name; the use of the professional title is a matter of conventional etiquette rather than a moral issue. Domain theory helps to explain why people often appear to be inconsistent in applying moral reasoning across different social contexts. It has also been applied by teachers at the high school level to help students distinguish between moral issues (e.g., cheating on tests or stealing from other students) and matters of convention (e.g., dress codes).

Sociological issues

One of the most frequent criticisms of Kohlberg's theory of moral development is that it draws universal implications from the life histories of a relatively privileged stratum of Western society, namely well-educated Caucasian males. As Carol Gilligan put it, Kohlberg's scheme

> hid the thoughts and feelings of all people who were considered to be lesser, less developed, less human, and we all know who these people are: women, people of color, gays and lesbians, the poor, and the disabled. . . . the only way you could be different within a hierarchical scheme was, you could be higher or you could be lower, and all the people who had historically been lower turned out—surprise, surprise—to be the people who did not create the scheme.

Gilligan herself is best known for her work in comparing Kohlberg's emphasis on justice and rationality to what she defined as an ethic of care. In a frequently cited example from *In a Different Voice*, Gilligan contrasts "Jake," an 11-year old who scores at Stage 4 on Kohlberg's scale, with "Amy," a girl of the same age who is rated a full stage lower on the grounds of her apparent "cognitive immaturity." ". . . her responses seem to reveal a feeling of powerlessness in the world, an inability to think systematically about the concepts of morality or law, a reluctance to challenge authority." Gilligan proceeds, however, to analyze "the different logic of Amy's response," based on the girl's concern to protect a network of relationships rather than to set up a hierarchical order of concepts regarding laws or duties.

> To the question, "What does he see that she does not?" Kohlberg's theory provides a ready response, manifest in the scoring of Jake's judgments a full stage higher than Amy's in moral maturity; to the question, "What does she see that he does not?" Kohlberg's theory has nothing to say.

Gilligan's later work represents a departure from standard methods of psychological research as well as a rejection of Kohlberg's specific theories.

Others have noted that Kohlberg's stage theory relies heavily on the verbal and conceptual skills of test subjects, to the disadvantage of younger or less well educated persons. Jerome Kagan, one of Kohlberg's colleagues at Harvard, thought that Kohlberg simply "didn't make sense" in maintaining that children below the age of four do not possess any moral reasoning abilities. Kagan attributed Kohlberg's position to his reliance on children's ability to respond verbally to moral dilemma stories. He said, "I could imagine a child who could not put into words, or into coherent sentences, his or her take on a moral problem, thus scoring at a lower stage [on Kohlberg's scale] than is actually the case." A similar problem surfaces with adult members of ethnic or racial minorities, in that some cultures do not place a high premium on verbal communication, abstract thought, or self-reflection; however, these characteristics hardly justify evaluating members of these cultures as morally underdeveloped or inferior. Anthony Cortese, a professor of sociology at Southern Methodist University, has pointed out that the scores of ethnics in the United States on Kohlberg's tests reflect their degree of assimilation into mainstream society rather than their level of moral development. "As ethnics enter middle and upper class in Western societies, they become more mainstream and their ties to [their] old culture tend to weaken."

Lastly, some studies of the moral development of educated professionals indicate that Kohlberg's scoring system favors those with some training in philosophy as well as highly developed general verbal skills. A study of Canadian medical students that was initially interpreted as suggesting that medical school actually hindered moral development was criticized for its overreliance on Kohlberg's stage theory. The critic remarked, "[According to Kohlberg], post-conventional stages are a rarity requiring philosophical sophistication. Is it fair or reasonable to expect medical education to provide a philosophical training as well?"

Character formation issues

Kohlberg has been criticized by representatives of two other contemporary philosophies of moral education, which may be roughly categorized as communitarian and character education approaches. Both groups of theorists point to several developments in American society since the early years of Kohlberg's career that have led to a revival of interest in moral education:

- The accelerating breakdown of family structure, reflected in the rising divorce rate and the number of children living in single-parent households.

- The growing influence of the mass media and their emphasis on materialism, violent behavior, immediate self-gratification, and deliberate violation of social standards, i.e., "pushing the envelope."

- An increased awareness that certain ethical values, such as respect, trustworthiness, responsibility, and the like, have objective worth in maintaining civilized societies.

- Troubling behavioral trends among young people, reflected in medical and psychiatric as well as criminal justice statistics.

Communitarian educators disagree with Kohlberg on the starting point of moral education; they begin with communication through language and social interactions rather than with reasoning ability. Communitarians also stress the importance of the specific religious, linguistic, ethnic, national, and other communities to which a child belongs in the formation of his or her identity. Helen Haste, a British educator in this group, has said, "Cultural narratives, traditions, and stories feed directly into our identity, signaling valued attributes and behaviors, and giving an explanation for our past and present." Beyond the child's sense of identity, communities are also sources of morality. "Social order rests on people's interdependence, and society only functions if people recognize and act upon their community responsibilities." From the communitarian perspective, Kohlberg's emphasis on rationality is built on an unrealistic concept of human nature, leading to "selfishness and egoism . . . a failure to see the individual as part of a whole, and the lack of subjective feeling of being part of something larger that would give the self meaning." The results of a Kohlbergian approach to parenting were summarized by a writer living in New York City:

> Since reason is so clearly ineffective when kids are being most kid-like, often my neighbors resort to a studied nonchalance in the face of a child's unruliness, refusing (so it seems to suffering bystanders) to train their children in public etiquette. We have all seen children careening around a crowded waiting room at the doctor's office, straining to get out of the shopping cart at the grocery store, or banging their spoons on the table in a restaurant. . . . In such situations one often notices on the parent's face an ironic smile, hiding. . .equal mixtures of rage and incompetence. It is the price you pay when you don't want to appear unreasonable.

The communitarian critique points to three specific gaps in Kohlberg's account of moral development: the gap between individual moral autonomy and deep commitment to a specific community; the gap between reason and such other aspects of human personality as emotion and imagination; and the gap between verbal expressions of moral conviction and actual behavior. With regard to the first issue, some observers have remarked on a noticeable tension between the individualism underlying Kohlberg's stage theory of development and the collectivist notions embedded in his concept of just communities. With regard to emotion, Kohlberg himself was compelled to acknowledge that in order for just communities to function adequately, individuals had to form emotional attachments to them as well as accept them on an intellectual basis. In terms of the gap between standards and conduct, some researchers found that some juvenile delinquents scored at higher stages on Kohlberg's tests than children who did not get into trouble with the law. This apparent anomaly was attributed to the fact that the lawbreakers had to develop a certain degree of cognitive sophistication in order to "con" authority figures.

Character education, which has received increasing attention since the early 1990s, is often associated with the work of Thomas Lickona, a professor of education who specializes in early childhood development. Lickona published a book in 1991 entitled *Educating for Character,* which urged cooperation among parents, schools, and local communities in teaching two aspects of moral character that Kohlberg deemphasized, namely the affective and moral action dimensions of character. Lickona retained Kohlberg's concept of the cognitive side of character—"Good character consists of knowing the good"—but added, "desiring the good, and doing the good." Lickona defines the affective side of character as including conscience, self-respect, empathy, loving the good, self-control, and a willingness to correct one's moral failings. Moral action, in his view, requires the three qualities of competence in listening, communicating, and cooperating; a will capable of mobilizing one's judgment and energy; and moral habit, understood as "A reliable inner disposition to respond to situations in a morally good way."

Philosophical issues

Some observers object to Kohlberg's theories of moral development because they disagree with his definition of goodness. Critics of Kohlberg have noted that his stage theory implicitly values questioning, challenging, and self-assertive behavior over

conformity, obedience, and compliance. One commentator has stated that

> No one goes further than Kohlberg in rejecting traditional moral education. . . . The whole moral inheritance of social norms and religious codes has nothing to offer the growing child; to the contrary, they run the risk of stifling his moral autonomy. Asked by parents and teachers why so many of his recommended lessons seemed to lead to the conclusion that children should resist authority, he scoffed, 'Such teachers do not believe moral behavior should be based on reasoning. . . .' [In Kohlberg's system] the healthy individual is the one who does not submit readily to his parents or rules. To become moral, the child has only to retreat in solitary meditation to the private monastery of his mind.

Another question in the minds of some of Kohlberg's critics is the source and stability of human moral goodness. Some maintain that it comes from within; that is, goodness is a basic human predisposition or potential. Others argue that it comes from the outside and must be imposed on a human nature that is innately flawed or vulnerable to its baser instincts. In their opinion, Kohlberg failed to offer an adequate account of moral evil. Kohlberg's faith in the civilizing power of education was contradicted by the recent history of Germany, which showed that scholars and other "reasonable people" could coexist quite comfortably with radical evil. Carol Gilligan said in 1993,

> There was an embarrassing fact—really embarrassing because I always think it was Larry who raised it. The fact that the Nazi Holocaust happened in the middle of Europe meant that the assumption that civilization led to . . . moral development could no longer be held. Education, social class, culture and civilization were not necessarily associated with higher stages of moral reasoning. . . . The Holocaust should not have occurred in Germany, according to the assumptions about development that Larry incorporated into his theory.

A third area of philosophical debate related to Kohlberg's theories is the centrality he accorded to the principle of justice and the way he defined that principle. Kohlberg explicitly took his definition of justice as fairness from the work of John Rawls (1921–2002), a political philosopher who also taught at Harvard. Rawls' best-known work, *A Theory of Justice,* was published in 1971. While Rawls' combination of Kantian and utilitarian lines of thought in his description of the social contract has been intensively discussed, his ideas are far from being universally accepted. For example, Kohlberg subscribed to Rawls' notion that justice is a "rationally objective moral principle" that any morally responsible adult would freely adopt. This premise, however, has been questioned by moral philosophers as well as political scientists.

Religious issues

Still another area of controversy is Kohlberg's view of the distinction between morality and religion insofar as it applies to specifically religious education. Few American religious educators, whether Christian or Jewish, have difficulty with the concept of a civic morality based on natural law, defined as the "law written on the hearts" of all people, in the words of St. Paul (Romans 2:15). Their critiques of Kohlberg are based partly on what they perceive as flaws in his research method, and partly on their views of the educative dimension of religious practices. For example, one commentator noted that Kohlberg failed to distinguish between "religion" and "religious affiliation" in defining morality as autonomous with respect to religion.

> Social scientists investigating religious behavior typically draw a sharp distinction between religiosity and religious affiliation. It is surprising and disappointing that . . . Kohlberg did not acquaint himself more assiduously with the corpus of empirical data and theorizing on the social-scientific study of religion.

In addition, this critic observed that Kohlberg's separation of morality from religion is incompatible with his notion of "the whole person developing as a whole." "Kohlberg . . . states that all human development is of a piece. Thus [religious practice] is intimately bound up with other areas of human development, including morality."

Another group of religious educators take issue with Kohlberg's theories from a communitarian perspective. Barry Chazan, a Jewish scholar, argues that Kohlberg's model of moral development is inadequate from the standpoint of maintaining Jewish identity in an increasingly secular and pluralistic society. "The Kohlberg model is ultimately too Platonic, too individualistic, and too traditionless to be applicable to the Jewish educational world, past, present, or future." Craig Dykstra, a Christian educator from a Dutch Reformed background, points out that such faith-related practices as prayer, worship, study of the Scriptures, giving hospitality to strangers, working for social justice, and similar actions are cooperative activities that form moral character in religious communities as well as in individuals. In addition, Dykstra maintains that the nature of faith itself distinguishes Christian religious education from other forms of education, because faith is not a human achievement; rather it is a "turn away from achievement and mastery toward receptivity and responsiveness."

In addition, some researchers in the field of religious education have compiled data suggesting that Elliott Turiel's domain theory offers a more adequate explanation of children's moral development in the context of specific religious communities than does Kohlberg's model. One study of children and adolescents from three distinctive religious traditions (Orthodox Jewish, Roman Catholic, and Mennonite [Anabaptist Protestant]) found that the young people distinguished between basic moral concerns (justice, compassion, and human well-being) and rules or practices specific to their respective faiths (fasting, keeping kosher, head coverings or prayer shawls, Sabbath observances, attendance at Mass, etc.). For example, one of the interviewers asked a nine-year-old Jewish girl whether it is all right for Christian boys not to wear kippot (head coverings worn by Jewish males). The girl answered that it is acceptable, "because that's not one of their rules. They don't show respect for God in the same way." "Is it okay that they respect God in a different way?" "Yes. The religion is different. What they do is not our business, and if they want to do that they can."

THEORIES IN ACTION

Research

Kohlberg's interest in field research   Kohlberg's theories not only unfolded from his doctoral research, but they were also field-tested by his Harvard graduate students. In fact, it was the work of one of these students, Moshe Blatt, which was credited with turning Kohlberg away from pure research toward applying his theory of moral development to actual educational practice. Blatt was the first to hypothesize that children could be stimulated to move more rapidly through the successive stages of moral development through systematic exposure to moral reasoning one step above their own. To test this hypothesis, Blatt interviewed a group of sixth-graders in a Jewish Sunday School over a period of 12 weeks. The students were tested at the beginning of the project to determine their current stage of moral development. Blatt then met with the students once a week to present a moral dilemma for discussion. In his own words, he then took "the 'solution' proposed by a child who was one stage above the majority of the children . . . and elaborated this solution until the children understood its logic and seemed convinced that its logic was reasonable or fair." At the end of the 12 weeks, Blatt retested the sixth-graders and found that 64% of them "had developed one full stage in their moral reasoning." Although Kohlberg was initially skeptical about the "Blatt effect," he later stated that "Blatt's venture launched cognitive-developmental moral education." In the period between

1975 and 1989, Kohlberg's students published seven reviews of "a large number" of studies that claimed to replicate Blatt's findings.

Although other educational psychologists question their findings, cognitive developmental theorists maintain that the body of research based on Kohlberg's work has proved three major contentions regarding moral education:

- A child's moral development can be influenced by educational interventions. Specifically, his or her progress through the various stages of moral development can be compressed into a shorter period of time.

- This accelerated development is not a temporary effect, but is maintained in the same way as "natural" moral development. In addition, the child is able to extend his or her progress to cover real-life moral dilemmas not discussed in the classroom.

- The educational interventions that have been shown to be most effective in promoting moral development include "providing opportunities for cognitive conflict," role-playing, and exposure to moral reasoning at the stage above one's own.

Measurement instruments   Kohlberg was frequently criticized in the 1960s and 1970s for psychometric weaknesses in the original version of his Moral Judgment Interview, or MJI, which he used in his dissertation research. As of the early twenty-first century, the MJI consisted of three forms, each containing three moral dilemmas. The test was administered as a 45-minute semi-structured interview recorded on tape. Subjects were presented with the three moral dilemmas included in their form. The interviewer then asked a series of open-ended probe questions intended to uncover the logical structure of the subject's moral reasoning. The MJI yields two scores: an overall score measuring the subject's moral maturity, and a stage score. In response to his critics, Kohlberg worked on standardizing his scoring system, which he then referred to as the Standard Issues Scoring System, or SIS. In 1987 *The Measurement of Moral Judgment* was finally published, shortly after Kohlberg's death. The scoring procedures for the MJI are time-consuming and require considerable training and sophistication on the interviewer's part; the scoring manual alone runs to 975 pages.

Another frequently administered test of moral reasoning based on Kohlberg's theories is the Defining Issues Test, or DIT, first published by James Rest in 1979. It incorporates Rest's "mixed stage"

modification of Kohlberg's stage theory. The DIT-1 is a multiple-choice self-administered test containing six moral dilemmas that require the subject to prioritize as well as agree or disagree with a set of questions following each dilemma. The DIT-1 short form contains only the first three dilemmas of the full DIT-1. The DIT-2 consists of five dilemmas related to contemporary social problems. To compare Kohlberg's instrument with Rest's, the MJI is more comprehensive, but the DIT is considerably easier to use and better documented. Another difference between the two tests is that the MJI can be used with children as young as seven, while the DIT cannot be used with subjects younger than 13. An excerpt from the DIT is included in the accompanying sidebar.

Case studies

Prison reform   Kohlberg's experiment with setting up a just community in a prison began in June 1971, when he and two colleagues started training and orientation meetings with line staff at a minimum-security prison for women in Niantic, Connecticut. The training sessions with the staff consisted of moral development theory, what Kohlberg described as "simple clinical practice," and group discussions. The researchers quickly found that the line staff felt hampered by having to enforce purely bureaucratic rules on the inmates, but they had no role definition as counselors or helpers. It was then decided to set up a model cottage in one of the cottages at the institution. The researchers selected a group of 20 women for the model program, along with six line staff, a supervisor trained in moral development theory, and a parole agent. The role of the line staff was redefined as one of helping the inmates through counseling and leading discussions. The inmates were divided into two groups of 10 each to participate in discussions of their personal issues and dilemmas.

The model cottage was to have some autonomy in determining parole and work release as well as in defining its own rules and policies. The researchers had some difficulty in persuading the staff and inmates to overcome their suspicions of each other, but eventually a workable form of self-government emerged. Kohlberg described its structure as follows:

> The entire discipline process of the cottage is handled through community meetings. . . . In these meetings, members are free to say anything they like. Occasionally, staff are put on the spot, as are inmates. The inmates generally make a great effort to explore all aspects of an incident (personalities, circumstances, etc.). A community meeting may be called at any time by any member of the community. . . . Both staff and inmates have a single vote.

What was innovative about the Niantic program, from Kohlberg's perspective, was that it conceived of the inmates' treatment in terms of moral justice rather than psychological or psychiatric categories and approaches. An article that he published in 1972, a year after the beginning of the program, was quite optimistic in its assessment:

> We have accomplished much. We have created a fair self-governing community which operates within the constraints of a larger total institution and correctional system. Half the original women have been placed in either work-release or parole programs. . . . None have failed as of this writing. . . . At present, two women are doing well in a local community college and others, hopefully, will enroll.

The participants in the Niantic model cottage program were not systematically tested on the MJI until several years after the beginning of the program; however, most staff and inmates felt that they learned important skills of moral reasoning, group discussion, and decision making. The inmates in particular felt that they were better prepared to return to the world outside the prison.

Secondary education Following his work at Niantic, Kohlberg then began to introduce his theories regarding the role of just communities in moral education into several alternative high schools in New York and Massachusetts. Alternative high schools in general were a product of the so-called free-school movement, which reached its peak of popularity in the United States in the early 1970s. The free-school movement, which was influenced by the wider countercultural trends of the period, was largely led by followers of John Dewey. Alternative schools, which are also referred to as democratic schools, may be either public or private institutions. Some public alternative high schools are offered as a choice to local students, while others are designed for students at risk of dropping out of school. Although there is no universally agreed-upon definition of a democratic school, most share the following characteristics:

- Decision-making is shared among the students and faculty.

- Staff and students relate to one another as equals.

- Learning is student-centered, allowing students to choose their daily activities.

- The surrounding community is regarded as an extension of the classroom in terms of providing further opportunities for learning.

An illustrative example of Kohlberg's approach is the second just community that he helped to establish within an alternative school, namely the Scarsdale Alternative High School (also known as SAS or the A School) in Scarsdale, New York. The A School was founded in 1972 as a democratic alternative to the public high school. As Scarsdale is a wealthy community in which students are pressured to do well in school in order to gain admission to prestigious colleges, some parents wanted their children to be able to attend a high school with a less competitive atmosphere. Unlike many alternative schools, the A School has its own building separate from the main high school. As of the early 2000s, SAS had 75 students and five full-time staff.

The A School declared itself a just community school in 1978, one year after the principal and two teachers attended a summer institute at Harvard. They were having difficulty building a sense of community within the school, and they asked Kohlberg to serve as a consultant at the end of the summer. One of the major issues that emerged during the first year of the A School's adoption of the just community model concerned the tension between personal freedom and membership in a community. The use of drugs and alcohol during a school retreat provided the occasion. While most of the students responded to the faculty's request not to use drugs during school hours or at school functions, they raised the question as to whether a majority in a participatory community has the right to make rules that limit the personal freedom of the minority. Eventually the students came to a position that Kohlberg described as follows:

> In the just community school the majority cannot, in general, limit personal rights of students; it can only limit them where the personal right cannot be held to be a moral right because it violates the more essential obligation to participate in a voluntary community. Smoking pot is not a basic right, like freedom of speech, but is rather a personal habit that can be restricted for the sake of the community and the individuals in it.

Another major issue that arose during Kohlberg's work as a consultant at the Scarsdale school was cheating. Cheating is a problem in many schools because it is harder to develop peer-supported opposition to it than to offenses like stealing. Whereas students can readily perceive that their peers are victims of unfairness when personal possessions are stolen, teachers appear to be the only victims of classroom cheating. Students, in other words, often regard themselves as a "we" group, with the teachers as a "they" group. As Kohlberg put it, "Strong collective norms against cheating can usually only develop if the peer and teacher groups are seen as parts of a common community with norms that are fair to teachers as well as students." What happened in A School community discussions when two incidents of cheating came before the group was that the students accepted the responsibility of confronting those among them who cheated; in other words, they instituted an honor code in which honesty became a rule, not simply a vague expectation, and students as well as teachers felt responsible to the community as a whole for enforcing the rule.

Kohlberg's involvement with high-school education was significant in that it led him to modify some of his early views on the process of moral development. In particular, his first writings emphasized the separation of form and content in moral reasoning; that is, he argued that the structure of the student's moral reasoning was more important than his or her specific answer. As Kohlberg dealt with adolescents at the stages he identified with conventional morality, however, he could no longer keep a safe academic distance from the content of their reasoning; in other words, the rules that a school community decides to institute and enforce are as important as the reasons guiding the decisions. At a minimum, life in any community requires adherence to some conventional moral norms. In Kohlberg's words,

> . . . if students decide—even democratically—that they can leave class whenever they feel bored, the teacher is not as likely to focus on the reasoning behind their decision as on how to impress upon them the virtues of patience and consideration for others.

In addition, the moral conventions that Kohlberg thought he could take for granted in the 1960s were more fragile than he recognized at the time; even a decade later it was obvious to most observers that commonly held beliefs had lost much of their force and authority.

The second major modification that Kohlberg made as a result of his experiences with alternative high schools was to rethink the distinction between making a moral judgment about a situation and assuming personal moral responsibility for one's actions. Some describe this distinction in terms of two questions: "What is right to do in this situation?" and "What should *I* do?" Kohlberg and a colleague reexamined the famous experiment conducted by Stanley Milgram in 1974, in which some subjects recruited as "teachers" were instructed to administer electric shocks to "learners." The experiment was designed to test the extent to which subjects would obey the experimenter's orders rather than their own conscience when the "learner" expressed pain. Kohlberg's reanalysis of Milgram's data indicated that very few of the subjects thought that it was "right" to continue administering the shocks. The experimenter, according

CHRONOLOGY

1927: Lawrence Kohlberg born in Bronxville, New York.

1945: Graduates from Phillips Academy in Andover, Massachusetts,

1948: Begins study at the University of Chicago,

1955: Marries Lucille Stigberg.

1958: Graduates from University of Chicago with a doctoral degree

1968: Becomes a full professor at Harvard University. Later founds the Center for Moral Devlopment and Education there.

1969: Studies moral development in an Israeli kibbutz.

1971: Coauthors "The Adolescent as Philosopher" with Carol Gilligan.

1971: Contracts parasitic illness in Central America. Kohlberg suffered the effects of the illness for 16 years.

1985: Officially obtains divorce from wife Lucille.

1987: Commits suicide by drowning in Winthrop, Massachusetts.

to Kohlberg, "did not influence their determination of what was right as much as excuse them from taking responsibility for the consequences of their actions." Although Kohlberg speculated that attaining higher stages of moral development is necessary for accepting personal moral responsibility, he came to recognize that it is not a sufficient condition.

Professional ethics and law enforcement One area in which Kohlberg's stage theory of moral development has received increased attention since the 1980s is the field of professional ethics, followed by that of law enforcement. In response to a number of much-publicized scandals, such professions as medicine, accounting, journalism, public relations, and business are making use of Kohlberg's tests of moral maturity for self-policing and self-evaluation. In some cases, the effects of professional education itself on students are investigated. For example, an article published in a Canadian accounting journal reported on recent research concerning the moral development of accounting students and professional accountants relative to that of other groups in Canadian society. The article mentioned such findings as the fact that women in the profession generally scored higher on Kohlberg's measures of moral development than did men. In addition, the researchers reported surprisingly high rates of ethical conflicts affecting their subjects; 66% told the researchers that they had experienced at least one moral conflict at work while 46% reported more than one.

In law enforcement, Kohlberg's stages are sometimes used to evaluate the motivations of lawbreakers. An interesting example of this application is an analysis of four identified categories of people (99% of whom are male) who write computer viruses, namely adolescents, college students, adults, and former virus writers. An analyst at IBM's Thomas J. Watson Research Center reported that of these four groups, only the adult virus writers "appeared to be ethically abnormal, appearing below the level of ethical maturity which would be considered normal [for their age group] on the Kohlberg scale." The analyst mentioned an additional disturbing finding, however; although early studies done of virus writers in 1994 had indicated that they tended to "age out" as their moral development continued, ". . . mixed messages from many different sources appeared to make virus writing appear 'less wrong,' pushing up the age of aging out, if the process occurred at all." Another area of research within law enforcement is the use of Kohlberg's stages to evaluate the level of moral development of police officers.

Relevance to modern readers

As of the early 2000s, Kohlberg's work was more directly relevant to educators than to psychologists. In addition, the so-called "culture wars" of the 1980s and the rise of the home schooling movement have tended to polarize educators; in general, Kohlberg's views are more congenial to teachers or parents involved in progressive education or alternative school programs than they are to those who regard themselves as traditionalists or neoclassicists. Some researchers aligned with the character education movement have attempted to reconcile their approach with Kohlberg's, but others consider cognitive developmentalism to be fundamentally incompatible with character education in terms of underlying assumptions and basic philosophy. Moreover, feminist educators have little patience with what they regard as the built-in sexism of Kohlberg's stage theory.

The area of research in which Kohlberg's contributions are most likely to affect contemporary readers outside the field of education is ethical analysis. Kohlberg's stage theory and his Moral Judgment Interview are still used to evaluate the moral maturity of students and practitioners in occupations ranging from finance and journalism to law enforcement and health care. Given ongoing concern about the trustworthiness of people in positions of public trust, one can predict that ethics research has a productive future.

BIBLIOGRAPHY

Sources

Books

Blatt, Moshe, and Lawrence Kohlberg. "The Effects of Classroom Moral Discussion on Children's Level of Moral Judgment." In Lawrence Kohlberg and Elliott Turiel, eds., *Recent Research in Moral Development.* New York: Holt, Rinehart and Winston, 1973.

Boyd, Dwight. "The Rawls Connection." In Brenda Munsey, ed., *Moral Development, Moral Education, and Kohlberg.* Birmingham, AL: Religious Education Press, 1980.

Chazan, Barry. "Jewish Education and Moral Development." In Brenda Munsey, ed., *Moral Development, Moral Education, and Kohlberg.* Birmingham, AL: Religious Education Press, 1980.

Crain, William C. *Theories of Development: Concepts and Applications,* Chapter 7, "Kohlberg's Stages of Moral Development." Englewood Cliffs, NJ: Prentice Hall, 1985.

Dykstra, Craig. *Growing in the Life of Faith: Education and Christian Practice.* Louisville, KY: Geneva Press, 1999.

Fowler, James. "Moral Stages and the Development of Faith." In Brenda Munsey, ed., *Moral Development, Moral Education, and Kohlberg.* Birmingham, AL: Religious Education Press, 1980.

Fowler, James. *Stages of Faith: The Psychology of Human Development and the Quest for Meaning.* San Francisco: Harper and Row, 1981.

Gilligan, Carol. *In a Different Voice: Psychological Theory and Women's Development.* Cambridge, MA: Harvard University Press, 1982.

Gilligan, Carol, Nona P. Lyons, and Trudy J. Hanmer, eds. *Making Connections: The Relational Worlds of Adolescent Girls at Emma Willard School.* Cambridge, MA: Harvard University Press, 1990.

Kohlberg, Lawrence. "Cognitive-Developmental Theory and the Practice of Collective Moral Education." In M. Wolins and M. Gottesman, eds., *Group Care: The Education Path of Youth Aliyah.* New York: Gordon and Breach, 1971.

Kohlberg, Lawrence. "Continuities and Discontinuities in Childhood and Adult Moral Development Revisited." In

Paul B. Baltes and K. Warner Schaie, eds., *Life-Span Developmental Psychology: Personality and Socialization.* New York: Academic Press, 1973.

Kohlberg, Lawrence. "Educating for a Just Society: An Updated and Revised Statement." In Brenda Munsey, ed., *Moral Development, Moral Education, and Kohlberg.* Birmingham, AL: Religious Education Press, 1980.

Kohlberg, Lawrence. "Education for Justice: A Modern Statement of the Platonic View." In Theodore R. Sizer, James M. Gustafson, and Nancy F. Sizer, eds., *Moral Education.* Cambridge, MA: Harvard University Press, 1970.

Kohlberg, Lawrence. "Moral and Religious Education and the Public Schools: A Developmental View." In Theodore R. Sizer, ed., *Religion and Public Education.* Boston: Houghton Mifflin, 1967.

Kohlberg, Lawrence. "Moral Education." In David L. Sills, ed., *International Encyclopedia of the Social Sciences.* Vol. 10. New York: Macmillan, 1968.

Kohlberg, Lawrence. "Stages of Moral Development as a Basis for Moral Education." In Brenda Munsey, ed., *Moral Development, Moral Education, and Kohlberg.* Birmingham, AL: Religious Education Press, 1980.

Kohlberg, Lawrence. "The Moral Atmosphere of the School." In Norman V. Overly, ed., *The Unstudied Curriculum: Its Impact on Children.* Washington, DC: Association for Supervision and Curriculum Development, 1970.

Kohlberg, Lawrence, and Elliott Turiel. "Moral Development and Moral Education." In G. Lesser, ed., *Psychology and Educational Practice.* Glenview, IL: Scott Foresman Educational Publishers, 1971.

Lee, James Michael. "Christian Religious Education and Moral Development." In Brenda Munsey, ed., *Moral Development, Moral Education, and Kohlberg.* Birmingham, AL: Religious Education Press, 1980.

Nucci, Larry. *Education in the Moral Domain.* Cambridge, UK: Cambridge University Press, 2001.

Nucci, Larry. "Moral Development and Character Formation." In H. J. Walberg and G. D. Haertel, eds., *Psychology and Educational Practice.* Berkeley, CA: MacCarchan, 1997.

Piaget, Jean. *The Moral Judgment of the Child.* Translated by Marjorie Gabain. New York: Simon and Schuster, 1997.

Power, F. Clark, Ann Higgins, and Lawrence Kohlberg. *Lawrence Kohlberg's Approach to Moral Education.* New York: Columbia University Press, 1989.

Rest, James. "Development Psychology and Value Education." In Brenda Munsey, ed., *Moral Development, Moral Education, and Kohlberg.* Birmingham, AL: Religious Education Press, 1980.

Rieff, Philip. *The Triumph of the Therapeutic: Uses of Faith After Freud.* New York: Harper and Row, 1966.

Taylor, Charles. *Sources of the Self: The Making of the Modern Identity.* Cambridge, MA: Harvard University Press, 1989.

Periodicals

Dewey, John. "My Pedagogic Creed." *The School Journal* 54 (January 1897): 77–80.

Dykstra, Craig. "A 'Post-Liberal' Christian Education?" *Theology Today* 42 (July 1985): 153–7.

Gilligan, Carol. "Remembering Larry." *Journal of Moral Education* 27 (February 1998): 227–42.

"Harvard Professor of Education Reported Missing Since Jan. 17." *New York Times,* 31 January 1987, 10.

Haste, Helen E. "Communitarianism and the Social Construction of Morality." *Journal of Moral Education* 25 (January 1996): 47–55.

Hunter, James Davison. "Leading Children Beyond Good and Evil." *First Things* 103 (May 2000): 36–42.

Hymowitz, Kay S. "Raising Children for an Uncivil Society." *City Journal* 7 (Summer 1997): 20–4.

Jang, Raymond W. "Does Medical Education Blunt Our Moral Reasoning? A Different Interpretation of the Sherbrooke Moral Development Study." *University of Toronto Medical Journal* 81 (December 2003): 55–7.

Kohlberg, Lawrence, and Carol Gilligan. "The Adolescent as a Philosopher: The Discovery of the Self in a Postconventional World." *Daedalus: Journal of the American Academy of Arts and Sciences* 100 (1971): 1051–86.

Kohlberg, Lawrence, and Rochelle Mayer. "Development as the Aim of Education." *Harvard Educational Review* 42 (November 1972): 449–96.

Kohlberg, Lawrence, Peter Scharf, and Joseph Hickey. "The Justice Structure of the Prison—A Theory and an Intervention." *Prison Journal* 11 (Autumn/Winter 1972): 3–14.

"Lawrence Kohlberg Is Dead." *New York Times* (8 April 1987): D30.

Lemon, W. Morley. "A Question of Ethics." *CA Magazine* (November 1996): 26–9.

Lickona, Thomas. "The Return of Character Education." *Educational Leadership* 51 (November 1993): 6–11.

Powers, Elizabeth. "Habermas on the Upper West Side." *First Things* 58 (December 1995): 39–44.

Snell, Robin S. "Studying Moral Ethos Using an Adapted Kohlbergian Model." *Organization Studies* 21 (Winter 2000).

Twemlow, Stuart, MD. "The Roots of Violence: Converging Psychoanalytic Explanatory Models for Power Struggles and Violence in Schools." *Psychoanalytic Quarterly* 69 (April 2000): 741–85.

Walsh, Catherine. "Reconstructing Larry: Assessing the Legacy of Lawrence Kohlberg." *Ed.: The Magazine of the Harvard Graduate School of Education* (October 2000).

Zalaznick, Edward. "The Just Community School: A Student Perspective." *Moral Education Forum* 5 (1980): 27–35.

Others

Campbell, Robert L. "Self and Values: An Interactivist Foundation for Moral Development." Paper presented at the annual conference of the Association for Moral Education in Ottawa, Canada, 15 November 1996.

Gordon, Sarah. "Virus Writers: The End of the Innocence?" Paper presented at the Virus Bulletin Conference, 2000. Yorktown Heights, NY: IBM Thomas J. Watson Research Center, 2000.

Rest, James. *Defining Issues Test (DIT)*. Minneapolis, MN: University of Minnesota Press, 1979.

Further readings

Brown, Lyn Mikel, and Carol Gilligan. *Meeting at the Crossroads: Women's Psychology and Girls' Development*. Cambridge, MA: Harvard University Press, 1992.

Cortese, Anthony Joseph Paul. *Ethnic Ethics: The Restructuring of Moral Theory*. Albany, NY: State University of New York Press, 1990.

Gilligan, Carol. *In a Different Voice: Psychological Theory and Women's Development*. Cambridge, MA: Harvard University Press, 1982.

Lickona, Thomas. *Educating for Character: How Our Schools Can Teach Respect and Responsibility*. New York: Bantam Books, 1991.

Modgil, Sohan, and Celia Modgil, eds. *Lawrence Kohlberg: Consensus and Controversy*. London: The Falmer Press, 1986.

Reed, Donald R. C. *Following Kohlberg: Liberalism and the Practice of Democratic Community*. South Bend, IN: University of Notre Dame Press, 1997.

Skinner, Ron. "Character Education." *Education Week*, 27 February 2004.

Walsh, Catherine. "Reconstructing Larry: Assessing the Legacy of Lawrence Kohlberg." *Ed.: The Magazine of the Harvard Graduate School of Education* (October 2000).